PROFESSIONAL WEB DESIGN: TECHNIQUES AND TEMPLATES, FIFTH EDITION

CLINT ECCHER

Cengage Learning PTR

CENGAGE
Learning®

Professional • Technical • Reference

Australia • Brazil • Japan • Korea • Mexico • Singapore • Spain • United Kingdom • United States

CENGAGE
Learning®

Professional • Technical • Reference

Professional Web Design: Techniques and Templates, Fifth Edition
Clint Eccher

Publisher and General Manager, Cengage Learning PTR: Stacy L. Hiquet

Associate Director of Marketing: Sarah Panella

Manager of Editorial Services: Heather Talbot

Senior Marketing Manager: Mark Hughes

Product Manager: Heather Hurley

Project/Copy Editor: Marta Justak

Technical Reviewer: Eric Hunley

Interior Layout Tech: MPS Limited

Cover Designer: Mike Tanamachi

Indexer: Valerie Perry

Proofreader: Michael Beady

> For product information and technology assistance, contact us at
> **Cengage Learning Customer & Sales Support, 1-800-354-9706**.
>
> For permission to use material from this text or product, submit all requests online at **cengage.com/permissions**.
>
> Further permissions questions can be emailed to
> **permissionrequest@cengage.com**.

Library of Congress Control Number: 2014937100

ISBN-13: 978-1-305-25752-8

ISBN-10: 1-305-25752-9

Cengage Learning PTR

20 Channel Center Street

Boston, MA 02210

USA

Cengage Learning is a leading provider of customized learning solutions with office locations around the globe, including Singapore, the United Kingdom, Australia, Mexico, Brazil, and Japan. Locate your local office at: **international. cengage.com/region**.

Cengage Learning products are represented in Canada by Nelson Education, Ltd.

For your lifelong learning solutions, visit **cengageptr.com**.

Visit our corporate website at **cengage.com**.

Printed in the United States of America
1 2 3 4 5 6 7 16 15 14

Mikayla—You are bursting with creativity and have wisdom and compassion beyond your years.

Lisa—I have never known such support from a non-family member as I have from you. I am grateful and humbled to have someone like you in my life.

ACKNOWLEDGMENTS

Chelsea Miller—You are truly an amazingly gifted photographer. Your work makes me look good.

Nancy Eccher—For all the photography that proves your father lives in you.

Daniel Yu—To the guy who started me down the Web road so many years ago. It's hard to believe this journey all started with the Lynx browser.

Mark Celano—For being my Italian coding Yoda.

Heather Hurley—To the acquisitions editor whose professionalism and follow-through over all the years has made my writing as painless as possible.

Marta Justak—For working with an author with no memory. I am grateful beyond words for all the help you provided with this edition.

For all of A5design's clients over the years—without you, none of this would have occurred.

ABOUT THE AUTHOR

Clint Eccher (Fort Collins, CO) is an award-winning Web designer with more than 18 years of experience designing and developing professional websites. He is the owner of A5design, a Web design company that not only subcontracts to various marketing, advertising, and IT organizations, but also is commissioned by Fortune 500 companies, local and national non-profit organizations, and small businesses for Web design and development. In addition to authoring *Professional Web Design: Techniques and Templates, Fourth Edition*, which has been published in five different languages, he also is the author of *Advanced Professional Web Design: Techniques and Templates*.

Contents

INTRODUCTION

The methods and processes in which professional websites are created have not changed much since the first edition of this book. Designers still need to understand requirements, realize the technical pros and cons of layouts, create comps, save images using the correct file types, and test sites similarly to how they have been tested for more than a decade. Some of the technical ways in which these processes are accomplished, however, have changed.

Probably the most significant change that has occurred since the original writing of this book is how the framework of sites is built. Table-based HTML (HyperText Markup Language), now XHTML (Extensible HyperText Markup Language), designs had been the staple for laying out websites for many years; however, this method started making a significant change after the second edition of this book, in favor of Cascading Stylesheet (CSS) based designs. Such design involves using stylesheets to style pages, instead of XHTML table structure, which requires more code. This book fully explains the essentials of using stylesheets to lay out sites.

In the fourth edition, search engine optimization (SEO) was explored, giving the reader a strong basic understanding of how to get sites to rank better in search engines. Conversion rate optimization (CRO) also was explained, hopefully, helping the designer create a more efficient site for the users who were already visiting them.

The goal of this book is still to educate beginning to intermediate Web designers on the various issues involved with Web design. The way in which this is accomplished is through general discussion, case studies, and specific tips and techniques. There are many ways in which designers today create sites. What is included in this design is how the A5design, the company owned by the author, has satisfied its clients since the late 1990s.

The book is written using as few technical terms as possible. While some technical terminology is always going to be necessary, a lot of it has been simplified or even excluded to help the reader understand the general concepts more easily and then apply them in an effective, quick manner. My premise is that learning is much easier once the reader gets some momentum going, which is *not* accomplished by tripping over technical terminology.

This is not to say that this book doesn't deal with specific issues that designers will likely run into, because it does. Many of the tips and techniques included in the book will be eventually experienced by the reader if he/she does enough Web design.

The tips and techniques included here come from many years of troubleshooting, pitfalls, and flat-out stupid mistakes. They have been fine-tuned, however, through creative solutions and technical common sense. After reading through this book, the reader will have a stronger understanding of what it takes to create a highly professional website.

Companion Website Downloads

You may download the companion website files from www.cengageptr.com/downloads.

Folder Contents

Code Examples: This folder contains code examples included in Chapters 6, 8, 9, 10, 11, 12, 13, 14, 15, 16.

- **Designs—First Edition:** This folder contains the files for each design, which includes at least one Photoshop file, XHTML file, and a CSS file.

    Designs 1–50

- **Designs—Third Edition:** This folder contains the files for each design, which includes at least one Photoshop file, XHTML file, and, in most cases, a CSS file.

    1–80-xhtml-web

    81–90-enewsletters

    91–100-signatures

    101–120-photoshop-web

    121–160-css-web

■ **Designs—Fourth Edition:** This folder contains the files for each design, which includes at least one Photoshop file, XHTML file, and a CSS file.

  161–180-xhtml-web

■ **Designs—Fifth Edition:** This folder contains the files for each design, which includes at least one Photoshop file, XHTML file, and a CSS file.

  181–190-xhtml-web

CHAPTER 1

OVERVIEW OF WEB DEVELOPMENT TODAY

Since the early- to mid-1990s, the Web design industry has undergone many changes that make life easier for the Web designer. Designers used to have to worry about the download time of a website and how it would render differently in various browsers. The goal used to be that a page with all its code and images should be downloaded in less than 50k. The designer would also have to employ many tricks to ensure that the page looked the same in both Netscape and Internet Explorer. To a large extent, these are no longer issues for the designer, which allows much more flexibility and time to focus on the design itself.

Other areas of Web design have also become more complex. Search Engine Optimization (SEO) is a perfect example. Increased competition and the ever-changing requirements employed by search engines, such as Google, have forced designers to continually stay on top of changes and be creative in how they get users to a site.

Design, however, is going through very similar issues. Depending on which designer you ask, the industry will have reached Nirvana either when websites for all users are loaded with multimedia functionality or when they are stripped of all "excess" graphics and functionality.

Oddly enough, as the industry has evolved, the benchmark for aesthetic design has not always moved forward in equal measure. While there have been some fads that have required designers to create more aesthetically appealing designs, that is not always the case. Instead, the quality of Web design has actually taken a step backward in recent years. Whether it's because of the designer's drive or the client's wishes, there is a mentality of playing it safe and designing sites exactly how most of the other sites are designed,

1

which makes everything look the same. This issue, however, is not always one of style. Many times, the designer simply doesn't know the technical methods to make a certain look-and-feel work. This is one of the main reasons why this book was written—to help designers create sites that allow them to do what they want and help their clients communicate as effectively as possible. For the designer who produces highly professional creative work, the market will always provide many opportunities. To be able to produce such sites, though, a Web designer needs to have a thorough understanding of the basics of Web design.

DEFINING WEB DESIGN

Web design is an ambiguous term. Web professionals define it differently all the time. While one person might define it as programming the back-end functionality of a site, another might define design as the development of the front-end look and feel that gives a sense of the company or individual it represents. The truth of the matter is that both of these definitions are correct.

In the "older" days of graphical Web development (circa 1995), Web design meant creating static HTML (Hypertext Markup Language) pages with linked text and graphics. All content and functionality was hard coded in each page. Today's environment, however, involves creating dynamic websites that use other programming languages to interact with databases and browsers, along with XHTML (Extensible Hypertext Markup Language) pages, graphics, and CSS (Cascading Style Sheets).

A well-rounded Web designer needs to understand many of the technical and artistic aspects of Web design, although not necessarily specializing in both. Today's technical standards, in many instances, involve creating dynamic database-driven sites that are versatile, scalable, efficient, and search-engine friendly. However, if such sites consist only of unformatted pages with black text on white screens, they will not communicate as effectively to the majority of their audiences. On the other hand, if a site uses the latest graphic design methods but consists of static pages that are difficult to update or that do not enhance or simplify the user's experience, then the site is going to be more inflexible and, depending on the site's requirements, impractical.

Many of the technical and artistic issues that Web designers should consider are discussed throughout this book. Here are a few examples and explanations of what a Web designer must consider before commencing.

Figure 1.1 is an example of a design that is easy to update. Unfortunately, it employs little artistic design to make the site attractive to most users.

Figure 1.2 is an example of the opposite situation. It is more graphically appealing, but this design cannot be easily maintained or expanded because the page is almost entirely made up of graphics. Such a design not only requires the designer to rework the code but also to do much more graphics work.

Figure 1.3 is an example of a nice blending of the two disciplines. Not only is it graphically appealing, but it is also a database-driven site that allows for text to be added without compromising the layout of the design when extended vertically.

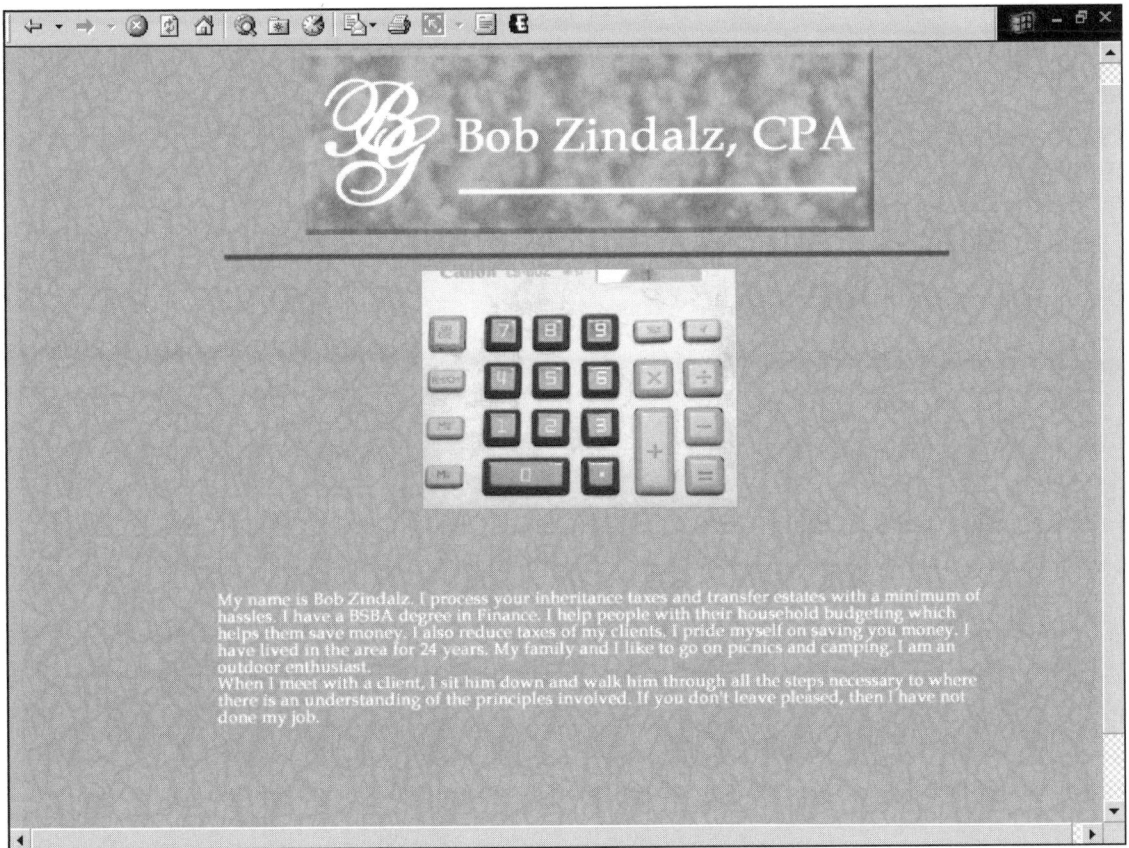

Figure 1.1
Site that focuses more on the technical aspects.

Figure 1.2
Site that focuses more on the aesthetic aspects.
© 2014 Cengage Learning.

For example, in Figure 1.3, the color and line to the left of the cow repeat vertically no matter how long the page runs, while the photos stay in their respective positions. This allows the original look and feel of the initial screen area to remain the same no matter how much content is added. The site also makes use of images in their most optimal formats and compression, which keeps the file sizes small and the download times fast.

Figure 1.3
Website that brings together both the aesthetic and technical aspects of design.
© 2014 Cengage Learning.

KNOWING THE SEVEN RULES OF WEB DESIGN

There are seven basic rules that, if followed, will help a beginning or intermediate designer become a professional:

1. **Just because you *can* does not mean you *should*.** Web technology offers many options and tools to build websites; however, just because the technology is there does not mean a designer should use that technology just for the sake of using it. Many times, adding technology can impede the performance of a site or irritate users, causing them to leave the site. For example, this might occur if you used Flash to animate a logo of a site. While the company may want to show off its new logo, the user probably does not care or want to see it move every time she hits a page. When using a new technology, the important question to ask is, "Does the technology add value to the site, or is it being added strictly as a novelty?"

2. **There is almost always an exception.** There rarely are absolutes in Web design. A designer should be careful of ruling out a technology or design method simply because it did not work for another site. Take, for example, the rotating logo. While it's not going to work for 99 percent of the world's websites, a corporation that is running an extremely expensive global rebranding campaign may want to use animation to show off its new logo for a month or two. It may even elect to show the animation on the homepage, which probably is a better approach to showing the new image without forcing it on the user too frequently.

3. **Users are the ultimate judges.** Opinions are never lacking when a site is in the design process. While an experienced designer may think a site should function or appear a certain way, the designer's boss may think differently. The bottom line is that the users *are* the bottom line. The site needs to make sense to them, so the site should be designed with them in mind.

4. **Crossover experience is something a designer needs to always strive for.** Professional Web design requires an understanding of the user's needs, regardless of how the designer personally believes the aesthetic and technical aspects of the site should be designed. Whatever the issue may be, a designer benefits from a comprehensive understanding of the many technical aspects of the site's design. A perfect example is that of forms. While it is important to make a form easy to use and attractive, the designer must also take technical considerations into mind. One pitfall a non-technical designer can fall into is creating a form field that may be layered above a down menu when it is expanded.

5. **Humility is the best approach.** Because there are so many intricacies to Web design, there are always going to be designers with more attractive sites, newer technology, or who use technology in a more creative way. If a designer does not let pride get in his way, learning from others can strengthen his skills.

6. **It is impossible to please everyone.** Whether it is the estimated 1.7 billion Web users around the world or three people in the office, a design is never going to make everyone happy. Everyone has an opinion. However, there is a fine line between making the majority happy and attempting to create a site that will actually be effective in communicating properly. A designer sometimes should take a stand to maintain certain functional and aesthetic aspects of a design.

7. **Try to stay on top of specifications and standards.** Web specifications and standards are constantly changing and will continue to do so. The designer should have a basic understanding of the latest techniques, which will affect future work.

CSS-driven Web design is one such example, which is what the revision of this book explains. While the previous editions explained how to create table-driven Web designs, this edition now focuses on creating sites that enable CSS position and style elements.

UNDERSTANDING THREE WEB-DESIGN PHILOSOPHIES

One helpful way of understanding the hundreds of millions of websites in the world today is to divide them into three distinct philosophies: usability, multimedia, and mortised. Depending on the designer, any of the three philosophies can do a good job of satisfying the goal of a website, which is to communicate to the user in the most effective manner. While multimedia and usability represent the proverbial argument between form and function, respectively, mortising represents the coming together of these two philosophies. When considering the pros and cons of each philosophy, a designer should take into account how each philosophy addresses the following three factors of any site:

- **Aesthetics:** How professional is the look and feel of the site? Is it consistent with the desired branding of the business or individual?

- **Usability:** How quickly and easily can a user find and process information while being able to perform necessary tasks?

- **Functionality:** Does programming enable the functional aspects of the site, such as forms and database-driven content?

Because of the vast array of hardware, software, and users on the Internet, no one philosophy is the perfect answer for everyone. However, by understanding each philosophy and its strengths and weaknesses, a designer can have a clear understanding of which one will best address the requirements of a particular site.

Usability Philosophy

Usability is a universal term that can be used when describing any site. It represents the ease with which the user can find and process information, as well as perform certain tasks.

The philosophy of usability takes this term to its most far-reaching scope. It attempts to make sites easily usable for all members of their Internet audience.

One method used to accomplish this goal is to strip down a site to its bare essentials, which includes deleting the majority, if not all, of its images. Some followers of the usability philosophy consider graphics to be a complication rather than a facilitation of the communication process. They also believe in designing sites that all browsers can view.

To better illustrate the philosophy of usability, Figure 1.4 shows an example of such a site. Notice that there is only HTML-generated color and no images. There is very little on this site that could be misconstrued by different browsers.

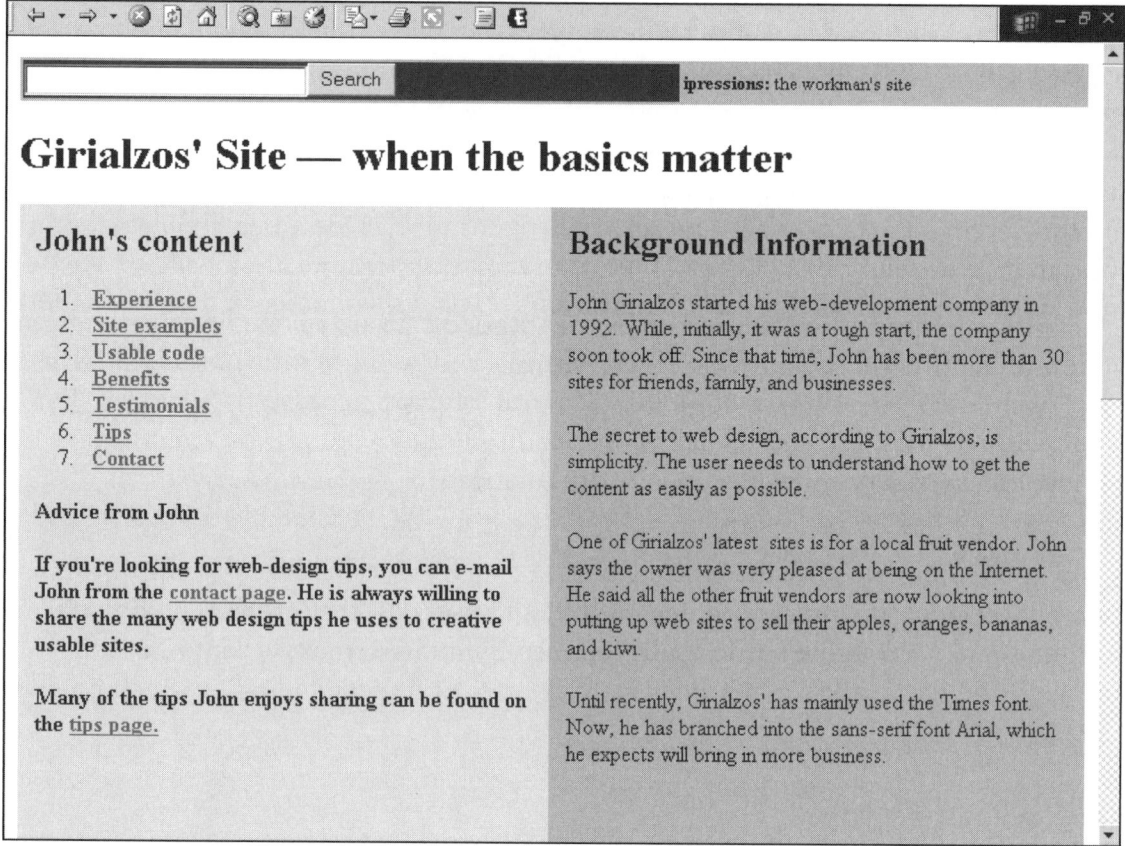

Figure 1.4
Site based on the usability philosophy.
© 2014 Cengage Learning.

Pros and Cons

As with any issue in life, there are always people with divergent views. Web design is no exception. The philosophy of usability falls at the most conservative side of the design spectrum, which, obviously, is going to have its detractors. Not all designers agree with this philosophy because of the simplicity of the designs, which resemble sites created in the 1990s. Visual usability is only one area that this philosophy addresses. There are also other technical and non-technical aspects that the usability philosophy takes into account. In accordance with the fourth rule of Web design, there are several practical points designers can and should take into consideration when designing:

- Download time should always be as minimal as possible.
- Navigation should be intuitive.
- Consistent Web terminology and metaphors, such as the shopping cart system, should be used (unless there is a valid reason for an exception).
- Writing should be clear and concise to expedite use.
- Sites should always be tested by a variety of users in a variety of browser environments.
- Accessibility for users with disabilities should be accounted for.

Anyone who has surfed the Internet would agree that finding information should be as easy as possible. No one likes to spend valuable time clicking all over a site to find a phone number or waste time with hyperlinks that do not go anywhere. This basis of the usability philosophy cannot be disputed for 99.9 percent of the world's sites.

One of the perceptions of usability is to appeal to everyone. This is simply not true. The sixth rule of Web design is that it is impossible to please everyone. As the number of users increases, a design quickly becomes "too complicated," "too simple," "too colorful," "too short," "too long," "too wild," or "too conservative," depending on the user.

This philosophy advocates limiting graphics to increase mass appeal. Graphics, however, often increase the usability of a site in four ways:

1. **The impression of a site, thus the identity of a business or individual, is first judged visually.** Most people form an immediate opinion when first coming to a site, if nothing more than at the subconscious level. If the site appears to be a five-minute design by an amateur, a user is going to question the professionalism and credibility of the business or individual and will very likely leave the site. The designer in Figure 1.5 valued aesthetics more than the designer of the site in Figure 1.4. Granted, the concept behind the site in Figure 1.4 is simplicity; however, the designer could have been more creative and used at least a couple of small 5KB to 10KB images to drastically improve the look of the site without noticeably increasing the download time.

2. **The brain processes images quicker than text.** Many traffic signs, called *ideograms*, are designed for quick, initial recognition of motor vehicle warnings, laws, and conditions. The reason is that the brain can process a sign, such as that in Figure 1.6, exponentially quicker than if the sign were to read, "It is illegal to make a left-hand turn at this intersection."

Web images work in the same way; they reduce the frustration of a user who is forced to read when a simple image will do. When a user looks at Figure 1.5, it is fairly obvious the site has something to do with shipping or a related industry. Whereas with Figure 1.4, there are no images cluing the user into the design's meaning. The user, therefore, has to spend time reading the page.

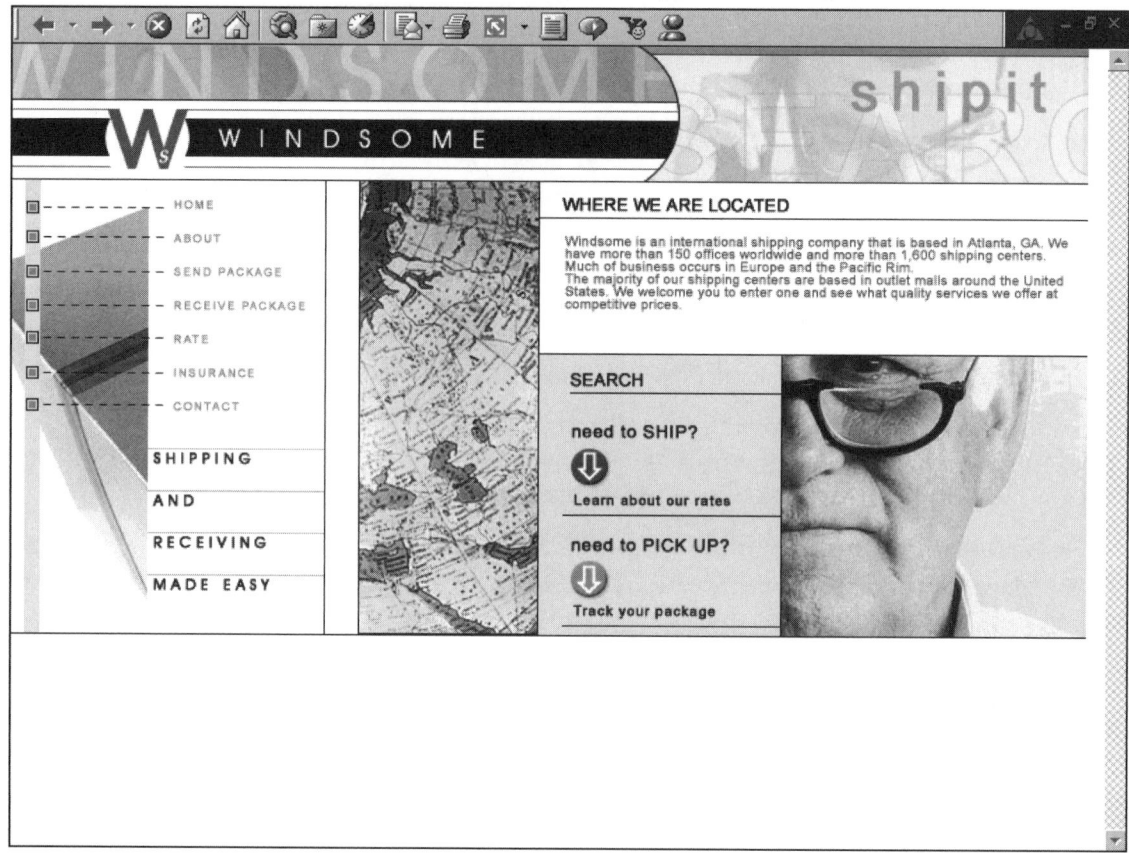

Figure 1.5
Site where the effort spent creating the design is apparent.
© 2014 Cengage Learning.

Figure 1.6
Ideogram that is more quickly processed by the brain than text.
© 2014 Cengage Learning.

3. **Graphics, along with color, help lead a person's eye.** Similar to using an image to help a user understand a concept quickly, graphics and colors can be used to help lead a user's eye to where the designer intended. This is useful when a designer has prioritized content that the user should see first. Although Figure 1.5 is printed in black/white, it uses colored buttons to catch the viewer's eye. The buttons are shortcuts to areas of the site that the two target audiences most likely come for: to ship or to pick up a shipment. The site in Figure 1.4 splits the site into two sides with no dominant color or images, leaving the user's eyes floating.

Designing for Accessibility

When designing for accessibility, a designer should not rely solely on color because some users might have color blindness, which will affect their perception of the site.

4. **Graphic technology can enhance functionality.** Immersive imagery (360-degree photos) is one example of technology that designers can use in certain instances to improve a user's experience and cognition. If a user were looking to spend $5,000 on a vacation to Mexico and wanted to view the rooms of hotels, would it be better to read about the rooms or look completely around them? If a picture is worth a thousand words, the entire page of Figure 1.4 would come up short when describing one room; the homepage, which stretches considerably farther than the figure depicts, has fewer than 900 words. It should be noted that in this example, immersive photos do require a longer download time. To make the site applicable to users with slow Internet connections, a designer should also provide traditional photographs as an alternative.

Multimedia Philosophy

On the other end of the design spectrum from the usability philosophy is the multimedia philosophy. Multimedia sites use animation, audio, and video to create more interactive sites, such as Figure 1.7, which changes the image with different breeds of dogs, while the site plays an upbeat tempo in the background. Many sites use vector-based graphics, which can be compressed smaller than bitmap images and generally resized without much degradation of the images, unlike bitmap images.

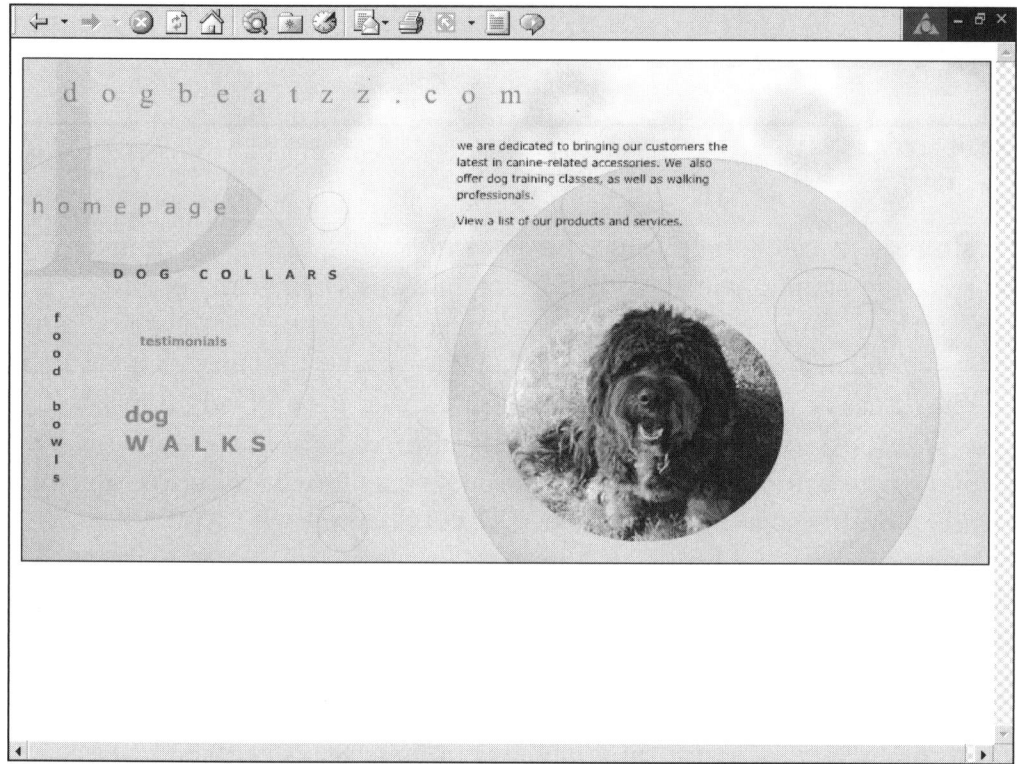

Figure 1.7
Site based on the multimedia philosophy.
© 2014 Cengage Learning.

Many of these multimedia sites are called Flash sites because they are created with Adobe's Flash animation software.

Pros and Cons

While many multimedia designers are still learning how to design effectively using this type of functionality, it is certainly an effective way to communicate via the Web. Some of the advantages of multimedia design include the following:

- Much of the technology is vector- and mathematics-based image technology, which allows for higher compression and the ability to resize images without much loss of image quality.

- It has a similar learning curve to XHTML and CSS. Most of the basic layout of simple content on a page can be easy to learn with programs like Flash; however, advanced capabilities of these programs can be a challenge.

- It communicates multidimensionally with graphics, animation, and audio.

Unfortunately, the technology for multimedia sites is not only a strength but also a weakness. Multimedia sites are still not practical for the majority of Internet users for several reasons:

- Browsers must have a plug-in for the user to view the graphics or site. While this isn't so much of an issue with PCs, many smart phones don't play Flash movies.

- Multimedia software still does not integrate with databases as easily as existing Web technology, such as .NET, PHP, and JavaServer Pages.

- Multimedia sites are usually more cost-prohibitive to the designer and to the client. In addition to graphics software, a designer needs animation and possibly audio-editing software to create a multimedia site, depending on the site's requirements. Because Flash sites generally aren't as easy to update as XHTML sites, it usually takes more time and costs more to do so.

- Many designers have yet to learn discretion when using the power of multimedia software. Although vector-based images compress well, the file sizes found on many multimedia sites are still considerably larger compared to traditional websites. This is because designers often use too much animation, graphics, and audio, which increases the download time of a page and which isn't always apparent when a user has broadband access. This goes back to Rule 1: Just because you can does not mean you should. The issue is not just with the download time of a page. It is also frustrating for users to go to a site where they have to see the same intro animation every time they visit. It should not be required to have to click past an intro to get into the site.

Mortised Philosophy

David Siegel, in his best-selling book *Creating Killer Web Sites* (Hayden Books, 1997), described *mortising* as piecing two images together using a table. Mortising, however, can be a much broader term, which represents the philosophy of piecing together graphics, text, and functionality, to build striking, graphically appealing sites that are fast, highly usable, and flexible.

Such sites bring together the best of both usability and multimedia worlds, combining them into professional designs that can be viewed by nearly all of today's Web users (see Figures 1.8 and 1.9). Mortising not only complements the functionality of a site, but it also enables designers to use techniques that the graphic design industry has spent decades perfecting without sacrificing download time.

Figure 1.8
Example of a mortised site.
Source: Onepartart.com.

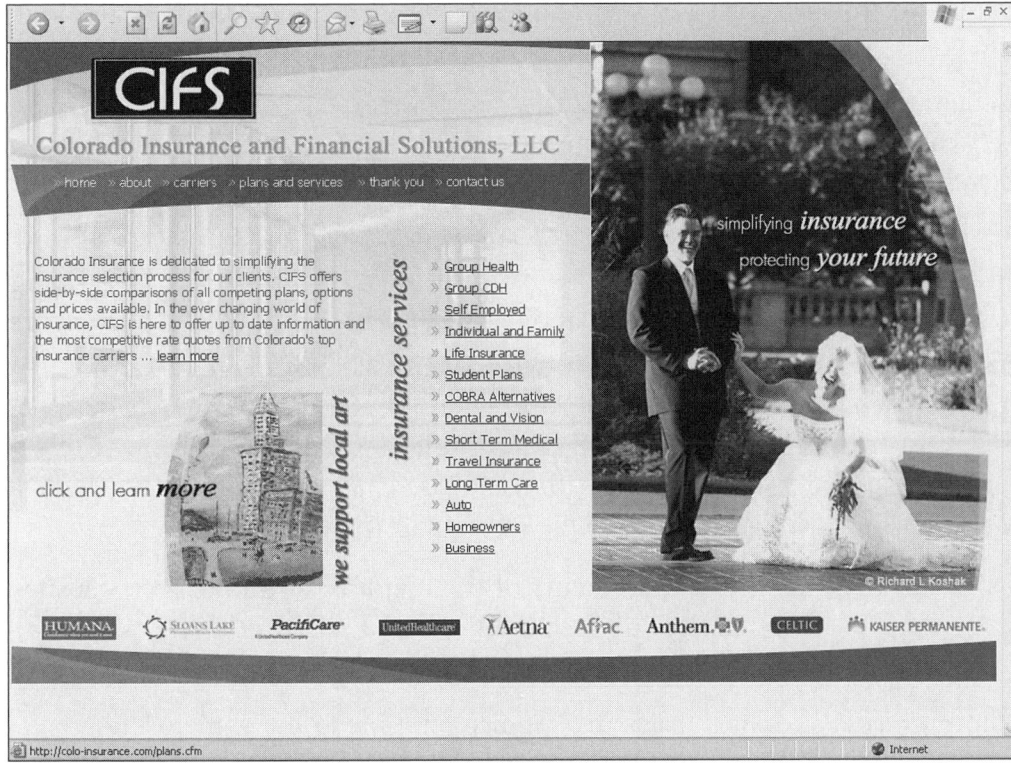

Figure 1.9
Site based on the mortised philosophy.

Source: colo-insurance.com.

Pros and Cons

While there is no "perfect" type of Web design, for many designers, mortised sites are the best current solution for communicating effectively to the largest possible audience on the Web. Following are some of the pros of this philosophy:

- Per Andre Agassi, "Image is everything." Mortised sites can be striking, fast, and highly usable, allowing clients to create powerful and lasting first impressions on their users.

- Because the designer can use more graphics and less text, the user can more quickly understand concepts, ideas, and emotions used in designs. The use of graphics also allows designers to take better advantage of traditional, time-tested graphic design aspects, including layout, color theory, and typography.

- Mortised sites not only work with static Web pages but also with dynamic database-driven sites. Because they use existing XHTML and CSS technology, such sites can be easily customized to work with Microsoft.NET, PHP technology, or Java technology, specifically JavaServer Pages.

- The learning curve to build such sites is extremely low for experienced Web designers because the technology is not new. Methods used in this book employ simple, creative, and practical ways to use XHTML and CSS in creative, useful ways.

- While they do not have to be, mortised sites can be easily designed to be scalable, database-driven sites. If a client or business wants to add three sections to a website, a well-designed mortised site can be easily expanded.

- Mortised sites are modular. This enables a designer to take advantage of various design options, such as Flash, in selected portions of a page. For example, a designer may not want to create an entire site in Flash but only want an advertisement of a new product in the center of the page. With a mortised site, adding such an element is easy when the site is designed with such flexibility in mind.

While mortised sites satisfy the site requirements of the majority of the world's websites, they are not the complete answer. They still face the same issues that usability and multi-media sites must contend with:

- Similar to multimedia sites, mortised sites require plug-ins to use some of their elements, such as animation and audio.

- Mortised sites are limited by the knowledge of the designer. A designer can create a similar-looking site in a WYSIWYG (What You See Is What You Get) editor, but such software is always going to limit the designer's full potential in one way or the other if he doesn't fully understand what goes on "under the hood."

Summary

There are seven rules of Web design that help a beginner develop into a professional designer: just because you *can* does not mean you *should;* there is almost always an exception; users are the ultimate judges; crossover experience is something a designer should always strive for; humility is the best approach; it is impossible to please everyone; and try to stay on top of specifications and standards. Each of these rules is applicable in certain instances when building a site.

The goal of a website is to communicate effectively to the largest audience possible. Any of these three design philosophies can be used to accomplish this goal: usability, multimedia, and mortised. Mortised sites typically offer the best of both worlds, which is why they are continually sought after by clients.

CHAPTER 2

DESIGNING FOR THE PAST, PRESENT, AND FUTURE

A common struggle for a Web designer is designing for the largest audience possible without sacrificing the desired graphical and functional aspects. Since the 1990s, and probably earlier, this struggle has been a common issue with designers; unfortunately, it will continue to be an issue as long as newer technology and design methods are constantly being introduced.

While a designer might want to take advantage of the latest technology, there should also be a concern that the audience will think usability implications were not taken into consideration if newer technology is employed that is not fully supported by all hardware and software. When designing for the past, present, and future, a professional should design for the needs of the site. When creating sites for the largest possible audience, the designer should become resolved to the fact that it is not always possible to use the latest technology in most cases. The designer must focus on making the best use of the most practical technology that is available. Fortunately, as the Web industry has progressed since the 1990s, it has become increasingly easy to build highly usable, fast, graphical sites with existing technology.

FEELING BROWSER PAIN

Since the 1990s, designers had to always worry about how various browsers, such as Netscape and Internet Explorer and then Internet Explorer and Firefox, would output pages. It was a constant battle to add and manipulate code to ensure the pages were consistent.

Figure 2.1 is a site in Firefox 1.5.0.6. Figure 2.2 is the same site in IE 6.0. Figure 2.2 shows how a bug in IE 6.0 drastically displays floated containers nested in floated containers. In other words, all the content in the right column is placed below that in the left column. As the content in the left column grows vertically, so will the content in the right column be dropped.

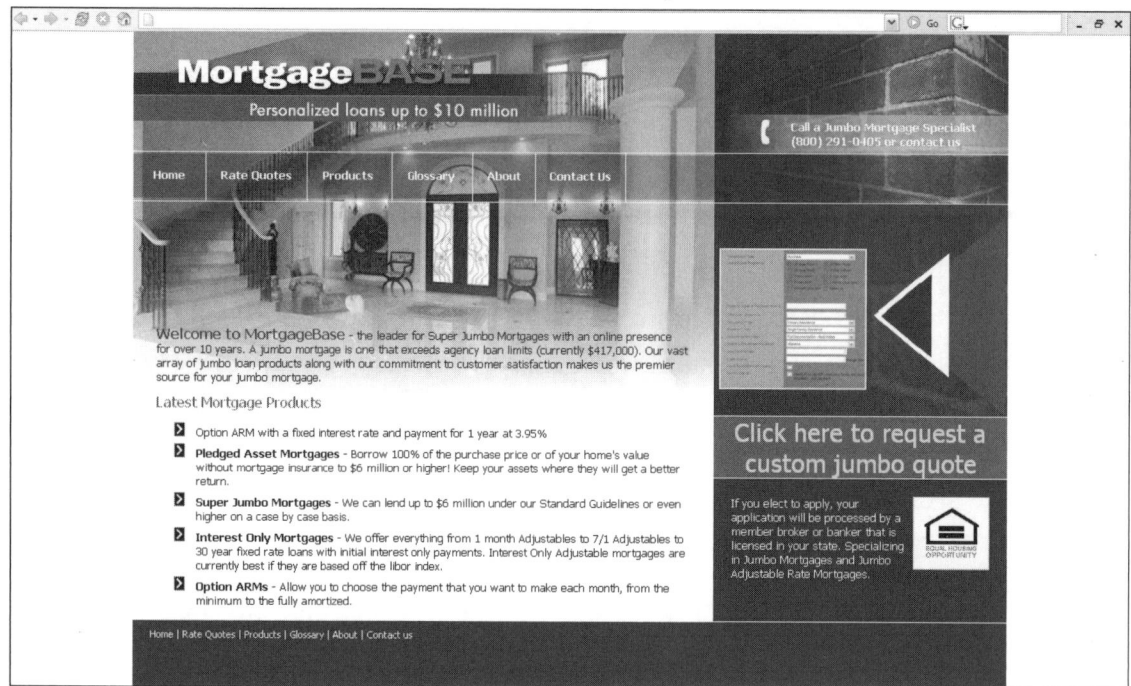

Figure 2.1
Site viewed in Firefox 1.5.0.6.
Source: mortgagebase.com.

While past issues, such as these, still exist as long as those versions of the browsers exist, the fact is that standards have now been employed among browsers to ensure they output code much more consistently. What used to involve hacks now only requires a slight tweaking of code, if issues ever appear.

Figure 2.2
Site viewed in IE 6.0.
Source: mortgagebase.com.

INCORPORATING USAGE STATISTICS

Because there is a growing discrepancy in the number of browser versions, as well as monitors with varying resolutions and bandwidth issues, the Web user with the most out-dated hardware and software continually lags behind. Therefore, it is nearly impossible to keep a user with the latest hardware and software satisfied while designing for those who might still be downloading sites with a dial-up modem, using IE 5.0, and viewing on a monitor with 800 × 600 resolution. This is why it is wise to base most Web design decisions on global usage statistics.

Global usage statistics give the designer useful information about the general population of Web users and allow the designer to create a site that will best suit as many users as possible. A designer can get usage statistics on browsers, versions of JavaScript used (if JavaScript is actually turned on), operating systems, and monitor resolution.

Basing a site's design on general usage statistics is always a smart way to begin a site design. Once the site is created, however, the designer can then also use statistics specific to that site. How this works on a Windows server, for example, is that a log file is collected every day. It collects data that includes everything from what browser the user was using to each individual page the user visited (see Figure 2.3).

Figure 2.3
Log file created on a Windows server.
© 2014 Cengage Learning.

After the log information has been saved, Web analysis software then analyzes and displays the data. One of the most commonly analyzed statistics is page visits. Figure 2.4 outputs such data from the log file in Figure 2.3.

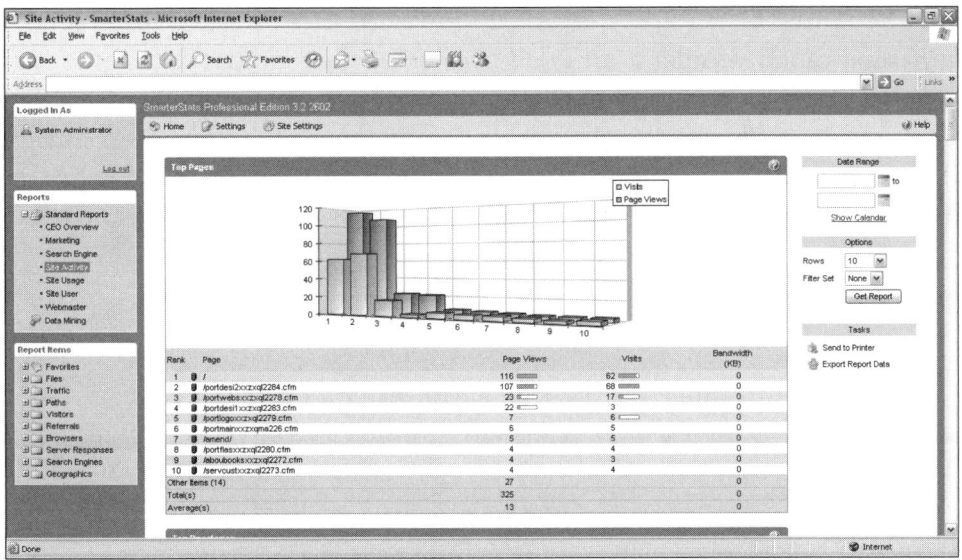

Figure 2.4
Page statistics captured for a website for one day.
© 2014 SmarterStats.

Another commonly used statistic is which search engines are hitting a site. This information allows the designer to track results and modify Search Engine Optimization efforts as needed (see Figure 2.5).

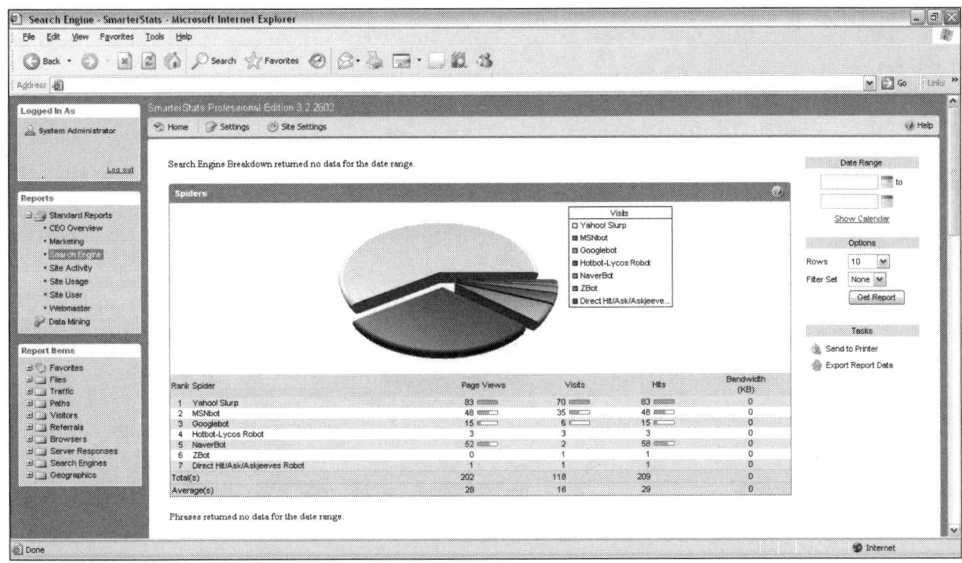

Figure 2.5
Search engine statistics for the image in Figure 2.3.
© 2014 SmarterStats.

The designer doesn't need to collect and analyze log files with software. Google Analytics allows for tracking with a much simpler method. The way it works is that a designer logs into the Google Analytics site, adds a site to the account, copies prepared lines of JavaScript code, and then adds the code to any page that is to be tracked. Google then collects and displays the data in the Analytics account. The software provides a lot of flexibility for the designer to then use the data to improve the site.

Branching Pages

The inconsistent support of XHTML, JavaScript, and CSS by IE and Netscape years ago made some developers resort to branching their code. In other words, once a user hits a page, a basic JavaScript code is used to determine a parameter, which then determines which code could be used for whichever condition.

In the past, prior to CSS-driven drop-down menus, branching was advantageous to use with JavaScript drop-down menus that only worked with Netscape's DOM (Document Object Model) or IE's DOM. These days, with so many varying resolutions, a good use of branching code can be to serve up varying design widths, depending on the resolution and if it's a mobile site.

Understanding Bandwidth

Bandwidth is the amount of data that is either uploaded or downloaded over a specified time. In other words, for designers, how quickly a site can be downloaded without losing the user. Studies over the years have shown that the number one complaint of users is that a site is too slow, which made speed a high priority when designing.

For someone who began designing in the 1990s, today's bandwidth standards are more than adequate when creating fast, striking sites. When the Internet first started becoming popular, the typical user usually had something comparable to a 9600bps (bits per second) modem.

As years passed, 14.4Kbps (kilobits per second) modems appeared and then the 28.8Kbps modems and 56Kbps modems arrived. Today, while there are still people using 14.4Kbps, 28.8Kbps, and 56Kbps modems, the majority of users have high-bandwidth connections, such as DSL or cable.

Because broadband is so prevalent today, designing sites with small downloads is not as important as it used to be, so the designer doesn't need to be quite as concerned about how quickly a site downloads. Even the download speeds of smart phones are faster. Still, perfection is always a great goal. And when seeking perfection, the designer should try to build sites that download as quickly as possible.

What is a large page download for a site? Some designers like to determine the speed of a site by the time it takes to download. The problem with this type of measurement is that it is relative. The same site that might take 10 seconds to load on a laptop might take 30 seconds to load on a smart phone, depending on the user's Internet connection, the total usage of the Internet at that time, or the usage of the site's server(s) at that time, among other factors.

A more comparable method of determining the speed of a site is by the weight of a page (the amount of kilobytes). The previous standard was to keep the site under 35KB. With the growth of CSS-based sites and Flash, this standard has grown considerably to where a 500KB site is not unreasonable. These sizes include CSS, graphics, possible multimedia components, and the output XHTML. (Output XHTML is the eventual XHTML a database-driven site returns to the browser. The actual page on the server with all the programming code will generally be larger.)

Some designers believe it is impossible to build graphical sites and keep them fast. This is simply not true. Many of the sites that require a large download are designed incorrectly. One way to design a site correctly for a small download is to compress its images properly. Take, for example, Figures 2.6 and 2.7. Figure 2.6 was taken with a digital camera using no compression. Figure 2.7 is the same image after being compressed. When resized to 250 × 214 pixels, it is possible to compress it more than 66 percent from its original 76.0KB to 14.5KB with very little visible difference.

Once a designer knows the tricks of keeping a site download small, it is important to keep the goal in mind when designing a site. Whenever designing, it is a good practice for a designer to keep the download calculator going in her head and constantly keep track of how big the site will eventually be. Once the goal of, say, 200KB is met, the designer should stop to make sure that all necessary content has been added. If it has not, the designer should try to take away or reduce in size a design element to make up for the additional download size of the required content.

Figure 2.6
Uncompressed JPG photo that is 76KB.
© 2014 Cengage Learning.

Figure 2.7
Compressed JPG photo that is 14.5KB.
© 2014 Cengage Learning.

BUILDING ON PREVIOUS DESIGN WEAKNESSES

A designer should continually strive toward making sites technically and aesthetically superior to previous designs—a goal that sounds like common sense, but, surprisingly, isn't always followed. Looking at Figure 2.8, it is fairly easy to find room for improvement—the color choice is too simple, the presentation of the artwork could be improved, and the layout does not make good use of space.

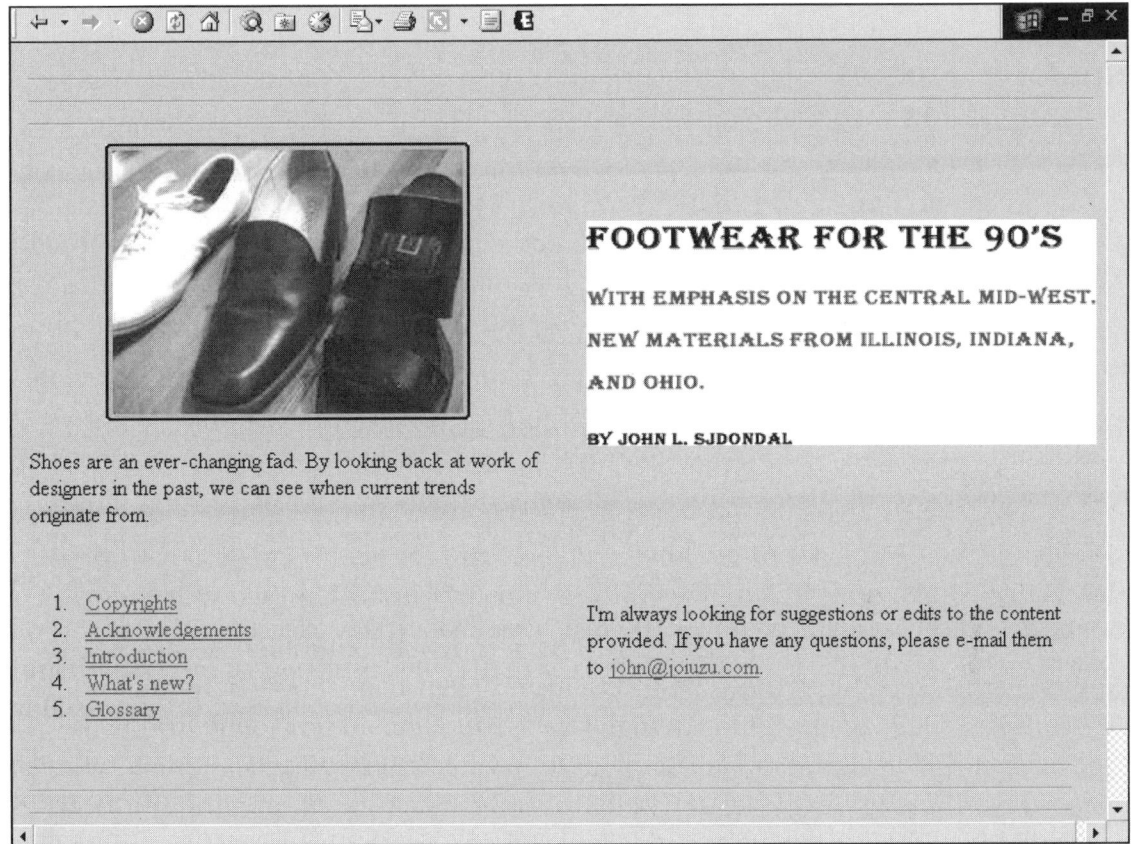

Figure 2.8
Site that could be designed to appear more professional.
© 2014 Cengage Learning.

When this book was first written, it was a naive assumption that design would get better over the years. This, however, is most definitely not the case. The standard of design is based more on each individual designer, rather than the collective consciousness. This is good news for the talented, discerning designer. Not only are there millions of sites that need to be redesigned, but as more businesses and individuals decide to put up new sites, there are also more opportunities to create sites that communicate more effectively.

Building more effective sites involves improving on past design weaknesses. The first step in accomplishing this is to understand and avoid such weaknesses. Following are some examples a designer should try to avoid.

IFrames and Frames

Multi-framed sites, for the most part, have gone the way of the dinosaur. IFrames, however, can still be beneficial to a designer. An IFrame is an individual frame that can be placed anywhere in a page, controlling how long a page could be. In other words, the designer can output a large amount of data, such as 150 countries with associated data for each, within 500 pixels of vertical space, without requiring the user to scroll down the screen many pages if the same data were output in a nonframed environment.

As for frames, although they are almost entirely extinct, clients may still occasionally ask about or request IFrames. Here are several reasons a designer could give a client as to why traditional framed sites should not be used:

1. Allowing a user to bookmark a site is impossible unless JavaScript is used. The problem is that when a user bookmarks a page, only one frame is bookmarked (usually, it is the last frame that was clicked in), rather than all the frames. As mentioned previously, this can be a benefit in some circumstances.

2. Targeting frames and passing programming variables is considerably more complicated than when using include files (that is, SSI, or Server Side include files).

3. Increasing the number of scrollbars decreases the amount of space a designer has to work with (see Figure 2.9).

4. Search engines do not like frames. Therefore the site will suffer in search-engine rankings, if it's ranked at all.

For the most part, to even discuss framed sites is a moot point. Still, excess knowledge only helps a designer.

Figure 2.9
Site that uses an IFrame to control how much space a large amount of data takes up.
Source: ACT Conferencing.

Image Buttons

Creating menu items as images, rather than text, can be attractive because the designer can use any desired font since the browser doesn't have to render it. However, simply for the advantage of a mouseover image, image buttons are not necessary or practical for four reasons:

1. **Download time:** A designer can drastically increase the download time of a site when using mouseover images as menu items, because the user has to download the images for both the On and Off states. In Figure 2.10, for example, the user has to download the eight images in the Off state and the eight images in the On state, which is shown in Figure 2.11.

   The entire download size of the images for the menu in Figure 2.10 is 20KB. This is already nearly half of the goal for the entire homepage, which is 50KB. Granted, while limiting download time is not nearly as crucial these days, unless the designer preloads the buttons in their On state, see Figure 2.11, they will still most likely show a delay, no matter the download speed.

2. **Maintenance:** Creating, editing, and adding such buttons to a site is time-consuming.

3. **Dynamic functionality:** The advantage of database-driven sites is their ability to create pages on the fly and allow menus to be created dynamically as well. When a designer creates menu items as static images, it defeats the purpose of being able to create such items dynamically.

4. **Search engines:** When text is saved as an image, search engines don't read it, although they can read the Alt tags. It's wise to make your site as search-engine friendly as possible.

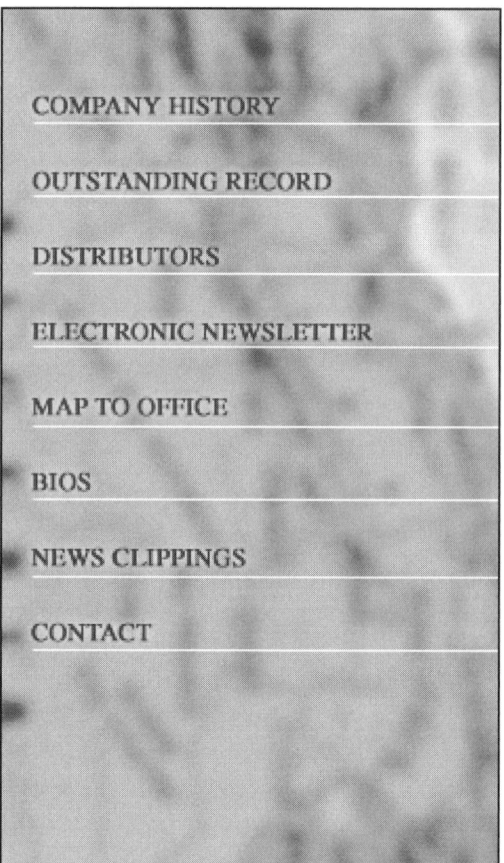

Figure 2.10
Menu items saved as images in the Off state.
© 2014 Cengage Learning.

Figure 2.11
Menu items saved as images in the On state (a white glow around the text).
© 2014 Cengage Learning.

Text-Driven CSS Menu Items

CSS menus can use background images in menu items. Using such a method also enables the designer to lay text over the image, allowing for more flexibility. Such usage of background images is incorporated in many designs included with this book.

Background Images

Background images can enhance a website to give it mood and depth. While the use of background images has changed slightly over the years, the concepts are fairly similar. There are several uses of background images that the designer can be creative with. The first of which is using a background image to serve as the majority or entire backdrop of a website while layering the HTML and graphics on top of it. While this wasn't advisable in the past, it now is much more acceptable with increased bandwidth and CSS-driven layouts, which require less download time. Figure 2.12 illustrates a site that uses one image to serve as the entire background.

Figure 2.13 is the background image that was used.

Another creative use of background images is giving the impression that a design has colors running down both sides of it indefinitely. Although this used to be an easy process with XHTML table sites, it now takes a little extra coding to accomplish the same result. Such a technique is explained in Chapter 12; however, Figure 2.14 illustrates the concept.

A third use of background images, as mentioned in the previous section, is using the images for menus. Using CSS, a designer can use an image for, say, a menu item, while not having to include the text with the image itself. In other words, the text is layered over the image. Figure 2.15 shows a site that does just that.

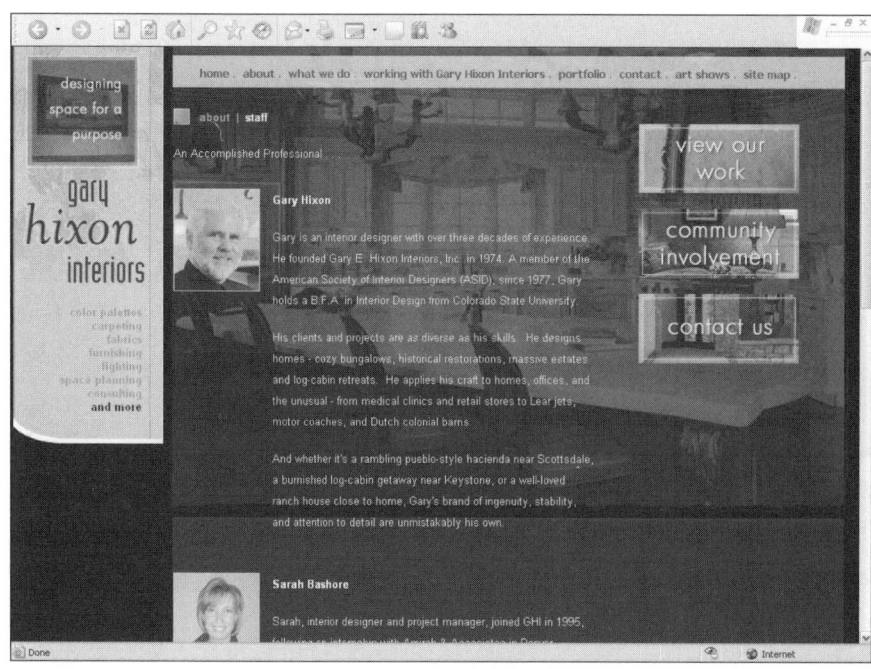

Figure 2.12
Site that uses a large image for its background.
Source: Gary Hixon Interiors.

Figure 2.13
Image that was used for the entire background of the site in Figure 2.12.
Source: Gary Hixon Interiors.

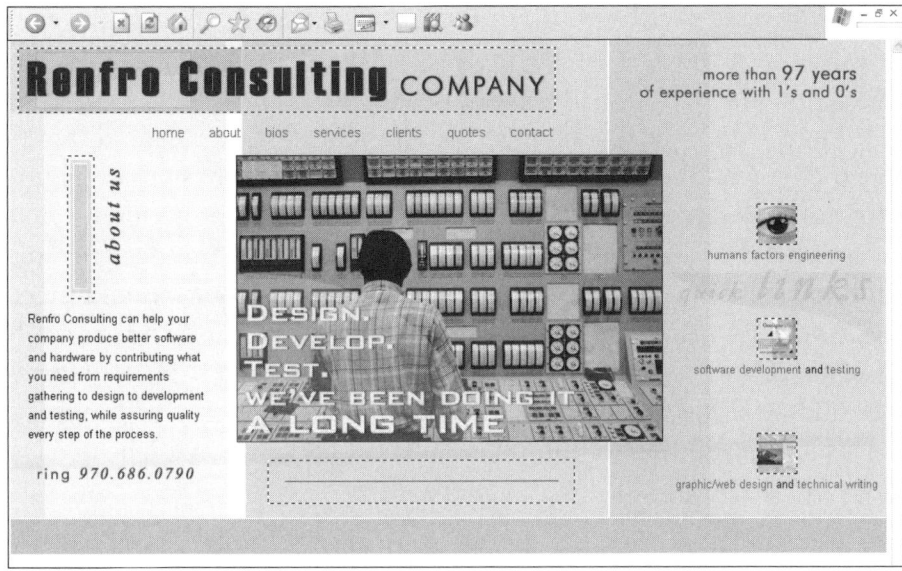

Figure 2.14
Site that uses background images to run colors down both sides of a design indefinitely, similar to how XHTML table designs work.

Source: renfroconsulting.com.

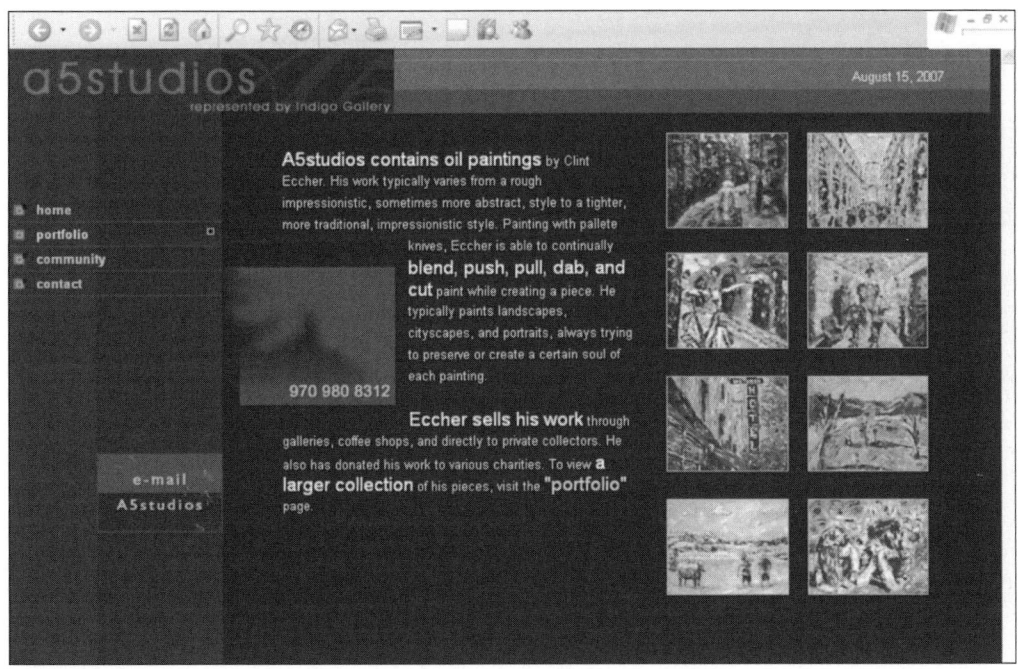

Figure 2.15
Background images that are used in a menu to show Over and Off states.

Source: a5studios.com.

Although many clients don't always like the width of their sites changing because the content shifts around, a background image can be used to easily expand the look and feel. The designer has to be careful to make sure that the background image is designed correctly for higher resolutions, though. Some designers even use branching code to use different versions of the background, depending on the resolution. While the design in Figure 2.16 doesn't expand horizontally, the background image does repeat horizontally at a higher resolution. Unfortunately, it does not look professional because the designer did not limit the background image from repeating. One instance that designers should probably stay away from is using a repeating background image endlessly, both horizontally and vertically. While it can work in certain situations, for the most part, it is amateurish looking. This is probably because it was so easy to do—since the dawning of graphical Web browsers, millions of sites used the technique, similar to glowing text. These days, sites similar to Figures 2.17 and 2.18 aren't designed very often.

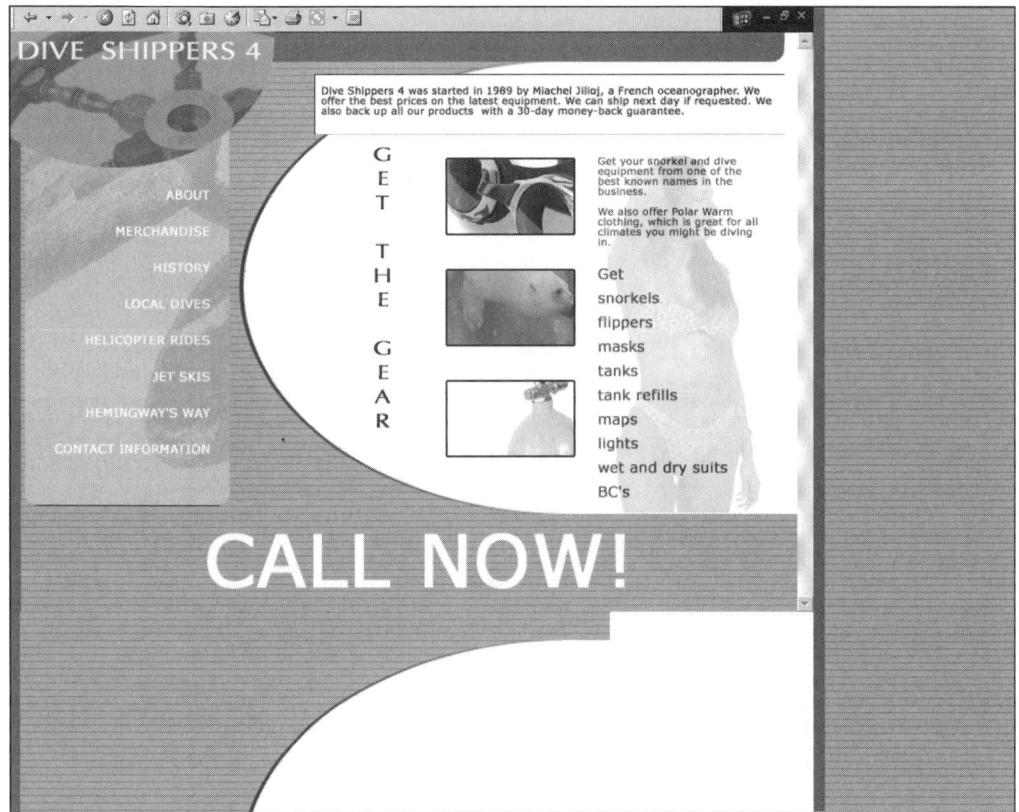

Figure 2.16
Page repeating an awkward-looking background image in a resolution higher than the design was created for.
© 2014 Cengage Learning.

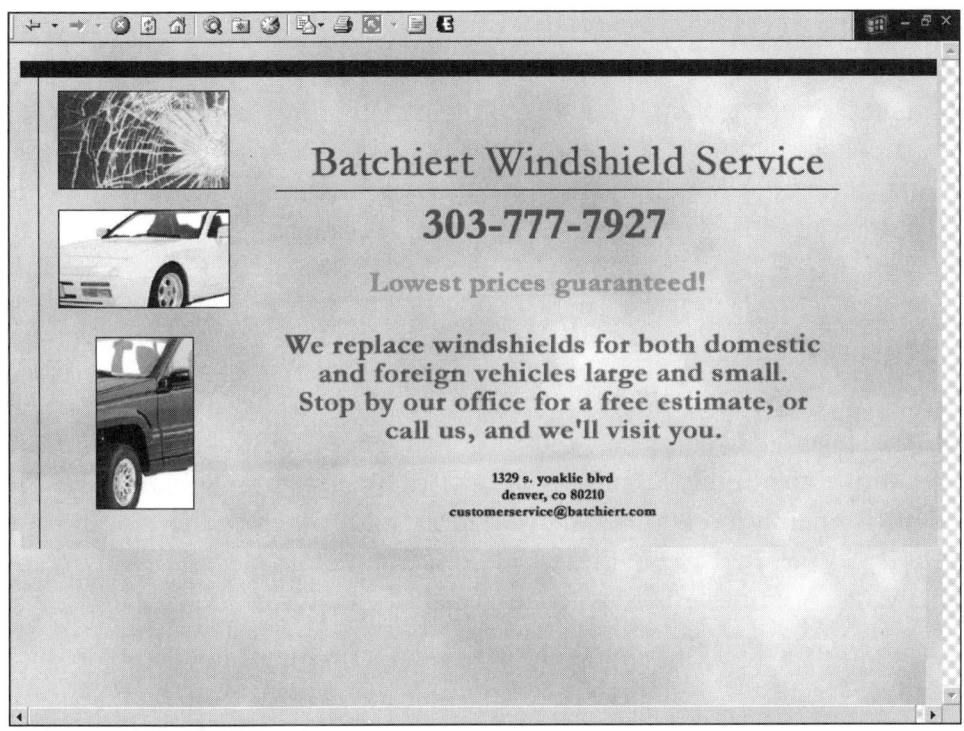

Figure 2.17
Site that infinitely repeats the background image of a cloud both horizontally and vertically.
© 2014 Cengage Learning.

Figure 2.18
Background image that is repeated in Figure 2.17.
© 2014 Cengage Learning.

Uncontrolled Color

Color can make or break a website. Not only should the colors be appropriate and appealing to the target audience, but they should also be used with intention and discretion. One of the strengths of using color is that a designer can help lead the user's eye. If a designer, on the other hand, uses too many colors, the user can quickly become confused as to what the most important information is. The user then has to start reading all the hyperlinks to find the desired content.

Uncompressed Images

Even with broadband, uncompressed images can still bog down a download. There are still designers who employ full-size images, but simply reduce their size on a website with the height and width attributes. Figure 2.19 shows a website that initially had the download size of 790KB, mainly because of the horizontal photo across the top and the image in the bottom left. With just two minutes of work, the designer could easily compress both those images to fit under 50KB, with no visual degradation.

In the early 1990s, the closest a designer could come to compressing an image was reducing the bit depth (2, 4, 8, 16, 32, 64, 128, or 256 colors) of a GIF or reducing the JPG compression percentage in increments of 10. Today, because of the vast improvement in graphics software, GIFs, for the most part, have been replaced with PNGs, which can be compressed one color at a time. And JPGs can even be compressed one percentage point at a time. With the power and ease of image-editing software, there is no reason for a designer not to drastically compress all images of a site.

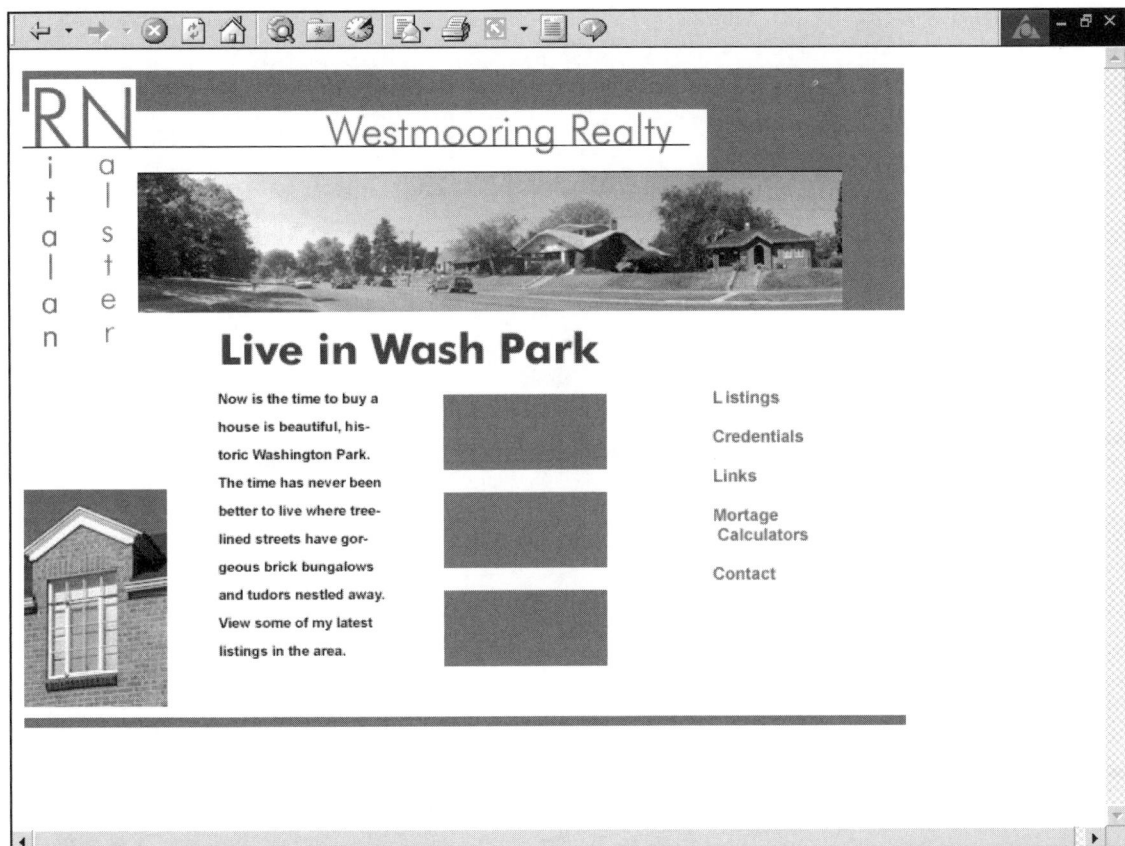

Figure 2.19
Site that does not use compressed images.
© 2014 Cengage Learning.

Thumbnails

A thumbnail is a smaller version of an image, which allows the user to preview the larger version without having to actually download the image until it is clicked. A mistake that beginning Web designers tend to make at least once is in resizing images to appear as thumbnail images. Figure 2.20 illustrates a Web page that includes many thumbnails of larger photos.

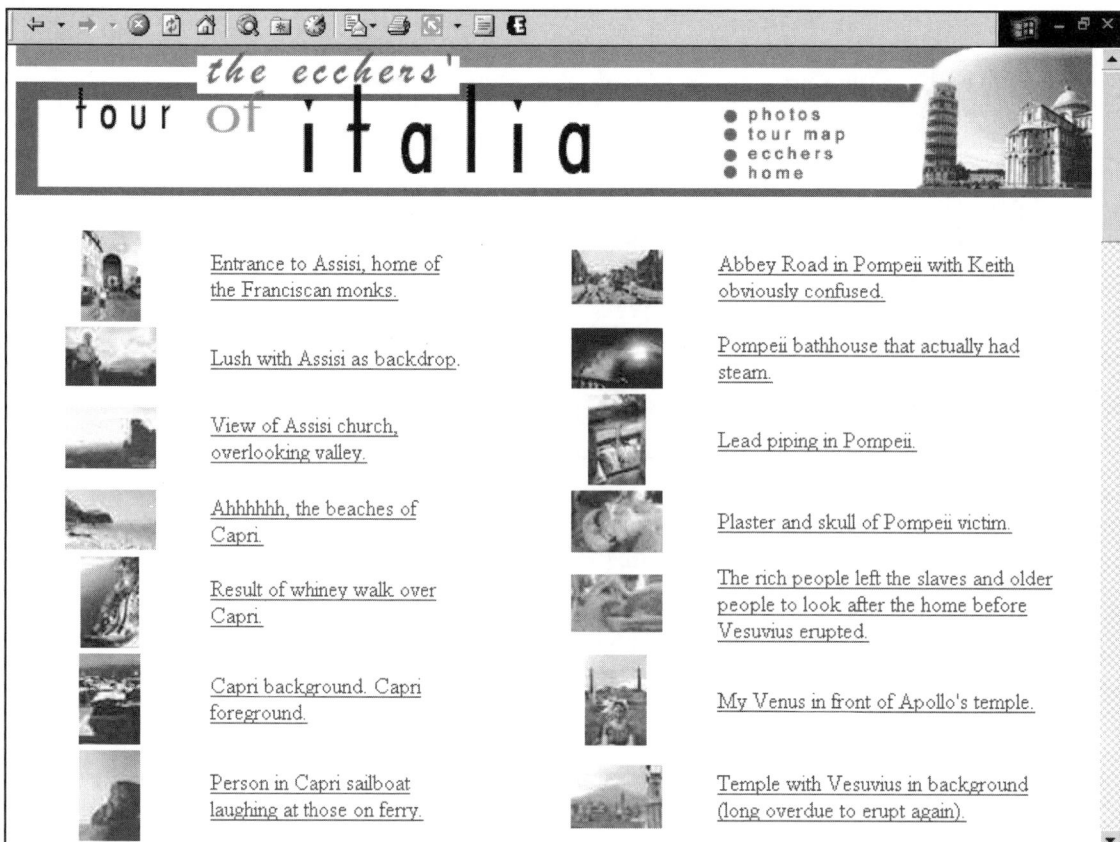

Figure 2.20
Site that makes use of thumbnail images.
© 2014 Cengage Learning.

When the user clicks a thumbnail, an enlarged copy of the image is displayed (see Figure 2.21).

When a designer places an image in HTML, the height and width attributes can be changed to tell the browser to resize the viewable size of the image. For example, the designer could tell the browser to display an image from 500 × 500 pixels to 20 × 20 pixels.

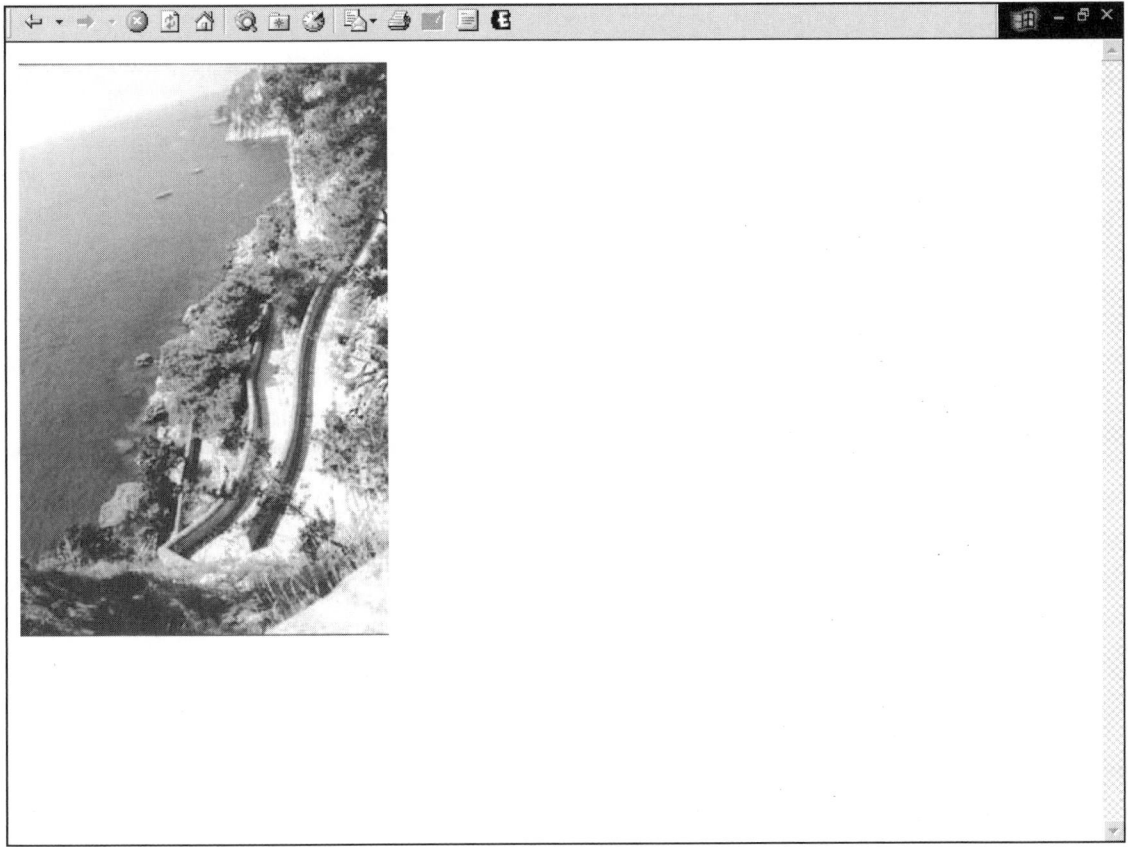

Figure 2.21
Larger version of a thumbnail image.
© 2014 Clint Eccher.

While it is possible to tell the browser to forcibly change the visual size of the image, it does not change the download size of the image. In other words, if the 500 × 500 image is 1000KB, it will remain 100KB when displayed at 20 × 20. If all 14 photos in Figure 2.20 were 1000KB, the download of the entire page would be nearly 1.4MB when it only needed to be 280KB if each image were compressed to be 20KB.

To create thumbnails correctly, a designer needs to make two images: the original photo and then the original photo resized smaller. While it is more work, the user will appreciate the increased speed of the download.

SUMMARY

Designers have been dealing with browser issues since the 1990s. While there are still some issues, they are comparatively minor and can be rectified fairly easily. A designer can and should determine design requirements based on usage statistics that not only provide browser information but also give information to monitor color depth, resolution, and JavaScript support, among other issues.

It is always smart to learn from the past. There are several mistakes that designers have made over the years that today's designers can learn from and improve on, such as frames, image buttons, background images, uncontrolled color, uncompressed images, and thumbnails.

CHAPTER 3

THINGS TO CONSIDER BEFORE BEGINNING

Working in a logical, practical manner is one of the keys to becoming a professional Web designer. It is particularly important to be logical and practical when working on the technical aspects of a site, such as collecting requirements, taking the client's concerns into mind, and designing for scalability and flexibility. While contemplating the design in depth beforehand requires more initial time and forethought, doing so can save many hours, if not days, addressing future problems.

USING REQUIREMENTS

Site requirements can best be compared to a recipe that tells a designer what needs to be included in the site, the steps required to complete each task, plus additional information, such as how to present the site and the types of people it will serve. Although every designer's or company's requirements might be different, they all share a common goal—an agreed-upon document that helps serve as a road map, as best as possible, to the completed site.

When constructing a site, some of the most important information a designer needs to document includes the following:

- **Look and feel requirements:** These include content placement, how the site conveys the company's message, the color palette, and fonts and image concepts to be presented.
- **Bandwidth requirements:** The way a site is designed will determine how large of a download the site will require. By understanding the bandwidth (download size) requirements, a designer can determine how many graphics to use.

- **Resolution requirements:** A site with improper resolution can hinder its usability or credibility.

- **Scalability requirements:** Because nearly all sites are in continual evolution, it is important for the designer to consider how the site can be expanded or changed in the future.

- **Content requirements:** The content volume of a site will influence nearly all other requirements, including the look and feel, the bandwidth, resolution, and scalability.

Depending on the size of a website, different levels of documentation are necessary. Many small sites (around 5 to 15 pages) only require the designer and client to email or call each other during the development process. Larger sites (more than 15 pages) often require more thorough documentation, which includes an official requirements document. Without such documentation, the designer could have a site nearly completed when the client says, "Oh, that's not what I meant. You actually need to do it this way." At that point, changes are not only time-consuming and painful, but the designer is left in the awkward position of whether to make the corrections pro bono or charge the client an additional fee. This mode of edits continually coming in with no foreseeable end is referred to as *scope creep*.

Because of documentation time, site requirements might increase the cost of the site. However, while initially taking more time and money, requirements can save considerable expense when the designer has everything planned prior to development.

Take, for example, a 20-field form. Without requirements, the form might start out at 20 fields. The client, though, after seeing the first draft, says, "Oh, I forgot a few items we need to add." They probably do not know that this involves making changes to not only the form, but also to the database and additional server-side scripted pages that complete the functionality. And that is just the first draft. The client might then run the form by a peer or boss who will have additional changes that the designer will have to incorporate. Before long, the same form could include 35 fields.

This may seem like a small-scale issue. However, it can become quite problematic, resulting in larger-scale meltdowns, such as major design problems. The designer might create a site with a horizontal navigation menu at the top. Then the client comes back with five additional sections to add to the site after weeks or months of development. What then? The initial solution would be to add the items to the menu. What if the menu already takes up the full width of the screen? One possibility would be to add another row of menu items. But this might look awkward or impede the usability of the site, or the design simply might not support a vertical stretch of the header area. Taking a very long step backward, the designer then realizes that the lacking requirements have drastically changed the scope of the project. A lot of the site is now going to need to be redesigned.

Collecting the Requirements

Requirements lacking detail can be just as detrimental as not having requirements at all. There are many different areas that should be addressed when documenting requirements. While many answers to questions are collected to help in the marketing and back-end (programming) development of the site, many can also be used by a designer to ensure that the design best supports current and future demands. Getting a feel for the areas that need to be addressed comes with experience; however, here is a minimal list of areas that will probably need to be documented. An in-depth requirements document should probably cover the following areas:

- **Site/client name:** Not all sites have the same name as the company they are designed for. Therefore, this is important to know before beginning a design.

- **Prepared by:** It is always helpful for your client to know who prepared the document and how to get in touch with that person.

- **Date:** While it might seem obvious, knowing the date helps the designer write future summary reports and track site-design efficiency.

- **Client contact(s):** The more contacts the better. A designer can never have too many people to call when various questions arise during development, although it is suggested that there be one final decision maker.

- **Version:** While the version of the requirements document should also be covered with the naming convention of the document (for example, requirements_v3.doc), it is also wise to include it in the document itself. Sometimes, the version number will remind the designer to save the current document as a new document.

- **Executive summary:** This summary gives the designer and design team the gist of the site. Half the battle of designing a site is getting "the big picture." An executive summary helps make more sense of the specifics.

- **Assumptions:** Many times the designer and client do not share the same assumptions. For example, the designer might not know that an intranet site also needs to serve as an extranet site, which could change the technical requirements. The fewer the presumptions, the more effective and efficient the development will be.

- **Dependencies:** While not all sites have dependencies, it is important to know if any exist. An example of one possible dependency could be if the site must rely on another company or site for live content, such as an RSS (Really Simple Syndication) feed.

- **Objectives:** It is easy for a designer to lose focus when getting into a project. Being able to revisit the objectives of a site can be helpful in regaining and clarifying that focus.

- **Action items:** Action items provide more detailed information on what specific steps need to be taken to accomplish various tasks.

- **Detailed requirements (includes front-end questions, functional requirements, and a site map/flowchart):** These are the heart of a requirements document, at least for a designer. They give the specific details on design, content, and functionality that a designer needs to include when creating the site. An example of such a requirement might read, "Include login form area on the homepage that includes the User ID and Password fields, along with a Submit button."

- **Proposed solution(s):** Talking about and documenting solutions are two different things. While the client may think one thing after a phone conversation, the solution actually written out may present another picture. Such documentation helps to prevent misunderstandings.

- **Possible future site considerations:** Because sites are in continual evolution, it is important to create a scalable design that can handle future additions. In other words, the client may say, "We need only 15 pages for this phase; however, the design will need to accommodate another 20 pages in phase 2."

- **Sign-off section:** Signing off on a document provides closure for the client and assurance for the designer, signifying that both sides are in agreement on the road map of a site.

Front-end requirements and flowcharts are usually more beneficial when designing comps for a site. It is from these two documents that a designer bases the design, site architecture, and navigation.

When collecting requirements, there are three rules a designer would be wise to follow:

- **Document everything:** One of the best methods for documenting things is for the designer to Cc or Bcc himself or herself on all emails. It is surprising how many of these emails are eventually referenced again.

- **Save each document as a different version:** Not only is it wise to back up all files in case of a hard-drive failure, but it is also smart to back up all files in case of human failure. Whether human failure means accidentally deleting a file or clarifying a point of confusion by going back to previous versions of a document, it is wise to save all files, whether graphics or text, as new versions. The first round of writing requirements, for instance, could possibly be saved as requirements_v1.doc, with the "v1" representing "version 1." When that document is revised, it should then be saved as requirements_v2.doc for version 2. It is just as important to save versions of graphics files. Many times a client will request changes, realize they do not work well, and then come back and say, "Well, I think we liked the first version better." At that point, it is much easier to open the original version of the file than to have to re-create it.

- **Receive a sign-off on the requirements before beginning work:** Until a designer receives the sign-off to begin work, whether it will be with an email or a deposit check, nothing is set in stone. One minute a client may say, "Yes, that is exactly what we want," and the next time the response may be, "Well, we just met, and we have some more changes we want to add before you start." At that point, precious time has not been spent working on a *comp* (or composite) that will need to satisfy completely different requirements.

A Photoshop Comp

A comp, as described in this book, is a graphics file that shows what the homepage will look like in terms of layout, color, images, text, functionality, and typography. Comps are generally created and edited in Adobe Photoshop (as PSD files) before eventually being broken up into XHTML, graphics, and CSS.

Obtaining Front-End Requirements

If the designer does not have the time or resources to collect in-depth requirements, a shorter version of a requirements document can be used to collect information. Such a document should provide the designer with enough information to enable him to create a design that supports the look and feel, architecture, and future possibilities of a site. Here are 13 questions a designer should try to have answered before beginning a site's comp:

1. Who is the audience, and what is the purpose of the site?

2. What is the feeling you want to convey to your audience with your website?

3. Will the site need to be expandable, in terms of sections, in the future?

4. What browser platform and resolution (for example, Chrome/Firefox or 1024 × 768 or higher) do you require?

5. How many levels, or "clicks," can the deepest information be?

6. What is the most important information that should be put on the homepage?

7. When can text and graphics (logo) samples be supplied for designing the comp?

8. Do the images and colors on the site need to be consistent with any existing branding?

9. Does it matter if the site scrolls vertically?

10. What kind of functionality (for example, forms, dynamic text, or multimedia elements) does your site need to have?

11. What is the desired download size of the homepage?

12. Does your company have a tagline?

13. What is the proposed deadline(s)?

The designer can send the document to the client to fill out or fill out the document himself over initial meetings, phone calls, or emails. Usually, having the designer fill out the document is the best choice simply because the client may not have enough design experience or savvy to answer all the questions. Once completed, the designer should reiterate and confirm the answers, as well as receive a sign-off before beginning the site's comp.

Creating a Flowchart

Smaller sites do not necessarily require a flowchart simply because it is not difficult to visualize a site with About Us, Services, Products, Testimonials, and Contact sections. Larger sites, especially application sites with 10 or more pages, are considerably easier to create when the designer has a flowchart. Not only is it easier to visualize the site, but it also saves a lot of time clarifying questions.

Figure 3.1 illustrates the possible complexity of an application site. When initially looking at the site, the user would see only six items on the menu, including a link back to the homepage. Surfing through the site, though, it quickly becomes apparent that the site contains more than 30 different pages.

Microsoft Visio

The flowchart in Figure 3.1 was created using Microsoft Visio. While flowcharts can be created in other programs, such as Microsoft PowerPoint, Visio contains functionality that not only easily creates but also easily edits documents. With Visio, a designer could select all the items under the Client Info section on the left, move them wherever desired, and have all the flow lines move with the boxes while automatically skipping over other stationary flow lines. This can save innumerable hours when working with a client that continually makes changes.

Figure 3.1
Flowchart showing a site that contains more than 30 different pages.

© 2014 Cengage Learning.

Another advantage to creating a flowchart is that it can be used to create a site map by taking out workflow lines, explanations, and back-end items. While it may not be necessary to include all sections in a sitemap, doing so only helps to increase the site usability.

Knowing Bandwidth Requirements

The amount of bandwidth a user can download determines how many graphical elements should be incorporated into a design. If the anticipated audience's bandwidth limitations are strict, the homepage design may possibly have to fit under 30–100KB. On the other hand, if the bandwidth limitations are liberal, the limit for the homepage design could be anywhere from 100KB to 1,000KB or even higher. As previously mentioned, user bandwidth is a relative term. No matter what the supposed connection speed is, many factors influence what that bandwidth really is. Some of those factors include the following:

- **How many users are concurrently hitting the same site?** The media used to occasionally report on sites going down because the sites' servers were not equipped to handle so many immediate users. While the problem of a server going down is an extreme example, a server does not need to go completely down to have its download speed compromised.

- **What is the overall usage of the Internet?** Whether it is a dial-up modem, DSL, or cable access, every user can fall victim to slow downloads as a result of a bogged down Internet. One hour the Internet could be pumping the bits like wildfire, and the next it could be spitting bits one at a time. A common example of slowing down of data transfer is when, during the school year and around 3 p.m. to 4 p.m., kids get home from school and log on to the Internet en masse.

- **What is the condition of the phone line coming into the computer?** A phone line can also slow down an Internet connection. A user could have a 56K modem but only receive 36K service because of the incoming line. Distance also can play into this problem, and DSL technology is limited to a certain distance it can pump bits. Generally speaking, this is a moot issue. However, there are still instances where a phone line can be an issue for people living in rural areas, whether in the U.S. or other countries.

Understanding various factors that affect the data transfer of a site is why it does not make sense to design a site totally on the basis of the actual time it takes to download. There are too many factors that may change the download time from minute to minute. It is better to build sites that meet a goal of so many kilobytes. This number includes everything—the Web page(s) used to build the homepage, the homepage itself, and the graphics used.

There are three general instances when a larger site might be designed without any band-width issues:

- **Intranet versus Internet site:** Intranet sites, which are internal business networks, usually offer a considerably higher bandwidth than the external Internet, which is subject to many more variables.

- **Corporate versus a more general audience:** Sometimes, a more advanced corporation, such as Cisco, will have an audience with higher bandwidth capability than a site designed for a more general audience, such as a mom-and-pop shop that sells homemade gift baskets.

- **High-bandwidth functionality versus purely content-driven:** Often, the purpose of a site also allows for a higher bandwidth flexibility. For instance, an online music store is going to have users with higher bandwidth than a site that is designed to offer pure text content.

DECIDING ON RESOLUTION

One of the biggest considerations with Web design is designing for resolution. Websites are designed for a certain monitor resolution. Monitors, however, have varying resolutions that are set independently of the site.

If the user's monitor resolution does not match the resolution the site was designed for, the site will appear differently than was originally intended. In other words, the way a monitor resizes a screen is similar to that of a television set. Whether a monitor screen size is 17 inches or 30 inches, the content will be dynamically resized to fill the entire screen the same way, at least horizontally. However, the problem is that computer moni-tors, unlike television sets, allow the user different resolutions. If the resolution of a moni-tor, for example, is set at 800×640 pixels, a site that is designed for 1024×768 resolution will appear too wide. If the resolution of the monitor is 1024×768, the same site will appear either too narrow and short, or it will be stretched horizontally.

Figures 3.2, 3.3, and 3.4 show how A5design's site, which was designed for 1024×768 resolution, appears on monitor resolutions of 800×600, 1024×768, and 1280×800, respectively.

The Web design industry for years designed sites for 640 × 480 resolution. Then around 1999, more sites began to be designed for 800 × 600 resolution. Since 2006, most sites have been designed for 1024 × 768 resolution.

It is difficult to say when or if another major expansion will occur. Most likely, it will take longer to reach that level because more and more baby boomers, who make up a growing segment of the Internet, are tired of not being able to read smaller text, which is usually a result of higher-resolution monitors. Although there are work-arounds, people, by nature, don't like change. This is only theory, though. Many times it's difficult to truly know how standards will evolve.

Figure 3.2
Site at 800 × 600 resolution.
Source: a5design.com.

Figure 3.3
Site at 1024 × 768 resolution.

Source: a5design.com.

Figure 3.4
Site at 1280 × 800 resolution.

Source: a5design.com.

The real question a designer needs to ask is "What is critical mass?" This ultimately determines what the newer resolution should be designed for. This is a call that, many times, a designer can leave to the client. Some people would say 75 percent of all users would be critical mass. Others might say 95 percent, claiming that taking the risk of losing 25 percent of a user base is not worth the benefit of going to a higher resolution. Making such a decision cannot be based solely on general statistics. It should also be based on the type of audience a site is geared toward. If the audience is high-tech, a site will likely be designed for the highest acceptable resolution much sooner than if the site were geared toward a more general audience, such as a search-engine site intended to satisfy the largest audience possible. It is the job of the designer to know the statistics, understand the implications of the various resolutions, and, if need be, make the call on the resolution if the client "doesn't care."

When going to a higher resolution, the designer must consider the quantity and ratio of content. As resolution increases, so does the screen real estate. Jumping from a resolution of 800 × 600 to 1024 × 768 increases the available screen area by nearly 40 percent. When designing for a content-intensive page, this extra space can be advantageous. The designer can either add more content or make current content look less busy by reworking the layout.

Designing for a higher resolution does not necessarily mean that the designer need disregard monitors with lower resolutions. One trick that designers frequently use is to design a site where the least important information is delegated to a column to the right. That way, the most important information, which is on the left, is still viewable by a user when the monitor is set to a lower resolution. Figures 3.5 and 3.6 are screenshots of a site designed specifically for this issue. Looking at the right-hand side of the screenshot in Figure 3.5, there is a column of advertisements that the user is probably not going to be as interested in.

When dropped down to a lower resolution, the column to the right is no longer visible. However, the main content to the left is still viewable.

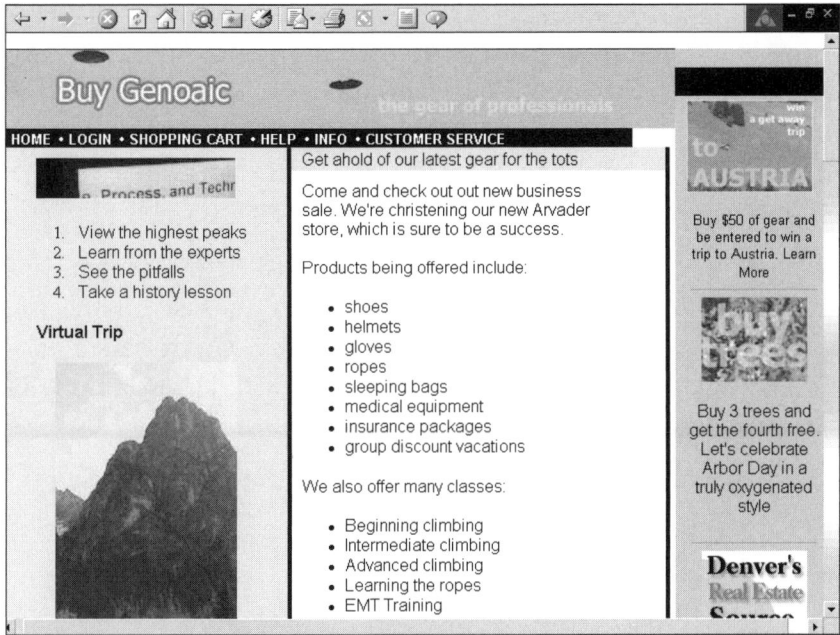

Figure 3.5
Site designed for a standard resolution.
© 2014 Cengage Learning.

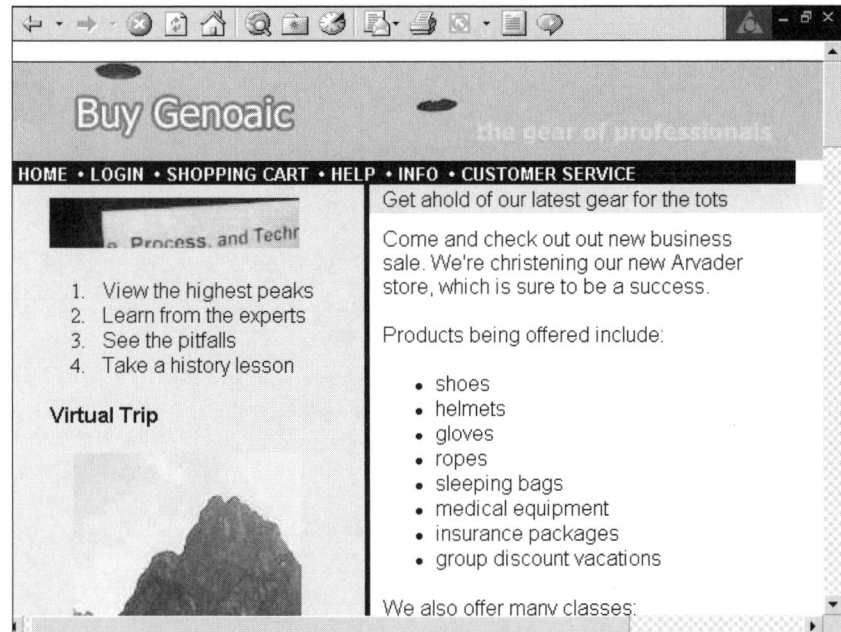

Figure 3.6
Same site as in Figure 3.5, but in a lower resolution.
© 2014 Cengage Learning.

Designing a site in this manner is a smart and easy way to address monitors with lower resolutions. It is generally good practice to show a little of the right-hand column so that the low-resolution user knows that there is more information available by scrolling to the right.

Designing Fixed Versus Relative Sites

A site designed for a lower resolution will not dynamically resize to fit the screen of a monitor with a larger resolution, but it can stretch horizontally to at least fill the full width. These kinds of pages, which use this relative resizing to fit a screen, are called *relative* or *jello* pages. Figures 3.7 through 3.9 are the same site viewed at the resolutions of 640 × 480, 800 × 600, and 1024 × 768.

The advantage of these sites is that they fill up the full width of the higher-resolution screen. It can be distracting to some users if the site does not at least fill the screen horizontally.

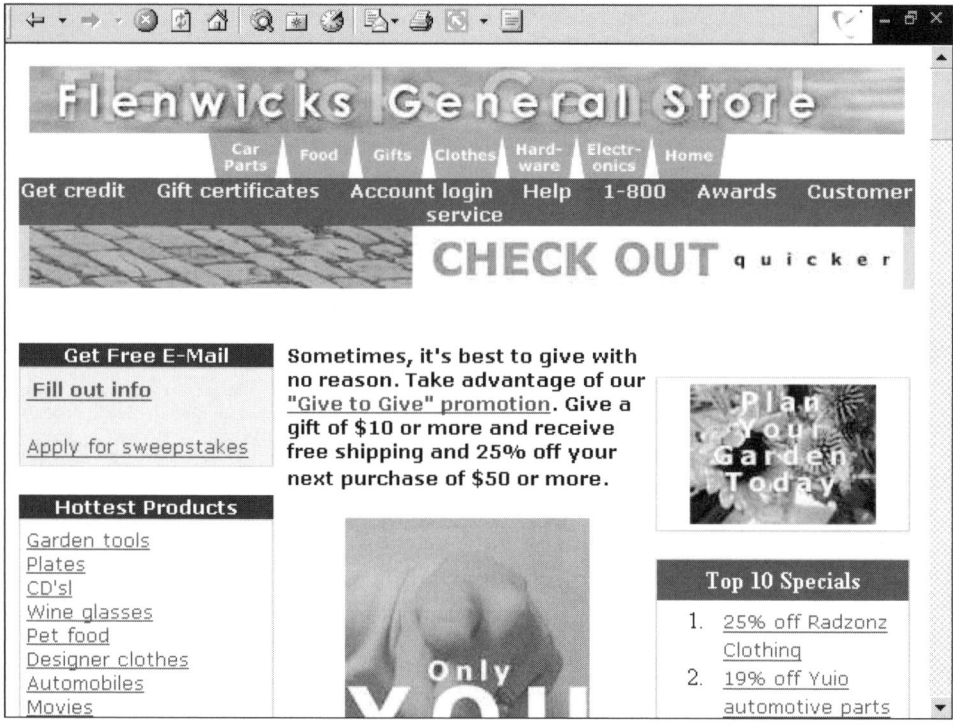

Figure 3.7
Relative site at 640 × 480 resolution.
© 2014 Cengage Learning.

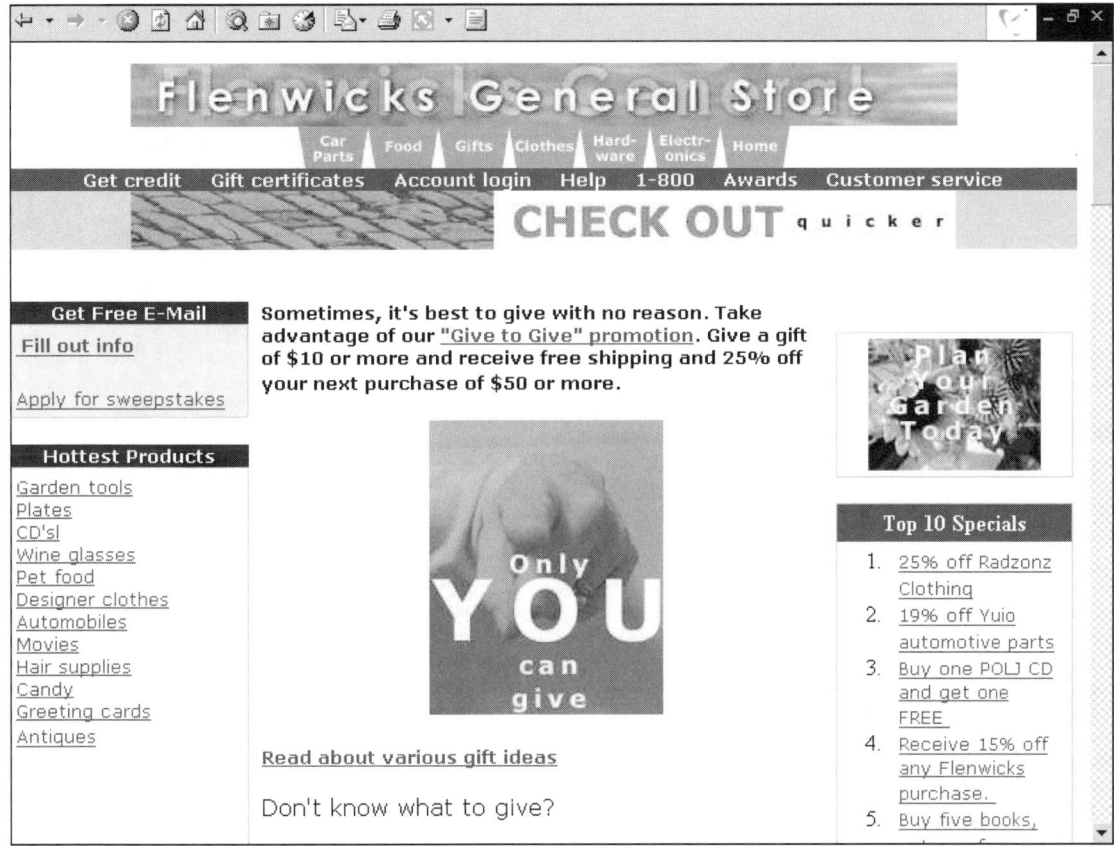

Figure 3.8
Relative site at 800 × 600 resolution.

© 2014 Cengage Learning.

Principle Remains the Same, Despite Resolution

While most of these site resolutions are antiquated, the principle remains the same in terms of varying sizes.

The disadvantage of relative sites is that the layout can be compromised, which can hurt the site's usability. As it stretches across the screen, the site will reposition certain text and images horizontally. Research has shown that after the text reaches a certain point in terms of width, the user will be less likely to continue reading it. Also, if the design was created to lead a user's eye to certain areas, those areas will not necessarily be in the same position at a higher resolution.

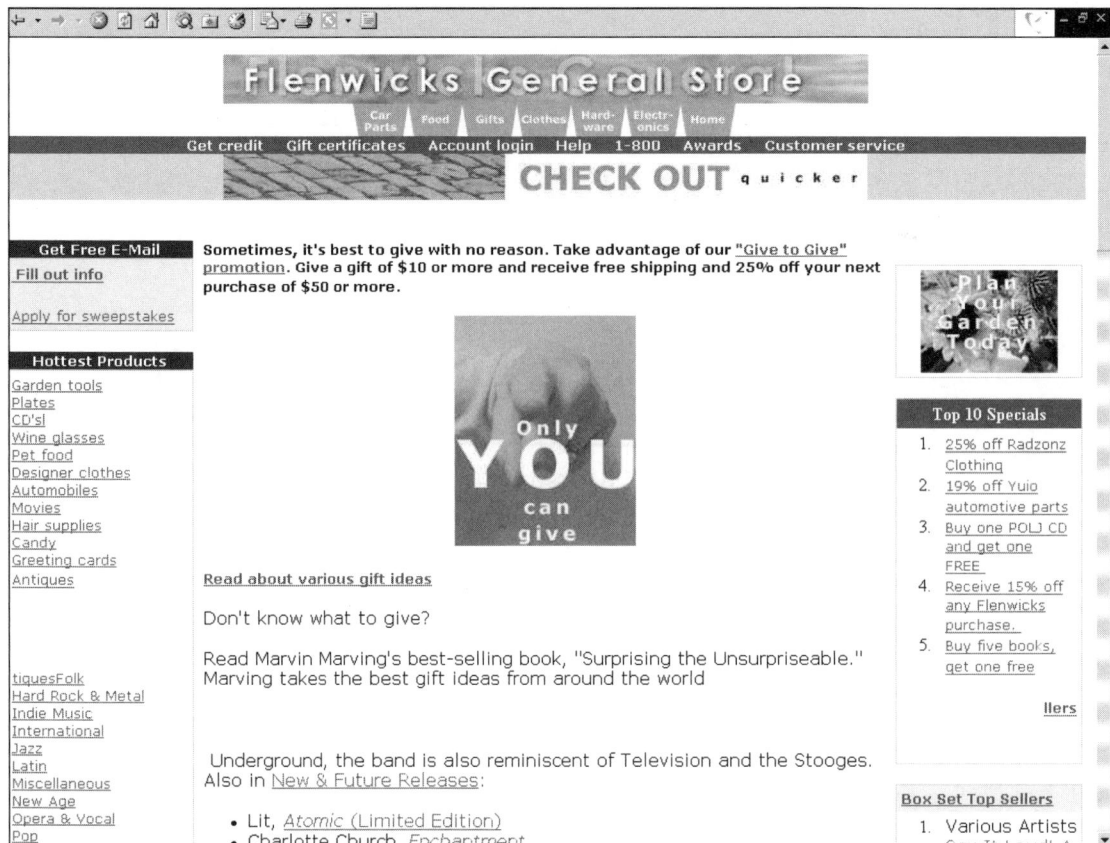

Figure 3.9
Relative site at 1024 × 768 resolution.
© 2014 Cengage Learning.

Most designers like to have control over the layout, which relative pages do not allow. Many designers spend time strategically, and sometimes artistically, placing text and images to be visually more effective. Relative pages, however, might distort the intended layout at difference resolutions. Special care must be taken when designing a page with fixed sizes on the tables to allow for expansion.

In order to tackle some of the resolution issues, designers can either force the width of the site or choose which columns will not expand by specifying a width in CSS for specific containers.

Creating Versions of a Site to Satisfy Differing Resolutions

If controlling the look and feel of a site for different resolutions is important enough, a designer can develop different versions of the same site for different resolutions. Branching JavaScript can be used to detect a user's resolution automatically and serve up the right code for a specific resolution. Such a solution involves much more time in creating and maintaining the site, but it also ensures a controlled look and feel for differing resolutions.

Deciding on Color Depth

Color depth is not nearly as complicated an issue as resolution is. Color depth refers to the number of colors a monitor can display. Similar to GIFs, the numbers increase exponentially, beginning with 2 (that is, 2, 4, 8, 16, 32, 64, 128, 256, and so on). After a certain bit depth, the human eye cannot detect a difference.

In the mid-1990s, there was a considerable break point in the number of colors a monitor provided, which designers needed to be aware of. The difference was between 8-bit (256 colors) and 16-bit (65,536 colors) depth. While saving an image as a GIF with 256 colors made it look very much like a normal photo, monitors did not offer the same quality. Figures 3.10 through 3.12 are the same JPG photo with the monitor resolution set to 8-bit, 16-bit, and 32-bit.

Using 16-bit resolution to view images is more than adequate. Today's monitors offer 32-bit color, which can display 16.7 million colors. But because the human eye can only detect approximately two million colors, 32-bit is somewhat overkill, as seen with Figures 3.11 and 3.12, which show no "visible" difference.

Why does this all matter? The truth is, it doesn't that much anymore. For the most part, it's included merely as a history lesson for the reader. Some designers still design for monitors with 256 colors, thus the color-safe palette, which is used to guarantee that browsers display colors the same, rather than providing their own versions of a "light blue." However, this is no longer necessary. Monitors have supported at least 16-bit color depth since 1996. Usage statistics confirm the fact that the majority of users have at least 16-bit color depth. A designer should still understand the issue because it occasionally comes up with other design jobs, such as creating icons.

Figure 3.10
Monitor color depth set to 8-bit color (256 colors).
© 2014 Cengage Learning.

Figure 3.11
Monitor color depth set to 16-bit color (65,536 colors).
© 2014 Cengage Learning.

Figure 3.12
Monitor color depth set to 32-bit color (16.7 million colors).
© 2014 Cengage Learning.

DESIGNING FOR SCALABILITY

Back in the mid-1990s there were very few extremely large sites (hundreds or thousands of pages). The majority of sites were small by today's standards and built with only static content. Because revising these small sites was so easy, it was common practice to redesign them every six months to a year. Today, sites are exponentially larger, more technically complicated, and more in tune with brand recognition. It is no longer easy or cost-effective to redesign a large site.

More importantly for some designers, a site must be easily maintainable. The fun part of Web design is creating a site. The real work begins when the client requests maintenance. This is why it is important that designers build sites that are scalable in two possible ways:

- **Editable sites:** A designer should be able to edit pages and sections of a site without any major rework of the design.

■ **Modular sites:** A homepage, for example, should be comprised of several files, or pieces put together, that can be easily replaced or edited. An analogy would be that of changing the oil in a car. If it were not possible to easily drain and refill the oil via a plug on the bottom and cap on the top, a mechanic would have to remove the engine, take it apart, drain and refill the oil, and then put the engine back into the vehicle.

Scalable sites are not difficult to create. They simply require a little more forethought by both the designer and client. In addition to the forethought that goes into creating a flexible design, two aspects are used to create scalable sites—nested containers and include files.

Using Include Files

Include files are used by developers to call code that is used repeatedly throughout a site. In other words, a single file could be reused by 10 different pages. Include files are commonly used to contain the footer information of the site, which would, very likely, be used on every single page. Such files are a blessing to designers. They reduce development and maintenance time, which can be considerable, depending on the size of a site. Another advantage of include files is that they make a site modular. In other words, they allow for one page, such as the homepage, to be built with various individual pages. Those same pieces can then be used to build other pages. Figure 3.13, which is a second-level page of a site, is a good example of modular functionality. The area on the right containing the oval circle is an include file. This file not only serves a functional purpose, but it also reduces the amount of space of the body if the content is not as long as other pages.

Figure 3.14 is a third-level page of the same site that requires the full width of the body for the map. To accommodate this space, the designer simply removed the include file on the right.

Figure 3.13
Modular site that uses an include file in the right section of the body.
Source: National Farmers Union.

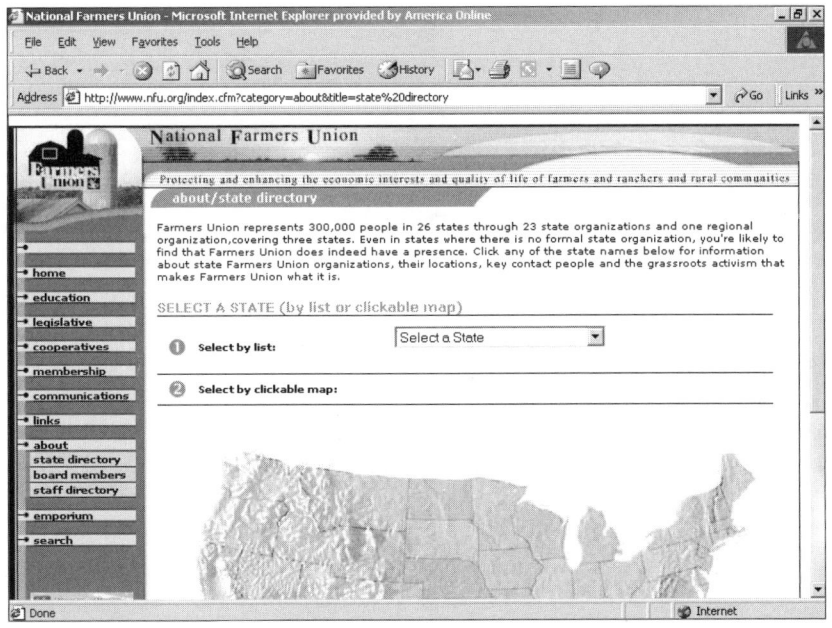

Figure 3.14
Third-level page of the site in Figure 3.13 where the right section was removed.
Source: National Farmers Union.

Creating a Flexible Design

The look and feel of a site is obviously a determining factor for its shelf life. If the site looks outdated, it will make the company or individual that the site represents appear outdated. Another factor that plays into the shelf life of a site is flexibility, which involves a designer's ability to add and delete pages and portions of pages.

If a designer needs to spend hours changing the layout of a site because the client wants to add two sections, but the menu will not support it, then the site has a poor, inflexible design. If the designer simply needs to add only a few rows of content in a nested container, then that is a flexible design.

Figure 3.15 is an example of an inflexible design. Notice the menu at the bottom center of the page. Not only are the items in an area that does not allow much vertical expansion, but the menu items are also images, which are easy to create but more difficult to maintain. Another weakness of this design is that the menu items have to be repositioned for subsequent pages, usually at the top or left of the main body.

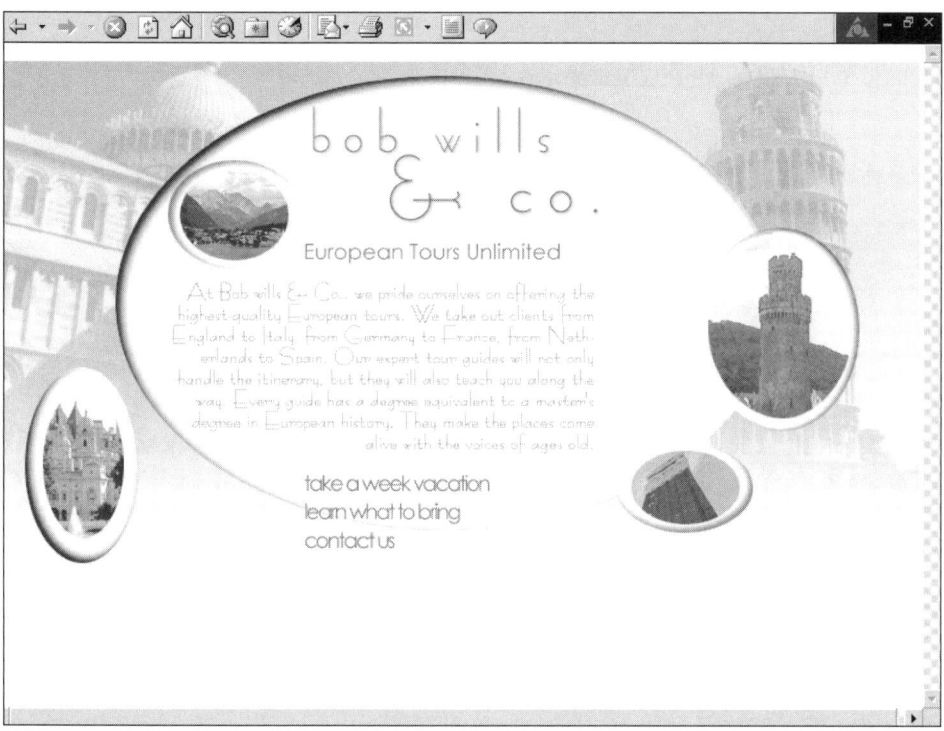

Figure 3.15
Example of an inflexible design.
© 2014 Cengage Learning.

There are three areas of a site that should be designed to be flexible:

- **Menu navigation:** This is probably the most common flexibility problem of designs. If a site undergoes edits, many times the client is going to add or delete menu items. While deleting is not as much of a problem, adding items is. The menu, therefore, needs to be able to have items added to it without requiring a redesign.

  Another flexibility problem is in making the menu too narrow, whether it is a vertical or horizontal menu. (Navigation and developing menus are discussed in Chapter 4.)

- **Content layout:** Whether a site has a low or high amount of content, there is almost always the possibility that new text or graphics will be added; therefore, the layout of the site should be able to accommodate such changes without being compromised. The site in Figure 3.15 would not be able to handle growth in the content area unless the font sizes were reduced, which might not be a wise decision because the entire site is very graphic-intensive. If the amount of text were increased, it would flow over the images to the right and to the bottom.

- **Title areas:** It is necessary for a user to be able to identify second- and third-level pages. One way to identify pages past the homepage is to include a text description, such as in Figure 3.16. It is wise to build an area that can handle some of the longer section names. The site in Figure 3.16 allows plentiful room to add even the longest of titles. As wide as "Application Development" is, it could be longer and still be supported by the design.

Per the seven rules of Web design (see Chapter 1, "Overview of Web Development Today"), there is nearly always an exception. So is the case for flexibility. The downside to flexibility is that it limits a designer in what can be done with the layout of a site. Many sites that do not require much, if any, maintenance are perfect candidates for designing flowing graphical designs that are comprised of minimal text. A perfect example would be a short-term site, such as a site of an upcoming movie that might be in existence for only six months, after which it probably would be taken down or left unmaintained. In a rare case like this, the designer does not need to worry as much about creating a site that can be easily managed.

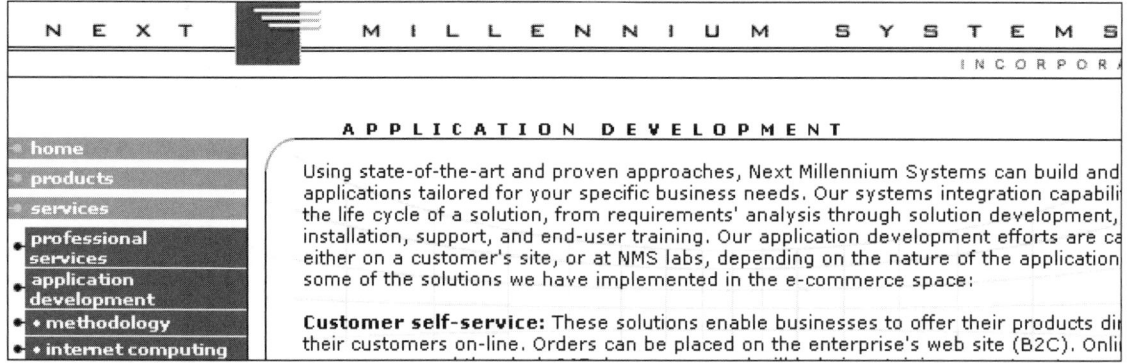

Figure 3.16
A design that supports long second- and third-level titles.

Source: Next Millennium Systems, Inc.

SUMMARY

A well-designed site is a well-thought-out site. Much of the work that goes into a design begins with collecting requirements so the designer understands the needs of the site. Such efforts can drastically reduce future time spent making corrections or redesigning.

A designer should take many requirements, such as bandwidth concerns, resolution, and color depth, into consideration before beginning the design. Once this information is collected, the designer should create flexible, scalable sites using include files.

CHAPTER 4

ENHANCING USABILITY

Users don't like being confused or having to wait when they go to a site. Studies have shown that visitors spend no longer than 10 to 20 seconds on the homepage, alone. This is not a lot of time to communicate a message. Usability, therefore, is king when trying to keep a user at the site—not only on the homepage, but also on subsequent pages.

Download time, resolution, and browser compatibility are three previously discussed areas that can make or break the usability of a site. There are, though, three areas that have not yet been discussed that are just as, if not more, important: site architecture, layout, and navigation.

SIMPLIFYING ARCHITECTURE

Architecture is the way a site is constructed and flows in terms of sections and pages. A site map is a visual representation of the site's architecture. As shown in Figure 4.1, a user can discover how this site is laid out by reading the Contents site map page. It is easy to see that the Sol-O-Matic page is in the Additional Products section, which, in turn, falls under the Coin-Op Equipment heading.

The designer should never rely solely on providing users with a site map for their understanding of how a site is constructed. Rather, the site should be intuitive in the way it is designed. Following are several aspects a designer should consider when creating the architecture of a site.

Use a Consistent Naming Convention

A designer typically should not try to get creative when naming sections and pages, unless they are unique to only that site. While it was more acceptable to be creative in the mid-1990s, this is no longer the case because certain usability standards have been set. In other words, users expect to see one thing, so why run the risk of losing them if they cannot find what they are expecting?

The company contact section in most sites is a perfect example; it is common practice to put contact information in a Contact, Contact Us, or Customer Service link on the site. This is an easily understandable, general, catchall term that can include the postal address, email address(es), and phone and fax numbers. If the designer, on the other hand, were to name the link Information Center, the user might not make the initial association.

Figure 4.1
Site map of a site.
Source: Clean Designs, Inc.

One instance where it is slightly more acceptable to be creative with naming conventions is when a site has a metaphorical theme, such as a town theme, for its sections. Naming the

Contact Us section as the Post Office is going to be fairly intuitive, as long as every section falls under a similar naming convention, such as Library, General Store, and Town Hall. Using metaphorical themes, though, can be risky. The designer is taking the chance that the majority of users will understand the theme and meanings of the sections. When designing a site for an international audience, the risk of confusion becomes even higher.

Limit the Clicking

Back in the mid-1990s, the standard number of clicks to get to any page from the homepage was as high as five or six. Today, however, it is generally wise to try to design a site so that a user can reach the majority of information within three clicks, although there are always exceptions to the rule. Limiting the number of clicks simply allows the user to get to the content more quickly, thus limiting the frustration of having to deal with numerous hyperlinks and waiting to download additional pages. There are certainly exceptions to this rule, such as forms and application sites with large amounts of content that require more clicks, but three clicks should always be the goal of a designer. Figure 4.1 demonstrates the value of limiting the number of clicks that a user must make. Note that all of the sections are within three clicks of the homepage.

Avoid Linking the User Out of the Section

Linking a user out of a section means that when a user clicks into, for example, the About Us section, and then clicks a subnavigation item Email Us, he ends up in the Contact Us section. It can be confusing to the user if the subnavigation of a site unexpectedly changes because the hyperlink is connected to another section.

Breadcrumbs Only Quick Fix

While using the *breadcrumbs* technique (showing the page path in the title, About Us/History/ Early Years) can be helpful, it does not eliminate the confusion of unexpectedly ending up in a new section of a site when the user expects to remain in that section.

While this particular example is not overly confusing, it becomes more so when the flow becomes circular. Take Figure 4.2 for an example. If a user came to this site and clicked the Professional Services bullet on the menu to the left, the hyperlink would take that user to the subpage displayed in the right-hand section of the figure. The subnavigation on that page, however, is where the confusing circular navigation begins. If the user were to click on RIZNA Consulting, the hyperlink would go to the RIZNA Consulting section, which also is in the left-hand menu area. If the user were to click on Running Consulting in the subnavigation menu, he would return to Professional Services, completely making a loop back to where the trip started. To confuse the issue even more, the subnavigation items Virtual Consulting and Technologies Used, which are on both of those pages, take the user to entirely different pages in different sections.

The problem of circular flow usually occurs when a client wants the site to appear to have more pages than it really has. Ultimately, this problem makes the site appear disorganized and should be avoided at all costs for the sake of usability.

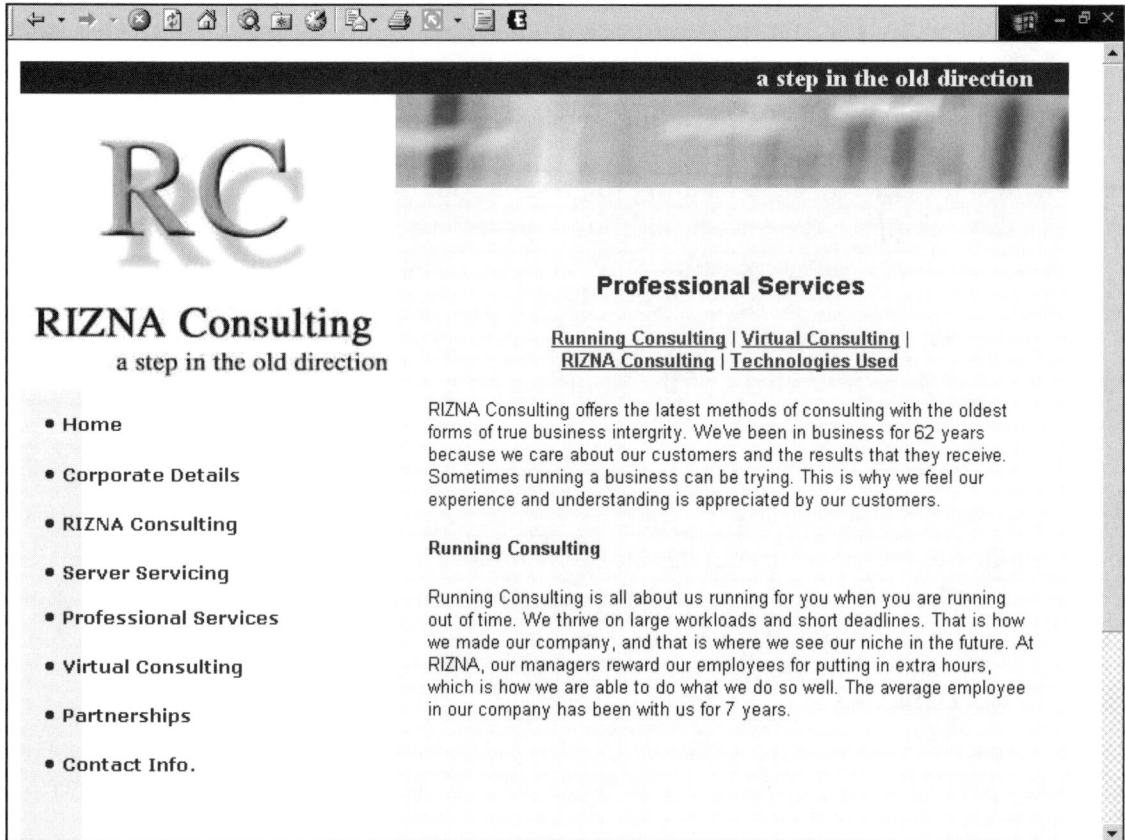

Figure 4.2
Site that confuses the user with its circular flow.
© 2014 Cengage Learning.

Create Cascading Architecture Versus Flat Architecture

Flat architecture has long been a staple of many sites. Flat architecture involves putting as much information on the homepage as possible so that the user only needs to click once or twice to find the desired page. The problem with a flat-architecture site, such as the one in Figure 4.3, is that the user becomes overwhelmed, confused, and frustrated with the difficult navigation. The site offers so much information that it is difficult for the user to find items without having to search the entire page slowly.

Cascading architecture, on the other hand, eliminates a lot of the confusion by organizing similar types of content in their own intuitive subsections of a site. Then when the user clicks, for example, on a link entitled Finance, similar items, such as tips, news, portfolio information, a stock ticker, and other financial areas, are all bundled on the same, concise Finance page. By combining consistent information on one "mini-homepage," the user does not have to drudge through all the submenus, lists, and shortcuts that are randomly included all over the homepage of a flat-architecture site.

Figure 4.3
Site that uses flat architecture to place as many links as possible on one page.
© 2014 Cengage Learning.

CREATING LAYOUT

A good layout is essential for the presentation of a professional image of a site. It also is important for the usability of a site. A user should be able to locate information with complete ease. Much of this is accomplished with the layout. Layout, in this instance, refers more to the positioning of elements, rather than the site's look and feel. Two areas a designer must consider when creating a layout are scrolling and positioning.

Scrolling Versus Not Scrolling

Everyone or every study on usability has an opinion on whether a site should scroll or not. It is one of those design issues that will never have a resolution, only trends advocating or opposing it. Because scrolling is always up for debate, it is smart for the designer to make it one of the required front-end questions for the client. Here are some of the pros and cons of scrolling.

Pros of Scrolling

- The design can fit more content on one page.
- The user does not have to click and wait for another page to load, which not only takes time, but the user must also refocus her eyes on a new area, most likely at or near the top of the screen.
- It is easy to navigate quickly if the user has a mouse with a scroller wheel or a stylus, which also allows for easy cursor movement.

Cons of Scrolling

- It takes less effort to click on a link that opens a new page than to mouseover to the scrollbar, click on it, and drag it up or down.
- Because scrollable pages are longer, their download time is typically larger.

One instance where scrolling is absolutely unacceptable is when the designer creates wide pages that force the user to scroll horizontally. Not only does it contradict accepted usability standards, but it also requires more motion than vertical scrolling because the Web page width is wider than its height.

Positioning Content

Perhaps the most important component of a professional, intuitive design is the positioning of content. The user should not have to go searching for the most relevant information of the site. Rather, it should be positioned where it is easy to find.

Probably the first item a designer must address is the positioning of the menu. Since the mid-1990s, designers have experimented with placing the menu on the left, right, top, center, or bottom of the page—anywhere a designer can imagine, a menu has been placed there.

Over the years, placing the menu to the left or on the top of the page has become the more traditional standard. There are technical reasons for this, which are explained in the next section.

The second area a designer should address is the header. This area typically includes any of the following items:

- Company logo
- Advertisements
- Links, such as "Login," for globally used functionality
- Company tagline
- Hyperlinks, such as "Save 20% today," which do not necessarily belong in the menu
- Content

When designing the header section of a site, a smart strategy is to use as much content that can be cached by the browser as possible. This decreases the download time of subsequent pages that use the same header file because content is already cached in the computer's memory. While it is tempting to create a unique header for every section of a site, the designer should ask the question, "Does it improve or hinder communication?" There is a difference between being creative to improve communication and being creative just to be different. Associating a color with a specific section might be beneficial, or it might just confuse the user, depending on the execution of the design elements.

When creating the header, a designer can take advantage of existing Web-usability standards. It is very common, for example, for a logo to be placed in the upper-left corner of a site. Because so many sites use this same design structure, users are accustomed to looking there for the logo. What a designer can do is place content in the upper-left corner that is deemed by the client to be more important than the logo. That way, the designer takes advantage of Web usability to increase the usability of that particular site.

The final area to consider when positioning is the body. Because designs can be shifted and shaped however desired, the best positioning location is not an easy call. Typically, the prime real estate of a site is the upper-center to upper-left section of the page(s). Users who come in at lower resolutions are going to lose the right side and bottom of a design before anywhere else; this, by default, makes the right and bottom areas less effective for communicating. This is not to say that these areas cannot be effectively used in a design. If the designer leads the user's eye with graphics or color, any section of the initial screen can be used.

The bottom line is that there are exceptions to every rule, and a designer should experiment with positioning. No site is perfect, and nearly all sites are in constant evolution. If Web designs became too similar and predictable, the user's eye would become lazy and less controllable.

Users, of course, are the ultimate judges. If a site does not compel them to stay, then the designer has not done a good job of communicating.

DEVELOPING NAVIGATION

Both usability and maintenance are issues to consider when creating the navigation, or menu(s), of a site. As mentioned previously, the menu is a key component of effective Web design. It should intuitively help a user find any item. If it doesn't, the designer runs the risk of losing the user who becomes frustrated and leaves the site. There also are technical reasons for designing a smart menu. Maintaining a site is not always easy or convenient. Therefore, a menu should be designed so that items can be easily added, edited, or deleted.

Creating Consistency

To confuse is to lose a user. Following an inconsistent menu is the same as using a map that constantly changes from minute to minute. There are three flaws a designer should avoid when creating the menu:

- **Moving the menu:** When inside the site, it is considered poor design to move the menu vertically or horizontally to accommodate other content that is added to the area. The user should be able to always look in the same area(s) for the same menu(s). A secondary menu is sometimes necessary for certain pages when the global menu (main menu included on all pages) will not support them. These menus should be placed in the same place on every page, rather than being placed wherever or whenever they may fit.

- **Changing the menu:** Once a menu is past the homepage, it should be set in stone. A designer should not be adding items unless there are pages or subcategories being added below parent sections that existed in the original menu on the homepage. For example, the designer can confuse the user by adding a section of an existing menu on one or two pages and then eliminating it from the menu on all other pages. The user is not always going to follow such changes.

- **Limiting the number of menus:** A menu serves as a convenient, concise listing of sections or pages of a site that a user can locate quickly. Once a designer begins adding mini-menus to other areas of a design, intuitive navigation is decreased. An example of such menus is shown in Figure 4.4. One menu is to the right of the global menu, which is in the upper-left corner of the page; the other menu is in the row below the World Tradeshow content.

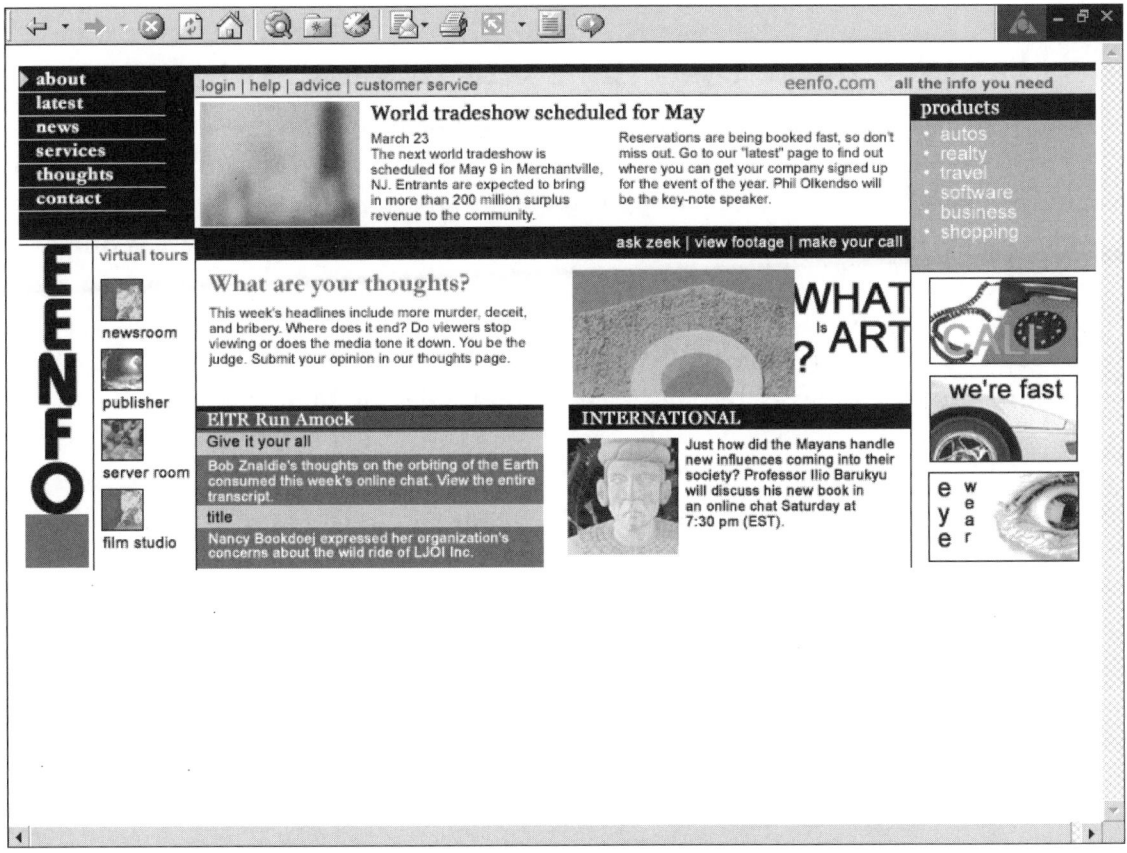

Figure 4.4
Site that includes two mini-menus in addition to a global menu.

Portal sites, which offer many resources and services, are usually the most common abusers of multiple-menu design. While there may be a menu for larger sections of the site, there may also be two or three other mini-menus that the user has to find. A well-designed site should rarely use more than two menus on any given page. Often, links or sections in mini-menus can be included in the global menu. Sometimes, they may fit very well in existing sections, or they might need to have a special subsection created.

Using Text for Menu Items

Creating images for menu items can add to the look of a site, but most of the time they require a lot more work on the designer's part to add or edit them in the future. Often, text with a simple mouseover image that can be repeated can be used in place of individual images for each item. Not only does this solution decrease the download size of a site, but it also makes a menu very easy to create and edit.

Deciding Whether to Use a Horizontal or Vertical Structure

Both horizontally and vertically structured menus have advantages and disadvantages. A horizontal menu structure allows the designer to use the full width of the screen for content. This is particularly useful for application sites that display large amounts of information in columns. Using a horizontal menu, though, has a drawback. There is only so much room to expand sideways. Therefore, if a design exceeds the width of the page, the designer will need to add another row for the menu, which can hurt usability, or the site will require a redesign. Another problem is that the menu can easily exceed the viewable area of monitors with lesser resolution. If, for example, the site is designed for 1024×768 resolution, a monitor with 800×600 resolution will lose 224 pixels on the right side of the screen. The advantages and disadvantages of a vertical menu are exactly opposite to those of a horizontal menu. An advantage is that vertical menus can be expanded easily because they stretch the page downward, which requires the user to simply scroll down. Because they take up horizontal space, vertical menus naturally minimize the amount of horizontal room the designer needs to work with. While this can be a disadvantage for an application site, it can actually be considered an advantage for a site that is lacking in content. A designer can use a wider vertical menu to take up the overall space of a low-content site.

Allowing Enough Width

Whether using a horizontal or vertical menu structure, the designer should always take the length of menu items into account before designing. If many of the items are long, then the menu might not even initially fit the width of the screen. Vertical menus also fall prey to this problem, although not as badly. If a menu item is too long in a vertical menu, it will either stretch the menu too wide or wrap around to the next line. Many times, the client will need to rename the menu items so they fit in a specified space.

Understanding the Different Types of Menus

There are four main types of menus that are used in websites, and each has its pros and cons. Many of the considerations for deciding which menu type to use are the same as those faced when designing an entire site: download time, browser support, and maintenance. Following are the various menus:

- **JavaScript or Java applets:** These menus can expand and contract when items are clicked. The advantages of these menus are that they allow the user to view the entire site by quickly scanning the navigation on one page, and they can be cached. The disadvantages are that they are more difficult to maintain (unless dynamically built on the fly using data from the database).

- **Macromedia Flash:** If the designer wants to build more creative menus, Flash is the way to go. It not only allows a designer with limited programming experience to build graphically animated menus, but Flash also allows audio to be added when a user mouses over or clicks on menu items. The disadvantages are that the user must have the Flash plug-in, these menus are more difficult to maintain, and they can annoy the user if not designed correctly. This last reason is similar to one of the overriding problems with multimedia sites—form precedes function. Users, for example, do not always want to see a round ball spin, shrink, expand, or change to a rectangle when each menu item is activated. The wow factor is great the first time, but quickly loses its appeal thereafter.

- **HTML text with mouseover:** These menus, which use text along with a couple of small mouseover images, are supported by all browsers, require only a small download, and can be dynamic. They still let the user know when an item has been selected, and they are extremely easy to maintain. A disadvantage is that while the designer can be creative with the mouseover images, the font types are limited to Web text unless embedded fonts are used, which requires a plug-in and the download of the font. Another disadvantage is that while they can be dynamically created with a database-driven site, each time a new menu is created, the user's browser cannot take advantage of caching the menu.

■ **CSS:** One of the most simple menu options is CSS menus. There are several different versions included with the designs in this book that run either horizontally or vertically. More importantly, there are CSS dropdown menus that are easy to update while also being search-engine friendly, not to mention that they also don't require JavaScript code that can be more complicated and code-intensive. Stu Nicholls with CSSplay (www.cssplay.co.uk/menus/) has come up with an incredibly flexible and easy-to-use system that is well supported. Figure 4.5 shows a site that uses CSSplay's menu system.

Figure 4.5
A simple yet powerful CSS menu provided for free by www.cssplay.co.uk.
© 2014 Stu Nicholls.

This CSS menu system is included online for the designer to use.

Because menus are so important to the usability of a site, it is important that the designer uses the right type of menu. If the audience is more advanced, Java, JavaScript, or Flash menus may be the way to go. If the audience contains both advanced and novice users, then HTML or CSS menus should probably be used, depending on how they're created.

Most of the designs included with this book use XHTML or CSS menus because of their limited download and ease of adding, editing, and deleting.

DESIGNING FOR ACCESSIBILITY

There are some Internet users who consider usability as much of a technical issue as a visual, navigational, or comprehensibility issue. In other words, can the content of a site actually be obtained and used—that is, is it accessible?

When planning a site, the designer needs to consider different issues, such as will the content need to be obtained by a voice browser? If a user has a slow connection, is it possible to read what an image is about before seeing it? Or is it wise to use server-side processing when client-side processing will suffice?

DESIGNING FOR CONTENT

The amount of content in a site usually determines how a site will be designed. Some clients simply need a couple of pages put up, while others need full-blown, database-driven sites that include thousands of pages. Therefore, the designer needs to understand the site's requirements before beginning. If a site has little content, then the remaining space can be supplemented with images. If a site requires more content, the designer will, most likely, use fewer images to keep the download smaller and the design less busy. Following are three types of sites a designer can create, based on content. (These are templates that are included in this book.)

■ **Low content:** These sites are usually designed for the client who only wants to have an "online brochure." Such sites generally include the basic information a user is looking for, such as information about the client, services and products offered, and contact information. Because these sites have a limited amount of content, they require more graphics to fill a page. This does not mean, however, that the entire page has to be filled with graphics. Much of it can also be white space, as shown in Figure 4.6. The ratio of content to images is generally around 20 percent to 80 percent, respectively.

Figure 4.6
Low-content design that uses graphics to supplement the limited amount of content.
© 2014 Cengage Learning.

■ **Medium content:** Many business sites created for the Web fall into this category. While clients for these sites may initially have a medium amount of content, they could be holding back on larger content so that they do not overwhelm the user on the homepage; such sites generally have three to five areas of limited content on the homepage. Figure 4.7 is an example of such a site. The content-to-images ratio is roughly 50 percent to 50 percent, respectively.

Figure 4.7
Medium-content design that has an even mix of content and graphics.
© 2014 Cengage Learning.

- **High content:** These sites are all about disseminating information or selling a product. Because they have so much content, the amount of images is limited, particularly large-size images. In other words, while images are used, they are generally smaller, such as the blurred images in the center of the site shown in Figure 4.8. These sites typically have more than five areas of content.

Figure 4.8
High-content design that offers a large amount of content and limited graphics.
© 2014 Cengage Learning.

Summary

No matter what the design philosophy is, usability should always be considered when creating a site. The user should not be confused by the naming of menu items or hyperlinks that go to unrelated sections, nor should he be overwhelmed by too much content.

A key factor in the usability and maintainability of a site is its navigation. Well-designed navigation will have items that can be easily added, edited, or deleted; download quickly; and are supported by the target users' browsers.

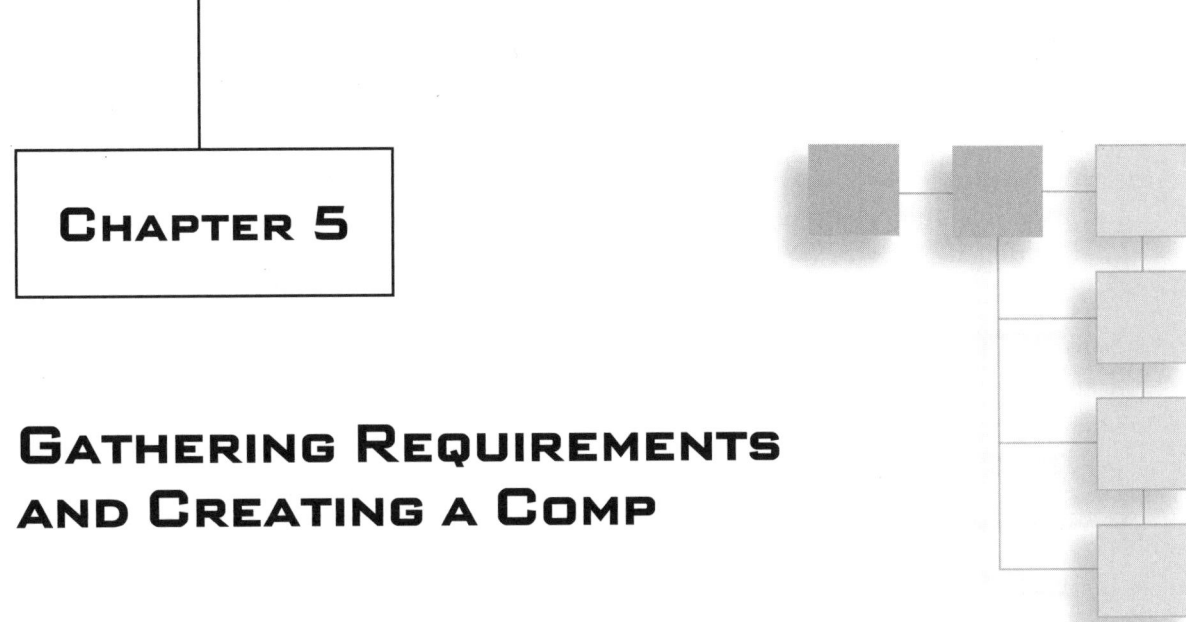

CHAPTER 5

GATHERING REQUIREMENTS AND CREATING A COMP

Once a designer understands the fundamentals of building a mortised site, then the fun begins—actually building the site. There are 10 general steps a designer should follow when building a mortised site:

1. **Gather and base a site on requirements.** Requirements determine, among other things, how many graphics the designer will use, what colors will be used, how fast the site must be, what future growth or changes the design must accommodate, and what content and functionality will be included on the homepage and subsequent pages.

2. **Create comp(s) for the client.** It's simpler and more efficient to build the look and feel of the site (that is, a *comp*) in Photoshop than to build the actual homepage piece by piece. Comps are also important because they can define many of the styles that are cascaded throughout the site.

3. **Receive a decision on the chosen comp and make edits.** Once a comp is decided upon, the client may very well request that a few changes be made to the design, such as "lighten the blue and replace the orange with yellow," or "replace this section of text with that one," or "use another photo in the upper-right corner." After the edits are received, the changes are made, and the selected comp is then resubmitted for approval. Sometimes, this process can take several iterations before the final comp is approved.

4. **Break up the comp into XHTML, graphics, and CSS.** At this point, the selected comp is sliced into different images and saved as compressed images. XHTML and CSS are then used to bring together the images, text, and possible functionality.

5. **Test the page in most commonly used browsers.** The designer should usually test a page in IE, Firefox, Chrome, and Safari as elements are added to it. Otherwise, after spending hours building a page, it might not function correctly in a browser that was not used during development. Sometimes, the browsers that need to be tested will change depending on site requirements or which browsers are most commonly used.

6. **Save components of the page as include files and test again.** To decrease the download time for subsequent pages and make maintenance considerably easier, the designer should save individual components, such as the menu, header, and footer, as separate include files. The design should then be tested again.

7. **Build second- and third-level pages from the homepage template.** Usually, the homepage design can be taken and reused as the general template structure for subsequent pages if it makes use of cached images and include files, which decrease download time. The designer then enters content into the body of each page of the site.

8. **Work with the client as the site is built.** The designer should have the client view the pages as they are built. Otherwise, if the requirements were misunderstood by either party, corrections could still be made before considerable time is wasted working on a site that will likely need redesigning. Another common issue with requirements is that while they may sometimes look good on paper, better ideas come about when the site is built.

9. **Test the entire site.** On larger sites where the budget allows, the designer can hire a professional tester(s) to test a site. However, on sites with limited budgets, it is usually the designer and client who test the site.

10. **Implement the site.** The designer uploads the site to the live server, whether it is an internal or external Web server.

GATHERING AND BASING A SITE ON REQUIREMENTS

Requirements are the roadmap for the designer to build upon. Misunderstandings between the client and designer are considerably less likely when requirements exist.

Requirements can be included in a couple of informal emails or phone calls, or they can be included in more involved documents that can be many pages long. Although requirements are not always gathered in the same way, the designer should always try to document as much as possible before beginning work.

While there is no set way to collect requirements, an example of how and what to collect is explained using the redesign of the Allos Therapeutics, Inc. site shown in Figure 5.1.

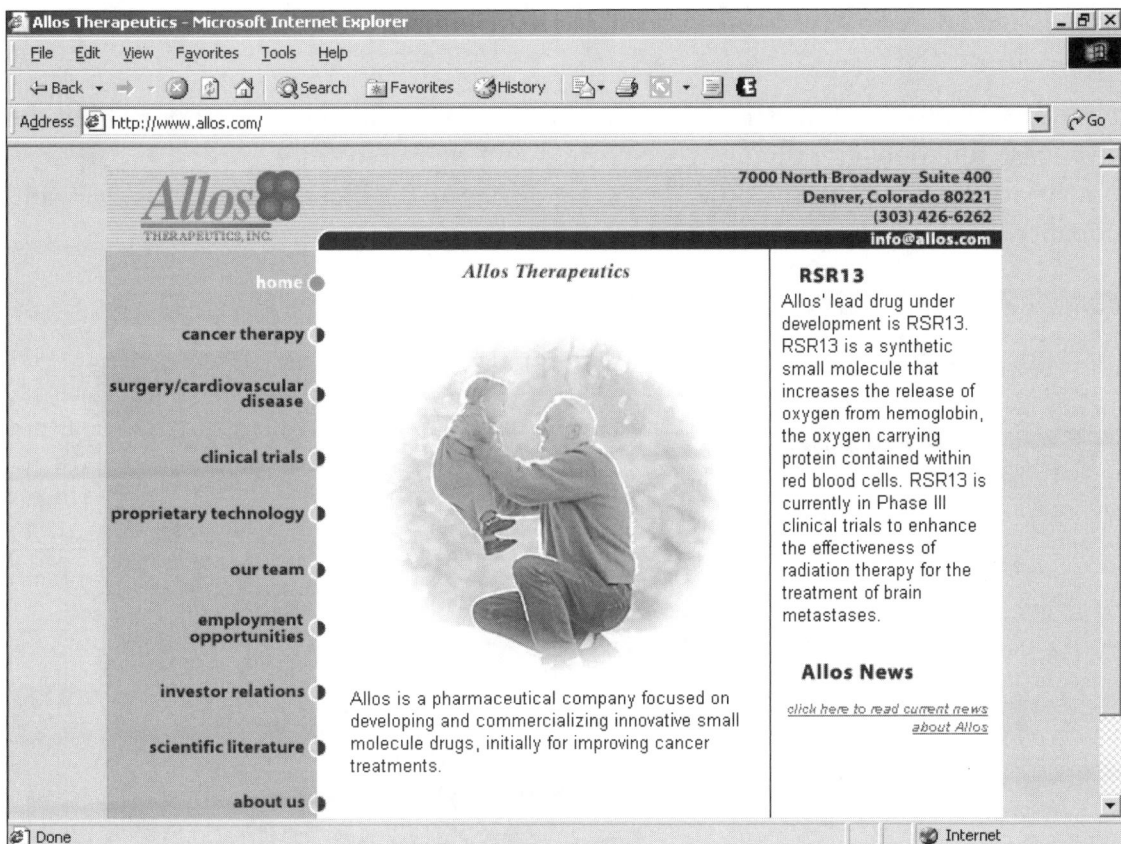

Figure 5.1
Allos Therapeutics, Inc.'s old design.
© 2014 Allos Therapeutics, Inc.

Under the guidance of the director of corporate communications, the company wanted to redesign its site to have a fresh, upbeat, professional look and be database-driven. The director wanted to incorporate Allos' new branding, as well as create a contemporary site that uses updated, relevant information.

The director and designer initially spoke together on the phone several times before scheduling a meeting. The director had a good idea of what she wanted. She had the entire site map laid out, along with several sentences describing the requirements for each page. She also knew the general look and feel that she was interested in. Having worked on many sites, the director knew the requirements would need input, revisions, and consensual agreement from her staff before beginning work on the site. Following a meeting with her peers, she and the designer discussed the various options and implications that the new site should address. At this point, the designer collected what is known as the *front-end requirements*.

Using the answers to those questions and specific requests made by the director about the site's database functionality, the designer created and delivered three comps. Incorporating some of the aspects from the other two designs, Figure 5.2 illustrates the look, feel, and functionality that were decided upon.

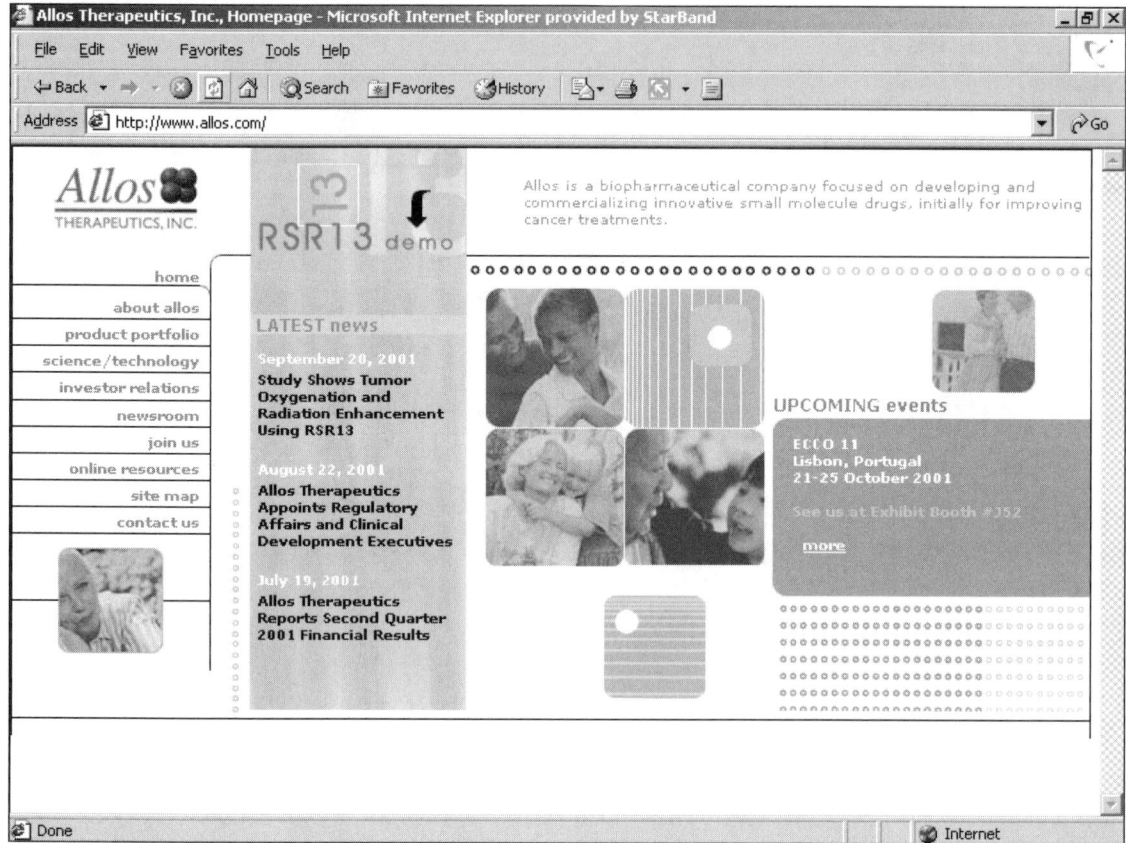

Figure 5.2
Redesigned site for Allos Therapeutics, Inc.
© 2014 Allos Therapeutics, Inc.

Following are some of the various attributes of the new design:

- There was a dominance of yellow, which gave the site the fresh, upbeat, professional look desired. However, because yellow is a color that can become overwhelming for some people, the majority of it was removed on subsequent pages.

- Since the client wanted the content to be dynamically generated from a database, each section was designed to be expandable without disrupting the design. This is why content containers were nested in each column.

- Because the second- and third-level pages had varying amounts of content, a nested container was designed into the right side of the page (see Figure 5.3). If a page had limited content, the area could be included to make the content area look fuller. If, on the other hand, a page had a lot of content, the container, which created an additional column, could be removed.

- To provide consistent navigation, the same expandable menu was saved as an include file in the left column for all pages. This also made future maintenance simple, enabling the designer to edit the entire site by changing only one file.

- The header was also saved as an include file to simplify maintenance.

Figure 5.3
Second-level page with right-hand container added to limit the amount of content that is necessary to fill a page.
© 2014 Allos Therapeutics, Inc.

The requirements process does not always end after a requirements document is approved. Throughout the building process, the director and designer added, deleted, and edited pages, as well as adjusted the functionality of the site. Fortunately, because many of the major requirements (such as the site's look and feel and site table structure) were finalized at the beginning of the project, future changes were minimal.

Many times with smaller sites, clients do not have the time, experience, or interest in discussing requirements. They simply want a site. In these cases, the client prefers to leave the decisions to the designer. The designer should still try, nonetheless, to provide options, explain the pros and cons of those options, and let the client make the decisions whenever possible. One example of such a decision is resolution. If a client recently purchased a computer with default resolution that is greater than the standard resolution of the average user's monitor, the designer should explain the situation to the client. By explaining the issue at hand, the client knows that if the site were created for her computer, it would probably be too wide for the majority of users with the standard resolution.

CREATING A COMP FOR THE CLIENT

Designing a comp is where the majority of the creative aspects of building a site occurs. It is where the designer lays out the text, images, possible functionality, and colors in a composition that will closely resemble the final product. The comp is then delivered to the client for possible editing and ultimate approval.

When creating a comp, the designer should take the technical as well as aesthetic aspects of a site into consideration. One thought process, for example, might be, "If I place this content in the header, will it remain there for the rest of the site, or will it be replaced by another element? If it is replaced by other content, what will that content be? Will it be text, or will it be a text-field box for testimonials?" In other words, at this point the designer considers what kind of programming will be required to get the page or site to function properly.

As previously mentioned, a comp is created in image editing software. For the purposes of this book, all examples use Adobe Photoshop (see Figure 5.4).

Figure 5.4
Comp being developed in Photoshop.
© 2014 Allos Therapeutics, Inc.

There are several advantages to creating a comp with Photoshop:

- A design can be created more quickly than when built as an actual Web page using XHTML, graphics, and CSS.

- Changes can be made quickly to a design during the comp process or in the future, once the site is live and the client requests a change.

- Because Photoshop uses layers, the design is extremely flexible. If a designer needs to replace one image that is on its own layer, only that layer needs to be changed.

■ The slicing technology included with Photoshop allows for the designer to add slices (boxes) on the file and then create and save many individual images from the one file. For example, if an older version of a logo is used in the comp while a newer one is being created, the designer can switch the logo eventually, save the new slice that creates the newer image, and then just upload that one particular file to the server.

Because the look, feel, and styles included in the comp will be cascaded down throughout the entire site, it is important to make sure the feeling and appearance they project is correct. This is why the designer, depending on the client's budget, should provide at least three different comps. It not only gives the client a choice of designs, but it also gives her the ability to mix and match certain pieces of the various designs. The client, for example, might say, "I like the black-and-white treatment you did to the photos in the first design. Can you add those to the third design?" Much of the designing of a comp is left to the creativity of the designer.

Varying Methods for Developing Comps

The way in which a designer delivers comps can vary. Sometimes, a lot of them will be delivered at once, or each one could be delivered after feedback is provided on the previous one. Many times, the latter works better because the designer can incorporate the latest edits more efficiently and effectively, along with earlier ones that remain pertinent.

Creating a Source Directory

There are many types of files (Web files, images, and source files) that go into creating a mortised site. If all files were saved together in one directory, individual files would be difficult to find, which is why a designer should use a consistent filing and naming system.

Creating a basic folder system before beginning a site takes at most a minute, but it saves the designer time and headaches when looking for files in the future. Here is one filing system method that requires four directories:

■ **Web project name:** This folder is usually named after a specific project. After years of creating and archiving many sites, it is easy to forget the specific site URL of the site, which is why it is sometimes wise to name the folder after the site itself. This is particularly helpful if the site URL doesn't match that of the company, or if the designer can't remember if the site is ".com" or ".net."

■ **Images:** This is where all the images used in the site are located. It is generally common practice to separate Web files from image files of websites.

- **Sources:** Because a designer may often have to refer back to the original PSD file(s), it is wise to keep them in a consistent area. A good place to store this folder is in a subdirectory under the Images folder. Some developers save the source files in a completely different area so the files are not accidentally copied over to a live server. Not only does a designer *not* want to allow access to such files, but they also can be an extremely large upload.

- **Stock:** While stock photos can be saved in the Sources folder, it is a good practice to save them in their own folder. Otherwise, if there are only three or four PSD files included in the Sources folder, they could be difficult to find if they are among all the other stock photo images.

In addition to using an organized folder system, a designer should also try to be consistent with the naming of files. This is particularly important for the Images folder. Because a mortised site can contain images used for spacing, backgrounds, and photos, it is generally helpful to use a naming convention that keeps such images in their respective families. One good method is to include the family of the image first in the name and then include the text that identifies that specific image in the second half of the file name. For example, if the image is a background for the menu, the name could be bg_menu.gif. The "bg_" classifies the image as a background image, and the "menu" identifies the image as the background behind the menu.

The advantage to this naming convention is that it is easy to find one file among many, especially if the designer knows what family the image is in. Figure 5.5 shows the Images folder for a site that has 35 images. Notice that all the background images are identified as "bg_," all the bullets as "bullet_," and all the photos as "photo_." If the designer uses an image for second- or third-level pages that has the same name as an image for the first level or homepage, an "_sl" (standing for "second level") can be added to the end of the image name. If the background image for a menu is different on the second level, for example, it could be named bg_menu_sl.gif.

Figure 5.5
Directory files using a consistent naming convention that identifies them in families.
© 2014 Cengage Learning.

Collecting and Documenting Stock Images

Using stock images is one way to make a site appear professional. Fortunately for the Web designer, stock photos can be much less expensive than for print designers. A high-resolution, print-ready image that costs $600 can cost around $150 for the low-resolution version (72 dpi)—exactly what is needed for Web design.

Prices generally range from $1 to more than $1,000, depending on which company the designer purchases from and whether the image is royalty-free. Generally, and depending on the company, royalty-free means that the image's number of uses and applications is unlimited by the designer once the image is purchased—as long as the image is not used in pornographic or defamatory ways. It is important to check the usage agreement before purchasing a photo because not all agreements are the same.

Images can usually be purchased online either individually or bundled together with other images. They also can be collectively downloaded, depending on the stock photo company. Buying an individual image is less expensive, and the image's subject matter (for example, the Amazon River dolphin) might be one that the designer will never need additional photos of. On the other hand, if the designer is going to be creating many high-tech websites, an online bundle of unique, high-tech images might be the way to go. Bundled stock collections are more expensive, but they contain many similar images for a subject, which dramatically drops the cost of each individual photo. One photo, for example, that costs $30 individually could be bundled with 100 similar images for $400, which drops the price to $4 per image. It simply depends on how much the designer anticipates using use such photos.

When collecting stock images for a design, it is a good practice to document all the images—that is, what the image is, which site it was found on, how much it costs, and the photo ID. (Most sites give a specific identifier or stock number for each image, such as #IE55648.) The designer can store this information in a text file in the Sources folder. That way, it is easy to know where to go when the image needs to be officially purchased for a site.

Because nearly all stock image companies allow the designer to download and temporarily use comp versions of images in their comp designs, the designer should not purchase the official image(s) until final approval and payment for the site has been received. Until that time, the designer should leave the watermarked (comp) version or thumbnail of the image(s) in the site—all the more incentive for the client to pay her bill.

Selecting Colors

Color plays an integral part in any website, which is why a professional Web designer should have a sound understanding of color theory. Color not only helps set the look and feel of a site, but it also can be used to increase the usability of a site by leading the user's eye and to help prioritize content.

Many color schemes are possible when designing a site. The designer can use a black-and-white scheme with one or two spot colors, a monochromatic scheme (different shades of one color), complementary schemes (colors that complement each other), or split-complementary schemes (two colors that are "one off" of a color that complements a color on the other side of a color wheel).

One of the questions a designer should ask a client before designing a site is what type of mood or feel the site should convey. The answer to this question can then be translated into the choice of colors used in a site, if the branding for the company hasn't already been determined. If, for instance, the client wanted a secure, conservative look, probably the best color to start with would be blue. It is a cool color that is used in many instances to convey a safe, reserved feeling.

The audience also comes into play when using color. Colors do not represent the same emotions in various countries. While white, for example, is used in weddings in the United States, it is used in funerals in China. The designer, therefore, might want to research colors when designing international sites. Another audience issue that the designer must consider is color blindness. The most common form is red/green color blindness; red and green look similar to someone with this blindness.

Color References for a Designer

Sites can be run through www.vischeck.com to determine how they will appear to color blind people. It also gives definitions and examples of the different types of color blindness.

Following are a couple of references that will give the designer a foundation for color theory:

- *Color Harmony: A Guide to Creative Color Combinations* by Hideako Chijiiwa (Rockport Publishers, 1987)

- *Color Bytes: Blending the Art and Science of Color* by Jean Bourges (Specialty Marketing Group, 1997)

- **Color wheel:** A good color wheel will show the designer different combinations, such as complementary and split-complementary colors. Color wheels can generally be found in art stores and online.

Deciding Layout

While there are obvious aesthetic considerations for the layout of a site, there are technical aspects as well. If the site is not designed correctly for the technical aspects, many repercussions can arise in the future for both the designer and, possibly, the programmer.

Depending on the design and site requirements, following are four aspects of layout that should be taken into consideration:

- **Vertical versus horizontal space:** A designer needs to consider the amount and type of content a site needs to support before designing the framework for the site. If the body requires a lot of room for content, then a wider design will be necessary. If the content is limited, then the designer is going to want to keep the body area narrow to avoid appearing as though it lacks substance. A good way to control the space of the content area is by using either a vertical or a horizontal menu. When placed in the header, a horizontal menu allows the designer to use the full area below it for space-intensive sites, such as Web applications that may include many columns of content. Vertical menus, on the other hand, can take up horizontal space and help supplement sites that lack content.

  If the screen simply does not offer enough room for content, the only other option, other than reducing font sizes, is to increase the required resolution of a site. A site with 1280×800 resolution has nearly 25 percent more screen space than a site with 1024×768 resolution.

  If the screen offers too much room, the designer has an alternative to using vertical menus—he can fill the space with fixed content. A designated space, such as that shown in the right side of Figure 5.3, can be used on any pages that do not have enough content. This space can either include photos or other content that has less priority.

- **Menu width:** If possible, a vertical menu should be wide enough so that menu items do not have to be carried over to a second line. Sometimes this involves renaming menu items to be shorter, and sometimes it requires making the menu area wider. If the designer needs to make the menu area wider, it should not take away valuable space in the body of the site. If it does take away valuable space, adding a tag to have the longer menu item(s) take up two lines instead of one is probably wiser.

- **Height of header:** The header area of a site generally remains the same throughout all pages of a site. If it is too high vertically, then valuable space is lost on pages that require large amounts of content. On the other hand, some sites have very limited content, which justifies using a header with more height. A good practice is to take the requirements of all the pages into consideration before building spatial areas, such as the header.

- **Placement of rounded edges and corners:** Many sites use rounded edges and corners. The advantage to rounded edges is that they soften the look of a site. Figure 5.6 uses a rounded corner just to the left of the upper part of the body of the page.

Figure 5.6
Design that uses a rounded edge for the upper-left corner of the page body.

Developing Layers

As previously mentioned, using layers in Photoshop saves a designer an inordinate amount of time when creating and editing a comp. Any item, whether text, shapes, or photos, can be saved on its own layer. That way, items cannot only be moved individually, but they can also be replaced individually without disrupting content on other layers. Figure 5.7, for example, is an image that consists of six layers, including the white background. The Photoshop Layers panel is shown in Figure 5.8.

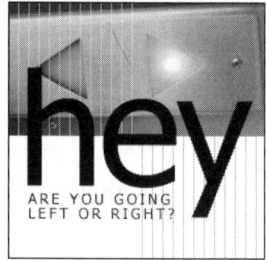

Figure 5.7
Image that is made up of layers.

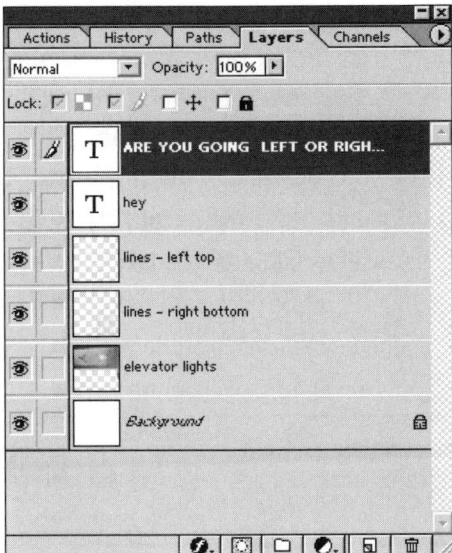

Figure 5.8
Layers panel in Photoshop.
© 2014 Cengage Learning.

If the client requested the text to be changed to "yo!," all the designer would need to do is open the file in Photoshop, click on the layer that says "hey," select the Text tool, click on the text in the file, and retype "hey" to read as "yo!"

While making this change, the designer could also move the lines or the "ARE YOU GOING LEFT OR RIGHT?" text, and reposition the newly retyped "yo!" text (see Figure 5.9). When creating comps for homepages, it is not unusual to create as many as 60 to 80 layers, which, additionally, can be nested within parent layers, called *Groups*—in other words, a layer can serve as a folder for additional layers.

Another advantage of layers is that they can be turned off easily so that if the client wanted to see the image in Figure 5.9 without the word "yo!," the designer could simply shut off that layer and save a new version of the Photoshop PSD file.

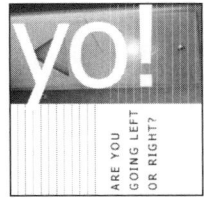

Figure 5.9
Same image as Figure 5.7 but with layers edited.
© 2014 Cengage Learning.

Layers can also be merged together for further editing. The "yo!" in Figure 5.9 could be merged with the elevator lights image. The two could then, for instance, have a motion blur added. When all the layers are merged together, the PSD file is flattened (the selected layers are merged to make one layer). Rarely will the designer ever want to flatten an image. If Figure 5.7 had been flattened, it would require considerable time and effort to cut "hey" out of the image, re-create the elevator image behind the word that was also cut out, and retype the word "yo!" Unfortunately, Photoshop PSD files can be flattened accidentally, which is why it is wise for a designer to back up all files. It usually takes only one accident and one experience with re-creating 70 layers of a comp for the designer to learn this lesson.

Making Copies of Layers

When merging several layers together at a time in Photoshop, the designer may want to make copies of the layers and turn them off before merging. This allows the designer to come back and edit pieces of the merged layer more easily in the future, if necessary.

Using Masks

Masks are extremely useful when a designer wants to control the shape or placement of an image. According to Adobe, a mask enables a designer to "isolate and protect areas of an image as you apply color changes, filters, or other effects to the rest of the image."

If a designer wanted to set an image inside the word "yo!" from Figure 5.9, the text could be rasterized (converted to a bitmapped image, which will not allow textual editing) and used as a mask. In Figure 5.10, the letters are used as a mask for an image of water. In other words, the water image is placed inside the letters. This can be advantageous when there is a photo or shape included in a design that cannot be moved, but the designer needs to replace it with another image. All the designer need do is use the original image as a mask, which the new image is then inserted into. Because the mask will initially be created as its own layer, the old layer can then be turned off or deleted to ensure that the edges of the image are smooth.

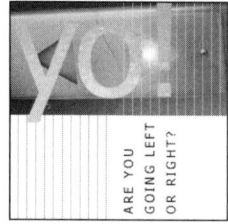

Figure 5.10
Image that uses the letters "yo!" as a mask for an image of water.
© 2014 Cengage Learning.

RECEIVING A DECISION ON THE CHOSEN COMP AND MAKING EDITS

Websites are in continual evolution. They especially evolve during the comp process. A design that works for a designer may not work for the person leading the project or that person's boss or peers. Frequently, the person in charge of the project will say, "It looks great to me. Let me just run it by so-and-so real quickly, and we'll be ready to go." While this sounds positive, there is usually a good chance that the next person will suggest additional changes.

The varying steps in the approval process make it wise for the designer to wait for approval on a comp before breaking it up into XHTML, graphics, and CSS. Because the breaking-up process can be time consuming and difficult to subsequently change, it is best to wait rather than begin, stop, and start all over again. Even though a design should be flexible, it can only be flexible for certain changes. If the client says, "My boss really wants you to move the menu from the left to the center," this edit will usually call for reworking the entire design.

Each site will go through its own unique process of approval. One site might require only one person's approval, while another site might require a committee's approval. There are several rules that the designer should follow when attempting to get approval:

- **Be patient.** There is a fine line between calling the client every day and showing the proper follow-through. Most companies, especially in corporate America, move slowly. While a client with a few people involved in approving a comp may do so quickly on the phone, it could take days to weeks for a corporate client to approve a certain desired look and feel.

- **Attempt to document all communications.** If the designer has the choice between calling or emailing a client, the wiser choice, many times, is to email. Not only is an email less intrusive, but it is also a good way of documenting communications. Whenever a client requests a change, the designer should ask for the change(s) to be submitted via email. That way, it protects both parties. Most disagreements or misunderstandings can be resolved by looking back at previous emails.

- **Offer alternatives.** Not all clients are going to be as technically or artistically minded as their designer. They may simply not know the various options a site can offer. Offering alternatives also lets the client know that the designer is keeping the client's best interests in mind. Color alternatives can be a good thing to offer a client if there is not a set palette. Because the slightest disproportion of a color can change the entire look and feel of a site, it is difficult to imagine changes without testing.

■ **Do not get attached to the work.** For every client who trusts the judgment of the designer, there are two who would prefer that a design look the way they desire. It is always amazing how quickly a design can change for the worse, at least in the designer's viewpoint. It is important, therefore, that the designer not become attached to a design. The paying client has the final say. If there is an affinity for a specific design look, the designer can always ask for permission to use the preferred version in a portfolio.

■ **Limit the number of changes from the outset.** Many times the approval process can get out of control. What once was one design can turn into three or four versions without the client's paying for the extra changes. This is why the designer should explain the approval process before beginning work on the designs. That way, there are no surprises when additional charges for excessive changes are incurred.

SUMMARY

There are 10 general steps to building a mortised site. One of the first and most important steps is gathering requirements and basing the site on those requirements. While requirements involve more work up front, defining requirements can make the development of a site considerably more time- and cost-efficient, as well as more effective.

Once the requirements are collected, the designer creates the comp(s) in Photoshop. There are several procedures a designer should follow to ensure that the comping process goes smoothly: create a source directory, collect and document stock images, and select colors.

After the first draft of a comp is completed, the designer works with the client to edit and finalize the site's functionality, appearance, and usability.

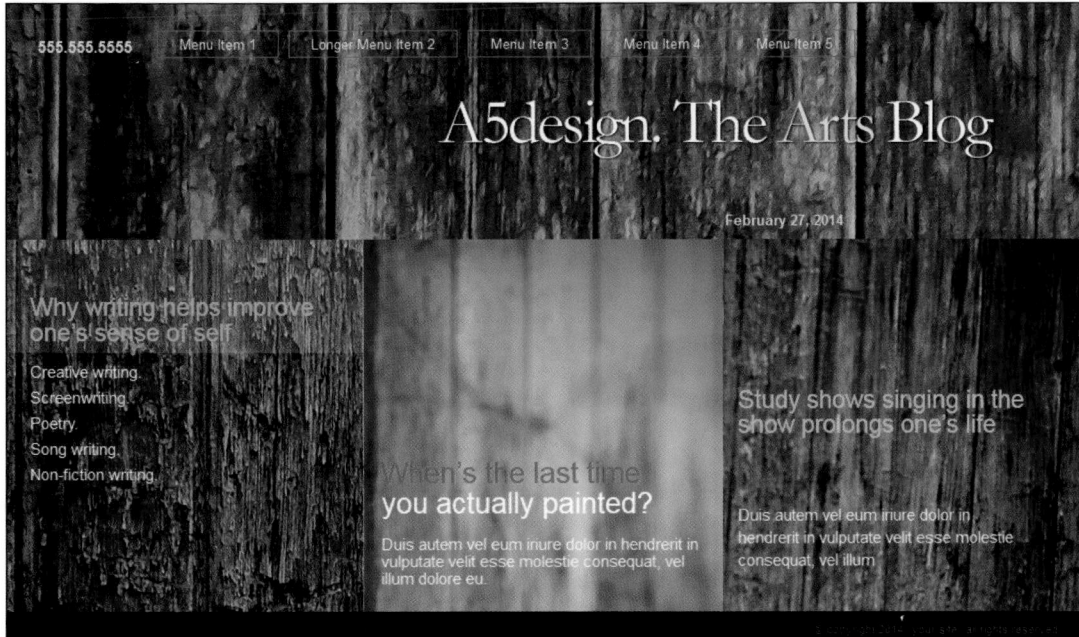

Design 190

555.555.5555 Menu Item 1 Longer Menu Item 2 Menu Item 3 Menu Item 4 Menu Item 5

a5design
dietary therapy

555.555.5555

Menu Item 1   **Longer Menu Item 2**   **Menu Item 3**   **Menu Item 4**   **Menu Item 5**

Duis autem vel eum iriure dolor in hendrerit in vulputate velit esse molestie consequat, vel illum dolore eu feugiat

Nulla facilisis at vero eros et accumsan et iusto odio dignissim qui blandit praesent luptatum zzril delenit augue duis dolore te feugait nulla facilisi. Lorem ipsum dolor sit amet, consectetuer adipiscing elit, sed diam nonummy nibh euismod tincidunt ut laoreet dolore magna aliquam erat volutpat Ut wisi enim ad minim veniam, quis nostrud exerci tation ullamcorper suscipit lobortis nisl ut aliquip ex ea commodo consequat.

Design 189

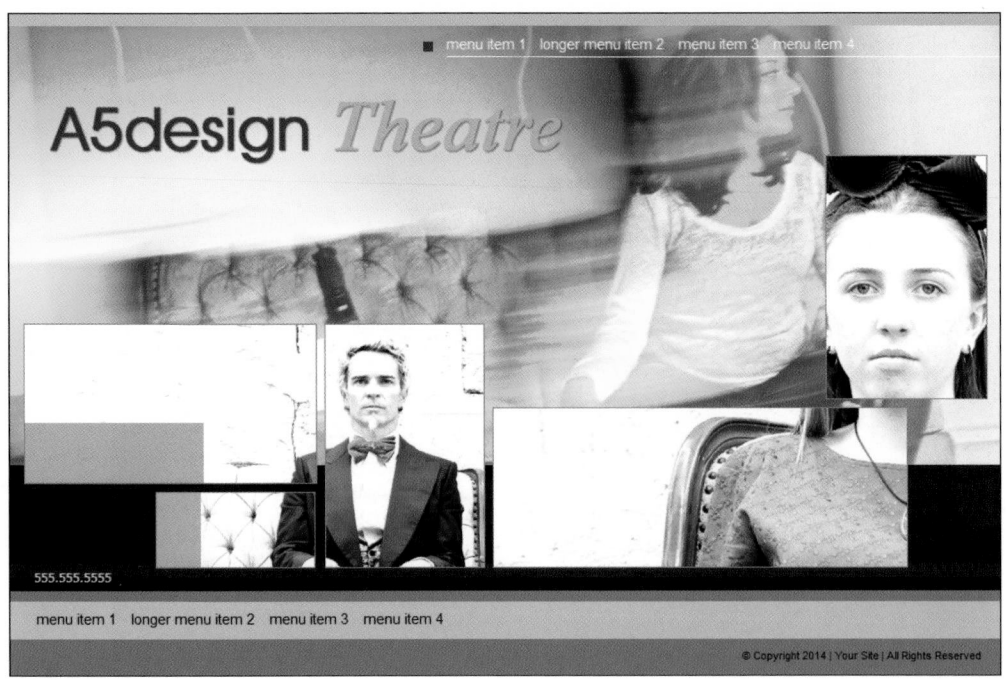

Design 188
© 2014 A5design. Photo Credit: Chelsea Miller Photography

Design 187
© 2014 A5design. Photo Credit: Chelsea Miller Photography

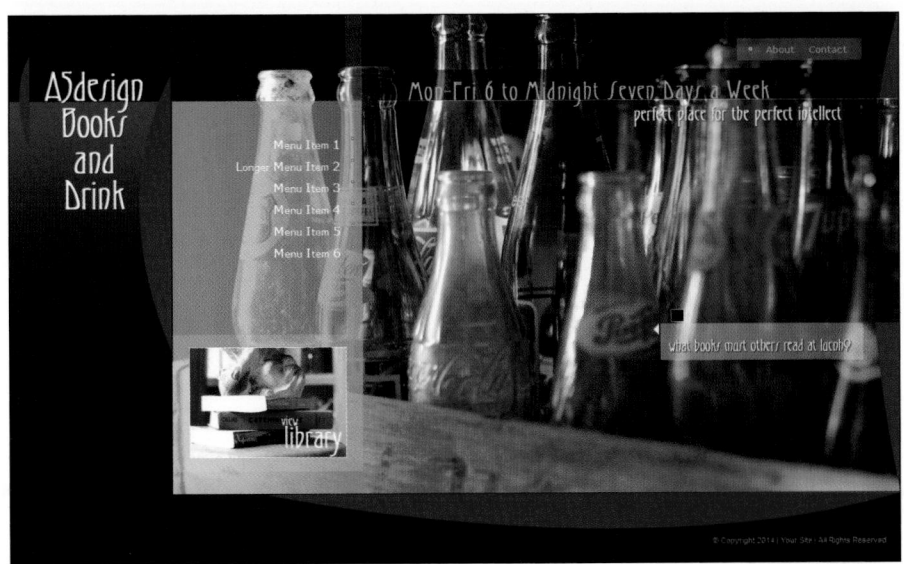

Design 186
© 2014 A5design. Photo Credit: Chelsea Miller Photography

Design 185
© 2014 A5design. Photo Credit: Chelsea Miller Photography

Design 184
© 2014 A5design. Photo Credit: Chelsea Miller Photography

Design 183
© 2014 A5design. Photo Credit: Chelsea Miller Photography

Design 182

Design 181

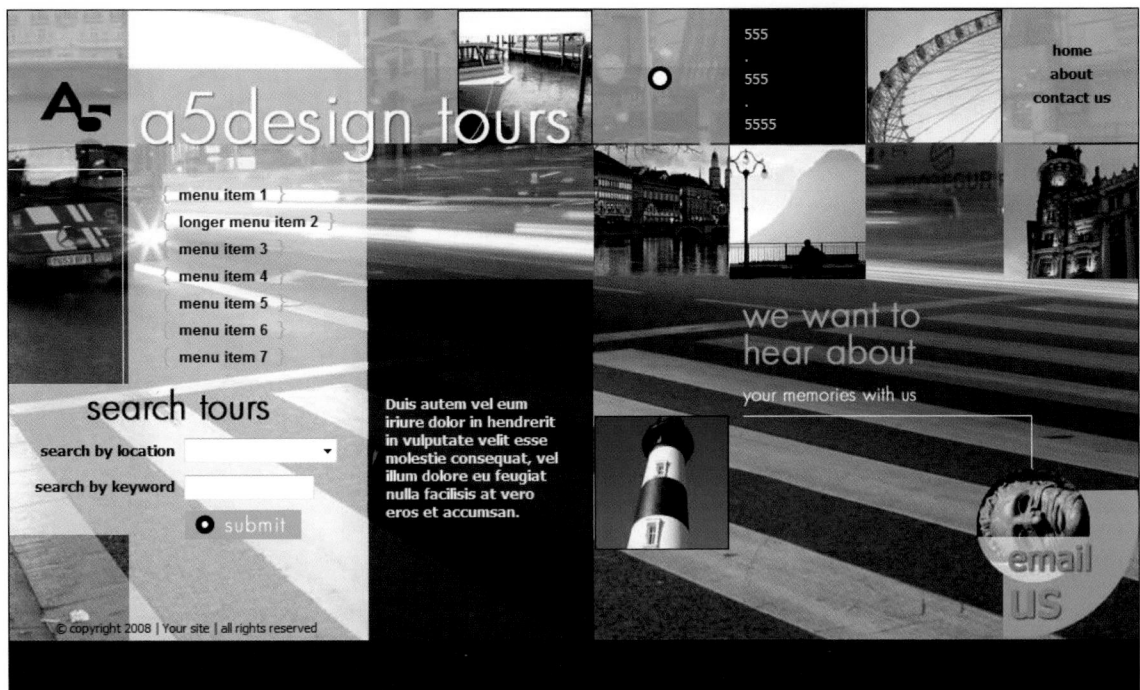

Design 146
© 2014 A5design. Photo Credit: ronsternimages.com

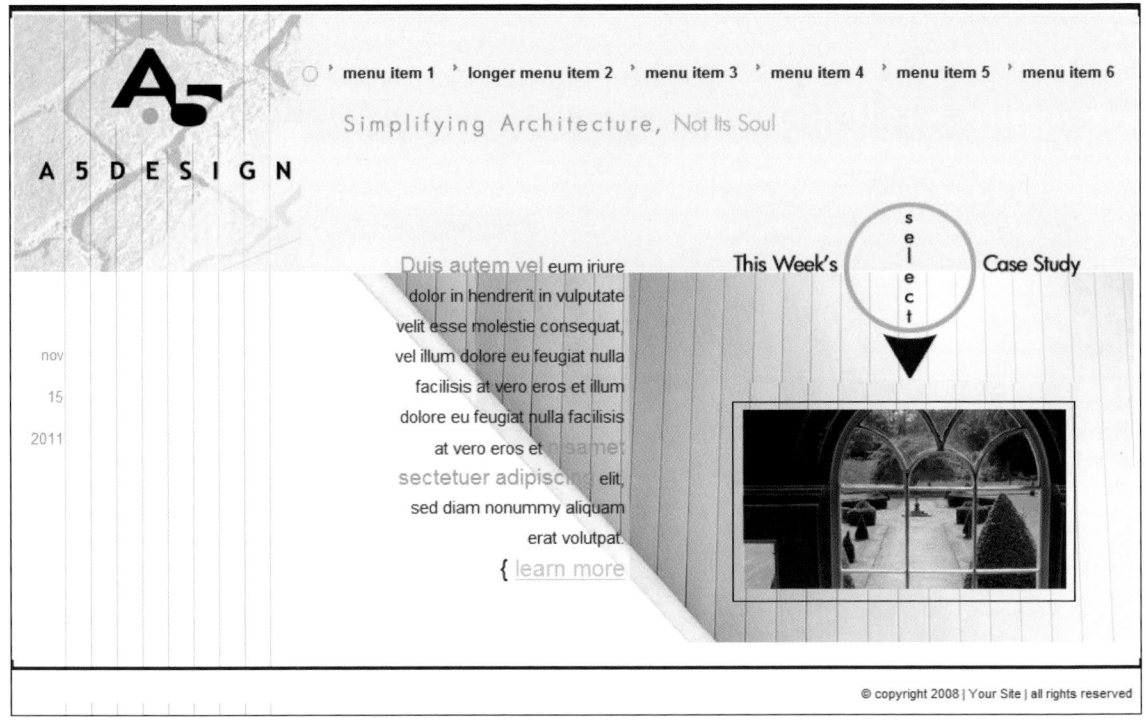

Design 143
© 2014 A5design. Photo Credit: ronsternimages.com and J&N Photography

Design 142
© 2014 A5design. Photo Credit: ronsternimages.com

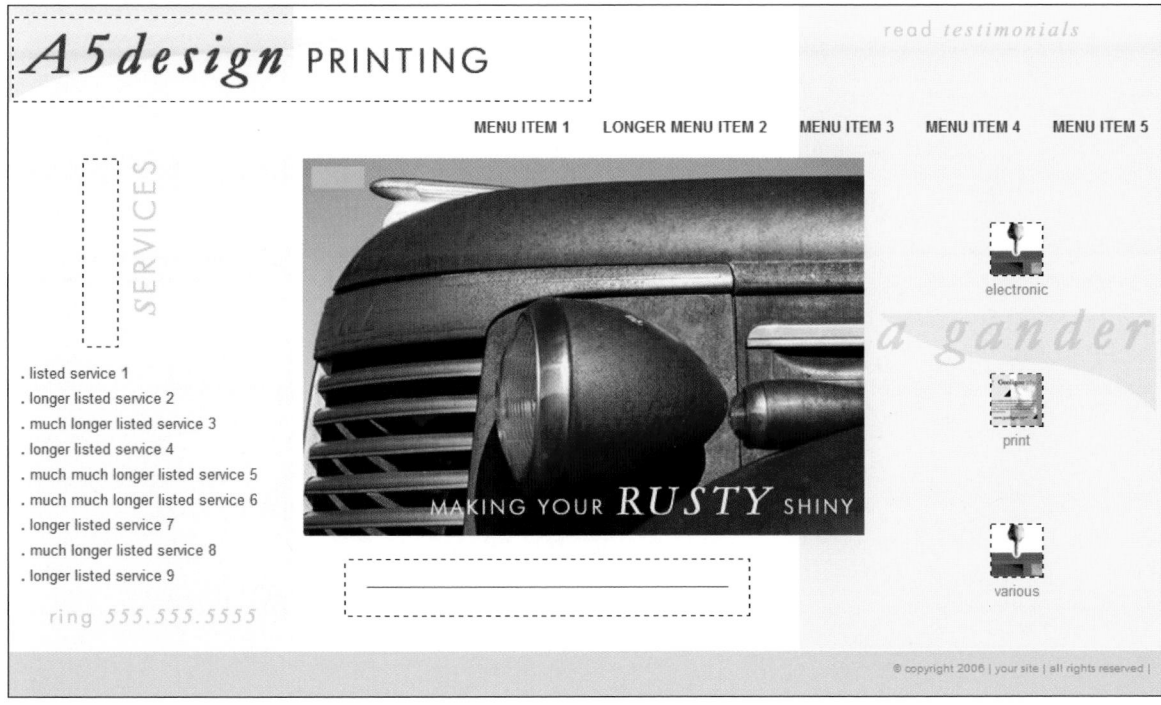

Design 134
© 2014 A5design. Photo Credit: idlerphotography.com

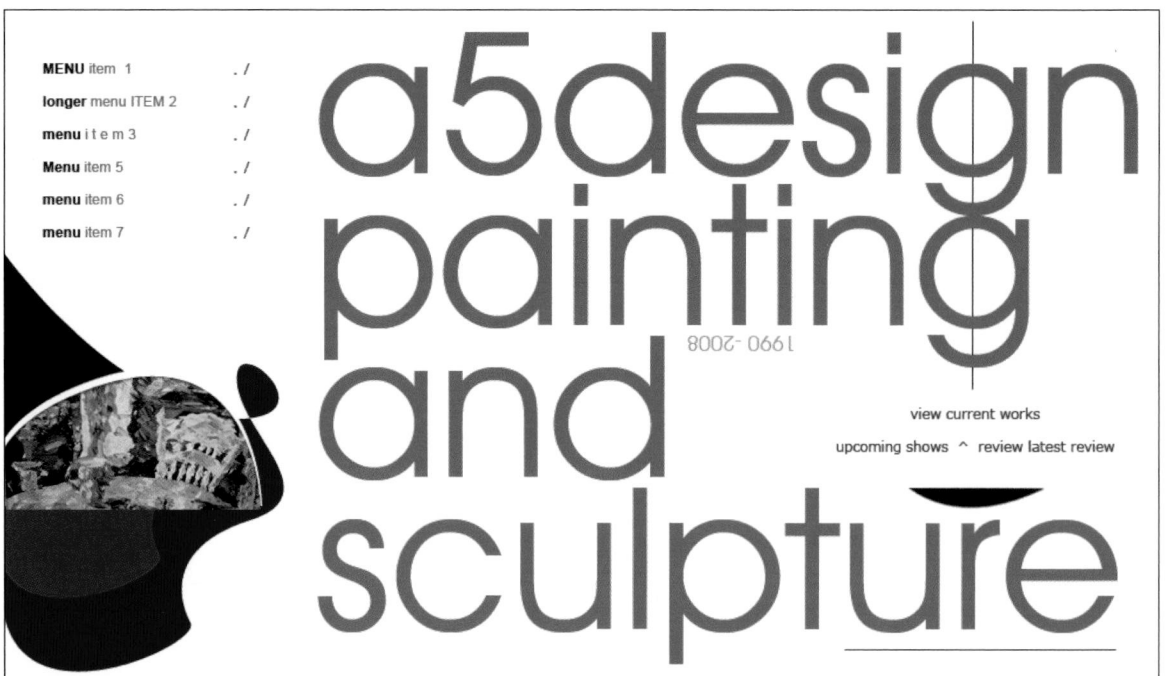

Design 120
© 2014 A5design. Photo Credit: A5design

Design 117
© 2014 A5design. Photo Credit: idlerphotography.com

CHAPTER 6

WHAT IS NEEDED TO BUILD MORTISED SITES

As an accomplished artist once said, "Everyone has the same tools. The only difference is how each person uses them." This statement epitomizes mortised sites. Building such sites is not difficult, especially for the experienced Web designer. There is, in fact, a very low learning curve for such designers because mortised sites do not introduce any new Web development technologies. Other than learning a graphics software program, such as Adobe Photoshop, the designer need only learn creative methods of using XHTML, graphics, and CSS—common tools for a Web designer. Of course, using JavaScript (scripting language), Flash, programming languages, and other tools can also enhance a mortised site.

The difference in the quality of a site is determined by a designer's knowledge of building sites and how the designer uses that knowledge. Two of the most important aspects to building such sites is using CSS to position the majority of content, rather than XHTML tables, and properly compressing and saving images. While CSS allows the designer to create nearly any layout possible, which may include additional programming, properly compressed and saved graphics make the site attractive and more usable. Together, they give the designer the means to build a homogenous site.

Before beginning to fully grasp these and other concepts, the designer should have an understanding of the big picture—that is, knowing the various steps that go into building a mortised site from conception to production. Following are 10 steps in the typical building of a mortised site:

1. Gathering and basing a site on requirements.
2. Creating comp(s) for the client.

3. Receiving a decision on the chosen comp and making edits.

4. Breaking up the comp into XHTML, graphics, and CSS.

5. Testing the page in the most widely used browsers.

6. Saving components of the page as include files and testing again.

7. Building second-level pages from the homepage template.

8. Working with the client as the site is built.

9. Testing the entire site.

10. Implementing or uploading the site.

This general overview helps a designer understand the entire process, which helps to make sense of the many specifics included in this book.

UNDERSTANDING THE CONCEPT OF MORTISING IMAGES

Building a mortised site is similar to piecing a puzzle together. The designer pieces images, content, and functionality together in a manner that allows form and function to complement each other rather than compete against each other.

Mortising can be accomplished at different levels. At the basic level, a designer can mortise just two images together. At the more advanced level, the designer can nest mortised containers (usually content in <SPAN> and <DIV> tags) inside mortised containers to accomplish complex designs. It all, however, begins with a basic understanding of how to piece together two or more images.

Figure 6.1 is an example of three images pieced together seamlessly. All of the images are compressed and saved in their best possible image format.

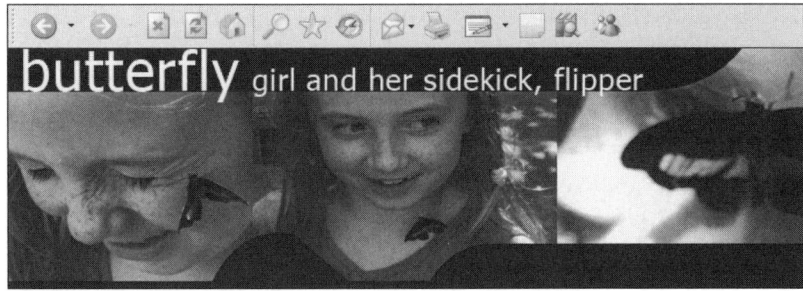

Figure 6.1
Three images mortised together.
© 2014 Cengage Learning.

While they appear to be one image, when spaces are added in between the images, it becomes apparent that there are three separate images (see Figure 6.2).

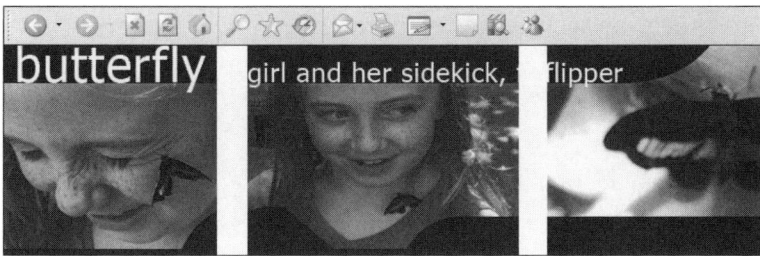

Figure 6.2
Three images that are mortised together to form the image in Figure 6.1.
© 2014 Cengage Learning.

Following is the code for this example. While there are more involved mortising examples throughout the book, this particular code can be reused in many different ways. It is especially important to note that all the spaces have been removed so the images aren't output incorrectly in some browsers, such as shown in Figure 6.3.

```
<div style="width:692px;"><span style="float:right;"><img src="images/photo-bottom-
center.jpg" width="266" height="209" alt="" border="0" /><img src=
"images/photo-bottom-right.jpg" width="213" height="209" alt=" " border="0" /></span>
<span style="float:left;"><img src="images/photo-bottom-left.jpg" width="213"
height="209" alt=" " border="0" /></span></div>
```

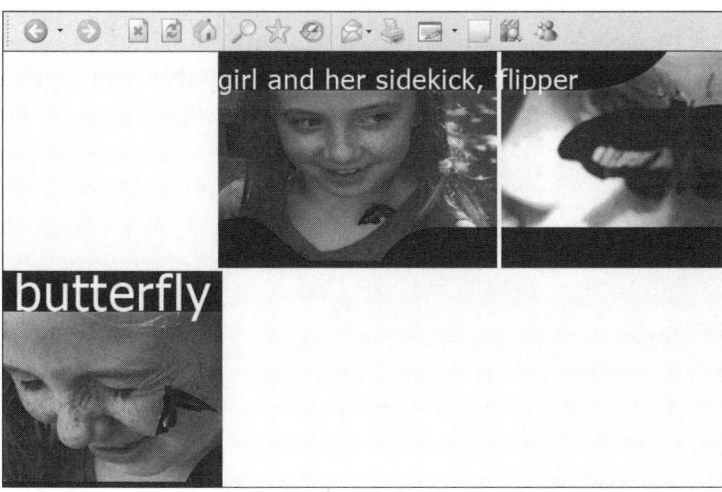

Figure 6.3
An example of how the images in Figure 6.2 will "fall apart" when normal spacing is added between the elements.
© 2014 Cengage Learning.

Notice how the first two images are nested together in a <SPAN> tag and then floated to the right of the left image. If the designer were to simply add all three images together or try floating them nearly any other way, they would not piece together seamlessly. It should also be noted that for this code to work, as well as other occasional CSS, it cannot have spaces in between it. Following is an example of how the code should *not* look:

```
<div style="width:692px;">
 <span style="float:right;">
 <img src="images/photo-bottom-center.jpg" width="266" height="209" alt=""
border="0" />
 <img src="images/photo-bottom-right.jpg" width="213" height="209" alt=""
border="0" /></span>
 <span style="float:left;">
 <img src="images/photo-bottom-left.jpg" width="213" height="209" alt=""
border="0" />
 </span>
</div>
```

There are several advantages to mortising:

■ The designer can save parts of images in their best respective image formats. For instance, in Figure 6.2, any of the three images could be saved as a PNG and placed among the other two JPG images, if the designer needed such flexibility. Or that image could be saved as a background image of a container that could have text layered over it.

■ The designer can have more freedom with layouts. Although everything is saved and structured in rigid, linear shapes in CSS Web design, the design does not have to appear that way. Instead, text, colors, and images can flow through a page, leading the user's eyes and creating a sense of motion or emotion with the design (see Figure 6.4).

■ The designer can be guaranteed of content and image placement because positioning is fixed.

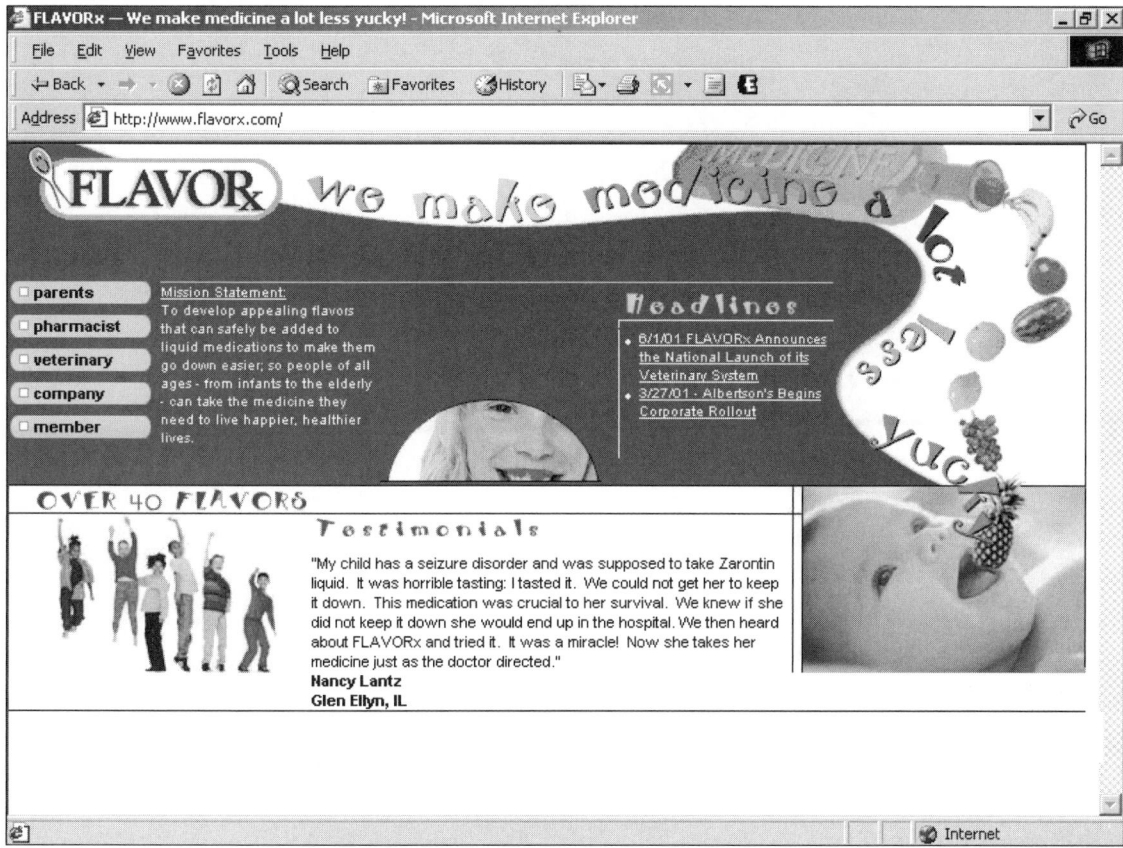

Figure 6.4
Site that uses images to create a sense of motion.
© 2014 FLAVORx.com.

Figure 6.5 represents another way to mortise three images together. It shows how to place images together with absolute or relative positioning. The designer can control placement of an image by wrapping a container around it and assigning the position, top, left, and right properties to it. Figure 6.5 shows how the first of three images is positioned in a container with the ID of a5-header. It is assigned absolute positioning, placing it 0 pixels from the top and 0 pixels from the left side.

Figure 6.5
The first of three images positioned in the container.
© 2014 Cengage Learning.

Background Color Helps with Differentiation

The 627-pixel-wide container is assigned a black background to differentiate it from the white background of the page.

After the first image has a `<DIV>` wrapped around it and is placed in the parent container, a second image is added. It also has a container wrapped around it. This image, however, is placed 247 pixels from the left, which positions the two images together (see Figure 6.6).

Figure 6.6
The second of three images positioned in the container.
© 2014 Cengage Learning.

The third image is positioned 304 pixels from the left, which is the sum total width of the first two images (247 + 57 = 304 pixels). Depending on the instance of mortising, the right property can be used in place of the left property. Listing 6.1 is the code to build the completed mortised images in Figure 6.7.

Figure 6.7
All three images positioned in the container.
© 2014 Cengage Learning.

Listing 6.1   Code for Figure 6.7

```
<!DOCTYPE html PUBLIC "-//W3C//DTD XHTML 1.0 Transitional//EN"
  "DTD/xhtml1-transitional.dtd">
<html><head><title>Mortised Images</title>
<style>
     #a5-header {
          position:relative;
          top:0px;
          left:0px;
          width:627px;
          height:400px;
          background:black;
     }
     #a5-photo-left {
          position:absolute;
          top:0px;
          left:0px;
     }
```

```
#a5-photo-center {
    position:absolute;
    top:0px;
    left:247px;
}
#a5-photo-right {
    position:absolute;
    top:0px;
    left:304px;
}
</style>
</head>
<body>
<div id="a5-header">
    <div id="a5-photo-left"><img src="images/photo-left.jpg"
        width="247" height="400" alt="" border="0" /></div>
    <div id="a5-photo-center"><img src="images/photo-center.jpg"
        width="57" height="400" alt="" border="0" /></div>
    <div id="a5-photo-right"><img src="images/photo-right.jpg"
        width="323" height="400" alt="" border="0" /></div>
</div>
</body>
</html>
```

Placing background images in a container is another way to mortise images together. One reason a designer may want to do so is to place text over the image. Figure 6.8 shows how the left image of a container is added.

Figure 6.8
The left image added to the container.

© 2014 Cengage Learning.

Background Color Helps with Differentiation

The 1,000-pixel-wide container is assigned a black background to differentiate it from the white background of the page.

Once the first image has been added, the second is inserted (see Figure 6.9). In this example, the left text is saved as an image, so the process of mortising the two images together is the same as the previous example.

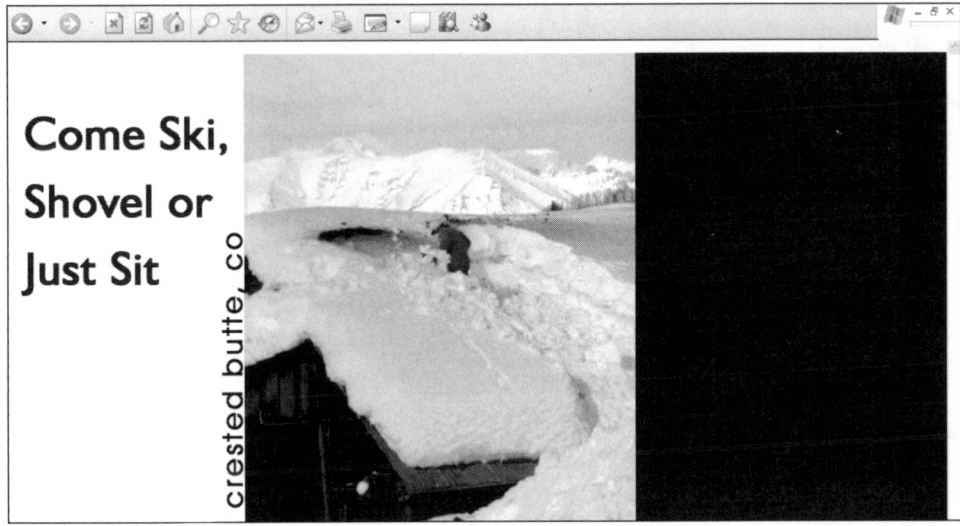

Figure 6.9
The center image added to the container.
© 2014 Cengage Learning.

Adding the right container is where this example becomes more complex. The designer is going to size and position the a5-text-right <DIV>; however, the text is going to be added to another <DIV> that is nested inside. This allows for padding and line-height properties and values to be added at a local level. Listing 6.2 is the code used to create the final layout (see Figure 6.10).

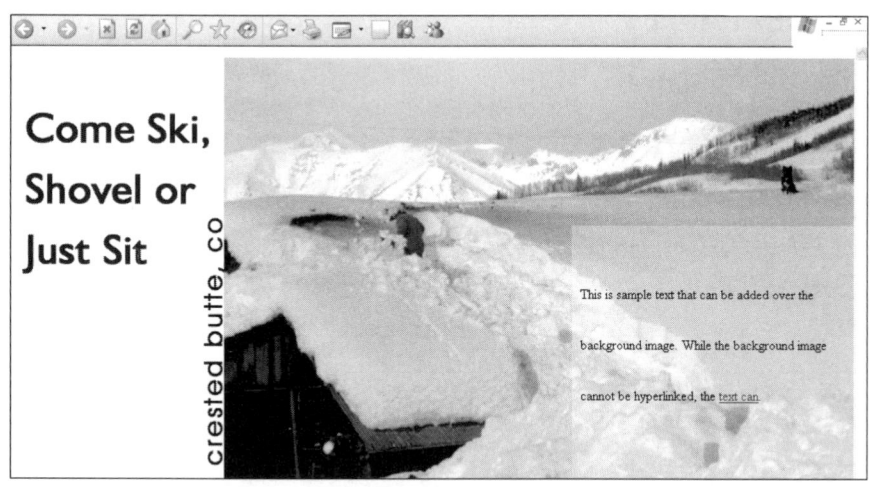

Figure 6.10
Background image and text added to the right column.
© 2014 Cengage Learning.

Listing 6.2   Code for Figure 6.10

```
<!DOCTYPE html PUBLIC "-//W3C//DTD XHTML 1.0 Transitional//EN"
  "DTD/xhtml1-transitional.dtd">
<html><head><title>Mortised Images</title>
<style>
  #a5-container {
     position:relative;
   `  top:0px;
     left:0px;
     width:1000px;
     height:500px;
     background:black;
  }
  #a5-image-left {
    position:absolute;
    top:0px;
    left:0px;
  }
  #a5-photo-center {
    position:absolute;
    top:0px;
    left:251px;
  }
```

```
     #a5-text-right {
        position:absolute;
        bottom:0px;
        right:0px;
        width:333px;
        height:500px;
        background:url("images/bg-right.jpg") no-repeat;
     }
  </style>
  </head>
  <body>
  <div id="a5-container">
      <div id="a5-image-left"><a href="x.htm"><img src="images/
        image-left.gif" width="251" height="500" alt="" border="0"
        /></a></div>
      <div id="a5-photo-center"><a href="x.htm"><img src="images/photo-
        center.jpg" width="416" height="500" alt="" border="0"
        /></a></div>
      <div id="a5-text-right">
        <div style="padding:250px 10px 10px 10px;line-height:60px;">
          This is sample text that can be added over the background
          image. While the background image cannot be hyperlinked,
          the <a href="x.htm">text can</a>.</div>
      </div>
  </div>
  </body>
  </html>
```

Understanding XHTML

XHTML used to be more involved with Web design when table-based designs were the standard and tables had to be nested within each other to mortise Web page elements together. Today, XHTML plays a much smaller, almost insignificant, roll in creating professional-looking sites.

In CSS-driven designs, XHTML mainly provides the framework for the page, which includes the `<HTML>`, `<HEAD>`, `<TITLE>`, and `<BODY>` tags; the structure of containers, which includes `<SPAN>` and `<DIV>` tags; and the general tags for page elements to be built, such as forms and embedded elements like hyperlinks and images.

The majority of positioning and layout is now controlled with CSS. This is not to devalue XHTML code. Its tags are still crucial in creating code that can be read by search engines and text readers, among other things. The good thing for the designer is that the `<TABLE>`, `<TR>`, and `<TD>` tags are now used mainly for displaying table data, such as in a spreadsheet.

Using a Limited Number of Tags

Out of more than 110 XHTML tags, a designer only needs to know a small number of them to build mortised sites with basic form functionality. Rather than spending time learning more tags, the designer can spend time logically and creatively manipulating this limited number of tags with CSS, rather than hundreds of lines of `<TABLE>` code. Included in Table 6.1 is a list of popular tags, along with some of their possible attributes and uses.

Table 6.1   Basic Tags for Building Mortised Sites

Tag	Description
`<html>`	Standard tag used in all pages, except include files. Closed at end of page with `</html>`.
`<head>`	Standard tag used in all pages, except include files. Closed at the end of the header information with `</head>`.
`<title>`	Standard tag used in all pages, except include files. Closed with `</title>`.
`<meta name="" content="">`	Standard tag used on pages. This tag provides information, determined by the designer, to be indexed by search engines. It is usually placed between the `<head>` and `</head>` tags.
`<body>`	Standard tag used in all pages. All content seen by the user falls within this tag set. Closed at the end of the page with `</body>`.
`<p>`, ` `	Essential for breaking lines in page layout. The `<p>` tag also can be used when applying a style to a block of text or images. The `<p>` tag is closed with a `</p>`, and the ` ` is simply closed within itself.
`<table>`	Essential tag for building tables. Closed at the end of the table with `</table>`.
`<tr>`	Essential tag for building table rows. Closed with `</tr>`.
`<td>`	Essential tag for creating table cells. Closed with a `</td>`.

`<img src="" width="" height="" alt="" border="" name="" />`	Essential for adding images to a page. The forward slash (/) is included in the tag so that it closes itself.
`<a href="" class="" target="">`	Essential for linking to pages, documents, and images. Closed with `</a>`.
`<div class="" style="">`	Used with CSS usually to control font size and color, images, multiple block-level elements, and content positioning. Closed with `</div>`.
`<span class="" style ="">`	Used to add styles to content. Closed with `</span>`.
`<strong>` or `<em>`	Used to bold text when it is not controlled using a style that is associated with text. Closed with `</strong>`.
`<!- comment ->`	Used to comment code. Used for all comments—single and multiple lines.
`<form id="" name="" action="" method="">`	Used to create forms in XHMTL. Closed with `</form>`.
`<input type="" id="" name="" value="" />`	Input is used to create form fields, such as "text," "radio," and "checkbox." The tag closes itself with a forward slash (/).
`<label for="" id="">`	Used for positioning elements with fields in a form.
`<textarea>`	Used for large text input entries. Closed with `</textarea>`.
`<select id="" name="" multiple="multiple">`	Used for dropdown form elements. Closed with `</select>`.
`<option selected="selected" value="" label="">`	Used to delineate individual items in a dropdown form field. Closed with `</option>`.

UNDERSTANDING GRAPHICS

Creating, using, saving, and compressing images in their best possible formats is essential to professional Web design. Because it is so important, the issue is addressed in depth in Chapter 7.

UNDERSTANDING CSS

Unlike in the past where CSS (Cascading Style Sheet) was used mainly to style text, it now plays, for the most part, the sole role in positioning and styling content, whether at the global, local, or inline level. Used to its greatest potential, one CSS document controls the styles of the entire site, similar to the concept of an include file (discussed later in this chapter). This book has been considerably rewritten to explain this new use of CSS and how it can be used to create highly professional websites. While Chapters 8 through 14 and 16 go into more specifics about this subject, the following sections are an overview a designer needs for a general understanding.

Understanding CSS Terminology

It is assumed that the designer has a working, if limited, knowledge of CSS. Recalling terminology, however, is not always the easiest thing to do, which is why Figure 6.11 was created. It provides a basic visual example of CSS elements and their terminology in a CSS style sheet.

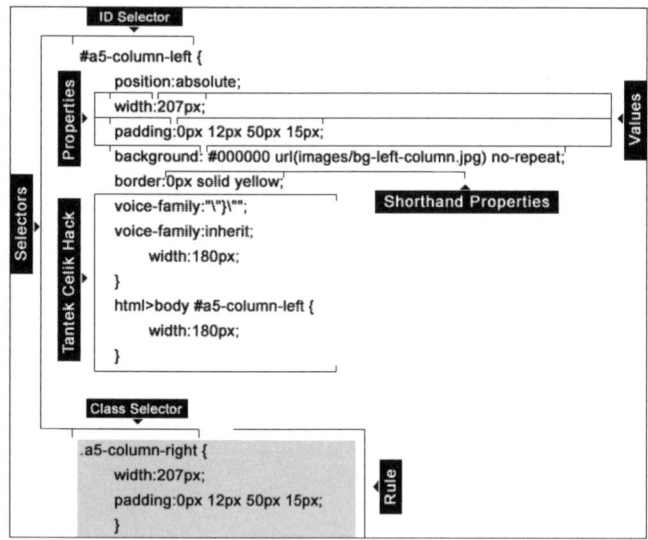

Figure 6.11
A visual reference of CSS terminology, including an example of the Tantek Celik Hack, which is no longer used.
© 2014 Cengage Learning.

Following are the various items to note about the code in Figure 6.11:

- **Selectors:** These are used when declaring and calling a particular rule. Figure 6.11 identifies two types of selectors, an ID selector and a Class selector, both of which can be used with XHTML tags, such as <P>, <DIV>, or <SPAN>.

- **Properties:** Various aspects of a selector that can be used for different styles.

- **Values:** The specific qualities of properties.

- **Shorthand Properties:** A method of combining multiple related values for a property under one general property. An example would be combining `padding-top: 10px; padding- right:15px; padding-bottom:25px; padding-left:30px` into one property that looks like `padding:10px 15px 25px 30px;`.

- **Rule:** The entire grouping of a selector, a property (or properties), and value(s).

- **Tantek Celik Hack:** While this is not necessarily considered CSS terminology, it was kept in this edition of the book as a historical reminder of how CSS has progressed over the years. In the past, the designer used to have to include such code to ensure IE 5/5.5 rendered the width of a `<DIV>` tag similarly to other browsers. Fortunately, this is no longer an issue.

CSS Used in This Book

The CSS coding philosophy used in this book is to be creative with a limited number of CSS properties and values, rather than use those that do not necessarily function under all conditions. In other words, the goal is to be the most flexible with the smallest number of properties and values that are proven to work in the widest range of browsers and their versions. While there is a much wider array of possibilities for a designer, it is left to the designer to expand upon what is discussed in this book. Table 6.2 lists many properties that are used in this book. Many of them are shorthand examples, meaning one property is used to set the various values that could be broken up into other properties.

Table 6.2   Some of the CSS Properties Used in This Book

Example Property	Usage
`margin:0px 0px 0px 0px;`	Used for setting the distance between the outside border of a container and what it is nested inside of it.
`padding:0px 0px 0px 0px;`	Used for setting the distance between the outside border of a container and what it is nested inside it.
`font:13px Arial, Helvetica, sans-serif;` `font-weight:bold;`	Used to set the size, face, and weight of a font. The bold value does not work in all situations, which is why it is sometimes separated out as `font-weight:bold;` or included in the XHTML code.

(Continued)

Table 6.2   Some of the CSS Properties Used in This Book (*Continued*)

Example Property	Usage
`color:#000000;`	Used to set the text color.
`a:link { color:#FF7800; }`	Used to set a hyperlink color.
`a:visited { color:#FF5A00; }`	Used to set the hyperlink color of a visited or previously clicked link.
`a:active { color:#FFC600; }`	Used for defining the color of a link while it is being clicked and has not yet been released.
`a:hover { color:#000000; }`	Used for changing the color of a hyperlink when it is moused over but has yet to be clicked.
`a.linklist:link { text-decoration: none;color:#308DAE;}`	Used for setting the color of a link with an assigned class (e.g., `class="linklist"`).
`a.linklist:visited { text-decoration: none;color:#308DAE;}`	Used for setting the visited color of a link with an assigned class (e.g., `class="linklist"`).
`a.linklist:active { text-decoration: none;color:#308DAE;}`	Used for setting the active color of a link with an assigned class (e.g., `class="linklist"`).
`a.linklist:hover { text-decoration: underline;color:#FF7800;}`	Used for setting the hover color of a link with an assigned class (e.g., `class="linklist"`).
`border: 1px solid #000000;`	Used for setting the border of a CSS element to 1, with a specified color.
`text-align:left;` `text-align:right;` `text-align:center;`	Used to control the horizontal placement of content, whether the value `left`, `right`, or `center` is used.
`position:relative;` `position:absolute;`	Used to define whether a box, or container, in the box model will be assigned relative or absolute positioning.
`float:right;` `float:left;` `float:center;`	Used to position elements to the left or right in content.
`clear:both;`	Used to remove floating elements from the left and right sides of a container.
`width:100%;`	Used to set the width of an element, such as a box.
`margin-left:auto;` `margin-right:auto;`	Used when centering a fixed-width Web page.

`left:0px;` `right:0px;`	Used for setting how many pixels from the left or right side of the body or a parent box an element is placed.
`top:0px;` `bottom:0px;`	Used for setting how many pixels from the top or bottom of the body or a parent box an element is placed.
`height:78px;`	Used for forcing the height of an element.

`width:88px;`
`voice-family:"\"}\"";`
`voice-family:inherit;`
`width:78px;`
`}`
`html>body #a5-header {`
`   width: 78px;`
`}`
	Used for setting various properties and values for different browsers. It is called the Tantek Celik hack, or Tantek hack.

`line-height:42px;` `vertical-align:30%;`	Used for forcing the vertical positioning of text in an element. The line-height property needs to be included for the vertical-align property to be interpreted by the browser. It also should appear after the font property to work for the various browsers.
`background:#000000 url(images/bg-menu.` `gif) repeat-x 0px 0px;`	Used for determining what background image is used, where it is placed, and how it is repeated. The HEX value sets what the background color of an element will be if the background does not fill the entire space.

BLOCK- AND LINE-LEVEL TAGS

Block- and inline-level tags are at the core of positioning and styling content in a website. The most common block-level element is the <DIV> tag. The most common line-level tag is the <SPAN> tag. Together, they are used similarly to how XHTML tables were used to create mortised sites. The <DIV> tag is used as a "box" to place content in, position, and style, similar to a table. The <SPAN> tag is used to style individual elements inside a block-level tag, although a <DIV> tag can be, and frequently is, used to do the same. Chapter 8 provides a basic understanding of how these tags are used, while Chapters 9, 10, 11, 12, 13, and 14 provide actual case studies on how to do so. A more technical explanation of these type of tags can be found on the World Wide Web Consortium (W3C) site at www.w3.org/TR/REC-CSS2/visuren.html#q5.

Understanding the DocType Declaration

A DocType Declaration (DTD) is a line of code that should be included in the first line of every Web page, barring include files. The most basic explanation of a DTD is that it defines the rules of how a browser should render a Web page, based on W3C's standards. Various types of declarations can be used, depending on how the designer wants a Web page to be interpreted by a browser and validated by the W3C. In other words, pages can be interpreted on their HTML, XHTML, or XML coding. The latest designs in this book are created using the following XHTML 1.0 transitional declaration:

```
<!DOCTYPE XHTML PUBLIC "-//W3C//DTD XHTML 1.0 Transitional//EN"
        "DTD/xhtml1-transitional.dtd">
```

Linking to CSS Style Sheets

While there are different ways to include a style sheet (such as linking, embedding, and including inline), imported style sheets offer one thing the others do not: they prevent older browsers that do not fully support CSS from crashing. In the past, style sheets were imported to keep browsers, such as Netscape 4.7, from choking on the CSS. Fortunately, this is more of a history lesson than a practical lesson, since Netscape is no longer a major player in the browser world. Listing 6.3 provides the code to import a style sheet:

Listing 6.3   Code Used to Import a Style Sheet

```
<style type="text/css" media="all">
    @import "mainstyle.css";
</style>
```

Including Print Style Sheets

A designer no longer has to create separate pages that are used specifically for printing a page. The following style sheet link simply needs to be added to the page's code.

```
<link rel="stylesheet" href="print.css" type="text/css"
        media="print"/>
```

Once this link has been added, the browser will call a separate style sheet that it will use for printing purposes. Usually, the style sheet is a copied version of the main style sheet, which is then modified to display the page how the designer desires. If the header, for example, does not need to be printed, the designer can change the style sheet to hide that element of the page. Following are several things a designer should consider changing to make a page more printer-friendly:

■ The font size could be changed to points for printing purposes. Otherwise, the page may not print sizes, such as pixels, clearly.

■ Any section can be turned off by adding the rule display:none; to any <DIV> or <SPAN> tag. For example, the following style would be completed hidden from a Web page when the rule was added to the style in the second version:

```
#a5-header {
  position:relative;
  top:0px;
  height:73px;
  background: red;}
```

```
#a5-header {
  position:relative;
  top:0px;
  height:73px;
  background: red;
  display:none;}
```

By making this change, anything in the container with the id value of a5-header would be hidden from the printer. To test what the page will look like, the designer can select Print Preview in the browser rather than actually having to print it.

■ The text to be printed can be resized easily to fit the screen however the designer chooses.

■ Colors that may not print very well in grayscale, such as yellow, can be changed to a darker color.

Figure 6.12 shows how a site is displayed in a browser. Figure 6.13 illustrates how drastically the same page can appear when reading a print style sheet. Many of the elements of the page, including the header, menu, and content columns, were removed so only the necessary information would be printed.

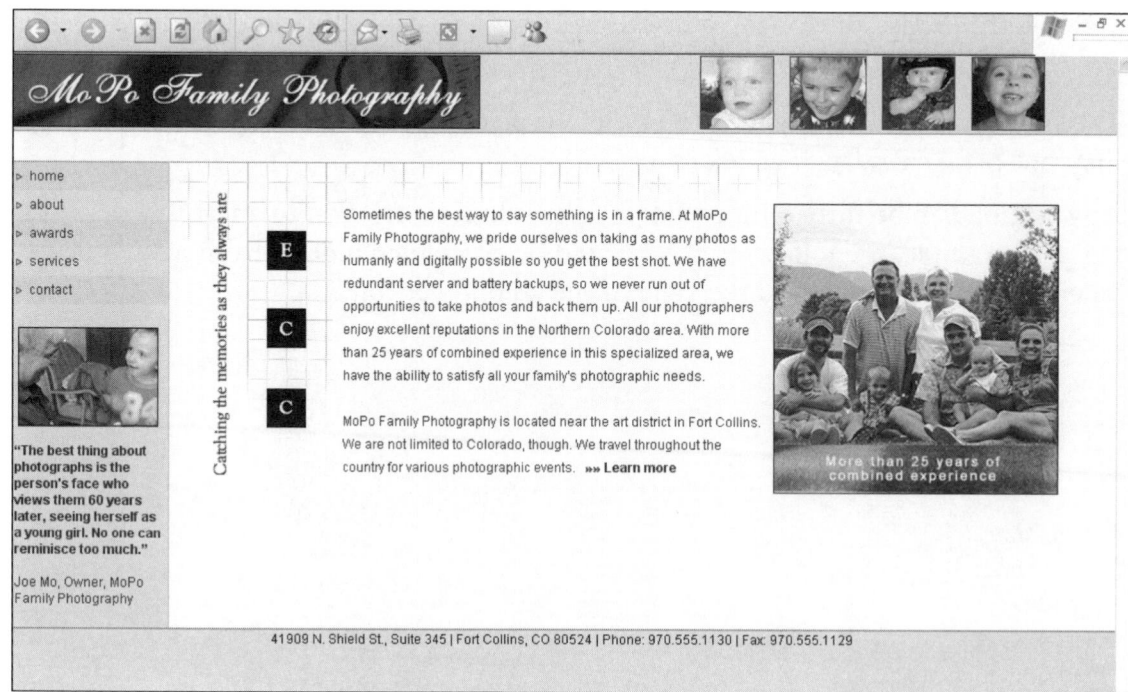

Figure 6.12
A Web page and how it appears with a nonprinting style sheet.
© 2014 Cengage Learning.

By simply selecting Print Preview in Internet Explorer, the browser will give the designer an idea of how the page will appear when it is printed. The great thing about this functionality is that the designer can test a page without actually having to print it.

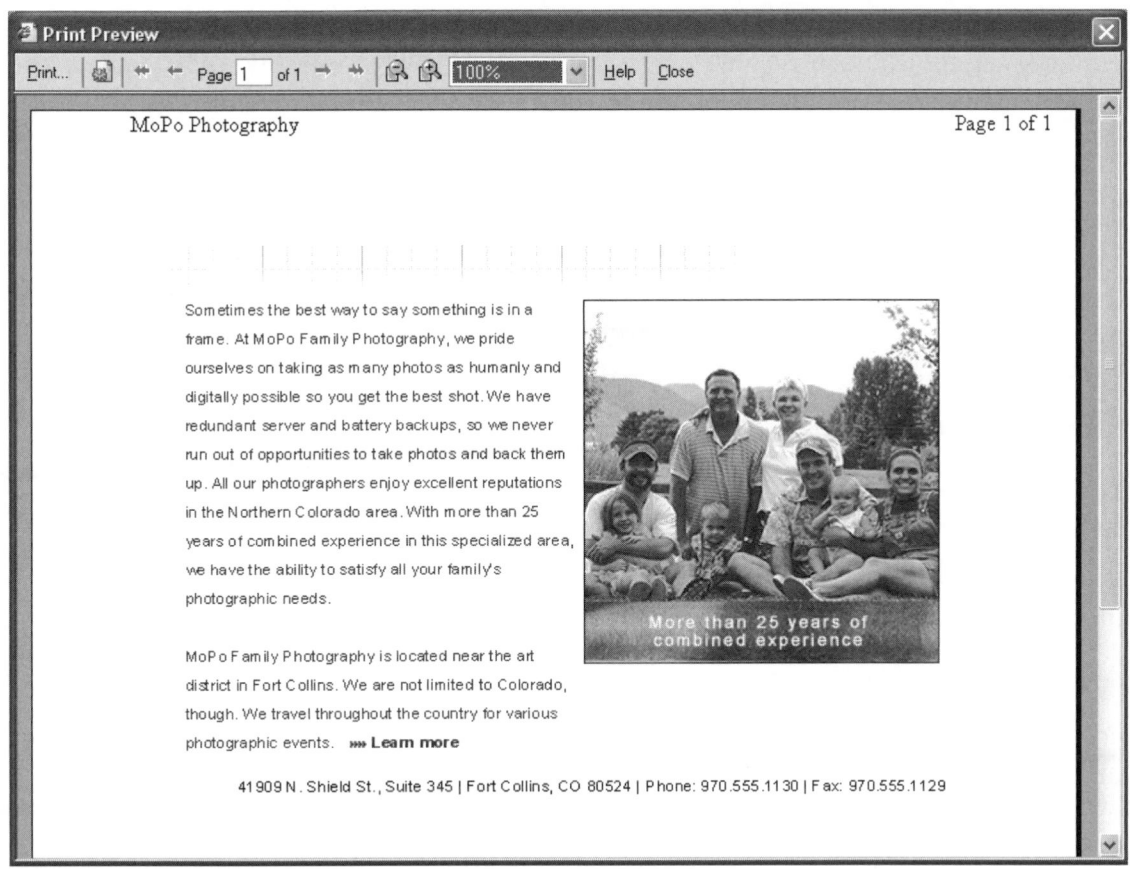

Figure 6.13
The same Web page as in Figure 6.12, but in Print Preview mode it uses a print style sheet to determine what is printed.
© 2014 Cengage Learning.

UNDERSTANDING INCLUDE FILES

Include files are individual files that can be repeatedly called into different pages (for example, PHP, .NET, or JSP pages). A blessing to Web designers, include files not only allow a site to be modular (various easily interchangeable pieces), but more importantly, they also reduce maintenance time. An example of an include file might be the footer text of a site. Instead of placing the text in every page, a designer might include one line of code in every page that calls that footer text, which is saved as its own file. Then, when the footer needs to be edited, the designer edits only one page.

To use include files, all a designer needs is to host a site on a server that offers server-side processing, such as Microsoft (.NET pages), Apache HTTP Server (SHTML pages), and JSP server (JSP pages), or an open-source server that runs PHP pages. Following are examples of code that are used to include files into other files:

Code to call include file in a .NET page:
```
<!- - #include file="menu.txt" - ->
```
Code to call include file in an SHTML page:
```
<!- -#include file="filename.shtml" - ->
```
Code to call include file in a PHP page:
```
<?php include("pagename.php"); ?>
```
Code to call include file in a JSP page:
```
<%@ include file="menu.jsp" %>
```

SUMMARY

The three components of building mortised sites are XHTML, CSS, and graphics. A designer, however, should also understand several concepts, such as mortising images, using block- and line-level tags, and taking advantage of include files. Mortised sites have a low learning curve because they do not require a Web designer to learn any new technologies—just a different coding methodology. Building such sites also requires a limited amount of XHTML and CSS. The designer, rather, needs to use existing tools and methods in new, creative ways to build fast, highly usable, professional sites.

CHAPTER 7

UNDERSTANDING GRAPHICS

One of the most important aspects of building mortised sites is to have properly saved and compressed graphics. Unlike working with XHTML, saving and compressing graphics leaves less to the imagination of the designer. Rather, the nature of the image will usually dictate how it should be saved, although there are times when the designer can be creative. This does not necessarily mean that the image will be saved as it should. The designer must understand how to best create, use, save, and compress images; and the first place to start is by understanding the two types of images used on the Web.

LEARNING ABOUT VECTOR AND BITMAP IMAGES

There are two general types of graphics used on the Web: vector and bitmap. Bitmap images, which are mainly composed of JPGs, PNGs, and GIFs, continue to be the most commonly used type of image on the Internet. The second type of graphics are vector images. These use mathematically based lines and curves to display images, as opposed to bitmap images, which use pixels to display images. The best way to understand the difference between the two types of images is to view an example. Figure 7.1 is an image of a circle.

Figure 7.1
Circle that could be created as both a vector or bitmap image.
© 2014 Cengage Learning.

A designer could create the same image in both a vector-based program, such as Adobe Illustrator, or a bitmap-based program, such as Adobe Photoshop. (More recent versions of Photoshop now also support vector-based images.) When zooming in on the left-bottom corner of the circle in both programs, the difference between vector and bitmap images is apparent. Figure 7.2 is the vector image, and Figure 7.3 is the bitmap image. The vector image is smooth, while the bitmap image is jagged.

Figure 7.2
Corner of a circle that was saved as a vector image.
© 2014 Cengage Learning.

Figure 7.3
Corner of a circle that was saved as a bitmap image.
© 2014 Cengage Learning.

When viewing each image at 100 percent in Photoshop, the two images look fairly similar because individual pixels make up the different shades of black used in the bitmap image. Shades of gray soften the edges (called *anti-aliasing*) to give the illusion of one color. Despite anti-aliasing, vector images still appear sharper.

Not only are lines in vector images crisper, but they also have smaller file sizes than bitmap images, as long as they are kept simple. Vector images are also more easily resized with less degradation to the image. There are, however, two advantages of bitmap images over vector images:

- Bitmap images compress and display images with millions of colors much better than vector images.

- Bitmap images are supported by all browsers, while most types of vector images still require a browser plug-in to view, unless they are saved as bitmap images.

Many multimedia sites are vector-based. One example of vector-based graphics is Scalable Vector Graphics (SVG). This is a language that allows a designer to create vector-based images, vector shapes, and text. In other words, instead of a designer having to create Figure 7.4 as a traditional image, ASCII text can actually be used for text. This not only makes maintenance easier, but it also allows search engines to be able to index the text. Unfortunately, SVG graphics also require a plug-in. Another example, more commonly known, is Adobe Flash. While you can also embed bitmap images in it, the vector aspect allows for a designer to create much larger movies with vector technology than if it were to be bitmap-based.

Figure 7.4
Text saved as an image.
© 2014 Cengage Learning.

Once again, however, when considering the differences between bitmap and vector images, a designer must consider Rule 1 of Web design: just because you *can* does not mean you *should*. Bitmap images continue to be the images of choice for Web developers. This is not something that will change soon; it will be difficult to get the critical mass of Web users to either upgrade to a browser that supports vector images or download plug-ins that support the images.

This makes it important for a designer to understand and use currently supported image formats. Once a designer has a full understanding of bitmap images, it is possible to use them to create striking, fast, usable sites. Fortunately, there are only three bitmap formats that are necessary to learn in order to build or customize mortised sites—JPGs, PNGs, and GIFs.

LEARNING ABOUT JPGS, PNGS, AND GIFS

With as much incompatibility as there is with Web software and hardware, it is refreshing to know that JPGs, PNGs, and GIFs are fully supported by all significant graphical browsers. It is important, though, that a designer learn the strengths and weaknesses of the formats. Otherwise, image quality and size can be drastically compromised.

Using PNGs and GIFs

There are two types of PNGs—8 bit and 24 bit. 8-bit PNGs are generally very comparable to GIFs because they both support up to 256 colors. There are two major differences between 8-bit and 24-bit PNGs:

■ 24-bit PNGs support as many colors as JPGs, except the PNG format is lossless, which means it maintains the actual colors and eliminates the issue of blurring of an image when it is overly compressed.

- 24-bit PNGs offer up to 256 transparent colors, compared with 8-bit PNGs or GIFs, which support only one color of transparency. This is extremely beneficial when layering images in a site because they don't have a jagged edge around the image area that isn't transparent.

While it doesn't sound impressive that 8-bit PNGs and GIFs support only 256 colors, these formats still have their benefits. Following are five advantages they offer over JPGs:

1. **PNGs and GIFs do a better job of compressing large areas of solid color.** They not only compress such images smaller, but the images also appear crisper.

2. **GIFs support animation.** Although animated GIFs have been overused and misused in the past and have been replaced mainly by Flash animation, there are still occasional, more obscure uses for them. One example would be using a "loading" image for an application site that doesn't use Flash. Without motion, users may believe that the site, their connection, or their systems are locked up.

3. **PNGs and GIFs allow for one color in an image to be transparent.** This is beneficial for a designer when layering an image over various background images, such as in Figures 7.5 and 7.6, where the text "bob's floral specials" is layered over the different floral JPGs.

   However, there is a disadvantage in using transparent images. Because 8-bit PNGs and GIFs allow only one color to be transparent, they do not display anti-aliased images very well. In other words, the images appear jagged. This is an instance where the designer might want to consider using a 24-bit PNG.

4. **PNGs and GIFs allow resizable color palettes.** Pulling colors out of the color palette the image is using can reduce GIF file sizes further. If the colors are not in the actual image, they are unnecessary data and can be tossed without any loss of quality.

5. **PNGs and GIFs maintain original color.** Unlike JPGs, PNGs and GIFs are lossless, meaning they maintain the original colors of an image better than JPGs. A good example of this is a JPG that is compressed too far. The white can turn to an off tint on different monitors, many times disrupting the consistent flow of white in a design. This, at least, was the case with older versions of Photoshop. It does not occur that often anymore.

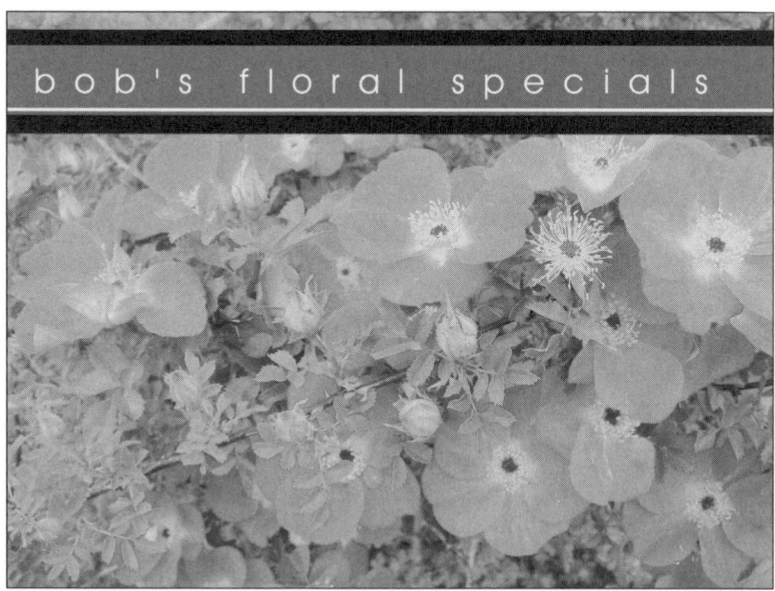

Figure 7.5
Image where the black strip and text on top is layered over a background image.
© 2014 Cengage Learning.

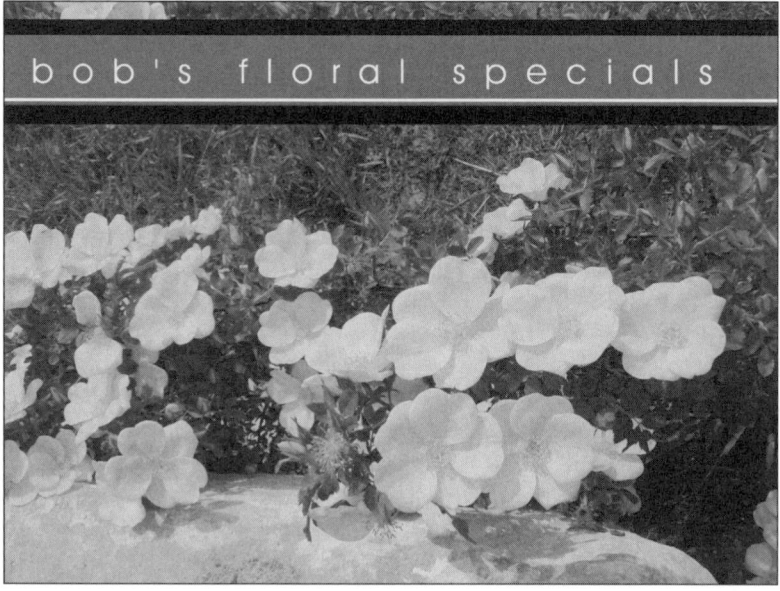

Figure 7.6
Image that uses the same layered black strip and text as in Figure 7.5.
© 2014 Cengage Learning.

Although a designer can save an 8-bit PNG or GIF with up to 256 colors, it is not always the wisest move. If that many colors are necessary to make a photo acceptable, then it is probably better to save the image as a JPG. Generally, it is good practice to save 8-bit PNGs or GIFs with a limited number of colors, anywhere from 2 to 64, depending on the physical size of the image. A designer should probably save an image as an 8-bit PNG or GIF when the following situations occur:

1. **The image has a limited number of solid colors**. The smaller the physical size of the image, the more colors a designer can use while maintaining an acceptable file size (see Figure 7.7).

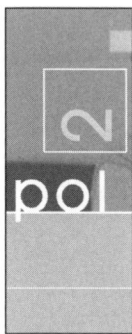

Figure 7.7
Image that should most likely be saved as a PNG or GIF because of its limited colors.
© 2014 Cengage Learning.

While larger images, such as the one in Figure 7.8, can be saved as a PNG or GIF, they usually should not have too many colors. Of course, you must remember Rule 2 of Web design: there nearly always is an exception to a rule.

When saving images as 8-bit PNGs or GIFs, a designer should be aware of the fact that gradations, such as drop shadows, will increase the file size or not be displayed with strong enough quality. Due to the fact that there are a fewer number of colors available, an effect called *banding* can occur. This causes the gradations to be represented by solid bands of color instead of flowing into one another. There is a process called *dithering*, which causes the bands to be broken into different patterns of tiny dots to imitate shades of color by placing certain colors beside one another. Unfortunately, it increases file size significantly. Figure 7.9 is a zoomed-in view of the curved edge of Figure 7.8. It takes many shades of gray to make the image appear to be raised. While it is still possible to adequately compress Figure 7.8, the additional colors will increase the file size of the image.

Figure 7.8
Image that uses a drop shadow to give the illusion of being raised.
© 2014 Cengage Learning.

Figure 7.9
Zoomed-in view of the drop shadow in Figure 7.8.
© 2014 Cengage Learning.

2. **The image is a line drawing.** Although this technically falls into the previous category, it is differentiated for one reason—when saving an image as a PNG or GIF, the white is guaranteed to stay white, unlike a JPG. Figure 7.10 is a cartoon that is sharper and whiter when saved as a GIF, as opposed to a JPG.

Figure 7.10
Line drawing that should be saved as a PNG or GIF.
© 2014 Cengage Learning.

3. **Text is saved as an image if it is not on a complex background, such as a photo.** Generally, to make a site smaller, a designer should try to save text separately from images like photographs, which should be saved as JPGs. If the text is separate, it should be saved as a PNG or GIF, such as in Figure 7.11. Saving the image as a GIF in this image keeps the text nearly as crisp as when it was in the image editing software.

Figure 7.11
Text that should be saved as a GIF (or PNG) image.
© 2014 Cengage Learning.

4. **The image is a thumbnail photo.** Depending on the physical size of the image and how many colors it uses, an 8-bit PNG or GIF will make a thumbnail appear sharper for about the same file size. If the number of colors is limited, such as in the photo of the house in Florence, Italy, shown in Figure 7.12, the image should be saved as an 8-bit PNG or GIF. If saved as a JPG at the same file size, the body of the house could become splotchy. Of course, this is not a hard and fast rule, especially with how the compression functionality of Photoshop has improved over the years.

In contrast, the photo of the Dover Cliffs shown in Figure 7.13 uses many gradations throughout the sky, cliffs, and channel, which makes it a better candidate to be saved as a JPG.

Figure 7.12
Thumbnail that should be saved as an 8-bit PNG or GIF because of the solid colors.
© 2014 Cengage Learning.

Figure 7.13
Thumbnail that should be saved as a JPG because of the many gradations.
© 2014 Cengage Learning.

5. **Small graphics are used.** One way to keep a website small is to use and reuse small graphics, whether in the layout of the page or as a mouseover. Strictly because of their size, such images, including buttons, bullets, and mouseovers, should generally be saved as PNGs or GIFs (see Figure 7.14). The reason is that PNG and GIF compression handle a small number of colors much better than JPG compression does.

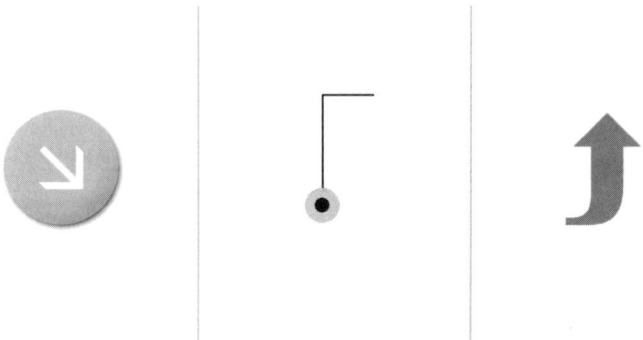

Figure 7.14
Small graphics that should be saved as PNGs or GIFs.
© 2014 Cengage Learning.

Knowing How PNG and GIF Compression Work

It is helpful for a designer to understand how PNG and GIF compression work. By creating and saving images a certain way, the designer can drastically reduce the download size of images. The secret of the two formats is that they compress as many pixels of one solid color at a time while running horizontally. In other words, if a designer creates an image where areas of one color run horizontally rather than vertically, the image will be compressed significantly smaller. Figure 7.15 is the exact same image as Figure 7.16; however, by rotating Figure 7.15 a mere 90 degrees and saving it so that the lines are horizontal, the image in Figure 7.16 can be compressed by more than 50 percent.

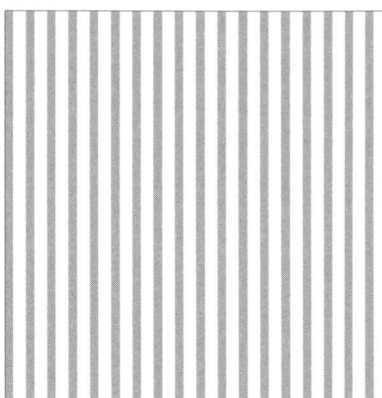

Figure 7.15
File size of image with vertical lines is 1KB.
© 2014 Cengage Learning.

Figure 7.16
File size of image with horizontal lines is .457KB.
© 2014 Cengage Learning.

Of course, this is a very specific example because not all images have lines. It does illustrate that the more you have solid colors run horizontally, the more the image can be compressed.

Unfortunately, if the image is already created, there is not much the designer can do. When starting a design from scratch, however, this can be helpful to know if the download size of the site is extremely critical. Figure 7.17 is a design that was created especially to benefit from GIF compression. Notice that nearly all the lines run horizontally. Not only does this take advantage of the GIF format's best compression, but it also takes advantage of using the ability to repeat background images. In other words, each line that cannot be saved just as a background color can be saved as a background image, which can be repeated infinitely across the X axis (horizontal) using CSS. That way, the design requires a download of only a few images. It is then up to the browser to repeat the images, rather than making it necessary to download larger images.

Figure 7.17
Design that takes advantage of GIF horizontal compression.
© 2014 Cengage Learning.

Using JPGs

While the GIF format is useful for saving images with limited colors, the JPG format is just as powerful when saving images with hundreds, thousands, or millions of colors. Unlike multiple benefits from the 8-bit PNG and GIF formats, this one advantage of the JPG format makes it remarkably valuable when building mortised sites.

A designer should typically save an image as a JPG in the following situations.

Saving a Photograph

Other than in certain instances when saving thumbnails or dealing with flat planes of color, as outlined in the "Using PNGs and GIFs" section, photographs should almost always be saved as JPGs. The image in Figure 7.18 was saved as a GIF with 128 colors.

The same image was saved as a JPG in Figure 7.19 with the quality (compression) level set to 41 in Photoshop. There is no visible difference in the two photos. Note that the JPG photo is compressed to be more than 80 percent smaller.

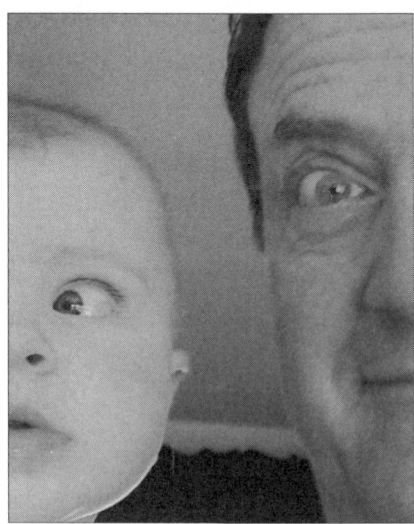

Figure 7.18
GIF photo saved at 25KB.
© 2014 Cengage Learning.

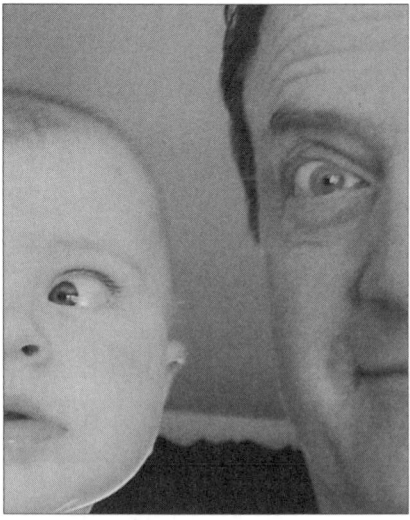

Figure 7.19
JPG photo saved at 5KB.
© 2014 Cengage Learning.

24-Bit PNG Lossless

The 24-bit PNG format can also save as many colors as JPG. Unlike the JPG format, the 24-bit PNG format will save the colors in a lossless method, which will maintain the original colors. The lossless method comes at a cost, though. The 24-bit PNG will typically be much larger than the JPG.

Saving an Image That Has Gradations

Although this is not an absolute rule, in most cases, the JPG format will compress images with gradations considerably better than the PNG and GIF formats, because gradations contain many colors. Depending on the area, gradations can range from a few colors to millions of colors. Figure 7.20 is an image of a tulip that is mainly comprised of gradations throughout the photo. Figure 7.21 is a zoomed-in view of the rectangle section shown in Figure 7.20.

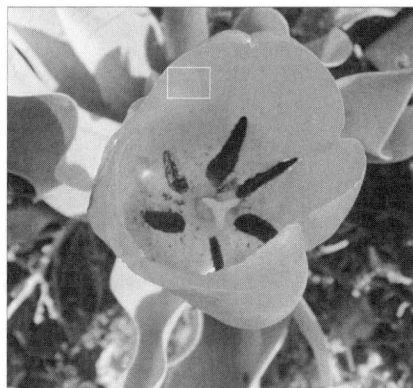

Figure 7.20
Photo of a tulip that is made up of many gradations.
© 2014 Cengage Learning.

Figure 7.21
Zoomed-in view of the rectangle area in Figure 7.20.
© 2014 Cengage Learning.

The human eye cannot physically detect that there are 167 colors used to create the area. A computer, however, can detect those colors, and, unless otherwise directed when saving the image, will try to save each of those colors, considerably increasing the file size.

Some gradations can also be saved as GIFs. The rectangle that makes up Figure 7.21 is an example of this situation. When saved with the entire photo, the rectangle would need to be saved as a JPG. However, if the rectangle were to be cropped and saved on its own, it could be saved as a PNG or GIF with only 16 colors, as opposed to 167. Once again, this is because the human eye cannot physically detect that many colors in that small of an area. Viewing the image at 100 percent, it is difficult to detect more than a handful of colors. Thus, when a color is subtracted from the image, it is replaced with a color that is still present in the image. Therefore, using 16 colors would be more than adequate.

Figure 7.22 is an example of a gradated design. The gradated circles (see Figure 7.23) at the top and bottom of the design are saved as GIFs rather than JPGs for two reasons:

- Because they are small, fewer colors are needed, which keeps the file size small.

- If they were saved as JPGs, the circles could lose their exact hue and the white in the image could have a pinkish tint, which would disrupt the design. This, though, is not that much of a problem anymore with the improvement of Adobe's compression functionality in Photoshop.

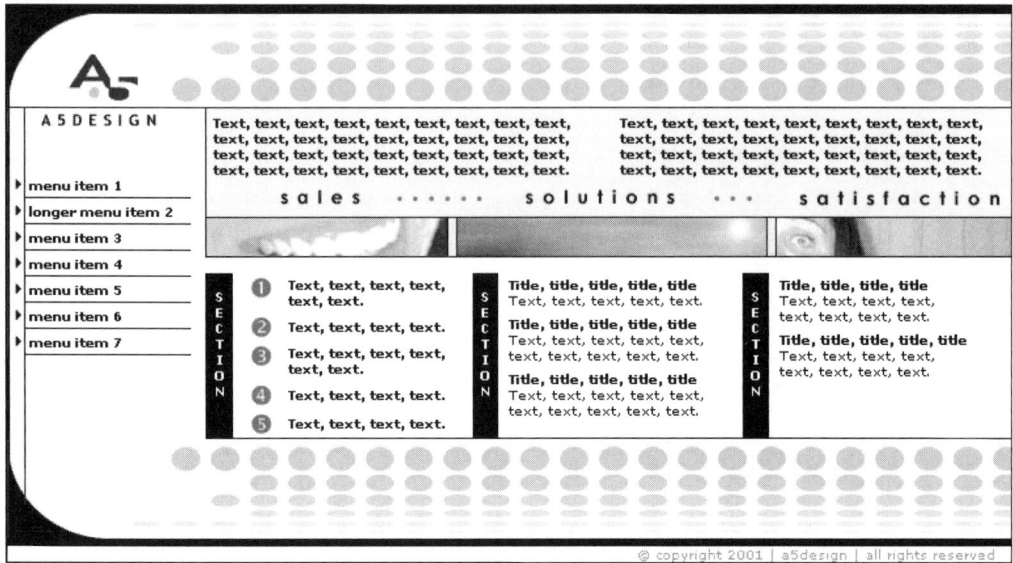

Figure 7.22
Design that uses gradated circles across the top and bottom of the image.
© 2014 Cengage Learning.

Figure 7.23
A zoomed-in view of some of the gradated circles in Figure 7.22.
© 2014 Cengage Learning.

Saving Text on Top of a Photo

When creating a mortised site, the goal is to make it as fast as possible. This usually means creating designs where elements can be saved in their best possible formats. In other words, generally save text as PNGs or GIFs and photographs as JPGs. But this is not always possible. One instance is when a designer saves an image with text on top of a background, such as a photo (see Figure 7.24). The problem the designer runs into with this example is that if the photo is saved as a GIF to keep the text crisp, it could be as large as 70KB. However, if the entire image were compressed as a JPG with a smaller size, the text could be blurred and splotchy. There are only two solutions. The first is to save the text as a separate image with a transparent color and layer it over the church, which would be used as a background image. The other solution would be to simply save the image as a higher quality JPG, which is usually the best decision. Saving it this way, the designer can compress the image to around 15KB without compromising the quality of the text too much.

Figure 7.24
Photo with text layered on top that should be saved as a JPG.
© 2014 Cengage Learning.

Using the JPG file format considerably broadens a designer's ability to build striking graphical sites. Figure 7.25 is a graphical site that has a total download of 35KB.

Figure 7.25
Graphical site that comes in under 35KB.
© 2014 House of Nutrition.

Misusing Image Formats

Properly creating, saving, and compressing images can make or break a site. Figure 7.25 was a perfect example of how small the download can be of a largely graphical site when properly using the JPG and GIF file formats. Figure 7.26, on the other hand, is at the other end of the spectrum. The site misuses images in enough instances to make the entire site download larger than 300KB.

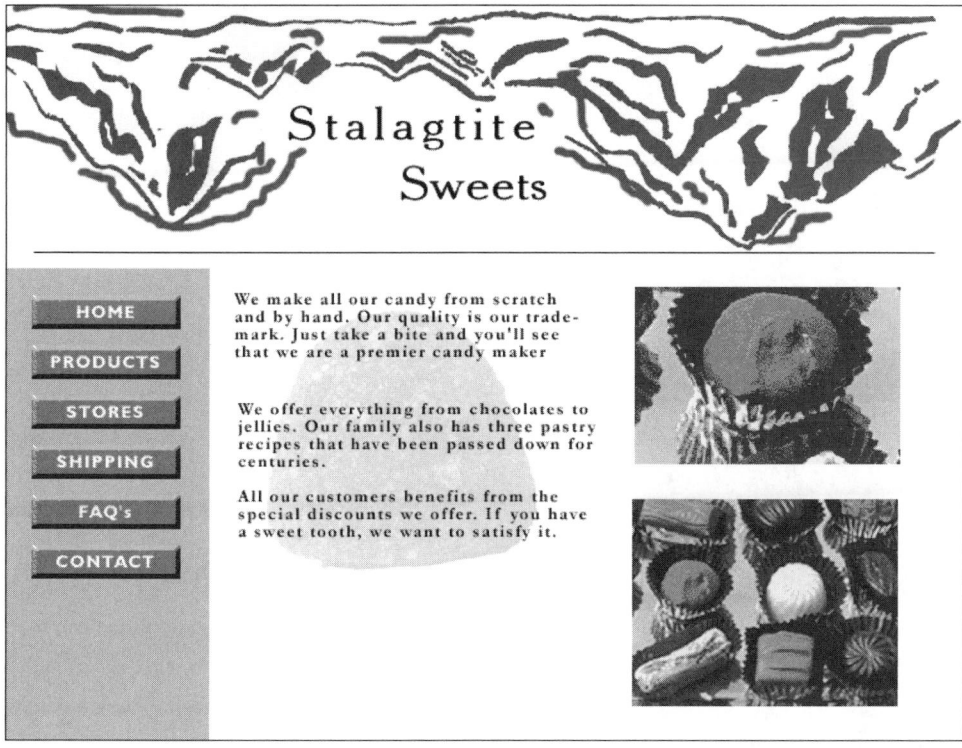

Figure 7.26
Site that misuses graphics; the entire page download is larger than 300KB.
© 2014 Cengage Learning.

With today's software and coding techniques, it is not always necessary, in most instances, to have a site come in at more than 50KB. Following are seven instances where a designer can compromise the quality of a site by incorrectly saving or compressing an image.

1. **Saving an uncompressed image.** This is the most common mistake made by designers. Just saving an image with the correct file format is not enough. The designer still needs to compress the image. Figure 7.27, for example, when saved at

the absolute lowest JPG compression setting in Photoshop, comes in at 65KB, while saving it with the absolute highest compression, the file size is reduced to 5KB. This allows a lot of room for variation. While the quality would be severely compromised at 5KB, saving the image at 65KB, too, is a mistake. Most JPGs need only be saved with so much compression. After a certain quality has been met, decreasing the compression only creates a larger file size; it does not improve the quality of the image.

PNGs and GIFs, too, can be compressed many times. Because each color that is eliminated from a PNG or GIF during compression is replaced by another color, images that are saved as GIFs can be drastically reduced many times.

Figure 7.27
Photo after being compressed.
© 2014 Cengage Learning.

2. **Photo saved as an 8-bit PNG or GIF.** While this was more of an issue in years past, designers still save photos as GIFs. Figure 7.28 is a photo that, when saved as a GIF, is 54KB. If the image were saved as a JPG, a file size of 14KB would provide acceptable image quality.

Figure 7.28
Image that should be saved as a JPG rather than a GIF.
© 2014 Cengage Learning.

3. **Solid colors saved as a JPG.** The JPG format is ironic. Because it can compress millions of colors so easily, it is easy for a designer to believe it can do the same for limited colors. This is not the case. Figure 7.29 shows an image that was saved as a GIF.

Figure 7.29
Image saved as a GIF.
© 2014 Cengage Learning.

Figure 7.30 is the same image saved as a JPG. Following are three problems with the latter image:

■ Although compressed nearly 80 percent, Figure 7.30 is still 4KB, as opposed to Figure 7.29, which is 2KB.

■ The lines on the right in Figure 7.30 are completely splotchy, unlike the lines in Figure 7.29, which are crisp.

■ The level at which the JPG is compressed slightly changes the background color.

Figure 7.30
Image from Figure 7.29 saved as a JPG.
© 2014 Cengage Learning.

4. **Mixing JPG, PNG, and GIF formats to maintain one color.** When compressing an image as a JPG, the image sometimes loses its color accuracy. In other words, the colors do not always remain the same after being compressed. In Figure 7.31, a clock with a colored border was saved on a background with the same color as the border. The clock with the border was saved as a JPG, while the background was saved as a GIF.

Figure 7.31
Example of color loss between a GIF and a JPG.
© 2014 Cengage Learning.

Taking a closer look at the seam where the two images were mortised together (Figure 7.32), it is apparent that the smoothness and clarity of the clock's border becomes splotchy.

Figure 7.32
Zoomed-in view of splotchiness in Figure 7.31.
© 2014 Cengage Learning.

5. **Overcompressing an image.** While compressing an image is not overly complicated, obtaining an eye for it takes a little experimenting for some designers. What initially may look good to a designer one day, may look overly compressed the next. When a JPG is overly compressed (see Figure 7.33) from its original state (Figure 7.34), the image loses its crispness.

One of the first places to show degradation is in solid colors, such as people's faces. All three faces and the lines on the floor in Figure 7.34 have lost their clarity.

Figure 7.33
Image saved as a JPG with proper compression.
© 2014 Cengage Learning.

Figure 7.34
Same image as Figure 7.33 saved as a JPG with too much compression.
© 2014 Cengage Learning.

When a GIF is overly compressed, the image becomes pixilated in areas with more colors. Figure 7.35 is the original image, while Figure 7.36 is an overly compressed version.

Figure 7.35
Image saved as a GIF with the correct number of colors.
© 2014 Cengage Learning.

Notice how spotty the drop shadow within the inner white circle becomes in Figure 7.36.

Figure 7.36
Image saved as a GIF with too few colors.
© 2014 Cengage Learning.

6. **Not saving images as PNGs, GIFs, or JPGs.** As previously mentioned, the three main image file formats used with the Internet today are PNGs, GIFs, and JPGs. However, a Web page can also use BMP files, and the browser will display them. The header image of Figure 7.26 was saved as a BMP. It is 159KB, but if it had been saved as a GIF, it could have been saved at around 14KB.

Figure 7.37 is a photo saved as a JPG that is 4KB, while the same image saved as a BMP file (Figure 7.38) is 166KB. It is included more for historical purposes, since BMP files preceded the major waves of GIFs and then PNGs.

Figure 7.37
Image saved as a JPG (4KB).
© 2014 Cengage Learning.

Figure 7.38
Image saved as a BMP (166KB).
© 2014 Cengage Learning.

7. **Saving large, animated GIFs.** The GIF format is versatile in that a designer can not only create a regular GIF and a GIF with a transparent color, but he can also save a GIF that is animated. Unfortunately, just because a designer can save an animated GIF does not necessarily mean it should be done (Web design Rule 1).

Using an animated GIF can, at times, increase the usability of a site if the file is typically under 10KB. However, when animated GIFs are used to display several photos, a designer is not only incorrectly saving the photos as GIFs, but two, three, or four of them are being saved into one animated GIF, amplifying the mistake.

UNDERSTANDING GRAPHICS/COMPRESSION SOFTWARE

Prior to the considerable growth of the Internet in the early to mid-1990s, the goal of graphics software was to create high-quality images, such as TIF, BMP, and EPS files. The reason was that the graphics created by the programs were mainly used for printers. Unfortunately, this created a problem for Web designers. Because a minimum of 300dpi (dots per inch) to 600dpi was required by printers, designers had to try to compress images to work with monitors, which mostly show only 72dpi. Anything in excess of 72dpi for images used to increase the file size without improving the quality of the image. (While this is still the case for many existing monitors, the trend is slowly changing to allow for higher resolution images.)

Large images coupled with slow modems severely handcuffed designers because it was difficult to create fast-downloading sites. Although the software gave the designer the ability to compress images, opportunities were limited. To compress a GIF, the designer could assign only a certain bit depth to an image. In other words, the designer had the choice of saving the image with only 2, 4, 8, 16, 32, 64, 128, or 256 colors. To compress a JPG, the designer could assign compression in only increments of 10. In other words, the designer had the choice to save an image only at a level of 0, 1, 2, 3, 4, 5, 6, 7, 8, 9, or 10.

Fortunately, software companies have made great strides in offering designers more flexibility in compressing images. Today, not only have these companies created and improved their own image-compression software, but they also have included this functionality in their image editing programs.

Compressing images has never been more flexible. Now, instead of determining the compression of a PNG or GIF in groups of numbers, a designer can select the specific number of colors and even the specific colors themselves to include in an image. For even more control, the designer can even select certain colors that must remain in an image as the total number of colors is reduced. Figure 7.39 illustrates the compression component included with Photoshop. It not only shows a designer which colors are selected for the particular image, but it also allows the designer to compare the original version with the compressed version as changes are made.

Figure 7.39
Image-compression window in Photoshop.
© 2014 Cengage Learning.

Compression Can Drastically Trim File Size

When choosing to compress an image with the JPG format, the designer now has the flexibility of increasing or decreasing compression by 1 percent instead of 10 percent at a time. This is incredibly useful because it allows the designer to take advantage of a unique characteristic of the JPG format. Sometimes when increasing the compression from, say, a quality level of 46 to 45, the quality of the image decreases. However, then when quality is dropped one more percent to 44, the image quality will shift enough to where it appears sharper than the lesser compression level of 45. This gives a designer the ability to trim the excess file size down to the bare-bones minimum.

SUMMARY

Much of the speed and quality of a site is determined by its graphics, which is why it is important for a designer to understand how to create, use, save, and compress images. While vector-based images are the newest technology available, traditional bitmap images, such as PNGs, GIFs, and JPGs, are the most widely and consistently supported.

PNGs, GIFs, and JPGs can do a good job of compressing images if the correct format is used. A designer can also use the formats incorrectly, which can compromise the quality of a site. If the designer understands how and when to use the formats along with compression software, sites can be highly graphical and yet fast at the same time.

CHAPTER 8

CREATING CSS DESIGNS

While back-end development such as db-driven programming and ecommerce functionality has made large strides over the years, so has the front-end design of sites. In the past, to create a website that had the look and feel of traditional graphic design, the designer had to resort to using nested HTML (now XHTML) tables for the majority of content placement. The tables not only allowed the designer to mortise images together, but they also allowed for the layout of XHTML text that was styled using CSS. With the evolution of browsers, nearly all layouts can now be accomplished using CSS. While Chapter 6, "What Is Needed to Build Mortised Sites," outlines essential basic information about CSS, this chapter explains the basics of how to use that code to create such sites. The chapter also explains the differences between XHTML table-based design and CSS-driven design.

THE BASICS OF CSS-BASED DESIGN WORKS VERSUS XHTML TABLE-BASED DESIGN

While a designer will very rarely use nested XHTML tables to lay out pages anymore, it's still good to have a rudimentary understanding if a page needs to be coded or if a page needs to be edited. Plus, a little history only makes us more knowledgeable in the present.

With table-based Web design, the content of a homepage is mortised, or pieced, together using XHTML tables. This content may include text, images, or both. No matter what is included in the design, a minimum of one table is typically used to position the elements.

CSS is then generally used to format the text. Figure 8.1 is an example of a site that uses one table to display the content. The table border is set to 3 to show how the page is constructed.

Figure 8.1
Mortised XHTML homepage, with the border's value set to 3, which uses one table to display both text and images.
Source: Onepartart.com.

Unfortunately, most XHTML sites that employ more visually and technically advanced design usually cannot be created with one table. The designer therefore must nest tables inside of tables to position the various elements of the site. Figure 8.2 is the combination of nested tables that are used to place all the elements together in a design.

Notice in Figure 8.2 that the tables are nested inside one another. The purpose of this method is to place the content in various positions, down to the specific pixel, in some cases. This design is created to be a "liquid" design, which means it can flex to wider resolutions. Figure 8.3 shows what the design looks like when the images and text are added, along with the basic CSS formatting.

Figure 8.2
Table structure of a more complex table-based design, with the nested tables' borders set to 3 to display the framework.
© 2014 Cengage Learning.

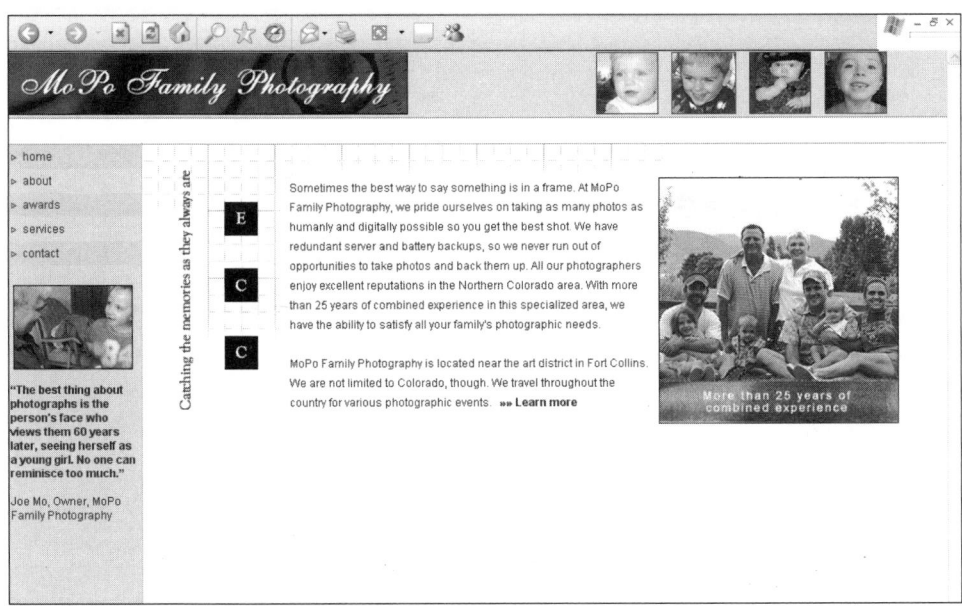

Figure 8.3
Design with table borders set to 0, and images, text, and CSS added to populate the table cells.
© 2014 Cengage Learning.

As complex as this design is, CSS can also be used to lay out the content. With relatively basic coding, a designer can make most sites look close, if not exact, to their table-based counterparts. Figure 8.4 is the same design as Figure 8.3, but it is laid out using a limited amount of CSS.

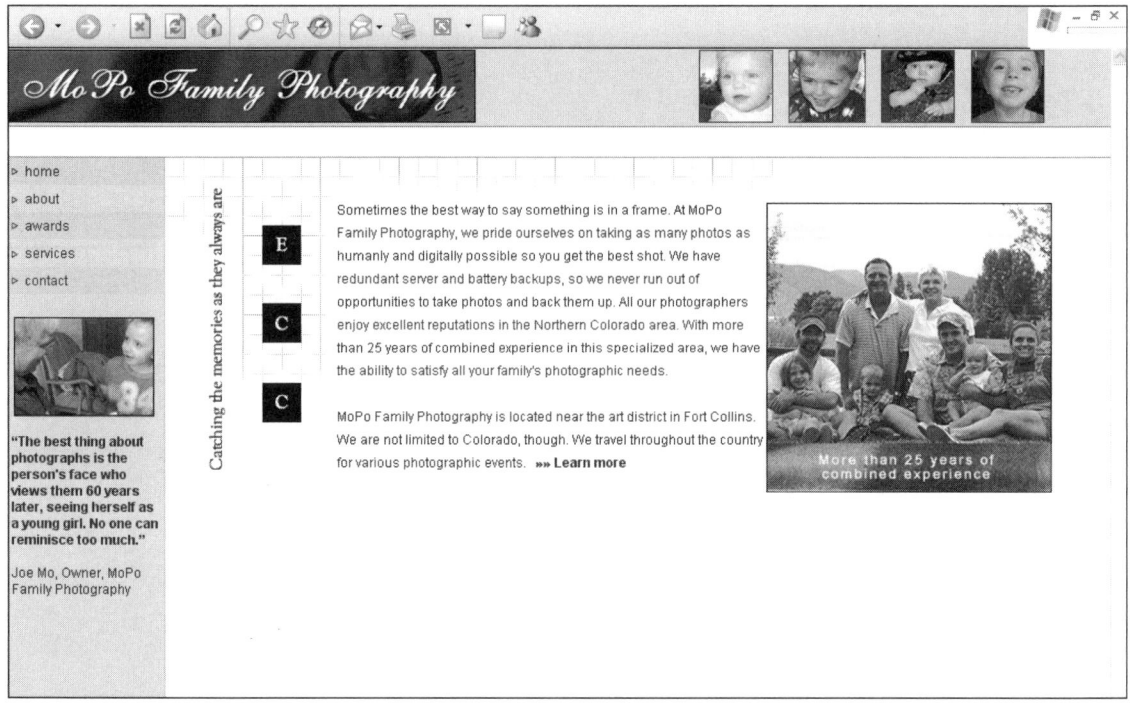

Figure 8.4
Design elements from Figure 8.3 laid out using CSS instead of XHTML tables.
© 2014 Cengage Learning.

In general, CSS sites work by using block- and line-level tags, such as <DIV> and <SPAN> tags, in addition to a few other XHTML tags, such as <BR /> and <H1>, to format and position the content. The <DIV> and <SPAN> tags are wrapped around individual elements of content and then assigned rules in a style sheet to position and style them. While the design in Figure 8.4 does not have tables that can have their borders set to 3 to show the layout, the borders or backgrounds of the tags can be set to 3 to differentiate them. Figure 8.5 shows the design with the borders "turned on" and the images and content removed.

Figure 8.5
Borders turned on and content removed to show the basic structure of the site.
© 2014 Cengage Learning.

One thing to note about CSS-based sites is they require considerably less coding. Listing 8.1 is the table-based code that is used to lay out the design in Figure 8.3.

Listing 8.1   XHTML Code for Figure 8.3

```
<!DOCTYPE html PUBLIC "-//W3C//DTD XHTML 1.0 Transitional//EN"
      "http://www.w3.org/TR/xhtml1/DTD/xhtml1-transitional.dtd">
   <html xmlns="http://www.w3.org/1999/xhtml" xml:lang="en" lang="en">
   <head>
      <title>MoPo Photography</title>
  -- enter meta data here for search engines, such as the following example -->
      <meta HTTP-EQUIV="Content-Type" CONTENT="text/html; charset=iso-8859-1" />
      <meta content="" name="keywords" />
      <meta content="" name="description" />
   <!-- link to javascript that enables any mouseovers on the page -->
   <script src="mouseovers.js" type="text/javascript"></script>
```

```
<!-- link to main stylesheet that controls text sizes and colors,
    among other things -->
<link rel="stylesheet" href="mainstyle.css" type="text/css" />
</head>
<body style="background-color: #ffffff; margin: 0px">
<!-- Note: To make this page stretch to resolutions higher than
    800 x 600 or remain fixed at 800 x 600, change the width of the
    below table tag from "770" to "100%" and vice versa -->
<table width="100%" cellspacing="0" cellpadding="0" border="0">
<tr>
<!-- ###### header start ###### -->
    <td colspan="3" align="left" valign="top" style="background-image:
        url(images/bg_header.gif); background-repeat: repeat-x">
        <table width="100%" cellspacing="0" cellpadding="0" border="0">
        <tr>
            <td align="left" valign="top"><img src="images/
                header_left.jpg" width="431" height="73" alt=""
                border="0" /></td>
            <td align="center" valign="top"><img src="images/
                header_right.jpg" width="329" height="73" alt=""
                border="0" /></td>
            <td><img src="images/spacer.gif" width="10" height="1"
                alt="" border="0" /></td>
        </tr>
        </table>
    </td>
<!-- ###### header end ###### -->
</tr>
<tr>
    <td colspan="3" bgcolor="#919191"><img src="images/spacer.gif"
        width="1" height="1" alt="" border="0" /></td>
</tr>
<tr>
<!-- ###### menu column start ###### -->
    <td align="left" valign="top" bgcolor="#EDEAD1">
        <table width="144" cellspacing="0" cellpadding="0" border="0">
        <tr>
            <td colspan="3" bgcolor="#ffffff"><img src="images/
                spacer.gif" width="1" height="1" alt="" border="0"
                /></td>
        </tr>
```

```
<tr>
    <td bgcolor="#ffffff"><img src="images/spacer.gif"
        width="1" height="1" alt="" border="0" /></td>
    <td align="left" valign="middle" bgcolor="#ffffff">
         </td>
    <td bgcolor="#ffffff"><img src="images/spacer.gif" name="menu_item_1"
        width="3" height="26" alt="" border="0" /></td>
</tr>
<tr>
    <td colspan="3" bgcolor="#909290"><img src="images/
        spacer.gif" width="1" height="1" alt="" border="0"
        /></td>
</tr>
<tr>
    <td align="left" valign="middle" bgcolor="#E4E1C6"><img
        src="images/bullet_menu_1_off.gif" name="homepage"
        width="17" height="24" alt="" border="0" /></td>
    <td align="left" valign="middle" bgcolor="#E4E1C6">
        <a href="index.htm" onmouseover="document.homepage.src=
        bullet_menu_1_on.src;"
onmouseout="document.homepage.src=bullet_menu_1_off.src" style=
        "text-decoration: none; color: #003366">home</a></td>

    <td bgcolor="#E4E1C6"><img src="images/spacer.gif"
        width="3" height="26" alt="" border="0" /></td>
</tr>
<tr>
    <td align="left" valign="middle" bgcolor="#EDEAD1"><img
        src="images/bullet_menu_2_off.gif" name="about"
        width="17" height="24" alt="" border="0" /></td>
        <td align="left" valign="middle" bgcolor="#EDEAD1"><a
            href="about.htm" onmouseover="document.about.src=
            bullet_menu_2_on.src;"
        onmouseout="document.about.src=bullet_menu_2_off.src"
        style="text-decoration: none; color: #003366">about
        </a></td>
    <td bgcolor="#EDEAD1"><img src="images/spacer.gif"
        width="3" height="26" alt="" border="0" /></td>
</tr>
<tr>
    <td align="left" valign="middle" bgcolor="#E4E1C6"><img
        src="images/bullet_menu_1_off.gif" name="bios"
        width="17" height="24" alt="" border="0" /></td>
```

```
        <td align="left" valign="middle" bgcolor="#E4E1C6"><a
            href="awards.htm" onmouseover="document.bios.src=
            bullet_menu_1_on.src;"
        onmouseout="document.bios.src=bullet_menu_1_off.src"
            style="text-decoration: none; color: #003366">awards
            </a></td>
        <td bgcolor="#E4E1C6"><img src="images/spacer.gif"
            width="3" height="26" alt="" border="0" /></td>
    </tr>
    <tr>
        <td align="left" valign="middle" bgcolor="#EDEAD1"><img
            src="images/bullet_menu_2_off.gif" name="services"
            width="17" height="24" alt="" border="0" /></td>
        <td align="left" valign="middle" bgcolor="#EDEAD1"><a
            href="services.htm" onmouseover="document.services.src=
            bullet_menu_2_on.src;"
onmouseout="document.services.src=bullet_menu_2_off.src"
    style= "text-decoration: none; color: #003366">services</a></td>
        <td bgcolor="#EDEAD1"><img src="images/spacer.gif"
            width="3" height="26" alt="" border="0" /></td>
    </tr>
    <tr>
        <td align="left" valign="middle" bgcolor="#E4E1C6"><img
            src="images/bullet_menu_1_off.gif" name="contact"
            width="17" height="24" alt="" border="0" /></td>
        <td align="left" valign="middle" bgcolor="#E4E1C6"><a
            href="contact.htm" onmouseover="document.contact.src=
            bullet_menu_1_on.src;"
            onmouseout="document.contact.src=bullet_menu_1_off.src"
            style="text-decoration: none; color: #003366">contact
            </a></td>
        <td bgcolor="#E4E1C6"><img src="images/spacer.gif"
            width="3" height="26" alt="" border="0" /></td>
    </tr>
    <tr>
        <td><img src="images/spacer.gif" width="17" height="20"
            alt="" border="0" /></td>
        <td><img src="images/spacer.gif" width="124" height="1"
            alt="" border="0" /></td>
        <td><img src="images/spacer.gif" width="3" height="1"
            alt="" border="0" /></td>
    </tr>
```

```
        <tr>
            <td colspan="3"><a href="index.htm"><img src="images/
                photo_bottom_left.jpg" width="144" height="92" alt=""
                border="0" /></a></td>
        </tr>
        <tr>
            <td><img src="images/spacer.gif" width="1" height="10"
                alt="" border="0" /></td>
        </tr>
        <tr>
            <td colspan="3" align="left" valign="top">
                <table width="100%" cellspacing="0" cellpadding="4"
                border="0">
                <tr>
                <td align="left" valign="top"><b>"The best thing about
                photographs is the person's face who views them 60
                years later, seeing herself as a young girl. No one
                can reminisce too much."</b><br /><br />Joe Mo, Owner,
                MoPo Family Photography
<br /><br /></td>
                </tr>
                </table>
            </td>
        </tr>
        </table>
    </td>
<!-- ###### menu column end ###### -->
<!-- ###### forces minimum height of body start ###### -->
    <td align="left" valign="top" bgcolor="#CAC9CA"><img src="images/
        spacer_white.gif" width="1" height="26" alt="" border="0"
        /></td>
<!-- ###### forces minimum height of body end ###### -->
<!-- ###### main content start ###### -->
    <td align="left" valign="top">
        <table width="100%" cellspacing="0" cellpadding="0" border="0">
        <tr>
<!-- ###### top center links start ###### -->
            <td colspan="3">
                <table width="100%" cellspacing="0" cellpadding="0"
                    border="0">
                <tr>
                    <td align="left"> </td>
```

```
                    <td><img src="images/spacer.gif" width="1"
                        height="26" alt="" border="0" /></td>
                </tr>
                <tr>
                <td><img src="images/spacer.gif" width="500" height="1"
                    alt="" border="0" /></td>
                    <td><img src="images/spacer.gif" width="1"
                        height="1" alt="" border="0" /></td>
                </tr>
                </table>
            </td>
<!-- ###### top center links end ###### -->
        </tr>
        <tr>
            <td colspan="3" bgcolor="#909290"><img src="images/
            spacer.gif" width="1" height="1" alt="" border="0" /></td>
        </tr>
        <tr>
            <td align="left" valign="top"><img src="images/tagline.gif"
                width="80" height="285" alt="" border="0" /></td>
            <td align="left" valign="top"><img src="images/image_left_
                of_text.gif" width="69" height="285" alt="" border="0"
                /></td>
<!-- ###### main text column start ###### -->
            <td align="left" valign="top">
                <table width="100%" cellspacing="0" cellpadding="0"
                    border="0">
                <tr>
                    <td colspan="5" align="left" valign="top"><img
                        src="images/image_above_text.gif" width="476"
                        height="36" alt="" border="0" /></td>
                </tr>
                <tr>
                    <td><img src="images/spacer.gif" width="1" height="1" alt=""
                        border="0" /></td>
                    <td align="left" valign="top" style="line-height:
                    16pt">
Sometimes the best way to say something is in a frame. At MoPo Family Photography, we
    pride ourselves on taking as many photos as humanly and digitally possible so you get
    the best shot. We have redundant server and battery backups, so we never run out of
    opportunities to take photos and back them up. All our photographers enjoy excellent
    reputations in the Northern Colorado area. With more than 25 years of combined
```

```
experience in this specialized area, we have the ability to satisfy all your family's
    photographic needs.
<br /><br />
MoPo Family Photography is located near the art district in Fort
    Collins. We are not limited to Colorado, though. We travel
    throughout the country for various photographic events.
      <a href="x.htm" style="text-decoration:none"><b>&raquo;
    &raquo; Learn more</b></a></td>
                        <td><img src="images/spacer.gif" width="1"
                            height="1" alt="" border="0" /></td>
                        <td align="left" valign="top"><a href="x.htm"><img
                            src="images/photo_middle_right.jpg" width="260"
                            height="265" alt="" border="0" /></a></td>
    <!-- ###### forces minimum height of body start ###### -->
                        <td><img src="images/spacer.gif" width="1"
                            height="257" alt="" border="0" /></td>
    <!-- ###### forces minimum height of body end ###### -->
                    </tr>
                    <tr>
                        <td><img src="images/spacer.gif" width="10"
                            height="1" alt="" border="0" /></td>
                        <td><img src="images/spacer.gif" width="146"
                            height="1" alt="" border="0" /></td>
                        <td><img src="images/spacer.gif" width="8"
                            height="1" alt="" border="0" /></td>
                        <td><img src="images/spacer.gif" width="260"
                            height="1" alt="" border="0" /></td>
                        <td><img src="images/spacer.gif" width="52"
                            height="1" alt="" border="0" /></td>
                    </tr>
                    </table>
                </td>
    <!-- ###### main text column end ###### -->
            </tr>
            <tr>
                <td colspan="3" style="background-image: url(images/
                    bg_bottom_line.gif); background-repeat: repeat-x"><img
                    src="images/bottom_left_square.gif" width="80"
                    height="9" alt="" border="0" /></td>
            </tr>
            <tr>
```

```
            <td colspan="3"><img src="images/spacer.gif" width="1"
                height="10" alt="" border="0" /></td>
        </tr>
        </table>
    </td>
<!-- ###### main content end ###### -->
</tr>
<tr>
    <td bgcolor="#7D7D7D"><img src="images/spacer.gif" width="144"
        height="1" alt="" border="0" /></td>
    <td bgcolor="#7D7D7D"><img src="images/spacer.gif" width="1"
        height="1" alt="" border="0" /></td>
    <td bgcolor="#7D7D7D"><img src="images/spacer.gif" width="625"
        height="1" alt="" border="0" /></td>
</tr>
<!-- ###### footer start ###### -->
<tr>
<td colspan="3" style="background-color: #CAC9CA;"><img src="images/
    spacer.gif" width="1" height="1" alt="" border="0" /></td>
</tr>
<tr>
    <td colspan="3" style="background-color: #EDEAD1;"><img
        src="images/spacer.gif" width="1" height="10" alt=""
        border="0" /></td>
</tr>
<!-- ###### footer end ###### -->
</table>
</body>
</html>
```

This code contains seven tables and 185 lines of code to lay out the elements of the page. CSS-based design has much cleaner XHTML code, reducing the weight, or download file size, of a page. The page contains only 67 lines of code. Listing 8.2 displays the code to produce the design in Figure 8.4.

Listing 8.2   CSS Code for Figure 8.4

```
<!DOCTYPE html PUBLIC "-//W3C//DTD XHTML 1.0 Transitional//EN"
"DTD/xhtml1-transitional.dtd">
<html xmlns="http://www.w3.org/1999/xhtml" xml:lang="en" lang="en">
<head>
<title>MoPo Photography</title>
```

```
!-- link to main stylesheet that controls text sizes and colors,
    among other things -->
<link rel="stylesheet" href="mainstyle.css" type="text/css" />
</head>
<body>
<div id="a5-header">
        <span class="toprightimage"><img src="images/header-right.jpg"
            width="329" height="73" alt="" border="0" id="toprightimage"
            /></span>
         <img src="images/header-left.jpg" width="431" height="73" alt=""
         border="0" />
    </div>
    <div id="a5-title">
         
    </div>
    <!-- ###### left column start ###### -->
    <div id="a5-column-left">
    <!-- ##### menu start ##### -->
        <div id="a5-menu">
            <div class="a5-menu-odd">
                <a href="index.htm">home</a>
            </div>
            <div class ="a5-menu-even">
                <a href="about.htm">about</a>
            </div>
            <div class ="a5-menu-odd">
                <a href="awards.htm">awards</a>
            </div>
            <div class ="a5-menu-even">
                <a href="services.htm">services</a>
            </div>
            <div class ="a5-menu-odd">
                <a href="contact.htm">contact</a>
            </div>
        </div>
    <!-- ##### menu end ##### -->
        <br />
        <div id="photo_bottom_left">
            <a href="index.htm"><img src="images/photo_bottom_left.jpg" width="144"
            height="92" alt="" border="0" /></a>
        </div>
```

```
        <div style="padding:12px 5px 0px 5px;"><b>"The best thing about
            photographs is the person's face who views them 60 years
            later, seeing herself as a young girl. No one can reminisce
            too much."</b><br /><br />Joe Mo, Owner, MoPo Family
            Photography</div>
    </div>
    <!-- ###### left column end ###### -->
    <div id="a5-column-left-center">
        <img src="images/tagline.gif" width="80" height="285" alt=""
            border="0" />
    </div>
    <div id="a5-column-right-center">
        <img src="images/image-left-of-text.gif" width="69" height="285"
            alt="" border="0" />
    </div>
    <!-- ###### right column start ###### -->
    <div id="a5-column-right">
        <img src="images/image-above-text.gif" width="476" height="36"
            alt="" border="0" />
        <div id="a5-column-right-bottom">
            <span class="photo"><img src="images/photo-middle-right.jpg"
                width="260" height="265" alt="" border="0" /></span>
Sometimes the best way to say something is in a frame. At MoPo Family Photography, we
    pride ourselves on taking as many photos as humanly and digitally possible so you
    get the best shot. We have redundant server and battery backups, so we never run out
    of opportunities to take photos and back them up. All our photographers enjoy
    excellent reputations in the Northern Colorado area. With more than 25 years of
    combined experience in this specialized area, we have the ability to satisfy all
    your family's photographic needs.
<br /><br />
MoPo Family Photography is located near the art district in Fort
    Collins. We are not limited to Colorado, though. We travel
    throughout the country for various photographic events.
      <a href="x.htm" style="text-decoration:none"><b>&raquo;
    &raquo; Learn more</b></a>
    </div>
    <div id="copyright">
        41909 N. Shield St., Suite 345 | Fort Collins, CO 80524 |
            Phone: 970.555.1130 | Fax: 970.555.1129
    </div>
</div>
```

```
<!-- ##### right column end ##### -->
</body>
</html>
```

Not only is the code much cleaner in Listing 8.2, but the file size is also dramatically reduced, coming in at approximately 3.2KB versus 11.2KB for the table-based design in Listing 8.1. Because there is more CSS added to a style sheet to create such a design, the style sheet is going to be larger, but not by much. The style sheet weight for Listing 8.1 is approximately 0.70KB, while the weight for Listing 8.2 comes in around 3.6KB. When the entire coding weight of each design is added up, the table-based design comes in around 12KB, while the CSS-based design comes in at 6.8KB, making a difference of nearly 50 percent. And this is only for one page. When the reduced file size for additional pages on the site is compounded, the reduction becomes much greater.

UNDERSTANDING THE BOX MODEL

To design a CSS-based design, such as Figure 8.4, the designer needs to use the box model method. This method involves wrapping `<DIV>` and `<SPAN>` (at least with the style used in this book) tags around page elements to position and place them. These tags are commonly referred to as *containers* because they are used to style elements that are contained within them.

When thinking in terms of a table-based design, the box model's containers are analogous to individual tables being nested inside one another. Positioning with CSS-based design is different than with table-based design. The latter uses table elements, such as table rows, columns, and cells, many times in association with spacer.gifs, to determine where items are placed. The former uses CSS's absolute or relative positioning to tell the boxes exactly where they will be in terms of any corner, usually at the top left or top right of the browser or in relation to a box or container in which it is nested.

Listing 8.3 displays a Web page with a style sheet that tells the box with the `id` value of `photo_bottom_left` where it needs to be positioned in relation to the top-left corner of the page, where the X,Y coordinates are 0,0.

Listing 8.3   Code for a Website That Uses the Box Model in Figure 8.4

```
<!DOCTYPE html PUBLIC "-//W3C//DTD XHTML 1.0 Transitional//EN"
      "DTD/xhtml1-transitional.dtd">
   <html xmlns="http://www.w3.org/1999/xhtml" xml:lang="en" lang="en">
   <head>
      <title>A5design</title>
```

```
<style>
    body {
        margin:0px;
        padding:0px;
        background:#ffffff;
        }
    #logo {
        position:absolute;
        top:245px;
        left:160px;
border:1px solid #000000;
        }
    </style>
</head>
<body>
    <div id="logo"><a href="index.htm"><img src="images/logo.jpg"
        width="144" height="92" alt="" border="0" /></a></div>
</body>
</html>
```

Figure 8.6 illustrates how the image is placed 245 pixels from the top and 160 pixels from the left. The property border has been added with a value of 1 and a color of #000000. This turns on the border to allow the designer to see the size of the box better.

Figure 8.6
Box placed inside a Web page with absolute positioning, forcing the image 245 pixels from the top and 160 pixels from the left.

© 2014 Cengage Learning.

When two other <DIV> tags are added, for example, they also can have either absolute or relative positioning assigned to them. In Listing 8.4, the <DIV> tag with the id of box2 is given absolute positioning outside the photo_bottom_left box (shown in Figure 8.7). The <DIV> tag with the id of box3 is given relative positioning inside the <DIV> tag with the id of box2.

Listing 8.4   Two Additional Boxes Added, One with Relative Positioning and the Other with Absolute Positioning for Figure 8.7

```
<!DOCTYPE html PUBLIC "-//W3C//DTD XHTML 1.0 Transitional//EN"
        "DTD/xhtml1-transitional.dtd">
    <html xmlns="http://www.w3.org/1999/xhtml" xml:lang="en" lang="en">
    <head>
        <title>A5design</title>
        <style>
            body {
                margin:0px;
                padding:0px;
                background:#ffffff;
                }
            #photo_bottom_left {
                position:absolute;
                top:245px;
                left:160px;
                border:1px solid #000000;
                }
            #box2 {
                position:absolute;
                top:400px;
                left:350px;
                width:100px;
                color:#ffffff;
                background:#000000;
                border:1px solid #000000;
                }
            #box3 {
                position:relative;
                top:0px;
                left:50px;
                height:100px;
                background:#D5C012;
                border:1px solid #000000;
                }
        </style>
    </head>
```

```
<body>
    <div id="photo_bottom_left"><a href="index.htm"><img src="images/
        photo_bottom_left.jpg" width="144" height="92" alt=""
        border="0" /></a></div>
    <div id="box2">
        This is box 2
        <div id="box3">This is box 3</div>
    </div>
</body>
</html>
```

Positioning Content in the Top-Left Corner with No Padding

The `margin:0px;` and `padding:0px` properties and values are added to the `<BODY>` tag in the style sheet to ensure that the content is positioned in the top-left corner of the browser. If these attributes are not added, content will not always begin at the X,Y attributes of 0,0 in a browser. Depending on the browser, this distance can change. Similar to XHTML table-based designs, it is necessary to declare background page colors when creating CSS-based designs, which is why the background property is added. This is included to ensure that all browsers use the same background color, not leaving the option to be declared by their default values.

When the page is displayed, box2 is located 100 pixels from the top and 350 pixels from the left. box3 is then placed inside the box2 tag and positioned 50 pixels from the left. Both boxes are assigned background colors, and they have their borders turned on to better illustrate their shapes and positions (see Figure 8.7).

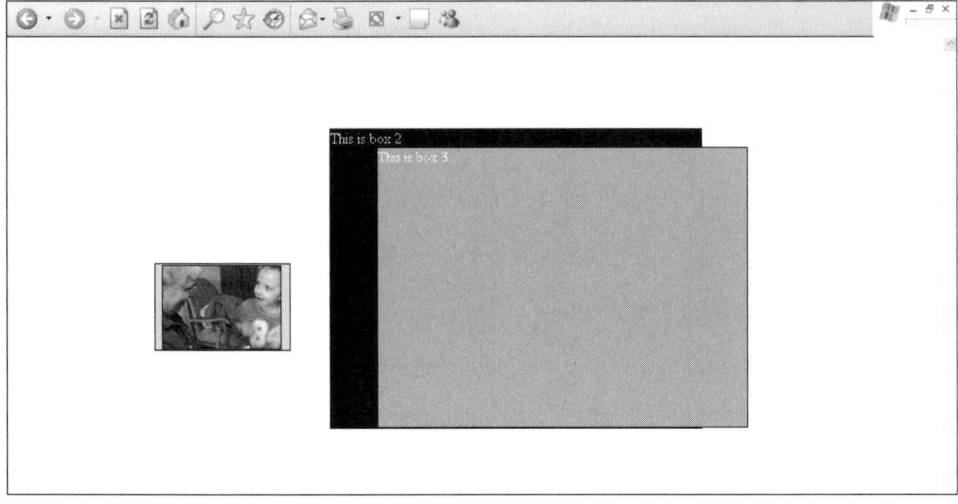

Figure 8.7
A box with relative positioning placed inside a box with absolute positioning.
© 2014 Cengage Learning.

Because box3 is positioned inside box2 using relative positioning, the latter stretches to the full height of both boxes. If, however, box3 is assigned absolute, instead of relative, positioning in the style sheet (see Listing 8.4), it will react differently (see Figure 8.8).

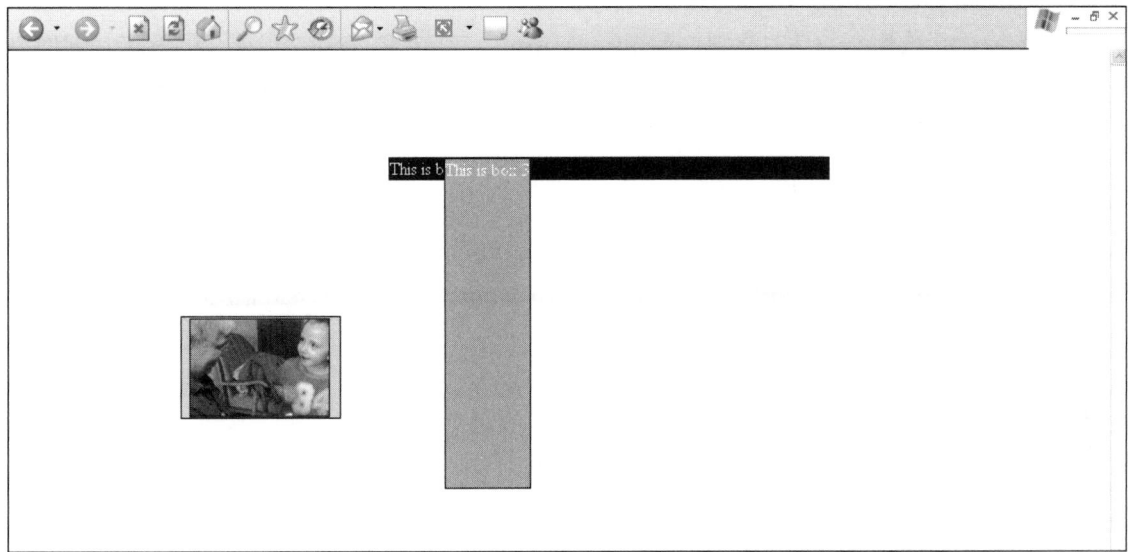

Figure 8.8
A box with absolute positioning placed inside another box with absolute positioning.
© 2014 Cengage Learning.

Following are three things to notice about how the relationship between the two boxes changes:

- Rather than position itself relative to box2, box3 positions itself from the top-left corner of box2.

- box2 will not recognize the combined height of the two boxes. Rather, it will recognize only its height. This is because absolute-positioned elements, similar to floating elements, fall outside the flow of relative-positioned elements. In other words, box2's border will not contain box3. This is important to keep in mind when nesting <DIV> tags in each other.

- The nested box does not inherit the width of the parent box. It will now need to be forced into the style sheet, using the width property.

These are just the overall concepts of the box model. Similar to XHTML tables, the box model, once understood at the basic level, can be used in more creative and advanced ways, such as the site shown in Figure 8.4. The case studies later in the book provide more detailed examples of building more advanced sites.

WHEN TO USE TABLES

Some CSS purists believe CSS Web designs should include very little, if any, XHTML tables. While there are more advantages than disadvantages to creating CSS-based sites over table-based designs, this does not mean that there is no longer a need for tables.

Tables serve a practical purpose in Web design: handling columns and rows of data. While there are ways to handle such content using CSS, there is no reason that XHTML cannot and should not be used in such circumstances, such as in Figure 8.9. In this example, 77 cells are used in the table. CSS would, in many cases, be too time-consuming to create and maintain.

First Name	Last Name	City	State	Zip	Phone	Fax
Mikayla	Missun	Wellington	CO	80550	555.555.5555	970.555.5555
Charlie	Joseph	Eaton	CO	80524	555.555.5555	970.555.5555
Kata	Anne	Fort Collins	CO	80524	555.555.5555	970.555.5555
Josh	Dogin	Phoenix	AZ	68798	555.555.5555	970.555.55555
Daniel	Yu	San Francisco	CA	89787	555.555.5555	970.555.5555
Susan	Jones	Boulder	CO	80540	555.555.5555	970.555.5555
William	Anderson	Denver	CO	80234	555.555.5555	970.555.5555
Josephie	Kuehl	Longmont	CO	80524	555.555.5555	970.555.5555
Jen	Marie	Crested Butte	CO	80113	555.555.5555	970.555.55555
Melissa	York	New York	NY	89747	555.555.5555	970.555.5555

Figure 8.9
Example Web page where using an XHTML table is more practical to position 77 cells of data than using CSS.
© 2014 Cengage Learning.

VALIDATING CODE

The W3C is the governing body when it comes to the creation of Web standards that help the Web "reach its true potential," according to the consortium. Over the years, an increasing number of designers and developers have begun adhering to such standards.

During Web page design, both XTHML and CSS should be validated, using the W3C's free online validating services. They not only help a developer understand what code is not compliant, but they also now provide explanations and examples of correctly written code. Following are the URLs for each validating service:

- **XHTML Markup Validation Service:** http://validator.w3.org/

- **CSS Validation Service:** http://jigsaw.w3.org/css-validator/

The W3C also offers a downloadable version of its CSS Validator. The software can be found at http://dev.w3.org/cvsweb/2002/css-validator/.

Using W3C to Validate Pages

Once a page is validated, the W3C provides and encourages designers and developers to include a W3C validation image on the page, which verifies that the page has been validated for either XHTML or CSS or both.

TESTING DESIGNS IN VARIOUS BROWSERS

Testing websites in various browsers used to be a major part of Web design because of how inconsistently the browsers rendered pages. These days, browsers do a great job of adhering to standards, which makes pages much more consistent. Still, it is wise for a designer to always test a page in the major browsers, which include Chrome, FireFox, Safari, and Internet Explorer. A good method for testing is to open the page in all the browsers and then to simply refresh the page (hitting the F5 button) in them when changes are made.

SUMMARY

While there is a learning curve that comes with changing a coding style from creating XHTML table-based designs to CSS-based designs, this chapter gives a basic understanding of the benefits of the CSS method and how it works (Chapters 9–14 then put these principles to use). The box model is explained, including how absolute and relative positioning are used to position block elements. As with all development, testing is encouraged. W3C validation services are included to give the designer a place to validate both the XHTML and CSS of a site.

CHAPTER 9

CASE STUDY: LOW-CONTENT CSS DESIGN

Since the introduction of CSS-based design, the majority of designs have taken a more simplistic look, similar to how they used to look before designers used more complex layouts using nested XHTML tables. As with the evolution of table-based layout, this most likely is simply just a result of the fact that most designers simply do not know how to technically create more complex designs that, many times, give a site a more professional unique look and feel that generally guarantee a longer shelf life. Instead, they simply replicate a few basic layouts that permeate the Web. This is the first chapter in this book that shows a designer how easy it is to create a more complex look by using CSS in more creative ways by breaking the "visual" confines of basic linear (rectangular and square) containers. In other words, this chapter explains how to make designs look how the designer wants them to look, rather than having to make a design look like images were merely placed in columns because that is all that could technically be done. The design in this chapter was created for 800×600 resolution; however, no matter the resolution, the same techniques apply to creating larger designs.

Design 121 Example

The design explained in this chapter is design 121 online (photo credits: www.idlerphotography.com).

UNDERSTANDING THE DESIGN'S STRUCTURE

Before beginning to build a design, it is important that the designer understand the page's infrastructure. The design shown in Figure 9.1 is a simple layout that uses a header and two columns below it to mortise the images together and therein place the content.

Figure 9.1
The low-content design explained in this chapter.
© 2014 Cengage Learning.

The Reasoning Behind Guides and Creating Slices in Photoshop Files

When building a design, you should usually create it first in image editing software, such as Photoshop, rather than spending time coding the actual design. While creating a *comp*, or sample design, is time-consuming, it will save time because most of the technical considerations are worked out during this phase of the process. It is also time-saving because the client is usually going to want to make changes to the design, and it is easier to make these changes when first creating the entire page. Then, once the design is approved, the designer simply needs to code it to appear as it does in the Photoshop file.

After a design is created in Photoshop, the designer is going to want to *break up*, or code, the design in XHTML and CSS. To begin this process, guides are placed to ensure that the elements are lined up in their correct positions. Slices, which are used to save areas of the design as images, can be fashioned easily once everything is positioned correctly.

Figure 9.2 shows how the guides and slices are positioned. The numbers added to the design are used to point out the 10 most important guides and slices.

Figure 9.2
Guides and slices strategically placed within the design.
© 2014 Cengage Learning.

There are several things to note about the guides and slices in Figure 9.2:

1. The horizontal guide just below number 1 is added to separate the header row from the lower part of the design.

2. The vertical guide to the left of number 2 separates the left column, which includes the menu, from the right column, which contains the main content for the page.

3. The three number 3s represent the slices that are used in the header area.

Slices

A slice is indicated by the small numbered rectangle in the top-left corner of each outlined rectangle or square.

4. The two number 4s indicate, to the left of them, the background images that are used in each menu item. The top number 4 represents the menu item when the user has

not selected that item. The lower number 4 represents the background when the hyperlinked menu item is in hover mode.

5. The two number 5s represent slices used to save images for the design that are not mortised together with any others. The right image, which says, "call for a free estimate," has the background image removed from it. This is accomplished by cropping out the background, and any other images, below the slice. When saving the Photoshop file, the designer can designate the checkered background, which is the background of the file, as a transparent background. This allows the image to be layered easily over any background in the file so that the background can appear through the area that is checkered. The advantage of this technique is that the image can then be moved anywhere over the background image of the woman, without the "estimate" image containing remnants of her checkered shirt. It is a coincidence that the Photoshop background and the woman's shirt are both checkered. If the image contained the woman's shirt, rather than that area being transparent, and was positioned differently, the image and background images would appear disjointed.

Anti-Aliasing Provides Smooth Curves

If the image had a curve and that image was saved with a transparent background, the curve would have a jagged edge because of anti-aliasing, which blends colors to give the perception of one color being curved.

6. The slice to the left of number 6 represents the background image that is used for the page title row for second-level pages (see Figure 9.3). Often, it is easier to save images that are not necessarily used on the homepage with the source file that is used for the homepage. This can eliminate the need to save a completely new PSD (Photoshop) file for just one image.

Figure 9.3
The page title area on second-level pages that uses a background image saved from the Photoshop file created for the homepage.

© 2014 Cengage Learning.

Because multiple images are layered and saved over the background image of the woman, it is helpful to duplicate the source PSD file and save it independently so the background can be saved. When the file has been duplicated, the extra images, all slices, and most guides can be removed, leaving only the background image. The designer then adds a slice around the portion of the file that will be saved as an individual image.

One advantage of duplicating the existing homepage file and deleting excess images is that the background image's placement remains the same. Because the main slice, represented by number 2 in Figure 9.2, is not removed, the designer knows exactly where to place the new slice. Figure 9.4 shows the homepage saved as a separate source file with all the original slices and excess images removed.

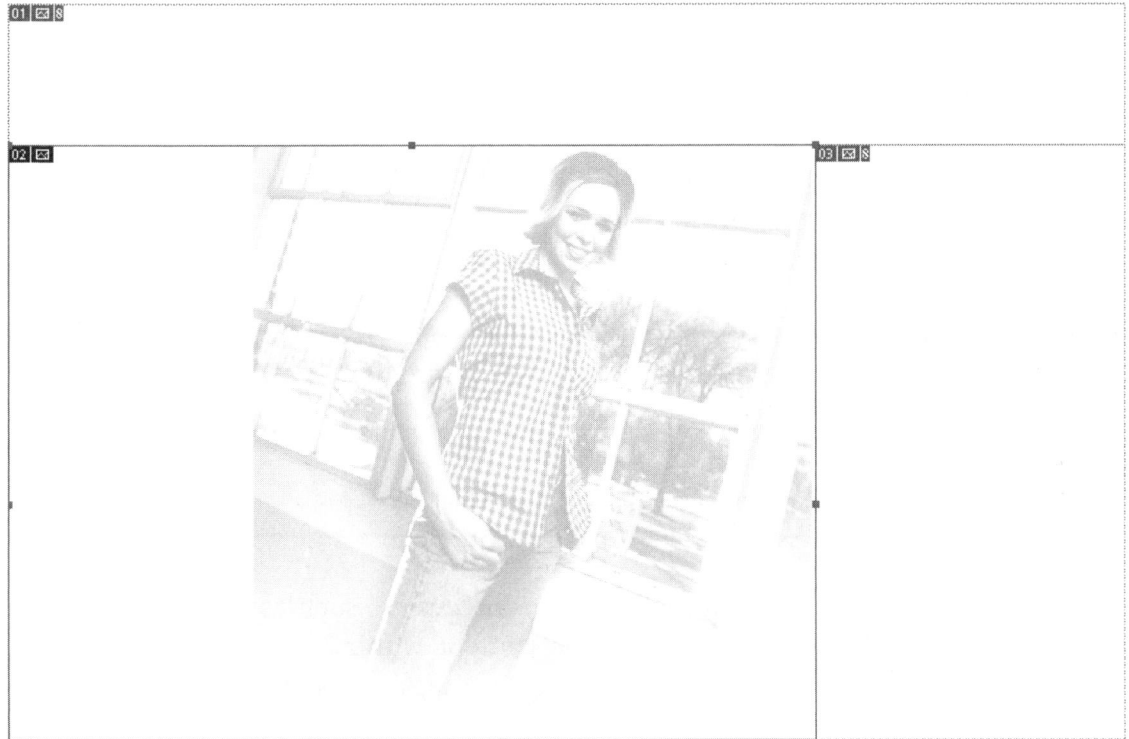

Figure 9.4
Homepage source file that is duplicated and saved as a separate file so the background image of the woman can be saved independently from the images layered over it.

Understanding the Placement of CSS Containers

More than 10 <DIV> tags are used to lay out the images saved from the Photoshop file and XHTML content. Figure 9.5 shows the <DIV> tags with all the images and content removed and their borders "turned on" by setting them to 1px.

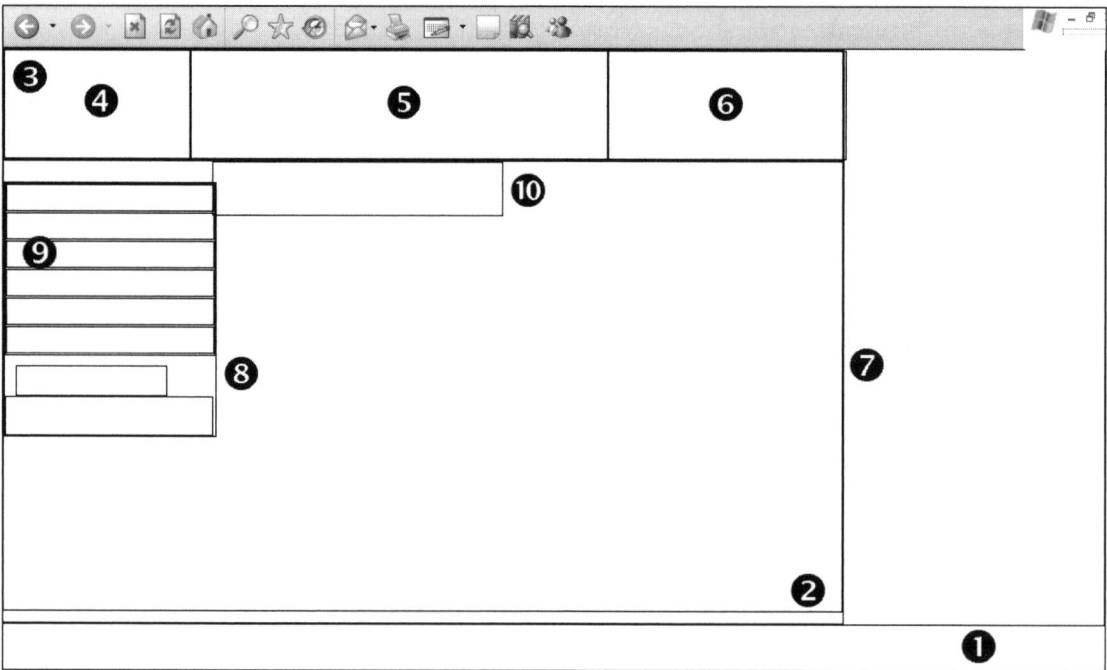

Figure 9.5
Design with images and content removed and various <DIV> tags turned on.
© 2014 Cengage Learning.

The <DIV> tags are used for different functions in the design, such as setting up its basic infrastructure, providing containers to position content within, and styling the content. Following are explanations of the 10 most useful <DIV> tags in Figure 9.5:

- The <DIV> tag above number 1 is used for centering the design in IE 5 and 5.5, if it is to have a fixed width. The container starts at the very top-left corner of the browser window. This style is no longer necessary for most sites, but it is mentioned here because it will still be included in designs from previous editions that are included online.

- The <DIV> tag below number 2 determines whether the design has a fixed width or is a liquid layout. It also begins in the top-left corner of the browser window.

- The <DIV> tag to the left of number 3 contains the images that are used in the header area.

- Numbers 4, 5, and 6 are images in the header area that are assigned absolute positioning.

- The <DIV> tag to the left of number 7 contains both the left and right columns of the body.

- Number 8 defines the left column, which contains, among other things, the menu.

- Number 9 represents the container that styles and positions the menu.

- Number 10 is the <DIV> that contains the content in the right column. It expands to the full width of the design when enough content is included to force the full width.

BUILDING THE STRUCTURE

Following are the steps for constructing the design, step by step. It is assumed that the Photoshop file has already been created or customized and the designer need only position the images and text.

Creating the XHTML and CSS Framework

The first step to building the design is to create the XHTML framework and initial CSS containers. Listing 9.1 is the code that is used to output the page in Figure 9.6.

Figure 9.6
Basic XHTML and CSS framework for the design.
© 2014 Cengage Learning.

Listing 9.1   Code for Figure 9.6

```
<!DOCTYPE html PUBLIC "-//W3C//DTD XHTML 1.0 Transitional//EN"
      "DTD/xhtml1-transitional.dtd">
   <html xmlns="http://www.w3.org/1999/xhtml" xml:lang="en"
lang="en"><head><title>Design 121</title>
   <meta http-equiv="Content-Type" content="text/html;
```

```
                 charset=iso-8859-1" />
       <style type="text/css">
       /* ++++++++++ global general styles start ++++++++++*/
       html, body {
           margin:0px;
           padding:0px;
           font: 13px Arial, Helvetica, sans-serif;
           color:#766D6D;
           background:#ffffff;
       }
       /* ++++++++++ global general styles end ++++++++++*/


       /* ++++++++++ global structure styles start ++++++++++*/
       #a5-body-center {
           text-align:left;
           border:1px solid #000000;
           }
       #a5-body {
           position: relative;
           width: 770px; /* change this to a specific amount for a fixed
               design or a relative amount if the design should expand to a percentage
of the screen. E.g., 770px or 100%, respectively. */
       /* remove these comment tags if the page is to be centered. The 'text-
           align' property in the 'a5-body-center' rule must also be changed
           from 'left' to 'center'
           margin-left: auto;
           margin-right: auto;*/
           text-align:left;
           padding-bottom:10px;
           border:1px solid #000000;
           }
       /* ++++++++++ global structure styles end ++++++++++*/
       </style>
       </head>
       <body>
       <div id="a5-body-center">
           <div id="a5-body">
               Enter text here.
           </div>
       </div>
       </body>
       </html>
```

There are several things to note about the code in Listing 9.1:

- The CSS style sheet is commented into a couple of different sections. The global general styles comment tags contain the general styles, such as the formatting of the <HTML> and <BODY> tags, hyperlinks, and fonts. The global structure styles comment tags include the styles used to define the structure of the design and elements included in that structure.

- Several rules define the <HTML> and <BODY> tags. The margin and padding properties are used to ensure that the design is placed in the very top-left corner of the browser, with no space between the design and the edges of the viewable area. The default font style for the site is set using the shorthand FONT property. The default font color is defined with the COLOR property. The background color also is assigned, even if it is only white (that is, #ffffff). This guarantees that all browsers display the site with the same background color because the default color is not always the same among browsers.

- The a5-body-center and a5-body rules are used to force the design to the left side of the browser screen with a fixed width of 770 pixels. If the designer wanted the design to fill the full width of the screen, the value of 770px would need to be changed to 100%. If, however, the designer wanted to center the design, the value of the text-align property in the a5-body-center rule would need to be changed from left to center. The margin-left and margin-right properties in the a5-body rule would only need to have the comment tags around them removed. This system gives the designer flexibility when more than one site is going to be built using this same default code. By adding this code to every design, it does not take much effort to quickly change a design to fit a client's needs.

- Both the a5-body-center and a5-body rules have their borders turned on using the following code: border:1px solid #000000;. For demonstration purposes, the code was added to both rules to show what the structure of the <DIV> tags looks like with no content added. Turning on the borders also helps when building a site because it is not always apparent where elements are placed or expanding to. Rather than remove these rules, it is easier to change the value of 1px to 0px, turning the borders off. Troubleshooting often involves turning the borders back on, thereby saving time and taking up very little download size by keeping them in the style sheet.

- Because the <div id="a5-body"> is nested inside the <div id="a5-body-center"> tag, it is indented. This allows for quicker recognition of nested tags, which becomes a useful technique when the page has more code added to it later.

Adding the Header Content

Once the XHTML and basic CSS framework have been added, the header area is then added into the code. Listing 9.2 is the code that is used to output the page in Figure 9.7.

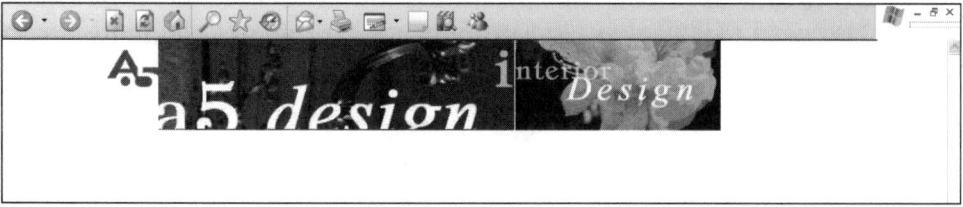

Figure 9.7
Design with all three header images added.
© 2014 Cengage Learning.

New Code Is in Bold

The newly added code is bolded to differentiate it from the existing code that is being built upon in this case study.

Listing 9.2   Code for Figure 9.7

```
<!DOCTYPE html PUBLIC "-//W3C//DTD XHTML 1.0 Transitional//EN"
     "DTD/xhtml1-transitional.dtd">
  <html xmlns="http://www.w3.org/1999/xhtml" xml:lang="en"
lang="en"><head><title>Design 121</title>
  <meta http-equiv="Content-Type" content="text/html;
     charset=iso-8859-1" />
  <style type="text/css">
  /* ++++++++++ global general styles start ++++++++++*/
  html, body {
     margin:0px;
     padding:0px;
     font: 13px Arial, Helvetica, sans-serif;
     color:#766D6D;
     background:#ffffff;
     }
  /* ++++++++++ global general styles end ++++++++++*/
  /* ++++++++++ global structure styles start ++++++++++*/
  #a5-body-center {
     text-align:left;
     border:0px solid #000000;
     }
```

```
#a5-body {
    position: relative;
    width: 770px; /* change this to a specific amount for a fixed
        design or a relative amount if the design should expand to a percentage
of the screen. E.g., 770px or 100%, respectively. */
/* remove these comment tags if the page is to be centered. The 'text-
    align' property in the 'a5-body-center' rule must also be changed
    from 'left' to 'center'
    margin-left: auto;
    margin-right: auto;*/
    text-align:left;
    padding-bottom:10px;
    border:0px solid #000000;
    }
/* ++++++++++ global structure styles end ++++++++++*/
#a5-header {
    position:relative;
    left:0px;
    top:0px;
    height:98px;
    border:0px solid #000000;
    }
    #a5-header-center {
        position:absolute;
        left:169px;
        top:0px;
        }
    #a5-header-right {
        position:absolute;
        left:553px;
        top:0px;
        }
</style>
</head>
<body>
<div id="a5-body-center">
    <div id="a5-body">
<!-- ###### header start ###### -->
        <div id="a5-header">
            <div><a href="index.htm"><img src="images/header-left.gif"
                width="169" height="98" alt="" border="0" /></a></div>
```

```
        <div id="a5-header-center"><img src="images/
            header-center.jpg" width="384" height="98" alt=""
            border="0" /></div>
        <div id="a5-header-right"><img src="images/
            header-right.jpg" width="217" height="98" alt=""
            border="0" /></div>
    </div>
<!-- ###### header end ###### -->
    </div>
</div>
</body>
</html>
```

There are several things to note about the code in Listing 9.2:

■ Three images are being mortised together in the header area, rather than just one (see Figure 9.8).

■ The a5-header rule is created to contain the three header images inside it. This container also allows the designer to easily move all those elements included inside it as one entity because their positioning is based off its top-left corner.

■ Because it is assigned relative positioning, with the left and top properties set to 0px, the a5-header container begins at the very top-left corner of the Web browser because the <DIV> tags it is nested inside also begin at the X,Y (0,0) coordinates of the page. The relative positioning also ensures that the <DIV> tag will stretch to the full width of the area it is occupying, which is 770 pixels. The height property of the rule, which is set to 98px, is added to ensure that the container collapses perfectly around the three images.

Otherwise, browsers may not structure the container similarly.

Figure 9.8
Three images that are mortised together in the header area.
© 2014 Cengage Learning.

<DIV> tags are wrapped around the header-left.gif image, which is the first image in the header area. This is to ensure that no additional space is added around the image, stretching the a5-header container too high, such as in Figure 9.9, which is a result of an entirely different cause, as noted.

To ensure that no space appears between the image and the container's border around the image, the code must look like the following:

```
<div><a href="index.htm"><img src="images/header-left.gif" width="169" height="98"
alt="" border="0" /></a></div>
```

Rather than like this:

```
<div><a href="index.htm"><img src="images/header-left.gif" width="169" height="98"
alt="" border="0" /></a> </div>
```

■ Both the a5-header-center and a5-header-right rules are added to the style sheet to position the other two images in the header area. Both of these rules use absolute positioning. This makes the left and top properties particularly important because they assign where the top-left corner of the container will be positioned. Because the first image is 169 pixels wide, the a5-header-center tag must start 169 pixels from the left—thus the 169px value. Because the center image is 384 pixels wide, that width added to the width of the first image determines that the third image must start 553 pixels from the left ($384 + 169 = 553$ pixels). This positioning works only if the borders are turned off, so they are not entered into the equation in some browsers. To guarantee that both images begin at the top of the a5-header container, the top property, with a value of 0px, is added to both rules.

Avoid Unnecessary Spaces

Sometimes, spaces or carriage returns in XHTML code can alter the way <DIV> tags are interpreted. The image located in the first <DIV> tag nested inside the a5-header <DIV> is a perfect example of this. If a space or carriage return is added after the closing </a> tag, the a5-header container will add extra space below the image(s) in IE 6 (see Figure 9.9). The background color of the container was set as black to show the difference in the image. It should be noted that one space in XHTML code will render one space in a design, if that space is in the content area. A space usually doesn't make a difference between lines of code. This note is one exception to this rule.

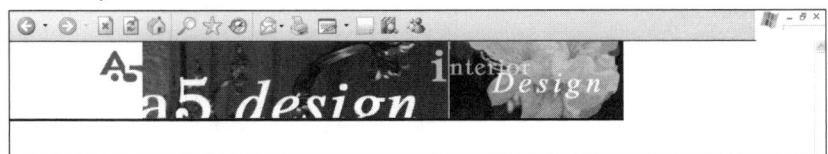

Figure 9.9
Extra space added below the header area because of a carriage return in the XHTML code.
© 2014 Cengage Learning.

Adding <DIV> in Which to Nest Left and Right Columns

Before the left and right columns of the design can be added, a <DIV> must be added that can contain the columns. In this case, the a5-body-content container serves two functions:

- Once the left and right columns are nested inside the <DIV>, the entire area can be moved easily in relation to the header area. If, for example, the design is customized to be 150 pixels high, the top property of the a5-body-center container would need to be changed to 150px.

- A background image can be applied specifically to this section. In this case, it is the image of the woman.

Positioning Background Images

The background image can also be applied to the HTML, BODY rule and have its location controlled by the shorthand background rule: background: #ffffff url(images/bg-body-content.jpg) no-repeat 0px 98px;. The left (0px) and top (98px) properties at the end of the rule tell the background image where it should be displayed in relation to the top-left corner of the browser window.

Figure 9.10 shows what the image looks like when the <DIV> is added. Without content in the <DIV>, it would normally collapse and not show the background. The a5-body-content rule, however, has been assigned a height of 410px, which will guarantee that the entire image always shows, whether or not there is enough content included in the <DIV> to make it expand to its full height.

Figure 9.10
The page with the a5-body-content container added, which will not only contain the left and right columns, but will also display a background image.

© 2014 Cengage Learning.

Creating the Left Column

After the `a5-body-content` container has been added, the left column can be created. This column will contain the menu, the Glance At box, and the copyright areas. Listing 9.3 shows what the code looks like, which then displays the design, as shown in Figure 9.11.

Figure 9.11
The design with the left column added to the `a5-body-content` container.
© 2014 Cengage Learning.

Listing 9.3   Code for Figure 9.11

```
<!DOCTYPE html PUBLIC "-//W3C//DTD XHTML 1.0 Transitional//EN"
        "DTD/xhtml1-transitional.dtd">
    <html xmlns="http://www.w3.org/1999/xhtml" xml:lang="en"
lang="en"><head><title>Design 121</title>
    <meta http-equiv="Content-Type" content="text/html;
        charset=iso-8859-1" />
    <style type="text/css">
    /* ++++++++++ global general styles start ++++++++++*/
    html, body {
        margin:0px;
        padding:0px;
        font: 13px Arial, Helvetica, sans-serif;
        color:#766D6D;
        background:#ffffff;
        }
    /* ++++++++++ global general styles end ++++++++++*/
    /* ++++++++++ global structure styles start ++++++++++*/
    #a5-body-center {
        text-align:left;
        border:0px solid #000000;
        }
    #a5-body {
        position: relative;
        width: 770px; /* change this to a specific amount for a fixed
            design or a relative amount if the design should expand to a percentage
of the screen. E.g., 770px or 100%, respectively. */
    /* remove these comment tags if the page is to be centered. The 'text-
        align' property in the 'a5-body-center' rule must also be changed
        from 'left' to 'center'
        margin-left: auto;
        margin-right: auto;*/
        text-align:left;
        padding-bottom:10px;
        border:0px solid #000000;
        }
    /* ++++++++++ global structure styles end ++++++++++*/
    #a5-header {
        position:relative;
        left:0px;
        top:0px;
```

```
        height:98px;
        background:#000000;
        }
    #a5-header-left {
        width:169px;
        }
    #a5-header-center {
        position:absolute;
        left:169px;
        top:0px;
        }
    #a5-header-right {
        position:absolute;
        left:553px;
        top:0px;
        }
  #a5-body-content {
      position:relative;
      background: #ffffff url(images/bg-body-content.jpg) no-repeat;
      height:410px;
margin-right:15px;
      border:0px solid #000000;
      }
    #a5-column-left {
        position:absolute;
        left:0px;
        top:19px;
        width:190px;
        }
        #a5-menu {
        font:bold 13px Arial, Helvetica, sans-serif;
            }
        #a5-menu a {
            display:block;
            text-align:left;
            line-height:23px;
            vertical-align:50%;
            padding-left:15px;
            margin-bottom:1px;
            text-decoration:none;
            background: url(images/bg-menu-off.gif) no-repeat 0px 0px;
            color:#E9F92C;
            }
```

```
        #a5-menu a:hover {
            background: url(images/bg-menu-on.jpg) no-repeat 0px 0px;
            margin-bottom:1px;
            color:#E9F92C;
            }
        #a5-bottom-left-content {
            width:136px;
            font:bold 12pt times, garamond, serif;
            line-height:26px;
            text-align:right;
            margin:9px 0px 0px 10px;
            color:#DF9B05;
            border:1px solid #999A8D;
            }
        #a5-copyright {
            font-size:8pt;
            padding:10px 50px 10px 10px;
            color:#766D6D;
            }
</style>
</head>
<body>
<div id="a5-body-center">
    <div id="a5-body">
<!-- ###### header start ###### -->
        <div id="a5-header">
            <div><a href="index.htm"><img src="images/header-left.gif"
                width="169" height="98" alt="" border="0" /></a></div>
            <div id="a5-header-center"><img src="images/
                header-center.jpg" width="384" height="98" alt=""
                border="0" /></div>
            <div id="a5-header-right"><img src="images/
                header-right.jpg" width="217" height="98" alt=""
                border="0" /></div>
        </div>
<!-- ###### header end ###### -->


<!-- ###### body content start ###### -->
        <div id="a5-body-content">
            <div id="a5-column-left">
                <div id="a5-menu">
                    <a href="index.htm">menu item 1</a>
```

```
                    <a href="menu-item-2.htm">longer menu item 2</a>
                    <a href="menu-item-3.htm">menu item 3</a>
                    <a href="index.htm">menu item 4</a>
                    <a href="index.htm">menu item 5</a>
                    <a href="index.htm">menu item 6</a>
                </div>

                <div id="a5-bottom-left-content">
                    <span style="font:bold 24pt times, garamond, serif;
                        ">Glance at</span><br />
                    some of the<br />
                    <span style="font:bold 13pt times, garamond, serif;
                        ">possibilities your</span><br />
                    house has to offer        <div style="padding-top:10px;">
                        <a href="index.htm"><img src="images/
                        photo-bottom-left.jpg" width="136"
                        height="93" alt="" border="0" /></a></div>
                </div>
                <div id="a5-copyright">
                    |  &copy; copyright 2006  
                        |<br />|  your company  |
                        <br />|  all rights reserved 
                         |
                </div>
            </div>
        </div>
<!-- ###### body content start ###### -->
        </div>
    </div>
    </body>
</html>
```

There are several things to note about the code in Listing 9.3:

- The a5-column-left container is assigned absolute positioning. This guarantees that it will always be in the same location. The one disadvantage to absolute positioning is the a5-column-left container will fall outside the flow of the document, meaning it can end up vertically longer than the a5-column-left container. Fortunately, for this design, this would not be visible if that were the case because the column does not have a background color or image that the content needs to remain over.

- The a5-menu container contains the menu items that are styled to enable easy mouseovers. The column is given a specific width to guarantee that the first element is positioned correctly in all browsers.

- The a5-menu a descendant rule is used to display and style each menu item. The display property with the block value will output each item in the <DIV> is in its own row. The text is then left justified, assigning the text-align property a value of left. The line-height and vertical-align properties, which need to be used together for the vertical-align property to be interpreted, force the height of the menu item and how the text will be vertically aligned. The padding-left:15px; rule forces the menu items 15 pixels from the left so they do not fall on the circular image at the very left of the row. Because the menu is layered over the a5-body-content background image to the right, the margin-bottom:1px; rule is added to ensure that there is transparent spacing between the menu items so the layering effect is noticeable (see Figure 9.12).

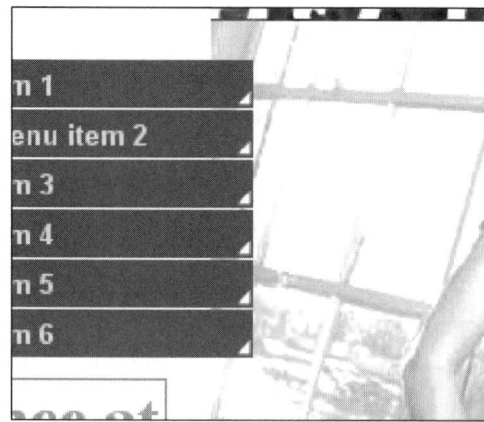

Figure 9.12
The menu items are assigned a margin-bottom value of 1px to ensure that it is apparent that the menu is layered over the background image in the a5-body-content rule.
© 2014 Cengage Learning.

One of the most important properties of this rule is the shorthand background property, which assigns a background image to a hyperlink and thus an item in the menu. This property works in conjunction with the a5-menu a:hover rule, which changes the background image when the user mouses over a menu item, avoiding the need for JavaScript (see Figure 9.13).

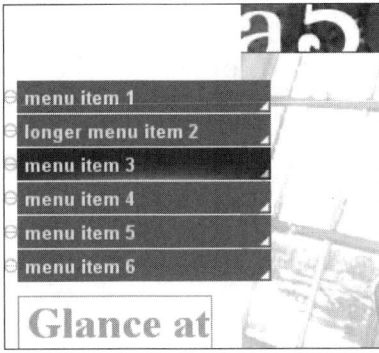

Figure 9.13
Background image that is switched using the code background: url(images/bg-menu-on.jpg) no-repeat 0px 0px;.
© 2014 Cengage Learning.

- The a5-bottom-left-content rule is added to create a separate text section below the menu. It employs many of the properties already discussed in this chapter. What gives it a different appearance is that the border is turned on and given a different color. While default font styling is included in the rule, additional styling is used at a local level in the <DIV> tag to resize text, such as "Glance at." The image in the container also is given local styling so that it has 10 pixels of padding between it and the text above it. If <DIV> tags are not added around the image, the border will not collapse around the image in some older browsers, such as IE 5, 5.5, and 6 browsers (see Figure 9.14).

- The only unique thing to note about the a5-copyright rule is where it is placed. If either the left or right columns or <DIV> tags nested in them are assigned absolute positioning, then the copyright should probably not be included in a footer row across the bottom of the entire site; this is because if the text runs too long in these absolute-positioned <DIV> tags, they can extend below the footer, either over or under it.

Figure 9.14
An image in a container that will not allow the border to collapse around the bottom, in all browsers, unless additional <DIV> tags are added.
© 2014 Cengage Learning.

Adding the Center (Right) Column

At this stage, most of the coding has been accomplished for the homepage. The designer needs to add only a column to the right. Because this design could always be turned into a three-column design, the column to the right is called a5-column-center, leaving the possibility of naming a right column a5-column-right. Listing 9.4 shows the completed code for the homepage design, which is shown in Figure 9.15.

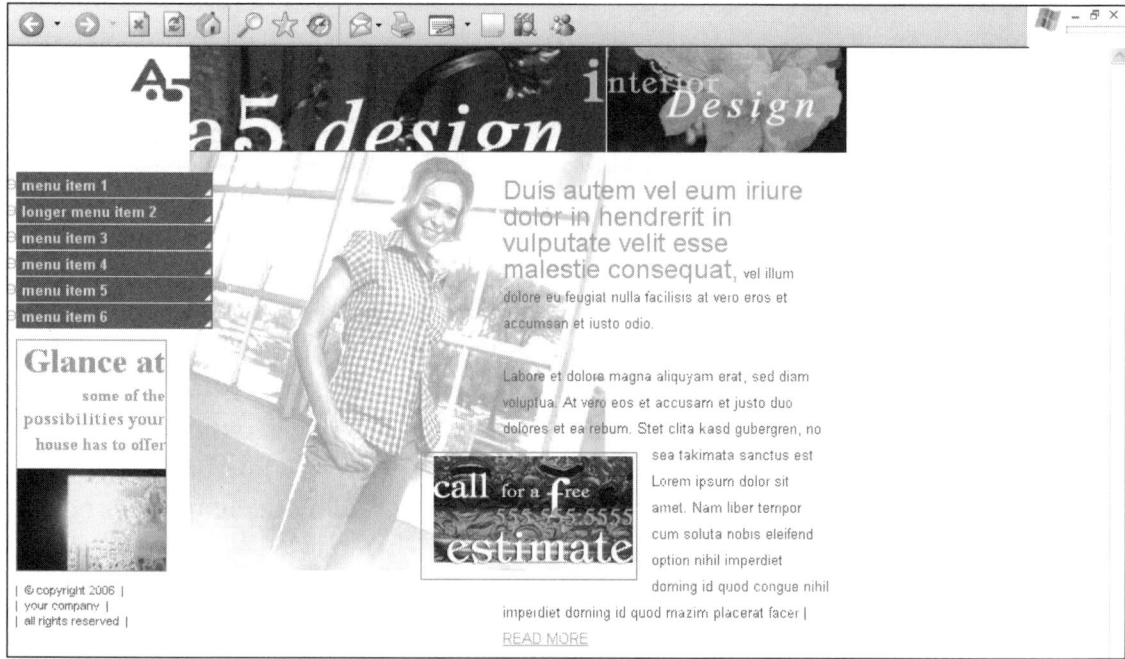

Figure 9.15
The completed design once the a5-column-right rule and content have been added.
© 2014 Cengage Learning.

New Code Is in Bold

The newly added code is bolded to differentiate it from the existing code that is being built upon in this case study.

Listing 9.4   Code for Figure 9.15

```
<!DOCTYPE html PUBLIC "-//W3C//DTD XHTML 1.0 Transitional//EN"
      "DTD/xhtml1-transitional.dtd">
   <html xmlns="http://www.w3.org/1999/xhtml" xml:lang="en"
lang="en"><head><title>Design 121</title>
   <meta http-equiv="Content-Type" content="text/html;
      charset=iso-8859-1" />
```

```css
<style type="text/css">
/* ++++++++++ global general styles start ++++++++++*/
html, body {
    margin:0px;
    padding:0px;
    font: 13px Arial, Helvetica, sans-serif;
    color:#766D6D;
    background:#ffffff;
    }
/* ++++++++++ global general styles end ++++++++++*/
/* ++++++++++ global structure styles start ++++++++++*/
#a5-body-center {
    text-align:left;
    border:0px solid #000000;
    }
#a5-body {
    position: relative;
    width: 770px; /* change this to a specific amount for a fixed
        design or a relative amount if the design should expand to a percentage
of the screen. E.g., 770px or 100%, respectively. */
    /* remove these comment tags if the page is to be centered. The
        'text-align' property in the 'a5-body-center' rule must also be
        changed from 'left' to 'center'
        margin-left: auto;
        margin-right: auto;*/
    text-align:left;
    padding-bottom:10px;
    border:0px solid #000000;
    }
/* ++++++++++ global structure styles end ++++++++++*/
#a5-header {
    position:relative;
    left:0px;
    top:0px;
    height:98px;
    background:#000000;
    }
    #a5-header-left {
        width:169px;
        }
```

```
    #a5-header-center {
        position:absolute;
        left:169px;
        top:0px;
        }
    #a5-header-right {
        position:absolute;
        left:553px;
        top:0px;
        }
#a5-body-content {
    position:relative;
    background: #ffffff url(images/bg-body-content.jpg) no-repeat;
    height:410px;
    margin-right:15px;
    border:0px solid #000000;
    }
    #a5-column-left {
        position:absolute;
        left:0px;
        top:19px;
        width:190px;
        }
        #a5-menu {
            font:bold 13px Arial, Helvetica, sans-serif;
            }
        #a5-menu a {
            display:block;
            text-align:left;
            line-height:23px;
            vertical-align: 50%;
            padding-left:15px;
            margin-bottom:1px;
            text-decoration:none;
            background: url(images/bg-menu-off.gif) no-repeat 0px 0px;
            color:#E9F92C;
            }
        #a5-menu a:hover {
            background: url(images/bg-menu-on.jpg) no-repeat 0px 0px;
            margin-bottom:1px;
            color:#E9F92C;
            }
```

```
                #a5-bottom-left-content {
                    width:136px;
                    font:bold 12pt times, garamond, serif;
                    line-height:26px;
                    text-align:right;
                    margin:9px 0px 0px 10px;
                    color:#DF9B05;
                    border:1px solid #999A8D;
                    }
                #a5-copyright {
                    font-size: 8pt;
                    padding:10px 50px 10px 10px;
                    color:#766D6D;
                    }
        #a5-column-center {
            position:absolute;
            left:190px;
            top:0px;
            line-height:18pt;
            padding:24px 0px 0px 268px;
            }
</style>
</head>
<body>
<div id="a5-body-center">
    <div id="a5-body">
<!-- ###### header start ###### -->
        <div id="a5-header">
            <div><a href="index.htm"><img src="images/header-left.gif"
                width="169" height="98" alt="" border="0" /></a></div>
            <div id="a5-header-center"><img src="images/
                header-center.jpg" width="384" height="98" alt=""
                border="0" /></div>
            <div id="a5-header-right"><img src="images/
                header-right.jpg" width="217" height="98" alt=""
                border="0" /></div>
        </div>
<!-- ###### header end ###### -->

<!-- ###### body content start ###### -->
        <div id="a5-body-content">
            <div id="a5-column-left">
```

```
        <div id="a5-menu">
            <a href="index.htm">menu item 1</a>
            <a href="menu-item-2.htm">longer menu item 2</a>
            <a href="menu-item-3.htm">menu item 3</a>
            <a href="index.htm">menu item 4</a>
            <a href="index.htm">menu item 5</a>
            <a href="index.htm">menu item 6</a>
        </div>

        <div id="a5-bottom-left-content">
            <span style="font:bold 24pt times, garamond,
                serif;">Glance at</span><br />
            some of the<br />
            <span style="font:bold 13pt times, garamond,
serif;">possibilities your</span><br />
            house has to offer
            <div style="padding-top:10px;"><a href="index.htm">
                <img src="images/photo-bottom-left.jpg"
                width="136" height="93" alt="" border="0" /></a></div>
        </div>
        <div id="a5-copyright">
        |  &copy; copyright 2006  |<br />|
                  your company  |<br />|
                  all rights reserved  |
        </div>
    </div>
    <div id="a5-column-center">
        <span class="color1text18">Duis autem vel eum iriure
                dolor in hendrerit in vulputate velit esse
                malestie consequat,</span> vel illum dolore eu
                feugiat nulla facilisis at vero eros et
                accumsan et iusto odio.<br /><br />
Labore et dolore magna aliquyam erat, sed diam voluptua. At vero eos et
        accusam et justo duo dolores et ea rebum. <span style="float:left;
        padding:10px; margin-left:-86px;"><a href="index.htm"><img src=
        "images/photo-center-middle.gif" width="199" height="117" alt=""
        border="0" /></a></span>Stet clita kasd gubergren, no sea takimata
        sanctus est Lorem ipsum dolor sit amet. Nam liber tempor cum
        soluta nobis eleifend option nihil imperdiet doming id quod congue
        nihil imperdiet doming id quod mazim placerat facer | <a href=
        "index.htm">READ MORE</a>
            </div>
```

```
        </div>
<!-- ###### body content start ###### -->
    </div>
</div>
</body>
</html>
```

There are several things to note about the code in Listing 9.4:

- Only one rule is added to style the right column: `a5-column-center`. It is given absolute positioning to ensure that the content does not fill the full width of the remaining screen. If the design were a liquid design, relative positioning would be the desired value.

- The `<DIV>` tag uses the `left` property to position the text 190 pixels from the left.

- The "call for a free estimate" image included in the container's text is assigned a local style that floats it to the left. The image is then assigned a `margin-left` property with the value of `-86px`. This forces the image to the left, partially outside the text flow (see Figure 9.16).

Figure 9.16
The design with the "call for a free estimate" image forced to the left, outside the main content flow.
© 2014 Cengage Learning.

This is where the transparency of the image between the border and the main part of the image becomes useful. This image can be added wherever the designer chooses within the content area. This is possible because the area between the border and the main part of the image will show the actual area over which it is layered.

CONSTRUCTING SECOND-LEVEL PAGES

A portion of the homepage design can be reused many times with other pages to maintain consistency and to limit the additional download necessary for second-level pages. (That is, the user's browser can cache certain images so they do not have to be downloaded again, making the page load faster.) When developing CSS sites, this process is much cleaner than with XHTML tables that can include many nested tables. Listing 9.5 shows the code used to create a second-level page after it has been customized from the homepage (see Figure 9.17).

Figure 9.17
A second-level page of the site constructed from the homepage design and code.
© 2014 Cengage Learning.

New Code Is in Bold

The newly added code is bolded to differentiate it from the existing code that is being built upon in this case study.

Listing 9.5   Code for Figure 9.17

```
<!DOCTYPE html PUBLIC "-//W3C//DTD XHTML 1.0 Transitional//EN"
        "DTD/xhtml1-transitional.dtd">
    <html xmlns="http://www.w3.org/1999/xhtml" xml:lang="en"
lang="en"><head><title>Design 121</title>
```

```
<meta http-equiv="Content-Type" content="text/html;
    charset=iso-8859-1" />
<style type="text/css">
/* ++++++++++ global general styles start ++++++++++*/
html, body {
    margin:0px;
    padding:0px;
    font: 13px Arial, Helvetica, sans-serif;
    color:#766D6D;
    background:#ffffff;
    }
a:link { color:#CB951D; }
a:visited { color:#A8B32D; }
a:active { color:#A8B32D; }
a:hover { color:#000000; }
.color1text18 {
    font-family: arial, geneva, sans-serif;
    font-size: 18pt;
    color: #A8B32D;
    }
/* ++++++++++ global general styles end ++++++++++*/
/* ++++++++++ global structure styles start ++++++++++*/
#a5-body-center {
    text-align:left;
    }
#a5-body {
    position: relative;
    width: 770px; /* change this to a specific amount for a fixed
        design or a relative amount if the design should expand to a percentage
of the screen. E.g., 770px or 100%, respectively. */
    /* remove these comment tags if the page is to be centered. The
        'text-align' property in the 'a5-body-center' rule must also be
        changed from 'left' to 'center'
    margin-left: auto;
    margin-right: auto;*/
    text-align:left;
    padding-bottom:10px;
    border:0px solid #000000;
    }
#a5-header {
    position:relative;
    left:0px;
```

```
        top:0px;
        height:98px;
        border:0px solid #000000;
        }
    #a5-header-center {
        position:absolute;
        left:169px;
        top:0px;
        }
    #a5-header-right {
        position:absolute;
        left:553px;
        top:0px;
        }
#a5-body-content {
    position:relative;
    background: #ffffff url(images/bg-body-content.jpg) no-repeat;
    height:410px;
    margin-right:15px;
    border:0px solid #000000;
    }
    #a5-column-left {
        position:absolute;
        left:0px;
        top:19px;
        width:190px;
        }
        #a5-menu {
            font:bold 13px Arial, Helvetica, sans-serif;
            }
        #a5-menu a {
            display:block;
            text-align:left;
            line-height:23px;
            vertical-align:50%;
            padding-left:15px;
            margin-bottom:1px;
            text-decoration:none;
            background: url(images/bg-menu-off.gif) no-repeat 0px 0px;
            color:#E9F92C;
            }
```

```
        #a5-menu a:hover {
            background: url(images/bg-menu-on.jpg) no-repeat 0px 0px;
            margin-bottom:1px;
            color:#E9F92C;
            }
        #a5-bottom-left-content {
            width:136px;
            font:bold 12pt times, garamond, serif;
            line-height:26px;
            text-align:right;
            margin:9px 0px 0px 10px;
            color:#DF9B05;
            border:1px solid #999A8D;
            }
        #a5-copyright {
            font-size: 8pt;
            padding:10px 50px 10px 10px;
            color:#766D6D;
            }
    #a5-column-center {
        position:absolute;
        left:190px;
        top:0px;
        line-height:18pt;
        padding:24px 0px 0px 268px;
        }
/* ++++++++++ global structure styles end ++++++++++*/
/* ++++++++++ second level start ++++++++++*/
#a5-body-content-sl {
    position:relative;
    background: #ffffff url(images/bg-body-content-sl.jpg) no-repeat;
    height:410px;
    margin-right:15px;
    border:0px solid #000000;
    }
    #a5-column-center-sl {
        position:absolute;
        left:190px;
        top:0px;
        line-height:18pt;
        padding:18px 0px 0px 18px;
        }
```

```
#a5-s1-title {
    height:24px;
    font:bold 14px Arial, Helvetica, sans-serif;
    background:#4E2124 url(images/bg-title.jpg) no-repeat
        left top;
    color:#ffffff;
    padding:3px 0px 0px 40px;
    margin-bottom:10px;
    border:0px solid #000000;
    voice-family:"\"}\"";
    voice-family:inherit;
        height:20px;
    }
    html>body #a5-s1-title {
        height:20px;
    }
/* ++++++++++ second level end ++++++++++*/
</style>
</head>
<body>
<div id="a5-body-center">
    <div id="a5-body">
<!-- ###### header start ###### -->
        <div id="a5-header">
            <div><a href="index.htm"><img src="images/header-left.gif"
                width="169" height="98" alt="" border="0" /></a></div>
            <div id="a5-header-center"><img src="images/
                header-center.jpg" width="384" height="98" alt=""
                border="0" /></div>
            <div id="a5-header-right"><img src="images/
                header-right.jpg" width="217" height="98" alt=""
                border="0" /></div>
        </div>
<!-- ###### header end ###### -->
<!-- ###### body content start ###### -->
        <div id="a5-body-content-s1">
            <div id="a5-column-left">
                <div id="a5-menu">
                    <a href="index.htm">menu item 1</a>
                    <a href="menu-item-2.htm">longer menu item 2</a>
                    <a href="menu-item-3.htm">menu item 3</a>
```

```
            <a href="index.htm">menu item 4</a>
            <a href="index.htm">menu item 5</a>
            <a href="index.htm">menu item 6</a>
        </div>
        <div id="a5-bottom-left-content">
            <span style="font:bold 24pt times, garamond,
                serif;">Glance at</span><br />
            some of the<br />
            <span style="font:bold 13pt times, garamond,
                serif;">possibilities your</span><br />
            house has to offer
            <div style="padding-top:10px;"><a href="index.htm">
                <img src="images/photo-bottom-left.jpg"
                width="136" height="93" alt="" border="0"
                /></a></div>
        </div>
        <div id="a5-copyright">
            |  &copy; copyright 2006  
                |<br />|  your company  |
                <br />|  all rights reserved 
                 |
        </div>
    </div>
    <div id="a5-column-center-s1">
<!-- ###### title start ###### -->
        <div id="a5-s1-title">longer menu item 2</div>
<!-- ###### title end ###### -->
            Nam liber tempor cum soluta nobis eleifend option
                congue nihil imperdiet doming id quod mazim
                placerat facer possim assum. Lorem ipsum dolor sit
                amet, consectetuer adipiscing elit, sed diam
                nonummy nibh euismod tincidunt ut laoreet dolore
                magna aliquam erat volutpat. Ut wisi enim ad minim
                veniam, quis nostrud exerci tation ullamcorper
                suscipit lobortis nisl ut aliquip ex ea commodo
                consequat.
    <br /><br />
Duis autem vel eum iriure dolor in hendrerit in vulputate velit esse molestie
consequat, vel illum dolore eu feugiat nulla facilisis.
    <br /><br />
At vero eos et accusam et justo duo dolores et ea rebum. Stet clita kasd gubergren,
no sea takimata sanctus est Lorem ipsum dolor sit amet. Lorem ipsum dolor sit amet,
consetetur sadipscing elitr, sed diam nonumy eirmod tempor invidunt ut labore et
```

```
dolore magna aliquyam erat, sed diam voluptua. At vero eos et accusam et justo duo
dolores et ea rebum. Stet clita kasd gubergren, no sea takimata sanctus est Lorem
ipsum dolor sit amet. Lorem ipsum dolor sit amet, consetetur sadipscing elitr, At
accusam aliquyam diam diam dolore dolores duo eirmod eos erat, et nonumy sed tempor
et et invidunt justo labore Stet clita ea et gubergren, kasd magna no rebum. Sanctus
sea sed takimata ut vero voluptua. est Lorem ipsum
            </div>
          </div>
    <!-- ###### body content end ###### -->
        </div>
      </div>
    </body>
    </html>
```

There are several things to note about the code in Listing 9.5:

■ The a5-body-content container is renamed a5-body-content-sl because it uses a different background image for the second-level pages that is lightened to help make the text more visible on the pages where it is layered over the woman. The a5-body-content-sl rule then calls this new image.

■ The margin-right:15px; code, as on the homepage, ensures that the text will never touch the right side of the browser window if it is a liquid design that expands to the full width of the screen.

■ The a5-sl-title rule is added to allow the designer to place a title on every page so the user knows which page is selected. The main thing to note about this code is that because the container is given padding, the Tantek hack is used so the height of the row is the same in the tested browsers, which included IE 5 and 5.5 for this design. A margin-bottom value of 10px is also added to provide space between the title area and the text for that page. It should be noted that this code is no longer necessary, so it can easily be deleted, and the rule modified. It is included in here because it is still included with older templates included with this book.

Adding a Floating Container for Additional Content

In the case study designs in Chapters 10, 11, 12, and 13, a third column is added to allow for more layout options. In this design, however, a new <DIV> is merely added and floated to the right side of the text to allow for similar functionality. Figure 9.18 illustrates what the new code (outlined in Listing 9.6) will look like.

Figure 9.18
A right text block area is added to second-level pages to allow for more layout possibilities.

© 2014 Cengage Learning.

New Code Is in Bold

The newly added code is bolded to differentiate it from the existing code that is being built upon in this case study.

Listing 9.6   Code for Figure 9.18

```
<!DOCTYPE html PUBLIC "-//W3C//DTD XHTML 1.0 Transitional//EN"
      "DTD/xhtml1-transitional.dtd">
   <html xmlns="http://www.w3.org/1999/xhtml" xml:lang="en"
lang="en"><head><title>Design 121</title>
   <meta http-equiv="Content-Type" content="text/html;
      charset=iso-8859-1" />
   <style type="text/css">
```

```css
/* ++++++++++ global general styles start ++++++++++*/
html, body {
    margin:0px;
    padding:0px;
    font: 13px Arial, Helvetica, sans-serif;
    color:#766D6D;
    background:#ffffff;
    }
a:link { color:#CB951D; }
a:visited { color:#A8B32D; }
a:active { color:#A8B32D; }
a:hover { color:#000000; }
.color1text18 {
    font-family: arial, geneva, sans-serif;
    font-size: 18pt;
    color: #A8B32D;
    }
/* ++++++++++ global general styles end ++++++++++*/
/* ++++++++++ global structure styles start ++++++++++*/
#a5-body-center {
    text-align:left;
    }
#a5-body {
    position: relative;
     width: 770px; /* change this to a specific amount for a fixed
            design or a relative amount if the design should expand to a percentage
of the screen. E.g., 770px or 100%, respectively. */
    /* remove these comment tags if the page is to be centered. The
        'text-align' property in the 'a5-body-center' rule must also be
        changed from 'left' to 'center'
        margin-left: auto;
        margin-right: auto;*/
    text-align:left;
    padding-bottom:10px;
    border:0px solid #000000;
    }
#a5-header {
    position:relative;
    left:0px;
    top:0px;
    height:98px;
    border:0px solid #000000;
    }
```

```
#a5-header-center {
    position:absolute;
    left:169px;
    top:0px;
    }
#a5-header-right {
    position:absolute;
    left:553px;
    top:0px;
    }
#a5-body-content {
position:relative;
background: #ffffff url(images/bg-body-content.jpg) no-repeat;
height:410px;
margin-right:15px;
border:0px solid #000000;
}
#a5-column-left {
    position:absolute;
    left:0px;
    top:19px;
    width:190px;
    }
    #a5-menu {
        font:bold 13px Arial, Helvetica, sans-serif;
        }
    #a5-menu a {
        display:block;
        text-align:left;
        line-height:23px;
        vertical-align:50%;
        padding-left:15px;
        margin-bottom:1px;
        text-decoration:none;
        background: url(images/bg-menu-off.gif) no-repeat 0px 0px;
        color:#E9F92C;
        }
    #a5-menu a:hover {
        background: url(images/bg-menu-on.jpg) no-repeat 0px 0px;
        margin-bottom:1px;
        color:#E9F92C;
        }
```

```css
        #a5-bottom-left-content {
            width:136px;
            font:bold 12pt times, garamond, serif;
            line-height:26px;
            text-align:right;
            margin:9px 0px 0px 10px;
            color:#DF9B05;
            border:1px solid #999A8D;
            }
        #a5-copyright {
            font-size: 8pt;
            padding:10px 50px 10px 10px;
            color:#766D6D;
            }
    #a5-column-center {
        position:absolute;
        left:190px;
        top:0px;
        line-height:18pt;
        padding:24px 0px 0px 268px;
        }
/* ++++++++++ global structure styles end ++++++++++*/
/* ++++++++++ second level start ++++++++++*/
#a5-body-content-sl {
    position:relative;
    background: #ffffff url(images/bg-body-content-sl.jpg) no-repeat;
    height:410px;
    margin-right:15px;
    border:0px solid #000000;
    }
    #a5-column-center-sl {
        position:absolute;
        left:190px;
        top:0px;
        line-height:18pt;
        padding:18px 0px 0px 18px;
        }
        #a5-sl-title {
            height:24px;
            font:bold 14px Arial, Helvetica, sans-serif;
            background:#4E2124 url(images/bg-title.jpg) no-repeat
                left top;
```

```
                color:#ffffff;
                padding:3px 0px 0px 40px;
                margin-bottom:10px;
                border:0px solid #000000;
                voice-family:"\"}\"";
                voice-family:inherit;
                    height:20px;
                }
                html>body #a5-sl-title {
                    height:20px;
                }
        #a5-content-right-sl {
                float:right;
                width:182px;
                font:bold 12pt times, garamond, serif;
                line-height:16px;
                text-align:right;
                padding:15px;
                margin:10px 10px 10px 15px;
                color:#ffffff;
                border:1px solid #999A8D;
                background:#C1C96A;
                voice-family:"\"}\"";
                voice-family:inherit;
                    width:150px;
                }
                html>body #a5-content-right-sl {
                    width:150px;
                }
/* ++++++++++ second level end ++++++++++*/
</style>
</head>
<body>
<div id="a5-body-center">
    <div id="a5-body">
<!-- ###### header start ###### -->
        <div id="a5-header">
            <div><a href="index.htm"><img src="images/header-left.gif"
                width="169" height="98" alt="" border="0" /></a></div>
            <div id="a5-header-center"><img src="images/
                header-center.jpg" width="384" height="98" alt=""
                border="0" /></div>
```

```
            <div id="a5-header-right"><img src="images/
                header-right.jpg" width="217" height="98" alt=""
                border="0" /></div>
        </div>
<!-- ###### header end ###### -->
<!-- ###### body content start ###### -->
        <div id="a5-body-content-sl">
            <div id="a5-column-left">
                <div id="a5-menu">
                    <a href="index.htm">menu item 1</a>
                    <a href="menu-item-2.htm">longer menu item 2</a>
                    <a href="menu-item-3.htm">menu item 3</a>
                    <a href="index.htm">menu item 4</a>
                    <a href="index.htm">menu item 5</a>
                    <a href="index.htm">menu item 6</a>
                </div>
                <div id="a5-bottom-left-content">
                    <span style="font:bold 24pt times, garamond,
                        serif;">Glance at</span><br />
                    some of the<br />
                    <span style="font:bold 13pt times, garamond,
                        serif;">possibilities your</span><br />
                    house has to offer
                    <div style="padding-top:10px;"><a href="index.htm">
                        <img src="images/photo-bottom-left.jpg"
                        width="136" height="93" alt="" border="0"
                        /></a></div>
                </div>
                <div id="a5-copyright">
                    |  &copy; copyright 2006  |
                        <br />|  your company  |
                        <br />|  all rights reserved 
                         |
                </div>
            </div>
            <div id="a5-column-center-sl">
<!-- ###### title start ###### -->
                <div id="a5-sl-title">longer menu item 2</div>
```

```
<!-- ###### title end ###### -->
                    Nam liber tempor cum soluta nobis eleifend option
                    congue nihil imperdiet doming id quod mazim
                    placerat facer possim assum. Lorem ipsum dolor sit
                    amet, consectetuer adipiscing elit, sed diam
                    nonummy nibh euismod tincidunt ut laoreet dolore
                    magna aliquam erat volutpat. Ut wisi enim ad minim
                    <div id="a5-content-right-sl">Nam liber tempor cum
                    soluta nobis eleifend option congue nihil imperdiet
                    doming id quod mazim placerat facer possim assum.
                    <br /><br />Duis autem vel eum iriure dolor in
                    hendrerit in vulputate velit esse molestie
                    consequat, vel illum dolore eu feugiat nulla
                    facilisis.<br /><br />Nam liber tempor cum soluta
                    nobis eleifend option congue nihil imperdiet doming
                    id quod mazim placerat facer possim assum.</div>
                    veniam, quis nostrud exerci tation ullamcorper
                    suscipit lobortis nisl ut aliquip ex ea commodo
                    consequat.
        <br /><br />
Duis autem vel eum iriure dolor in hendrerit in vulputate velit esse molestie
consequat, vel illum dolore eu feugiat nulla facilisis.
        <br /><br />
At vero eos et accusam et justo duo dolores et ea rebum. Stet clita kasd gubergren,
no sea takimata sanctus est Lorem ipsum dolor sit amet. Lorem ipsum dolor sit amet,
consetetur sadipscing elitr, sed diam nonumy eirmod tempor invidunt ut labore et
dolore magna aliquyam erat, sed diam voluptua. At vero eos et accusam et justo duo
dolores et ea rebum. Stet clita kasd gubergren, no sea takimata sanctus est Lorem
ipsum dolor sit amet. Lorem ipsum dolor sit amet, consetetur sadipscing elitr, At
accusam aliquyam diam diam dolore dolores duo eirmod eos erat, et nonumy sed tempor et
et invidunt justo labore Stet clita ea et gubergren, kasd magna no rebum. Sanctus sea
sed takimata ut vero voluptua. est Lorem ipsum
                    </div>
                </div>
        <!-- ###### body content end ###### -->
            </div>
        </div>
    </body>
</html>
```

There is one key thing to note about the code in Listing 9.6:

■ The `a5-content-right-s1` rule uses the Tantek hack to ensure that the width is the same among all tested browsers. While none of the CSS is new at this point in the design, floating a `<DIV>` in the text can have varied results. Depending on where the container is included in the text, various browsers will render the line wraps and the line height (at least for one or two lines) differently. The designer should definitely test pages that use this layout technique.

SUMMARY

The design built in this chapter is a two-column layout that allows for including a floating `<DIV>` area on second-level pages. The chapter explains how the design could work as a liquid design or as a fixed design. Other techniques, such as using switching background images for mouseovers, mortising images, and using transparent PNGs or GIFs in a layout, are discussed. While a designer may not follow this exact coding method, all the techniques can be applied independently when creating other designs.

CHAPTER 10

CASE STUDY: MEDIUM-CONTENT CSS DESIGN

The complexity of a Web design can be deceptive. A design that looks simple can require more complex CSS coding, while a visually complex design may merely involve simple coding to achieve the proper mortising of images and content placement. The design in this chapter, while its look and feel appear similar to the design in Chapter 9, is more complex because it uses a three-column rather than a two-column design. Also, it is centered in the browser and uses mortised images on the top half of the homepage so the user can not only view the images but also click on them. The second level uses a screened version as the background image, which allows the design to add content freely over the image.

Design 122 Example

The design explained in this chapter is design 122 online (photo credits: www.idlerphotography.com).

UNDERSTANDING THE DESIGN'S STRUCTURE

Figure 10.1 shows the design that is explained in this chapter. It involves two basic overall columns, one for the left side, which includes the menu, and one for the right, which includes additional nested <DIV> tags to position and style the content on the right. This includes the In the News and Purchase Online text areas.

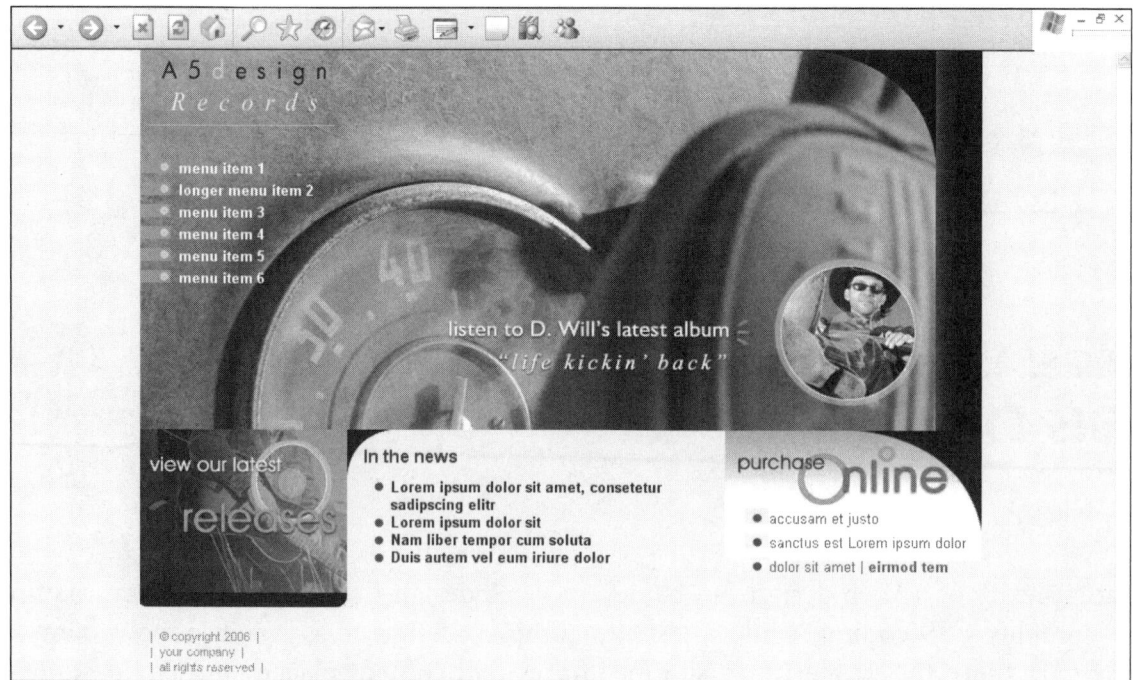

Figure 10.1
The medium-content CSS design explained in this chapter.

© 2014 Cengage Learning.

Reasoning Behind Guides and Creating Slices in a Photoshop File

There are 11 slices included in this design, all deriving their positioning from the numerous guides that were added. Understanding these is the first step toward visualizing how to structure and style the various containers more efficiently.

Figure 10.2 outlines 10 of the most important slices and guides that the designer needs to understand. While some of them are used similarly in the design in Chapter 9, others offer additional ways to build mortised CSS sites.

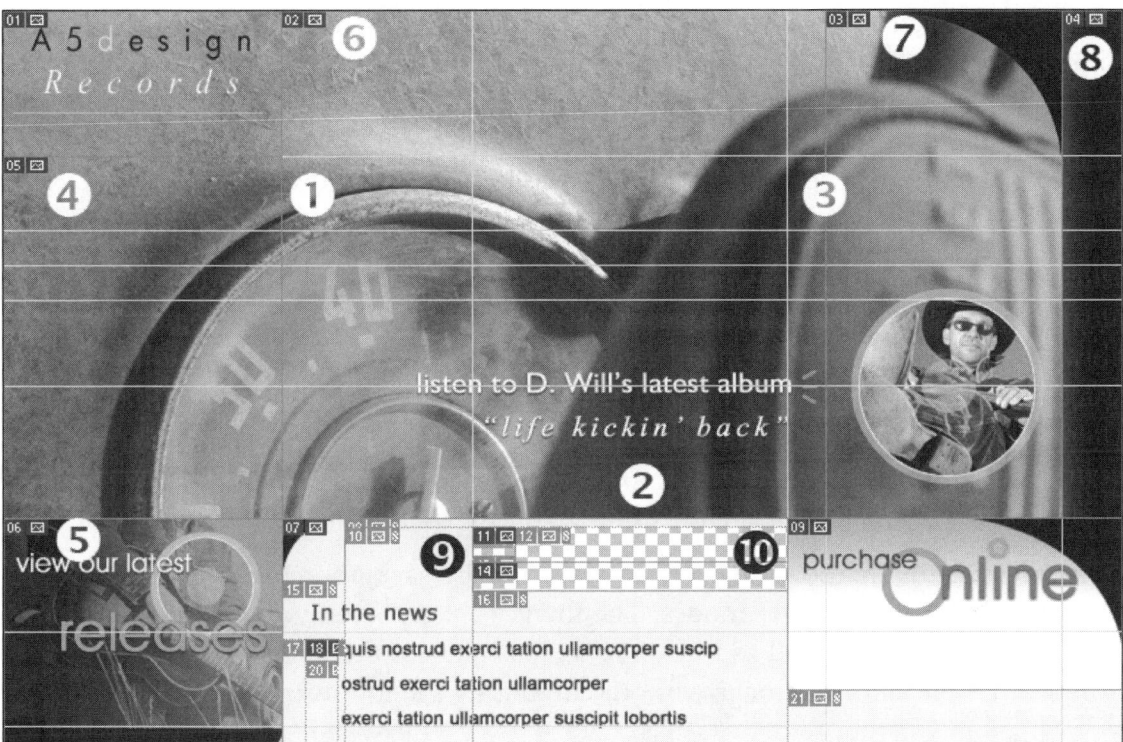

Figure 10.2
Guides and slices strategically placed within the design.
© 2014 Cengage Learning.

- The guide to the left of number 1 is used to separate the design into left and right columns. The left column includes the menu, and the right column is a parent column that will have two columns, the center and right columns, nested inside it.

- The guide below number 2 represents the guide that is used not only to outline the bottom of the background image in the menu, but also to separate the main graphical area on the right from the XHTML text (In the News and Purchase Online content) that is included below.

- The guide to the left of number 3 is used to separate the center and right columns, both of which are nested inside the parent right column.

- The slice indicated by number 4 is the background image that is used for the menu area of the design. One consideration in this type of design is that you don't want the background to repeat vertically because it was not designed to do so. This caveat forces the designer to work within a specified height, which includes any height taken up by submenu items. By using a nonrepeatable background image, the designer can mortise it with the slice illustrated by number 5. If, however, the design were altered visually so that it did not matter if the two images were mortised together, the menu could be changed structurally to stretch down as far as the designer wanted.

■ Number 5 shows the slice that creates an image placed below the menu in the left column.

■ The images represented by numbers 6, 7, and 8 are mortised together to form the large image area of the right column. All three images are saved, so they can be hyperlinked or, for example, replaced by a Flash movie. Because they are nested in a fixed <DIV>, if the design were changed to be liquid, the background color on the right, which is black, would extend to the right of the images. The extension would be seamless because the right image is gradated into solid black.

■ The slices to the right of number 9 are used for the background images of each menu item in Normal and Hover modes. The images are cut from them so their backgrounds can be saved as transparent. This enables the items to be moved over the menu's background image without containing the top image. This technique is explained in Chapter 9.

■ Number 10 indicates the image that is used as the background of the bottom-right column text area. While text is layered over it, it cannot be hyperlinked because it is a background image.

Understanding the Placement of CSS Containers

The number of <DIV> tags used in this design is similar to the design in Chapter 9. The main difference is in how they are used. Figure 10.3 shows the structure of the designs with the borders of the <DIV> tags turned on.

Figure 10.3
Ten of the most important containers used to build the design in this chapter.
© 2014 Cengage Learning.

The <DIV> tags are used for different functions in the design, such as setting up the basic infrastructure of the design, providing containers to position content within the infrastructure, and styling the content within the containers. Following are explanations for the 10 most useful containers in Figure 10.3:

1. The <DIV> tag to the left of number 1 is used for centering the design in IE 5 and 5.5. It extends the full width of the screen.

2. The <DIV> tag above number 2 determines whether the design has a fixed width or is a liquid layout.

3. The <DIV> tag to the left of number 3 contains both the left and right parent columns of the body. They are considered parent columns because the right column contains the code for the visual center and right columns of the design. This container extends to the right edges of the <DIV> outlined by number 2.

4. The <DIV> to the left of number 4 defines the right column. This contains everything to the right of the left column, which in this example, is for the sake of visual simplicity.

5. The menu column lies to the left of number 5, which is included in the left column.

6. Number 6 represents a <DIV> that contains the "view our latest releases" image in the left column below the menu.

7. Number 7 identifies the <DIV> that contains the top nested images in the right column.

8. The <DIV> to the left of number 8 is used to contain the center and right content columns that begin below the <DIV> that includes numbers 8, 9, and 10.

9. Number 9 shows the bottom-center content column that is nested inside number 8.

10. Number 10 represents the bottom-right content column nested inside number 8.

BUILDING THE STRUCTURE

Here are the step-by-step instructions for building the design. It is assumed that the Photoshop file has already been created or customized and the designer only needs to position the images and text.

Creating the XHTML and CSS Framework

The first step for building the design is to create the XHTML framework and initial CSS containers. Listing 10.1 is the code that is used to output the page shown in Figure 10.4.

Figure 10.4
Basic XHTML and CSS framework for the design.
© 2014 Cengage Learning.

Listing 10.1   Code for Figure 10.4

```
<!DOCTYPE html PUBLIC "-//W3C//DTD XHTML 1.0 Transitional//EN"
    "DTD/xhtml1-transitional.dtd">
<html xmlns="http://www.w3.org/1999/xhtml" xml:lang="en"
lang="en"><head><title>Design 122</title>
<meta http-equiv="Content-Type" content="text/html; charset=iso-8859-1" />
<style type="text/css">
/* ++++++++++ global general styles start ++++++++++*/
html, body {
    margin:0px;
    padding:0px;
    font: 13px Arial, Helvetica, sans-serif;
    color:#766D6D;
    background:#F8F4EB;
    }
/* ++++++++++ global general styles end ++++++++++*/
/* ++++++++++ global structure styles start ++++++++++*/
#a5-body-center {
    text-align:center;
    border:1px solid #000000;
    }
#a5-body {
    position: relative;
    width: 770px; /* change this to a specific amount for a fixed
        design or a relative amount if the design should expand to a percentage
of the screen. E.g., 770px or 100%, respectively. */
    margin-left: auto;
    margin-right: auto;
    text-align:left;
    padding-bottom:10px;
    border:1px solid #000000;
    }
/* ++++++++++ global structure styles end ++++++++++*/
</style>
</head>
<body>
<div id="a5-body-center">
    <div id="a5-body">
     
    </div>
</div>
</body>
</html>
```

There are several things to note about the code in Listing 10.1:

- The CSS style sheet is commented into a couple of different sections. The global general styles comment tags contain the general styles, such as the formatting of the <HTML> and <BODY> tags, hyperlinks, and fonts.

- Several rules define the <HTML> and <BODY> tags. The margin and padding properties are used to ensure that the design is placed in the very top-left corner of the browser, with no space between the design and the edges of the viewable area. The default font style is set using the shorthand FONT property. The default font color is defined with the COLOR property. The background color also is assigned (that is, #F8F4EB). This guarantees that all browsers display the site with the same background color because they would not otherwise always necessarily be the same.

- The a5-body-center and a5-body rules are used to force the design to the side of the browser screen with a fixed width of 770 pixels. If the designer wanted to fill the full width of the screen, the value of 770px would need to be changed to 100%. If, however, the designer wanted to simply justify the design to the left, the value of the text-align property in the a5-body-center rule would need to be adjusted from center to left. The margin-left and margin-right properties in the a5-body rule ensure that the extra white space is evenly split on both sides. This system allows more than one site to be built with ease and flexibility, using the same default code, allowing the designer to adjust quickly to a client's needs.

- Both the a5-body-center and a5-body rules have their borders turned on using the following code: border:1px solid #000000;. For demonstration purposes, the code was added to both rules to show what the structure of the <DIV> tags looks like with no content added in them. Turning on the borders also helps a designer when building a site because it is not always apparent where elements are placed or where they are expanding. Rather than removing these rules, it is easier to change the value of 1px to 0px, turning the borders off. Troubleshooting often involves turning the borders back on because it saves times and takes up little download size to keep them in the style sheet.

- Because the <div id="a5-body"> tag is nested inside the <div id="a5-bodycenter"> tag, it is indented. This allows for quicker recognition of tags that are nested inside each other, which becomes useful when the page has more code added later.

Adding the Left Column

After the framework has been built, the left column needs to be added. This section includes the logo, menu, and bottom-left image of the design. Figure 10.5 shows what the design looks like after the code in Listing 10.2 has been added.

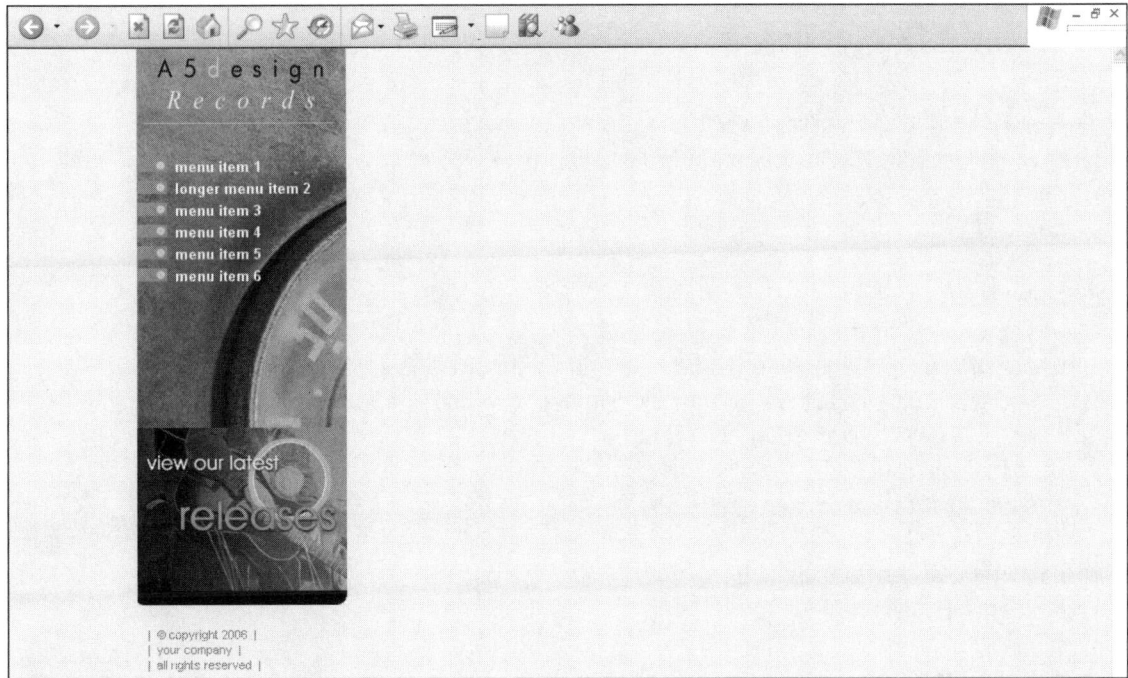

Figure 10.5
The design with the left column added.

New Code Is in Bold

The newly added code is bolded to differentiate it from the existing code that is being built upon in this case study.

Listing 10.2   Code for Figure 10.5

```
<!DOCTYPE html PUBLIC "-//W3C//DTD XHTML 1.0 Transitional//EN"
    "DTD/xhtml1-transitional.dtd">
<html xmlns="http://www.w3.org/1999/xhtml" xml:lang="en"
lang="en"><head><title>Design 122</title>
    <meta http-equiv="Content-Type" content="text/html;
        charset=iso-8859-1" />
```

```css
<style type="text/css">
/* ++++++++++ global general styles start ++++++++++*/
html, body {
    margin:0px;
    padding:0px;
    font: 13px Arial, Helvetica, sans-serif;
    color:#766D6D;
    background:#F8F4EB;
    }
/* ++++++++++ global general styles end ++++++++++*/
/* ++++++++++ global structure styles start ++++++++++*/
#a5-body-center {
    text-align:center;
    }
#a5-body {
    position: relative;
    width: 770px; /* change this to a specific amount for a fixed
        design or a relative amount if the design should expand to a percentage
of the screen. E.g., 770px or 100%, respectively. */
    margin-left: auto;
    margin-right: auto;
    text-align:left;
    padding-bottom:10px;
    border:0px solid #000000;
    }
#a5-column-left {
    position:absolute;
    left:0px;
    top:0px;
    width:191px;
    border:0px solid #000000;
    }
    #a5-menu {
        font:bold 13px Arial, Helvetica, sans-serif;
        height:249px;
        background:url(images/bg-left-column.jpg) no-repeat;
        }
    #a5-menu a {
        display: block;
        text-align:left;
        line-height:20px;
        vertical-align: 30%;
```

```
        height:20px;
        padding-left:35px;
        text-decoration:none;
        background: url(images/bg-menu-off.gif) no-repeat 0px 0px;
        color:#ffffff;
        }
    #a5-menu a:hover {
        background: url(images/bg-menu-on.gif) no-repeat 0px 0px;
        color:#F9F68C;
        }
        #a5-menu-sl {
            width:191px;
            color:#000000;
            font:bold 12px Arial, Helvetica, sans-serif;
            text-align:left;
            }
        #a5-menu-sl a {
            display: block;
            text-align:left;
            line-height:18px;
            vertical-align: 50%;
            height:18px;
            padding-left:40px;
            font-weight:normal;
            text-decoration:none;
            background: url(images/bg-menu-off-sl.gif) no-repeat
                0px 0px;
            color:#000000;
            }
        #a5-menu-sl a:hover {
            background: url(images/bg-menu-on-sl.gif) no-repeat
                0px 0px;
            color:#4C5C6B;
            }
    #a5-copyright {
        font-size: 11px;
        padding:20px 50px 10px 10px;
        color:#978872;
        }
/* ++++++++++ global structure styles end ++++++++++*/
</style>
</head>
```

```
<body>
<div id="a5-body-center">
    <div id="a5-body">
<!-- ###### left column start ###### -->
        <div id="a5-column-left">
            <div><a href="index.htm"><img src="images/header-left.jpg"
                width="191" height="100" alt="" border="0" /></a></div>
            <div id="a5-menu">
                <a href="index.htm">menu item 1</a>
                <a href="menu-item-2.htm">longer menu item 2</a>
                <a href="menu-item-3.htm">menu item 3</a>
                <a href="index.htm">menu item 4</a>
                <a href="index.htm">menu item 5</a>
                <a href="index.htm">menu item 6</a>
            </div>
            <div><a href="index.htm"><img src="images/image-bottom-
                left.jpg" width="191" height="162" alt=""
                border="0" /></a></div>
            <div id="a5-copyright">
                |  &copy; copyright 2006  |<br />
                |  your company  |<br />
                |  all rights reserved  |
            </div>
        </div>
<!-- ###### left column end ###### -->
    </div>
</div>
</body>
</html>
```

There are several things to note about the code in Listing 10.2:

■ The `a5-column-left` rule has absolute positioning assigned to it. Its left and top properties are both assigned `0px` to force the `<DIV>` into the top-left corner of the `a5-body` container it is nested within. The width of the column is fixed at 191 pixels, using the `width` property. This ensures that the column's width will not change, no matter what other content is included in the right column. It also forces the width of the left column so the menu items fill in its full width.

■ When the logo is added as the first item in the `a5-column-left` container, it needs to have `<DIV>` tags wrapped around it to eliminate extra space between it and the menu area below in some older browsers, such as IE 5, 5.5, and 6 (see Figure 10.6). While these are antiquated browsers, it's still necessary to understand the code because it's included in older designs included with the book.

Figure 10.6
Space that is added between the logo and the menu area in IE 5, 5.5, and 6 because <DIV> tags were not wrapped around the image.
© 2014 Cengage Learning.

■ The a5-menu rule is assigned the height of 249 pixels, which forces it to be the full height of the background image, which is also 249 pixels. To call the background image, a version of the shorthand property for backgrounds is used: background:url(images/bg- left-column.jpg) no-repeat;. Font size, bolding, and family also are assigned to this <DIV>, which will then cascade down to any nested or child containers.

■ The a5-menu a descendant rule is used to display and style each menu item. The display property with the block value will output each item in the <DIV> in its own row. The line-height is set to 20 pixels. Unlike the design in Chapter 9, the vertical-align property is not assigned here because it will move the text in relation to the background image, which is declared using the following shorthand code: background: url(images/bg-menu-off.gif) no- repeat 0px 0px;.

■ The a5-menu a:hover rule is used to reassign the background image from bg-menu-off.gif to bg-menu-on.gif and the color of the text from #ffffff to #F9F68C when the user mouses over the text.

Reasoning for Case Difference

There is a case difference between the color of a link and the hover link (that is, #ffffff and #F9F68C). The reason for this is that #ffffff was entered manually while building the site, and #F9F68C was copied from the Color Picker in Photoshop when grabbing the exact HEX color (see Figure 10.7).

Figure 10.7
HEX color #F9F68C, which was pulled from the Color Picker in Photoshop.

© 2014 Cengage Learning.

- The `image-bottom-left.jpg` image below the menu is added after the `a5-menu` `<DIV>` in the code. It has no styling added to it other than the `<DIV>` tags wrapped around it.

- The `a5-copyright` rule positions the copyright text below the `image-bottom-left.jpg` image, using padding around the text. The `padding:20px 50px 10px 10px;` code adds 20 pixels of padding to the top of the text, 50 pixels to the right, 10 pixels to the bottom, and 10 pixels to the left.

Adding <DIV> to Nest Center and Inside-Right Columns

An `a5-body-content` `<DIV>` is added to create a right column inside which the top-right images, bottom-left content area, and bottom-right content area will be nested. Figure 10.8 shows what the design looks like with the `a5-body-content` `<DIV>` border turned on.

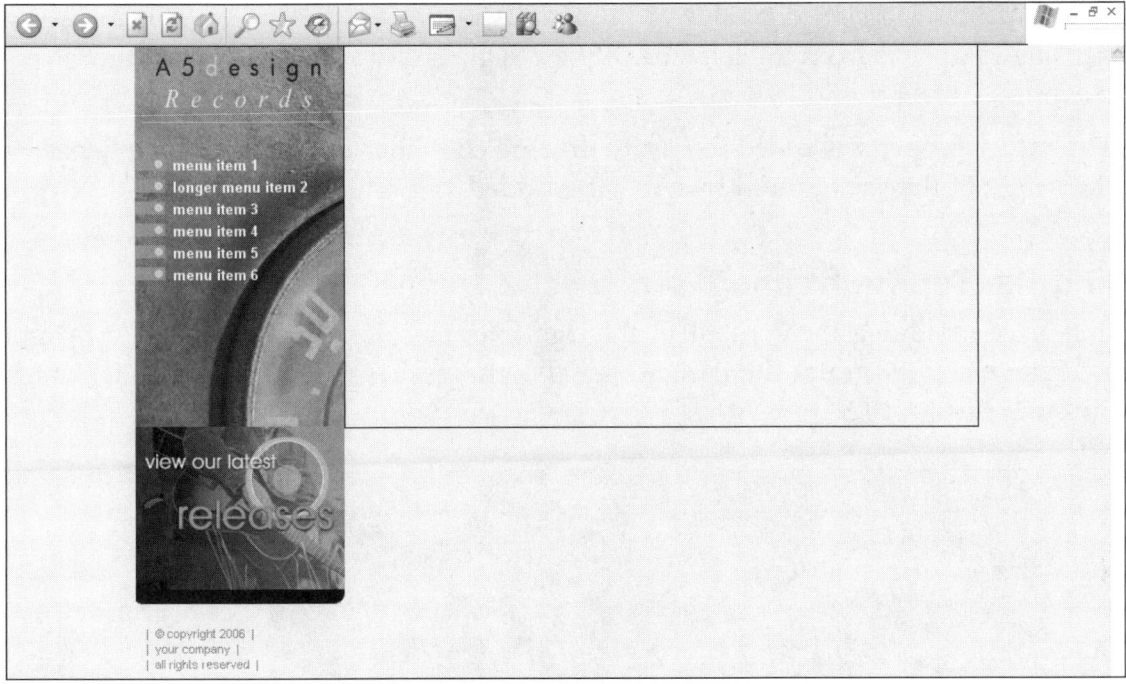

Figure 10.8
Page with the a5-body-content <DIV> added to form the right column.
© 2014 Cengage Learning.

This container is added because it will contain a background image in the second-level pages. By building the design around it in the homepage, the second-level pages, which are built from the homepage, are easier to construct because the base foundation of the code is already incorporated into the code. Following is the rule once it is added to the style sheet:

```
#a5-body-content {
    position:relative;
    margin-left:191px;
    height:349px;
    border:1px solid #000000;
    }
```

There are three things to note about the preceding code:

- The code has relative positioning so that it will flex to the full width of the a5-body container within which it is nested. This helps ensure that the design can also serve as a liquid design if the width of the a5-body rule is changed to 100%.

- The container is assigned a value of 191px to its margin-left property. This forces its left side 191 pixels from the left side of the design, so it is placed just past the left column.

- The height property is added to ensure that the container is 349 pixels high, which is the height of the background image that is added.

Adding the Top-Right Images

The first stage in adding the content in the right parent column is to add the top-right images. Figure 10.9 illustrates the design once the images are added into the code, which is included in Listing 10.3.

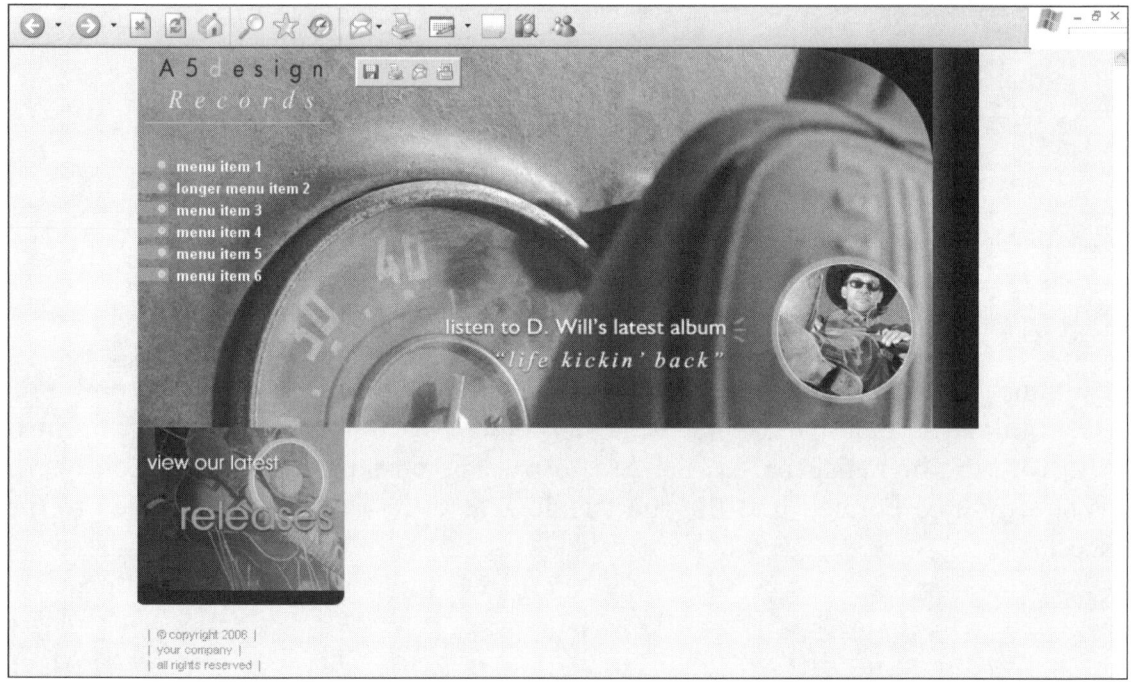

Figure 10.9
The first step to adding content to the right parent column is to add the mortised images.
© 2014 Cengage Learning.

New Code Is in Bold

The newly added code is bolded to differentiate it from the existing code that is being built upon in this case study.

Listing 10.3   Code for Figure 10.9

```
<!DOCTYPE html PUBLIC "-//W3C//DTD XHTML 1.0 Transitional//EN"
    "DTD/xhtml1-transitional.dtd">
<html xmlns="http://www.w3.org/1999/xhtml" xml:lang="en"
lang="en"><head><title>Design 122</title>
<meta http-equiv="Content-Type" content="text/html; charset=iso-8859-1" />
<style type="text/css">
/* ++++++++++ global general styles start ++++++++++*/
html, body {
    margin:0px;
    padding:0px;
    font: 13px Arial, Helvetica, sans-serif;
    color:#766D6D;
    background:#F8F4EB;
    }
/* ++++++++++ global general styles end ++++++++++*/
/* ++++++++++ global structure styles start ++++++++++*/
#a5-body-center {
    text-align:center;
    }
#a5-body {
    position: relative;
    width: 770px; /* change this to a specific amount for a fixed
        design or a relative amount if the design should expand to a percentage
of the screen. E.g., 770px or 100%, respectively. */
    margin-left: auto;
    margin-right: auto;
    text-align:left;
    padding-bottom:10px;
    border:0px solid #000000;
    }
#a5-column-left {
    position:absolute;
    left:0px;
    top:0px;
    width:191px;
    border:0px solid #000000;
    }
    #a5-menu {
        font:bold 13px Arial, Helvetica, sans-serif;
        height:249px;
```

```
        background:url(images/bg-left-column.jpg) no-repeat;
        }
    #a5-menu a {
        display: block;
        text-align:left;
        line-height:20px;
        vertical-align: 30%;
        height:20px;
        padding-left:35px;
        text-decoration:none;
        background: url(images/bg-menu-off.gif) no-repeat 0px 0px;
        color:#ffffff;
        }
    #a5-menu a:hover {
        background: url(images/bg-menu-on.gif) no-repeat 0px 0px;
        color:#F9F68C;
        }
        #a5-menu-sl {
            width:191px;
            color:#000000;
            font:bold 12px Arial, Helvetica, sans-serif;
            text-align:left;
            }
            #a5-menu-sl a {
            display: block;
            text-align:left;
            line-height:18px;
            vertical-align: 50%;
            height:18px;
            padding-left:40px;
            font-weight:normal;
            text-decoration:none;
            background: url(images/bg-menu-off-sl.gif) no-repeat
                0px 0px;
            color:#000000;
            }
        #a5-menu-sl a:hover {
            background: url(images/bg-menu-on-sl.gif) no-repeat
                0px 0px;
```

```
color:#4C5C6B;
                }
        #a5-copyright {
            font-size: 11px;
            padding:20px 50px 10px 10px;
            color:#978872;
                }
    #a5-body-content {
        position:relative;
        margin-left:191px;
        border:0px solid #000000;
        }
    #a5-top-row {
        position:relative;
        left:0px;
        top:0px;
        background:#000000;
        border:0px solid #000000;
        }
    /* ++++++++++ global structure styles end ++++++++++*/
    </style>
    </head>
    <body>
    <div id="a5-body-center">
        <div id="a5-body">
    <!-- ###### left column start ###### -->
            <div id="a5-column-left">
                <div><a href="index.htm"><img src="images/header-left.jpg"
                    width="191" height="100" alt="" border="0" /></a></div>
                <div id="a5-menu">
                <a href="index.htm">menu item 1</a>
                    <a href="menu-item-2.htm">longer menu item 2</a>
                    <a href="menu-item-3.htm">menu item 3</a>
                    <a href="index.htm">menu item 4</a>
                    <a href="index.htm">menu item 5</a>
                    <a href="index.htm">menu item 6</a>
                </div>
                <div><a href="index.htm"><img src="images/image-bottom-
                    left.jpg" width="191" height="162" alt="" border="0"
                    /></a></div>
                <div id="a5-copyright">
```

```
                        |  &copy; copyright 2006  |<br />
                            |  your company  |<br />| 
                             all rights reserved  |
                    </div>
                </div>
    <!-- ###### left column end ###### -->
    <!-- ###### body content start ###### -->
            <div id="a5-body-content">
                <div id="a5-top-row">
                    <div><a href="x.htm"><img src="images/photo-center-
                        top.jpg" width="373" height="349" alt=""
                        border="0" /></a></div>
                    <div style="position:absolute;left:373px;top:0px">
                        <a href="x.htm"><img src="images/photo-right-
                        top.jpg" width="164" height="349" alt=""
                        border="0" /></a></div>
                    <div style="position:absolute;left:537px;top:0px;">
                        <a href="x.htm"><img src="images/image-right-
                        top.gif" width="42" height="349" alt="" border="0"
                        /></a></div>
                </div>
            </div>
    <!-- ###### body content end ###### -->
        </div>
    </div>
    </body>
    </html>
```

There are several things to note about the code in Listing 10.3:

■ The only rule that is added to the page-level style sheet is a5-top-row. This rule
provides a container for the three images to be nested inside it. Because it is assigned
relative positioning and a background value of #000000, a black background will
expand to the right if the page is turned into a liquid design (see Figure 10.10).

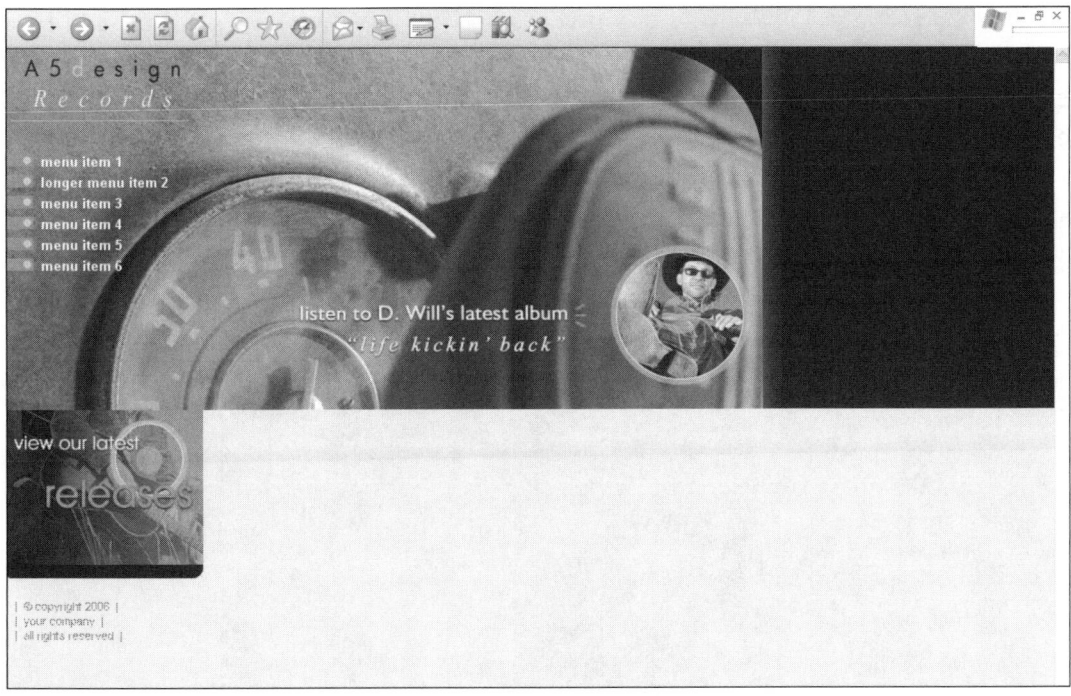

Figure 10.10
The a5-top-row rule can be expanded to the full width of the page if the design is changed to a liquid format.
© 2014 Cengage Learning

- Most of the styling in the a5-top-row container occurs at the local level. The first image is wrapped with <DIV> tags to ensure that no additional space is added to the bottom of the container in IE 5, 5.5, and 6, such as in Figure 10.11.

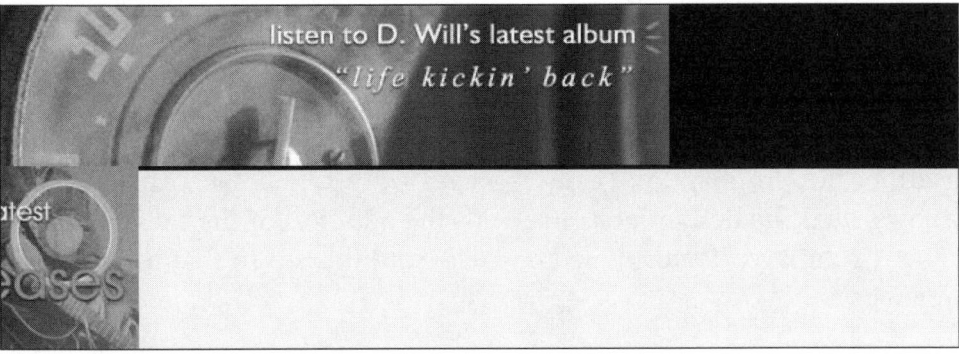

Figure 10.11
Additional space added to the bottom of the container in IE 5, 5.5, and 6 when <DIV> tags are not wrapped around the first image when it is added.
© 2014 Cengage Learning.

The other two images, however, are given absolute positioning, so they are mortised together. The first image is positioned 373 pixels from the left by adding the following style in the local <DIV> tag: `style="position:absolute;left:373px;top:0px"`. This is 373 pixels because the coordinates of all images are based off the top-left corner of the `a5-top-row` <DIV> in which they are nested. Since the first image is 373 pixels wide, the second image must begin 373 pixels from the left (see Figure 10.12).

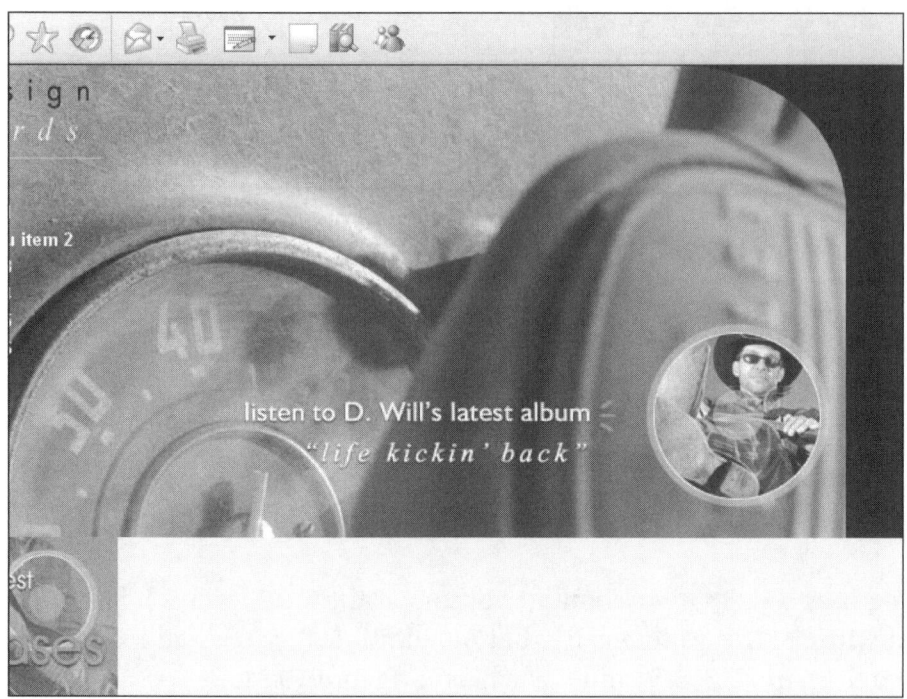

Figure 10.12
The top-right area after the second image is added 373 pixels from the left side of the container.
© 2014 Cengage Learning.

The third image is given absolute positioning that forces it 537 pixels from the left, which is the total width of the left image and center image: 373 pixels + 164 pixels = 537 pixels. Figure 10.9 shows what the design looks like with the addition of the third image, which, as with the other two images, is positioned 0 pixels from the top so that they all touch the top of the browser window.

Adding the Bottom, Center, and Right Content Areas

The final step in creating the homepage is to add the `a5-bottom-row` container and its contents. Figure 10.13 shows what the design looks like when the final code is added to the page (see Listing 10.4).

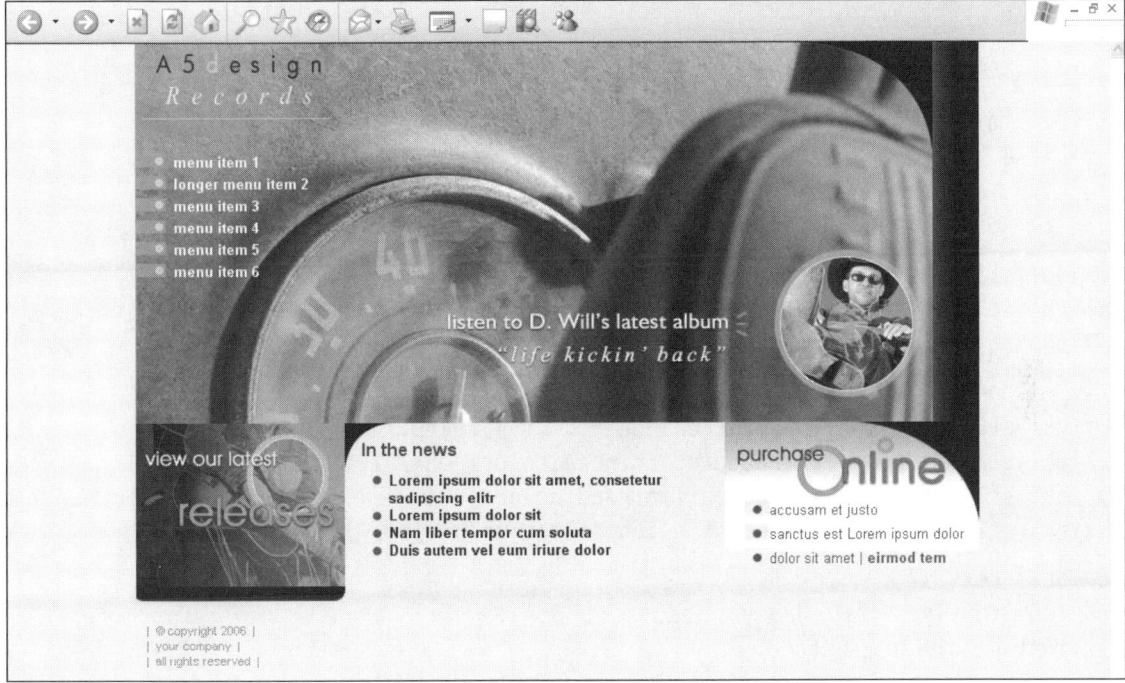

Figure 10.13
The design once the `a5-bottom-row` container and its contents are added.
© 2014 Cengage Learning.

New Code Is in Bold

The newly added code is bolded to differentiate it from the existing code that is being built upon in this case study.

Listing 10.4   Code for Figure 10.13

```
<!DOCTYPE html PUBLIC "-//W3C//DTD XHTML 1.0 Transitional//EN"
"DTD/xhtml1-transitional.dtd">
<html xmlns="http://www.w3.org/1999/xhtml" xml:lang="en"
lang="en"><head><title>Design 122</title>
<meta http-equiv="Content-Type" content="text/html;
    charset=iso-8859-1" />
```

```
<style type="text/css">
/* ++++++++++ global general styles start ++++++++++*/
html, body {
    margin:0px;
    padding:0px;
    font: 13px Arial, Helvetica, sans-serif;
    color:#766D6D;
    background:#F8F4EB;
    }
a:link { color:#CB951D; }
a:visited { color:#A8B32D; }
a:active { color:#A8B32D; }
a:hover { color:#000000; }

a.linklist1:link { text-decoration:none;color:#191718;}
a.linklist1:visited { text-decoration:none;color:#064791;}
a.linklist1:active { text-decoration:none;color:#064791;}
a.linklist1:hover { text-decoration:underline;color:#0781E1;}

a.linklist2:link { text-decoration:none;color:#0762AD;}
a.linklist2:visited { text-decoration:none;color:#064791;}
a.linklist2:active { text-decoration:none;color:#064791;}
a.linklist2:hover { text-decoration:underline;color:#191718;}

.color-1-text-12 {
    font-family: arial, geneva, sans-serif;
    font-size: 12pt;
    color: #044465;
    }
/* ++++++++++ global general styles end ++++++++++*/
/* ++++++++++ global structure styles start ++++++++++*/
#a5-body-center {
    text-align:center;
    }
#a5-body {
    position: relative;
    width: 770px; /* change this to a specific amount for a fixed
        design or a relative amount if the design should expand to a percentage
of the screen. E.g., 770px or 100%, respectively. */
    margin-left: auto;
    margin-right: auto;
    text-align:left;
    padding-bottom:10px;
```

```
        border:0px solid #000000;
        }
#a5-column-left {
        position:absolute;
        left:0px;
        top:0px;
        width:191px;
        border:0px solid #000000;
        }
        #a5-menu {
            font:bold 13px Arial, Helvetica, sans-serif;
            height:249px;
            background:url(images/bg-left-column.jpg) no-repeat;
            }
        #a5-menu a {
            display: block;
            text-align:left;
            line-height:20px;
            vertical-align: 30%;
            height:20px;
            padding-left:35px;
            text-decoration:none;
            background: url(images/bg-menu-off.gif) no-repeat 0px 0px;
            color:#ffffff;
            }
        #a5-menu a:hover {
            background: url(images/bg-menu-on.gif) no-repeat 0px 0px;
            color:#F9F68C;
            }
            #a5-menu-sl {
                width:191px;
                color:#000000;
                font:bold 12px Arial, Helvetica, sans-serif;
                text-align:left;
                }
            #a5-menu-sl a {
                display: block;
                text-align:left;
                line-height:18px;
                vertical-align: 50%;
                height:18px;
                padding-left:40px;
```

```css
            font-weight:normal;
            text-decoration:none;
            background: url(images/bg-menu-off-sl.gif) no-repeat
                0px 0px;
            color:#000000;
            }
        #a5-menu-sl a:hover {
            background: url(images/bg-menu-on-sl.gif) no-repeat 0px 0px;
            color:#4C5C6B;
            }
    #a5-copyright {
        font-size: 11px;
        padding:20px 50px 10px 10px;
        color:#978872;
        }
#a5-body-content {
    position:relative;
    margin-left:191px;
    border:0px solid #000000;
    }
#a5-top-row {
    position:relative;
    left:0px;
    top:0px;
    background:#000000;
    border:0px solid #000000;
    }
#a5-bottom-row {
    position:relative;
    left:0px;
    top:0px;
    height:100%;
    border:0px solid #000000;
    }
    #a5-column-middle {
        position:relative;
        left:0px;
        top:0px;
        margin:0px 230px 0px 0px;
        font-weight:bold;
```

```
            background: url(images/bg-curve-bottom-middle.gif) no-repeat
                top left;
            border:0px solid #000000;
            }
        #list-1 {
            margin-top:10px;
            line-height:16px;
            vertical-align:top;
            list-style-image: url(images/bullet.gif);
                }
    #a5-column-right {
        position:absolute;
        right:-1px;/*explain this is a bug with IE */
        top:0px;
        width:230px;
        background: url(images/bg-right-column.jpg) no-repeat 0px 0px;
        border:0px solid #000000;
        voice-family:"\"}\"";
        voice-family:inherit;
            right:-1px;
            width:230px;
        }
        html>body #a5-column-right {
            right:0px;
            width:230px;
        }
        #list-2 {
            line-height:22px;
            vertical-align:top;
            list-style-image: url(images/bullet.gif);
                }
/* ++++++++++ global structure styles end ++++++++++*/
</style>
</head>
<body>
<div id="a5-body-center">
    <div id="a5-body">
<!-- ###### left column start ###### -->
        <div id="a5-column-left">
            <div><a href="index.htm"><img src="images/header-left.jpg"
                width="191" height="100" alt="" border="0" /></a></div>
            <div id="a5-menu">
```

```
                <a href="index.htm">menu item 1</a>
                <a href="menu-item-2.htm">longer menu item 2</a>
                <a href="menu-item-3.htm">menu item 3</a>
                <a href="index.htm">menu item 4</a>
                <a href="index.htm">menu item 5</a>
                <a href="index.htm">menu item 6</a>
            </div>
            <div><a href="index.htm"><img src="images/image-bottom-
                left.jpg" width="191" height="162" alt="" border="0"
                /></a></div>
            <div id="a5-copyright">
                |  &copy; copyright 2006  |<br />
                    |  your company  |<br />| 
                     all rights reserved  |
            </div>
        </div>
    </div>
<!-- ###### left column end ###### -->
<!-- ###### body content start ###### -->
        <div id="a5-body-content">
            <div id="a5-top-row">
                <div><a href="x.htm"><img src="images/photo-center-
                    top.jpg" width="373" height="349" alt=""
                    border="0" /></a></div>
                <div style="position:absolute;left:373px;top:0px">
                    <a href="x.htm"><img src="images/photo-right-
                    top.jpg" width="164" height="349" alt="" border="0"
                    /></a></div>
                <div style="position:absolute;left:537px;top:0px;">
                    <a href="x.htm"><img src="images/image-right-
                    top.gif" width="42" height="349" alt=""
                    border="0" /></a></div>
            </div>
            <div id="a5-bottom-row">
                <div id="a5-column-middle">
                    <div class="color-1-text-12" style="padding:15px
                    0px 0px 15px;"><b>In the news</b></div>
                    <ul id="list-1">
                        <li><a href="x.htm" class="linklist1">Lorem
                            ipsum dolor sit amet, consetetur sadipscing
                            elitr</a></li>
                        <li><a href="x.htm" class="linklist1">Lorem
                            ipsum dolor sit</a></li>
```

```
                    <li><a href="x.htm" class="linklist1">Nam
                        liber tempor cum soluta</a></li>
                    <li><a href="x.htm" class="linklist1">Duis
                        autem vel eum iriure dolor</a></li>
                </ul>
            </div>
            <div id="a5-column-right">
                <ul id="list-2" style="margin-top:70px;">
                    <li><a href="x.htm" class="linklist2">accusam
                        et justo </a></li>
                    <li><a href="x.htm" class="linklist2">sanctus
                        est Lorem ipsum dolor</a></li>
                    <li><a href="x.htm" class="linklist2">dolor sit
                        amet</a> | <a href="x.htm" class=
                        "linklist2"><b>eirmod tem</b></a></li>
                </ul>
            </div>
        </div>
    </div>
<!-- ###### body content end ###### -->
    </div>
</div>
</body>
</html>
```

There are several things to note about the code in Listing 10.4:

- Rules are added between the `global general styles` comment tags for three types of links: the default links, the list in the bottom-center content area, and the list in the bottom-right content area. The default link style is added for all links without a specific class assigned to them. The `a.linklist1:link` rule is applied to the bottom-left list links, and the `a.linklist2:link` is assigned to the bottom-right list links. Both custom link rules were given general naming conventions so they could be assigned to lists that might be added elsewhere in the site.

- The `color-1-text-12` rule is added between the `global general styles` comment tags. It is used to style the In the News headline of the bottom-center content area.

- The `a5-bottom-row` rule and container are added to position the bottom-center and bottom-right content areas. They are assigned relative positioning with both the left and right properties set to `0px`, which positions the container below the `a5-top-row` `<DIV>`. It is assigned the `height` property with a value of `100%` so larger amounts of content can be added to the column. Otherwise, the text will be cut off in IE 5, 5.5, and 6.

■ The `a5-column-middle` rule provides the container for the bottom-center content area. Because it is assigned relative positioning, it will stretch to the far right edge of the design. A larger body of text is included in the area for Figure 10.14 to show how the text could fill the design without any padding or margin values set.

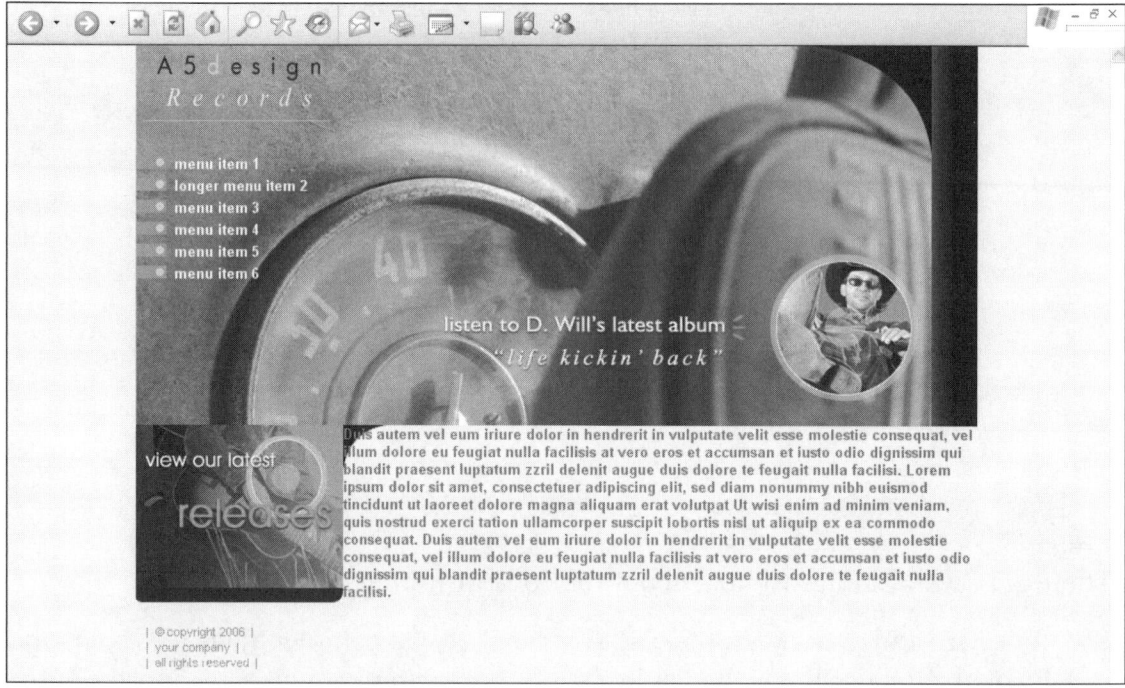

Figure 10.14
If given no constraints, the `a5-column-middle` rule would allow content to stretch the full width of the design, such as in this example, which includes a larger amount of dummied content.
© 2014 Cengage Learning.

The advantage of this structure is that the center column can stretch if the design is changed to a liquid design. Because the bottom-right column is 233 pixels wide, the `a5-column-middle` rule is assigned 240 pixels of margin to the right. This guarantees that the text in the center column will not only stop before it reaches the right column's area, but it will have 7 pixels of space between the two containers.

The `a5-column-middle` rule also has a background image declared in it, which provides the black curve in the top-left corner of the design.

- The `list-1` rule provides styling to the list that is included in the `a5-column-middle` container. The `list-style-image` is used in conjunction with the `line-height` rule and `vertical-align` rule to position the bullets in somewhat similar positions among the various tested browsers.

- Adding the `a5-column-right` rule and content is the final step in completing the design. The container is assigned the Purchase Online background image. Because of a positioning bug in IE 6, the Tantek hack is used to position the container 1 pixel to the right of its default location so the entire container, and thus the background image, lines up with the image in the top row. If the hack is not used, the page will be positioned incorrectly, as shown in Figure 10.15.

- To prevent the list in the `a5-column-right` container from covering the text portion of the background image (that is, the Purchase Online image), the `list-2` rule is assigned a local style. This style sets the top margin to 70 pixels. The `margin-top` rule is separated from the `list-2` rule in the page-level style sheet to enable the designer to control the positioning of the list if the rule is reused elsewhere in the site. If the two rules were combined, this list would always be forced down 70 pixels from the top wherever it was included.

Figure 10.15
The Tantek hack is used to position the bottom-right content area 1 pixel to the right or else there will be a 1-pixel difference between it and the image above in IE 6. This code can be easily removed because it is no longer necessary for contemporary browsers.

© 2014 Cengage Learning.

CONSTRUCTING SECOND-LEVEL PAGES

As with most sites, the second-level pages are based on the homepage design. This structure allows images from the homepage to be reused for subsequent pages, not only to provide visual consistency in the design, which improves usability, but also to allow browsers to cache the original images, making the page download quicker. In this design, two second-level templates are created: one that contains three columns and one that contains two columns.

Constructing a Second-Level Page with Three Columns

The first second-level template that is created is the page that appears when the designer clicks on the menu item titled Longer Menu Item 2. This page contains three columns. Such a design offers the ability to supplement pages with less content with a right column that could contain repetitive information, such as photos, announcements, and specials. Of course, this is not the only reason for a three-column design. The purpose, for example, could also be to provide a more advanced visual layout by adding another element, which, in turn, could have more elements added to it. Figure 10.16 shows what the design looks like when the final code (see Listing 10.5) is added to the page.

Figure 10.16
The three-column second-level template that is derived from the homepage design.

New Code Is in Bold

The newly added code is bolded to differentiate it from the existing code that is being built upon in this case study.

Listing 10.5   Code for Figure 10.16

```
<!DOCTYPE html PUBLIC "-//W3C//DTD XHTML 1.0 Transitional//EN"
    "DTD/xhtml1-transitional.dtd">
<html xmlns="http://www.w3.org/1999/xhtml" xml:lang="en"
lang="en"><head><title>Design 122</title>
<meta http-equiv="Content-Type" content="text/html;
    charset=iso-8859-1" />
<!-- link to main stylesheet that control text sizes and colors, among
    other things -->
<link rel="stylesheet" href="mainstyle.css" type="text/css" />
<style>
/* +++++++++ global sl structure styles start +++++++++++*/
#a5-body-content-sl {
    position:relative;
    margin-left:191px;
    height:100%;
    background: url(images/bg-body-content-sl.jpg) no-repeat 0px 0px;
    border:0px solid #000000;
    }
    #a5-top-row-sl {
        position:relative;
        left:0px;
        top:0px;
        height:100%;
        border:0px solid #000000;
        }
    #a5-sl-title {
        height:24px;
        font:bold 14px italic Arial, Helvetica, sans-serif;
        background: #000000 url(images/bg-title.gif) no-repeat 0px 0px;
        color:#ffffff;
        padding:4px 0px 0px 40px;
        margin-bottom:10px;
        border:0px solid #000000;
        voice-family:"\"}\"";
        voice-family:inherit;
            height:20px;
        }
```

```
html>body #a5-s1-title {
    height:20px;
}
#a5-column-middle-s1 {
    position:relative;
    left:0px;
    top:10px;
    margin:0px 230px 0px 10px;
    padding-right:10pt;
    border:0px solid #000000;
    }
#a5-column-right-s1 {
    position:absolute;
    right:-1px;
    top:11px;
    width:230px;
    height:800px;
    text-align:right;
    background: url(images/bg-right-column-s1.gif) repeat-y
        0px 0px;
    border:0px solid #000000;
    voice-family:"\"}\"";
    voice-family:inherit;
        right:-1px;
        top:10px;
        width:230px;
    }
    html>body #a5-column-right-s1 {
        right:0px;
        top:10px;
        width:230px;
    }
    #a5-column-right-content-s1 {
        position:relative;
        right:0px;
        top:15px;
        width:230px;
        font: 14px italic Arial, Helvetica, sans-serif;
        color:#044465;
        padding:80px 30px 10px 20px;
```

```
                border:0px solid #000000;
                voice-family:"\"}\"";
                voice-family:inherit;
                    width:180px;
                }
                html>body #a5-column-right-content-sl {
                    width:180px;
                }
/* ++++++++++ global sl structure styles end ++++++++++*/
</style>
</head>
<body>
<div id="a5-body-center">
    <div id="a5-body">
<!-- ###### left column start ###### -->
        <div id="a5-column-left">
            <div><a href="index.htm"><img src="images/header-left.jpg"
                width="191" height="100" alt="" border="0" /></a></div>
            <div id="a5-menu">
                <a href="index.htm">menu item 1</a>
                <a href="menu-item-2.htm">longer menu item 2</a>
                <a href="menu-item-3.htm">menu item 3</a>
                <a href="index.htm">menu item 4</a>
                <a href="index.htm">menu item 5</a>
                <a href="index.htm">menu item 6</a>
            </div>
            <div><a href="index.htm"><img src="images/image-bottom-
                left.jpg" width="191" height="162" alt="" border="0"
                /></a></div>
            <div id="a5-copyright">
                |  &copy; copyright 2006  |<br />
                    |  your company  |<br />| 
                     all rights reserved  |
            </div>
        </div>
<!-- ###### left column end ###### -->
<!-- ###### body content start ###### -->
        <div id="a5-body-content-sl">
            <div id="a5-top-row-sl">
                <div id="a5-sl-title">longer menu item 2</div>
                <div id="a5-column-middle-sl">
```

```
<span class="color-1-text-12"><b>Duis autem vel eum iriure dolor in
    hendrerit in vulputate velit esse molestie consequat, vel illum
    dolore eu feugiat nulla facilisis at vero eros et accumsan et iusto
    odio dignissim</b></span> qui blandit praesent luptatum zzril
    delenit augue duis dolore te feugait nulla facilisi. Lorem ipsum
    dolor sit amet, consectetuer adipiscing elit, sed diam nonummy nibh
    euismod tincidunt ut laoreet dolore magna aliquam erat volutpat
<br /><br />
Ut wisi enim ad minim veniam, quis nostrud exerci tation ullamcorper
    suscipit lobortis nisl ut aliquip ex ea commodo consequat. Duis
    autem vel eum iriure dolor in hendrerit in vulputate velit esse
    molestie consequat, vel illum dolore eu feugiat nulla facilisis at
    vero eros et accumsan et iusto odio dignissim qui blandit praesent
    luptatum zzril delenit augue duis dolore te feugait nulla facilisi.
<br /><br />
Lorem ipsum dolor sit amet, consetetur sadipscing elitr, sed diam
    nonumy eirmod tempor invidunt ut labore et dolore magna aliquyam
    erat, sed diam voluptua. At vero eos et accusam et justo duo
    dolores et ea rebum. Stet clita kasd gubergren, no sea takimata
    sanctus est Lorem ipsum dolor sit amet. Lorem ipsum dolor sit amet,
    consetetur sadipscing elitr, sed diam nonumy eirmod tempor invidunt
    ut labore et dolore magna aliquyam erat, sed diam voluptua. At vero
    eos et accusam et justo duo dolores et ea rebum. Stet clita kasd
    gubergren, no sea takimata sanctus est Lorem ipsum dolor sit amet.
    Lorem ipsum dolor sit amet, consetetur sadipscing elitr, sed diam
    nonumy eirmod tempor invidunt ut labore et dolore magna aliquyam
    erat, sed diam voluptua. At vero eos et accusam et justo duo
    dolores et ea rebum. Stet clita kasd gubergren, no sea takimata
    sanctus est Lorem ipsum dolor sit amet.
                </div>
                <div id="a5-column-right-sl">
                    <div id="a5-column-right-content-sl">
    <b>Duis autem vel eum iriure dolor in hendrerit in vulputate</b> velit
        esse molestie consequat, vel illum dolore eu feugiat nulla
        facilisis at vero eros et accumsan et iusto odio dignissim qui
        blandit praesent luptatum zzril delenit augue duis dolore te
        feugait nulla facilisi. Lorem ipsum dolor sit amet, consectetuer
        adipiscing elit, sed diam nonummy nibh euismod tincidunt ut laoreet
        dolore magna aliquam erat volutpat
                    </div>
                </div>
            </div>
        </div>
```

```
<!-- ###### body content end ###### -->
    </div>
</div>
</body>
</html>
```

There are several things to note about the code in Listing 10.5:

- A second style sheet has been added for the second-level pages. For demonstration purposes, the style sheet for the homepage has been saved as `mainstyle.css` and includes a link to the page. The style sheet for the second-level pages has been included as a page-level style sheet, which will be interpreted after the first style sheet.

- The `a5-body-content` rule has been renamed as the `a5-body-content-sl` rule. This enables the designer to include the background image `bg-body-content-sl.jpg` for the container. While the container was initially built into the homepage design, it is not assigned a background image until this page because the top-right images in the homepage need to be hyperlinked but do not need to have text flow over them. Saving the images together as one image and using it as a background image for this page maintains the look and feel of the top-right area of the homepage. It is assigned 100% height to ensure that the text will fill its full height. Otherwise, it could get cut off in IE 5, 5.5, and 6.

Reasoning for "-sl" Being Appended

The rules added in the second-level template have `-sl` appended to their names to signify that they are to be used for secondary pages. Otherwise, if the rules contain the same name in both the `mainstyle.css` and `mainstyle-sl.css` files, a browser may use the incorrect style for that page.

- Because the content is now nested inside what was the `a5-top-row` container, it has to be renamed `a5-top-row-sl` and have its background color of #000000 removed. The background image is now more transparent, so this <DIV> does not necessarily need to have a background color if it is changed to a liquid format.

- The `a5-sl-title` rule is added to include the page title for secondary pages at the top of the page. The height of the <DIV> is set at 24 pixels to guarantee that it expands to the specified height of the background image. Padding is used to position the title vertically in the container and 40 pixels from the left, which is taken up by the background image `bg-title.gif`. To ensure that the color of the `bg-title.gif` is continued across the screen, the shorthand background property is assigned a background color value of #000000. Because padding is used to position the text within the container, the Tantek hack is added to ensure that the height of the container is the same for both compliant and noncompliant browsers.

■ Similar to the bottom two nested containers that were used in the homepage (a5-column-middle and a5-column-right), the a5-column-middle-sl and a5-column-right-sl <DIV> tags were added to provide the two right columns of the design.

Because the a5-column-right-sl container is assigned an absolute positioning value, it also is assigned a height of 800 pixels to ensure that the text does not run beyond the container—not that there would be a visible difference because there is no repeating background image or color the text would run beyond. If the text were to run farther down the page than 800 pixels and the column were to include a background color, for example, the designer might want to change the forced height of the column so that the text did not pass the color.

■ The content included in the a5-column-right-sl container is nested inside the a5-column-right-content-sl <DIV> tag. The main thing to note about this rule is that it is assigned padding that forces it 80 pixels from the top, which guarantees the text will not be placed over the background image bg-right-column-sl.gif in the a5-column-right-sl column. This is done to avoid black text running over the black background of the image, which would make it appear invisible.

Constructing a Second-Level Page with Two Columns

The full-width second-level template included with this design is the page the designer comes to when clicking on the Menu Item 3 link in the menu. The purpose of this template is to provide a page where more content can be added. The designer, of course, may also choose to use the extra space to include a more customized layout on the page. Whatever the reason for using this template, the page allows more visual real estate with which to work. Figure 10.17 shows what the design looks like when the final code is added to the page (see Listing 10.6).

Figure 10.17
The two-column second-level template that is based on the homepage design.
© 2014 Cengage Learning.

New Code Is in Bold

The newly added code is bolded to differentiate it from the existing code that is being built upon in this case study.

Listing 10.6   Code for Figure 10.17

```
<!DOCTYPE html PUBLIC "-//W3C//DTD XHTML 1.0 Transitional//EN"
    "DTD/xhtml1-transitional.dtd">
<html xmlns="http://www.w3.org/1999/xhtml" xml:lang="en"
lang="en"><head><title>Design 122</title>
<meta http-equiv="Content-Type" content="text/html;
    charset=iso-8859-1" />
<!-- link to main stylesheet that control text sizes and colors, among
    other things -->
<link rel="stylesheet" href="mainstyle.css" type="text/css" />
<style>
/* ++++++++++ global sl structure styles start ++++++++++*/
```

```
#a5-body-content-sl {
    position:relative;
    margin-left:191px;
    height:100%;
    background: url(images/bg-body-content-sl.jpg) no-repeat 0px 0px;
    border:0px solid #000000;
    }
#a5-top-row-sl {
    position:relative;
    left:0px;
    top:0px;
    border:0px solid #000000;
    }
#a5-sl-title {
    height:24px;
    font:bold 14px italic Arial, Helvetica, sans-serif;
    background: #000000 url(images/bg-title.gif) no-repeat 0px 0px;
    color:#ffffff;
    padding:4px 0px 0px 40px;
    margin-bottom:10px;
    border:0px solid #000000;
    voice-family:"\"}\"";
    voice-family:inherit;
        height:20px;
    }
html>body #a5-sl-title {
        height:20px;
    }
#a5-column-middle-sl {
        position:relative;
        left:0px;
        top:10px;
        margin:0px 230px 50px 10px;
        padding-right:10pt;
        padding-bottom:20px;
        border:0px solid #000000;
        }
#a5-column-right-sl {
        position:absolute;
        right:-1px;
        top:11px;
        width:230px;
```

```
            height:800px;
            text-align:right;
            background: url(images/bg-right-column-sl.gif) repeat-y
                0px 0px;
            border:0px solid #000000;
            voice-family:"\"}\"";
            voice-family:inherit;
                right:-1px;
                top:10px;
                width:230px;
            }
            html>body #a5-column-right-sl {
                right:0px;
                top:10px;
                width:230px;
                }
                #a5-column-right-content-sl {
                position:relative;
                right:0px;
                top:15px;
                width:230px;
                font: 14px italic Arial, Helvetica, sans-serif;
                color:#044465;
                padding:80px 30px 10px 20px;
                border:0px solid #000000;
                voice-family:"\"}\"";
                voice-family:inherit;
                    width:180px;
                }
                html>body #a5-column-right-content-sl {
                    width:180px;
                }
        #a5-column-full-sl {
            position:relative;
            left:0px;
            top:10px;
            margin:0px 20px 0px 10px;
            padding-right:10pt;
            border:0px solid #000000;
            }
/* ++++++++++ global sl structure styles end ++++++++++*/
</style>
</head>
```

```
<body>
<div id="a5-body-center">
    <div id="a5-body">
<!-- ###### left column start ###### -->
        <div id="a5-column-left">
            <div><a href="index.htm"><img src="images/header-left.jpg"
                width="191" height="100" alt="" border="0" /></a></div>
            <div id="a5-menu">
                <a href="index.htm">menu item 1</a>
                <a href="menu-item-2.htm">longer menu item 2</a>
                <a href="menu-item-3.htm">menu item 3</a>
                <a href="index.htm">menu item 4</a>
                <a href="index.htm">menu item 5</a>
                <a href="index.htm">menu item 6</a>
            </div>
            <div><a href="index.htm"><img src="images/image-bottom-
                left.jpg" width="191" height="162" alt="" border="0"
                /></a></div>
            <div id="a5-copyright">
                |  &copy; copyright 2006  |<br />
                    |  your company  |<br />| 
                     all rights reserved  |
            </div>
        </div>
<!-- ###### left column end ###### -->
<!-- ###### body content start ###### -->
        <div id="a5-body-content-sl">
            <div id="a5-top-row-sl">
                <div id="a5-sl-title">menu item 3</div>
                <div id="a5-column-full-sl">
<span class="color-1-text-12"><b>Duis autem vel eum iriure dolor in
    hendrerit in vulputate velit esse molestie consequat, vel illum
    dolore eu feugiat nulla facilisis at vero eros et accumsan et
    iusto odio dignissim</b></span> qui blandit praesent luptatum
    zzril delenit augue duis dolore te feugait nulla facilisi. Lorem
    ipsum dolor sit amet, consectetuer adipiscing elit, sed diam
    nonummy nibh euismod tincidunt ut laoreet dolore magna aliquam
    erat volutpat
<br /><br />
Ut wisi enim ad minim veniam, quis nostrud exerci tation ullamcorper
    suscipit lobortis nisl ut aliquip ex ea commodo consequat. Duis
    autem vel eum iriure dolor in hendrerit in vulputate velit esse
```

```
        molestie consequat, vel illum dolore eu feugiat nulla facilisis at
        vero eros et accumsan et iusto odio dignissim qui blandit praesent
        luptatum zzril delenit augue duis dolore te feugait nulla facilisi.
<br /><br />
Lorem ipsum dolor sit amet, consetetur sadipscing elitr, sed diam
        nonumy eirmod tempor invidunt ut labore et dolore magna aliquyam
        erat, sed diam voluptua. At vero eos et accusam et justo duo
        dolores et ea rebum. Stet clita kasd gubergren, no sea takimata
        sanctus est Lorem ipsum dolor sit amet. Lorem ipsum dolor sit
        amet, consetetur sadipscing elitr, sed diam nonumy eirmod tempor
        invidunt ut labore et dolore magna aliquyam erat, sed diam
        voluptua. At vero eos et accusam et justo duo dolores et ea rebum.
        Stet clita kasd gubergren, no sea takimata sanctus est Lorem ipsum
        dolor sit amet. Lorem ipsum dolor sit amet, consetetur sadipscing
        elitr, sed diam nonumy eirmod tempor invidunt ut labore et dolore
        magna aliquyam erat, sed diam voluptua. At vero eos et accusam et
        justo duo dolores et ea rebum. Stet clita kasd gubergren, no sea
        takimata sanctus est Lorem ipsum dolor sit amet.
                    </div>
                </div>
            </div>
<!-- ###### body content end ###### -->
        </div>
    </div>
    </body>
    </html>
```

There are several things to note about the code in Listing 10.6:

- The only rule added to the second-level style sheet is `a5-column-full-sl`. This rule forces the container to fill the full width of the page, barring the assigned padding and margin values.

- After the rule is added, the actual container replaces the `a5-column-middlesl` and `a5-column-right-sl` `<DIV>` tags in the code. Because it is assigned margin and padding settings, the text does not touch the right image.

Summary

The design in this chapter is very different from the one in Chapter 9. It not only contains three columns in the homepage, but it also uses mortised images in the top-right section of the page. These images are then saved as one lighter background image that is included in the second-level pages. These pages use a second style sheet that is assigned specifically to them. To avoid any interpretation issues between the two style sheets, the rules in the second-level style sheet have -sl appended to the end. The two- and three-column structures in the second-level pages offer the designer more content layout flexibility, depending on the amount of content included in the design.

CHAPTER 11

CASE STUDY: HIGH-CONTENT CSS DESIGN

The design explained in this chapter uses many of the same techniques as the layouts in Chapters 9 and 10; the key difference is that it contains more content. The technical structure is a hybrid of the two designs in that it uses a header <DIV> across the top, as in Chapter 9, and incorporates a three-column layout below, as does the design in Chapter 10. It is designed to display more content than many sites, whether the purpose is to sell product, provide large amounts of content, or even a combination of the two.

Design 123 Example

The design explained in this chapter is design 123 online (photo credits: www.idlerphotography.com).

UNDERSTANDING THE DESIGN'S STRUCTURE

Figure 11.1 illustrates the design explained in this chapter. It is designed to work easily as either a fixed or a liquid design. Because the header area stretches across the entire design, elements can be added, edited, or removed without having to modify other areas of the site.

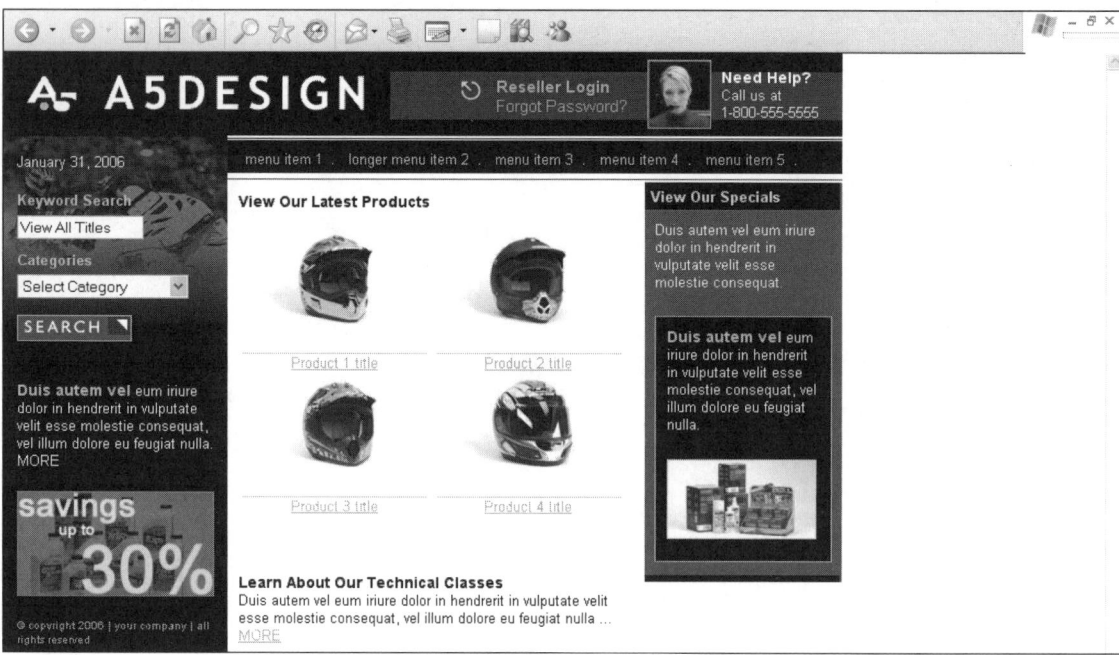

Figure 11.1
The high-content CSS design explained in this chapter.

© 2014 Cengage Learning.

Design Width

This design, along with those in Chapters 9 and 10, was written at a time when the resolution for which designers created sites was 800 × 600. The principles of this design are still the same, no matter what the resolution or width of the design is. The width from 770 pixels would simply need to be changed to 1,000 pixels. The designer would merely need to widen any or all of the columns to take on the additional 230 pixels (1,000 − 770 = 230).

Reasoning Behind Guides and Creating Slices in Photoshop Files

There are 15 slices used in the main Photoshop file and one in a secondary file to create the images for the homepage design. Figure 11.2 shows all the slices used in the homepage file and outlines the 10 most important guides and slices necessary in constructing the design with XHTML and CSS.

Figure 11.2
Ten of the most important guides and slices used to build the design in this chapter.
© 2014 Cengage Learning.

Following are explanations of the 10 most important guides and slices used in Figure 11.2:

1. The guide above number 1 is used to separate the header row from the bottom portion of the design, which includes the left, center, and right columns.

2. The guide to the left of number 2 is used to separate the left column, which includes the menu, from the right column, which includes the nested center and right columns.

3. The guide above number 3, which is difficult to differentiate from the black line it abuts, is used to separate the menu area from the content below.

4. The slice to the top left of number 4 is used to save the `header-left` image, which includes the company's logo.

5. The two images in the header row to the far right of number 5 are mortised together, along with their text. The first image found to the right of number 5 is the background image that is repeated horizontally across the header file. This works even if the design is changed to a liquid format.

6. Number 6 does not represent a slice in the homepage file shown in Figure 11.2 but highlights the image behind the form that is saved as a background image in a separate file (see Figure 11.3). Similar to the Chapter 9 and 10 designs, a separate Photoshop file is used to save such an image. Although a slice could be created to save this background image in the main Photoshop file, a designer may want the image to run down the left column behind content other than the form. For this reason, the image was created in a separate Photoshop file. Number 1 represents this slice in Figure 11.3.

Figure 11.3
A Photoshop file that includes the background image behind the form, saved separately from the homepage file.
© 2014 Cengage Learning.

7. The slice to the top left of number 7 is used to save the Search button. If the designer were to continue building this ecommerce site, it would require additional buttons that would, most likely, be consistent with this image. Therefore, the designer might want to crop and save the button in a separate Photoshop file, which would make saving separate files easier.

8. The slice to the top left of number 8 represents a banner ad saved from the homepage file. The important thing to note about this image is that it is saved with extra space to the left and right sides, which gives the designer room to be flexible if the image needs to be moved to the left or right down the road or if a larger image needs to be added.

9. Number 9 represents a product used in the homepage design. Although each of the four products is saved individually in this homepage file, they could be saved as their own separate Photoshop files for the same reason the button image could be saved individually.

10. Number 10 represents two slices. The slice to the top left of the number is used to provide a line at the bottom of the right column to give it a sense of closure. Because the column is assigned absolute positioning, it will not automatically maintain the same height as the center column. This line could also be created by simply adding a bottom border to the area with CSS. The slice to the bottom left of number 10 is used as the background image of the title area for the second-level pages.

Understanding the Placement of CSS Containers

Slightly more <DIV> tags are used in this design than in the designs explained in Chapters 9 and 10 because more individual content elements are used here. Structurally, all three designs require the same number of <DIV> tags to build their infrastructures. They are merely placed differently. As mentioned earlier, this design, as shown in Figure 11.4, is a hybrid of those two designs in that it uses a horizontal header container and a three-column format below the header.

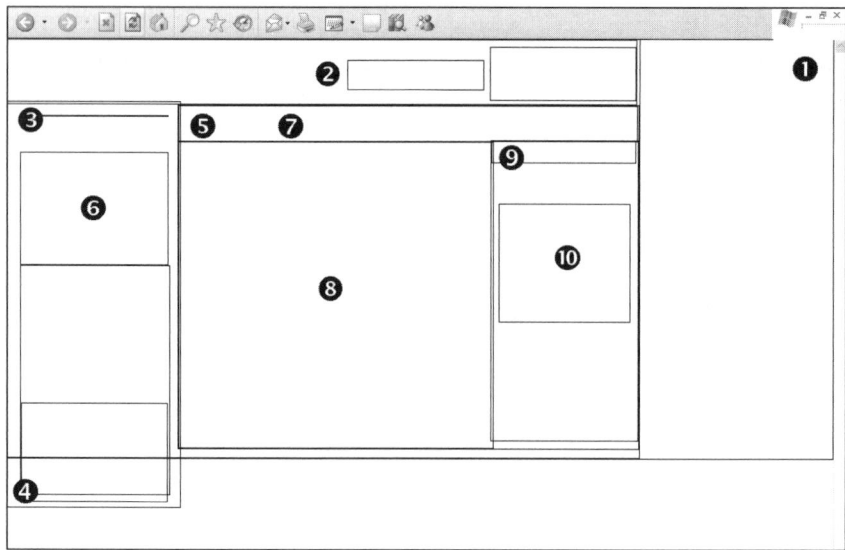

Figure 11.4
Ten of the most important containers used to build the design.
© 2014 Cengage Learning.

Following are explanations for 10 of the most useful containers in Figure 11.4:

- The <DIV> tag to the right of number 1 is used for centering the design in IE 5 and 5.5.

- Number 2 represents the header <DIV>, which contains the nested content to the right of the number.

- The <DIV> tag to the top left of number 3 represents the left column's container.

- Number 4 represents the banner ad that is saved for the left column. It also shows how the left column, which is assigned absolute positioning, extends past the boundaries of the containers within which it is nested.

- The <DIV> to the top left of number 5 is the a5- column-right container, which includes the menu row and center and right columns.

- Number 6 points out the <DIV> in the left column that contains the search form.

- Number 7 represents the container within which the menu is nested.

- The center column of content is nested inside the container indicated by number 8.

- The right column container begins at the top-left corner of number 9.

- Number 10 represents a <DIV> tag that is used to nest additional content in the right column.

BUILDING THE STRUCTURE

Following are the step-by-step instructions for building the design. It is assumed that the Photoshop file has already been created or customized and that the designer only needs to position the images and text.

Creating the XHTML and CSS Framework

The first step to build the design is to create the XHTML framework and initial CSS containers. Listing 11.1 is the code that is used to output the page shown in Figure 11.5.

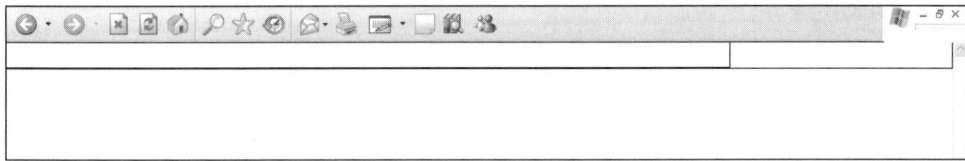

Figure 11.5
Basic XHTML and CSS framework for the design.
© 2014 Cengage Learning.

Listing 11.1   Code for Figure 11.5

```
<!DOCTYPE html PUBLIC "-//W3C//DTD XHTML 1.0 Transitional//EN"
    "DTD/xhtml1-transitional.dtd">
<html xmlns="http://www.w3.org/1999/xhtml" xml:lang="en"
lang="en"><head><title>Design 123</title>
<meta http-equiv="Content-Type" content="text/html;
    charset=iso-8859-1" />
<style type="text/css">
/* ++++++++++ global general styles start ++++++++++*/
html, body {
    margin:0px;
    padding:0px;
    font: 13px Arial, Helvetica, sans-serif;
    color:#000000;
    background:#ffffff;
    }
/* ++++++++++ global general styles end ++++++++++*/
/* ++++++++++ global structure styles start ++++++++++*/
#a5-body-center {
    text-align:left;
    border:1px solid #000000;
    }
```

```
#a5-body {
    position: relative;
    width: 770px; /* change this to a specific amount for a fixed
        design or a relative amount if the design should expand to
a percentage of the screen. E.g., 770px or 100%, respectively. */

    /* remove these comment tags if the page is to be centered
    margin-left: auto;
    margin-right: auto;*/
    text-align:left;
    padding-bottom:10px;
    border:1px solid #000000;
    }
    /* ++++++++++ global structure styles end ++++++++++*/
</style>
</head>
<body>
<div id="a5-body-center">
    <div id="a5-body">
         
    </div>
</div>
</body>
</html>
```

There are several things to note about the code in Listing 11.1:

■ The CSS style sheet is commented into a couple of different sections. The `global general styles` comment tags contain the general styles, such as the formatting of the `<HTML>` and `<BODY>` tags, hyperlinks, and fonts. The `global structure styles` comment tags include the styles used to define the structure of the design and elements included in that structure.

■ Several rules define the `<HTML>` and `<BODY>` tags. The `margin` and `padding` properties are used to ensure that the design is placed in the very top-left corner of the browser, with no space between the design and the edges. The default font style for the site is set using the shorthand `FONT` property. Defining the default font color is accomplished with the `COLOR` property. The background color is assigned to ensure that all browsers display the same color because not all browsers show the same color.

■ The `a5-body-center` and `a5-body` rules are used to force the design to the left side of the browser screen with a fixed width of 770 pixels. If the designer wanted to fill the full width of the screen, the value of 770px would need to be changed to 100%. If, however, the designer wanted to simply justify the design to the left, the value of the text-align property in the a5-body-center rule would need to be changed from center to left. The margin-left and margin- right properties in the a5-body rule ensure that the extra white space is split evenly on both sides. While this system tends to be more complex, it allows the designer flexibility when more than one site is going to be built. By adding this code to every design, it does not take much work to quickly modify a design to fit a client's needs.

■ Both the a5-body-center and a5-body rules have their borders turned on using the following code: border:1px solid #000000;. For demonstration purposes, the code was added to both rules to show what the structure of the <DIV> tags looks like without content added. Turning on the borders helps a designer when building a site because it is not always apparent where elements are placed or expanding. Rather than removing these rules, it is easier to change the value of 1px to 0px, turning the borders off instead. Troubleshooting often involves turning the borders back on, so it saves time and takes up very little download size to keep them in the style sheet.

■ Because the <div id="a5-body"> is nested inside the <div id="a5-body-center"> tag, it is indented. This allows for quicker recognition of tags that are nested inside each other, which becomes a useful technique when the page has more code added to it.

Adding the Header Row

Once the XHTML and basic CSS framework have been added, the header area is then added into the code. Listing 11.2 is the code that is used to create the updated page in Figure 11.6.

Figure 11.6
The header row that is added to the design.
© 2014 Cengage Learning.

New Code Is in Bold

The newly added code is bolded to differentiate it from the existing code that is being built upon in this case study.

Listing 11.2   Code for Figure 11.6

```
<!DOCTYPE html PUBLIC "-//W3C//DTD XHTML 1.0 Transitional//EN"
    "DTD/xhtml1-transitional.dtd">
<html xmlns="http://www.w3.org/1999/xhtml" xml:lang="en"
lang="en"><head><title>Design 123</title>
<meta http-equiv="Content-Type" content="text/html;
    charset=iso-8859-1" />
<style type="text/css">
/* ++++++++++ global general styles start ++++++++++*/
html, body {
    margin:0px;
    padding:0px;
    font: 13px Arial, Helvetica, sans-serif;
    color:#000000;
    background:#ffffff;
    }
a:link { color:#FF7800; }
a:visited { color:#FF5A00; }
a:active { color:#FFC600; }
a:hover { color:#000000; }

a.linklist1:link { text-decoration:none;color:#0EC0FF;}
a.linklist1:visited { text-decoration:none;color:#0EC0FF;}
a.linklist1:active { text-decoration:none;color:#0EC0FF;}
a.linklist1:hover { text-decoration:none;color:#D5EE03;}

/* ++++++++++ global general styles end ++++++++++*/
/* ++++++++++ global structure styles start ++++++++++*/
#a5-body-center {
    text-align:left;
    }
#a5-body {
    position: relative;
    width: 770px; /* change this to a specific amount for a fixed
            design or a relative amount if the design should expand to
a percentage of the screen. E.g., 770px or 100%, respectively. */
    /* remove these comment tags if the page is to be centered
```

```
            margin-left: auto;
            margin-right: auto;*/
vvtext-align:left;
            padding-bottom:10px;
            border:0px solid #000000;
            }
    #a5-header {
        position:relative;
        left:0px;
        top:0px;
        height:78px;
        background: #000000 url(images/bg-header.gif) repeat-x;
        border:0px solid #000000;
        }
        #a5-login {
            position:absolute;
            top:24px;
            right:186px;
            width:165px;
            font: 15px Arial, Helvetica, sans-serif;
            border:0px solid #ffffff;
            }
        #a5-call {
            position:absolute;
            top:8px;
            right:0px;
            width:177px;
            font: 13px Arial, Helvetica, sans-serif;
            color:#ffffff;
            border:0px solid #000000;
            }
    /* ++++++++++ global structure styles end ++++++++++*/
    </style>
    </head>
    <body>
    <div id="a5-body-center">
        <div id="a5-body">
    <!-- ##### header start ##### -->
            <div id="a5-header">
                <div><a href="index.htm"><img src="images/logo.gif"
                    width="357" height="78" alt="" border="0" /></a></div>
```

```
            <div id="a5-login">
                <span style="float:left;"><a href="x.htm"><img
                    src="images/reseller-button.gif" width="33"
                    height="23" alt="" border="0" /></a></span>
                <a href="x.htm" class="linklist1"><b>Reseller Login
                    </b><br />
                Forgot Password?</a>
            </div>
            <div id="a5-call">
                <span style="float:left;padding-right:6px;"><a href=
                    "x.htm"><img src="images/photo-header-right.jpg"
                    width="58" height="64" alt="" border="0"
                    /></a></span>
                <div style="margin-top:8px;">
                    <span style="font: 14px Arial, Helvetica, sans-
                        serif;"><b>Need Help?</b></span><br />
                    Call us at<br />
                    1-800-555-5555
                </div>
            </div>
        </div>
    </div>
<!-- ╫╫╫╫╫ header end ╫╫╫╫╫ -->
    </div>
</div>
</body>
</html>
```

There are several things to note about the code in Listing 11.2:

- Both the default link colors and linklist1 link rules are added. While the default colors are added before they will actually be used, the linklist1 style is used for the Reseller Login link.

- The a5-header rule and code are added to provide a container for the nested elements. The rule has relative positioning assigned to it, so it expands to the full width of the screen. It is assigned a height of 78 pixels, which is the height of the images in the header. Using the background property, the bg-header.gif is repeated horizontally across the header.

- The logo.gif file is included in a <DIV> tag. This ensures that the image will appear at the top-left corner of the header with no additional space around it in some browsers, such as IE 5, 5.5, and 6 (see Figure 11.7).

Figure 11.7
Header after the `logo.gif` image is added to the left side of the container.
© 2014 Cengage Learning.

■ The `a5-login` container is added after the `logo.gif` image in the header. The rule is given absolute positioning, locating the container 186 pixels from the right. This allows space for the final `<DIV>` to be added within those 186 pixels between it and the right side (see Figure 11.8).

Figure 11.8
The header after the `a5-login` container has been added to the right of the `logo.gif` image.
© 2014 Cengage Learning.

■ The `reseller-button.gif` image is floated to the left of the "Reseller Login. Forgot Password?" text. In this instance, the `float` property is assigned to the image using a `<SPAN>` tag at the local level in the code. Because the button image does not take up the full height of the header, the container is positioned 24 pixels from the top of the header, using the `top` property.

■ The final container in the header is included using the `a5-call` rule (see Figure 11.9). This rule is assigned absolute positioning, similar to the `a5-login` container. The former, however, is located 0 pixels from the right, with a width of 177 pixels. This not only guarantees that the `<DIV>` will abut the right side of the container, but it will also have 9 pixels of padding between it and the `a5-login` container because the `a5-login` `<DIV>` is located 186 pixels from the right (186 − 177 = 9 pixels).

Figure 11.9
After the final container `a5-call` is added, the header has all the elements added to it.
© 2014 Cengage Learning.

The layout of this content is a bit more involved than the previous containers in the `a5-header` row. It has two nested elements: the `photo-header-right.jpg` (which is floated to the left of the text, including 6 pixels of padding to the right) and a `<DIV>` that contains the text (which also has a `<SPAN>` tag styling the "Need Help" text). Barring the default font color and size, the majority of styling is completed at the local level.

Creating the Left Column

After the `a5-header` container has been added, the left column needs to be added. This column includes a search form, a content area, and the image used as a banner ad. Figure 11.10 shows what the design looks like after the code in Listing 11.3 has been added.

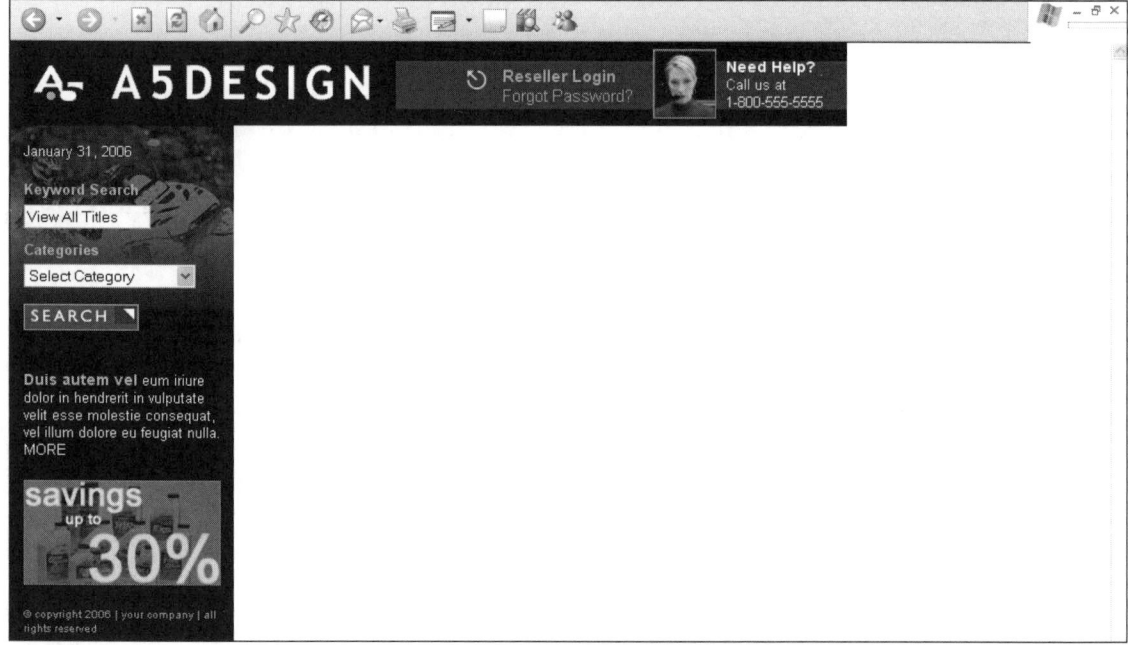

Figure 11.10
The design after the left column has been added under the header row.
© 2014 Cengage Learning.

New Code Is in Bold

The newly added code is bolded to differentiate it from the existing code that is being built upon in this case study.

Listing 11.3   Code for Figure 11.10

```
<!DOCTYPE html PUBLIC "-//W3C//DTD XHTML 1.0 Transitional//EN"
"DTD/xhtml1-transitional.dtd">
<html xmlns="http://www.w3.org/1999/xhtml" xml:lang="en"
lang="en"><head><title>Design 123</title>
<meta http-equiv="Content-Type" content="text/html;
    charset=iso-8859-1" />
<style type="text/css">
/* ++++++++++ global general styles start ++++++++++*/
html, body {
    margin:0px;
    padding:0px;
    font: 13px Arial, Helvetica, sans-serif;
    color:#000000;
    background:#ffffff;
    }
a:link { color:#FF7800; }
a:visited { color:#FF5A00; }
a:active { color:#FFC600; }
a:hover { color:#000000; }

a.linklist1:link { text-decoration:none;color:#0ECOFF;}
a.linklist1:visited { text-decoration:none;color:#0ECOFF;}
a.linklist1:active { text-decoration:none;color:#0ECOFF;}
a.linklist1:hover { text-decoration:none;color:#D5EE03;}

.color-1-text-13 { font-family: arial, geneva, sans-serif; font-size:
    13px; color: #FFAE00;}
.color-1-text-14 { font-family: arial, geneva, sans-serif; font-size:
    14px; color: #FFAE00;}

.color-2-text-14 { font-family: arial, geneva, sans-serif; font-size:
    14px; color: #000000;}
/* ++++++++++ global general styles end ++++++++++*/
/* ++++++++++ global structure styles start ++++++++++*/
```

```css
#a5-body-center {
    text-align:left;
    }
#a5-body {
    position: relative;
    width: 770px; /* change this to a specific amount for a fixed
            design or a relative amount if the design should expand to
a percentage of the screen. E.g., 770px or 100%, respectively. */

    /* remove these comment tags if the page is to be centered
        margin-left: auto;
        margin-right: auto;*/
        text-align:left;
        padding-bottom:10px;
        border:0px solid #000000;
        }
#a5-header {
    position:relative;
    left:0px;
    top:0px;
    height:78px;
    background: #000000 url(images/bg-header.gif) repeat-x;
    border:0px solid #000000;
    }
    #a5-login {
        position:absolute;
        top:24px;
        right:186px;
        width:165px;
        font: 15px Arial, Helvetica, sans-serif;
        border:0px solid #ffffff;
        }
    #a5-call {
        position:absolute;
        top:8px;
        right:0px;
        width:177px;
        font: 13px Arial, Helvetica, sans-serif;
        color:#ffffff;
        border:0px solid #000000;
        }
```

```
#a5-column-left {
    position:absolute;
    left:0px;
    top:78px;
    width:207px;
    color:#ffffff;
    padding:0px 12px 50px 15px;
    background: #000000 url(images/bg-left-column.jpg) no-repeat;
    border:0px solid yellow;
    voice-family:"\"}\"";
    voice-family:inherit;
        width:180px;
    }
    html>body #a5-column-left {
        width:180px;
    }
    #date {
        position:relative;
        top:16px;
        left:0px;
        color:#ffffff;
        border:0px solid #ffffff;
        }
    #formsearch {
        position:relative;
        top:35px;
        left:0px;
        border:0px solid yellow;
        }
    #a5-column-left-content {
        position:relative;
        left:0px;
        top:35px;
        color:#ffffff;
        border:0px solid #ffffff;
        }
        #a5-copyright {
            position:relative;
            left:0px;
            top:10px;
            bottom:5px;
            font: 10px Arial, Helvetica, sans-serif;
```

```
                color:#9D9D9D;
                text-align:left;
                border:0px solid #000000;
                }
    /* ++++++++++ global structure styles end ++++++++++*/
    </style>
    </head>
    <body>
    <div id="a5-body-center">
        <div id="a5-body">
    <!-- ###### header start ###### -->
            <div id="a5-header">
                <div><a href="index.htm"><img src="images/logo.gif"
                    width="357" height="78" alt="" border="0" /></a></div>
                <div id="a5-login">
                    <span style="float:left;"><a href="x.htm"><img src=
                        "images/reseller-button.gif" width="33"
                        height="23" alt="" border="0" /></a></span>
                    <a href="x.htm" class="linklist1"><b>Reseller Login
                        </b><br />
                    Forgot Password?</a>
                </div>
                <div id="a5-call">
                    <span style="float:left;padding-right:6px;"><a href=
                        "x.htm"><img src="images/photo-header-right.jpg"
                        width="58" height="64" alt="" border="0" /></a>
                        </span>
                    <div style="margin-top:8px;">
                        <span style="font: 14px Arial, Helvetica,
                            sans-serif;"><b>Need Help?</b></span><br />
                        Call us at<br />
                        1-800-555-5555
                    </div>
                </div>
            </div>
    <!-- ###### header end ###### -->
    <!-- ###### left column start ###### -->
                <div id="a5-column-left">
                    <div id="date">
                        January 31, 2006
                    </div>
                    <div id="formsearch" class="color-1-text-13">
```

```
                    <form method="post" action="x.htm" name="search"
                        style="margin-top:0px;">
                        <b>Keyword Search</b>
                        <div style="padding:5px 0px 10px 0px;"><input
                            type="text" size="15" name="keywords"
                            value="View All Titles" /></div>
                        <b>Categories</b>
                        <div style="padding:5px 0px 15px 0px;">
                        <select name="categories" size="1">
                            <option value="All">Select Category</
                                option>
                            <option value="sample">This is a sample
                                entry</option>
                        </select>
                        </div>
                        <input type="image" src="images/button-
                            search.gif" />
                    </form>
                </div>
                    <div id="a5-column-left-content">
                        <div style="padding:15px 0px 10px 0px;color:
                            #ffffff;"><span class="color-1-text-14"><b>
                            Duis autem vel</b></span> eum iriure dolor in
                            hendrerit in vulputate velit esse molestie
                            consequat, vel illum dolore eu feugiat nulla.
                            MORE</div>
                        <div style="padding:10px 0px 10px 0px;color:
                            #ffffff;"><a href="x.htm"><img src="images/
                            banner-left-bottom.jpg" width="180"
                            height="96" alt="" border="0" /></a></div>
                        <div id="a5-copyright">
                            &copy; copyright 2006 | your company | all
                                rights reserved
                        </div>
                    </div>
                </div>
<!-- ###### left column end ###### -->
        </div>
</div>
</body>
</html>
```

There are several things to note about the code in Listing 11.3:

- The `a5-column-left` container, which contains all the content in the left column, is assigned absolute positioning. It remains on the left side of the design and begins 78 pixels from the top of the page, exactly below the header. It is assigned a width of 207 pixels. Using the `padding` property, the entire column is given padding on the left and right sides. Because the box model bug used to be prevalent, the Tantek hack was included so that the `left` and `right` padding is interpreted properly and similarly by both compliant and noncompliant browsers. Fortunately, for the most part, this is no longer necessary. This is why the width is changed to 180 pixels for compliant browsers, because 17 pixels need to be subtracted from the original specified width.

- The date container is the first content added. Although in this design the date is static text, scripts to output the date using JavaScript or a database-driven programming language can be added easily. Two more things to note about this container are that it is assigned relative positioning, which makes it take up the entire width of the column, and it is positioned 16 pixels from the top of the column using the `top` property.

- After the date container has been added, the `formsearch` `<DIV>` is added. It contains all the form elements, such as the "Keyword Search" text and input field, "Categories" text and drop-down menu, and the Search button. The positioning of the elements in the form occurs at the local level. One style to note is `style="margin-top:0px;"`, which is included in the parent `<FORM>` tag. This helps override the default margin settings of some browsers so the form is positioned similarly among browsers. The `color-1-text-13` rule is added to style the text in the `formsearch` `<DIV>`.

- The `a5-column-left-content` `<DIV>` is added after the `formsearch` `<DIV>`. The first three words are not only styled with the `color-1-text-14` rule that was added to the style sheet, but also the container is assigned local padding to the top and bottom.

Adding the Center Column

After the left column is completed, the right column is added to the design, completing it. Figure 11.11 shows what the design looks like after it has been completed (see Listing 11.4).

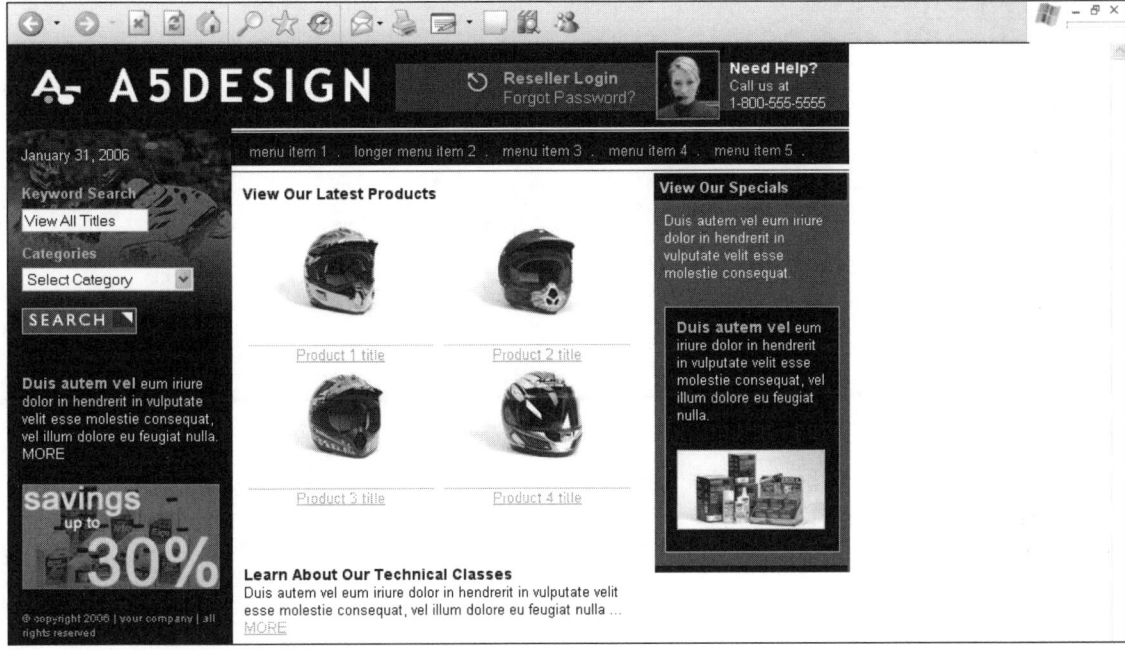

Figure 11.11

The design after the entire right column has been added.

© 2014 Cengage Learning.

New Code Is in Bold

The newly added code is bolded to differentiate it from the existing code that is being built upon in this case study.

Listing 11.4   Code for Figure 11.11

```
<!DOCTYPE html PUBLIC "-//W3C//DTD XHTML 1.0 Transitional//EN"
    "DTD/xhtml1-transitional.dtd">
<html xmlns="http://www.w3.org/1999/xhtml" xml:lang="en"
lang="en"><head><title>Design 123</title>
<meta http-equiv="Content-Type" content="text/html;
    charset=iso-8859-1" />
<style type="text/css">
/* ++++++++++ global general styles start ++++++++++*/
html, body {
    margin:0px;
    padding:0px;
    font: 13px Arial, Helvetica, sans-serif;
```

```
        color:#000000;
        background:#ffffff;
        }
    a:link { color:#FF7800; }
    a:visited { color:#FF5A00; }
    a:active { color:#FFC600; }
    a:hover { color:#000000; }

    a.linklist1:link { text-decoration:none;color:#0EC0FF;}
    a.linklist1:visited { text-decoration:none;color:#0EC0FF;}
    a.linklist1:active { text-decoration:none;color:#0EC0FF;}
    a.linklist1:hover { text-decoration:none;color:#D5EE03;}

    .color-1-text-13 { font-family: arial, geneva, sans-serif; font-size:
        13px; color: #FFAE00;}
    .color-1-text-14 { font-family: arial, geneva, sans-serif; font-size:
        14px; color: #FFAE00;}

    .color-2-text-14 { font-family: arial, geneva, sans-serif; font-size:
        14px; color: #000000;}
    /* ++++++++++ global general styles end ++++++++++*/
    /* ++++++++++ global structure styles start ++++++++++*/
    #a5-body-center {
        text-align:left;
        }
    #a5-body {
        position: relative;
        width: 770px; /* change this to a specific amount for a fixed
                design or a relative amount if the design should expand to
a percentage of the screen. E.g., 770px or 100%, respectively. */

    /* remove these comment tags if the page is to be centered
        margin-left: auto;
        margin-right: auto;*/
        text-align:left;
        padding-bottom:10px;
        border:0px solid #000000;
        }
    #a5-header {
        position:relative;
        left:0px;
        top:0px;
        height:78px;
        background: #000000 url(images/bg-header.gif) repeat-x;
        border:0px solid #000000;
        }
```

```
      #a5-login {
          position:absolute;
          top:24px;
          right:186px;
          width:165px;
          font: 15px Arial, Helvetica, sans-serif;
          border:0px solid #ffffff;
          }
      #a5-call {
          position:absolute;
          top:8px;
          right:0px;
          width:177px;
          font: 13px Arial, Helvetica, sans-serif;
          color:#ffffff;
          border:0px solid #000000;
          }
#a5-column-left {
      position:absolute;
      left:0px;
      top:78px;
      width:207px;
      color:#ffffff;
      padding:0px 12px 50px 15px;
      background: #000000 url(images/bg-left-column.jpg) no-repeat;
      border:0px solid yellow;
      voice-family:"\"}\"";
      voice-family:inherit;
          width:180px;
      }
      html>body #a5-column-left {
          width:180px;
      }
      #date {
          position:relative;
          top:16px;
          left:0px;
          color:#ffffff;
          border:0px solid #ffffff;
          }
```

```css
#formsearch {
    position:relative;
    top:35px;
    left:0px;
    border:0px solid yellow;
    }
#a5-column-left-content {
    position:relative;
    left:0px;
    top:35px;
    color:#ffffff;
    border:0px solid #ffffff;
    }
    #a5-copyright {
        position:relative;
        left:0px;
        top:10px;
        bottom:5px;
        font: 10px Arial, Helvetica, sans-serif;
        color:#9D9D9D;
        text-align:left;
        border:0px solid #000000;
        }
#a5-column-right {
    position:relative;
    right:0px;
    top:0px;
    margin-left:207px;
    border:0px solid #000000;
    }
#a5-menu-box {
    position:relative;
    top:0px;
    left:0px;
    height:42px;
    width:100%;
    color:#ffffff;
    line-height:42px;
    vertical-align:30%;
    background:url(images/bg-menu.gif) repeat-x 0px 0px;
    border:0px solid #000000;
    }
```

```
        #a5-menu a {
            display:inline;
            text-decoration:none;
            color:#94CCDE;
            font-weight:normal;
            }
        #a5-menu a:hover {
            font-weight:normal;
            color:#ffffff;
            }
    #a5-column-right-left {
        position:relative;
        left:0px;
        top:0px;
        padding:10px 10px 10px 10px;
        margin-right:177px;
        border:0px solid #000000;
        }
        .a5-products {
        height:300px;
        border: 0px solid #000000;
        }
        .a5-individual-product {
        float: left;
        margin:0px 2px 0px 2px;
        border:0px solid #000000;
        }
        .a5-individual-product p {
        border-top:1px solid #BFBFBF;
        width:170px;
        text-align: center;
        }
#a5-column-right-right {
        position:absolute;
        right:0px;
        top:42px;
        width:177px;
        height:365px;
        color:#ffffff;
        padding:0px 9px 0px 9px;
        background:#215F5F url(images/bg-bottom-line-right-column.gif)
            no-repeat left bottom;
```

```
            border:0px solid red;
            voice-family:"\"}\"";
            voice-family:inherit;
                width:159px;
            }
            html>body #a5-column-right-right {
                width:159px;
            }
            .a5-title-right {
                font-family: arial, geneva, sans-serif;
                font-size: 13px;
                color: #D5EE03;
                line-height:25px;
                font-weight:bold;
                margin:0px -9px 0px -9px;
                padding-left:5px;
                margin-bottom:10px;
                background:#000000;
                border:0px solid #000000;
                }
        #a5-right-nested-box {
                position:relative;
                right:0px;
                top:23px;
                width:159px;
                padding:10px 10px 0px 10px;
                background:#000000;
                color:#ffffff;
                border:1px solid #0EC0FF;
                voice-family:"\"}\"";
                voice-family:inherit;
                    width:139px;
                }
            html>body #a5-right-nested-box {
            width:139px;
                }
/* ++++++++++ global structure styles end ++++++++++*/
</style>
</head>
<body>
<div id="a5-body-center">
    <div id="a5-body">
```

```
<!-- ###### header start ###### -->
    <div id="a5-header">
        <div><a href="index.htm"><img src="images/logo.gif" width=
            "357" height="78" alt="" border="0" /></a></div>
        <div id="a5-login">
            <span style="float:left;"><a href="x.htm"><img
                src="images/reseller-button.gif" width="33"
                height="23" alt="" border="0" /></a></span>
            <a href="x.htm" class="linklist1"><b>Reseller Login
                </b><br />
            Forgot Password?</a>
        </div>
        <div id="a5-call">
            <span style="float:left;padding-right:6px;"><a
                href="x.htm"><img src="images/photo-header-
                right.jpg" width="58" height="64" alt=""
                border="0" /></a></span>
            <div style="margin-top:8px;">
                <span style="font: 14px Arial, Helvetica,
                    sans-serif;"><b>Need Help?</b></span><br />
                Call us at<br />
                1-800-555-5555
            </div>
        </div>
    </div>
<!-- ###### header end ###### -->
<!-- ###### left column start ###### -->
        <div id="a5-column-left">
            <div id="date">
                January 31, 2006
            </div>
            <div id="formsearch" class="color-1-text-13">
                <form method="post" action="x.htm" name="search"
                    style="margin-top:0px;">
                    <b>Keyword Search</b>
                    <div style="padding:5px 0px 10px 0px;"><input
                        type="text" size="15" name="keywords"
                        value="View All Titles" /></div>
                    <b>Categories</b>
                    <div style="padding:5px 0px 15px 0px;">
                    <select name="categories" size="1">
                        <option value="All">Select Category
                            </option>
```

```
                        <option value="sample">This is a sample
                            entry</option>
                    </select>
                    </div>
                    <input type="image" src="images/
                        button-search.gif" />
                </form>
            </div>
            <div id="a5-column-left-content">
                <div style="padding:15px 0px 10px 0px;color:
                    #ffffff;"><span class="color-1-text-14"><b>
                    Duis autem vel</b></span> eum iriure dolor in
                    hendrerit in vulputate velit esse molestie
                    consequat, vel illum dolore eu feugiat nulla.
                    MORE</div>
                <div style="padding:10px 0px 10px 0px;color:
                    #ffffff;"><a href="x.htm"><img src="images/
                    banner-left-bottom.jpg" width="180"
                    height="96" alt="" border="0" /></a></div>
                <div id="a5-copyright">
                    &copy; copyright 2006 | your company | all
                        rights reserved
                </div>
            </div>
        </div>
<!-- ###### left column end ###### -->
<!-- ###### right column start ###### -->
        <div id="a5-column-right">
            <div id="a5-menu-box">
            <div id="a5-menu">
                   
                <a href="index.htm">menu item 1</a>  
                    .  
                <a href="menu-item-2.htm">longer menu item 2
                    </a>  .  
                <a href="menu-item-3.htm">menu item 3</a> 
                     .  
                <a href="index.htm">menu item 4</a>  
                    .  
                <a href="index.htm">menu item 5</a>  
                    .  
            </div>
            </div>
```

```html
<!-- ###### column right left start ###### -->
                <div id="a5-column-right-left">
            <span class="color-2-text-14" style="padding-
                bottom:5px;"><b>View Our Latest Products</b></span>
            <br /><br />
            <div class="a5-products">
                <div class="a5-individual-product">
                    <a href="x.htm"><img src="images/
                        product-1.jpg" width="175" height="95"
                        alt="" border="0" /></a><br />
                    <p><a href="x.htm">Product 1 title</a></p>
                </div>
                <div class="a5-individual-product">
                    <a href="x.htm"><img src="images/
                        product-2.jpg" width="175" height="95"
                        alt="" border="0" /></a><br />
                    <p><a href="x.htm">Product 2 title</a></p>
                </div>
                <div class="a5-individual-product">
                    <a href="x.htm"><img src="images/
                        product-3.jpg" width="175" height="95"
                        alt="" border="0" /></a><br />
                    <p><a href="x.htm">Product 3 title</a></p>
                </div>
                <div class="a5-individual-product">
                    <a href="x.htm"><img src="images/
                        product-4.jpg" width="175" height="95"
                        alt="" border="0" /></a><br />
                    <p><a href="x.htm">Product 4 title</a></p>
    </div>
        </div>
        <br />

        <div class="color-2-text-14"><b>Learn About Our
            Technical Classes</b></div>
        Duis autem vel eum iriure dolor in hendrerit in
            vulputate velit esse molestie consequat, vel
            illum dolore eu feugiat nulla ... <a href=
            "x.htm">MORE</a>


        </div>
```

```
<!-- ##### column right left end ##### -->
<!-- ##### column right right start ##### -->
                <div id="a5-column-right-right">
                    <div class="a5-title-right">
                        <b>View Our Specials</b>
                    </div>
                    <div>Duis autem vel eum iriure dolor in hendrerit
                        in vulputate velit esse molestie consequat.
                        </div>
                    <div id="a5-right-nested-box"><span class="color-1-
                        text-14"><b>Duis autem vel</b></span> eum
                        iriure dolor in hendrerit in vulputate velit
                        esse molestie consequat, vel illum dolore eu
                        feugiat nulla.
                        <div style="margin:24px 0px 20px 0px;"><img
                            src="images/banner-right-middle.jpg"
                            width="136" height="73" alt="" border="0"
                            /></div>
                    </div>
                </div>
<!-- ##### column right right end ##### -->
            </div>
<!-- ##### right column end ##### -->
        </div>
    </div>
    </body>
</html>
```

There are several things to note about the code in Listing 11.4:

■ All the content in the right column, including the menu, the center column (which
includes the products), and the right column, are nested inside the a5-column-right
container. It is assigned relative positioning, with a margin-left value of 207 pixels.
This guarantees that the container will be positioned 207 pixels from the left, which is
the width of the left column.

■ To ensure that the menu occurs consistently on every page, including the different
second-level pages, the a5-menu-box container is added with relative positioning above
the rest of the content in the <DIV>. Figure 11.12 shows what the design looks like
with just the menu added.

Figure 11.12
The menu is the first element to be added to the right column.
© 2014 Cengage Learning.

- The content in the right column is nested inside the a5-column-right container. Because it is assigned absolute positioning, it is placed 42 pixels from the top of the container. These 42 pixels force the column down past the menu area. Otherwise, the column would begin in the area where the menu runs (see Figure 11.13).

Figure 11.13
An image of how the right column would look if it were not positioned 42 pixels from the top.
© 2014 Cengage Learning.

Because the container is assigned absolute positioning, it is given a height value of 365 pixels to ensure that the nested content inside it does not run below the container. The <DIV> is assigned the bg-bottom-line-right-column.gif background image, which is the black line at the bottom of the column. No matter what the height of the column is, the background image will automatically place itself at the bottom because of the bottom value included in the shorthand background property.

- The a5-title-right <DIV>, which is the first item nested in the right column, is placed at the top of the column. One of the most useful properties assigned to the rule is margin- bottom, which has a value of 10 pixels. This creates some visual space between the title area and the text below it.

■ The `a5-right-nested-box` rule is added to create the nested `<DIV>` in the column, which contains the text and image. Because padding is added to the container, the width of the `<DIV>` needs to be adjusted for various browsers using the Tantek hack. The image is positioned using a local style that is included in the `<DIV>` tags wrapped around it.

One thing to consider about such a menu is it is limited in the amount of items that can be added because of limited horizontal space. This is where drop-down CSS, JavaScript, or Flash menus can become useful because more menu items can be added when the user mouses over a menu item. The menu in this instance works fine because the site is created to be driven by the search form on the left, which can be used to navigate hundreds or thousands of pages. The menu itself is designed more for general sections, such as About, Customer Service, and Specials.

While the menu code looks the same as that in the designs in Chapters 9 and 10, it is styled slightly differently. The display property in the `a5-menu` rule in this design is assigned a value of `inline` instead of `block`, meaning the items will be output horizontally across a line, as opposed to vertically.

The `a5-column-right-left` rule is used to output the content in the center column of the design. It is assigned relative positioning, with a `margin-right` value of 177 pixels, which keeps it from crossing over into the right column. One unique aspect of this container, compared to any others in this design or in Chapters 9 or 10, is that it includes repeated floating `<DIV>` tags, which contain each product. Normally handled with an XHTML table, these products wrap around to form separate columns and rows. If the width of the design were expanded to fill 1024×768 resolution, three products would appear in the first row, as opposed to two in the 800×600 version. While they do not have to expand, by doing so, they fill the extra whitespace of the design that would normally exist because only two products are used to fill it. This function is accomplished by adding a container that is assigned the `a5-products` rule. The one thing to note about this rule is that it is assigned a height of 300 pixels. If this height is not set, the text below the images will randomly reposition itself in different browsers at 1024×768 resolution. Because the height value is assigned, the developer cannot output more products than the height will allow, which is four in this example. Each product is positioned and styled inside the `a5-products` container, using the `a5-individual-product` and `a5-individual-product p` rules. Figure 11.14 shows the design with the center column added with the border of the products table turned on to show the space it takes up.

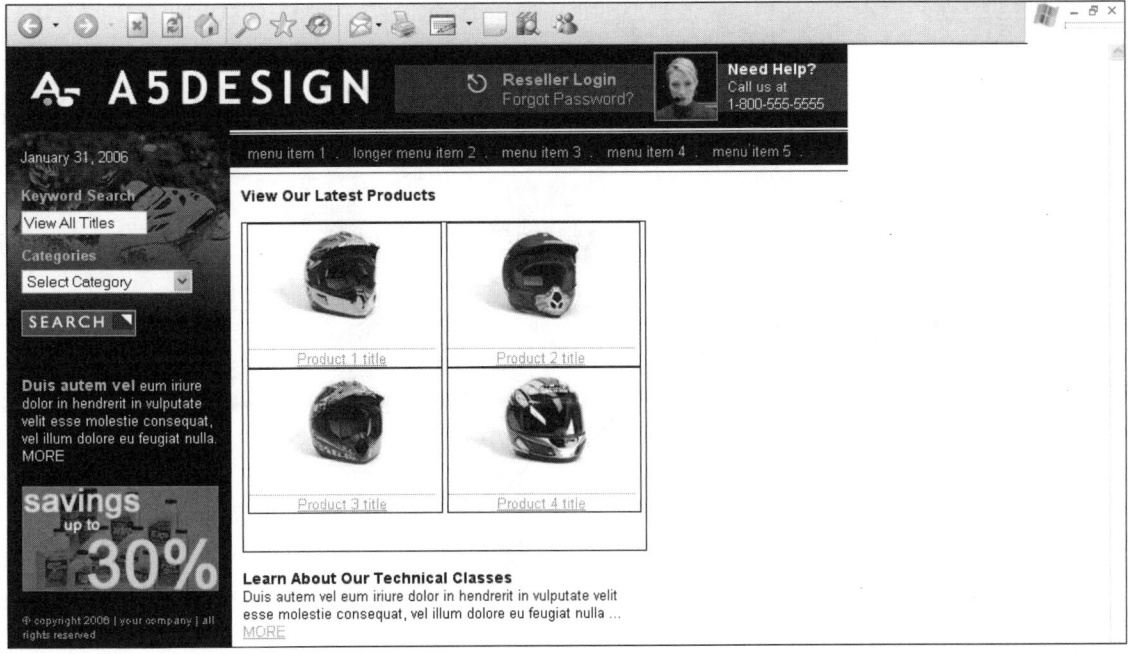

Figure 11.14
The center column added to the design with the border of the products table turned on.

Using Comment Tags in an Intuitive Way

Using comment tags to separate code makes finding particular sections much easier. Using an intuitive system is important for designers to understand their code. In this section of code, the "right column" is the parent column, while "column right left" represents the left column of the right section. Visually, though, in the design, this column is the center column. A designer could also name this section the "center column," or name the "right column" the "parent right column," signifying that there will be a child right column.

CONSTRUCTING SECOND-LEVEL PAGES

Similar to the designs in Chapters 9 and 10, the homepage is duplicated and modified for second-level templates. This design includes both three- and two-column versions to provide the design layout with more flexibility.

Constructing a Second-Level Page with Three Columns

The first second-level template created is the page that appears when the designer clicks on the menu item titled Longer Menu Item 2. This page contains three columns. Such a design offers the designer the ability to supplement content with a right column that could contain information that could be included on more than one page, such as photos and descriptions. Figure 11.15 shows what the design looks like when the final code is added to the page (see Listing 11.5).

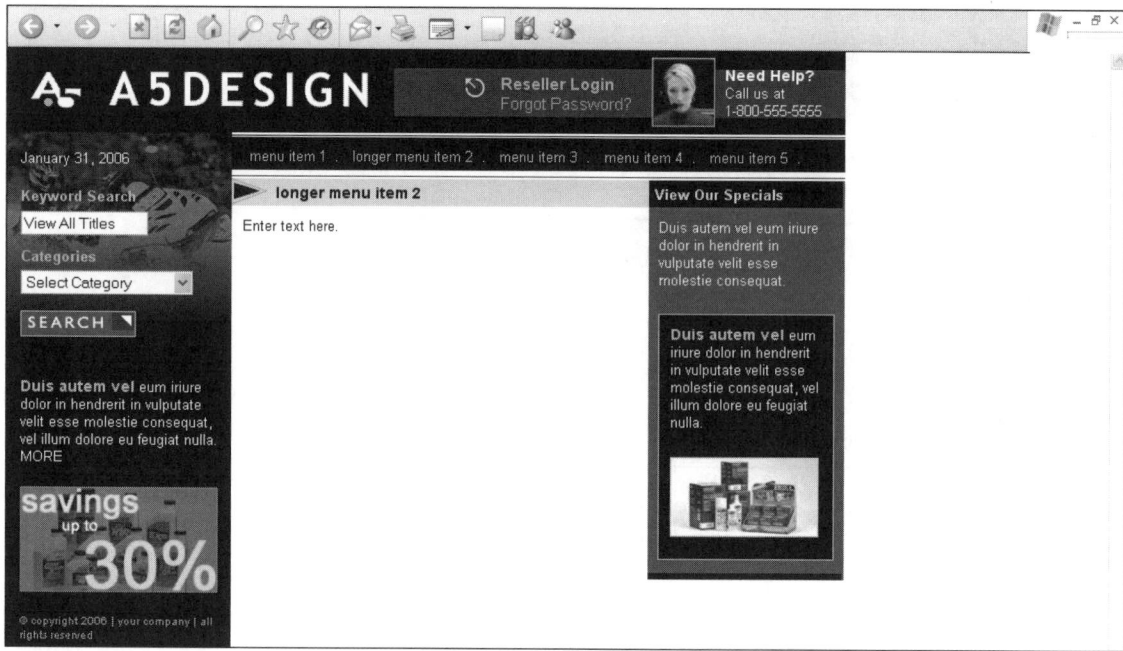

Figure 11.15
A three-column second-level template created from a customized version of the homepage design.
© 2014 Cengage Learning.

New Code Is in Bold

The newly added code is bolded to differentiate it from the existing code that is being built upon in this case study.

Listing 11.5   Code for Figure 11.15

```
<!DOCTYPE html PUBLIC "-//W3C//DTD XHTML 1.0 Transitional//EN"
    "DTD/xhtml1-transitional.dtd">
<html xmlns="http://www.w3.org/1999/xhtml" xml:lang="en"
lang="en"><head><title>Design 123</title>
<meta http-equiv="Content-Type" content="text/html;
    charset=iso-8859-1" />
<style type="text/css">
/* ++++++++++ global general styles start ++++++++++*/
```

```
html, body {
    margin:0px;
    padding:0px;
    font: 13px Arial, Helvetica, sans-serif;
    color:#000000;
    background:#ffffff;
    }
a:link { color:#FF7800; }
a:visited { color:#FF5A00; }
a:active { color:#FFC600; }
a:hover { color:#000000; }

a.linklist1:link { text-decoration:none;color:#0ECOFF;}
a.linklist1:visited { text-decoration:none;color:#0ECOFF;}
a.linklist1:active { text-decoration:none;color:#0ECOFF;}
a.linklist1:hover { text-decoration:none;color:#D5EE03;}

.color-1-text-13 { font-family: arial, geneva, sans-serif; font-size:
    13px; color: #FFAE00;}
.color-1-text-14 { font-family: arial, geneva, sans-serif; font-size:
    14px; color: #FFAE00;}

.color-2-text-14 { font-family: arial, geneva, sans-serif; font-size:
    14px; color: #000000;}
/* ++++++++++ global general styles end ++++++++++*/
/* ++++++++++ global structure styles start ++++++++++*/
#a5-body-center {
    text-align:left;
    }
#a5-body {
    position: relative;
    width: 770px; /* change this to a specific amount for a fixed
            design or a relative amount if the design should expand to
a percentage of the screen. E.g., 770px or 100%, respectively. */
    /* remove these comment tags if the page is to be centered
    margin-left: auto;
    margin-right: auto;*/
    text-align:left;
    padding-bottom:10px;
    border:0px solid #000000;
    }
#a5-header {
    position:relative;
    left:0px;
```

```
        top:0px;
        height:78px;
        background: #000000 url(images/bg-header.gif) repeat-x;
        border:0px solid #000000;
        }
    #a5-login {
        position:absolute;
        top:24px;
        right:186px;
        width:165px;
        font: 15px Arial, Helvetica, sans-serif;
        border:0px solid #ffffff;
        }
    #a5-call {
        position:absolute;
        top:8px;
        right:0px;
        width:177px;
        font: 13px Arial, Helvetica, sans-serif;
        color:#ffffff;
        border:0px solid #000000;
        }
#a5-column-left {
    position:absolute;
    left:0px;
    top:78px;
    width:207px;
    color:#ffffff;
    padding:0px 12px 50px 15px;
    background: #000000 url(images/bg-left-column.jpg) no-repeat;
    border:0px solid yellow;
    voice-family:"\"}\"";
    voice-family:inherit;
        width:180px;
    }
    html>body #a5-column-left {
        width:180px;
    }
    #date {
        position:relative;
        top:16px;
        left:0px;
```

```
            color:#ffffff;
            border:0px solid #ffffff;
            }
        #formsearch {
            position:relative;
            top:35px;
            left:0px;
            border:0px solid yellow;
            }
        #a5-column-left-content {
            position:relative;
            left:0px;
            top:35px;
            color:#ffffff;
            border:0px solid #ffffff;
            }
            #a5-copyright {
                position:relative;
                left:0px;
                top:10px;
                bottom:5px;
                font: 10px Arial, Helvetica, sans-serif;
                color:#9D9D9D;
                text-align:left;
                border:0px solid #000000;
                }
#a5-column-right {
    position:relative;
    right:0px;
    top:0px;
    margin-left:207px;
    border:0px solid #000000;
    }
    #a5-menu-box {
        position:relative;
        top:0px;
        left:0px;
        height:42px;
        width:100%;
        color:#ffffff;
        line-height:42px;
        vertical-align:30%;
```

```
            background:url(images/bg-menu.gif) repeat-x 0px 0px;
            border:0px solid #000000;
            }
        #a5-menu a {
            display:inline;
            text-decoration:none;
            color:#94CCDE;
            font-weight:normal;
            }
        #a5-menu a:hover {
            font-weight:normal;
            color:#ffffff;
            }
    #a5-column-right-left {
        position:relative;
        left:0px;
        top:0px;
        padding:10px 10px 10px 10px;
        margin-right:177px;
        border:0px solid #000000;
        }
        .a5-products {
        height:300px;
        border: 0px solid #000000;
        }
        .a5-individual-product {
        float: left;
        margin:0px 2px 0px 2px;
        border:0px solid #000000;
        }
        .a5-individual-product p {
        border-top:1px solid #BFBFBF;
        width:170px;
        text-align: center;
        }
#a5-column-right-right {
        position:absolute;
        right:0px;
        top:42px;
        width:177px;
        height:365px;
```

```css
        color:#ffffff;
        padding:0px 9px 0px 9px;
        background:#215F5F url(images/bg-bottom-line-right-column.gif)
            no-repeat left bottom;
        border:0px solid red;
        voice-family:"\"}\"";
        voice-family:inherit;
            width:159px;
        }
        html>body #a5-column-right-right {
            width:159px;
        }
        .a5-title-right {
            font-family: arial, geneva, sans-serif;
            font-size: 13px;
            color: #D5EE03;
            line-height:25px;
            font-weight:bold;
            margin:0px -9px 0px -9px;
            padding-left:5px;
            margin-bottom:10px;
            background:#000000;
            border:0px solid #000000;
            }
        #a5-right-nested-box {
            position:relative;
            right:0px;
            top:23px;
            width:159px;
            padding:10px 10px 0px 10px;
            background:#000000;
            color:#ffffff;
            border:1px solid #0ECOFF;
            voice-family:"\"}\"";
            voice-family:inherit;
                width:139px;
        }
        html>body #a5-right-nested-box {
                width:139px;
            }
/* ++++++++++ global structure styles end ++++++++++*/
```

```
/* ++++++++++ second level start ++++++++++*/
#a5-column-right-left-sl {
    position:relative;
    left:0px;
    top:0px;
    padding:0px 10px 0px 10px;
    margin-right:177px;
    border:0px solid #000000;
    }
#a5-sl-title {
    margin:0px -10px 10px -10px;
    padding:5px 0px 0px 40px;
    height:25px;
    color:#000000;
    background:#DBDBDB url(images/bg-sl-title.gif) no-repeat left top;
    border:0px solid #000000;
    font:bold 14px italic Arial, Helvetica, sans-serif;
    voice-family:"\"}\"";
    voice-family:inherit;
        height:20px;
    }
    html>body #a5-sl-title {
        height:20px;
    }
#a5-column-left-full {
    position:relative;
    left:0px;
    top:1px;
    color:#000000;
    padding:0px 10px 0px 10px;
    }
/* ++++++++++ second level end ++++++++++*/
</style>
</head>
<body>
<div id="a5-body-center">
    <div id="a5-body">
<!-- ###### header start ###### -->
        <div id="a5-header">
            <div><a href="index.htm"><img src="images/logo.gif"
                width="357" height="78" alt="" border="0" /></a></div>
            <div id="a5-login">
```

```
                <span style="float:left;"><a href="x.htm"><img
                    src="images/reseller-button.gif" width="33"
                    height="23" alt="" border="0" /></a></span>
                <a href="x.htm" class="linklist1"><b>Reseller Login
                    </b><br />
                Forgot Password?</a>
            </div>
            <div id="a5-call">
                <span style="float:left;padding-right:6px;"><a href=
                    "x.htm"><img src="images/photo-header-right.jpg"
                    width="58" height="64" alt="" border="0" /></a>
                    </span>
                <div style="margin-top:8px;">
                    <span style="font: 14px Arial, Helvetica,
                        sans-serif;"><b>Need Help?</b></span><br />
                    Call us at<br />
                    1-800-555-5555
                </div>
            </div>
        </div>
<!-- ###### header end ###### -->
<!-- ###### left column start ###### -->
        <div id="a5-column-left">
        <div id="date">
            January 31, 2006
            </div>
            <div id="formsearch" class="color-1-text-13">
                <form method="post" action="x.htm" name="search"
                    style="margin-top:0px;">
                    <b>Keyword Search</b>
                    <div style="padding:5px 0px 10px 0px;"><input
                        type="text" size="15" name="keywords"
                        value="View All Titles" /></div>
                    <b>Categories</b>
                    <div style="padding:5px 0px 15px 0px;">
                    <select name="categories" size="1">
                        <option value="All">Select Category
                            </option>
                        <option value="sample">This is a sample
                            entry</option>
                    </select>
                    </div>
```

```
                    <input type="image" src="images/
                            button-search.gif" />
                </form>
            </div>
            <div id="a5-column-left-content">
                <div style="padding:15px 0px 10px 0px;color:
                    #ffffff;"><span class="color-1-text-14"><b>
                    Duis autem vel</b></span> eum iriure dolor in
                    hendrerit in vulputate velit esse molestie
                    consequat, vel illum dolore eu feugiat nulla.
                    MORE</div>
                <div style="padding:10px 0px 10px 0px;color:
                    #ffffff;"><a href="x.htm"><img src="images/
                    banner-left-bottom.jpg" width="180"
                    height="96" alt="" border="0" /></a></div>
                <div id="a5-copyright">
                    &copy; copyright 2006 | your company | all
                        rights reserved
                </div>
            </div>
        </div>
    </div>
<!-- ###### left column end ###### -->
<!-- ###### right column start ###### -->
        <div id="a5-column-right">
            <div id="a5-menu-box">
                <div id="a5-menu">
                       
                    <a href="index.htm">menu item 1</a> 
                         .  
                    <a href="menu-item-2.htm">longer menu item 2
                        </a>  .  
                    <a href="menu-item-3.htm">menu item 3</a> 
                         .  
                    <a href="index.htm">menu item 4</a>  
                        .  
                    <a href="index.htm">menu item 5</a>  
                        .  
                </div>
            </div>
```

```
<!-- ###### column right left start ###### -->
              <div id="a5-column-right-left-sl">
                  <div id="a5-sl-title">
                      longer menu item 2
                  </div>
                  Enter text here.
              </div>
<!-- ###### column right left end ###### -->
<!-- ###### column right right start ###### -->
              <div id="a5-column-right-right">
                  <div class="a5-title-right">
                      <b>View Our Specials</b>
                  </div>
                  <div>Duis autem vel eum iriure dolor in hendrerit
                  in vulputate velit esse molestie consequat.</div>
                  <div id="a5-right-nested-box"><span class="color-
                      1-text-14"><b>Duis autem vel</b></span> eum
                      iriure dolor in hendrerit in vulputate velit
                      esse molestie consequat, vel illum dolore eu
                      feugiat nulla.
                  <div style="margin:24px 0px 20px 0px;"><img
                      src="images/banner-right-middle.jpg"
                      width="136" height="73" alt="" border="0"
                      /></div>
                  </div>
              </div>
<!-- ###### column right right end ###### -->
          </div>
<!-- ###### right column end ###### -->
      </div>
</div>
</body>
</html>
```

There are several things to note about the code in Listing 11.5:

- The second level start and second level end comment tags are added to separate the rules specifically added for the second-level area from the rest of the style sheet. Unlike the design in Chapter 9, the two style sheets are included as one in this chapter, which is more an issue of preference. Sometimes a designer may include everything in one style sheet to keep all the code together or may want to break it up into separate style sheets for more of a distinct separation.

Rules for Secondary Pages

The rules added in the second-level template have `-sl` appended to their names to signify that they are to be used for secondary pages.

- The `a5-column-right-left-sl` rule is added to the style sheet for the second-level template. It replaces the `a5-column-right-left` rule, which is the container for the center column on the homepage. The only difference between the two styles is that the content on the second-level page, which is styled by the `a5-column-right-left-sl` rule, adds 10 pixels of padding to the top and bottom of the container to position itself with the menu and to add extra spacing on the bottom.

- The `a5-sl-title` rule is added to include the page title for secondary pages at the top of the page. This rule sets the height of the `<DIV>` at 25 pixels, using the `height` property. Padding also is used to position the title from the top and left sides in the container. To ensure that the color of the `bg-title.gif` is continued across the screen, the shorthand `background` property is assigned a background color value of #DBDBDB. Because padding is used to position the text within the container, the Tantek hack is added to ensure that the height of the container is the same for both compliant and noncompliant browsers.

Constructing a Second-Level Page with Two Columns

The full-width second-level template included with this design is the page the designer comes to when clicking on the Menu Item 3 link in the menu. The purpose of this template is to provide a page with more white space for the designer to work with. Figure 11.16 shows what the design looks like when the final code is added to the page and the right column is removed from the design (see Listing 11.6).

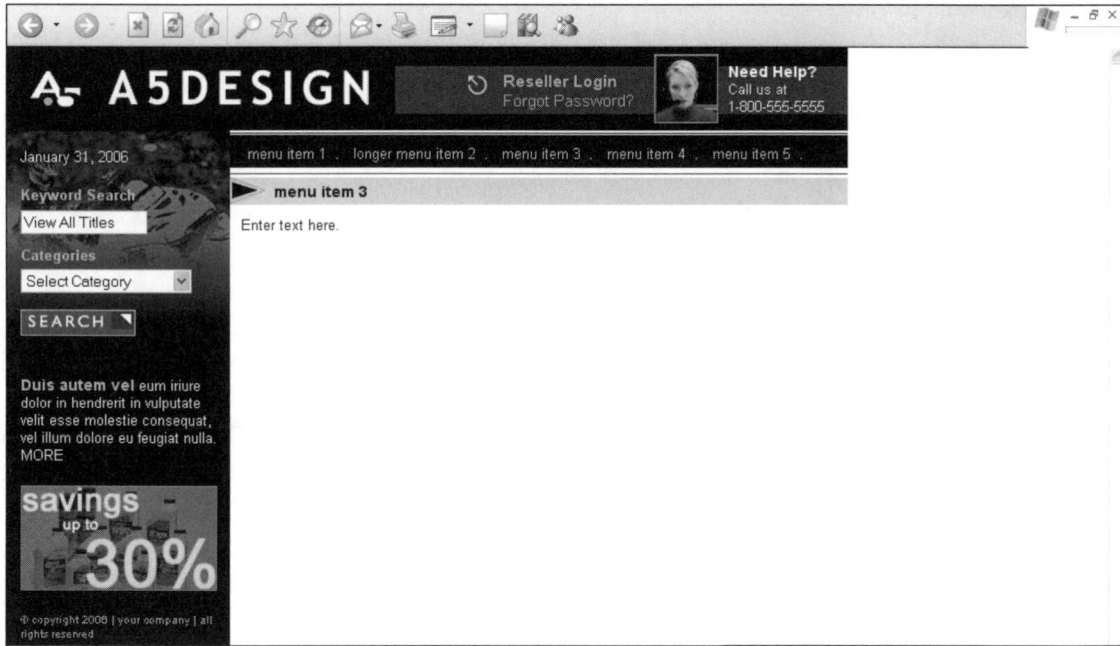

Figure 11.16

A two-column second-level template created from a customized version of the homepage design.

New Code Is in Bold

The newly added code is bolded to differentiate it from the existing code that is being built upon in this case study.

Listing 11.6   Code for Figure 11.16

```
<!DOCTYPE html PUBLIC "-//W3C//DTD XHTML 1.0 Transitional//EN"
    "DTD/xhtml1-transitional.dtd">
<html xmlns="http://www.w3.org/1999/xhtml" xml:lang="en"
lang="en"><head><title>Design 123</title>
<meta http-equiv="Content-Type" content="text/html;
    charset=iso-8859-1" />
<style type="text/css">
/* ++++++++++ global general styles start ++++++++++*/
    html, body {
    margin:0px;
    padding:0px;
    font: 13px Arial, Helvetica, sans-serif;
```

```
        color:#000000;
        background:#ffffff;
        }
a:link { color:#FF7800; }
a:visited { color:#FF5A00; }
a:active { color:#FFC600; }
a:hover { color:#000000; }

a.linklist1:link { text-decoration:none;color:#0EC0FF;}
a.linklist1:visited { text-decoration:none;color:#0EC0FF;}
a.linklist1:active { text-decoration:none;color:#0EC0FF;}
a.linklist1:hover { text-decoration:none;color:#D5EE03;}

.color-1-text-13 { font-family: arial, geneva, sans-serif; font-size:
        13px; color: #FFAE00;}
.color-1-text-14 { font-family: arial, geneva, sans-serif; font-size:
        14px; color: #FFAE00;}

.color-2-text-14 { font-family: arial, geneva, sans-serif; font-size:
        14px; color: #000000;}
/* ++++++++++ global general styles end ++++++++++*/
/* ++++++++++ global structure styles start ++++++++++*/
#a5-body-center {
        text-align:left;
        }
#a5-body {
        position: relative;
        width: 770px; /* change this to a specific amount for a fixed
                design or a relative amount if the design should expand to
a percentage of the screen. E.g., 770px or 100%, respectively. */

    /* remove these comment tags if the page is to be centered
        margin-left: auto;
        margin-right: auto;*/
        text-align:left;
        padding-bottom:10px;
        border:0px solid #000000;
        }
#a5-header {
        position:relative;
        left:0px;
        top:0px;
        height:78px;
        background: #000000 url(images/bg-header.gif) repeat-x;
        border:0px solid #000000;
        }
```

```
        #a5-login {
            position:absolute;
            top:24px;
            right:186px;
            width:165px;
            font: 15px Arial, Helvetica, sans-serif;
            border:0px solid #ffffff;
            }
        #a5-call {
            position:absolute;
            top:8px;
            right:0px;
            width:177px;
            font: 13px Arial, Helvetica, sans-serif;
            color:#ffffff;
            border:0px solid #000000;
            }
#a5-column-left {
    position:absolute;
    left:0px;
    top:78px;
    width:207px;
    color:#ffffff;
    padding:0px 12px 50px 15px;
    background: #000000 url(images/bg-left-column.jpg) no-repeat;
    border:0px solid yellow;
    voice-family:"\"}\"";
    voice-family:inherit;
        width:180px;
    }
    html>body #a5-column-left {
        width:180px;
    }
    #date {
        position:relative;
        top:16px;
        left:0px;
        color:#ffffff;
        border:0px solid #ffffff;
        }
```

```
#formsearch {
    position:relative;
    top:35px;
    left:0px;
    border:0px solid yellow;
    }
#a5-column-left-content {
    position:relative;
    left:0px;
    top:35px;
    color:#ffffff;
    border:0px solid #ffffff;
    }
    #a5-copyright {
        position:relative;
        left:0px;
        top:10px;
        bottom:5px;
        font: 10px Arial, Helvetica, sans-serif;
        color:#9D9D9D;
        text-align:left;
        border:0px solid #000000;
        }
#a5-column-right {
    position:relative;
    right:0px;
    top:0px;
    margin-left:207px;
    border:0px solid #000000;
    }
    #a5-menu-box {
        position:relative;
        top:0px;
        left:0px;
        height:42px;
        width:100%;
        color:#ffffff;
        line-height:42px;
        vertical-align:30%;
        background:url(images/bg-menu.gif) repeat-x 0px 0px;
        border:0px solid #000000;
        }
```

```
    #a5-menu a {
        display:inline;
        text-decoration:none;
        color:#94CCDE;
        font-weight:normal;
        }
    #a5-menu a:hover {
        font-weight:normal;
        color:#ffffff;
        }
#a5-column-right-left {
    position:relative;
    left:0px;
    top:0px;
    padding:10px 10px 10px 10px;
    margin-right:177px;
    border:0px solid #000000;
    }
    .a5-products {
    height:300px;
    border: 0px solid #000000;
    }
    .a5-individual-product {
    float: left;
    margin:0px 2px 0px 2px;
    border:0px solid #000000;
    }
    .a5-individual-product p {
    border-top:1px solid #BFBFBF;
    width:170px;
    text-align: center;
    }
#a5-column-right-right {
    position:absolute;
    right:0px;
    top:42px;
    width:177px;
    height:365px;
    color:#ffffff;
    padding:0px 9px 0px 9px;
    background:#215F5F url(images/bg-bottom-line-right-column.gif)
        no-repeat left bottom;
```

```
        border:0px solid red;
        voice-family:"\"}\"";
        voice-family:inherit;
            width:159px;
        }
        html>body #a5-column-right-right {
            width:159px;
        }
        .a5-title-right {
            font-family: arial, geneva, sans-serif;
            font-size: 13px;
            color: #D5EE03;
            line-height:25px;
            font-weight:bold;
            margin:0px -9px 0px -9px;
            padding-left:5px;
            margin-bottom:10px;
            background:#000000;
            border:0px solid #000000;
            }
        #a5-right-nested-box {
            position:relative;
            right:0px;
            top:23px;
            width:159px;
            padding:10px 10px 0px 10px;
            background:#000000;
            color:#ffffff;
            border:1px solid #0ECOFF;
            voice-family:"\"}\"";
            voice-family:inherit;
                width:139px;
            }
        html>body #a5-right-nested-box {
                width:139px;
            }
/* ++++++++++ global structure styles end ++++++++++*/
/* ++++++++++ second level start ++++++++++*/
#a5-column-right-left-sl {
    position:relative;
    left:0px;
    top:0px;
```

```
            padding:0px 10px 0px 10px;
            margin-right:177px;
            border:0px solid #000000;
            }
    #a5-sl-title {
            margin:0px -10px 10px -10px;
            padding:5px 0px 0px 40px;
            height:25px;
            color:#000000;
            background:#DBDBDB url(images/bg-sl-title.gif) no-repeat left top;
            border:0px solid #000000;
            font:bold 14px italic Arial, Helvetica, sans-serif;
            voice-family:"\"}\"";
            voice-family:inherit;
                height:20px;
            }
            html>body #a5-sl-title {
                height:20px;
            }
    #a5-column-left-full {
            position:relative;
            left:0px;
            top:1px;
            color:#000000;
            padding:0px 10px 0px 10px;
            }
    /* ++++++++++ second level end ++++++++++*/
    </style>
    </head>
    <body>
    <div id="a5-body-center">
        <div id="a5-body">
    <!-- ###### header start ###### -->
        <div id="a5-header">
                <div><a href="index.htm"><img src="images/logo.gif"
                    width="357" height="78" alt="" border="0" /></a></div>
                <div id="a5-login">
                    <span style="float:left;"><a href="x.htm"><img src=
                        "images/reseller-button.gif" width="33"
                        height="23" alt="" border="0" /></a></span>
```

```
                    <a href="x.htm" class="linklist1"><b>Reseller Login
                        </b><br />
                    Forgot Password?</a>
                </div>
                <div id="a5-call">
                    <span style="float:left;padding-right:6px;"><a
                        href="x.htm"><img src="images/photo-header-
                        right.jpg" width="58" height="64" alt=""
                        border="0" /></a></span>
                    <div style="margin-top:8px;">
                        <span style="font: 14px Arial, Helvetica,
                            sans-serif;"><b>Need Help?</b></span><br />
                        Call us at<br />
                        1-800-555-5555
                    </div>
                </div>
            </div>
        </div>
    <!-- ###### header end ###### -->
    <!-- ###### left column start ###### -->
                <div id="a5-column-left">
                    <div id="date">
                        January 31, 2006
                    </div>
                    <div id="formsearch" class="color-1-text-13">
                        <form method="post" action="x.htm" name="search"
                            style="margin-top:0px;">
                            <b>Keyword Search</b>
                            <div style="padding:5px 0px 10px 0px;"><input
                                type="text" size="15" name="keywords"
                                value="View All Titles" /></div>
                            <b>Categories</b>
                            <div style="padding:5px 0px 15px 0px;">
                            <select name="categories" size="1">
                                <option value="All">Select Category
                                    </option>
                                <option value="sample">This is a sample
                                    entry</option>
                            </select>
                            </div>
                            <input type="image" src="images/
                                button-search.gif" />
                        </form>
                    </div>
```

```
            <div id="a5-column-left-content">
                <div style="padding:15px 0px 10px 0px;color:
                    #ffffff;"><span class="color-1-text-14"><b>
                    Duis autem vel</b></span> eum iriure dolor in
                    hendrerit in vulputate velit esse molestie
                    consequat, vel illum dolore eu feugiat nulla.
                    MORE</div>
                <div style="padding:10px 0px 10px 0px;color:
                    #ffffff;"><a href="x.htm"><img src="images/
                    banner-left-bottom.jpg" width="180"
                    height="96" alt="" border="0" /></a></div>
                <div id="a5-copyright">
                    &copy; copyright 2006 | your company | all
                        rights reserved
                </div>
            </div>
        </div>
<!-- ###### left column end ###### -->
<!-- ###### right column start ###### -->
        <div id="a5-column-right">
            <div id="a5-menu-box">
                <div id="a5-menu">
                       
                    <a href="index.htm">menu item 1</a>  
                        .  
                    <a href="menu-item-2.htm">longer menu item 2
                        </a>  .  
                    <a href="menu-item-3.htm">menu item 3</a> 
                         .  
                    <a href="index.htm">menu item 4</a>  
                        .  
                    <a href="index.htm">menu item 5</a>  
                        .  
                </div>
            </div>
<!-- ###### column right left start ###### -->
            <div id="a5-column-left-full">
                <div id="a5-sl-title">
                    menu item 3
                </div>
                    Enter text here.
            </div>
```

```
<!-- ###### column right left end ###### -->
            </div>
<!-- ###### right column end ###### -->
        </div>
    </div>
    </body>
    </html>
```

There are two things to note about the code in Listing 11.6:

■ The right column is removed by eliminating all the code between the `column right right start` and `column right right end` comment tags.

■ Once the right column is removed, the center column can expand to the full width of the screen. Before it can do this, though, the `a5-column-rightleft-sl` container needs to be duplicated and named `a5-column-left-full`. The style then needs to be changed by removing the `margin-right` property so the new container can expand all the way to the right edge of the screen. The `left` and `right` padding properties and values need to remain in the rule so the text in the container does not touch the left and right edges.

SUMMARY

Overall, the structure and CSS used in this design is a hybrid of the designs explained in Chapters 9 and 10. Several characteristics make it unique, though. Because it contains considerably more content, this design requires more rules to be created. Another difference is the homepage outputs products, which use a wrapping <DIV> technique that can be used in various sites and circumstances to output content in a similar "portfolio" manner. The final major difference of this design from the other chapters is that the menu is given a limited amount of space and is aligned horizontally rather than vertically. Therefore, the design relies on the search form in the left column to drive the majority of content. While not all sites will look and function similarly to the one in this chapter, elements of it can always be copied and modified to work in another design.

CHAPTER 12

CASE STUDY: FULL-HEIGHT THREE-COLUMN LAYOUT

Since the mid-1990s, creating a three-column table-based layout in XHTML, where all three columns have their own background colors that run the same height, has been an easily accomplished, widely used technique. As one column is increased in height, the other two change accordingly, maintaining the same colors. In CSS, however, it takes some maneuvering to modify the code because elements that are assigned absolute positioning or are floated fall outside the normal document flow, meaning they are not controlled by parent elements. In other words, the background colors/images in each column won't necessarily be at the same height, depending on whether additional content is added to any column. Fortunately, there is a solution to this problem.

This chapter outlines the design structure that A5design has created for its clients. It is a simple, clean, hack-free solution that is used in many of the CSS designs included in this book. Following are some of the requirements it satisfies:

- The design can be changed easily from a fixed to a liquid design and vice versa. The design explained in this chapter was created for a 1024 × 768 resolution.

- A footer is included at the bottom of the three columns.

- No matter the height of any column, the colors of all three columns will run from the top of the page down to the footer.

Design 131 Example

The design explained in this chapter is design 131 online (photo credits: www.idlerphotography.com and www.gooligoo.com).

UNDERSTANDING THE DESIGN'S STRUCTURE

Figure 12.1 illustrates the design explained in this chapter. As with the previous three case studies, it is created to function as a fixed or liquid design. Basic fundamental differences, however, allow it to work unlike many other CSS templates. These differences, which include a couple more <DIV> containers and a new core framework, are explained later in this chapter.

Figure 12.1
The full-height three-column design explained in this chapter.
© 2014 Cengage Learning.

Reasoning Behind Guides and the Creating of Slices in the Photoshop File

There are 13 slices used from the Photoshop file to create the images for the homepage design. Figure 12.2 shows all the slices used in the file. It also outlines the 10 most important guides and slices necessary for constructing the design with XHTML and CSS.

Following are explanations of the guides and slices illustrated in Figure 12.2:

- The guide to the left of number 1 is used to separate the left column from the center column.

- The guide to the left of number 2 is used to separate the center column from the right column.

Figure 12.2
Ten of the most important guides and slices used to build the design in this chapter.
© 2014 Cengage Learning.

- The guide below number 3 is used to differentiate the header from the content below it.

- The slice to the left of number 4 is very important in understanding this new design technique because it will be repeated as a background image for the entire height of the left column.

- The slice to the right of number 5 is similar to the slice represented in number 4. It will be repeated on the right side from the top of the design all the way to the footer. It illustrates the flexibility of this design technique because the background color does not necessarily have to extend the full column width, which is represented by number 2. This technique allows for the text to appear as though it is layered over the center column's color, even though, technically, it is included in the right column.

- The two slices below number 6 are used as the background images of the On and Off states of the menu items.

- The slice to the right of number 7 creates an image that is included in the right column. This image is noteworthy because it includes the background image, so when the image is layered over the background, the change between the two is seamless.

- The slice represented by number 8 is used to save a background image for the header. It repeats horizontally in the design for both fixed and liquid formats.

- The slice to the left of number 9 is similar to the slice to the right of number 7 in that it includes the background image, which is repeated for the full height of the left column.

- The slice to the right of number 10 is used as the background image in the title area for the second-level pages (see Figure 12.3).

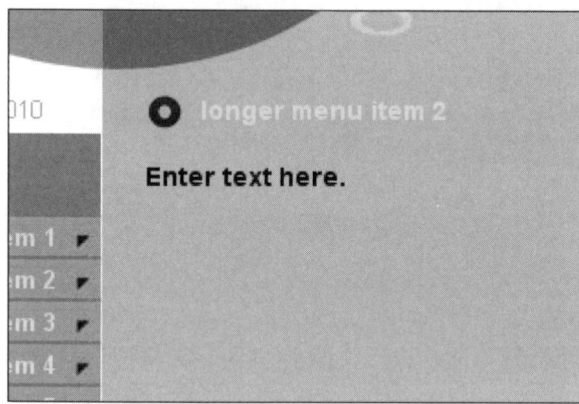

Figure 12.3
The background image of second-level titles that is saved from the homepage design.
© 2014 Cengage Learning.

Understanding the Placement of CSS Containers

There are 20 <DIV> tags used in this design. The number is higher than in the previous case studies in this book, mainly because this design structure requires a few more to accomplish its flexibility and functionality.

Following are explanations of the 10 most useful containers, shown in Figure 12.4:

1. The <DIV> tag to the top left of number 1 is used for centering the design in IE 5 and 5.5.

2. The <DIV> nested inside number 1, represented by number 2, illustrates the a5-body container that is used to control, among other things, the width of the design.

3. Number 3 illustrates the a5-bg-left <DIV> that is nested inside the a5-body <DIV>. This container is used to run a background image down the left side of the entire design, no matter what element is layered over it.

4. Number 4 represents the a5-bg-right container that runs a background image down the right side of the entire design.

5. The <DIV> that contains number 5 represents the header row that is positioned across the top of the design.

6. Number 6 illustrates the left column of the design.

7. Number 7 points out the <DIV> that is used for the entire area to the right of the left column. This area contains both the center and right columns.

8. Number 8 is the right column that is nested inside the number 7 container. It is then floated to the right.

9. The container represented by number 9 is used as the footer area.

10. Number 10 represents a <DIV> tag that is used for the most complex nested container, which is used for the menu.

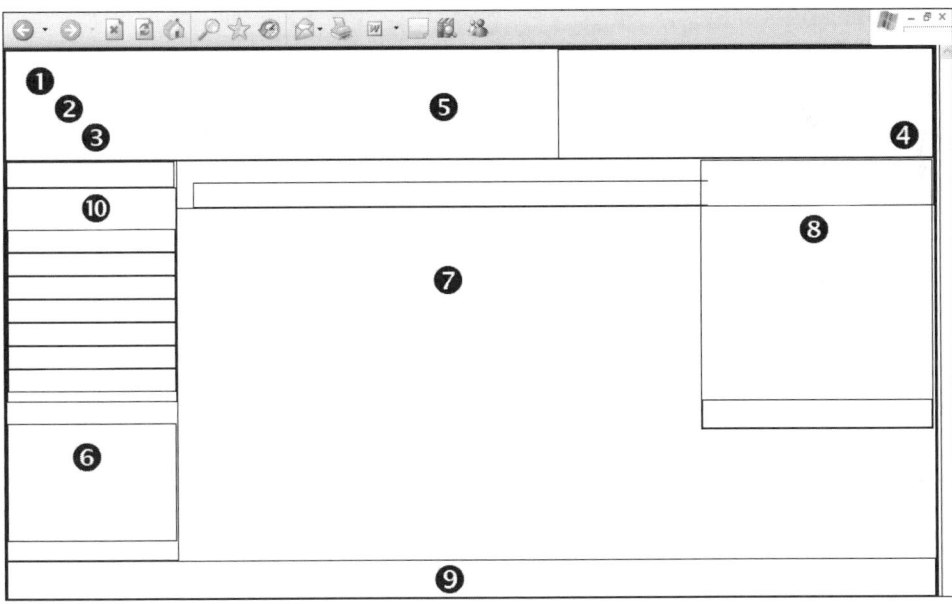

Figure 12.4
Ten of the most important containers used to build the design.
© 2014 Cengage Learning.

Building the Structure

Following are the steps for building the design. It is assumed that the Photoshop file has already been created or customized and the designer needs only to position the images and text.

Creating the XHTML and CSS Framework

The first step in building the design is to create the XHTML framework and initial CSS containers. Listing 12.1 is the code that is used to output the page shown in Figure 12.5.

Figure 12.5
Basic XHTML and CSS framework for the design.

© 2014 Cengage Learning.

Listing 12.1   Code for Figure 12.5

```
<!DOCTYPE html PUBLIC "-//W3C//DTD XHTML 1.0 Transitional//EN"
    "DTD/xhtml1-transitional.dtd">
<html xmlns="http://www.w3.org/1999/xhtml" xml:lang="en"
lang="en"><head><title>Design 131</title>
<meta http-equiv="Content-Type" content="text/html;
    charset=iso-8859-1" />
<style type="text/css">
/* ++++++++++ global general styles start ++++++++++*/
html, body {
    margin:0px;
    padding:0px;
    font: 12.8pt arial, helvetica, sans-serif;
    color:#000000;
    }
/* ++++++++++ global general styles end ++++++++++*/
/* ++++++++++ global structure styles start ++++++++++*/
.a5-bg-left {
    width:100%;
    margin-bottom:-10px;
background:url(images/bg-left-column.gif) repeat-y left top;
    }
```

```css
.a5-bg-right {
    width:100%;
    background:url(images/bg-right-column.gif) repeat-y right top;
    }
#a5-body-center {
    text-align:left;
    }
#a5-body {
    position: relative;
    width: 1000px; /* change this to a specific amount for a fixed
    design. E.g., 1000px. Or, it can be changed to a percentage, which
    will allow the design to be liquid */

/* remove these comment tags if the page is to be centered
    margin-left: auto;
    margin-right: auto;*/
    text-align:left;
    background:#7ED0D4 url(images/bg-right-column.gif) repeat-y right
        top;
    border:0px solid #000000;
    }
/* ++++++++++ global structure styles end ++++++++++*/
</style>
</head>
<body>
<div id="a5-body-center">
    <div id="a5-body">
        <div class="a5-bg-left">
        <div class="a5-bg-right">
            <b><span style="color:#ffffff;">The<br />
            content<br />
            will<br />
            be<br />
            added<br />
            here.</b><br /> </span>
        </div>
    </div>
</div>
</body>
</html>
```

There are several things to note about the code in Listing 12.1:

- The CSS style sheet is commented into two sections. The global general styles comment tags contain the general styles, such as the formatting of the <HTML> and <BODY> tags, hyperlinks, and fonts. The global structure styles comment tags include the styles used to define the structure of the design and elements included in that structure.

- Several rules define the <HTML> and <BODY> tags. The margin and padding properties are used to ensure that the design is placed in the very top-left corner of the browser with no space between the design and the edges. The default font style for the site is set using the shorthand FONT property. Defining the default font color is accomplished with the COLOR property. The background color also is assigned to ensure that all browsers display the same color, which is not always the case.

- The a5-body-center and a5-body rules are used to force the design to the left side of the browser screen with a fixed width of 1000 pixels. If the designer wants to fill the full width of the screen, the value of 1000px needs to be changed to 100%. However, if the designer wants to justify the design to the left, the value of the text-align property in the a5-body-center rule needs to be changed from center to left. The margin-left and margin-right properties in the a5-body rule ensure that the extra white space is split evenly on both sides.

- The big difference at this stage, compared to the previous case studies in Chapters 9, 10, and 11, is the addition of the a5-bg-left and a5-bg-right classes and <DIV> containers. These provide relatively positioned containers for the entire site to be nested within. The a5-bg-left <DIV> runs its background image down the left side, while the a5- bg-right runs its background image down the right side. Thus, rather than using browser-generated colors, the background images, which are found at the bottom-left and bottom-right corners (see Figure 12.6) of the Photoshop design, are repeated.

- A background color is added to the a5-body container to give the center column color.

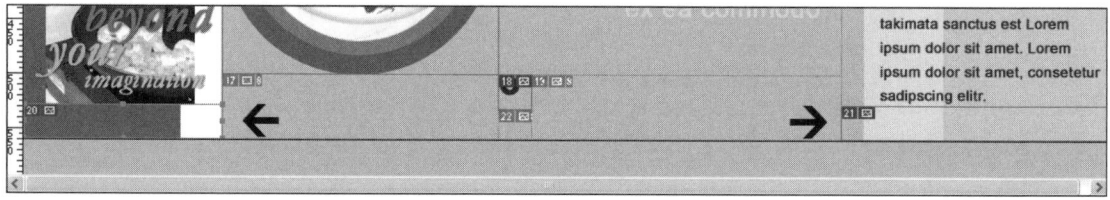

Figure 12.6
Slices, indicated by the left and right arrows, are used to create the left and right background images that repeat down the design.
© 2014 Cengage Learning.

The `a5-bg-left` rule has the `margin-bottom` property added with a value of `-10px`. This ensures that the background images will not extend past the footer in some browsers. When the content is added to the core area, without any columns or positioning, it shows that the background images repeat vertically (refer to Figure 12.5). If the length of the content is increased, the background images repeat accordingly (see Figure 12.7).

Figure 12.7
Text added to the design to illustrate how both background images will repeat vertically.
© 2014 Cengage Learning.

Adding the Rows and Columns to the Framework

Unlike the previous case studies, the row and column framework of this design is explained up front because it all works together to create a flexible design. Once understood, the content just needs to be added into these containers. Listing 12.2 is the code that is added to create the updated page in Figure 12.8.

Bold Text = New Code

The newly added code is bolded to differentiate it from the existing code that is being built upon in this case study.

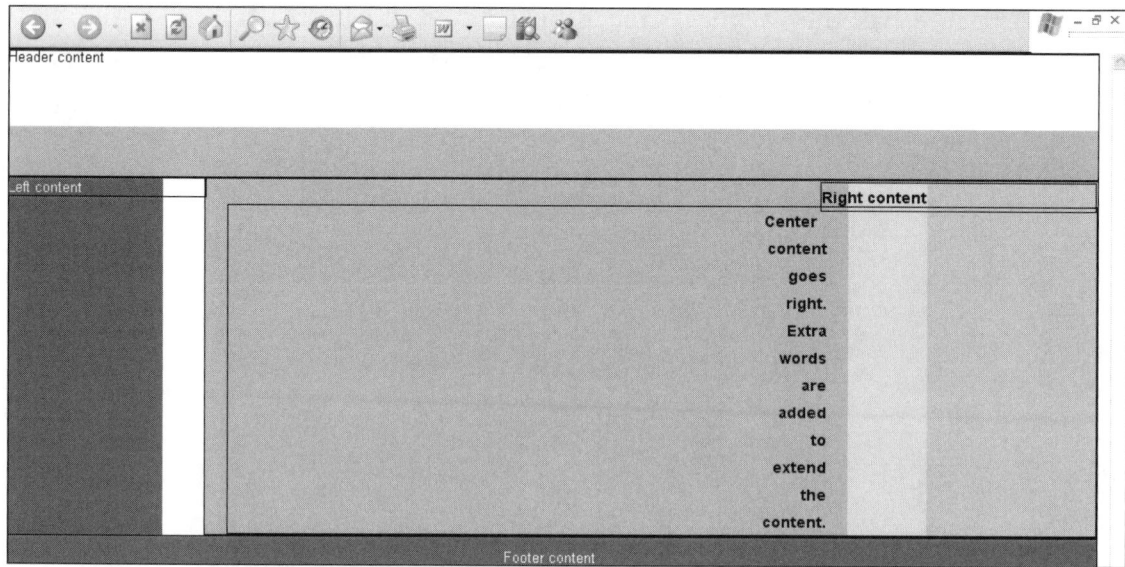

Figure 12.8
Row and column framework without content added to it.

© 2014 Cengage Learning.

Listing 12.2   Code for Figure 12.8

```
<!DOCTYPE html PUBLIC "-//W3C//DTD XHTML 1.0 Transitional//EN"
    "DTD/xhtml1-transitional.dtd">
<html xmlns="http://www.w3.org/1999/xhtml" xml:lang="en"
lang="en"><head><title>Design 131</title>
<meta http-equiv="Content-Type" content="text/html;
    charset=iso-8859-1" />
<style type="text/css">
/* ++++++++++ global general styles start ++++++++++*/
html, body {
    margin:0px;
    padding:0px;
    font: 12.8pt arial, helvetica, sans-serif;
    color:#000000;
    }
/* ++++++++++ global general styles end ++++++++++*/
/* ++++++++++ global structure styles start ++++++++++*/
.a5-bg-left {
    width:100%;
    margin-bottom:-10px;
    background:url(images/bg-left-column.gif) repeat-y left top;
    }
```

```
.a5-bg-right {
    width:100%;
    background:url(images/bg-right-column.gif) repeat-y right top;
    }
#a5-body-center {
    text-align:left;
    }
#a5-body {
    position: relative;
    width: 1000px; /* change this to a specific amount for a fixed
        design. E.g., 1000px. Or, it can be changed to a percentage,
        which will allow the design to be liquid */

/* remove these comment tags if the page is to be centered
    margin-left: auto;
    margin-right: auto;*/
    text-align:left;
    background:#7ED0D4 url(images/bg-right-column.gif) repeat-y right
        top;
    border:0px solid #000000;
    }
#a5-header {
    position:relative;
    left:0px;
    top:0px;
    height:117px;
    background: url(images/bg-header.gif) repeat-x;
    border:1px solid #000000;
    }
#a5-column-left {
    float:left;
    width:181px;
    height:auto;
    border:1px solid #000000;
    }
#a5-body-content {
    position:relative;
    margin-left:181px;
    border:1px solid #000000;
    }
    #a5-column-center {
        position:relative;
```

```
                left:0px;
                top:0px;
                margin:23px 0px 0px 20px;
                font: bold 10.8pt arial, helvetica, sans-serif;
                line-height:19pt;
                border:1px solid #000000;
                }
        #a5-column-right {
                float:right;
                width:250px;
                margin-top:-23px;
                text-align:left;
                border:1px solid #000000;
                }
    #a5-footer {
            clear:both;
            text-align:center;
            line-height:35px;
            background:#4A7A7D;
            border:1px solid #000000;
            }


    /* ++++++++++ global structure styles end ++++++++++*/
    </style>
    </head>
    <body>
    <div id="a5-body-center">
        <div id="a5-body">
            <div class="a5-bg-left">
            <div class="a5-bg-right">
<!-- ###### header start ###### -->
                <div id="a5-header">
                Header content
                </div>
<!-- ###### header end ###### -->
<!-- ###### left column start ###### -->
                <div id="a5-column-left">
                    <span style="color:#ffffff;">Left content</span>
                </div>
<!-- ###### left column end ###### -->
<!-- ###### body content start ###### -->
```

```
                <div id="a5-body-content">
                    <div id="a5-column-center">
                        <div id="a5-column-right">
                            Right content
                        </div>
                        <div style="margin-right:246px;text-align:right;">
                            Center<br />content<br />goes<br />right.<br />
                                Extra<br />words<br />are<br />added<br />
                                to<br />extend<br />the<br />content.
                        </div>
                    </div>
                </div>
<!-- ##### footer start ##### -->
                    <div id="a5-footer"><span style="color:#ffffff;">Footer
                        content</span></div>
<!-- ##### footer end ##### -->
<!-- ##### body content end ##### -->
            </div>
            </div>
        </div>
    </div>
    </body>
    </html>
```

There are several things to note about the code in Listing 12.2:

- The `a5-header` row is the first structural element to be added. It is given relative positioning so it expands the full width of the page. It also is assigned a height of 117 pixels so the container collapses perfectly around the contents in all browsers. A horizontally repeating background is added to fill the space between the images and fill extra space if the design is changed to a liquid format.

- The `a5-column-left` rule floats the left column to the left side under the header row. The width of the column is set to 181 pixels.

Borders Set to 1 for Demonstration Purposes

The border of the various containers is set to 1 for demonstrational purposes for this step. They are reset to 0 in the final code.

- The `a5-body-content` is added under the header area to contain the center and right columns. It is given relative positioning to fill the width of the page. It is assigned a left margin of 181 pixels, so any content in it abuts the left column. One of the tricks to this design is to set the right margin of the center content at the local level. This ensures that the content does not cross over into the right column because it is nested inside this container. The right margin for the center area is set at 246 pixels. To position the content that will be added to this container, the top margin is set to 23 pixels, and the left is set to 20 pixels.

Right Column Set to 250 Pixels

Technically, the right column is 250 pixels wide, so the right margin of the center content should be set to 250, instead of 246, to avoid overlapping. In this design, however, 246 pixels is acceptable.

- As mentioned in the previous note, the a5-column-right container is floated to the right inside the a5-column-center <DIV>. By floating it to the right and positioning the bg-right-column.gif image in the a5-bg-right container to the right, the background image of the column and the background of the image will always align with one another, whether the design is fixed or liquid. Because the center container is given a top margin of 23 pixels, the right column has the top margin set to −23 pixels, so it will be mortised with the header row. This is why the words "center content" and "right content" are set at different heights in Figure 12.8. The words also are not aligned vertically because the right column is set to 250 pixels, while the right margin of the center content is set to 246 pixels, as mentioned earlier.

- The a5-footer row is added outside the a5-body-content container, with the clear property set to both. This keeps the content in the a5-left-column and a5-center-column containers from crossing over the row.

Populating the Header, Footer, and Columns with Content

Once the framework of the design has been added, the designer need only populate the areas with the appropriate content. Because this styling is very similar to the previous three case studies, the discussion for Listing 12.3 is limited to unique aspects of this design. Figure 12.9 is the completed homepage design that is outlined in Listing 12.3.

Figure 12.9
The completed design after the various containers have been populated and styled.

Bold Text = New Code

The newly added code is bolded to differentiate it from the existing code that is being built upon in this example.

Listing 12.3   Code for Figure 12.9

```
<!DOCTYPE html PUBLIC "-//W3C//DTD XHTML 1.0 Transitional//EN"
    "DTD/xhtml1-transitional.dtd">
<html xmlns="http://www.w3.org/1999/xhtml" xml:lang="en"
lang="en"><head><title>Design 131</title>
<meta http-equiv="Content-Type" content="text/html;
    charset=iso-8859-1" />
<style type="text/css">
/* ++++++++++ global general styles start ++++++++++*/
html, body {
    margin:0px;
    padding:0px;
    font: 12.8pt arial, helvetica, sans-serif;
    color:#000000;
    }
```

```
a:link { color:#D0FAFC; }
a:visited { color:#D0FAFC; }
a:active { color:#D0FAFC; }
a:hover { color:#000000; }

a.linklist1:link { text-decoration:none;color:#E9DF40;}
a.linklist1:visited { text-decoration:none;color:#E9DF40;}
a.linklist1:active { text-decoration:none;color:#E9DF40;}
a.linklist1:hover { text-decoration:underline;color:#ffffff;}
 .color-1-text-98 {
    font-family:arial, helvetica, sans-serif;
    font-size:9.8pt;
    color: #16C7C1;
    }
 .color-2-text-8 {
    font-family:arial, helvetica, sans-serif;
    font-size:8pt;
    color: #D0FAFC;
    }
 .color-2-text-10 {
    font-family:arial, helvetica, sans-serif;
    font-size:10pt;
    color: #D0FAFC;
    }
 .color-2-text-18 {
    font-family:arial, helvetica, sans-serif;
    font-size:18pt;
    color: #D0FAFC;
    }
 .color-3-text-88 {
    font-family:arial, helvetica, sans-serif;
    font-size:8.8pt;
    color: #ffffff;
    }
/* ++++++++++ global general styles end ++++++++++*/
/* ++++++++++ global structure styles start ++++++++++*/
.a5-bg-left {
    width:100%;
    margin-bottom:-10px;
    background:url(images/bg-left-column.gif) repeat-y left top;
    }
.a5-bg-right {
    width:100%;
```

```
    background:url(images/bg-right-column.gif) repeat-y right top;
    }
#a5-body-center {
    text-align:left;
    }
#a5-body {
    position: relative;
    width: 1000px; /* change this to a specific amount for a fixed
            design. E.g., 1000px. Or, it can be changed to a percentage,
            which will allow the design to be liquid */
/* remove these comment tags if the page is to be centered
    margin-left: auto;
    margin-right: auto;*/
    text-align:left;
    background:#7ED0D4 url(images/bg-right-column.gif) repeat-y right
        top;
    border:0px solid #000000;
    }
#a5-header {
    position:relative;
    left:0px;
    top:0px;
    height:117px;
    background: url(images/bg-header.gif) repeat-x;
    border:0px solid #000000;
    }
    #a5-header-right {
        position:absolute;
        right:0px;
        top:0px;
        height:117px;
        border:0px solid #000000;
        }
#a5-column-left {
    float:left;
    width:181px;
    border:0px solid #000000;
    }
        #a5-date {
            text-align:center;
            background:#ffffff;
            vertical-align:50%;
            line-height:26px;
            }
```

```
#a5-menu {
    width:181px;
    padding:44px 0px 10px 0px;
    font:bold 12.8pt arial, helvetica, sans-serif;
    background: url(images/bg-menu.gif) repeat-y 0px 0px;
    }
#a5-menu a {
    display:block;
    text-align:left;
    line-height:23px;
    vertical-align:50%;
    text-align:right;
    padding:0px 25px 0px 10px;
    text-decoration:none;
    background: url(images/bg-menu-off.jpg) no-repeat 0px 0px;
    color:#DEEFF0;
    }
#a5-menu a:hover {
    background: url(images/bg-menu-on.jpg) no-repeat 0px 0px;
    color:#ffffff;
    }
#a5-photo-bottom-left {
    margin:23px 0px 20px 0px;
    border:0px solid #000000;
    }
#a5-body-content {
    position:relative;
    margin-left:181px;
    border:0px solid #000000;
    }
#a5-column-center {
    position:relative;
    left:0px;
    top:0px;
    margin:23px 0px 0px 20px;
    font: bold 10.8pt arial, helvetica, sans-serif;
    line-height:19pt;
    border:0px solid #000000;
    }
#a5-column-right {
    float:right;
    width:250px;
```

```
            margin-top:-23px;
            text-align:left;
            border:0px solid #000000;
            }
    #a5-bottom-right-text {
            font: bold 12.8pt arial, helvetica, sans-serif;
            line-height:14pt;
            padding:0px 10px 10px 30px;
            }
#a5-footer {
    clear:both;
    text-align:center;
    line-height:35px;
    background:#4A7A7D;
    border:0px solid #000000;
    }
/* ++++++++++ global structure styles end ++++++++++*/
</style>
</head>
<body>
<div id="a5-body-center">
    <div id="a5-body">
        <div class="a5-bg-left">
        <div class="a5-bg-right">
<!-- ###### header start ###### -->
            <div id="a5-header">
                <div><img src="images/header-left.jpg" width="557"
                    height="117" alt="" border="0" /></div>
                <div id="a5-header-right"><a href="index.htm"><img
                    src="images/header-right.gif" width="403"
                    height="117" alt="" border="0" /></a></div>
            </div>
<!-- ###### header end ###### -->
<!-- ###### left column start ###### -->
            <div id="a5-column-left">
                <div id="a5-date" class="color-1-text-98">September
                    31, 2010</div>
                <div id="a5-menu">
                    <a href="index.htm">menu item 1</a>
                    <a href="menu-item-2.htm">longer menu item 2</a>
                    <a href="menu-item-3.htm">menu item 3</a>
                    <a href="index.htm">menu item 4</a>
```

```
                <a href="index.htm">menu item 5</a>
                <a href="index.htm">menu item 6</a>
                <a href="index.htm">menu item 7</a>
            </div>
            <div id="a5-photo-bottom-left"><a href="index.htm">
                <img src="images/photo-bottom-left.jpg"
                width="180" height="125" alt="" border="0"
                /></a></div>
        </div>
<!-- ###### left column end ###### -->
<!-- ###### body content start ###### -->
                <div id="a5-body-content">
                    <div id="a5-column-center">
                        <div id="a5-column-right">
                            <div><img src="images/image-right-column-
                                top.gif" width="250" height="88" alt=""
                                border="0" /></div>
                            <div><img src="images/image-right-column-
                                middle.jpg" width="250" height="169"
                                alt="" border="0" /></div>
                            <div id="a5-bottom-right-text">
At vero eos et accusam et justo duo dolores et ea rebum. Stet clita
    kasd gubergren, no sea takimata sanctus est Lorem ipsum dolor sit
    amet. Lorem ipsum dolor sit amet, consetetur sadipscing elitr.
                            </div>
                        </div>
                        <div style="margin-right:246px;text-align:right;">
<span class="color-2-text-18">Duis autem vel eum iriure dolor in
    </span> hendrerit in vulputate velit esse molestie consequat, vel
    illum dolore eu feugiat nulla facilisis at vero eros et accumsan
    et iusto odio dignissim qui blandit praesent luptatum <span
    style="float:left;padding:10px 10px 10px 0px;margin-left:-20px;">
    <img src="images/photo-center-middle.jpg" width="256" height="256"
    alt="" border="0" /></span>zzril delenit augue duis dolore te
    feugait nulla facilisi. Lorem ipsum dolor sit amet, consectetuer
    adipiscing elit, sed diam nonummy nibh euismod tincidunt ut
    laoreet dolore magna aliquam erat olutpat. <span class="color-2-
    text-18">Ut wisi enim ad minim eniam, quis nostrud exerci tation
    ullamcorper suscipit lobortis nisl ut aliquip ex ea commodo</span>
                        </div>
                    </div>
                </div>
```

```
<!-- ###### footer start ###### -->
            <div id="a5-footer"><div style="margin:0px 0px 10px 0px;
                font-weight:bold;" class="color-2-text-10">
                    <a href="index.htm" class="linklist1">menu item 1
                        </a>  .  <a href="menu-
                        item-2.htm" class="linklist1">longer menu item
                        2</a>  .  <a href="menu-
                        item-3.htm" class="linklist1">menu item 3</a>
                          .  <a href="index.htm"
                        class="linklist1">menu item 4</a>  
                        .  <a href="index.htm" class=
                        "linklist1">menu item 5</a>  . 
                         <a href="index.htm" class="linklist1">
                        menu item 6</a>  .  <a
                        href="index.htm" class="linklist1">menu
                        item 7</a><br />
        <span class="color-2-text-8">&copy; copyright 2006 | your company |
            all rights reserved</span></div></div>
<!-- ###### footer end ###### -->
<!-- ###### body content end ###### -->
            </div>
          </div>
        </div>
    </div>
    </body>
    </html>
```

There are several things to note about the code in Listing 12.3:

- The linklist1 rules are added to style the second menu that runs horizontally in the footer. This is the same menu that is included in the left column. It is added to increase usability of the design by providing navigation at the bottom of the page so the user does not have to scroll back up the page.

- The a5-menu container is given a background image that is layered over the image that is repeated for the entire left column. Then each menu item is assigned yet another background image when an item is moused on and off. Not only is this layering seamless, but it also requires less download time because all three images are of nominal file size.

- The a5-bottom-right-text container is assigned a left margin of 30 pixels to position the text to the right of the background color in the center column. Because this color is included in the right column background, which creates an overlapping effect, the text needs to be positioned differently if it is to remain over just the right two colors.

CONSTRUCTING SECOND-LEVEL PAGES

Similar to the previous three case studies, the homepage is reused and customized for secondary pages. The technique is the same, except for a couple of differences. One difference is that the 246-pixel right margin of the center column is removed so the text will run the full width of the content area. The second modification is that the a5-bg-right container is renamed a5-bg-right-sl for the full-page version, which is the Menu Item 3 page. Once it is renamed, the a5-bg-right-sl rule is added, which uses a background color, rather than an image, to populate the body of the page (see Figure 12.10).

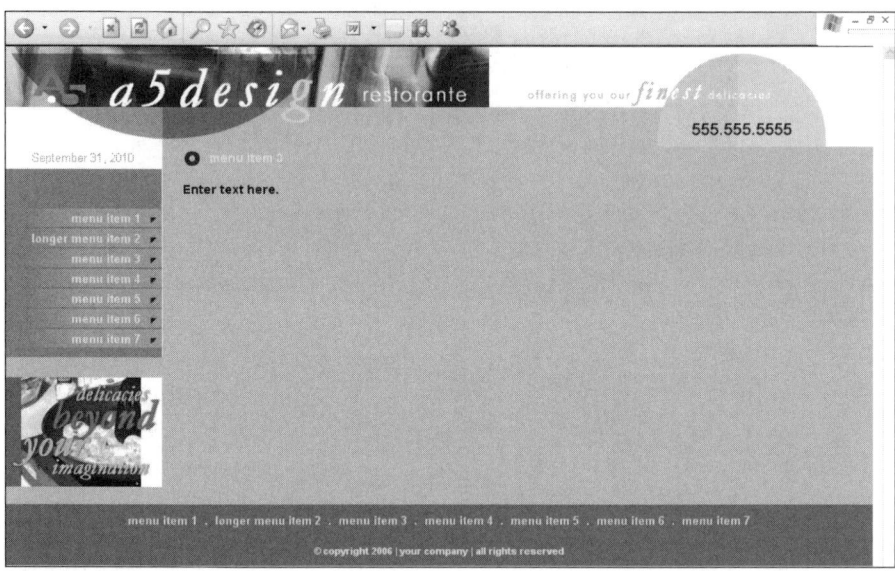

Figure 12.10
The Menu Item 3 template that has the repeating right background image replaced with a CSS-generated color that fills the page.
© 2014 Cengage Learning.

SUMMARY

The design explained in this case study is a succinct way to create a new design that has the background colors extended throughout all three columns. The coding is simple to understand and use, requiring no hacks or JavaScript. Not only are background images used to accomplish this technique, but also the core structure of the design is written to allow for content that is scalable and will not run beyond the footer. As with other designs in this book, it allows for the page to be either a fixed-width or a liquid design. Of all the design structures explained and included in this book, this one will, most likely, be the most widely used because of its flexibility and scalability.

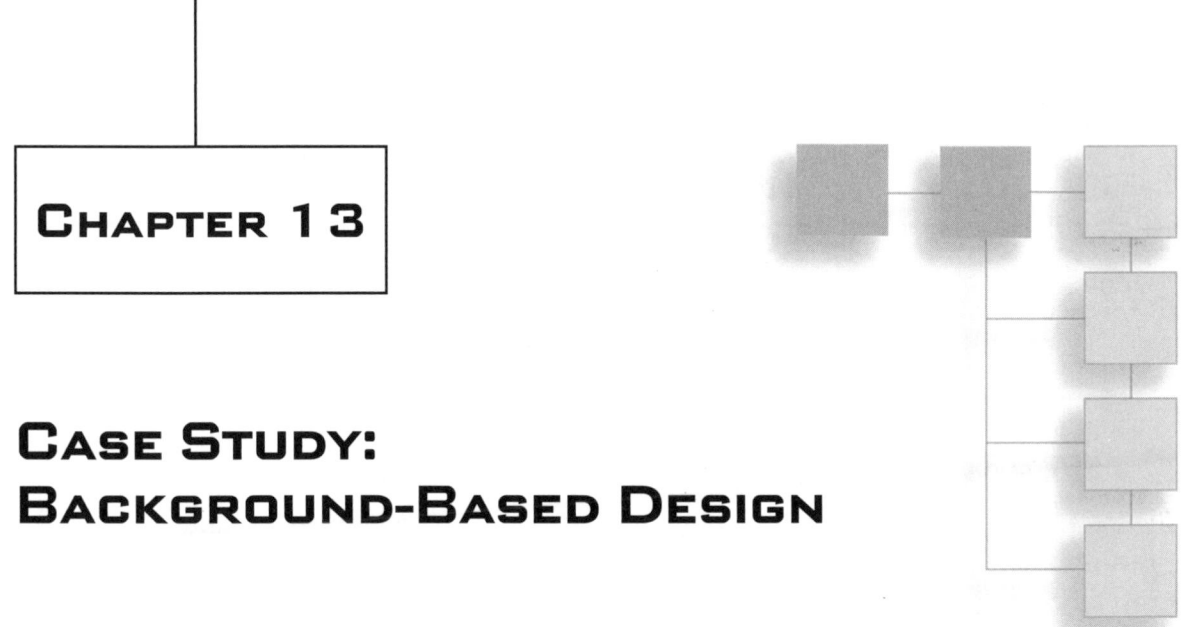

CHAPTER 13

CASE STUDY:
BACKGROUND-BASED DESIGN

Another method that allows a designer to be creative is to base a design largely around a background image. With such a design, the majority of graphical elements are included with the image itself. The main disadvantage to such a design is that the background image can be a larger download size. The advantage to this method is that the designer has more flexibility in terms of creating imagery and a layout that isn't limited as much by XHTML or CSS. Another advantage is that a designer can create designs that can have their look and feel easily modified by replacing only one image, whether on the homepage or on second-level pages.

The design in this chapter is not only used to create a mood with the graphics, but the homepage image also provides for the boxes in which to place the content. The downside to this design is that the sections are not scalable. In other words, if the client wants to expand the content, the imagery, along with the XHTML and CSS, would need to be modified so that the text did not flow outside of the boxes. The upside is the boxes can look much more attractive because the designer isn't constricted as much by having to use various images, such as background or nested images, to create the look and feel.

This design structure isn't robust or flexible enough for many sites. There are, however, an increasing number of clients who request that their sites use large, powerful graphics to communicate, rather than relying just on text. For clients such as these, this type of design may very well satisfy their needs.

Background Image Can Have Everything Layered Over It

The use of background image designs is not limited to the technique used in this chapter. Another possibility is to simply place a background image in the page and to layer images and text over it. The graphical elements can have their opacity changed so they appear somewhat transparent, and thus a part of the image. But, even better, the design can also use 24-bit PNG images over it, which allows for very clean transparent images over the background image. This not only allows for the layered images to be easily replaced, but the background image can also be easily replaced without affecting the layered elements.

Design 141 Example

The design explained in this chapter is design 141 online (photo credits: www.ronsternimages.com and www.a5design.com).

UNDERSTANDING THE DESIGN'S STRUCTURE

Figure 13.1 represents the background-based design explained in this chapter. Unlike the previous case studies in this book, the homepage of this design not only uses a background image for the majority of the imagery of the design, but it also uses fixed boxes for the content. Because the boxes are not scalable, the text inside them has absolute positioning assigned to it. Normally, such positioning might be a problem because it does not adhere to document flow, which can change how the text in other areas relates to increased or decreased content.

The majority of the text is still provided as XHTML text so that search engines can read it. Because most elements of the imagery, including photos layered over photos and the larger text, are part of the background image, the user will not be able to click on them. This is why another design trick is employed. Spacer GIFs, friend of the table-based designer, are sized, positioned, and hyperlinked accordingly over the areas of the design that need to be clickable. It's similar to the older method of creating "hot spots" with image mapping.

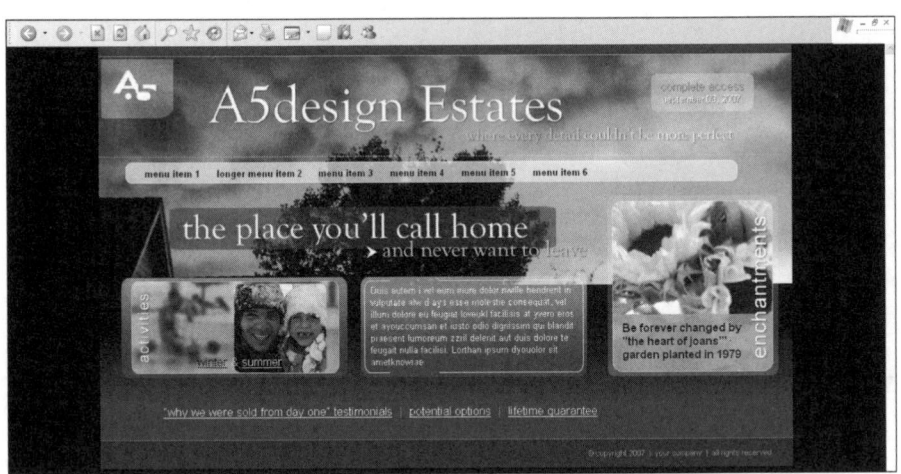

Figure 13.1
The background-based design explained in this chapter.
© 2014 Cengage Learning.

Reasoning Behind Guides and the Creating of Slices in the Photoshop File

There is only one slice used for the homepage file of the design and two slices used for the secondary page design. Slice number 1 in Figure 13.2 illustrates the file that is used to provide the homepage images.

The goal of this design is to create a more graphically advanced design than with the designs in the previous case studies. To attain this for the current site, the design uses transparent images and curved corners coupled with various layered images. While much of this design could be accomplished using techniques explained previously in this book, a more simple design structure was used to provide the reader with another possibility.

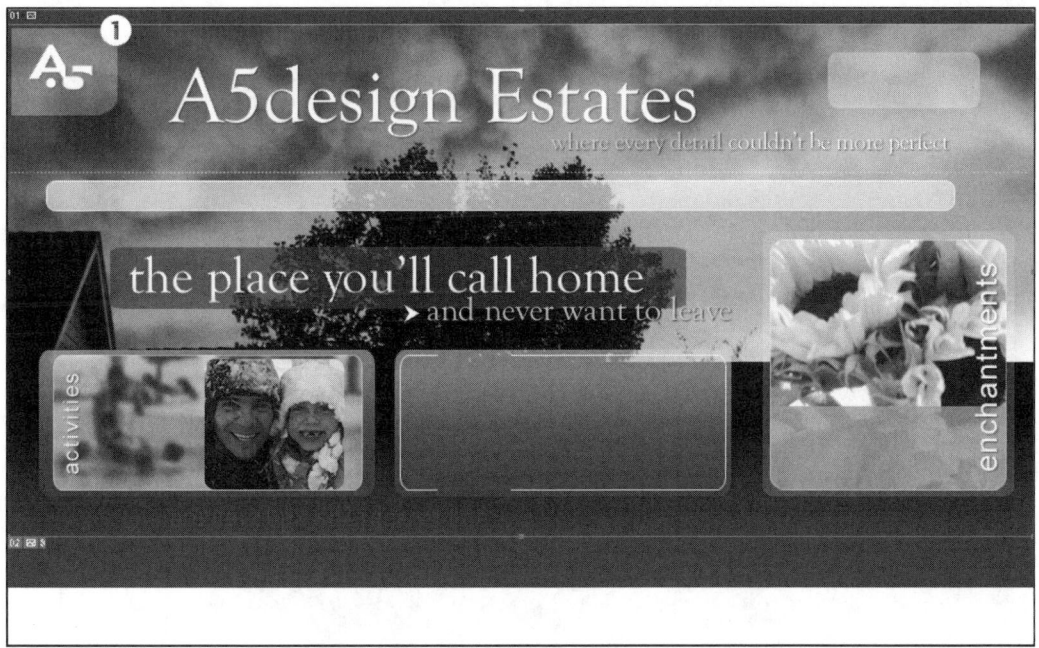

Figure 13.2
The only slice, identified by number 1, that is used to build the homepage design.
© 2014 Cengage Learning.

The one thing to note about Figure 13.2, other than there is only one slice, is that the bottom of the design uses a gradation that eventually turns into the color that is used for the background color of the design. This layout method allows the designer to simply set the background color of the page, identified by number 2 in Figure 13.3, to coincide with the color that is set just before the bottom of the slice is reached, identified by number 1 in the same figure.

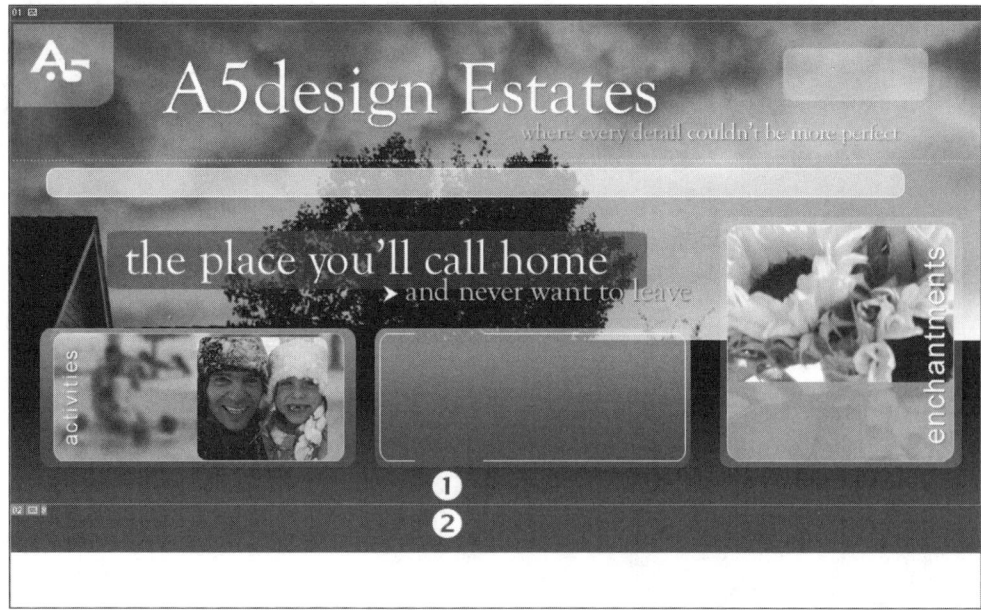

Figure 13.3
The colors on both sides of the bottom of the slice, represented by numbers 1 and 2, are designed
to be the same color, providing a seamless transition of images.

© 2014 Cengage Learning.

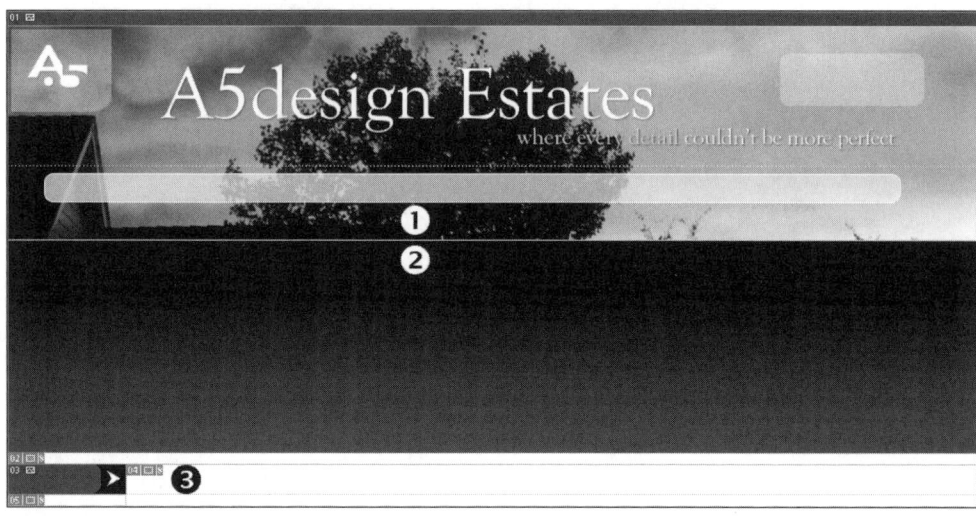

Figure 13.4
The blending technique used for the homepage in Figure 13.3 is employed exactly the same way for the
second-level design.

© 2014 Cengage Learning.

This method of blending colors of an image into the background color is also used for the secondary page. Figure 13.4 shows how the colors were blended into the black below the trees, number 1, with the background color of the page, number 2.

The other slice to note in the secondary-level page (see Figure 13.4) is just to the left of number 3. This slice is used as a background image for the page title <DIV>.

Understanding the Placement of CSS Containers

There are 18 <DIV> tags that are used to create the homepage layout of this design. Many of them serve the same basic purpose for the structure of the site, as they do in the case study in Chapter 12. The thing to note about this design is that the majority of them are assigned absolute positioning.

Following are explanations of the 10 most useful containers, shown in Figure 13.5:

- The <DIV> tag to the top left of number 1 is used for centering the design in IE 5 and 5.5. It also represents the top-left corner of the a5-body container that is used to control, among other things, the width of the design. Number 1 also points out where the "complete access" code is included for the top-right portion of the design.

- Number 2 is placed right above the a5-menu-box <DIV> it represents. This container not only controls the absolute placement of the menu, but it also includes a <DIV>, a5-menu, that is nested inside to provide the style for each menu item.

- The top-right <DIV> tag, a5-header-right, is illustrated by the number 3. This is a fixed area that is used for the login area of the site.

- Number 4 represents the header <DIV>, which contains the <DIV> tags that are illustrated by numbers 2 and 3.

- The top-left corner of the left column begins at number 5.

- Number 6 represents the right column of the design.

- Number 7 shows the container that includes the hyperlinked spacer.gif and "winter & summer" text in the left column. This container, as well as the ones used for the center column content (represented by number 8) and the right column content (represented by number 9), are assigned absolute positioning.

- The bottom text area is positioned using the <DIV> to the right of number 10.

Figure 13.5
Ten of the most important containers used to build the design.
© 2014 Cengage Learning.

BUILDING THE STRUCTURE

Following are the steps for building the design. It is assumed that the Photoshop file has already been created or customized and the designer just needs to position the images and text.

Creating the XHTML and CSS Framework

The first step in building the design is to create the XHTML framework and initial CSS containers. Listing 13.1 is the code that is used to output the page shown in Figure 13.6.

Figure 13.6
Basic XHTML and CSS framework for the design.

© 2014 Cengage Learning.

Listing 13.1   Code for Figure 13.6

```
<!DOCTYPE html PUBLIC "-//W3C//DTD XHTML 1.0 Transitional//EN"
DTD/xhtml1-transitional.dtd">
<html xmlns="http://www.w3.org/1999/xhtml" xml:lang="en"
lang="en"><head><title></title>
<meta http-equiv="Content-Type" content="text/html; charset=iso-8859-1" />
<style type="text/css">
  /* ++++++++++ global general styles start ++++++++++*/
  html, body {
    margin:0px;
    padding:0px;
    font:10pt arial, helvetica, sans-serif;
    background:#000000;
    color:#ffffff;
    }
  /* ++++++++++ global general styles end ++++++++++*/
  /* ++++++++++ global structure styles start ++++++++++*/
  #a5-body-center {
    text-align:center;
    }
  #a5-body {
    position:relative;
    width:1000px;
    margin-left:auto;
    margin-right:auto;
    text-align:left;
    background:#6A4203 url(images/bg-body.jpg) no-repeat;
    border:0px solid #ffffff;
    }
```

```
/* ++++++++++ global structure styles end ++++++++++*/
</style>
</head>
<body>
<div id="a5-body-center">
  <div id="a5-body">
  This is the main body area.
  </div>
</div>
</body>
</html>
```

There are several things to note about the code in Listing 13.1:

- The CSS style sheet is commented into two sections. The `global general styles` comment tags contain the general styles, such as the formatting of the `<HTML>` and `<BODY>` tags, hyperlinks, and fonts. The `global structure styles` comment tags include the styles used to define the structure of the design and elements included in that structure.

- Several rules define the `<HTML>` and `<BODY>` tags. The `margin` and `padding` properties are used to ensure that the design is placed in the very top-left corner of the browser, with no space between the design and the edges. The default font style for the site is set using the shorthand `FONT` property. Defining the default font color is accomplished with the `COLOR` property. The background color also is assigned to ensure that all browsers display the same color, which is not always the case.

- How this design differs from the others is that the majority of graphical elements are created using the background image. This image, `bg-body.jpg`, is declared in the `a5-body` rule. Figure 13.7 illustrates that when more content is added to the design, this image will begin to appear. The background color of `#6A4203` also is added to the rule. This is the color that is at the bottom of the `bg-body.jpg` image, which enables the two to blend into each other.

- The `a5-body-center` and `a5-body` rules are used to center the design in the browser window and to give it a fixed width of 1,000 pixels. If the designer wants to fill the full width of the screen for higher resolutions, the value of `1000px` needs to be changed to `100%`. If, however, the designer wants to simply justify the design to the left, the value of the `text-align` property in the `a5-body-center` rule needs to be changed from `center` to `left`. The `margin-left` and `margin-right` properties in the `a5-body` rule ensure that the extra white space is split evenly on both sides.

Figure 13.7
When content is added to the base code, the background image will begin to appear.
© 2014 Cengage Learning.

Adding the Header Area to the Framework

Depending on the design, the header area is usually the first area of content that needs to be added. This is certainly true for this case study. The header area not only contains the menu and the code for the login area, but it also takes up 220 pixels of vertical space with the design. Figure 13.8 shows the design with the header content, XHTML, and CSS added, which is included in Listing 13.2.

Figure 13.8
The design with the header content, XHTML, and CSS added.
© 2014 Cengage Learning.

New Code Is in Bold

> The newly added code is bolded to differentiate it from the existing code that is being built upon in this case study.

Listing 13.2   Code for Figure 13.8

```
<!DOCTYPE html PUBLIC "-//W3C//DTD XHTML 1.0 Transitional//EN" "DTD/xhtml1-
transitional.dtd">
<html xmlns="http://www.w3.org/1999/xhtml" xml:lang="en"
lang="en"><head><title></title>
<meta http-equiv="Content-Type" content="text/html; charset=iso-8859-1" />
<style type="text/css">
  /* ++++++++++ global general styles start ++++++++++*/
  html, body {
    margin:0px;
    padding:0px;
    font:10pt arial, helvetica, sans-serif;
    background:#000000;
    color:#ffffff;
    }
  a:link { text-decoration:none;color:#FF8037; }
  a:visited { text-decoration:none;color:#FF8037; }
  a:active { text-decoration:none;color:#FF8037; }
  a:hover { text-decoration:underline;color:#ffffff; }

.color-1-text-10 {
  font: 10pt arial, helvetica, sans-serif;
  color: #ffffff;
  }
.color-1-text-10 {
  font: 10pt arial, helvetica, sans-serif;
  color: #ffffff;
  }
.color-1-text-13 {
  font: 13pt arial, helvetica, sans-serif;
  color: #ffffff;
  }
.color-2-text-10 {
  font: 10pt arial, helvetica, sans-serif;
  color: #92684B;
  }
.color-2-text-13 {
  font: 13pt arial, helvetica, sans-serif;
  color: #92684B;
  }
```

```
.color-3-text-8 {
  font: 8pt arial, helvetica, sans-serif;
  color: #A48B65;
  }
.color-4-text-12 {
  font: 12pt arial, helvetica, sans-serif;
  color: #000000;
  }
  /* ++++++++++ global general styles end ++++++++++*/
  /* ++++++++++ global structure styles start ++++++++++*/
  #a5-body-center {
    text-align:center;
    }
  #a5-body {
    position:relative;
    width:1000px;
    margin-left:auto;
    margin-right:auto;
    text-align:left;
    background:#6A4203 url(images/bg-body.jpg) no-repeat;
    border:0px solid #ffffff;
    }
#a5-header {
  position:relative;
  left:0px;
  top:0px;
  height:220px;
  border:0px solid #000000;
  }
  #a5-header-right {
    position:absolute;
    top:52px;
    right:30px;
    height:60px;
    width:200px;
    text-align:center;
    border:0px solid #000000;
    }
  #a5-header-right-bg {
    position:absolute;
    top:53px;
    right:29px;
    height:60px;
```

```
        width:200px;
        text-align:center;
        border:0px solid #000000;
        }
   #a5-menu-box {
        position:absolute;
        top:175px;
        left:65px;
        line-height:40px;
        vertical-align:50%;
        color:#ffffff;
        font:bold 10pt arial, helvetica, sans-serif;
        border:0px solid #000000;
        }
     #a5-menu a {
          display:inline;
          text-decoration:none;
          color:#030303;
          }
   #a5-menu a:hover {
          text-decoration:underline;
          color:#97370C;
          }
    /* ++++++++++ global structure styles end ++++++++++*/
</style>

</head>
<body>
<div id="a5-body-center">
   <div id="a5-body">
<!-- ###### header start ###### -->
     <div id="a5-header">
         <div><a href="index.htm"><img src="images/spacer.gif"
width="770" height="157" alt="" border="0" /></a></div>
         <div id="a5-header-right-bg" class="color-3-text-13">complete
access<br /><span class="color-3-text-10">september 09, 2007</span></div>
         <div id="a5-header-right" class="color-1-text-13"><a
href="index.htm">complete access</a><br /><span class="color-1-text-
10">september 09, 2007</span></div>
<!-- ###### menu start ###### -->
     <div id="a5-menu-box">
        <div id="a5-menu">
             <a href="index.htm">menu item 1</a>
                 
```

```
            <a href="menu-item-2.htm">longer menu item 2</a>
                
            <a href="menu-item-3.htm">menu item 3</a>
                
            <a href="menu-item-4.htm">menu item 4</a>
                
            <a href="index.htm">menu item 5</a>
                
            <a href="index.htm">menu item 6</a>
          </div>
        </div>
<!-- ###### menu end ###### -->
      </div>
<!-- ###### header end ###### -->
   </div>
 </div>
</body>
</html>
```

There are several things to note about the code in Listing 13.2:

The basic hyperlink rules have been added to the design. These are used to style the "complete access" text in the top-right corner. They are also used to hyperlink the spacer.gif, which is the first of several such images that are layered over their respective visual elements in the background image. This method allows the designer to create more attractive and integrated graphics elements, while also enabling them to be hyperlinked easily. Figure 13.9 shows the header area with the spacer.gif layered over the area. The border of the image has been turned on and set to 2px to show how it's positioned in the code.

Figure 13.9
The header area with a spacer.gif layered over the title area, which enables the designer to hyperlink the area.
© 2014 Cengage Learning.

- The "complete access september 9, 2007" text and code in the top-right corner is duplicated so it can be layered on top of itself. This enables the designer to create an XHTML-based drop shadow and removes the need to create an image that not only takes more time to create and implement, but also isn't search-engine and text-reader friendly. Both the a5-header-right and a5-header-right-bg styles that are used to create these duplicate styles are assigned absolute positioning. The latter moves the lower layer to the right and down 1 pixel. The important thing to note is the way that browsers position the <DIV> containers. The a5-header- right-bg container needs to come first in the XHTML code. The reason is because it is rendered, and then the layer that has a hyperlink assigned to it is rendered on top of it. If it is not positioned this way in the XHTML, the hyperlink will not work properly among the various browsers.

- The a5-menu-box selector uses absolute positioning to place the menu area. The a5-menu a rule is then applied to every hyperlinked menu item that is included in the container. The display:inline; property/value combination determines that the menu items will be output horizontally in a line. The a5-menu a:hover; property/value combination changes the color of the hyperlink when it is moused over and turns on the underline below the link (see Figure 13.10).

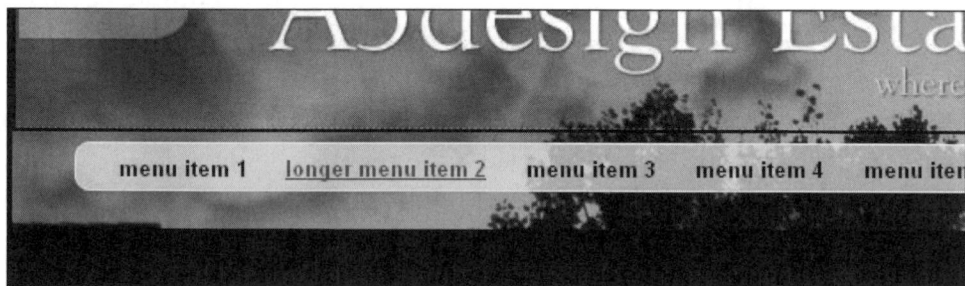

Figure 13.10
The Longer Menu Item 2 link when it is moused over.
© 2014 Cengage Learning.

Adding the Body Content and Footer

The structure of this design's body content is not overly complicated compared to the previous designs. While it has left and center columns, they aren't used for the majority of the placement of items, unlike the previous case studies. Rather, most of the content is positioned autonomously of other content because it is assigned absolute positioning. Listing 13.3 is all the code that is used to create the full design in Figure 13.11.

Figure 13.11
Design with the body content and footer added.

© 2014 Cengage Learning.

New Code Is in Bold

The newly added code is bolded to differentiate it from the existing code that is being built upon in this case study.

Listing 13.3   Code for Figure 13.11

```
<!DOCTYPE html PUBLIC "-//W3C//DTD XHTML 1.0 Transitional//EN" "DTD/xhtml1-
transitional.dtd">
<html xmlns="http://www.w3.org/1999/xhtml" xml:lang="en"
lang="en"><head><title></title>
<meta http-equiv="Content-Type" content="text/html; charset=iso-8859-1" />
<style type="text/css">
/* ++++++++++ global general styles start ++++++++++*/
```

```
html, body {
  margin:0px;
  padding:0px;
  font: 10pt arial, helvetica, sans-serif;
  background:#000000;
  color:#ffffff;
  }
a:link { text-decoration:none;color:#FF8037; }
a:visited { text-decoration:none;color:#FF8037; }
a:active { text-decoration:none;color:#FF8037; }
a:hover { text-decoration:underline;color:#ffffff; }

a.a5-right-column:link { text-decoration:none;color:#ffffff;}
a.a5-right-column:visited { text-decoration:none;color:#ffffff;}
a.a5-right-column:active { text-decoration:none;color:#ffffff;}
a.a5-right-column:hover { text-decoration:none;color:#809ED6;}

a.a5-link-light:link { text-decoration:underline;color:#ffffff;}
a.a5-link-light:visited { text-decoration:underline;color:#ffffff;}
a.a5-link-light:active { text-decoration:underline;color:#ffffff;}
a.a5-link-light:hover { text-decoration:underline;color:#92684B;}

a.a5-link-dark:link { text-decoration:underline;color:#000000;}
a.a5-link-dark:visited { text-decoration:underline;color:#000000;}
a.a5-link-dark:active { text-decoration:underline;color:#000000;}
a.a5-link-dark:hover { text-decoration:underline;color:#92684B;}
 .color-1-text-10 {
  font: 10pt arial, helvetica, sans-serif;
  color: #ffffff;
  }
 .color-1-text-10 {
  font: 10pt arial, helvetica, sans-serif;
  color: #ffffff;
  }
 .color-1-text-13 {
  font: 13pt arial, helvetica, sans-serif;
  color: #ffffff;
  }
 .color-2-text-10 {
  font: 10pt arial, helvetica, sans-serif;
  color: #92684B;
  }
```

```
.color-2-text-13 {
  font: 13pt arial, helvetica, sans-serif;
  color: #92684B;
  }
.color-3-text-8 {
  font: 8pt arial, helvetica, sans-serif;
  color: #A48B65;
  }
.color-4-text-12 {
  font: 12pt arial, helvetica, sans-serif;
  color: #000000;
  }
/* ++++++++++ global general styles end ++++++++++*/
/* ++++++++++ global structure styles start ++++++++++*/
#a5-body-center {
  text-align:center;
  }
#a5-body {
  position: relative;
  width: 1000px;
  margin-left: auto;
  margin-right: auto;
  text-align:left;
  background:#6A4203 url(images/bg-body.jpg) no-repeat;
  border:0px solid #ffffff;
  }
#a5-header {
  position:relative;
  left:0px;
  top:0px;
  height:220px;
  border:0px solid #000000;
  }
  #a5-header-right {
    position:absolute;
    top:52px;
    right:30px;
    height:60px;
    width:200px;
    text-align:center;
    border:0px solid #000000;
    }
```

```
#a5-header-right-bg {
  position:absolute;
  top:53px;
  right:29px;
  height:60px;
  width:200px;
  text-align:center;
  border:0px solid #000000;
  }
#a5-menu-box {
  position:absolute;
  top:175px;
  left:65px;
  line-height:40px;
  vertical-align:50%;
  color:#ffffff;
  font:bold 10pt arial, helvetica, sans-serif;
  border:0px solid #000000;
  }
  #a5-menu a {
    display:inline;
    text-decoration:none;
    color:#030303;
    }
  #a5-menu a:hover {
    text-decoration:underline;
    color:#97370C;
    }
#a5-left-middle-text {
  position:absolute;
  left:139px;
  top:443px;
  border:0px solid #ffffff;
  }
#a5-left-middle-image {
  position:absolute;
  left:0px;
  top:311px;
  border:0px solid #ffffff;
  }
#a5-center-middle-text {
  position:absolute;
  left:390px;
```

```
    top:342px;
    width:297px;
    line-height:17px;
    color:#ffffff;
    border:0px solid #ffffff;
    }
#a5-right-middle-image {
    position:absolute;
    right:28px;
    top:225px;
    border:0px solid #ffffff;
    }
#a5-column-left {
    float:left;
    width:750px;
    margin:15px 0px 0px 0px;
    border:0px solid #ffffff;
    }
    #a5-column-left-text {
        margin:280px 0px 0px 90px;
        border:0px solid #000000;
        }
    #a5-column-center {
        position:relative;
        left:0px;
        top:0px;
        border:0px solid #000000;
        }
        #a5-column-center-text {
            margin:177px 65px 0px 730px;
            line-height:18px;
            border:0px solid #000000;
            }
#a5-footer-separator {
    clear:both;
    height:30px;
    }
#a5-footer {
    clear:both;
    padding:0px 30px 0px 0px;
    height:40px;
    line-height:40px;
```

```
  vertical-align:80%;
  text-align:right;
  border-top:1px solid #A48B65;
  background:#482C01;
  }
/* ++++++++++ global structure styles end ++++++++++*/
</style>
</head>
<body>
<div id="a5-body-center">
   <div id="a5-body">
<!-- ###### header start ###### -->
     <div id="a5-header">
        <div><a href="index.htm"><img src="images/spacer.gif"
width="770" height="157" alt="" border="0" /></a></div>
        <div id="a5-header-right-bg" class="color-2-text-
13">complete access<br /><span class="color-2-text-10">september 09,
2007</span></div>
        <div id="a5-header-right" class="color-1-text-13"><a
href="index.htm">complete access</a><br /><span class="color-1-text-
10">september 09, 2007</span></div>
<!-- ###### menu start ###### -->
         <div id="a5-menu-box">
           <div id="a5-menu">
             <a href="index.htm">menu item 1</a>
                 
             <a href="menu-item-2.htm">longer menu item 2</a>
                 
             <a href="menu-item-3.htm">menu item 3</a>
                 
             <a href="menu-item-4.htm">menu item 4</a>
                 
             <a href="index.htm">menu item 5</a>
                 
             <a href="index.htm">menu item 6</a>
           </div>
         </div>
<!-- ###### menu end ###### -->
     </div>
<!-- ###### header end ###### -->
```

```
<!-- ###### left text box start ###### -->
      <div id="a5-left-middle-text" class="color-1-text-13"><a
href="x.htm" class="a5-link-dark">winter</a> &amp; <a href="x.htm"
class="a5-link-light">summer</a></div>

      <div id="a5-left-middle-image"><a href="x.htm"><img
src="images/spacer.gif" width="355" height="130" alt="" border="0"
/></a></div>
<!-- ###### left text box end ###### -->

<!-- ###### center text box start ###### -->
      <div id="a5-center-middle-text">Duis autem i vel eum iriure
dolor nwille hendrerit in vulputate alw d ays esse molestie consequat, vel
illum dolore eu feugiat loveukl facilisis at yvero eros et ayouccumsan et
iusto odio dignissim qui blandit praesent lumoreum zzril delenit aut duis
dolore te feugait nulla facilisi. Lorthan ipsum dyouolor sit
ametknowrae</div>

      <div id="a5-right-middle-image"><img src="images/spacer.gif"
width="231" height="161" alt="" border="0" style="border:1px solid #ffffff;"
/></div>
<!-- ###### center text box end ###### -->

<!-- ###### left column start ###### -->
      <div id="a5-column-left">
        <div id="a5-column-left-text" class="color-1-text-13">
          <a href="x.htm" class="a5-link-light">"why we were
sold from day one" testimonials</a>  <span
style="color:#AD8B28;">|</span>  <a href="x.htm" class="a5-link-
light">potential options</a>  <span
style="color:#AD8B28;">|</span>  <a href="x.htm" class="a5-link-
light">lifetime guarantee</a>
        </div>
      </div>
<!-- ###### left column end ###### -->

<!-- ###### center column start ###### -->
      <div id="a5-column-center">
        <div id="a5-column-center-text">
          <span class="color-4-text-12"><strong>Be forever
changed by
          "the heart of joans'" garden
          planted in 1979</strong></span>
        </div>
      </div>
```

```
<!-- ###### center column end ###### -->

<!--########## footer start ##########-->
     <div id="a5-footer-separator"> </div>
     <div id="a5-footer" class="color-3-text-8">© copyright
2007  |  your company  |  all rights
reserved</div>
<!--########## footer end ##########-->

  </div>
</div>

</body>
</html>
```

Following are things to note about the code in Listing 13.3:

- Several custom hyperlink rules (for example, `a.a5-right-column:link { text-decoration:none;color:#ffffff;}`), along with various text rules (for example, `color-4-text-12`), have been added to the style sheet to stylize the content throughout the page.

- The `a5-left-middle-text` and `a5-left-middle-image` <DIV> tags are added to create the box that appears in the left column, although the visual aspect of it is assigned in the code. The container is positioned 139 pixels from the left side and 443 pixels from the top. The Winter and Summer hyperlinks are then styled with the `a5-link-dark` and `a5-link-light` styles, respectively. Figure 13.12 illustrates what the design looks like with only the left column added and with the border turned on for the `spacer.gif` that is added to make that section clickable. Because the text is in an absolutely positioned container, it does not push the footer down until code is later added into the `a5-column-left` <DIV>—at least in IE 6.

- Once the left box has been populated, the `a5-center-middle-text` container is added. This container is positioned 390 pixels from the left and 443 pixels from the top, similar to the container for the left box (that is, `a5-leftmiddle-text`). The width is set to 297 pixels to force the text to remain within the "visible" confines of the center box. The length of the text would need to be controlled by the designer, whether that means hand coding or controlling the number of output characters from a database. Figure 13.13 shows what the design looks like with the content added for the container.

- The `a5-right-middle-image` container is added to allow for the flowers area to be clickable. The "be forever changed" text on top of the flower image is added to the `a5-column-center-text` container, which is nested inside the `a5-column-center` <DIV>. The code that enables this can be found farther down the page. One advantage of adding this content, along with the "why we were sold from day one testimonials | potential options | lifetime guarantee" text in the `a5-column-left` column (refer back to Figure 13.1), is that it populates the left and center columns, which forces the footer to its desired position.

- As mentioned in the previous bullet, the "why we were sold from day one testimonials | potential options | lifetime guarantee" text is added to the `a5-column-left` container. The text is then nested inside the `a5-columncenter-text` container. This nesting allows for the text area to have margins applied to the `a5-column-center-text` <DIV> without affecting the width of the `a5-column-left` container.

- The `a5-footer-separator` container is added to provide a margin between the bottom of the content and the top of the footer.

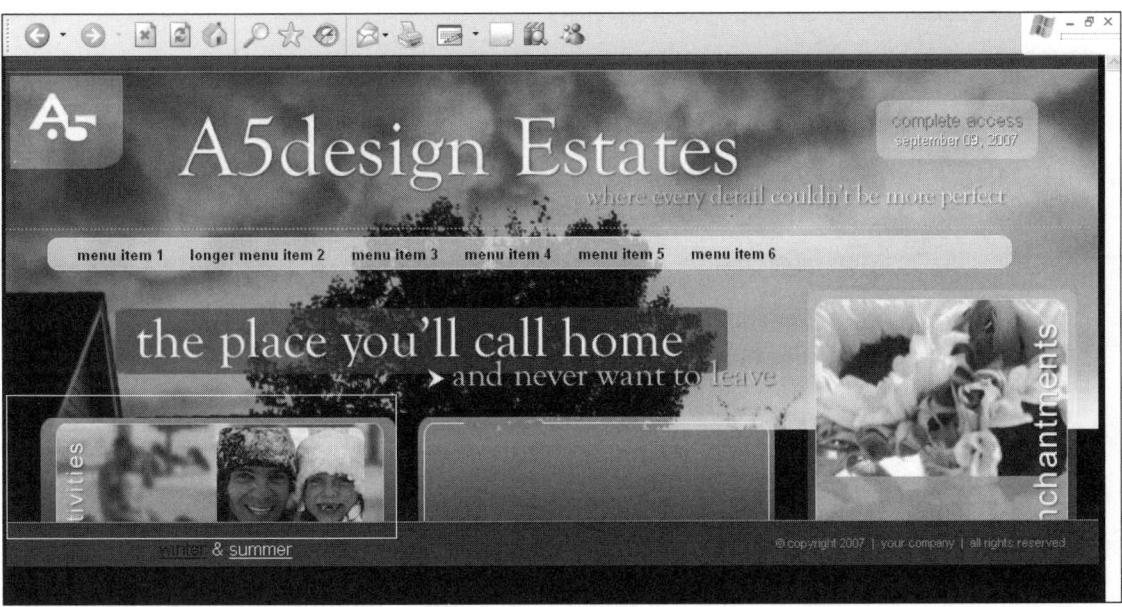

Figure 13.12
Design with the text for the left box added.
© 2014 Cengage Learning.

Figure 13.13
Design with the text for the center box added.
© 2014 Cengage Learning.

CONSTRUCTING SECOND-LEVEL PAGES

Similar to the previous three case studies, the homepage is reused and customized for secondary pages (see Figure 13.14). There are only a few changes that need to be made to create a modified version of the homepage:

- Once the homepage is saved as `menu-item-2.htm`, the containers that have absolute positioning added to them are removed. This is yet one more reason the left and center columns were included with the homepage design. They can now be easily used to their full potential by just adding content to them.

- The `a5-column-left-text` and `a5-column-center-text` containers are renamed to `a5-column-left-text-sl` and `a5-column-center-text-sl`, respectively. A rule for each is added to the style sheet to modify the placement of the content that each contains.

- A second Photoshop file is created to provide a modified version of the background image. The `a5-body-sl` rule is added to the style sheet that calls this new image, titled `bg-body-sl.jpg`.

- To provide a secondary page title, the `a5-sl-title` <DIV> is added at the top of the `a5-column-left-text-sl` container. A rule is added to the style sheet to stylize the text in that <DIV>.

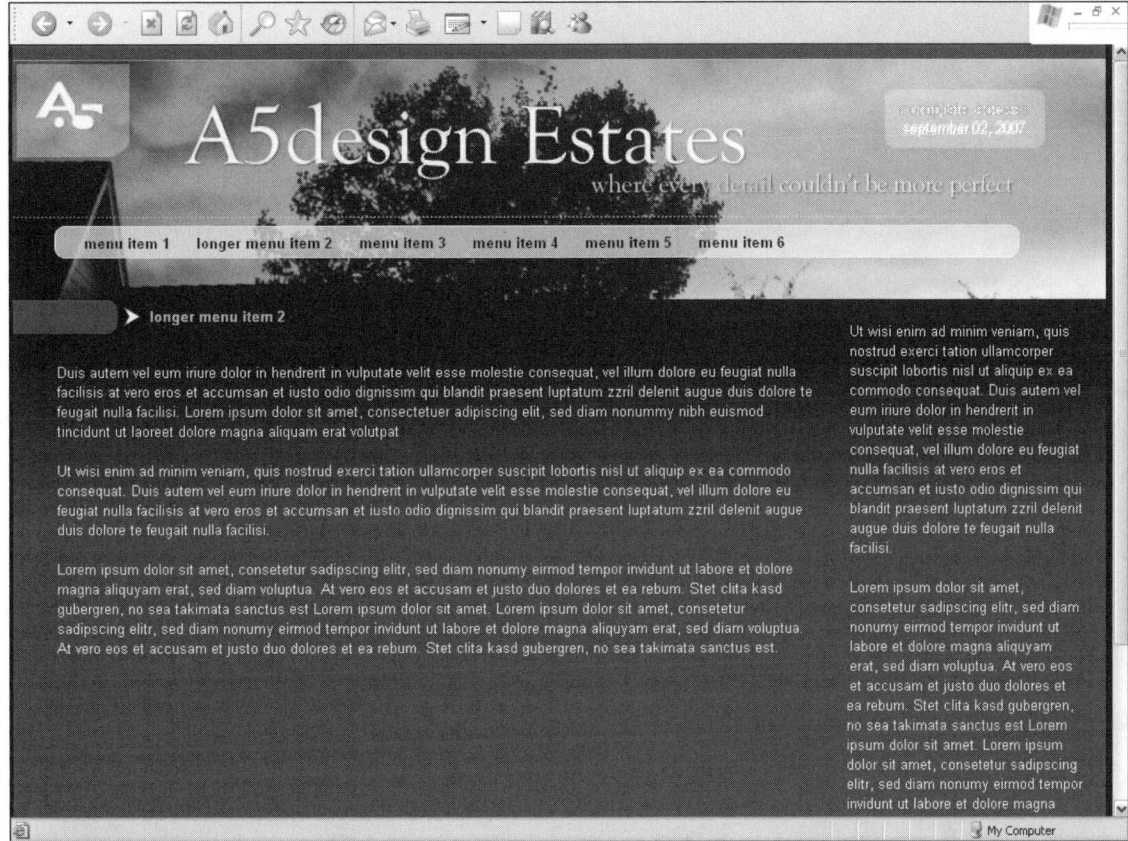

Figure 13.14
A second-level template that is created from the homepage design.
© 2014 Cengage Learning.

SUMMARY

The purpose of this design is to offer the designer the ability to create more graphical sites. Rather than providing a flexible, scalable design, the XHTML and CSS are used to place content over the background image, which provides the majority of graphical elements. The majority of items on the homepage are assigned absolute positioning. The secondary pages, however, provide a more traditional way of placing and stylizing content, considering they will need to be much more flexible. While this design is limited in its flexibility, it gives an alternative for design that the other case studies cannot provide because this design uses the graphics and content placement in entirely different ways.

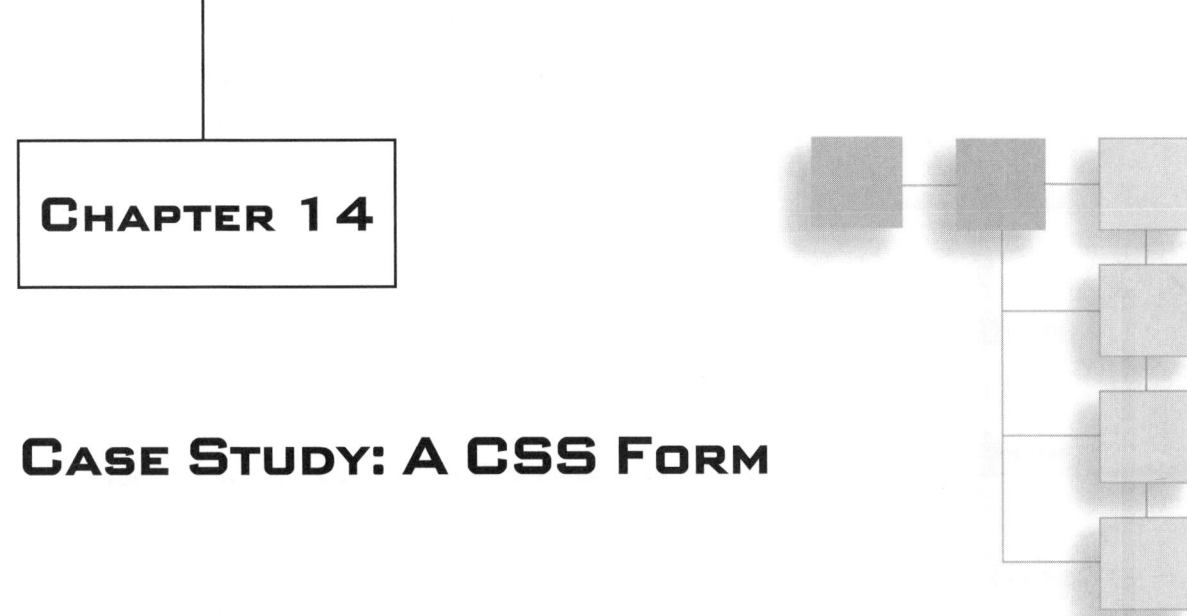

CHAPTER 14

CASE STUDY: A CSS FORM

Building a CSS-based form is not overly difficult. Once the style sheet rules have been created, the XHTML is very simple to employ. A form, in fact, is much easier to build because it reuses much of the CSS, making it more of a process of repeating and possibly tweaking the code.

As with Web design, there are little tricks a designer should be aware of. The form in this chapter was built to show many of the challenges a designer may run into. Each row, in fact, illustrates a completely different element to consider.

The form is added initially to the design explained in Chapter 12 (see Figure 14.1) to provide a visual for how it will eventually look in a page. For the sake of simplicity, however, the form is later explained on its own. It could be added to any design, as long as it is not too wide for the allotted area on a page.

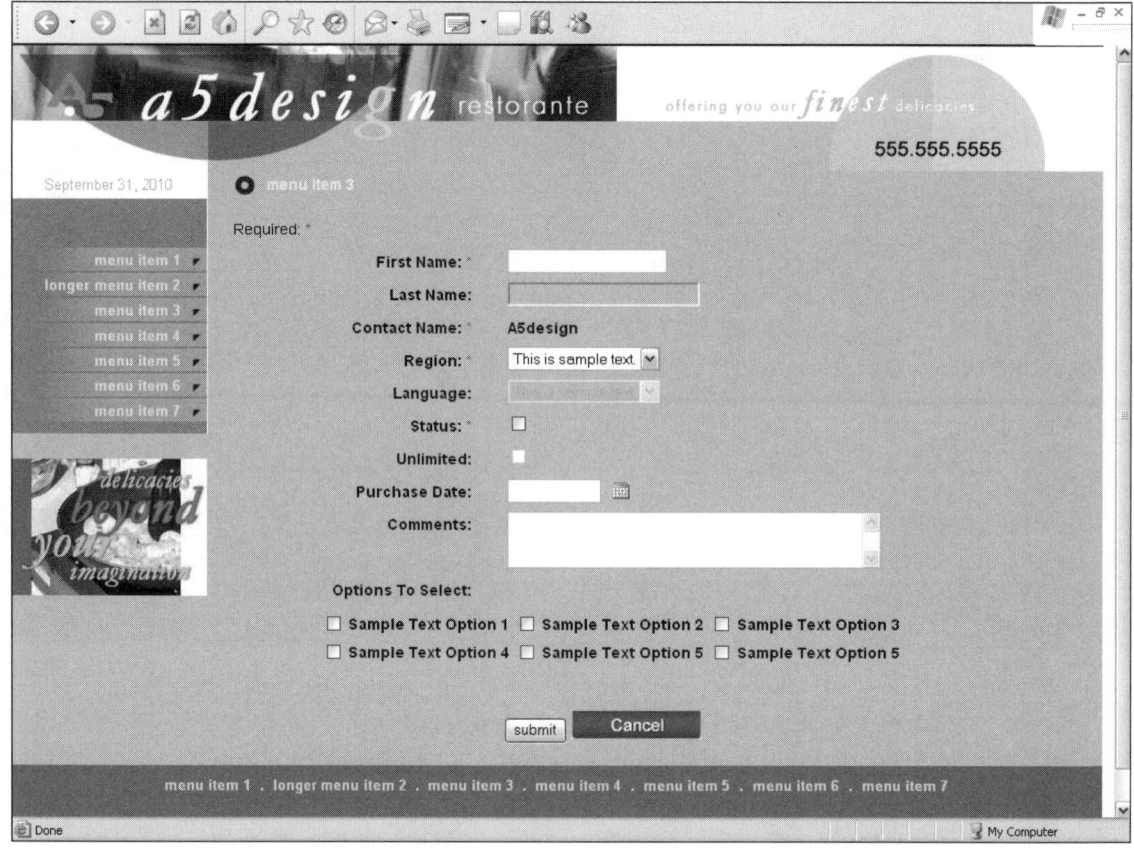

Figure 14.1
The sample form explained in this chapter.
© 2014 Cengage Learning.

UNDERSTANDING THE FORM'S STRUCTURE

The structure of this form is relatively simple. It is a two-column format nested inside opening and closing <FORM> tags. It is made into a two-column format by floating the form field's label, such as First Name, to the left of the actual form field. The background colors of the form elements are changed in Figure 14.2 to show the columns.

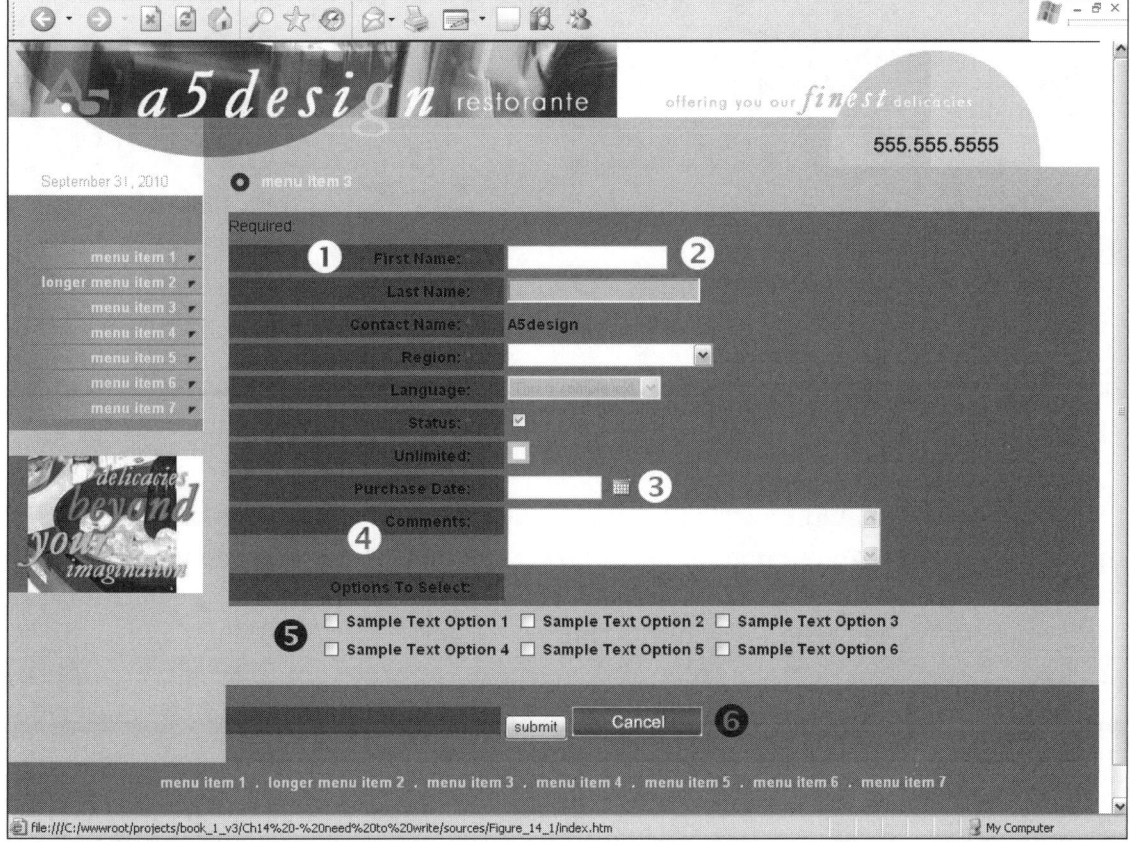

Figure 14.2
The background colors changed in the form to show how the two-column format is accomplished.
© 2014 Cengage Learning.

There are five things to note about the form's structure, shown in Figure 14.2:

1. The left column, shown by number 1, is set to 220 pixels wide. Because every label has the same width and is floated to the left, the entire column looks like it is the same width. If, however, the designer were to change the width of the label in one of the rows, it becomes apparent that each label is technically autonomous, unlike elements structured in a traditional XHTML table layout (see Figure 14.3).

Figure 14.3
Example of how the width of each label is autonomous.
© 2014 Cengage Learning.

2. The right column is composed of the form fields. As shown in number 2, if the width of the left label were widened, the form field in the right column would change accordingly, but only for that row.

3. The right column could be styled or modified however necessary, as long as the row has space to the right. Number 3 shows how a calendar image has been positioned to the right of the Purchase Date form field. The rule declaring the background color of the entire form has been changed to a different color, which would make the entire area look like one color if the color of the left column were not different. Figure 14.4 illustrates how the background color of the entire Last Name row could be changed if need be.

Figure 14.4
Example of how the background color of the Last Name row could be stylized separately from the other rows.
© 2014 Cengage Learning.

4. The height of the left column for each row is autonomous from the height of the right column because it is floated to the left, making it fall outside of the document flow. Number 4 represents how the height of the Comments label does not change when the height of the field in the right column increases the height of the row.

5. Because of the more involved layout of the row to the right of number 5, an XHTML table is used to position the form fields. The <DIV> nested inside is not assigned a class, which allows for the full width of the row to be used.

EXPLAINING THE STYLE SHEET USED FOR THE FORM

Because the global CSS rules are reused for nearly every form item, they are explained up front to give the reader a better overall understanding of what is happening. Listing 14.1 shows all the rules used in the style sheet.

Listing 14.1   CSS Rules That Comprise the Style Sheet

```
margin:0px 0px 0px 0px;
  }
.a5-required-field {
  color:#D60000;
  }
.a5-disabled-field {
  background:#7ED0D4;
  }
.a5-disabled-checkbox {
  background:#7ED0D4;
  voice-family:"\"}\"";
  voice-family:inherit;
  }
  html>body .a5-disabled-checkbox {
    padding-top:3px;
  }
.a5-row-1 {
  height:30px;
  }
.a5-row-1 label {
  float: left;
  width: 220px;
  text-align: right;
  padding:0px 30px 0px 0px;
  }
```

There are several things to note about the styles used for the form. Following are explanations for each of the rules:

- **.a5-form:** Because browsers do not all apply the same default margin value for a form, the designer should declare it in order to provide consistency. One way this is accomplished is by setting the margins to 0.

- **.a5-required-field:** There are several ways to show a user which field is required. Creating an asterisk next to the form label is one of the most common. This rule simply makes the asterisk red.

- **.a5-disabled-field:** The form, when placed in the design (see Figure 14.1), has a background color behind it. Because of this, a background color for disabled fields is added to make the field look like it blends more into the background, visually representing the fact it's disabled. To complete this usability, or lack thereof, the designer must also include code in the XHTML disabled="true" to disable the field.

- **.a5-disabled-checkbox:** This rule is added to consistently show the background color of a disabled checkbox in all browsers. Otherwise, some browsers render the background image entirely behind a checkbox or just partially behind it.

- **.a5-row-1:** This rule, along with the next, are the most commonly used in the form. This particular rule is added to set the default height of the row.

- **.a5-row-1 label:** This rule can be used to make the most sweeping changes in the form because it controls the default width of the left column. In this example, the width is set to 220 pixels. The rule also floats the column to the left side of the form, while forcing the label text to the right side of that column. A right padding value of 30 pixels is added to position the label text in from the right side, providing some visual space between the labels and the form fields.

Building the Form Row by Row

It is probably easiest to understand how to build the form if you see it built row by row. For demonstration purposes, the form is removed from the design and built separately. Following are explanations of how each row is built.

Test, Test, Test

The important thing to remember is to always test the form in various browsers. Sometimes, there are more cross-browser anomalies that arise when building a form than when building a Web page.

Adding the <FORM> Tag and Required Row

The first code to be added is the <FORM> tag. As with most forms, the main three attributes to add to the <FORM> tag are method, which tells the form to "post" or "get" the data; action, which in this case tells the form where to post the data; and the name attribute, which assigns a name to the form, uniquely identifying it. The final attribute added to this example is class, which calls the rule a5-form. This rule, declaring the default margin value as 0, defines the spacing outside the <FORM> tag, ensuring that all browsers display it the same rather than depending on their default values, which are not always the same.

The second section of code added is that which lays out the Required row. This row is added to let the user know that the red asterisk included for certain rows indicates that a particular row is required. This row has a local style added to create a top margin of 10 pixels in order to provide a little spacing between the form and the content it follows. Listing 14.2 displays this initial code added to the form.

Listing 14.2   Initial XHTML and CSS Code Added to Form

```
<form action="menu-item-3.cfm" method="post" name="sample_form" class="a5-form">
<div class="a5-row-1" style="margin:10px 0px 0px 0px;">
  Required: <span class="a5-required-field">*</span>
</div>
</form>
```

Adding the First Name Row

The First Name row is the next item to be added to the form. Figure 14.5 illustrates how the form looks when the row is added to the form.

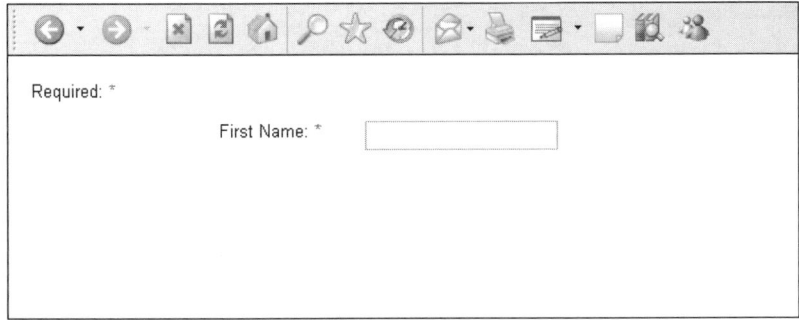

Figure 14.5
The form with the First Name row added to the form.
© 2014 Cengage Learning.

There are several things to note about this code:

- The row is created by the `<DIV>` that has an `id` value of `a5-row-1` assigned to it. As stated earlier, this row is assigned a height of 30 pixels.

- The `<LABEL>` tag gives the designer the means to place a name next to the field it is identifying. While a `<LABEL>` tag is not necessary, doing so not only makes the content accessible, but it also allows the user to be able to click on that text, which will make the field the focus of the cursor. In other words, if the user clicks on the text First Name, the cursor will appear blinking in the First Name field. The `<LABEL>` tag knows where to place the cursor because of the for attribute, which is assigned a value of first_name. The designer then adds the id value of first_name in the form field. So, when the <LABEL> text is clicked, the browser knows to match the for value of the tag with the same id value of whichever form field has that value associated with it.

■ The <LABEL> tag is styled by the a5-row-1 label rule in the style sheet. This rule assigns a width of 220 pixels to the tag, floating it to the left of the form field, aligning its text to the right, and creating 30 pixels of padding to the right.

■ A <SPAN> tag, with the class a5-required-field assigned to it, is wrapped around an asterisk. The sole purpose of this style is to make the asterisk red to help it stand out visually.

Much of what is discussed with this example row is reused for many of the items in the form. Listing 14.3 shows the text that is added.

Listing 14.3   XHTML Code for First Name Row

```
<div class="a5-row-1">
    <label title="First Name" for="first_name">First Name: <span class="a5-required-
field">*</span></label>
    <input type="text" name="first_name" id="first_name" />
</div>
```

Adding the Last Name Row

The Last Name row uses much of the same code as the First Name line. The main difference is that this row is added to provide an example of a disabled row. Figure 14.6 shows how the disabled version appears when the a5-disabled-field class is added to the code in Listing 14.4. It is important to note that if the class were not added to the form field, it would still be disabled, but it would appear nearly the same as the First Name field. This is why the a5-disabled-field rule has a background color added to it.

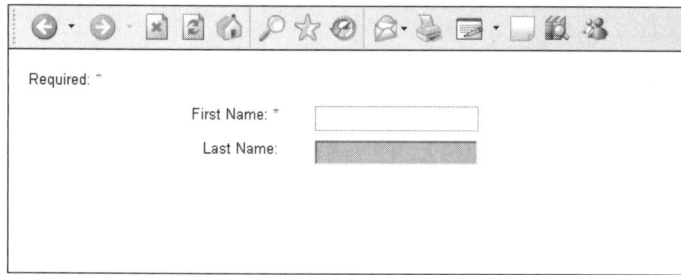

Figure 14.6
The form with the Last Name row added.
© 2014 Cengage Learning.

Listing 14.4 XHTML Code for Last Name Row

```
<div class="a5-row-1">
    <label title="Last Name" for="last_name">Last Name:</label>
  <input type="text" name="last_name" id="last_name" disabled="disabled" class="a5-
disabled-field" />
</div>
```

Adding the Contact Name Row

This row is added to show that text could be added in the right column instead of a form field (see Listing 14.5). This code is useful because dynamic forms often output just text in spaces generally allocated for fields, which, ultimately, are not submitted with the form, unless the data is also contained within a hidden form field (see Figure 14.4). The code, however, also shows that the right column area provides a lot of flexibility for the designer. An image or instructional text, for instance, could be added, if need be.

Listing 14.5 XHTML Code for Contact Name Row

```
<div class="a5-row-1">
    <label title="Contact Name">Contact Name: <span class="a5-required-field">*
</span></label>
    <strong>A5design</strong>
</div>
```

Adding the Region and Language Rows

The Region and Language rows are added to show how a drop-down menu would appear if it were added to a row. The Language element is different from the Region element in that it has been assigned the a5-disabled-field class. Similar to the Last Name field, it is assigned this class to change its background color to show it has been disabled. Unlike the <INPUT> tag, though, when the <SELECT> tag is disabled, it visually appears disabled by the way the browser renders it. Figure 14.7 shows how the four form elements appear when a background color is not assigned. Listing 14.6 shows the results of the code for the Region and Language rows.

Figure 14.7
An example of how the `<INPUT>` and `<SELECT>` fields appear differently when they are enabled and disabled.
© 2014 Cengage Learning.

Listing 14.6   XHTML Code for Region and Language Rows

```
<div class="a5-row-1">
    <label title="Region" for="region">Region: <span class="a5-required-field">*
</span></label>
  <select name="region" id="region">
    <option value="This is sample text">This is sample text.</option>
    <option>This is longer sample text</option>
  </select>
</div>
<div class="a5-row-1">
    <label title="Language" for="language">Language:</label>
  <select name="language" id="language" disabled="disabled">
    <option value="This is sample text">This is sample text.</option>
  </select>
</div>
```

Adding the Status and Unlimited Rows

Similar to the Region and Language rows, the Status and Unlimited rows are included to show how a different form element would look when it was enabled and disabled. The Unlimited checkbox is the same as the Status checkbox, except it has been disabled. The slight difference in this example, as with the Last Name and Language examples of disabled form elements, is that this type of form field employs a different disabled class (i.e., `a5-disabled-checkbox`). Figure 14.8 shows how the checkbox looks in different browsers if it is merely assigned a background color, as with the `a5-disabled-field` class. It illustrates how the background color does not make up a consistent height in the left and right examples. This is why the `a5-disabled-field` class was created. It adds three pixels of padding to the top of the checkbox field for compliant browsers, so it appears like the left example in Figure 14.8 for all browsers. Listing 14.7 shows the code that is added to build the two rows.

Figure 14.8
How the checkbox appears in different browsers if it is not assigned the `a5-disabled-checkbox` class.
© 2014 Cengage Learning.

Listing 14.7   XHTML Code for Status and Unlimited Rows

```
<div class="a5-row-1">
    <label title="Unlimited" for="unlimited">Unlimited: </label>
  <input type="checkbox" name="status" id="status" />
</div>
<div class="a5-row-1">
    <label title="Unlimited" for="unlimited">Unlimited:</label>
  <span class="a5-disabled-checkbox"><input type="checkbox" name="unlimited"
id="unlimited" disabled="disabled" /></span>
</div>
```

Adding the Purchase Date Row

The Purchase Date row shows how an image can be included to the right of the form field. It is simply placed to the right of the field, as opposed to being floated to the right. If the designer were to get more technical, it could be assigned a few pixels of padding to the top so it is placed at the same height for all browsers. A `<SPAN>` container is wrapped around the image to provide 10 pixels of padding to the left. Listing 14.8 shows the code used to render the row.

Listing 14.8   XHTML and CSS Code for Purchase Date Row

```
<div class="a5-row-1">
    <label title="Purchase Date" for="purchase_date">Purchase Date:</label>
  <input type="text" name="purchase_date" id="purchase_date" style="width:70px;" />
<span style="padding-left:10px;"><img src="images/icon-calendar.gif" width="16"
height="15" alt="" border="0" /></span>
</div>
```

Adding the Comments Row

The code required to produce the Comments row is almost identical to several of the other rows, barring one difference—the row includes the <TEXTAREA> tag, which does not force the height of the row for compliant browsers, such as Firefox. The designer, therefore, needs to force the height of the row. One way to do so is to add a local style to the parent <DIV>, shown in Listing 14.9. Without declaring the height of the row, the row would look like the right side of Figure 14.9. The left side illustrates what the row looks like if a height is defined.

Figure 14.9
The Comments row and how it will appear in compliant browsers when a height is and isn't defined when using the <TEXTAREA> tag.
© 2014 Cengage Learning.

Listing 14.9   XHTML and CSS Code for Comments Row

```
<div class="a5-row-1" style="height:80px;">
    <label title="Comments" for="comments">Comments:</label>
  <textarea name="comments" id="comments" rows="3" cols="40"></textarea>
</div>
```

Adding the Options to Select Rows

The Options to Select rows add two more situations a designer may or may not come across. The first is to include only a section title and nothing more in a row. This is accomplished by merely not including a form field. The second is a little more involved. It requires two things: (1) define appropriate margins for positioning in the parent <DIV>, which, in this case, sets the bottom margin to 20 pixels and the left margin to 80 pixels; and (2) use a table to lay out the form fields in columns and rows. While the latter could be accomplished with CSS, the more simple and straightforward route is to use a table. The code in Listing 14.10 shows how simple the table needs to be.

Listing 14.10   XHTML and CSS Code for Options to Select Row

```
<div class="a5-row-1">
    <label>Options To Select:</label>
</div>
<div style="margin:0px 0px 20px 80px;">
  <table cellspacing="0" cellpadding="3" border="0">
  <tr>
  <td>
      <input type="checkbox" name="sample_text_1" id="sample_text_1" />
      <label title="Sample Text Option 1" for="sample_text_1">Sample Text
Option 1</label>
    </td>
    <td>
      <input type="checkbox" name="sample_text_2" id="sample_text_2" />
      <label title="Sample Text Option 2" for="sample_text_2">Sample Text
Option 2</label>
    </td>
    <td>
      <input type="checkbox" name="sample_text_3" id="sample_text_3" />
      <label title="Sample Text Option 3" for="sample_text_3">Sample
Text Option 3</label>
    </td>
  </tr>
  <tr>
  <td>
      <input type="checkbox" name="sample_text_4" id="sample_text_4" />
      <label title="Sample Text Option 4" for="sample_text_4">Sample Text
Option 4</label>
    </td>
  <td>
      <input type="checkbox" name="sample_text_5" id="sample_text_5" />
      <label title="Sample Text Option 5" for="sample_text_5">Sample Text
Option 5</label>
    </td>
    <td>
      <input type="checkbox" name="sample_text_6" id="sample_text_6" />
      <label title="Sample Text Option 6" for="sample_text_6">Sample Text
Option 6</label>
    </td>
  </tr>
  </table>
</div>
```

Adding the Submit and Cancel Buttons

The final row contains the Submit and Cancel buttons. There are several things to note about this section of code: (1) a local style is added to the <DIV> to provide 20 pixels of padding on the top and bottom, (2) the <LABEL> tag has   added so that all browsers recognize the tag and account for its width, and (3) the two buttons are placed side by side without any additional styling. The Cancel button calls an image, while the Submit button is generated with XHTML (see Listing 14.11).

Listing 14.11   XHTML and CSS Code for Submit and Cancel Buttons

```
<div class="a5-row-1" style="padding:20px 0px 20px 0px;">
    <label> </label>
  <input type="submit" value="submit" />
  <input type="image" src="images/button-cancel.gif" />
</div>
```

The Final Product

When all the code and images are added, the final 13-row form only needs the back-end functionality added to it. Figure 14.10 is the visual representation of the final code, which is shown in Listing 14.12.

Figure 14.10
How the final form appears prior to being added to the design (see Figure 14.1).

Listing 14.12   XHTML and CSS Code for Completed Form

```
<!DOCTYPE html PUBLIC "-//W3C//DTD XHTML 1.0 Transitional//EN" "DTD/xhtml1-
transitional.dtd">
<html xmlns="http://www.w3.org/1999/xhtml" xml:lang="en"
lang="en"><head><title></title>
<style type="text/css">
html, body {
  margin:0px;
  padding:10px;
  font: 9.8pt arial, helvetica, sans-serif;
  color:#000000;
  }
.a5-form {
  margin:0px 0px 0px 0px;
  }
.a5-required-field {
  color:#D60000;
  }
.a5-disabled-field {
  background:#7ED0D4;
  }
.a5-disabled-checkbox {
  background:#7ED0D4;
  voice-family:"\"}\"";
  voice-family:inherit;
  }
  html>body .a5-disabled-checkbox {
    padding-top:3px;
  }
.a5-row-1 {
  height:30px;
  }
.a5-row-1 label {
  float: left;
  width: 220px;
  text-align: right;
  padding:0px 30px 0px 0px;
  }
</style>
</head>
```

```
<body>
<form action="menu-item-3.cfm" method="post" name="sample_form" class="a5-form">
<div class="a5-row-1" style="margin:10px 0px 0px 0px;">
  Required: <span class="a5-required-field">*</span>
</div>
<div class="a5-row-1">
    <label title="First Name" for="first_name">First Name: <span class="a5-required-
field">*</span></label>
    <input type="text" name="first_name" id="first_name" />
</div>
<div class="a5-row-1">
    <label title="Last Name" for="last_name">Last Name:</label>
  <input type="text" name="last_name" id="last_name" disabled="disabled" class="a5-
disabled-field" />
</div>
<div class="a5-row-1">
    <label title="Contact Name">Contact Name: <span class="a5-required-field">*
</span></label>
  <strong>A5design</strong>
</div>
<div class="a5-row-1">
    <label title="Region" for="region">Region: <span class="a5-required-field">*
</span></label>
  <select name="region" id="region">
    <option value="This is sample text">This is sample text.</option>
    <option>This is longer sample text</option>
  </select>
</div>
<div class="a5-row-1">
    <label title="Language" for="language">Language:</label>
  <select name="language" id="language" disabled="disabled" class="a5-disabled-
field">
    <option>This is sample text.</option>
  </select>
</div>
<div class="a5-row-1">
    <label title="Status" for="status">Status: <span class="a5-required-field">*
</span></label>
  <input type="checkbox" name="status" id="status" />
</div>
```

```
<div class="a5-row-1">
    <label title="Unlimited" for="unlimited">Unlimited:</label>
  <span class="a5-disabled-checkbox"><input type="checkbox" name="unlimited"
id="unlimited" disabled="disabled" /></span>
</div>
<div class="a5-row-1">
    <label title="Purchase Date" for="purchase_date">Purchase Date:</label>
  <input type="text" name="purchase_date" id="purchase_date" style="width:70px;" />
<span style="padding-left:10px;"><img src="images/icon-calendar.gif" width="16"
height="15" alt="" border="0" /></span>
</div>
<div class="a5-row-1" style="height:80px;">
    <label title="Comments" for="comments">Comments:</label>
  <textarea name="comments" id="comments" rows="3" cols="40"></textarea>
</div>
<div class="a5-row-1">
    <label>Options To Select:</label>
</div>
<div style="margin:0px 0px 20px 80px;">
  <table cellspacing="0" cellpadding="3" border="0">
  <tr>
  <td>
      <input type="checkbox" name="sample_text_1" id="sample_text_1" />
      <label title="Sample Text Option 1" for="sample_text_1">Sample Text
Option 1</label>
    </td>
    <td>
      <input type="checkbox" name="sample_text_2" id="sample_text_2" />
      <label title="Sample Text Option 2" for="sample_text_2">Sample Text
Option 2</label>
  </td>
  <td>
      <input type="checkbox" name="sample_text_3" id="sample_text_3" />
      <label title="Sample Text Option 3" for="sample_text_3">Sample Text
Option 3</label>
    </td>
  </tr>
  <tr>
  <td>
      <input type="checkbox" name="sample_text_4" id="sample_text_4" />
      <label title="Sample Text Option 4" for="sample_text_4">Sample Text
Option 4</label>
    </td>
```

```
    <td>
        <input type="checkbox" name="sample_text_5" id="sample_text_5" />
        <label title="Sample Text Option 5" for="sample_text_5">Sample Text
Option 5</label>
      </td>
    <td>
        <input type="checkbox" name="sample_text_6" id="sample_text_6" />
        <label title="Sample Text Option 6" for="sample_text_6">Sample
Text Option 6</label>
      </td>
    </tr>
    </table>
</div>
<div class="a5-row-1" style="padding:20px 0px 20px 0px;">
    <label> </label>
  <input type="submit" value="submit" />
  <input type="image" src="images/button-cancel.gif" />
</div>
</form>
</body>
</html>
```

SUMMARY

Creating a form with CSS is not difficult once the designer understands the basic structure of the layout. After rules have been created for each row and the <LABEL> text, there are only a few nuances that need to be learned to control the form fields and the <DIV> tags that contain them. When these are understood, it becomes much easier for the designer to satisfy the majority of form requests he will come across using the methods discussed in this chapter. Even if a form needs to be more involved, the basics that are explained will provide a strong foundation for such a request.

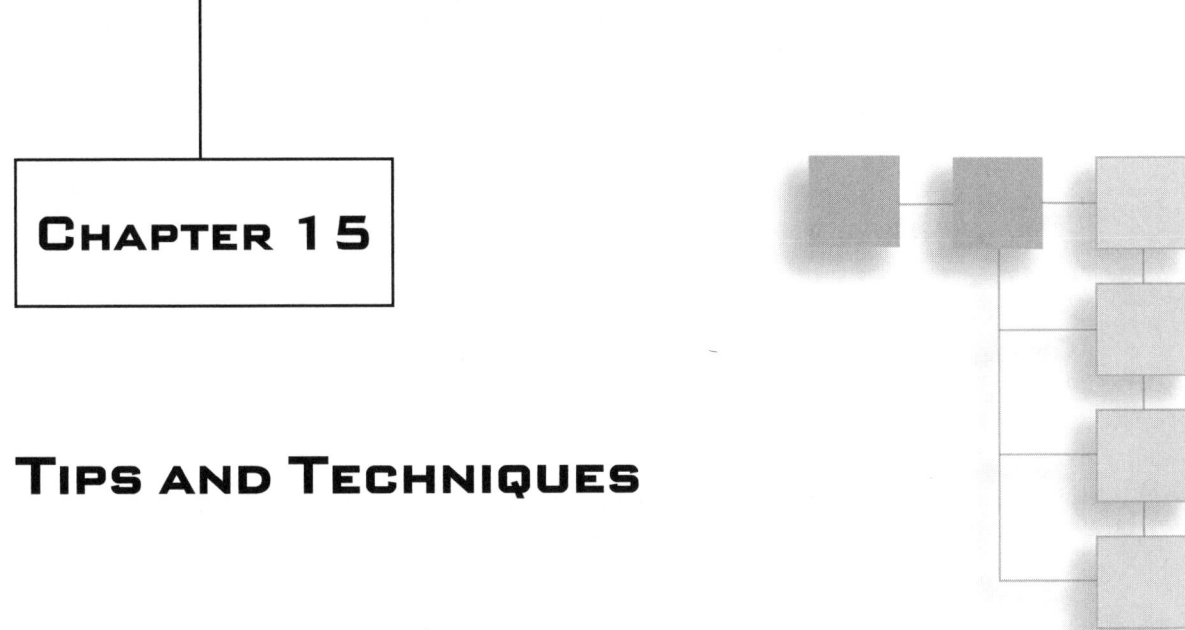

CHAPTER 15

TIPS AND TECHNIQUES

When learning how to build websites, the most time-consuming aspect is not always creating the look and feel of the site in image editing software, such as Photoshop. Rather, more time is usually spent figuring out how to code the site. The tips and techniques included in this chapter will help the designer understand methods and work-arounds that he will probably need to learn when creating sites. While not all the tips will be useful while building one site, many of them will eventually arise if the reader builds many sites over time.

NAMING RULES AND PROPERTIES CORRECTLY

Occasionally, the designer may add a style and either the page does not reflect the proper styling or the styling is incorrect. A few common errors can occur:

■ The style on the page does not match the correct spelling in the style sheet.

```
<style type="text/css">
    #samplestyle {
    color:#ffffff;
    }
</style>
<div id="sample_style">
    This is sample text
</div>
```

Should read as

```
<style type="text/css">
    #samplestyle {
    color:#ffffff;
    }
</style>
<div id="samplestyle">
    This is sample text
</div>
```

■ The style on the page may be referencing an ID selector when the selector in the style sheet is actually a class or vice versa.

```
<style type="text/css">
    .samplestyle {
    color:#ffffff;
    }
</style>
<div id="samplestyle">
    This is sample text
</div>
```

Should read as

```
<style type="text/css">
    .samplestyle {
    color:#ffffff;
    }
</style>
<div class="samplestyle">
    This is sample text
</div>
```

■ The syntax of a style may not be correct. Missing semicolons are an occasional reason for this error.

```
<style type="text/css">
    #samplestyle {
    color:#ffffff;
    background:red
    }
</style>
```

Should read as

```
<style type="text/css">
    #samplestyle {
    color:#ffffff;
    background:red;
    }
</style>
```

Class Can Be Called by Only One Tag

Although it does not have anything to do with styling, another naming error a designer can make is to call the same ID class with two separate tags in the XHTML. While the page may still display correctly, the XHTML will not validate because an ID class can be referenced only once in a document.

Two other naming issues are more difficult to find. Sometimes, without removing code to test the problem, the designer will not find where the error is occurring.

- Two rules could have the same selector name. Because it is easy to copy a rule and simply modify it to serve as another rule, the designer can sometimes forget to rename the new rule. If a new rule has been added but its properties are not being applied in the browser, the problem could be that it has the same name as another rule.

```
<style type="text/css">
        #style1 {
        color:yellow;
        background:black;
        }
        #style2 {
        color:white;
        background:blue;
        }
        #style1 {
        color:green;
        background:purple;
        }
</style>
```

```
<div id="style1">
    This is sample text
</div>
<div id="style3">
    This is sample text
</div>
```

Should read as

```
<style type="text/css">
    #style1 {
    color:yellow;
    background:black;
    }
    #style2 {
    color:white;
    background:blue;
    }
    #style3 {
    color:green;
    background:purple;
    }
</style>
<div id="style1">
    This is sample text
</div>
<div id="style3">
    This is sample text
</div>
```

REMOVING BODY MARGINS AND PADDING

By default, browsers add top and left space between the browser window and the content that is output (see Figure 15.1). This space varies depending on the browser.

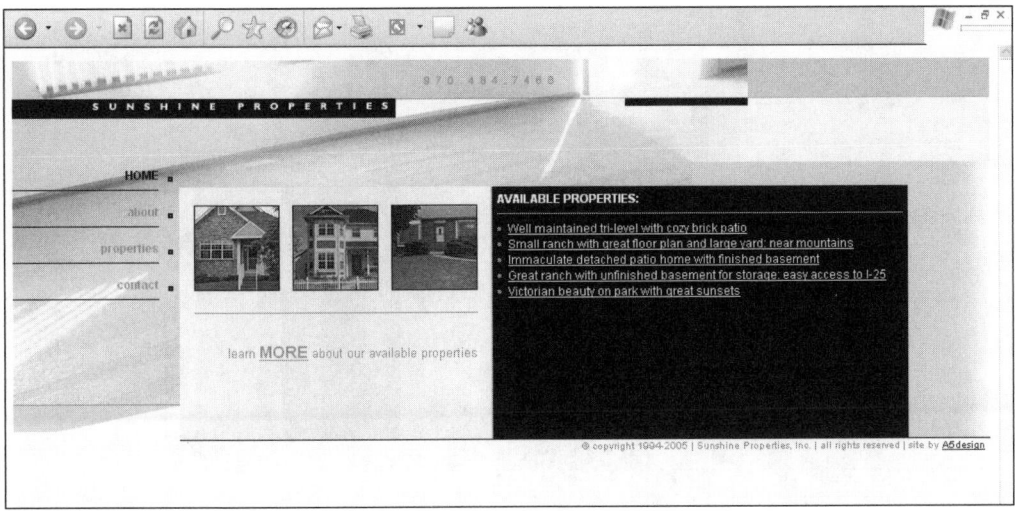

Figure 15.1
Website with default margins that add space between the top and left edges of the Web window and the design.
© 2014 Cengage Learning.

Removing the space is easily accomplished. The designer needs only to assign the style to the HTML and BODY selectors in the main style sheet:

```
html, body {
        margin:0px;
        padding:0px;
        background:#ffffff;
        }
```

Remove the Spacing

For most browsers, setting the margin to 0px removes the spacing.

Adding the margin and padding properties will make the page begin in the very top-left corner of the browser's window (see Figure 15.2). It is also always good form to define the background color.

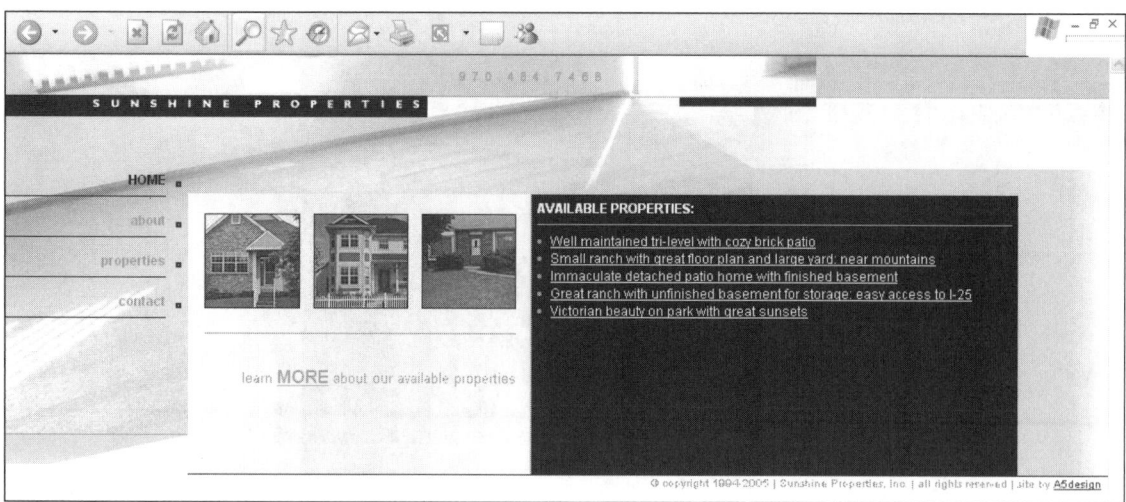

Figure 15.2
Page with the `margin` and `padding` properties for the `<html>` and `<body>` tags set to `0px`.
© 2014 Cengage Learning.

CREATING THE FRAMEWORK FOR A FIXED-WIDTH CSS DESIGN

The five case studies in Chapters 9, 10, 11, 12, and 13 go into the specifics of creating fixed designs that can also be easily modified to be liquid layouts. This section explains the basics of creating the framework for such a design. Following are the various stages of creating such a design:

1. Add basic XHTML framework and initial style rule.

Things to note about the code in step 1:

- As with table-based designs, the code in Listing 15.1 provides the basic structure that contains the `DocType`, character encoding labeling, embedded or linked style sheet, and the code and content that are to be displayed on the page. A rule then defines the margins, padding, font, font color, and background color for the `<HTML>` and `<BODY>` tags.

Listing 15.1   Code for Step 1

```
<!DOCTYPE html PUBLIC "-//W3C//DTD XHTML 1.0 Transitional//EN"
    "DTD/xhtml1-transitional.dtd">
<html><head><title>Fixed-Width Design</title>
<meta http-equiv="Content-Type" content="text/html;
    charset=iso-8859-1" />
```

```
<style type="text/css">
html, body {
    margin:0px;
    padding:0px;
    font: 13px Arial, Helvetica, sans-serif;
    color:#000000;
    background:#ffffff;
    }
</style>
</head>
<body>
</body>
</html>
```

2. Create body and header rules in the style sheet and add code to the XHTML body (see Figure 15.3).

Figure 15.3
Design with header area added, along with a tag that restrains the width of the design to 770 pixels.
© 2014 Cengage Learning.

Things to note about the code in step 2:

- The a5-body rule is used as a container to restrain the width of the entire page to 770 pixels. The advantage of being able to control the width is that if the designer wants the design to expand to the full width of the screen, the value of the width property simply needs to be set to 100%.

Default Width of DIV Tags Depends on Assigned Positioning

<DIV> tags, by default, will stretch to 100% width of the screen when assigned relative positioning. If absolute positioning is assigned, the tag, by default, will expand only as wide as the content expands the container.

- The a5-header rule sets the basic properties of the <DIV> tag that will be assigned to the content inside the tag (see Listing 15.2).

Listing 15.2   Code for Step 2

```
<!DOCTYPE html PUBLIC "-//W3C//DTD XHTML 1.0 Transitional//EN"
      "DTD/xhtml1-transitional.dtd">
    <html><head><title>Fixed-Width Design</title>
    <meta http-equiv="Content-Type" content="text/html;
      charset=iso-8859-1" />
    <style type="text/css">
    html, body {
        margin:0px;
        padding:0px;
        font: 13px Arial, Helvetica, sans-serif;
        color:#000000;
        background:#ffffff;
        }
    #a5-body {
        position: absolute;
        left:0px;
        top:0px;
        width: 770px;
        text-align:left;
        }
    #a5-header {
        position:absolute;
        left:0px;
        top:0px;
        text-align:center;
        color:#ffffff;
        width:100%;
        background:red;
        height:180px;
        }
    </style>
    </head>
    <body>
    <div id="a5-body">
        <div id="a5-header">
            Header content goes here.
        </div>
    </div>
    </body>
    </html>
```

3. Create rules in the style sheet that not only create the left and right columns but also the rule they are nested inside of. Then add the code to the XHTML body (see Figure 15.4).

Figure 15.4
Design with the left and right columns added to a `<DIV>` tag that positions the content 180 pixels below the header `<DIV>`.
© 2014 Cengage Learning.

Things to note about the code in step 3:

- The `a5-main-content` rule is added to force the positioning of the left and right columns. It is positioned below the header, which is set to 180 pixels high. Therefore, the rule positions the `<DIV>` tag 180 pixels from the top. It also separates the nested left and right columns from the bottom footer area that will be added.

- The `a5-column-left` rule is created to force the `<DIV>` to the top-left corner of the `a5-main-content` `<DIV>` tag. The `left` property tells the `<DIV>` tag to position itself 0 pixels from the left side. The `margin-right` property of the rule restricts its positioning by telling it that it must end its width at 232 pixels from the right-hand side of the page or `<DIV>` tag in which it is nested.

- The `a5-column-right` rule is added to position the column on the right side of the page and force its width to 232 pixels. The `right` property tells the `<DIV>` tag that it is to be 0 pixels from the right side of the page.

Columns Extend Vertically When Using Background Images

Nesting `<DIV>` tags do not always function the same as nesting tables. Figure 15.4 shows that the background color of the right column does not stretch to the full height of the `a5-main-content` tag in which it is nested. While the designer can force the height of the right column, if the left column grows, the right column will not change its height. This situation presents a problem when repeating a background color or image. The figure shows how the background of the `a5- main-content` extends vertically beyond the right column but not the left column because the left column is forcing the height. Unlike with table-based design, this changes the way a designer can control the look and feel of the site (see Listing 15.3).

Listing 15.3   Code for Step 3

```
<!DOCTYPE html PUBLIC "-//W3C//DTD XHTML 1.0 Transitional//EN"
        "DTD/xhtml1-transitional.dtd">
    <html><head><title>Fixed-Width Design</title>
    <meta http-equiv="Content-Type" content="text/html;
        charset=iso-8859-1" />
    <style type="text/css">
    html, body {
        margin:0px;
        padding:0px;
        font: 13px Arial, Helvetica, sans-serif;
        color:#000000;
        background:#ffffff;
        }
    #a5-body {
        position: absolute;
        left:0px;
        top:0px;
        width:770px;
        text-align:left;
        }
    #a5-header {
        position:absolute;
        left:0px;
        top:0px;
        text-align:center;
        color:#ffffff;
        width:100%;
        background:red;
        height:180px;
        }
    #a5-main-content {
        position:absolute;
        left:0px;
        top:180px;
        color:#ffffff;
        width:100%;
        background:green;
        border:0px solid #ffffff;
        }
```

```
    #a5-column-left {
        position:relative;
        left:0px;
        top:0px;
        color:#ffffff;
        margin-right:232px;
        border:0px solid #ffffff;
        background:blue;
        }
    #a5-column-right {
        position:absolute;
        right:0px;
        top:0px;
        color:#ffffff;
        width:232px;
        background:black;
        border:0px solid #ffffff;
        }
</style>
</head>
<body>
<div id="a5-body">
    <div id="a5-header">
        Header content goes here.
    </div>
    <div id="a5-main-content">
        <div id="a5-column-left">
            Left column content goes here.<br /><br />And here.
        </div>
        <div id="a5-column-right">
            Right column content goes here.
        </div>
    </div>
</div>
</body>
</html>
```

4. Create a footer rule in the style sheet and add the code to the XHTML body (see Figure 15.5).

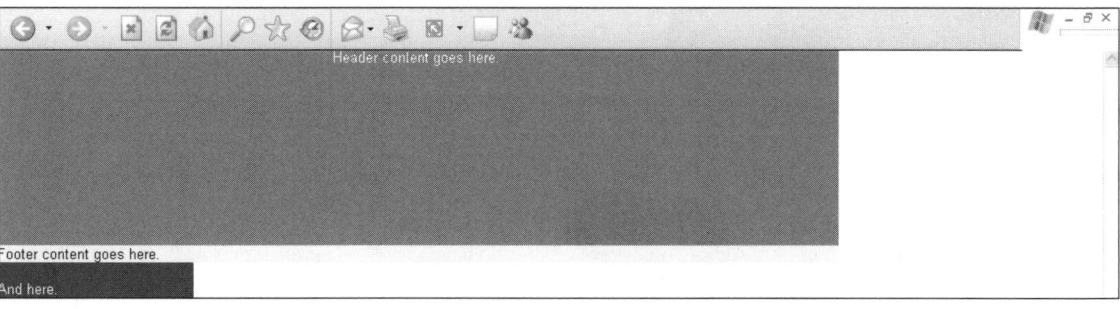

Figure 15.5
Design with the footer rule added.
© 2014 Cengage Learning.

Things to note about the code in step 4:

■ The a5-footer rule is nested inside the a5-main-content tag. When the rule is assigned relative positioning, it is forced to the next line because the left and right columns fill the entire width of the page. If the a5-column-left rule were assigned absolute positioning without a width, the left and right columns together would not fill the entire width of the page, which would bump up the positioning of the a5-footer area, making the page look jumbled (see Figure 15.6).

■ The a5-footer rule does not need a width assigned because it is assigned relative positioning, which makes it fill 100% of the width by default (see Listing 15.4).

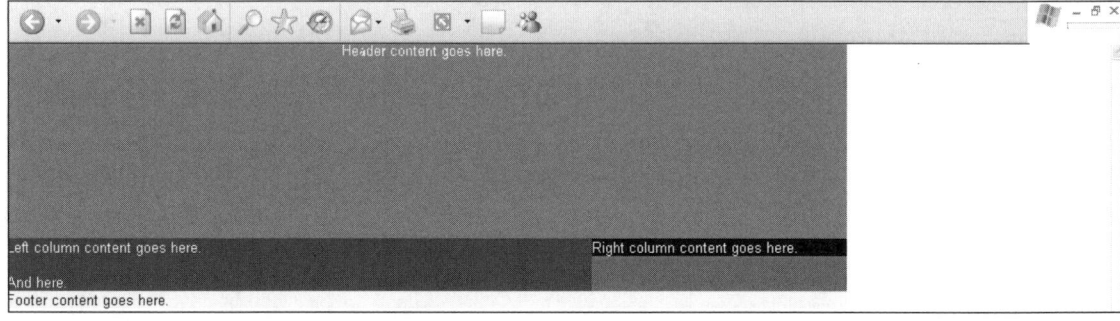

Figure 15.6
Completed framework of fixed-width design that includes two nested columns in a <DIV> tag that is positioned between the header and footer areas.
© 2014 Cengage Learning.

Listing 15.4   Code for Step 4

```
<!DOCTYPE html PUBLIC "-//W3C//DTD XHTML 1.0 Transitional//EN"
        "DTD/xhtml1-transitional.dtd">
    <html><head><title>Fixed-Width Design</title>
    <meta http-equiv="Content-Type" content="text/html;
        charset=iso-8859-1" />
    <style type="text/css">
    html, body {
        margin:0px;
        padding:0px;
        font: 13px Arial, Helvetica, sans-serif;
        color:#000000;
        background:#ffffff;
        }
    #a5-body {
        position: absolute;
        left:0px;
        top:0px;
        width:770px;
        text-align:left;
        }
    #a5-header {
        position:absolute;
        left:0px;
        top:0px;
        text-align:center;
        color:#ffffff;
        width:100%;
        background:red;
        height:180px;
        }
    #a5-main-content {
        position:absolute;
        left:0px;
        top:180px;
        color:#ffffff;
        width:100%;
        background:green;
        border:0px solid #ffffff;
        }
```

```
        #a5-column-left {
            position:absolute;
            left:0px;
            top:0px;
            color:#ffffff;
            margin-right:232px;
            border:0px solid #ffffff;
            background:blue;
            }
        #a5-column-right {
            position:absolute;
            right:0px;
            top:0px;
            color:#ffffff;
            width:232px;
            background:black;
            border:0px solid #ffffff;
            }
    #a5-footer {
        position:relative;
        left:0px;
        top:0px;
        color:#000000;
        background:yellow;
        border:0px solid #ffffff;
        }
</style>
</head>
<body>
<div id="a5-body">
    <div id="a5-header">
        Header content goes here.
    </div>
    <div id="a5-main-content">
        <div id="a5-column-left">
            Left column content goes here.<br /><br />And here.
        </div>
        <div id="a5-column-right">
            Right column content goes here.
        </div>
```

```
            <div id="a5-footer">
                Footer content goes here.
            </div>
        </div>
    </div>
    </body>
    </html>
```

Typically, the designer adds text, images, and additional code to the framework as it is being built. Figure 15.7 is a simplified example of how the page would look with content added and the style sheet modified to not only make the page more attractive but to also customize various <DIV> tags.

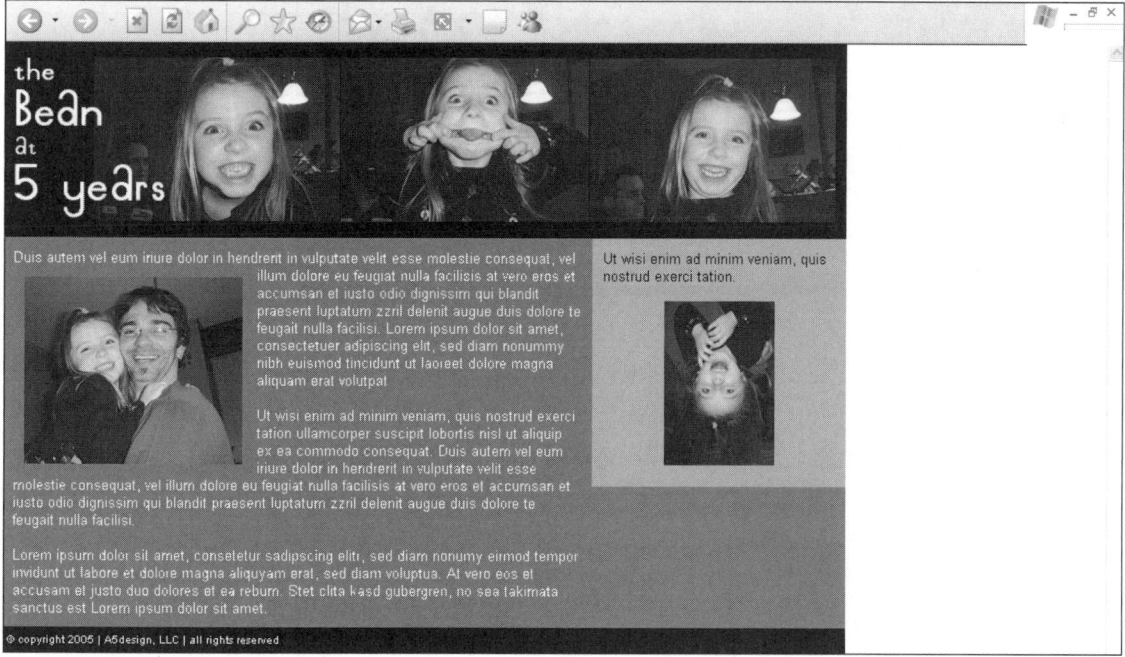

Figure 15.7
Sample content added to framework of the site, which was modified to accompany the content and to make it more attractive.
© 2014 Cengage Learning.

TAKING INTO ACCOUNT INCREASING AND DECREASING COLUMN HEIGHTS

Although it is nice to include the footer row at the bottom of the design in Figure 15.7, there are a couple of caveats to this layout, at least when including containers that use absolute positioning:

- Because the positioning of the right column is set to `absolute`, if the content in the column were to be increased, it would not only stretch lower than the left column, but because the footer also has relative positioning assigned to it, the right column would also flow above or below it, depending on the browser (see Figure 15.8).

Figure 15.8
A problem with a container with absolute positioning (right column) running past a container with relative positioning (footer) that should, visually, remain below it.

© 2014 Cengage Learning.

- If the content in the left column were to be decreased, not only would the right column extend below both it and the footer `<DIV>`, but the footer `<DIV>` would also move up past the `a5-main-content` `<DIV>` (see Figure 15.9).

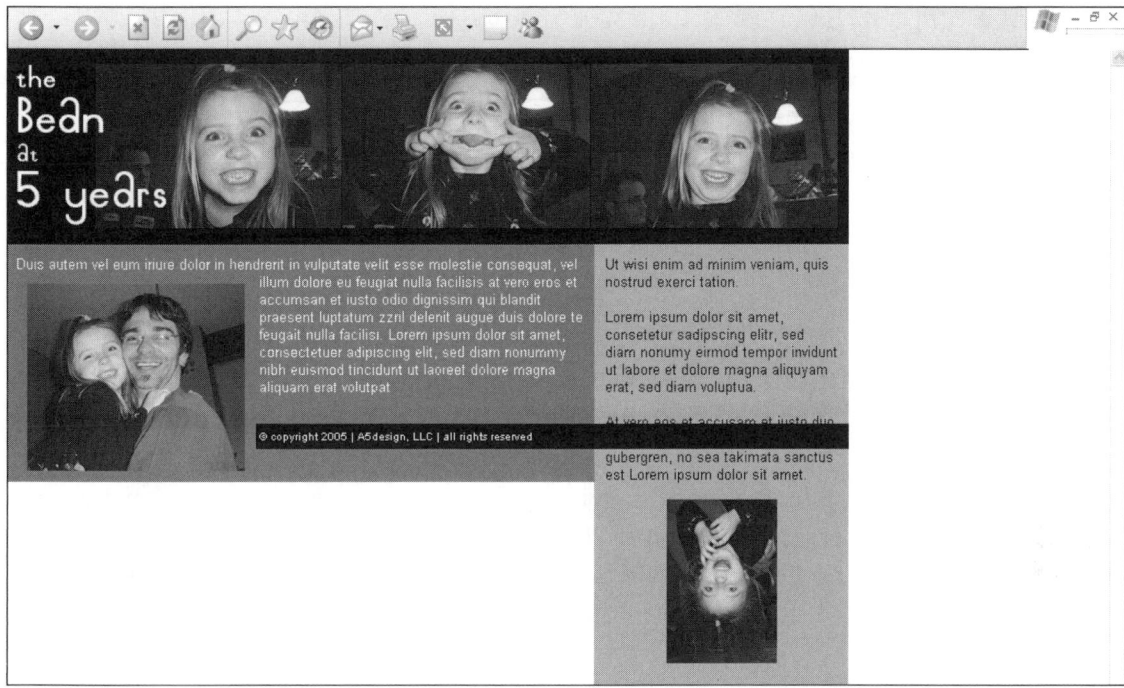

Figure 15.9
If content is decreased in the left column, not only does the right column move below the footer but the footer also moves up.

© 2014 Cengage Learning.

Content Flows Around Floated Images

Because the photo in the left column of Figure 15.9 is floated, it is not included in the document flow, meaning other elements could pass above and below it, as well as in front of and behind it.

If the amount of content is going to change dynamically, this design structure may not be the best solution. The designer may consider not including a footer area and assigning different positions to the <DIV> tags, or the designer may want to use the design technique described in Chapter 12 or 13 that provides a solution to creating equal column designs.

CENTERING A FIXED-WIDTH DESIGN

Depending on the requirements, some sites need to be designed with liquid layouts—that is, they fill the full width of the screen. Yet others require a fixed width. HTML and XHTML used to make the process simple, but with the varied browser support of CSS, the process is a little more involved. One way requires wrapping two different <DIV> tags around the body. Following are the steps to accomplish this task:

1. Add a rule to the style sheet that centers the fixed-width design, which is set at 770 pixels for this example. This rule centers the body for IE 5 and 5.5. It would be extremely rare for this code still to be necessary, but it doesn't hurt to explain its use.

```
#a5-body-center {
        text-align:center;
        }
```

2. Add a second rule that sets the text-align property to left, assigns the left and right margins to auto, and defines the positioning as relative. Setting the positioning to relative will allow the design to be positioned relative to the <DIV> tag in which it is nested. The auto value of the margins will tell the browser to set the margins evenly on both sides, thus centering the code. The text-align:left; code is added because the a5-body-center rule that was added centers not only the body, but also the text in that container, by inheritance.

```
#a5-body-center {
        text-align:center;
        }
    #a5-body {
        position: absolute;
        left:0px;
        top:0px;
        width:770px;
        text-align:left;
        }
```

3. Add the two <DIV> tags around the code between the <BODY> tags in the XHTML page. Listing 15.5 is the code that was used to create Figure 15.7.

Listing 15.5   Code for Figure 15.7

```
<!DOCTYPE html PUBLIC "-//W3C//DTD XHTML 1.0 Transitional//EN"
        "DTD/xhtml1-transitional.dtd">
    <html><head><title>Fixed-Width Design</title>
    <meta http-equiv="Content-Type" content="text/html;
        charset=iso-8859-1" />
    <style type="text/css">
    html, body {
```

```
        margin:0px;
        padding:0px;
        font: 13px Arial, Helvetica, sans-serif;
        color:#000000;
        background:#ffffff;
        }
#a5-body-center {
        text-align:center;
        }
#a5-body {
        position: relative;
        margin-left:auto;
        margin-right:auto;
        width:770px;
        text-align:left;
        }
#a5-header {
        text-align:center;
        color:#ffffff;
        width:100%;
        padding-top:15px;
        background:black;
        height:180px;
        }
#a5-main-content {
        position:absolute;
        left:0px;
        top:180px;
        color:#ffffff;
        width:100%;
        background:#89766F;
        border:0px solid #ffffff;
        }
    #a5-column-left {
            position:relative;
            left:0px;
            top:0px;
            color:#ffffff;
            padding:10px;
            margin-right:232px;
            background:#7A7878;
            border:0px solid #ffffff;
        }
```

```
        #a5-column-right {
            position:absolute;
            right:0px;
            top:0px;
            color:#000000;
            height:100%;
            width:232px;
            background:#B0ADAD;
            border:0px solid #ffffff;
            }
    #a5-footer {
        position:relative;
        left:0px;
        top:0px;
        font: 10px Arial, Helvetica, sans-serif;
        padding:5px;
        color:#ffffff;
        background:#000000;
        border:0px solid #ffffff;
        }
</style>
</head>
<body>
<div id="a5-body-center">
    <div id="a5-body">
        <div id="a5-header">
                <div><img src="images/photo_beanie_faces.jpg"
                width="750" height="150" alt="" border="0" /></div>
        </div>
        <div id="a5-main-content">
            <div id="a5-column-left">
                Duis autem vel eum iriure dolor in hendrerit in
                    vulputate velit esse <span style="position:
                    relative;float:left;padding:10px;"><img
                    src="images/photo_beanie_daddy.jpg" width="200"
                    height="171" alt="" border="0" /></span>molestie
                consequat, vel illum dolore eu feugiat nulla
                facilisis at vero eros et accumsan et iusto odio
                dignissim qui blandit praesent luptatum zzril
                delenit augue duis dolore te feugait nulla
```

```
                            facilisi. Lorem ipsum dolor sit amet, consectetuer
                            adipiscing elit, sed diam nonummy nibh euismod
                            tincidunt ut laoreet dolore magna aliquam erat
                            volutpat
            <br /><br />
            Ut wisi enim ad minim veniam, quis nostrud exerci tation
                    ullamcorper suscipit lobortis nisl ut aliquip ex ea commodo
                    consequat. Duis autem vel eum iriure dolor in hendrerit in
                    vulputate velit esse molestie consequat, vel illum dolore eu
                    feugiat nulla facilisis at vero eros et accumsan et iusto
                    odio dignissim qui blandit praesent luptatum zzril delenit
                    augue duis dolore te feugait nulla facilisi.
            <br /><br />
            Lorem ipsum dolor sit amet, consetetur sadipscing elitr, sed diam
                    nonumy eirmod tempor invidunt ut labore et dolore magna
                    aliquyam erat, sed diam voluptua. At vero eos et accusam et
                    justo duo dolores et ea rebum. Stet clita kasd gubergren, no
                    sea takimata sanctus est Lorem ipsum dolor sit amet.
                </div>
                <div id="a5-column-right">
                    <div style="padding:10px;">
            Ut wisi enim ad minim veniam, quis nostrud exerci tation.
                    <br />
                    <div style="text-align:center;padding:15px 0px 10px
                            0px;"><img src="images/photo_beanie_right.jpg"
                            width="100" height="150" alt="" border="0"
                            /></div>
                    </div>
                </div>
                <div id="a5-footer">
                    &copy; copyright 2005 | A5design, LLC | all rights
                        reserved  
                </div>
            </div>
        </div>
    </div>
    </body>
    </html>
```

When the page is rendered, it would look like Figure 15.10. Notice that there is an even amount of space on both sides of the design.

Figure 15.10
Fixed-width design that is centered using CSS.
© 2014 Cengage Learning.

CREATING A LIQUID DESIGN

Because of the way the fixed design was created, modifying it to be a liquid design is very simple. All the designer needs to do is change the 770px value of the a5-body rule to 100%. This is because the left column will always try to fill the screen because it is assigned relative positioning and it is included in a <DIV> tag, which together defaults to 100% width. There are two main reasons the design works the way it does:

■ The left column has relative positioning assigned to it, so it can expand and contract, depending on the resolution or width of the screen.

■ While the positioning will stretch to 100% by default, it can also be controlled with the margin property. In this case, the margin-right property is set to 232px, which means the column will stretch within 232 pixels of the right side of the screen but no further.

Figure 15.11 shows how the page shown in Figure 15.10 expands when the value of the a5-body rule is changed from 770px to 100%.

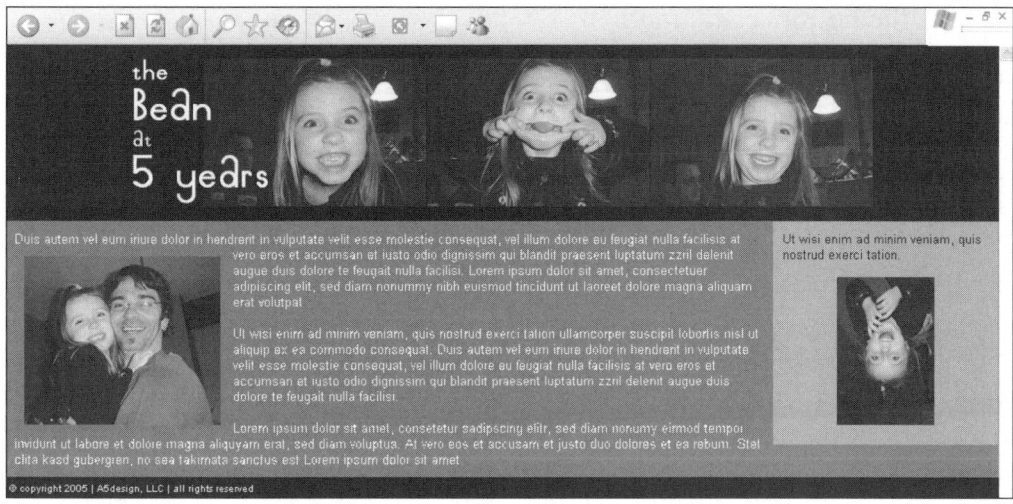

Figure 15.11
Liquid design that fills the full width of the screen.
© 2014 Cengage Learning.

Chapters 9, 10, 11, 12, and 13 provide additional examples and explanations of how designs can be created to be liquid.

CREATING A LINE

When XHTML tables were used to add lines in content, the designer could repeat a background image sideways along a table row or simply place an image in the table row, among other solutions. CSS-based layout made this much more simple. Because <DIV> tags are used so frequently in page layout, the tool for which to create a line, many times, is already there, and if it's not, it's easy to add. The code in Listing 15.6 shows two lines of text, representing paragraphs, which are separated by two <BR /> tags (see Figure 15.12).

```
This text represents the top paragraph.

This text represents the bottom paragraph.
```

Figure 15.12
Two paragraphs separated by <br /> tags.
© 2014 Cengage Learning.

Listing 15.6   Code Before <DIV> Tag Is Wrapped Around

This text represents the top paragraph.

```
<br /><br />
```

This text represents the bottom paragraph.

For a designer to add the line that is between the two paragraphs in Figure 15.13, a `<DIV>` tag can simply be wrapped around the top or bottom paragraph, with a basic style assigned to it (see Listing 15.7).

```
This text represents the top paragraph.
This text represents the bottom paragraph.
```

Figure 15.13
Line that is added between the two paragraphs in Figure 15.12.

© 2014 Cengage Learning.

Listing 15.7   Code that Creates a Line Using a `<DIV>` Tag

```
<div style="width:260px;margin:0px 0px 5px 0px;padding:0px 0px 10px 0px;border-bottom:1px
solid #000000;">
This text represents the top paragraph.
</div>
```

This text represents the bottom paragraph. Things to note about the style that is added to the `<DIV>` tag, resulting in the layout in Figure 15.13:

- The width rule is added to control the width of the content. If the width is not set, the `<DIV>` tag would run as wide as the page allowed.

- The margin rule is added to provide 5 pixels of separation between the line and the second paragraph. It basically is setting half the height that was created when the two `<BR/>` tags were added.

- The padding rule sets the space between the first paragraph and the line, which is really the bottom border of the paragraph.

- The border-bottom rule sets the border width to 1 px and the color to black.

USING BACKGROUND IMAGES AS DESIGN ELEMENTS

Back when Netscape 4.7 was the standard, there were all types of issues when designing with background images. These days, however, CSS-based design allows for the full use of background images, which includes layering nested background images on top of one another. This change allows for more design possibilities. One example is to use a background image for the entire site.

Figure 15.14 shows how background images can be used more extensively. There are four things to note about the design:

- The background in the right column (right side of the infinity loop) is broken up from the background in the left column (left side of the loop, along with the woman). This is because the right image is best saved as a GIF file, while the left image should be saved as a JPG.

- The entire left column of color is repeated as a background image in the page's `<BODY>` tag, so it will repeat endlessly down the left-hand side. It repeats underneath the background image of the left column. Because the bottom of the left background image looks exactly like the page background image, there is seamless repeating.

- Each menu item is assigned a background image to its left that serves as a bullet.

- The bullet changes when the menu item is moused over, which is explained in the next section.

Figure 15.14
Design that uses background images as menu bullets, images for the left and right columns, and a repeating image for the entire page.

Source: Innergy Coaching, LLC.

CODING CSS MOUSEOVERS

Menu mouseovers used to require JavaScript to perform a simple image switch. Now, CSS allows the designer to simply replace the background image by assigning a different image when the user mouses over an item (see Figure 15.15). The three-step process is as follows:

Figure 15.15
CSS-driven mouseover in the menu section of the site.
Source: Innergy Coaching, LLC.

1. The designer creates a rule that will be used to display the menu item when it is not moused over. The two main properties to pay attention to in the following code are display and background. The display property, when assigned a block value, tells the browser to vertically stack each hyperlinked menu item when it is included inside the a5-menu container. The background property, with its values, determines what image will be used for the menu item, including how it will be positioned and whether it will be repeated. In this example, the image will not be repeated, and it will be positioned in the top-left corner of the block.

```
#a5-menu a {
        display: block;
        background: url(images/bg-menu-off.gif) no-repeat 0px 0px;
        text-decoration:none;
        color:#ffffff;
        font-weight:normal;
        padding: 3px 5px 2px 25px;
    }
```

2. The designer then adds the hover element to the hyperlinks. When the user mouses over a link, the background image is changed from bg-menu-off.gif to bg-menu-on.gif,

with the same positioning of the image. The font is turned bold, so not only the image, but also the changing text color, identifies the link.

```
#a5-menu a:hover {
        background: url(images/bg-menu-on.gif) no-repeat 0px 0px;
        font-weight:bold;
        color:#ffffff;
    }
```

3. The menu items need to be added to a container with the ID value of a5-menu.

```
<div id="a5-menu">
    <a href="index.htm">home</a>
    <a href="about.htm">about</a>
    <a href="services.htm">services</a>
    <a href="ezine.htm">ezine</a>
    <a href="contact.htm">contact</a>
</div>
```

CSS Menu Code Online

A more complex CSS menu that provides drop-down menus is available online. It allows for multi-level flyouts and customization possibilities.

Using JavaScript Drop-down Menus

Often, a site requires more than a flat menu. Rather, it requires drop-down menus so the user can access the various levels of key pages easily by perusing the menu on one page. Figure 15.16 provides an example of such a menu.

Figure 15.16
Example of a drop-down JavaScript menu.
© 2014 Cengage Learning.

CSS Menus Easier to Code Than JavaScript

Unless the designer or developer understands JavaScript, creating such a menu can be time-intensive. This is one reason why CSS drop-down menus are quickly becoming the standard for many designers.

REMEMBERING THE ORDER OF MARGIN AND PADDING SHORTCUTS

Writing shorthand CSS properties and values makes designing and managing sites much easier. Sometimes remembering the order of the shorthand methods, however, is not always as easy. There is a visual reminder for the value order of the two most commonly used properties: margin and padding. Because the values are ordered in clockwise motion, they can be visualized as being positioned around a box, starting with the top border (see Figure 15.17).

Figure 15.17
A visual reminder of how the values are ordered with the shorthand versions of the margin and padding properties.

© 2014 Cengage Learning.

USING THE BORDER AND BACKGROUND PROPERTIES FOR TROUBLESHOOTING

When developing CSS designs where containers of images and text are mortised together, it is important to know exactly where the boundaries of each box are. If this is not known, a simple process of adding a background color to a container can turn into a time-consuming task. Looking at Figure 15.18, it appears that the containers are properly positioned.

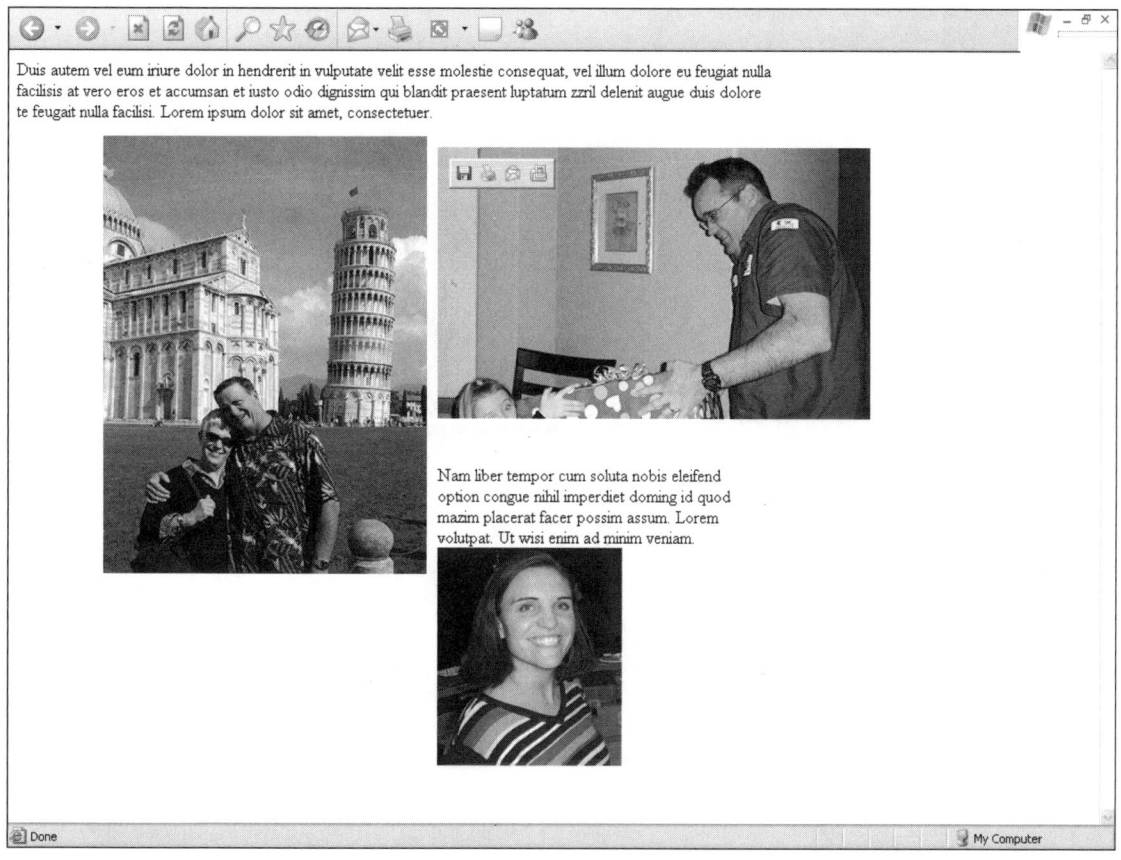

Figure 15.18
A page with three boxes laid out so that no overlap or misplacement appears.
© 2014 Cengage Learning.

The truth, however, is while the text and images may be properly positioned, this does not mean the boxes that contain them are designed to be edited easily. Adding a background color to the top paragraph makes it readily apparent that the page's infrastructure is not positioned as properly as it may appear without the background color (see Figure 15.19).

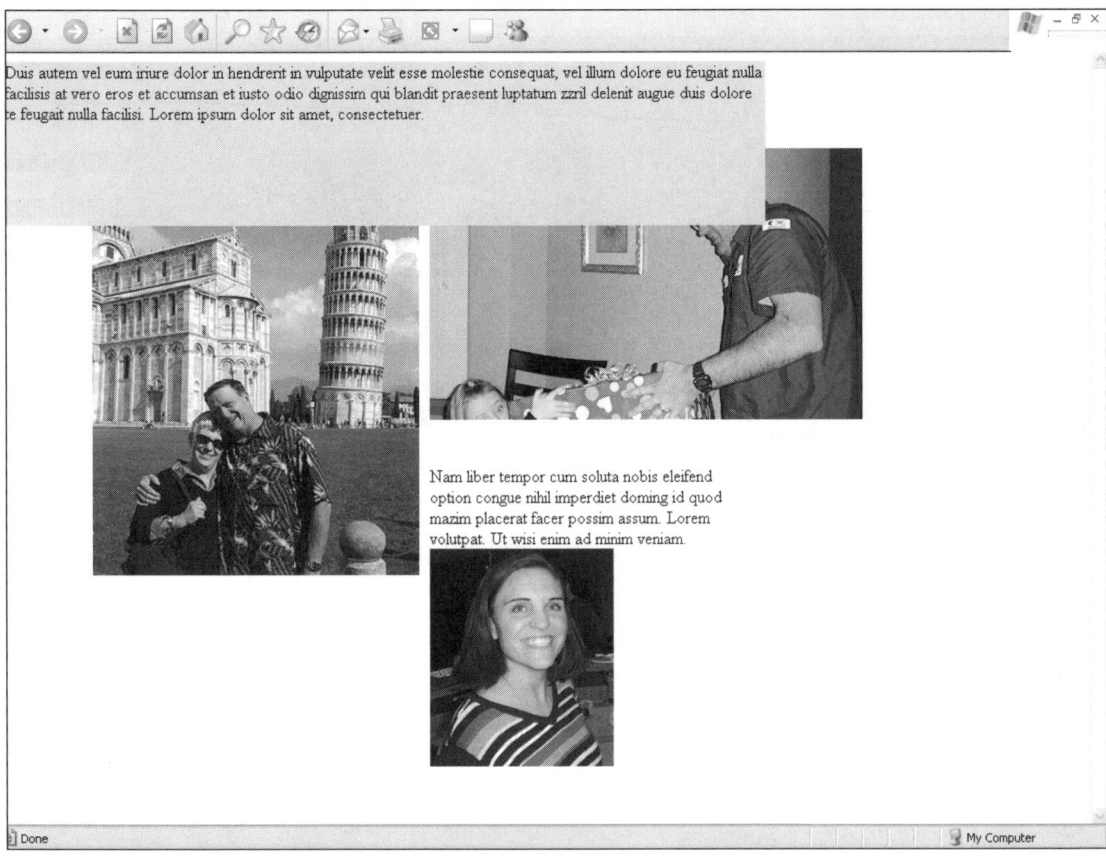

Duis autem vel eum iriure dolor in hendrerit in vulputate velit esse molestie consequat, vel illum dolore eu feugiat nulla facilisis at vero eros et accumsan et iusto odio dignissim qui blandit praesent luptatum zzril delenit augue duis dolore te feugait nulla facilisi. Lorem ipsum dolor sit amet, consectetuer.

Nam liber tempor cum soluta nobis eleifend option congue nihil imperdiet doming id quod mazim placerat facer possim assum. Lorem volutpat. Ut wisi enim ad minim veniam.

Figure 15.19
Results of adding a background color to the top container, which includes the text.
© 2014 Cengage Learning.

Before a designer can correct such a problem with a design, it is necessary to understand where the boundaries are for the elements that are going to be modified. Two methods can be used to view the borders:

■ Turn on the border of the elements by setting it to at least one pixel (see Figure 15.20). The code to do so is `border:1px solid #000000;`. When the designer is done testing the container, the value of the border size can be set to 0, such as `border:0px solid #000000;`. Much of the code in this book contains such lines. Because the extra code takes up a nominal amount of file size, it is easier to turn the border off than to remove the code. One advantage to this is that the designer can view the shapes of the containers and what is layered behind them because, other than the borders, they are transparent.

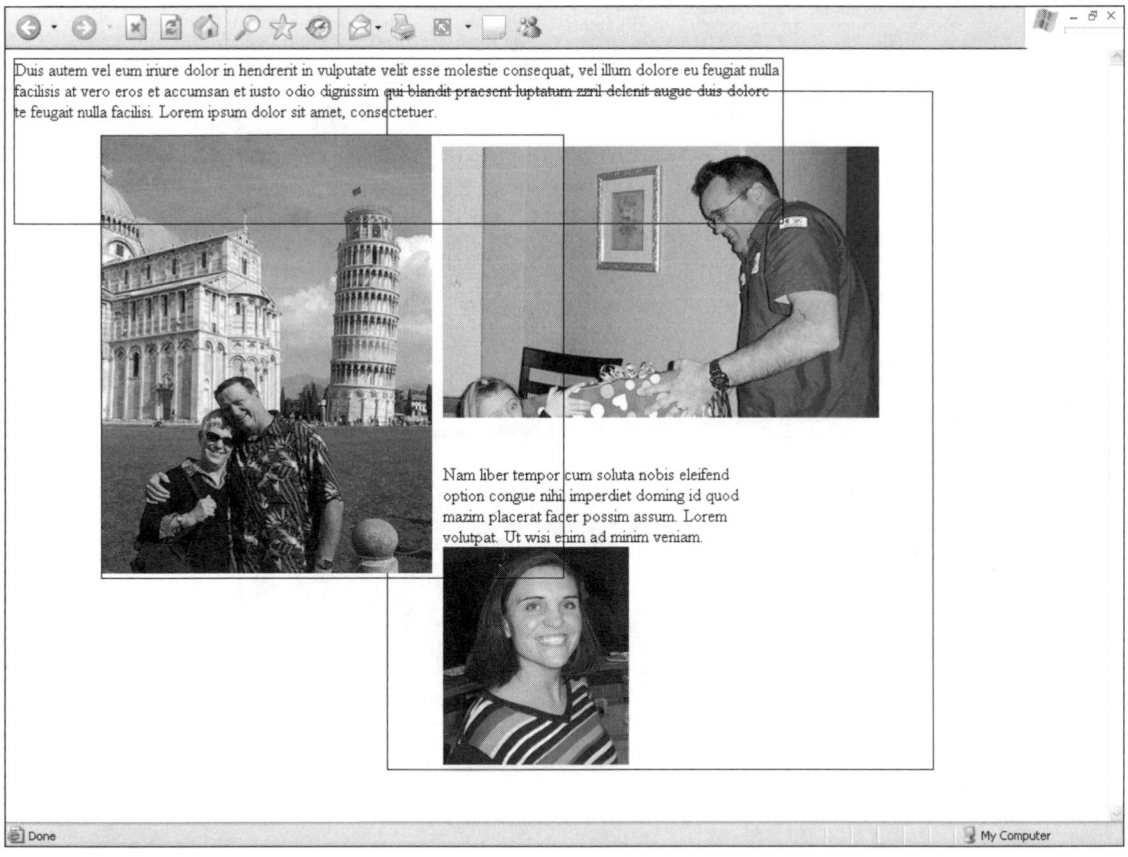

Figure 15.20
A page with the containers' borders set to 1 to view their boundaries.
© 2014 Cengage Learning.

- Similar to the example in Figure 15.19, the background color can be set to contrast with the background of adjacent containers (see Figure 15.21). The code to do so is `background: red;`. The advantage of this method is that the designer understands the exact width a container will take up. If, on the other hand, a designer is trying to position two boxes to the exact pixel, turning on the borders of the boxes will be confusing because compliant browsers will add the extra width to the total width. Thus, if a box is 200 pixels wide, it will grow to 202 if the border is set to 1, because one pixel will be added to both the left and right sides.

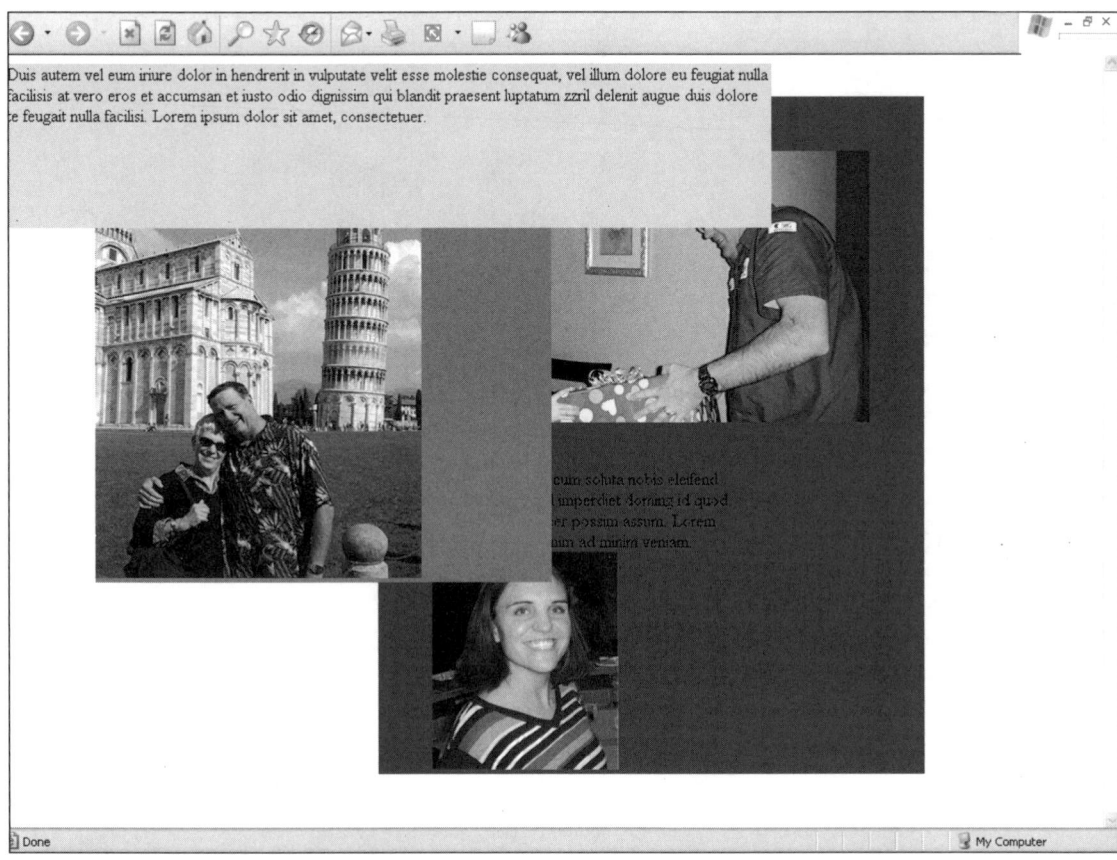

Figure 15.21
A page with the containers' backgrounds set to various colors to view their locations.
© 2014 Cengage Learning.

COMMENTING OUT CODE FOR TROUBLESHOOTING

Any novice designer or developer can create code. An experienced designer or developer, however, can fix things "under the hood." Being able to troubleshoot a page, whether it is XHTML, CSS, or a programming language, is a very necessary skill to have. One helpful method for testing pages is to remove code to either see how a page will react in terms of layout or to see if the problem disappears when the code is removed.

While code can be cut and the page can be saved to perform such testing, the code can be lost if the computer crashes before the code can be reinserted and resaved. A safer method is to comment out the code. This is accomplished by using comment tags, which tell the browser or server to hide the code inside them from the user. For most languages, comment tags work similarly to XHTML tags, where an opening tag is added to the beginning and a closing tag is added to the end of the code that is to be excluded. Comment tags vary depending on the language, and the following are three examples of commonly used tags:

- **XHTML:** The opening tag is <! - -. The closing tag is - ->. The second line of the following code would be output by the server but not displayed by the browser:

```
This is a sample line of text. <br />
<!-- This is the line that would be commented out <br /> -->
This is the line of code the browser would begin displaying again.
```

Comment Tags Must Have Correct Syntax to Validate

An XHTML page will not validate if the comment tags do not have the correct syntax. If the developer, for instance, has too many hyphens in a comment tag, it will not validate.

- **CSS:** The opening tag is /*. The closing tag is */. The second property of the following rule would not be interpreted by the browser:

```
#photo2 {
    position:absolute;
    /* width:90px; */
    height:80px;
    }
```

- **JavaScript:** This is one exception for using comment tags when the designer does not necessarily need to include a closing tag. The opening tag would merely be //. The second line of the following code would be output by the server but not interpreted by the browser:

```
bullet_text_on = new Image
// bullet_text_off = new Image
bullet_text_on.src = "http://www.a5design.com/images/
    bullet_text_on.gif"
```

If, however, the designer wanted to comment out the entire section of code, an opening /* could be used, along with a closing */. Following is how the code would look if it all were to be commented out:

```
bullet_text_on = new Image
// bullet_text_off = new Image
bullet_text_on.src = "http://www.a5design.com/images/
    bullet_text_on.gif"
```

USING UNIQUE NAMING CONVENTIONS

When designing and developing code, whether it is XHTML, CSS, or a programming language, it is usually a smart practice to come up with a unique naming convention because there will be times when a developer's code has to be integrated with another developer's code. If naming conventions conflict, then errors will occur that will require time to troubleshoot.

When creating ID and class selectors in CSS, for example, most of the rules in this book will begin with a5-, which is short for A5design. This helps prevent integrating a style sheet with another site's style sheet. If both style sheets contain a selector for the header, odds are that the other one will not be named a5-header. Instead, it may likely be header.

AVOIDING HORIZONTAL SCROLLBARS

When designing a page, it is usually best to avoid use of a horizontal scroll bar (see Figure 15.22). While some users already feel bothered about scrolling vertically, scrolling horizontally, in many circles, is considered a cardinal sin. This is why a designer often wants to avoid making a page that is too wide, even if just by a few pixels, to make sure that a design does not activate the horizontal bar.

Figure 15.22
A page with the horizontal scrollbar activated because the page was made too wide.
© 2014 Cengage Learning.

Higher Monitor Resolution May Not Activate Horizontal Bar

The one exception to this rule is if the designer is creating a site for a higher resolution that some users will not have their monitors set to access.

While page width must obviously be taken into consideration, a more subtle consideration is the browser the site is being designed in. Compliant browsers do not include the right scroll bar until the height of the page requires it, unlike older versions of IE, which always include it. This means that if the designer creates a page in a compliant browser, an extra 18 pixels will be added to the page, which means the designer has 18 pixels less horizontal space to work with. This is why, in certain situations, it is smart to design sites initially in IE to ensure that the extra pixels are already included in the width.

USING CSS SHORTCUTS

The goal of this book is not necessarily to produce the most efficient CSS coding possible. Rather, it is to make the examples as simple as possible, thus ensuring that the concepts are understood more easily. If the designer wanted to create more efficient code, one way is to use CSS shortcuts. One example of such a shortcut is using an abbreviated HEX number, such as #fff instead of #ffffff. This, however, is just the beginning of many options. More shortcuts can be easily found by using a search engine.

UNDERSTANDING FONT UNITS

There are many considerations when it comes to what type of unit to use when sizing fonts on the Web. The options include pixels, points, ems, and percentages. Following are some things to consider when selecting a font:

- Will the text be viewed in a browser, printed, or both?
- What type of operating system is the design primarily meant for?
- Do you want users to be able to resize the fonts using their browsers?

This subject requires thorough discussion, but it is being noted here for the designer to be aware of the various options for further possible investigation.

USING GLOBALLY DRIVEN <SPAN> AND <DIV> TAGS FOR PRINTING PURPOSES

Sometimes using local or in-line styles can benefit the designer if an element on that page, for example, is the only item in the site that needs to be modified. For example, if a warning on a page needs to be colored red, such an in-line style would work best.

One disadvantage of using local or in-line styles is if the designer wants to add a printing style sheet. Because a printing style sheet enables, and sometimes requires, a designer to be able to set the `display` property to `none`, if those styles cannot be controlled from one document, then the designer will have to modify each of those pages, which not only takes time, but also creates the unnecessary risk of possibly missing a style without thorough testing.

USING INTERCHANGEABLE ELEMENTS WHEN DESIGNING REBRANDABLE SITES

Rebrandable sites often require a designer to create elements that can be easily customizable for various clients. Figure 15.23 is an example of such a site.

Figure 15.23
A rebrandable site with various reusable elements.

Following are five simple tricks being used to create more visual, reusable elements in Figure 15.23:

1. **Layered CSS text that could serve as a drop shadow.** By duplicating XHTML and CSS code, the designer can layer one element over the other. The CSS rule, of course, would need a unique name, but once it's renamed, it can be positioned under the other. This method is used for menu text in the top-right corner in Figure 15.23. The top layer of text is saved as white, while the lower layer is saved as black. The lower layer is simply moved one pixel to the right and one pixel down.

2. **In-line characters that are produced by XHTML code.** There are many XHTML characters that can be used in sites as bullets or other elements to provide easy visual recognition by the user. The arrows to the left of the Services page title are created by the following code: ».

3. **Icons that can be layered over any element without the risk of anti-aliasing affecting their quality.** This element is not unique to Web design. Nearly all software uses it with its icons. The secret is to create clean edges that don't blend into the background (see Figure 15.24).

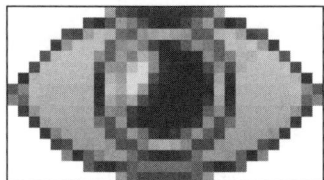

Figure 15.24
An icon that can stand on its own without requiring anti-aliasing.
© 2014 Cengage Learning.

By not blending into the background, the icon can be moved anywhere on the page or have the background image changed without any consequences, other than the colors possibly not popping off the page. Figure 15.25 shows what the icon would look like on the page if its background were changed to black.

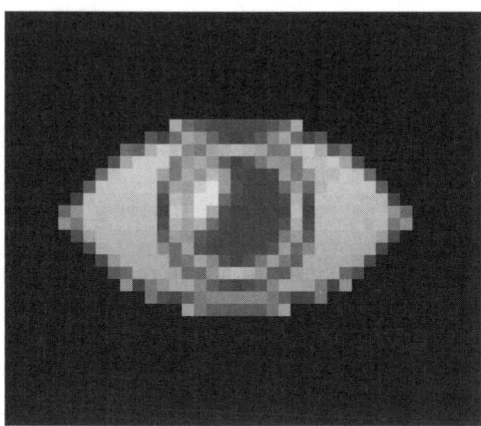

Figure 15.25
The same icon in Figure 15.24 with the background color changed to black.
© 2014 Cengage Learning.

4. **Using 24-bit PNGs.** A trick that is easier than creating icons with clean edges is simply saving images as 24-bit PNGs. This way they can have edges that blend in with the background. The only downside is the file size of these images will tend to be larger.

5. **Using linear shapes.** With curves comes anti-aliasing, which makes it more difficult to change background colors of websites or portions of them. While curves are used in the icon, the designer is able to get away with that because the icon is small, making it more difficult to see the pixilation along the edges. This is why many sites use linear shapes that do not require any new images to be created. Instead, the background image is simply changed in the style sheet. All of the shapes in the header in Figure 15.23, barring the logo and the "Rebrandable Site" text, use CSS layered <DIV> tags to provide the design. It is a simple example, but one that illustrates the possibilities if the designer were to get creative.

INCLUDING HIDDEN <DIV> TAGS FOR FUTURE USE

When creating rebrandable sites, it is necessary sometimes for the designer to prepare for content that may be added to the source code down the road. One way to do this is to create containers in the code. When the `display` property is set to `none`, the container will then be "invisible" until the property is removed. Figure 15.26 shows how Figure 15.23 would look if the rule had its display property removed from the style sheet.

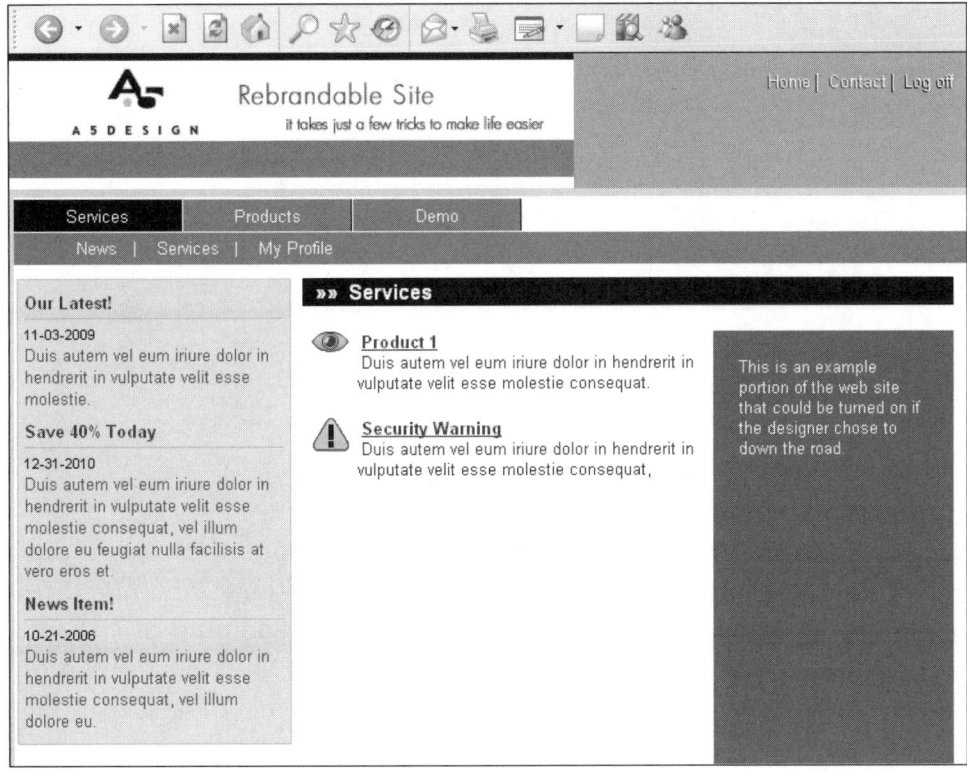

Figure 15.26
The same design as in Figure 15.23 but with a container in the right portion of the body made visible.
© 2014 Cengage Learning.

For a lot of sites, it is not overly difficult to go into the code to add elements after the site is live. However, some sites require more involved coding that may make it too time-consuming or difficult to add elements after the fact. This is a quick solution for sites with such future needs.

POSITIONING THE LINE-HEIGHT PROPERTY CORRECTLY

Using the line-height property allows the designer to not only play with a site's typography, but also have the ability to increase or decrease the height of a text area for structural purposes. To do this, the following code is all that needs to be added to a rule: `line-height:14px;`. This property, however, will not be read by browsers if it is positioned above the `font` property. Following are examples of the incorrect and correct placement of the `line-height` property.

Incorrectly positioned `line-height` property:

```
#a5-column-left-text {
  line-height:60px;
  font: 10pt tahoma, arial, helvetica, sans-serif;
  }
```

Correctly positioned `line-height` property:

```
#a5-column-left-text {
  font: 10pt tahoma, arial, helvetica, sans-serif;
  line-height:60px;
  }
```

TESTING CONTINUALLY AND CONSISTENTLY

It is a good practice to continually test pages as they are being created, rather than waiting until the coding is completed, because coding problems can quickly compound themselves. If a container, for example, is assigned the wrong width, padding, or margins, other related <DIV> or <SPAN> tags may also be adjusted incorrectly. Once the initial problem is discovered, any number of changes may need to be made to make the design flow correctly.

Testing should also be done consistently. One method of testing is to always open the same browsers in the same order. The designer can then easily click on each browser and refresh it to see how the site appears. By using some method of consistency, the designer will recall more readily how each browser handles the nuances of CSS.

CREATING SOURCE IMAGE FILES THAT CAN BE EASILY CUSTOMIZED AND RESAVED

Most websites are in continual evolution. That is, they are constantly undergoing changes and revisions. While physically making changes to the source code of Web pages is not overly time-consuming, tweaking image files is an entirely different matter. There are two issues a designer should be aware of when editing images:

- The quality of an image can only be maintained or degraded but not improved. Once an image is compressed, certain aspects of that file are permanently lost.

- Images that are flattened (reduced to one layer) are difficult and sometimes impossible to edit, depending on the type of edits required.

For any designer who has had a client request that the "colors in an image or comp be replaced" or "this object be moved closer to that object," understanding the importance of source files quickly becomes necessary. If the client wants these changes made to a flattened image, many times the task is difficult, if not impossible, without re-creating the image.

This is why the designer should always save source files for the images created. They can be the original photos or images used to create images, the final images fully uncompressed, or layered Photoshop files that can be edited easily. Each of these options offers the designer the ability to easily resave or edit a file—and usually with very little effort.

Whenever a designer creates a Photoshop file for an image or a design comp, that file should be saved in its original format without any flattening of the layers. If the designer needs to make revisions, then a new version of the file should be saved. While each Photoshop file for a Web page can easily reach 5MB, the disk space used for each version is more than a fair trade-off when the designer needs to create a website that uses two images less than 1KB each to serve as the mouseover images. For instance, what if the client asks that a file be cropped by 60 percent? Then, a day later, the client says the file was actually better the way it was. What then? If the original version of the file was not saved, the only option is to re-create the image. Take, for example, the comp shown in Figure 15.27. Considering that there are 64 layers in this image, reconstituting it could take hours.

Figure 15.27
Photoshop design that has 64 layers.
© Adobe® Systems Incorporated.

BREAKING OUT SECTIONS OF SOURCE IMAGE FILES

Saving source image files provides flexibility and ease in editing website images down the road. Some pieces can even be saved separately from their original files for added convenience. Figure 15.28, for example, shows a screenshot of a second-level page that uses such images. In the site, nearly all second- and third-level pages use the oval image on the right. In this example, the U.S. Capitol building is included in the oval. Each section, however, has its own image.

Figure 15.28
Site that uses a different photo in the right-hand oval for each section.
Source: National Farmers Union.

To make creating and editing these photos easier, the oval area was cropped from the source PSD file and saved as its own individual source file (see Figure 15.29). This allows the designer to apply that specific file to create or edit photos, rather than having to open the entire page and save the one desired image from that file.

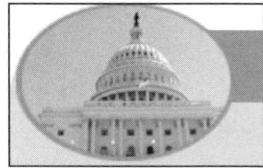

Figure 15.29
Image used in Figure 16.28, which is saved from a source PSD file for all similar such images.
Source: National Farmers Union.

CREATING SMART NAVIGATION

Navigation can and should, in most cases, satisfy two requirements:

- Enhance the usability of a site so that a user can find desired items or information easily and consistently.

- Allow for easy and efficient creation, editing, deletion, and downloading of individual menu items.

The first of these two requirements depends more on the architecture of a site than anything else. If the positioning, hierarchy, and naming conventions of sections and sub-sections of the site's architecture are intuitive, then the menu will only help capitalize on such planning and forethought.

The second requirement, however, is not always a given. It sometimes is less burdensome to create attractive menu items by saving them as images rather than as text. Doing so, though, limits the designer's flexibility when maintaining menus, and it increases the download. Editing menu items as text is not only simpler, but it also helps facilitate easy maintenance of the site; source menu files need not be found, edited, and resaved. Text menu items also allow for a menu to be dynamically generated from a database. Because they are made up of XHTML text, such menu items also require a considerably smaller download.

Another aspect of navigation a designer must consider is whether to use horizontal or vertical menus. Each has its benefits. Horizontal navigation allows for the entire width of a screen to be used for a site that, for example, uses tables that require many columns of data. Vertical menus, though, offer the ease of unlimited growth. While horizontal menus eventually run out of space for items, adding more items to a vertical menu simply requires the user to scroll up and down, rather than forcing a redesign of the page. Horizontal menus, however, often employ drop-down menus to allow for more menu items to be included.

REUSING IMAGES

Using browser caching is an easy way to decrease a site's download. The way it works is that once a browser downloads an image, it stores it in a temporary folder on the user's computer. That way, if the image is called again from another page or even on the same page, the browser uses the image stored on the computer, rather than downloading another copy.

Following are three instances where graphics can be reused:

1. **Framework graphics:** Graphics that are included in the homepage design can, many times, easily be reused in the framework of subsequent pages if the containers are built and mortised correctly.

   Figure 15.30 is a site that reuses the left and top images for the second- and third-level templates, such as the second-level page shown in Figure 15.31.

Figure 15.30
Site that reuses the left and top images on second- and third-level templates.
Source: Knowledge Workers, Inc.

Figure 15.31
Second-level page that reuses the left and top graphics of Figure 15.30.
Source: Knowledge Workers, Inc.

2. **Menu mouseover images:** Menu mouseovers are essential to designs that are created with the goal of high usability. Mouseovers allow a user to easily determine exactly where the cursor is pointing, something that is not always easy to do, due to the shape or size of a cursor. Using images for the text is not a wise choice when XHTML text can be used as the menu item and two images less than 1KB can each be reused as the On and Off states of the mouseovers. Figure 15.32 is a site that reuses two images for the mouseovers.

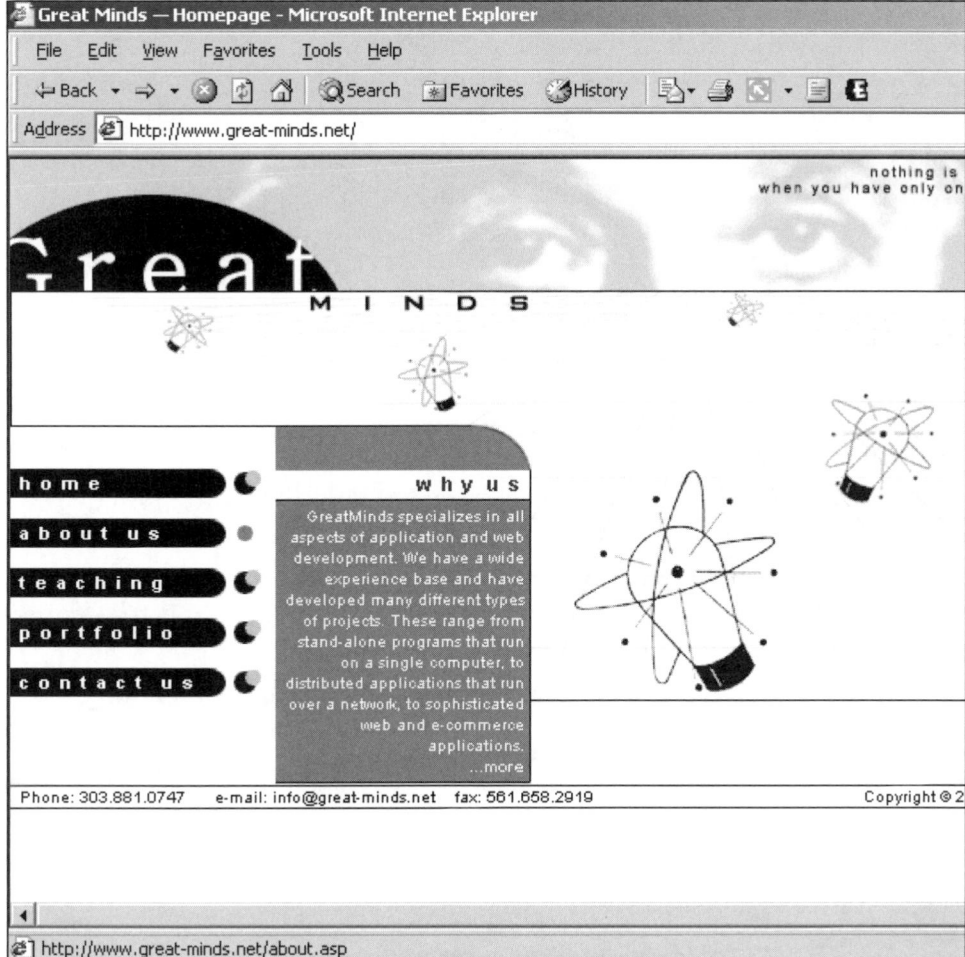

Figure 15.32
Website that uses two images less than 1KB each to serve as the mouseover images.
Source: Great Minds, Inc.

3. **Corners:** A good way of rounding the edges of a container is to use small corner images. While the rest of the area can be colored with the XHTML's background color, an image can be reused for as many corners as necessary. Figure 15.33 is an example of such a corner.

Figure 15.33
Corner image that can be reused.
© 2014 Cengage Learning.

INDENTING AND COMMENTING CODE

Sometimes, it is difficult to tell which table is nested in which when building, editing, or troubleshooting complex mortised sites. Indenting and commenting code, however, can help alleviate this problem. Discovering the nesting order of containers is easier when the code for each nested container is indented farther to the right than the higher-level (parent) containers. Comments also help a designer locate a single piece of code from within the entire page. Following is a sample of code that uses both indenting and comments to identify sections:

```
<!-- ###### left column start ###### -->
  <div id="a5-column-left">
    <!--########## left column text start ##########-->
    we create reasonably priced, highly professional web
designs, web sites, web applications, e-newsletters, and other visual, usable, and
functional work. while we create various custom designs for our clients, our best-
selling, internationally published designs are a good place to start to not only
understand our design skills but also to discover we're not a flash-in-the-pan
design firm. following are a few shortcuts to more commonly requested information:
    <!--########## left column text end ##########-->
  </div>
<!-- ###### left column end ###### -->
```

REMOVING SPACES AND COMMENTS

Often, the designer's goal is to find code easily for future editing. Sometimes, however, the goal is entirely about download speed. If the designer is more concerned about download, then removing extra spaces or comments will help decrease the file size of the page.

XHTML compression software can be found on download sites, such as www.tucows.com and www.download.com, which automates this process. The only thing the designer needs to remember is to save the original source page for easy editing in the future. Otherwise, having to edit the compressed code could be quite cumbersome.

The code for the site shown in Figure 15.34 before removing the spaces and comments was nearly 18KB. After removing the extraneous code, the size was reduced by nearly 2KB. Although it could have been decreased even more by eliminating all the spaces, the text would have been jumbled, and the programming code would not have worked properly.

Figure 15.34
Site that could have nearly 2KB trimmed by removing spaces and comments.
Source: The Moore Real Estate Group.

Removing Extraneous Spaces Only Helps

As mentioned in various examples in this book, while spacing in XHTML should not affect a CSS-driven design, it does do so in certain circumstances. In most cases, though, removing spaces only makes the browser interpret the code more accurately.

SUMMARY

Understanding common roadblocks and issues with designing websites can make a designer or developer much more efficient. If a designer creates enough sites, she will run into most of the issues outlined and hopefully be able to easily work through them with the help of this chapter. Some of the tips and techniques in this chapter included coding CSS mouseover menus, controlling content layout, using unique naming conventions, and learning basic testing tricks. If nothing else, the content in this chapter should help the designer imagine code in a more structured, forward-thinking way.

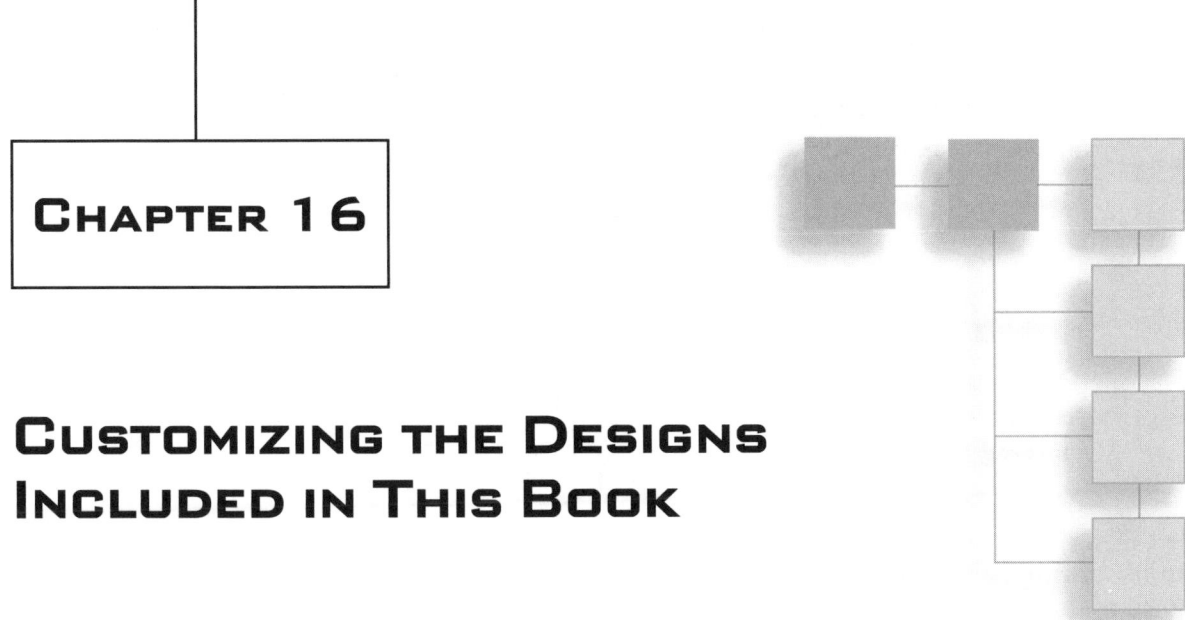

CHAPTER 16

CUSTOMIZING THE DESIGNS INCLUDED IN THIS BOOK

There are 260 templates included with this book, which contain both pure CSS and table-based XHTML Web designs, email signatures, e-newsletters, and Photoshop designs, which do not have code written for them. All the files are constructed in similar fashions, respectively, which makes understanding and customizing them a fairly consistent process. This chapter not only explains how to customize such templates, but it also provides basic Photoshop tips that can be used to customize the templates quickly.

STEPS TO CUSTOMIZING A TEMPLATE

There are six basic steps to customizing a template. The basic process involves customizing and saving a Photoshop file, which outputs PNG, GIF, and JPG files that are then displayed, along with any text, by preprogrammed XHTML (HTML), Cascading Style Sheets, and possibly JavaScript files. Following are the six steps:

1. Open the main Photoshop file. The design used for this chapter is design 57 (see Figure 16.1).

2. Customize the images and colors in the Photoshop file(s).

3. Optimize and save the necessary images that will be used by precoded XHTML, CSS, and possibly JavaScript files.

4. Open XHTML, CSS, or JavaScript files with an HTML editor.

5. Customize the text and any other code.

6. Test the design.

Figure 16.1
The design that is customized in this chapter.
© 2014 Cengage Learning.

Step 1: Open the Main Photoshop File

After copying the online files and pasting them into a directory, the designer needs to locate and open the main design file (design_57.psd) in Photoshop (see Figure 16.2).

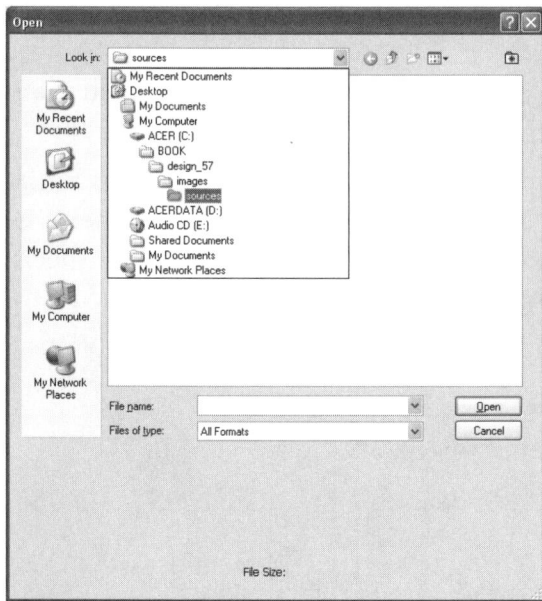

Figure 16.2
The location of the files after being saved to the hard drive.
© 2014 Cengage Learning.

How Files Look on a Hard Drive

Figure 16.2 represents one example of how the files would look on a hard drive after being downloaded. This is all relative to the individual's system.

Updating Photoshop Files

The templates included with this book are saved in Photoshop version 6 or higher. Adobe has continually changed how its software handles text, and the newer versions are no exception. When opening a file in a more recent version, Photoshop will ask if the reader wants to update the file (see Figure 16.3). Selecting Update will cause the vector-based text to have its positioning slightly readjusted.

Figure 16.3
Photoshop dialog box asking if a file should have text updated.
© 2014 Cengage Learning.

Step 2: Customize Images and Colors

Making and saving changes in Photoshop will change all the images in a design and many of the colors as well (see Figure 16.4). Colors that are not changed when saving a Photoshop file can be changed in the XHTML or CSS files.

Step 3: Optimize and Save Necessary Images

Once changes have been made to the Photoshop file, the designer will need to save the file so that the necessary PNG, GIF, and JPG images are saved from the sliced Photoshop file. Following are the steps to do so:

1. Select the Save For Web option from Photoshop's File menu (see Figure 16.5).

Figure 16.4
Design in Photoshop with customized colors and photos.
© 2014 Cengage Learning.

Figure 16.5
Design being optimized with Photoshop's Save For Web function.
© 2014 Cengage Learning.

2. Click on the Slice Select tool from the menu on the left (see Figure 16.6).

Figure 16.6
Slice Select tool in the Save For Web window.
© 2014 Cengage Learning.

3. Select a slice to be optimized and select the compression on the right side of the window (see Figure 16.7).

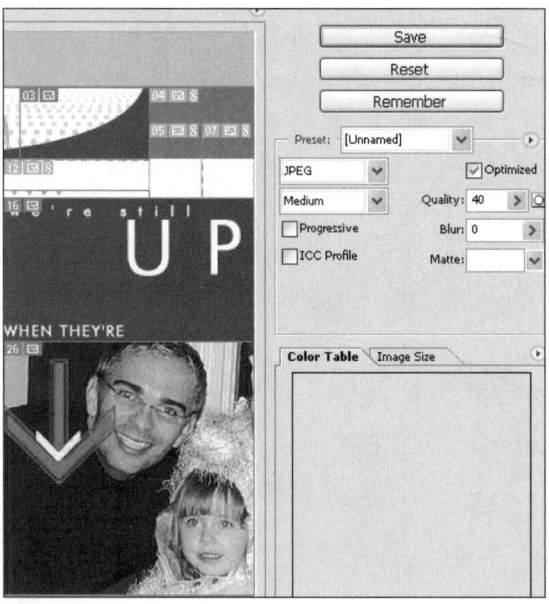

Figure 16.7
The slice that has its file type and compression assigned in the Save For Web window.
© 2014 Cengage Learning.

Changing File Extension in Code

If the designer changes the type of image a slice is saved as, such as GIF to JPG, the file extension must be changed in the CSS or XHTML template as well. For example, if `photo_middle_right` is changed from a JPG file to a GIF file, all references to `photo_middle_right.jpg` in the template must be changed to `photo_middle_right.gif`.

4. Ensure that all changed slices of the template are still compressed to the best level possible.

5. Select Save in the top-right area of the Save For Web window.

6. Select Replace in the Replace Files window.

Photoshop Replaces All Files in Images Subdirectory

Once a user clicks on Replace, Photoshop will save all slices as either PNGs, GIFs, or JPGs from the file and place them in an Images subdirectory below where the `design_57.html` file is saved.

Step 4: Open an XHTML (HTML), CSS, or JavaScript File

All three file types can be opened in any HTML editor. In Figure 16.8, the sample file is opened in Adobe's ColdFusion Studio. This software is pretty much extinct in Web development; however, any quality software will be somewhat similar in style. It also shows that the designer does not need the latest and greatest software for such development. A reader, in fact, could even use basic text editing software, such as Notepad, which is included with Microsoft operating systems.

Step 5: Customize Text and Code

Once a template file has been opened in an HTML editor, it can be easily modified and saved however the designer may choose. Following are suggestions for customizing such files:

■ Always save a backup to revert to or pull original pieces of code from, if necessary.

■ Check pages in a browser frequently (refer to step 6).

Figure 16.8
A file opened in Adobe's ColdFusion Studio HTML editing software.
© Adobe® Systems Incorporated.

- Switch the CSS or border value to 1 where the code is being customized. This allows the designer to understand better how the design is constructed.

- Ensure that the location and image name for each menu item is consistent when working with XHTML templates that use mouseovers in the menu (see Listing 16.1). No two menu items can have the same location and image names.

Listing 16.1   Unique JavaScript Names for Mouseover Code

```
<tr>
<td valign="top"><img src="images/bullet_menu_off.gif" width="18"
height="20" alt="" border="0" name="menu_item_1"></td>
<td class="white2"><a href="index.htm" style="text-decoration:
none; color: #ffffff" onmouseover="document.menu_item_1.src=
bullet_menu_on.src;"

onmouseout="document.menu_item_1.src=bullet_menu_off.src"><b>menu
item 1</b></a></td>
</tr>
```

Only for XHTML Templates

This suggestion is only applicable to the table-based XHTML templates included with the book.

Step 6: Test the Design

As soon as a designer makes a change to a template, it should be opened in a browser or, better yet, in various browsers, depending on how thoroughly the designer wants to test the code. Then, as changes are made to the template from the HTML editor, the designer should refresh the browser(s) continually to ensure that the changes were made correctly. To open a design in IE, for example, the designer follows six steps:

1. Click the browser's File menu.
2. Click Open.
3. Click Browse.
4. Click on `index.htm`, which is the homepage for the design in Figure 16.9.

Figure 16.9
A locally saved `index.htm` file to be opened in IE 6.
© 2014 Cengage Learning.

5. Click Open to open the file in a browser.

6. Click OK to confirm opening the file.

PHOTOSHOP TUTORIALS

This section includes tutorials on basic techniques a designer or developer will usually need to know in order to customize a design. They include replacing photos, resizing photos, changing colors, and undoing or redoing actions.

Replacing Photos

Not all designs can have photos simply replaced in the code. With many mortised designs, the process of replacing a photo first begins with the Photoshop file, using masks. Following are instructions on replacing a photo in a Photoshop template, using the original photo as a mask.

1. Make sure that the Layers panel is visible (see Figure 16.10).

Figure 16.10
The Layers panel in Photoshop where different layers may be selected.
© Adobe® Systems Incorporated.

2. Click on the Window menu in the top menu bar.

3. Click on the Layers option (see Figure 16.11).

Figure 16.11
The Layers panel can be accessed from the Window menu.
© 2014 Cengage Learning.

4. Make sure that the Layers tab is selected in the panel. If it is not, click on it (refer to Figure 16.11).

5. Open the image to be inserted into the existing image.

6. Select the entire image (Ctrl-A for Windows; Cmd-A for Macintosh) and then copy that image (Ctrl-C for Windows or Cmd-C for Macintosh; see Figure 16.12).

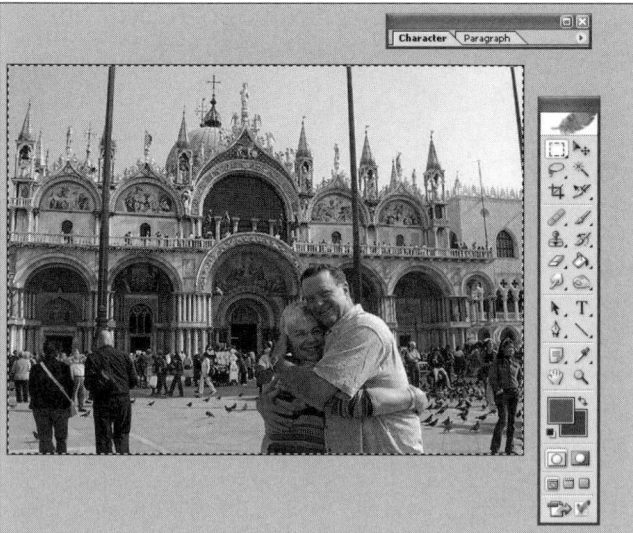

Figure 16.12
The image selected that will be used in the design.
© 2014 Cengage Learning.

7. Select the layer of the photo in the design (in this example, it is the upside-down photo of the man) that is going to be replaced.

Right-Clicking Image to Find Layer Name

Windows users can right-click the photo to be replaced and then select the layer's name, which will send the user directly to that layer (see Figure 16.13). The user may have more than one option to select, so if they are not already named, it might be necessary to click on the various layers until the correct one is selected.

Figure 16.13
Possible layers to select if the user right-clicks on an image.
© 2014 Cengage Learning.

8. Click on the layer in the Layers panel. Once this layer has been selected, the content on the layer will be available for editing.

Making Layers Visible and Invisible

A layer can be made visible or invisible by clicking the eye icon on and off, located to the left of the layer name (see Figure 16.14). Toggling the eye on and off is a good way to test if the correct layer has been selected.

Figure 16.14
Toggling the eye icon on a layer will turn it off and on in the Photoshop file.
© 2014 Cengage Learning.

9. Activate the layer's image by selecting the entire layer area (Ctrl-A for Windows; Cmd-A for Macintosh) and move the layer up one pixel (one click) and down one pixel by using the up and down arrow keys (see Figure 16.15).

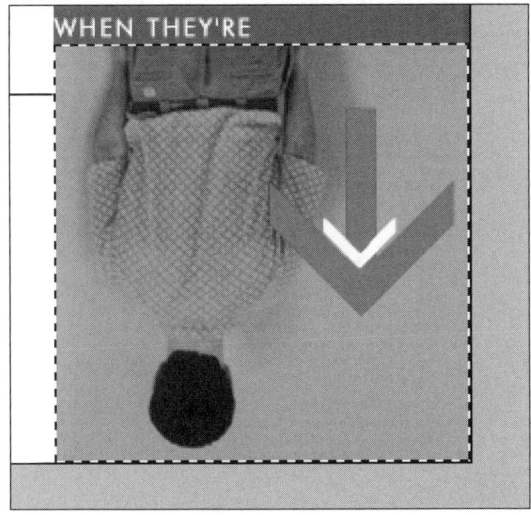

Figure 16.15
The image that will be used as a mask must first be selected.
© 2014 Cengage Learning.

Using Marching Ants to Detect a Mask

The image is selected when the marching ants (moving dotted lines) are marching around that specific image or at least the part of the image that is viewable within the borders of the Photoshop file. Prior to moving the image up and down one pixel, ants will be marching around the border of the entire Photoshop file. If the marching ants are displayed in a square or rectangular shape that is larger than the image (see Figure 16.16), then the image is already set as a mask. If this occurs, the user must turn off the photo by turning off the eye for its layer and restarting this tutorial at step 3, this time selecting the correct layer (the square image that contains the actual photo).

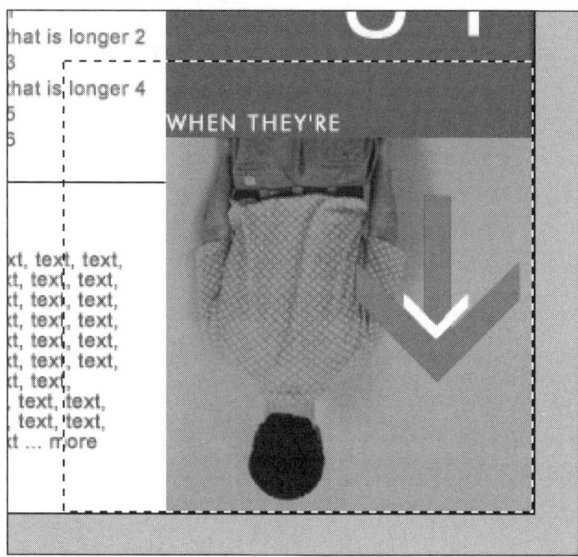

Figure 16.16
How the marching ants would appear if the image were already saved as a mask.
© 2014 Cengage Learning.

10. Insert the image already copied in step 6 (see Figure 16.12) by pressing Shift-Ctrl-V for Windows or Shift-Cmd-V for Macintosh. The image will then be placed inside the existing image (see Figure 16.17).

Figure 16.17
The design after both the selected image and the one in the center have been added into their respective masks.
© 2014 Cengage Learning.

Resizing Photos

Following are instructions for resizing a photo in Photoshop. Although this tutorial explains how to resize a photo in a mask, the same process occurs when resizing any photo or image on any layer.

1. Make sure that the Layers panel is visible (refer to Figure 16.10).

2. Select the layer of the photo in the design (in this example, it is the couple hugging) that is going to be resized (refer to Figure 16.13).

3. Click on the layer in the Layers panel. Once this layer has been selected, the content will be available for editing.

4. Activate the layer's image by selecting the entire layer area (Ctrl-A for Windows; Cmd-A for Macintosh) and move the layer up one pixel (one click) and down one pixel by using the up and down arrow keys (see Figure 16.18).

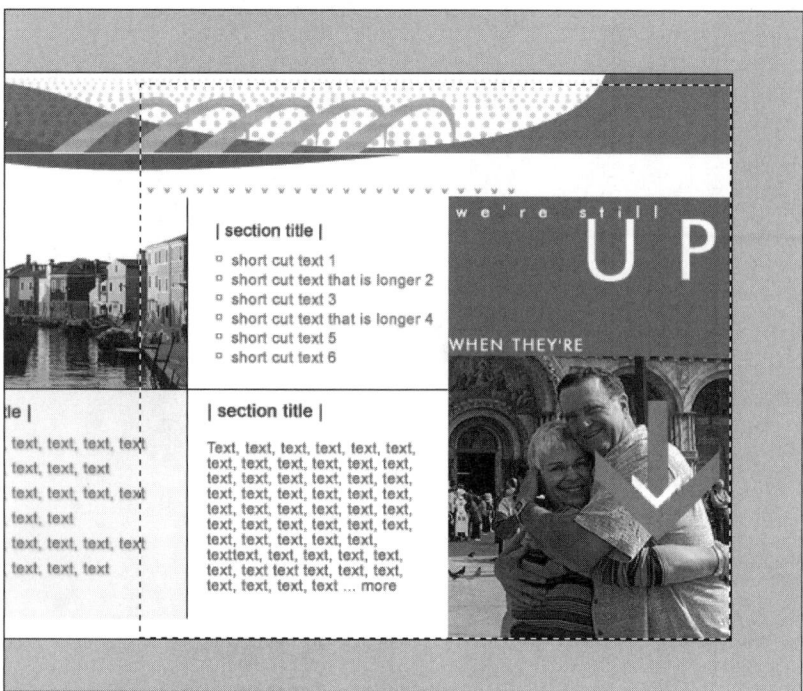

Figure 16.18
The photo after it has been activated in the window.
© 2014 Cengage Learning.

Marching Ants Remain Inside Photoshop File

The image in Figure 16.18 extends below and to the right of the design. The marching ants, however, will remain inside the Photoshop file.

5. Activate the outer frame of the image by pressing Ctrl-T for Windows or Cmd-T for Macintosh. Once the outer frame is active, small square handles in the corners will appear (see Figure 16.19).

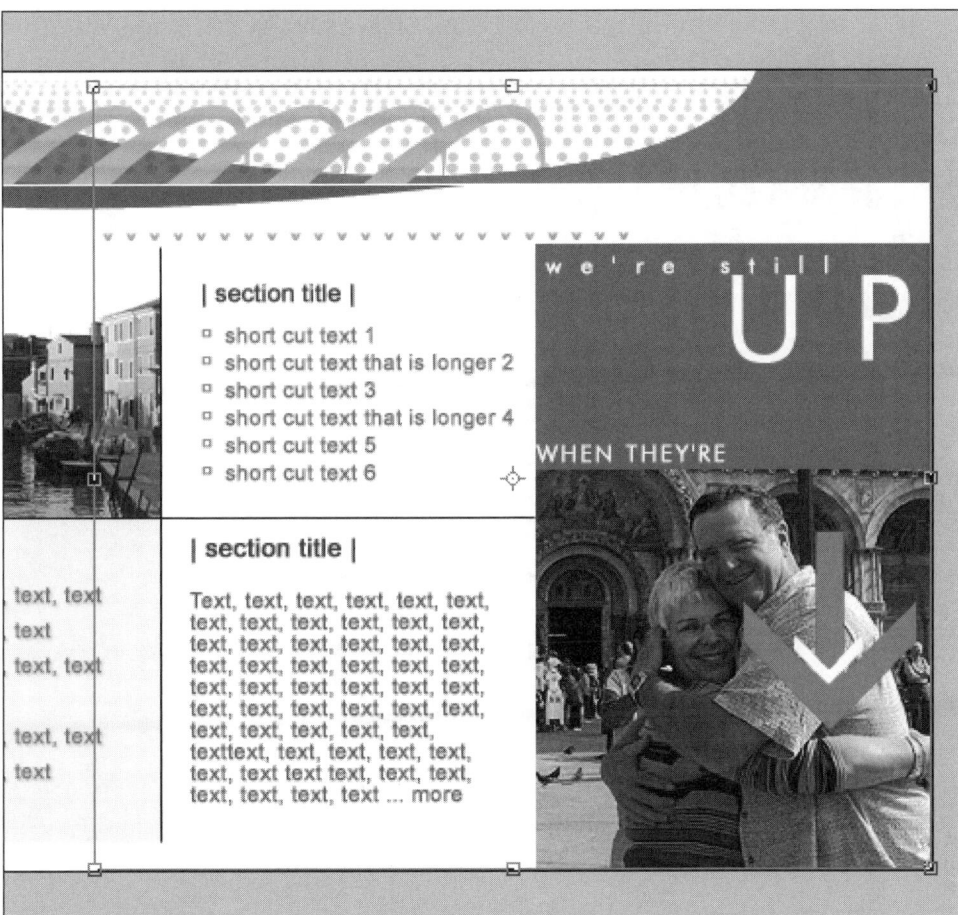

Figure 16.19
Small handles will appear when the image is ready to be resized.
© 2014 Cengage Learning.

6. Resize the image by clicking and dragging any of the corners on the frame that turn the mouse into an up or down arrow.

Maintaining Proportions When Resizing

Often, the image will need to be resized proportionately. Holding the Shift key and the handles simultaneously while dragging will ensure that the image's proportions remain the same.

7. During the resizing process, the image can also be moved. To do so, select the Move tool in the toolbar and click and drag the image rather than the handles (see Figure 16.20).

Figure 16.20
The Move tool included in the menu bar.
© 2014 Cengage Learning.

8. Deactivate the marching ants by pressing Ctrl-D for Windows or Cmd-D for Macintosh after the image has been resized and located correctly (see Figure 16.21). The border and corners will then disappear.

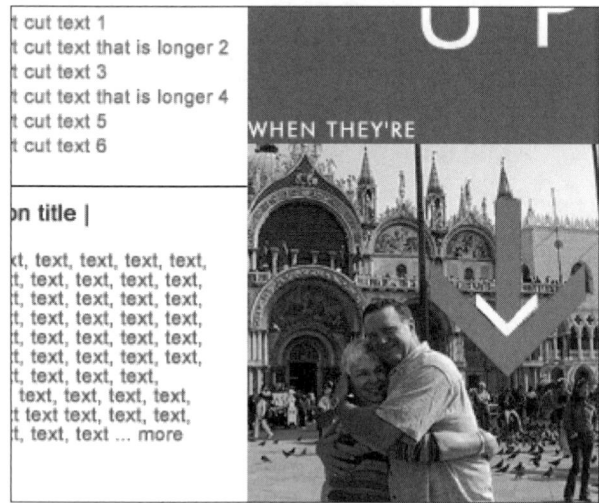

Figure 16.21
The photo after it has been resized and moved.
© 2014 Cengage Learning.

Changing Colors

Changing the colors of a design often begins with the Photoshop file because the colors are saved as images, rather than browser-generated colors. Following are instructions on changing colors of solid objects in a Photoshop template:

1. Make sure that the Layers panel is visible.

2. Select the layer of the photo in the design (in this example, it is the couple hugging) that is going to be changed.

3. Click on the layer in the Layers panel. Once this layer has been selected, content on the layer will be available for editing.

4. Select the layer of the photo in the design (in this example, the top-right corner) that is going to be changed (see Figure 16.22).

Figure 16.22
The layer, which represents the top-right curve of the design, to be recolored.
© 2014 Cengage Learning.

5. Click on the layer in the Layers panel. After this layer has been selected, the content on the layer will be available for editing.

6. Activate the layer's image by selecting the entire layer area (Ctrl-A for Windows; Cmd-A for Macintosh) and move the layer up one pixel (one click) and down one pixel by using the up and down arrow keys (see Figure 16.23).

Figure 16.23
The image that will be re-colored after it has been activated.
© 2014 Cengage Learning.

7. Click the Color Picker in the toolbar to open the Color Picker dialog box and select a replacement (see Figure 16.24).

Figure 16.24
The Color Picker dialog box.
© 2014 Cengage Learning.

8. Click OK to close the Color Picker dialog after the replacement color has been selected.

9. Select Fill from the Edit menu (see Figure 16.25).

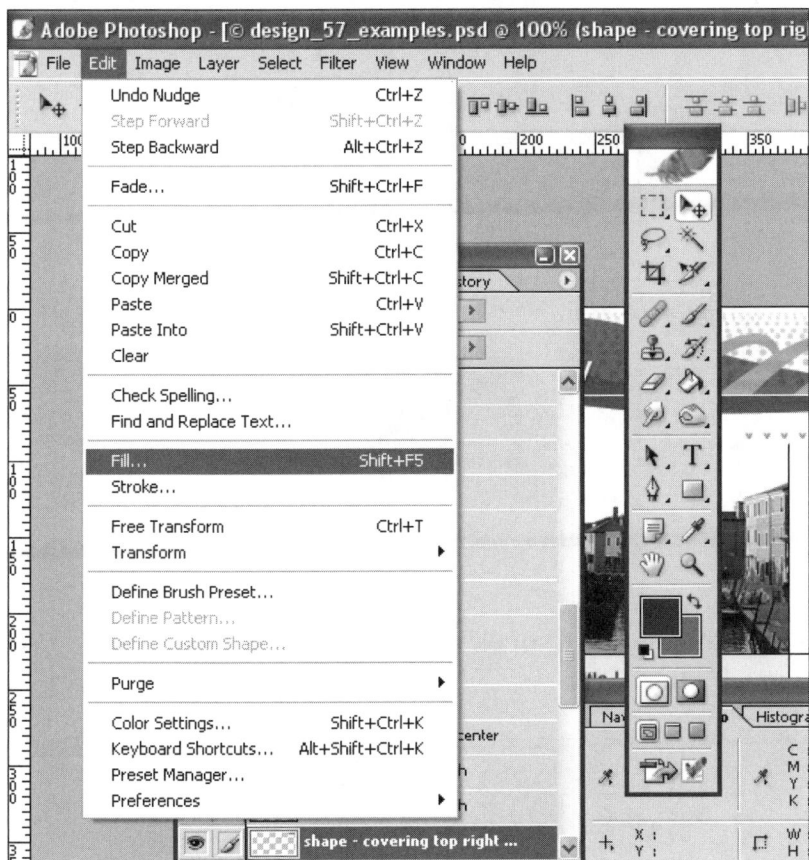

Figure 16.25
The Fill option in the Edit menu.
© 2014 Cengage Learning.

10. Click OK to confirm the fill (see Figure 16.26).

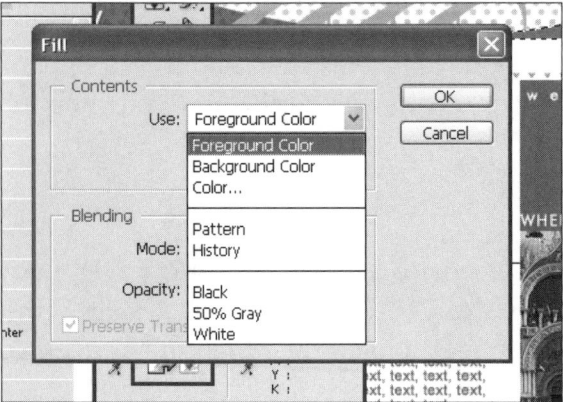

Figure 16.26
The Fill dialog box and the various possibilities the Use drop-down menu offers.
© 2014 Cengage Learning.

11. Deactivate the marching ants by pressing Ctrl-D for Windows or Cmd-D for Macintosh once the color has been replaced or "filled." Figure 16.27 shows the design with many of the colors changed. Because it is a black-and-white image, the changes will appear mainly as tonal differences.

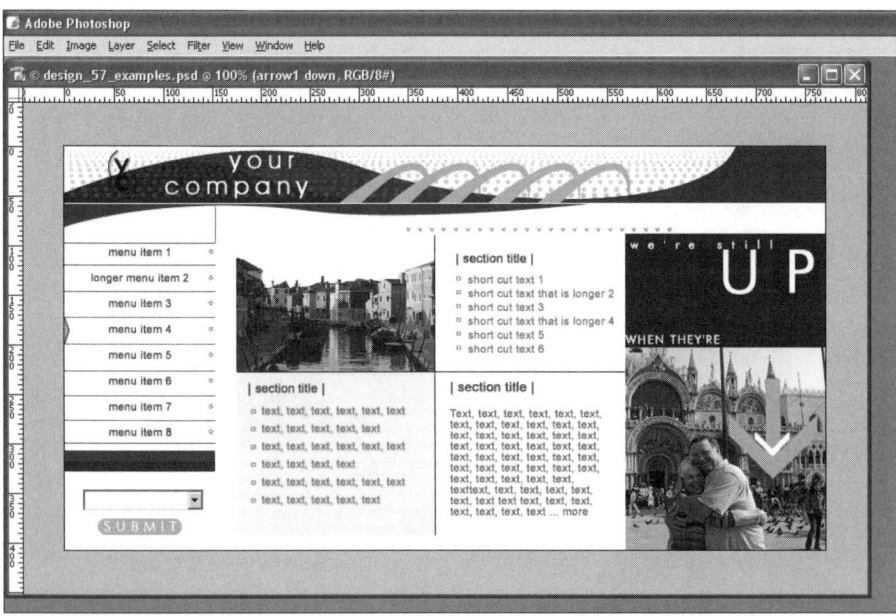

Figure 16.27
The design once many of the colors have been changed. Because the figure is black and white, the changes will appear only as tonal differences.
© 2014 Cengage Learning.

Undoing and Redoing Actions

The designer can undo and redo actions in Photoshop. This tutorial outlines the hot keys for undoing actions, but, more importantly, it shows how to configure Photoshop to allow for actions to be undone.

Undoing Actions

To undo an action using hot keys, the user needs to select Ctrl-Alt-Z for Windows or Cmd-Alt-Z for Macintosh. By holding down the Ctrl (or Cmd) and Alt keys, the user can repeatedly click the letter Z to undo as many actions as the program has been configured to allow.

Redoing Actions

After undoing actions, the user can click Ctrl-Z for Windows and Cmd-Z for Macintosh to redo all the actions. By repeatedly pressing this key combination, the user can toggle between the two different states of change, which is useful when deciding how a certain image or color will look compared to the older version.

Configuring the Undo Actions (History States) Setting

Undoing actions has a limit with the default settings of Photoshop, so the user needs to change the settings first to ensure that the settings will allow a certain number of changes. Following are instructions on how to do so:

1. Select Preferences, General under the Edit menu (see Figure 16.28). The Preferences dialog box will appear.

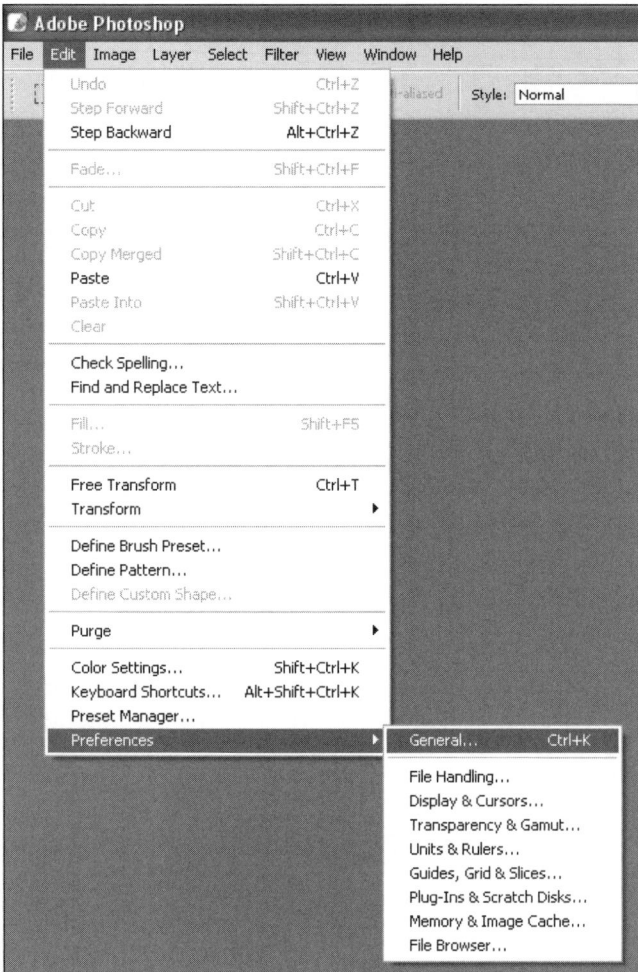

Figure 16.28
Selecting Preferences, General from the Edit menu.
© 2014 Cengage Learning.

2. Change the History States setting to the number of changes Photoshop should be able to revert back to. The number of changes in this example is 20 (see Figure 16.29).

Figure 16.29
The History States option in the Preferences dialog box, which is set at 20.
© 2014 Cengage Learning.

3. Click OK to confirm the changes.

SUMMARY

Because all the designs included in this book are built similarly, whether they use an XHTML table- or CSS-based design, they also are customized in very much the same way. This chapter not only explains the steps for customizing a design, but it also provides brief Photoshop tutorials on how to make changes in the software. These tutorials include replacing photos, resizing photos, changing colors, and undoing and redoing actions. Because it is filled with images, this chapter offers a quick read for fundamental Photoshop skills.

CHAPTER 17

TEMPLATES INCLUDED ONLINE

There are 240 designs included with this book. Because this book was first published in 2001, the designs have evolved graphically and technically over the years. Although designs become antiquated in terms of coding standards or hardware standards (for example, screen resolution), there are elements that can still be used, studied, or modified from older designs. This is why older templates are included with the newer ones.

Also important for the reader to keep in mind is that templates can and, in most cases, should be modified for specific projects. A5design's clients don't always realize that colors and images can be easily modified to turn a real-estate template into a photography template or a wild magenta abstract template into a conservative blue business template. The layout of a design should be the driving force behind selecting it. Layout considerations include whether the title and logo are given the correct placement and prominence, if the menu is horizontal or vertical, how many text sections are provided, and how scalable the design is for future functionality and growth.

The various types of designs online include XHTML table-based templates, XHTML e-newsletter templates, XHTML signature templates, Photoshop templates, and CSS-based templates. Barring the Photoshop templates, all designs include a source Photoshop file(s) along with the slices and code already completed. The Photoshop templates are the one exception because they do not have slices or code included.

The templates are broken up into four folders online: Designs—First Edition, Designs—Third Edition, Designs—Fourth Edition, and Designs—Fifth Edition. The 50 templates in the Designs—First Edition folder are XHTML-based and designed for 800×600

resolution with fixed widths. The 160 templates in the Designs—Third Edition folder are much more diverse. Some are XHTML-based designed for 800 × 600 resolution but with the ability to make the width liquid or relative; some are e-newsletters or email templates; some are CSS-based designed for 800 × 600 resolution; some are pure Photoshop templates; and some are CSS-based designed for 1024 × 768 resolution. The templates in the Designs— Fifth Edition folder are CSS-based for 1024 × 768 resolution. Following is a breakdown of the folders and the templates included in them:

Designs—Fifth Edition Folder

■ **Designs 181–190:** CSS designs that were created for 1024 × 768 resolution.

Designs—Fourth Edition Folder

■ **Designs 161–180:** CSS designs that were created for 1024 × 768 resolution. These designs use a repeating background image to expand for monitors with higher resolutions.

Designs—Third Edition Folder

■ **Designs 1–80:** XHTML table-based designs that were originally created for 800 × 600 resolution but were also coded as liquid designs, which, if the designer chooses, allows for them to expand to greater widths.

■ **Designs 81–90:** XHTML e-newsletters that can be either emailed from a browser or embedded into an email and then emailed.

■ **Designs 91–100:** XHTML signatures that can be embedded into email messages, many times working in conjunction with a website and/or e-newsletter to provide consistent branding.

■ **Designs 101–110:** Photoshop designs that were created for 800 × 600 resolution but could be easily modified for 1024 × 768 resolution. These designs have not been coded.

■ **Designs 111–120:** Photoshop designs that were created for 1024 × 768 resolution. These designs have not been coded.

■ **Designs 121–130:** CSS designs that were created for 800 × 600 resolution. Because the designs are liquid, they can be modified easily to fit higher resolutions, or they can be centered within the browser in a fixed format.

- **Designs 131–160:** CSS designs that were created for 1024 × 768 resolution. Because the designs are liquid, they can be modified easily to fit higher resolutions, or they can be centered within the browser in a fixed format.

Designs—First Edition Folder

- **Designs 1–50:** XHTML table-based designs that were created for 800 × 600 resolution. They have fixed widths.

DESIGNS—FIFTH EDITION FOLDER

The designs are coded for 1024 × 768 resolution.

Design 190

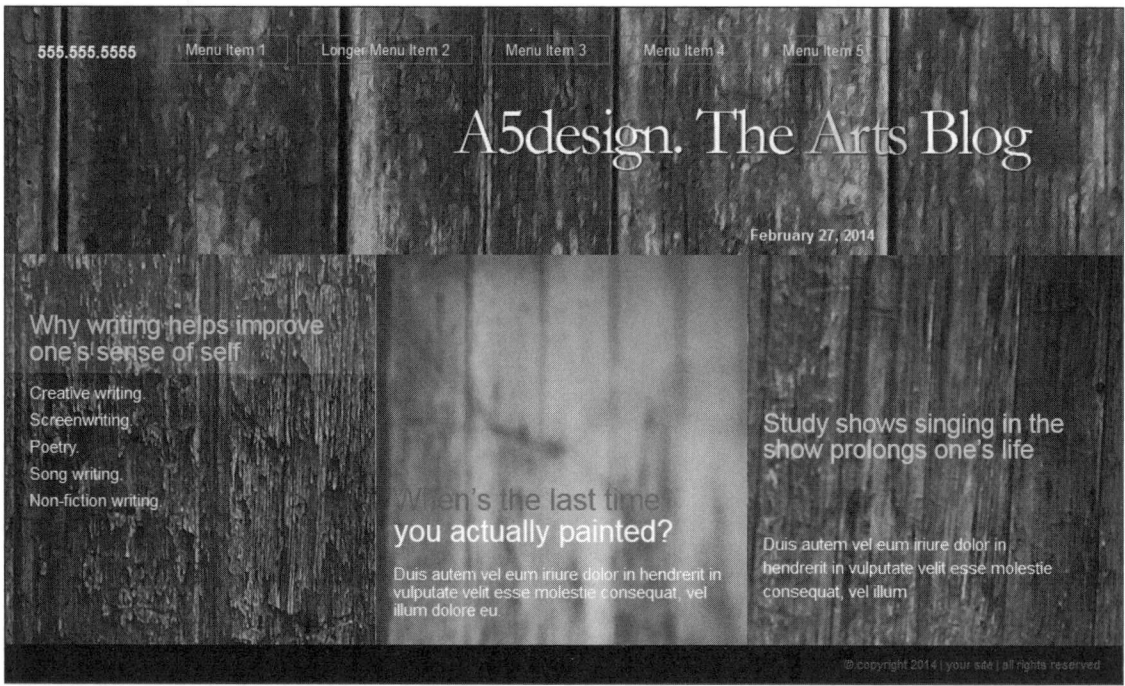

© 2014 Cengage Learning.

Homepage design.

Photoshop source file names: Designs—Fifth Edition/181-190-css/design_190/design_190.psd

XHTML pages: index.htm, menu-item-2.htm, menu-item-3.htm

Photo credits: Chelsea Miller Photography

Design 189

© 2014 Cengage Learning.

Homepage design.

Photoshop source file names: Designs—Fifth Edition/181-190-css/design_189/design_189.psd

XHTML pages: index.htm, menu-item-2.htm, menu-item-3.htm

Photo credits: Chelsea Miller Photography

Design 188

© 2014 Cengage Learning.

Homepage design.

Photoshop source file names: Designs—Fifth Edition/181-190-css/design_188/design_188.psd, bg-main.psd, bg-main-sl.psd

XHTML pages: index.htm, menu-item-2.htm, menu-item-3.htm

Photo credits: Chelsea Miller Photography

Design 187

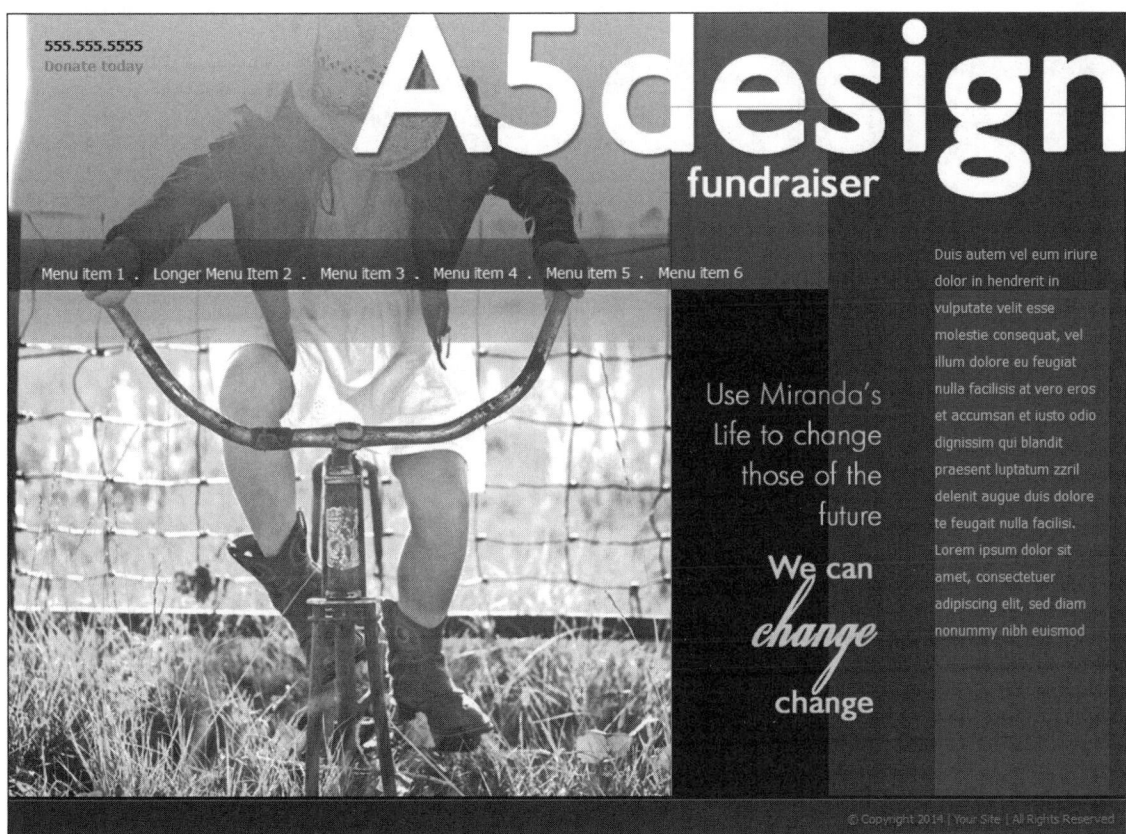

© 2014 Cengage Learning.

Homepage design.

Photoshop source file names: Designs—Fifth
Edition/181-190-css/design_187/design_187.psd, main-bg.psd, main-bg-sl.psd

XHTML pages: index.htm, menu-item-2.htm, menu-item-3.htm

Photo credits: Chelsea Miller Photography

Design 186

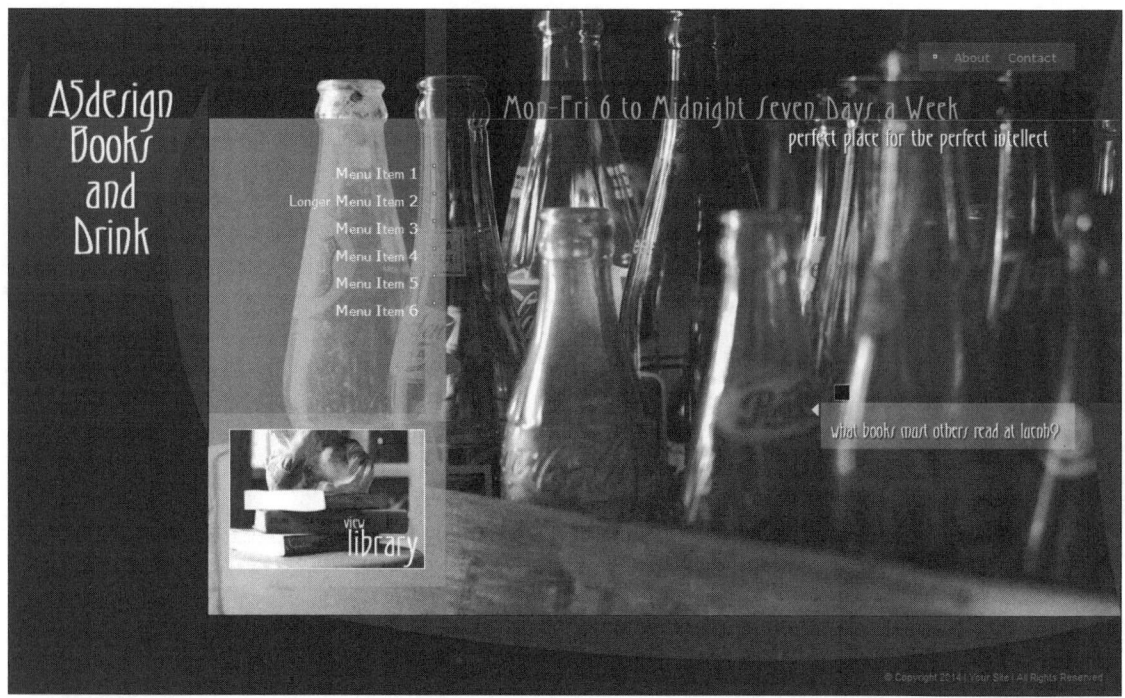

Homepage design.

Photoshop source file names: Designs—Fifth Edition/181-190-css/design_186/design_186.psd, main-bg.psd, main-bg-sl.psd

XHTML pages: index.htm, menu-item-2.htm, menu-item-3.htm

Photo credits: Chelsea Miller Photography

Design 185

© 2014 Cengage Learning.

Homepage design.

Photoshop source file names: Designs—Fifth Edition/181-190-css/design_185/design_185.psd, main-sl.psd

XHTML pages: index.htm, menu-item-2.htm, menu-item-3.htm

Photo credits: Chelsea Miller Photography

Design 184

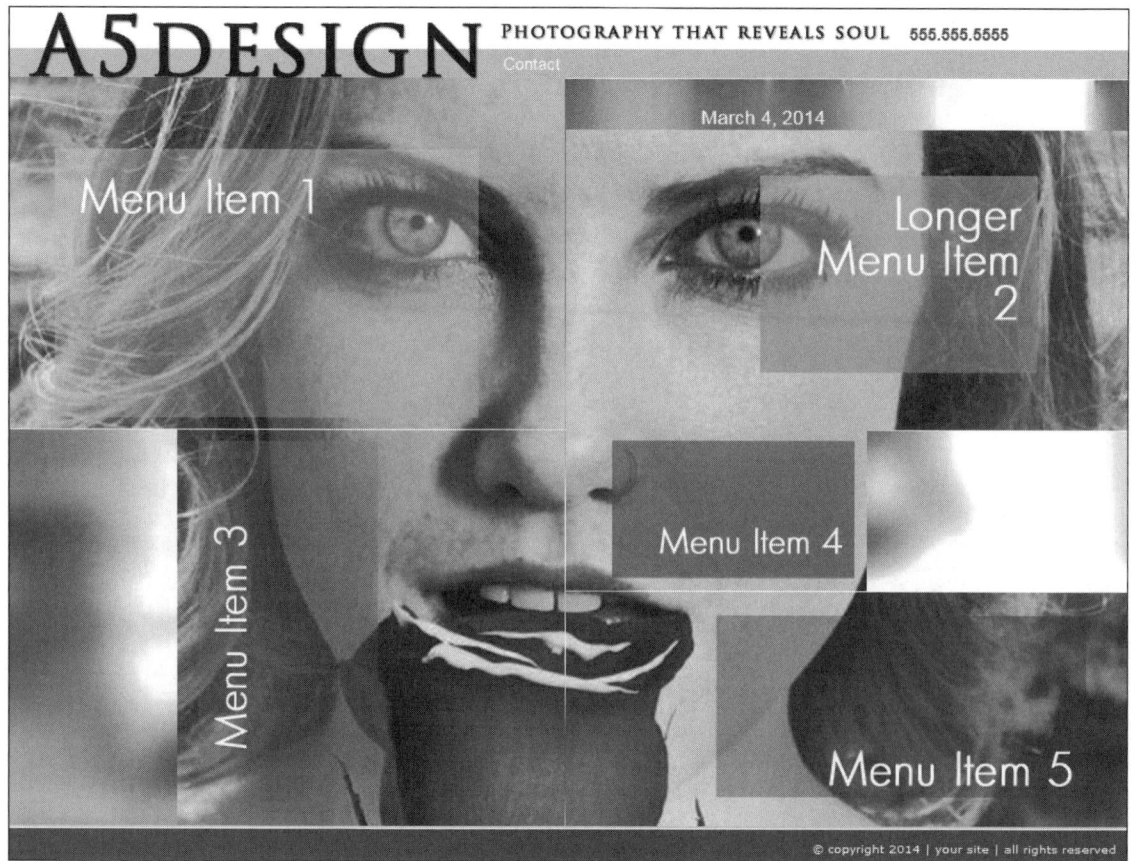

Homepage design.

Photoshop source file names: Designs—Fifth Edition/181-190-css/design_184/design_184.psd, bg-body.psd, bg-body-sl.psd

XHTML pages: index.htm, menu-item-2.htm, menu-item-3.htm

Photo credits: Chelsea Miller Photography

Design 183

© 2014 Cengage Learning.

Homepage design.

Photoshop source file names: Designs—Fifth Edition/181-190-css/design_183/design_183.psd, bg-body.psd, bg-body-sl.psd

XHTML pages: index.htm, menu-item-2.htm, menu-item-3.htm

Photo credits: Chelsea Miller Photography

Design 182

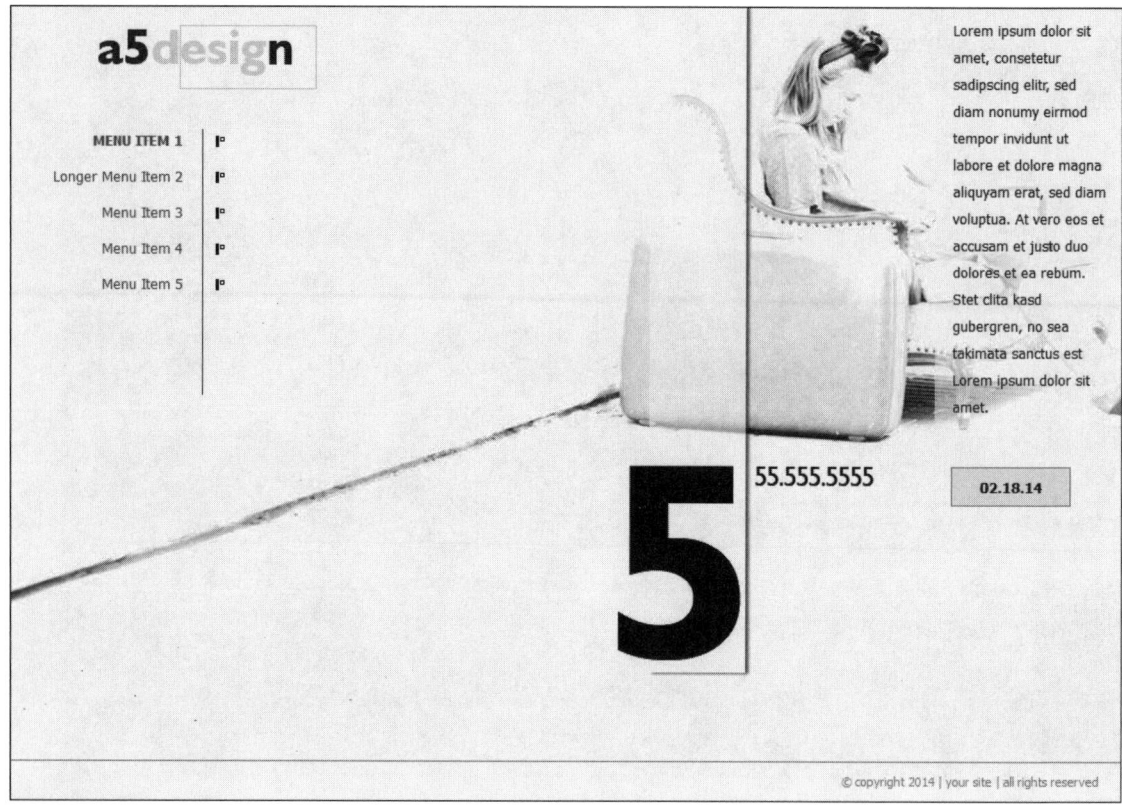

Homepage design.

Photoshop source file names: Designs—Fifth Edition/181-190-css/design_182/design_182.psd, main_bg.psd, main_bg_sl.psd

XHTML pages: index.htm, menu-item-2.htm, menu-item-3.htm

Photo credits: Chelsea Miller Photography

Design 181

© 2014 Cengage Learning.

Homepage design.

Photoshop source file names: Designs—Fifth Edition/181-190-css/design_181/design_181.psd, bg-main-sl.psd

XHTML pages: index.htm, menu-item-2.htm, menu-item-3.htm

Photo credits: A5design

DESIGNS—FOURTH EDITION FOLDER

The designs are coded for 1024 × 768 resolution. Because many users view the designs at high resolution, repeating backgrounds are incorporated into most of the designs in this folder. The code can be easily copied and applied to most of the designs in the Third Edition folder.

Design 180

© 2014 Cengage Learning.

Homepage design.

Photoshop source file names: Designs—Fourth Edition/161-180-css/design_180/main.psd, bg-main.psd

XHTML pages: index.htm, menu-item-2.htm, menu-item-3.htm

Photo credits: J&N Photography

Design 179

© 2014 Cengage Learning.

Homepage design.

Photoshop source file names: Designs—Fourth Edition/161-180-css/design_179/main.psd, bg-main.psd

XHTML pages: index.htm, menu-item-2.htm, menu-item-3.htm

Photo credits: J&N Photography

Design 178

Homepage design.

Photoshop source file names: Designs—Fourth Edition/161-180-css/design_178/main.psd, bg-main.psd

XHTML pages: index.htm, menu-item-2.htm, menu-item-3.htm

Photo credits: J&N Photography

Design 177

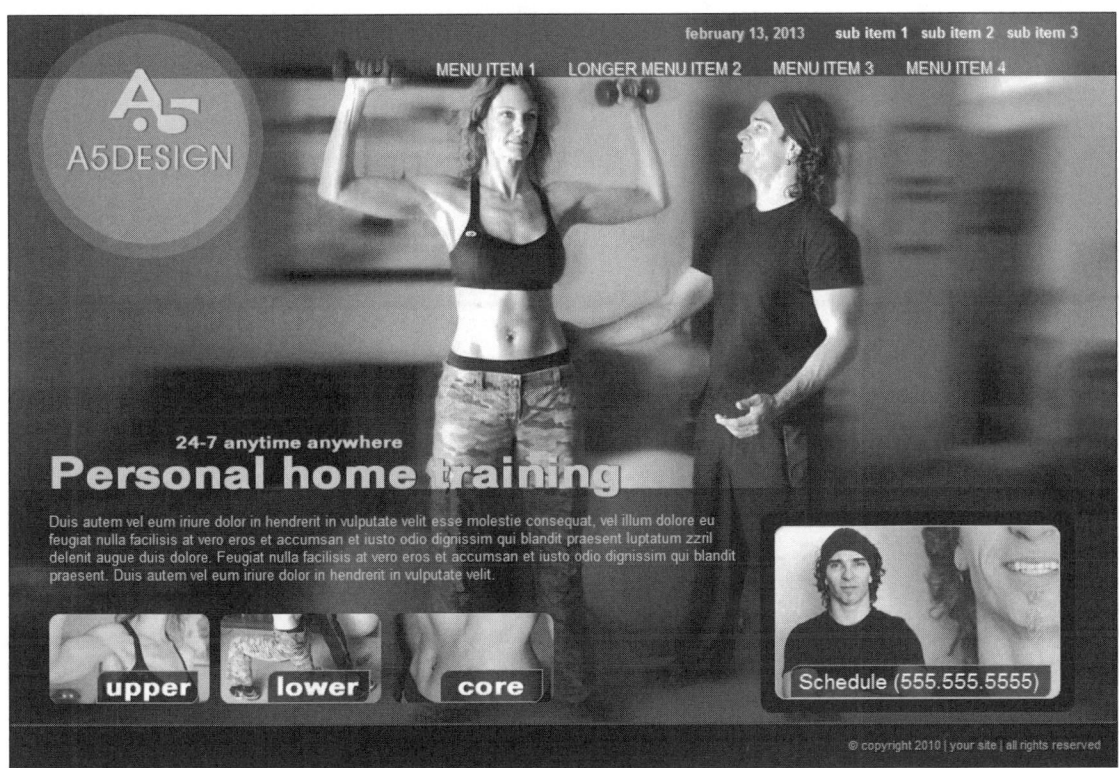

Homepage design.

Photoshop source file names: Designs—Fourth Edition/161-180-css/design_177/main.psd, bg-main.psd

XHTML pages: index.htm, menu-item-2.htm, menu-item-3.htm

Photo credits: J&N Photography

Design 176

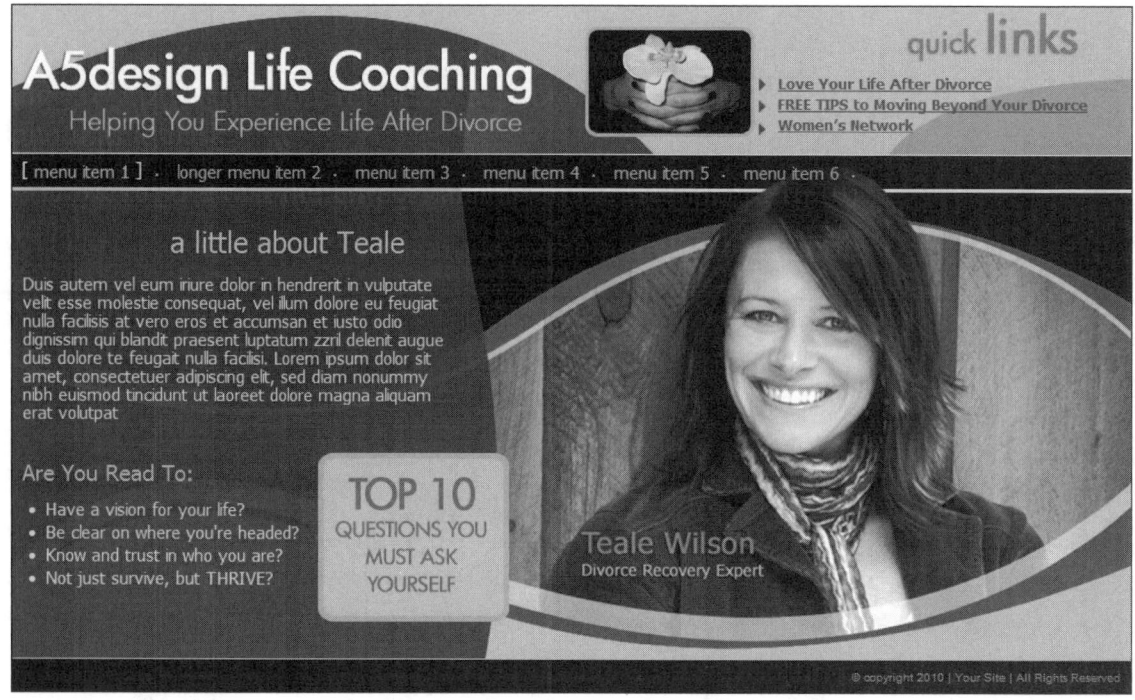

Homepage design.

Photoshop source file names: Designs—Fourth Edition/161-180-css/design_176/main.psd, bg-main.psd

XHTML pages: index.htm, menu-item-2.htm, menu-item-3.htm

Photo credits: Sara Hunter

Design 175

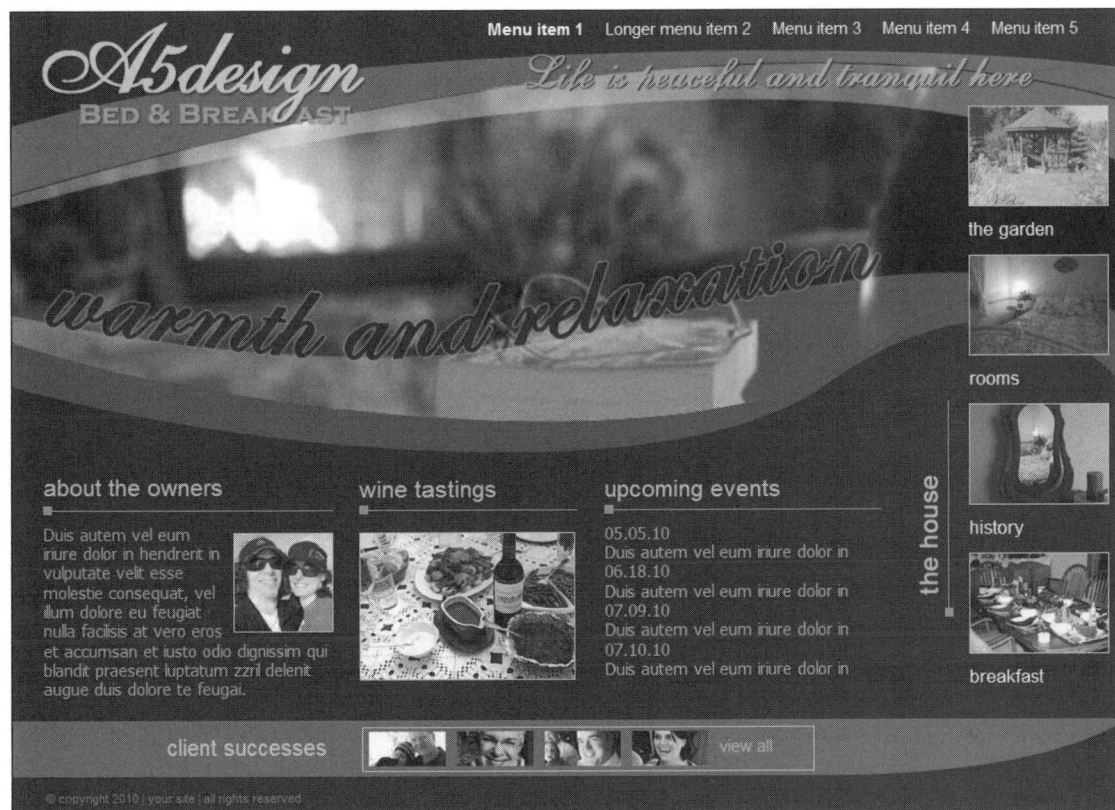

© 2014 Cengage Learning.

Homepage design.

Photoshop source file names: Designs—Fourth Edition/161-180-css/design_175/main.psd, bg-main.psd

XHTML pages: index.htm, menu-item-2.htm, menu-item-3.htm

Photo credits: J&N Photography, A5design

Design 174

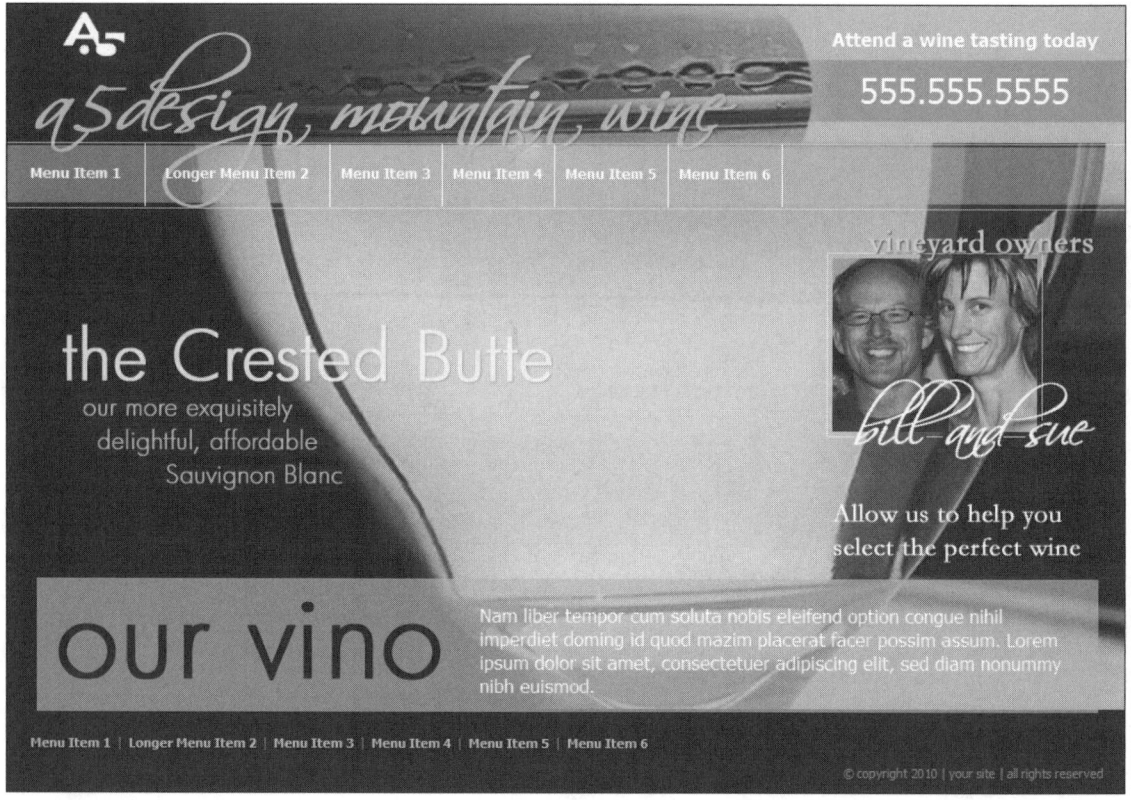

Homepage design.

Photoshop source file names: Designs—Fourth Edition/161-180-css/design_174/main.psd, bg-main.psd

XHTML pages: index.htm, menu-item-2.htm, menu-item-3.htm

Photo credits: Carol Prince

Design 173

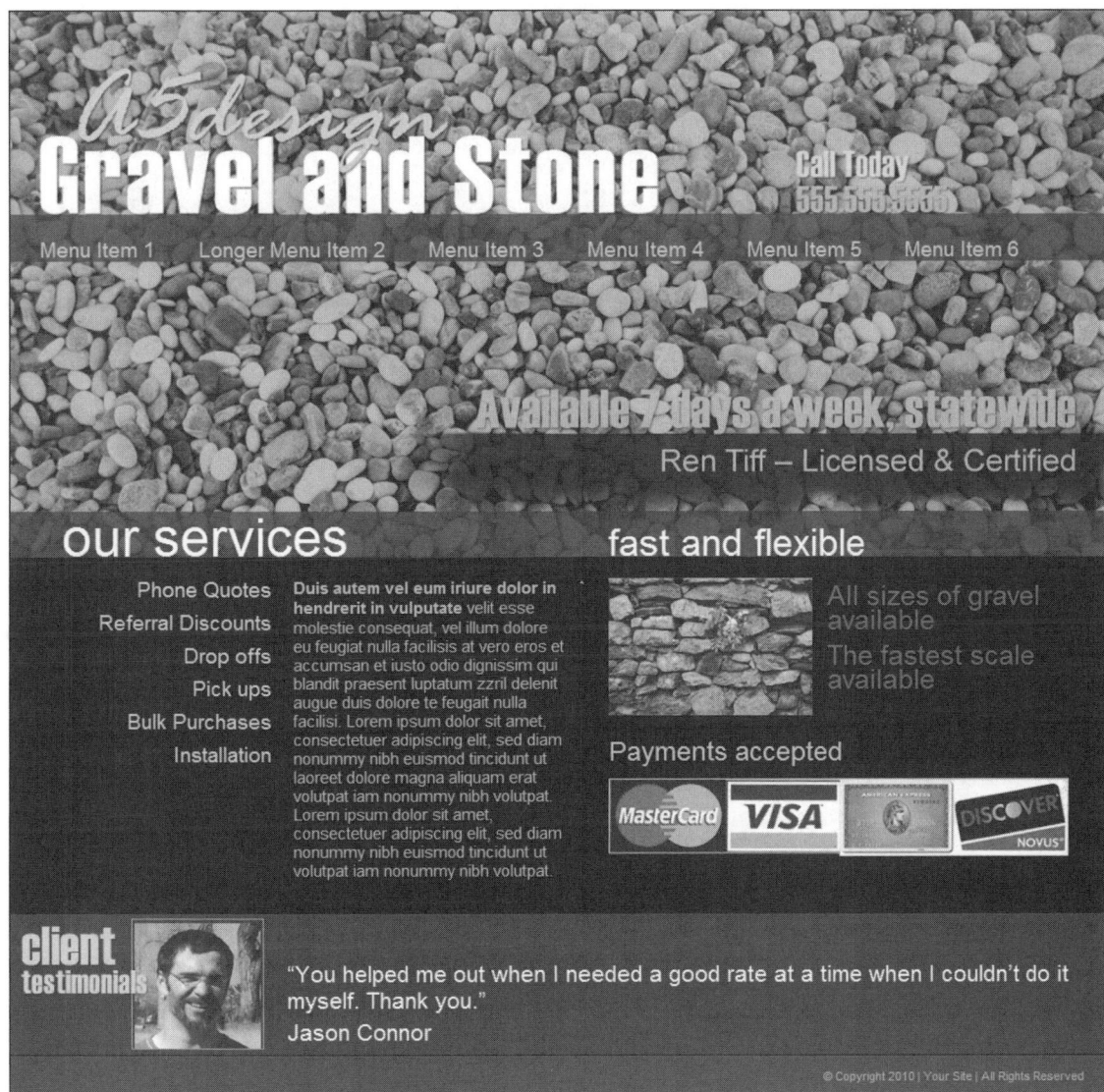

© 2014 Cengage Learning.

Homepage design.

Photoshop source file names: Designs—Fourth Edition/161-180-css/design_173/main.psd, bg-main.psd

XHTML pages: index.htm, menu-item-2.htm, menu-item-3.htm

Photo credits: J&N Photography

Design 172

© 2014 Cengage Learning.

Homepage design.

Photoshop source file names: Designs—Fourth Edition/161-180-css/design_172/main.psd, bg-main.psd

XHTML pages: index.htm, menu-item-2.htm, menu-item-3.htm

Photo credits: J&N Photography, A5design

Design 171

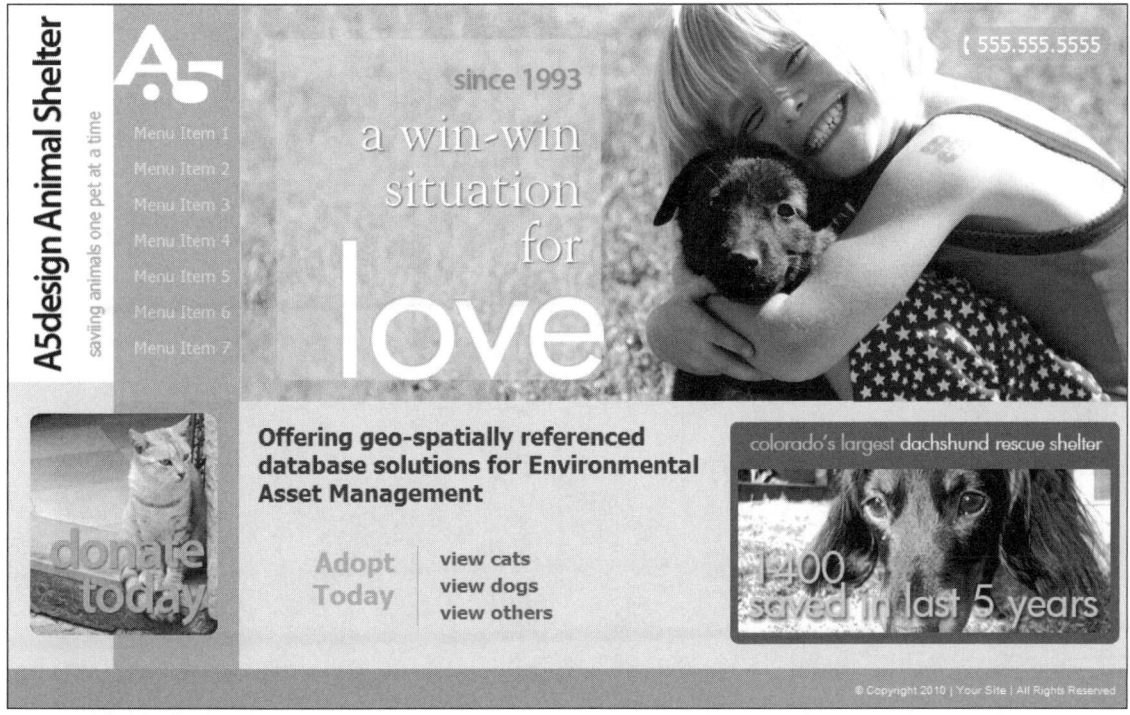

© 2014 Cengage Learning.

Homepage design.

Photoshop source file names: Designs—Fourth Edition/161-180-css/design_171/main.psd, bg-main.psd

XHTML pages: index.htm, menu-item-2.htm, menu-item-3.htm

Photo credits: J&N Photography, A5design

Design 170

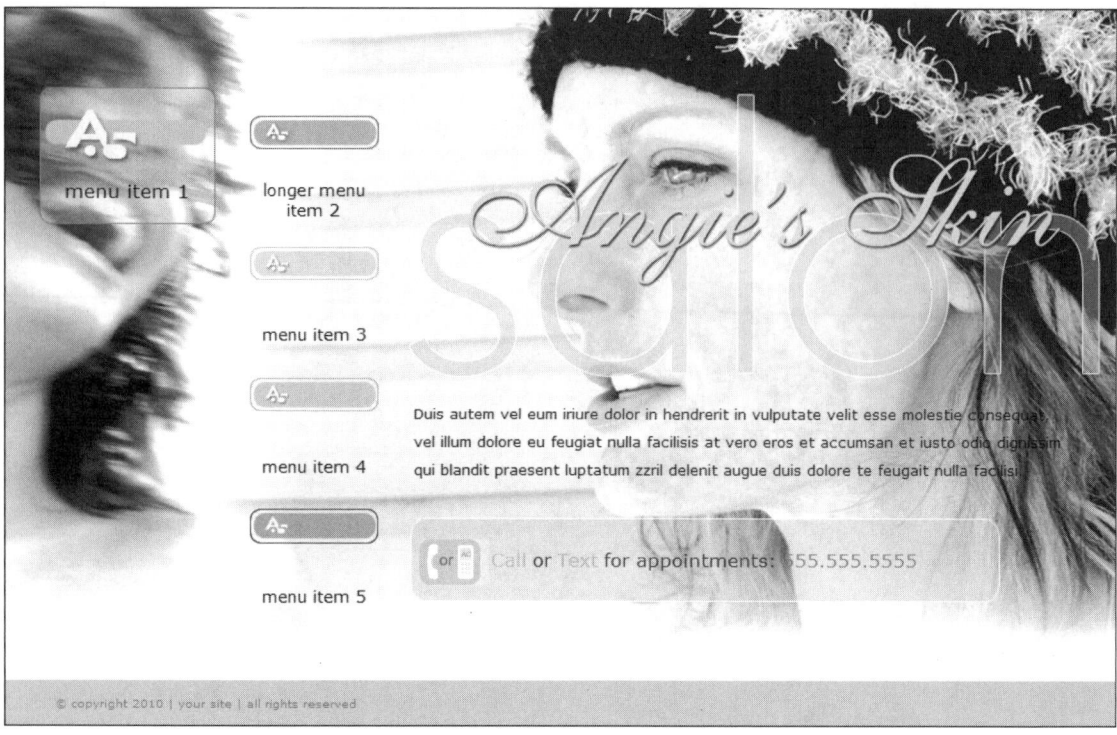

Homepage design.

Photoshop source file names: Designs—Fourth Edition/161-180-css/design_170/main.psd, bg-main.psd

XHTML pages: index.htm, menu-item-2.htm, menu-item-3.htm

Photo credits: A5design

Design 169

Homepage design.

Photoshop source file names: Designs—Fourth Edition/161-180-css/design_169/main.psd, bg-main.psd

XHTML pages: index.htm, menu-item-2.htm, menu-item-3.htm

Photo credits: www.oddmomoutdesigns.com

Design 168

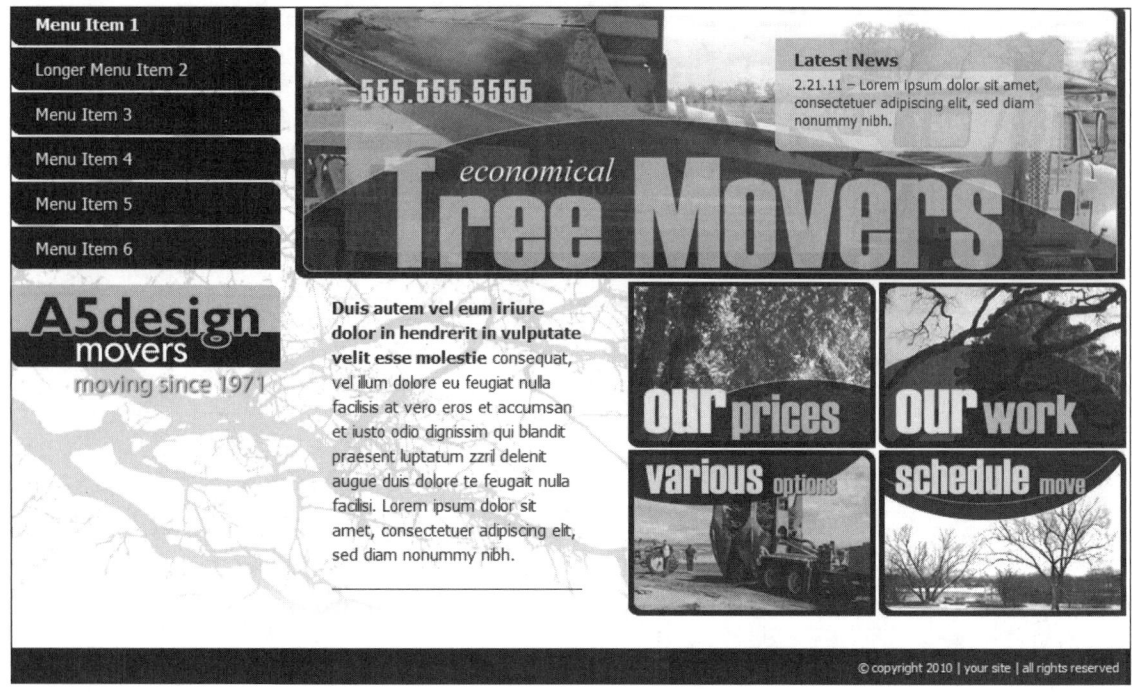

Homepage design.

Photoshop source file names: Designs—Fourth Edition/161-180-css/design_168/main.psd, bg-main.psd

XHTML pages: index.htm, menu-item-2.htm, menu-item-3.htm

Photo credits: J&N Photography

Design 167

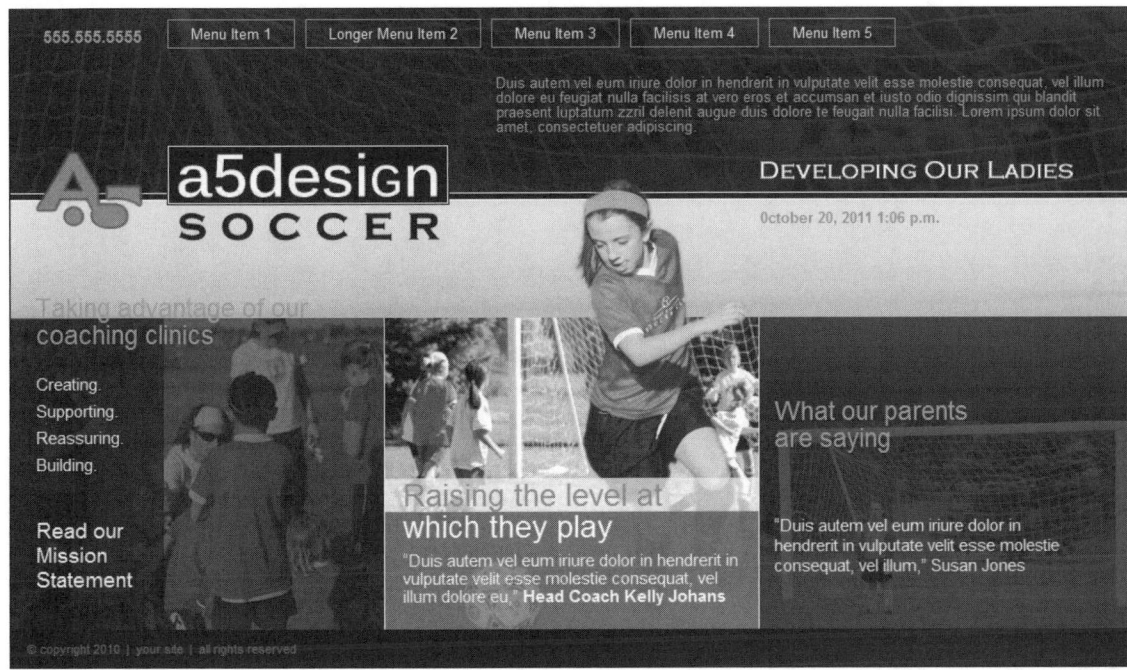

© 2014 Cengage Learning.

Homepage design.

Photoshop source file names: Designs—Fourth Edition/161-180-css/design_167/main.psd, bg-main.psd

XHTML pages: index.htm, menu-item-2.htm, menu-item-3.htm

Photo credits: J&N Photography

Design 166

Homepage design.

Photoshop source file names: Designs—Fourth Edition/161-180-css/design_166/main.psd, bg-main.psd

XHTML pages: index.htm, menu-item-2.htm, menu-item-3.htm

Photo credits: J&N Photography

Design 165

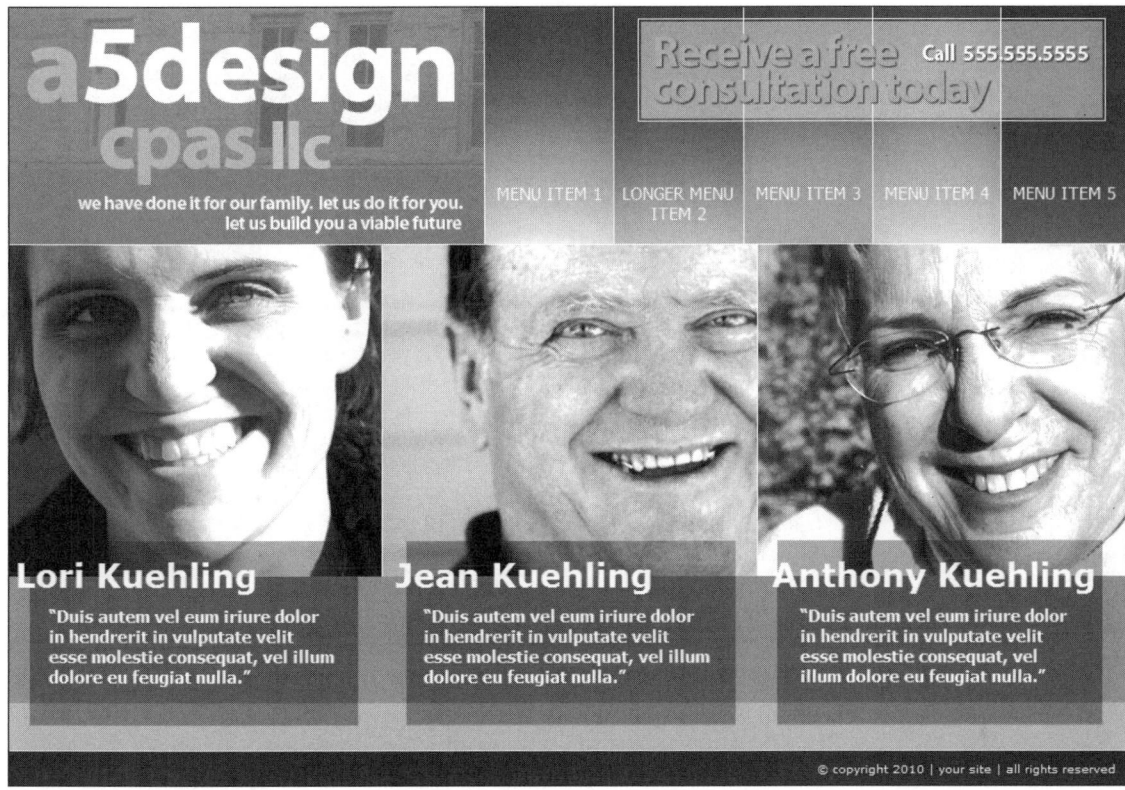

© 2014 Cengage Learning.

Homepage design.

Photoshop source file names: Designs—Fourth Edition/161-180-css/design_165/main.psd, bg-main.psd

XHTML pages: index.htm, menu-item-2.htm, menu-item-3.htm

Photo credits: J&N Photography

Design 164

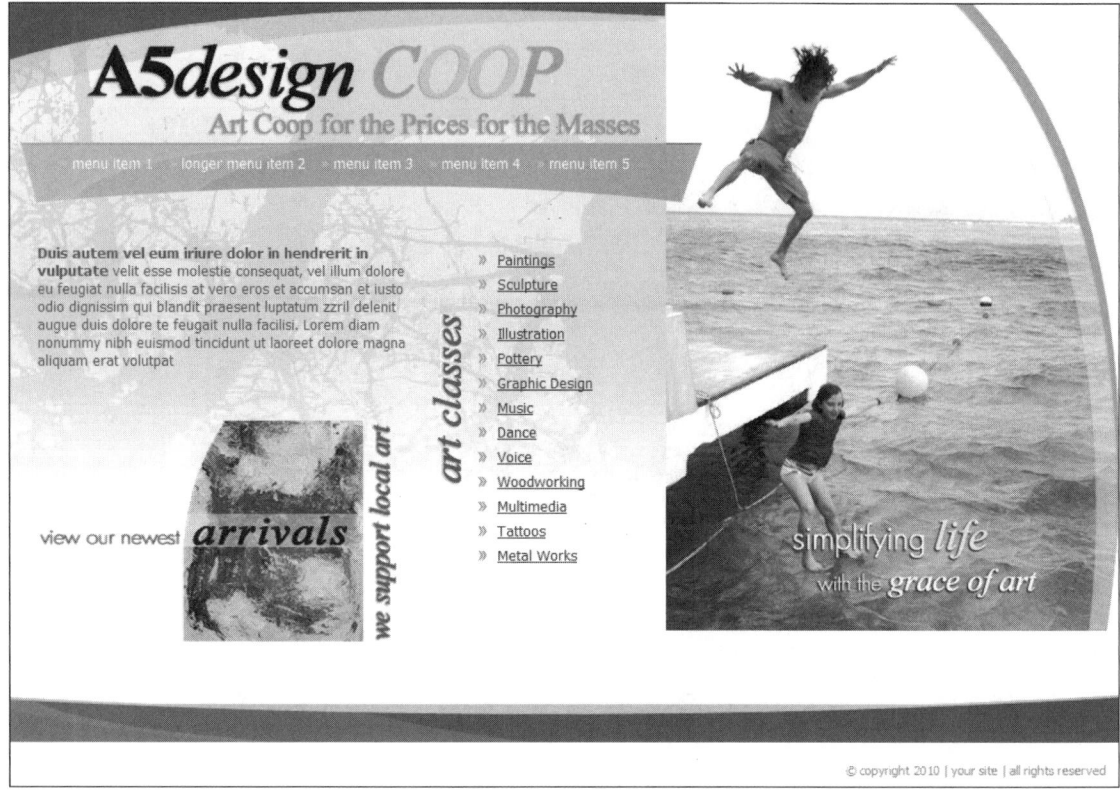

Homepage design.

Photoshop source file names: Designs—Fourth Edition/161-180-css/design_164/main.psd, bg-main.psd

XHTML pages: index.htm, menu-item-2.htm, menu-item-3.htm

Photo credits: Lori Discoe

Design 163

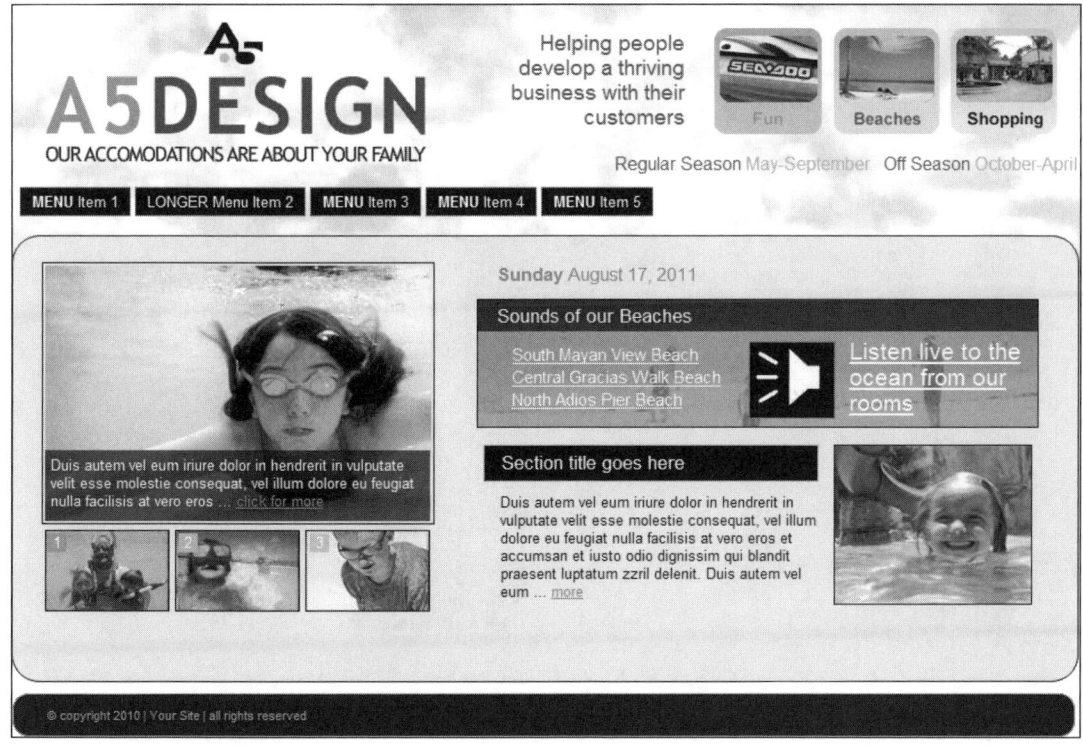

© 2014 Cengage Learning.

Homepage design.

Photoshop source file names: Designs—Fourth Edition/161-180-css/design_163/main.psd, bg-main.psd

XHTML pages: index.htm, menu-item-2.htm, menu-item-3.htm

Photo credits: J&N Photography, A5design

Design 162

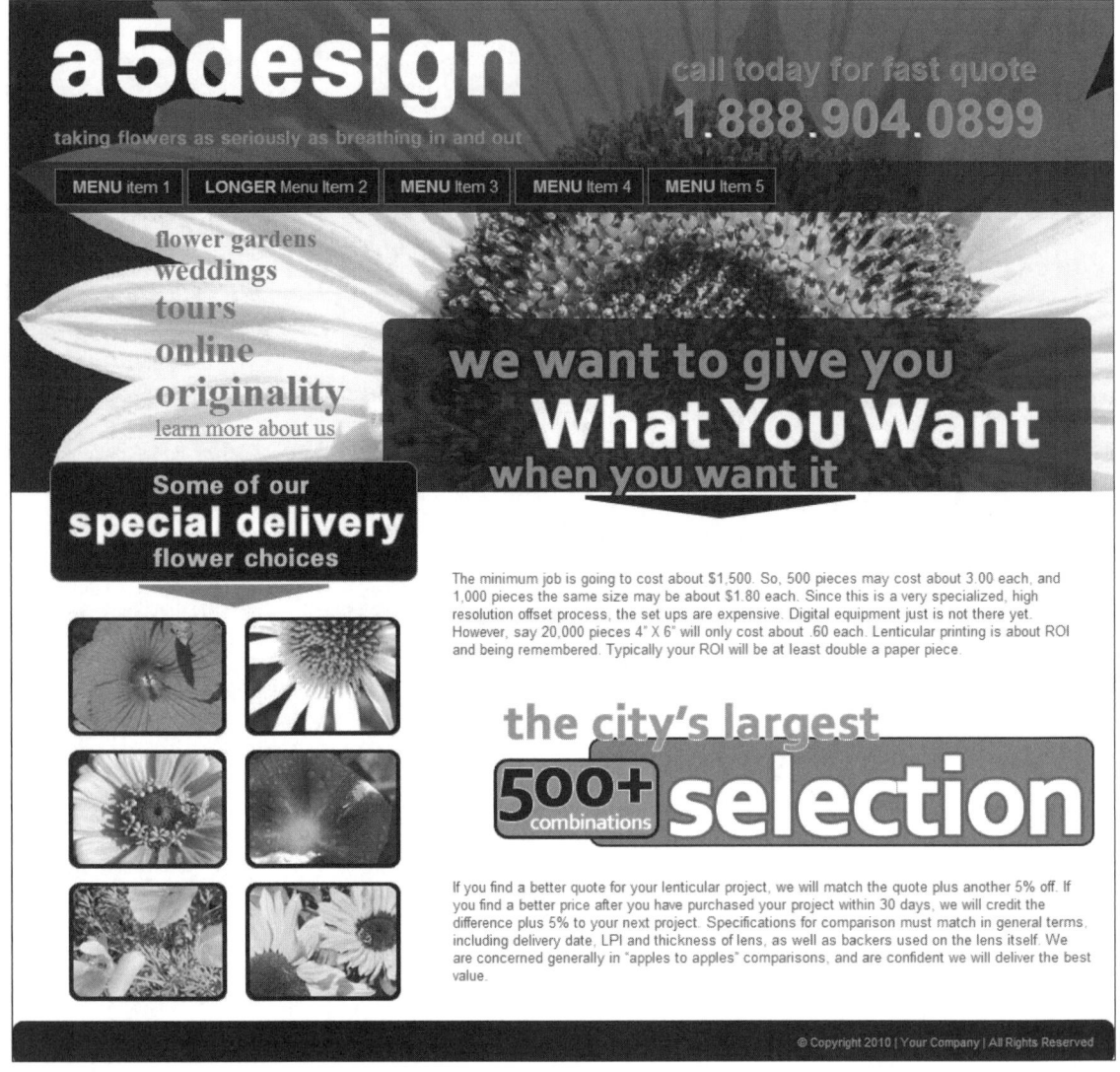

© 2014 Cengage Learning.

Homepage design.

Photoshop source file names: Designs—Fourth Edition/161-180-css/design_162/main.psd, bg-main.psd

XHTML pages: index.htm, menu-item-2.htm, menu-item-3.htm

Photo credits: J&N Photography

Design 161

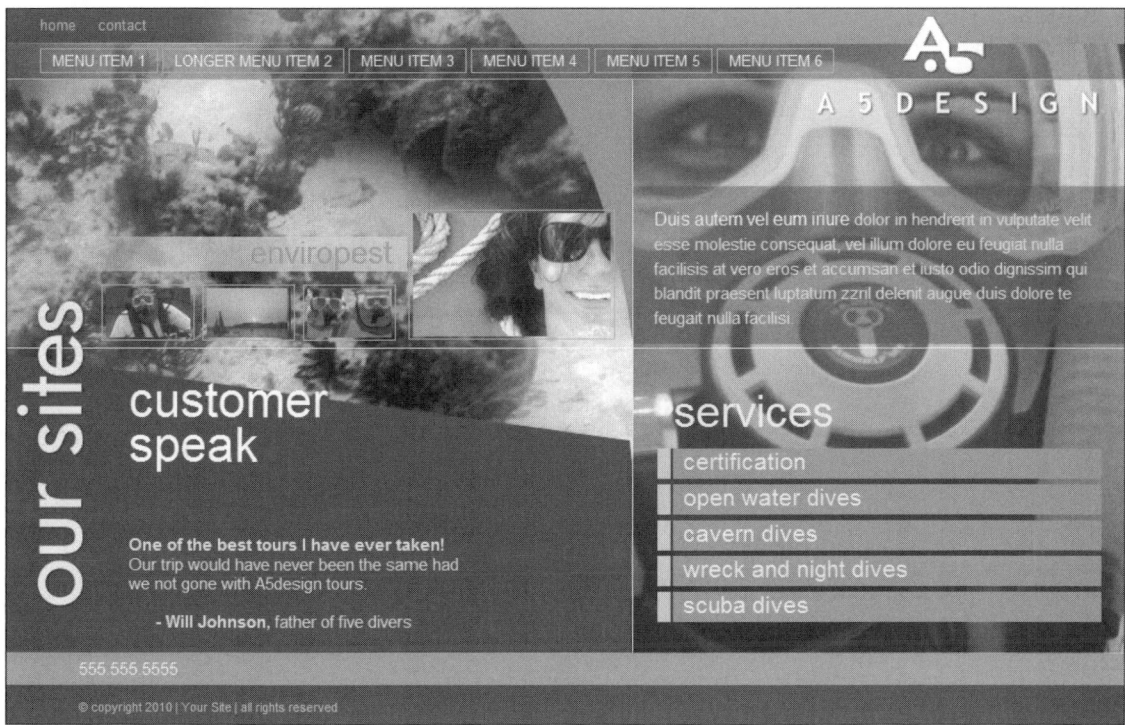

Homepage design.

Photoshop source file names: Designs—Fourth
Edition/161-180-css/design_161/main.psd, bg-main.psd

XHTML pages: index.htm, menu-item-2.htm, menu-item-3.htm

Photo credits: Lori Discoe, A5design

DESIGNS—THIRD EDITION FOLDER

The designs in this folder decrease in numerical order. The most recent designs are shown first. These are CSS-based designs created for 1024 × 768 resolution. As the design numbers decrease, so does the resolution and coding method used. In other words, the resolution for which the designs are created eventually decreases to 800 × 600 resolution, and the coding method eventually becomes XHTML table-based designs, as opposed to CSS-based designs. The purpose of the older designs serves more as creative inspiration for readers to create their own designs or even to modify more recent templates included with the book.

Design 160

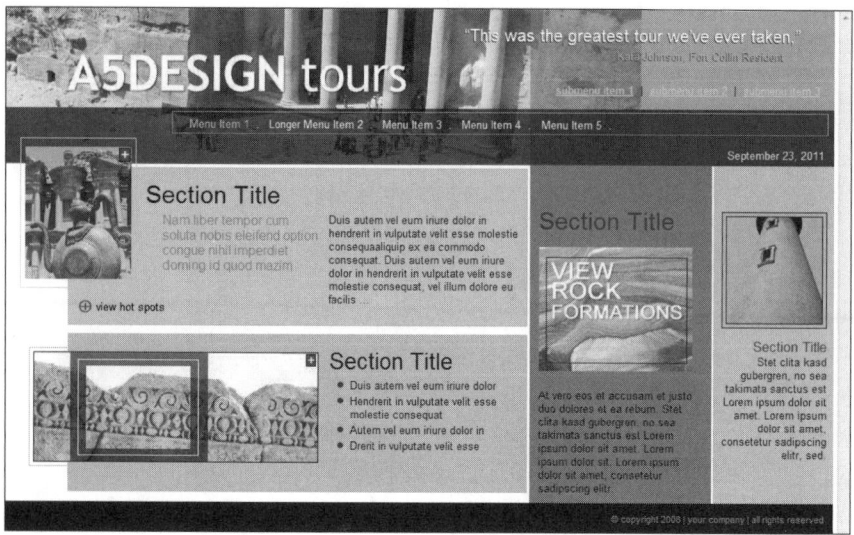

Homepage design.

Photoshop source file names: Designs—Third Edition/121-160-css/design_160/main.psd, bg-main.psd

XHTML pages: index.htm, menu-item-2.htm, menu-item-3.htm

Photo credits: ronsternimages.com

Design 159

Homepage design.

Photoshop source file names: Designs—Third
Edition/121-160-css/design_159/main.psd, bg-main.psd, bg-main-sl.psd

XHTML pages: index.htm, menu-item-2.htm

Design 158

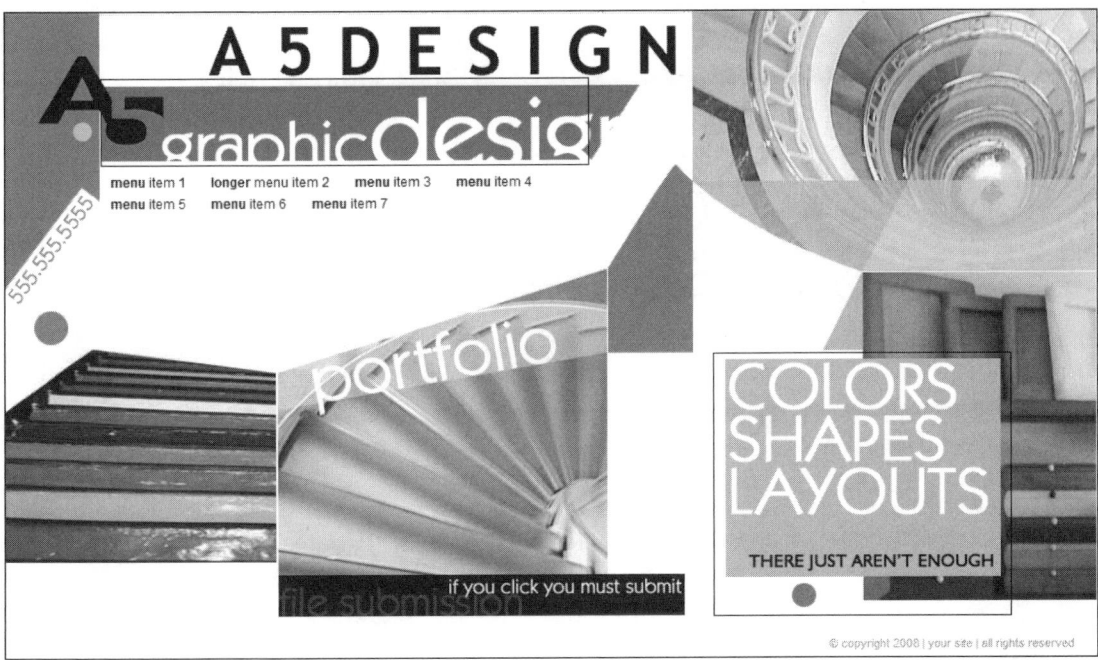

© 2014 Cengage Learning.

Homepage design.

Photoshop source file names: Designs—Third
Edition/121-160-css/design_158/main.psd

XHTML pages: index.htm, menu-item-2.htm, menu-item-3.htm

Photo credits: ronsternimages.com

Design 157

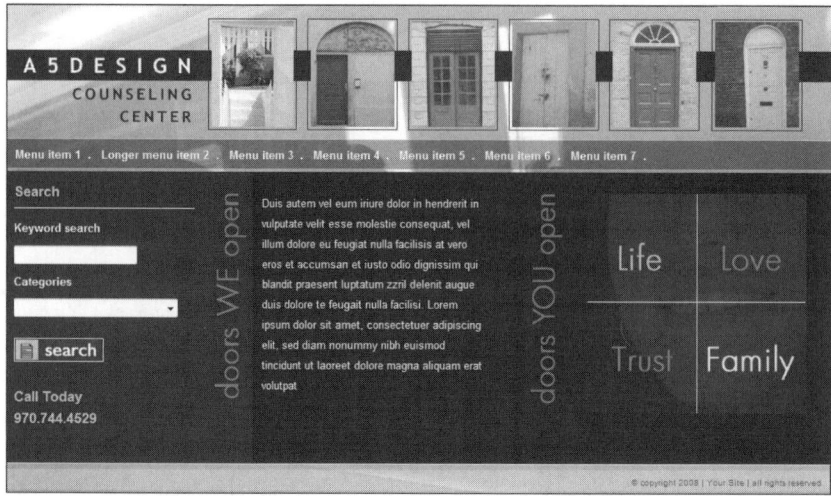

© 2014 Cengage Learning.

Homepage design.

Photoshop source file names: Designs—Third Edition/121-160-css/design_157/main.psd

XHTML pages: index.htm, menu-item-2.htm, menu-item-3.htm

Photo credits: ronsternimages.com

Design 156

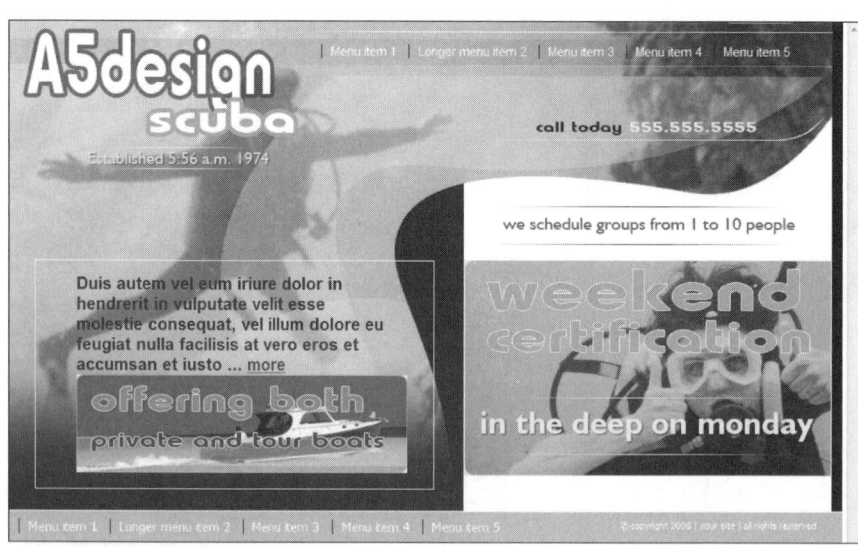

© 2014 Cengage Learning.

Homepage design.

Photoshop source file names: Designs—Third Edition/121-160-css/design_156/main.psd, main-sl.psd

XHTML pages: index.htm, menu-item-2.htm, menu-item-3.htm

Photo credits: ronsternimages.com, J&N Photography

Design 155

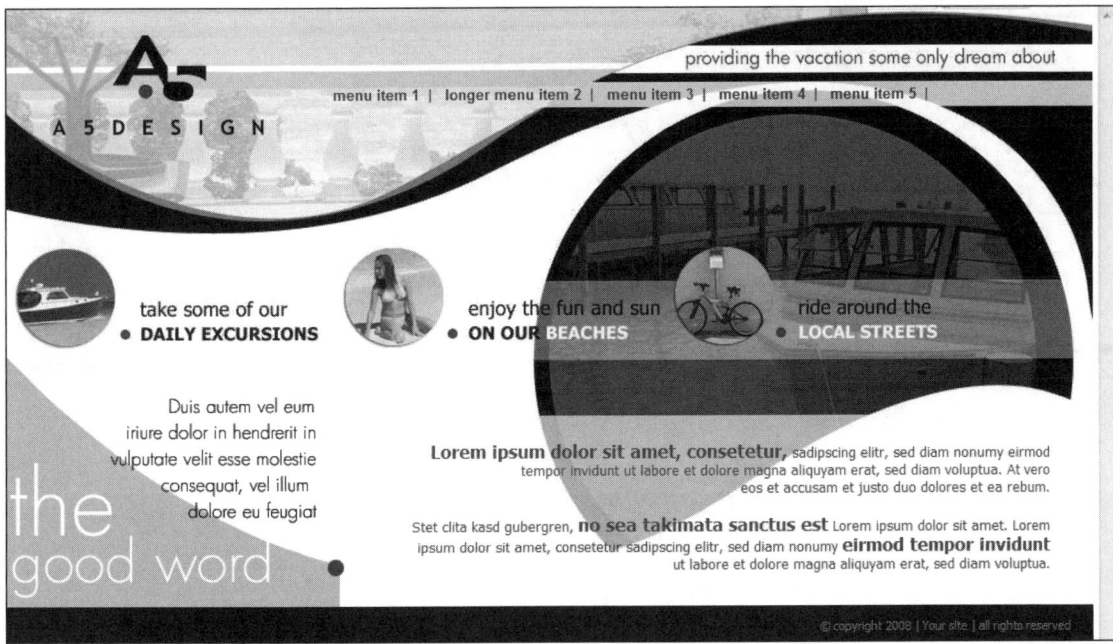

© 2014 Cengage Learning.

Homepage design.

Photoshop source file names: Designs—Third Edition/121-160-css/design_155/main.psd, main-bg.psd, main-bg-sl.psd

XHTML pages: index.htm, menu-item-2.htm, menu-item-3.htm

Photo credits: ronsternimages.com

Design 154

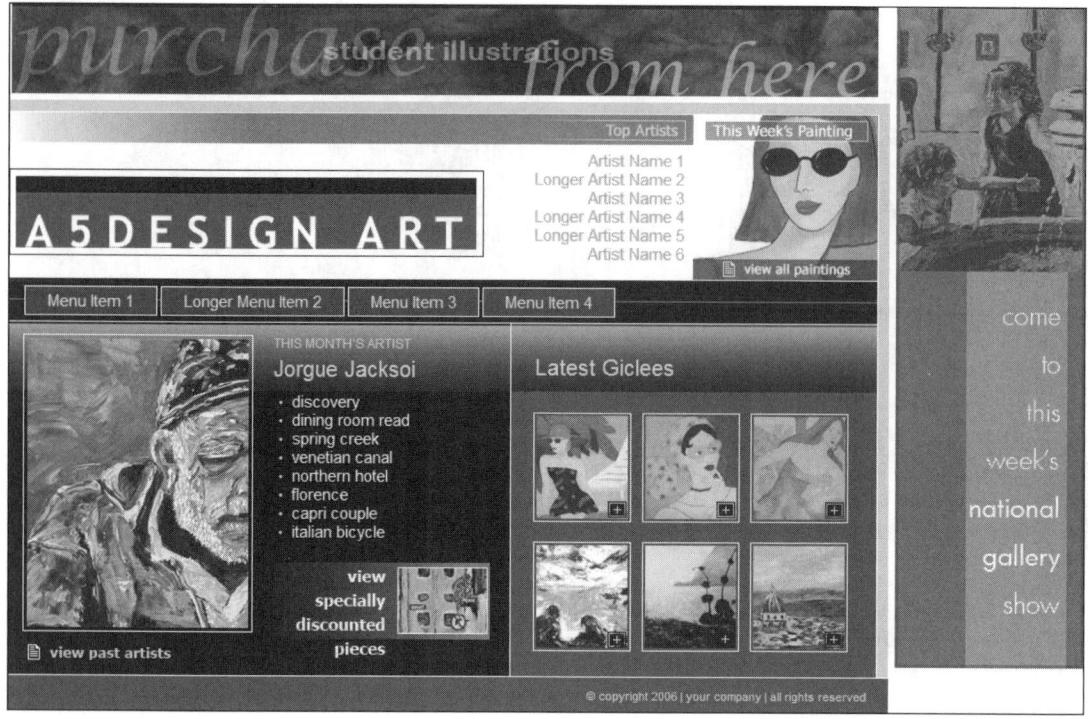

© 2014 Cengage Learning.

Homepage design.

Photoshop source file names: Designs—Third Edition/121-160-css/design_154/main.psd

XHTML pages: index.htm, menu-item-2.htm, menu-item-3.htm

Photo credits: ronsternimages.com, A5design, onepartart.com

Design 153

Homepage design.

Photoshop source file names: Designs—Third Edition/121-160-css/design_153/main.psd, bg-main.psd, bg-main-sl.psd

XHTML pages: index.htm, menu-item-2.htm, menu-item-3.htm

Photo credits: ronsternimages.com, A5design

Design 152

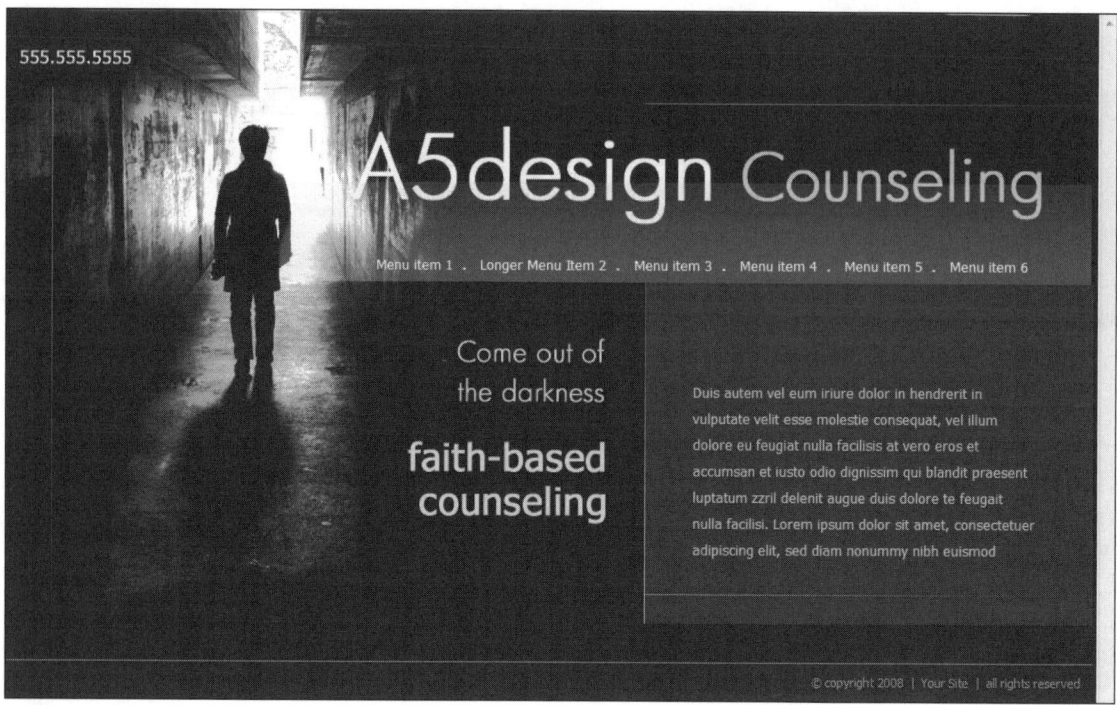

Homepage design.

Photoshop source file names: Designs—Third Edition/121-160-css/design_152/main.psd, main-bg.psd, main-bg-sl.psd

XHTML pages: index.htm, menu-item-2.htm, menu-item-3.htm

Photo credits: ronsternimages.com

Design 151

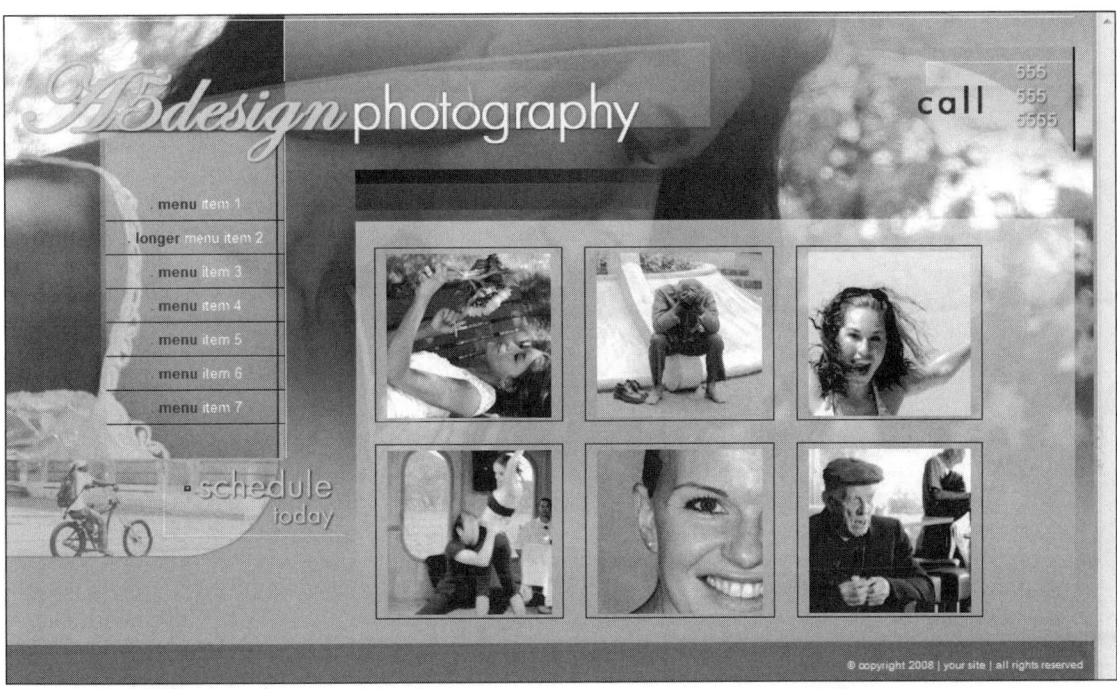

© 2014 Cengage Learning.

Homepage design.

Photoshop source file names: Designs—Third Edition/121-160-css/design_151/main.psd, bg-main.psd

XHTML pages: index.htm, menu-item-2.htm

Photo credits: ronsternimages.com

Design 150

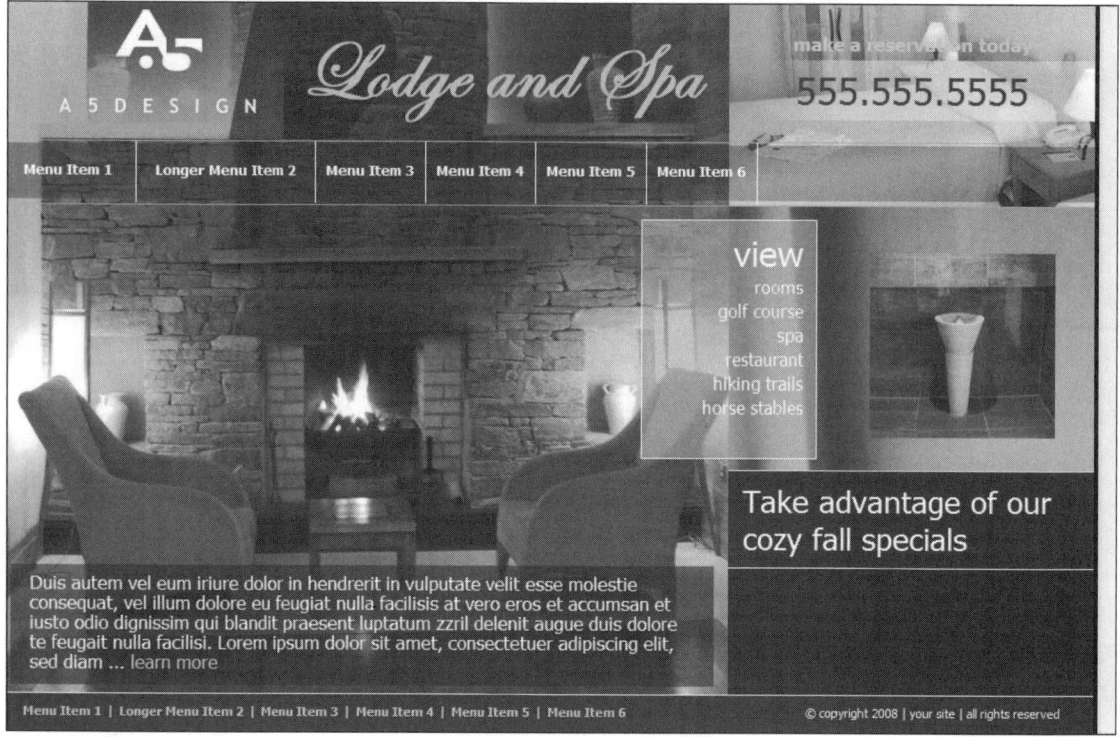

Homepage design.

Photoshop source file names: Designs—Third Edition/121-160-css/design_150/main.psd, bg-main.psd, bg-main-sl.psd

XHTML pages: index.htm, menu-item-2.htm, menu-item-3.htm

Photo credits: ronsternimages.com

Design 149

Homepage design.

Photoshop source file names: Designs—Third Edition/121-160-css/design_149/main.psd

XHTML pages: index.htm, menu-item-2.htm, menu-item-3.htm

Photo credits: ronsternimages.com

Design 148

Homepage design.

Photoshop source file names: Designs—Third Edition/121-160-css/design_148/main.psd, bg-main.psd, bg-main-sl.psd

XHTML pages: index.htm, menu-item-2.htm, menu-item-3.htm

Photo credits: ronsternimages.com, A5design

Design 147

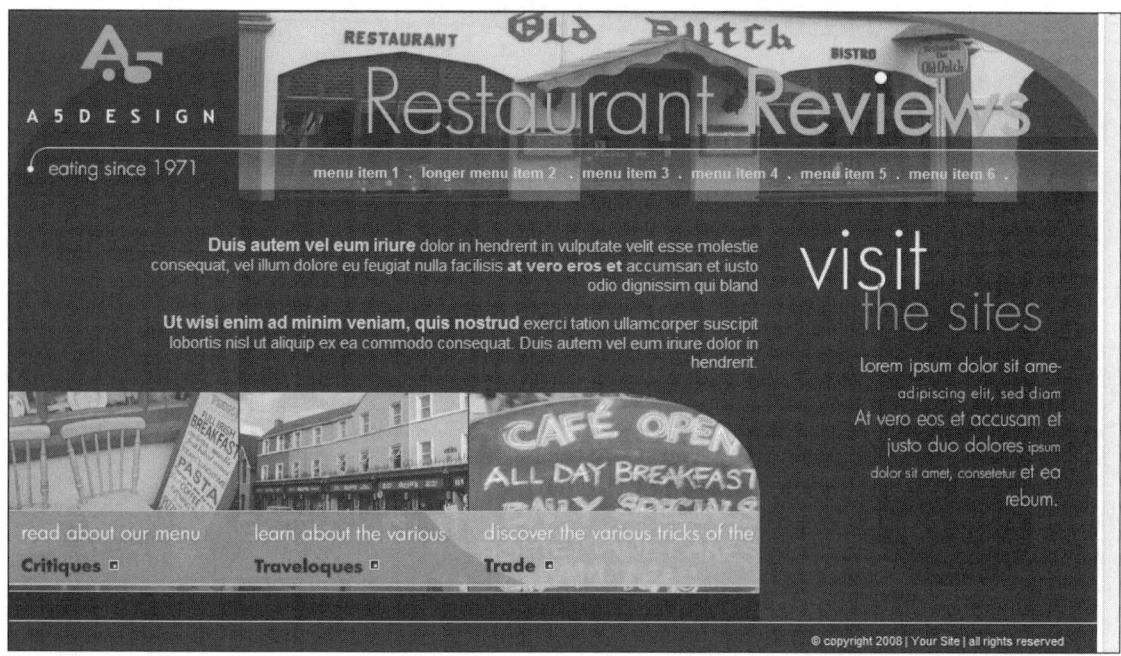

© 2014 Cengage Learning.

Homepage design.

Photoshop source file names: Designs—Third Edition/121-160-css/design_147/main.psd

XHTML pages: index.htm, menu-item-2.htm, menu-item-3.htm

Photo credits: ronsternimages.com

Design 146

Homepage design.

Photoshop source file names: Designs—Third
Edition/121-160-css/design_146/main.psd, bg-main.psd, bg-main-sl.psd

XHTML pages: index.htm, menu-item-2.htm

Photo credits: ronsternimages.com

Design 145

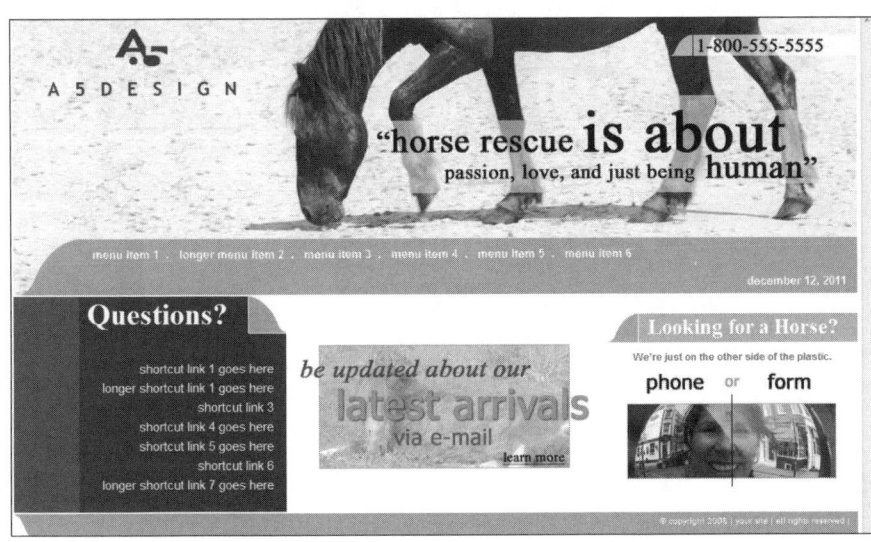

Homepage design.

Second-level template for more content.

Photoshop source file names: Designs—Third Edition/121-160-css/design_145/main.psd, main-sl.psd

XHTML pages: index.htm, menu-item-2.htm, menu-item-3.htm, menu-item-4.htm

Photo credits: ronsternimages.com

Design 144

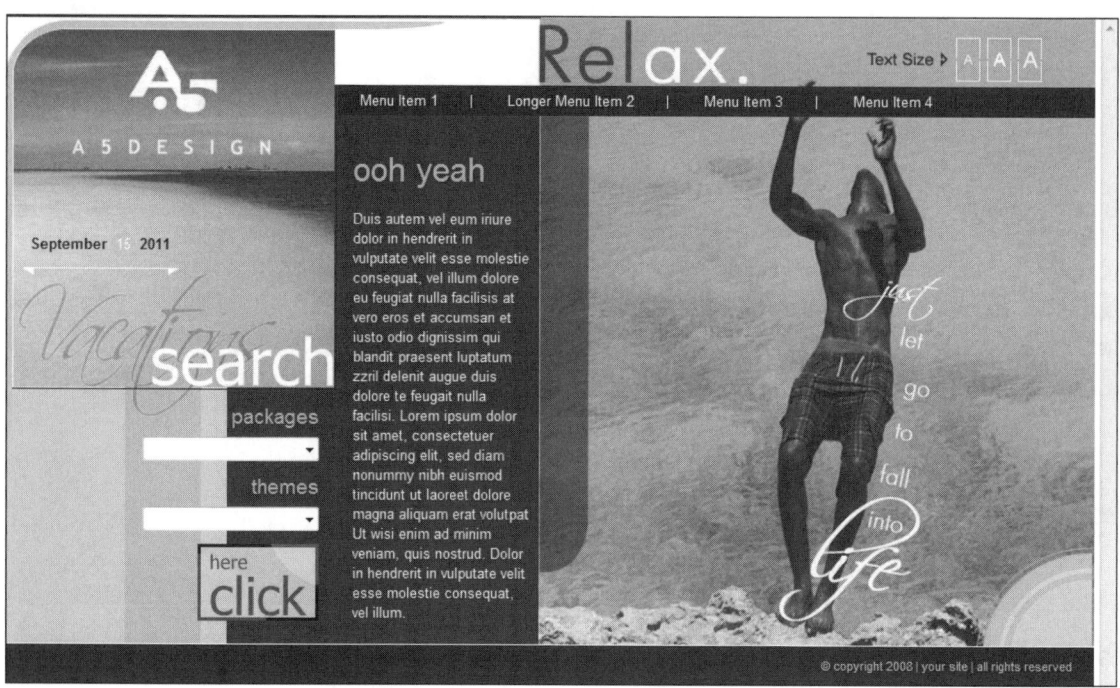

Homepage design.

Photoshop source file names: Designs—Third Edition/121-160-css/design_144/main.psd, main-sl.psd

XHTML pages: index.htm, menu-item-2.htm

Photo credits: ronsternimages.com

Design 143

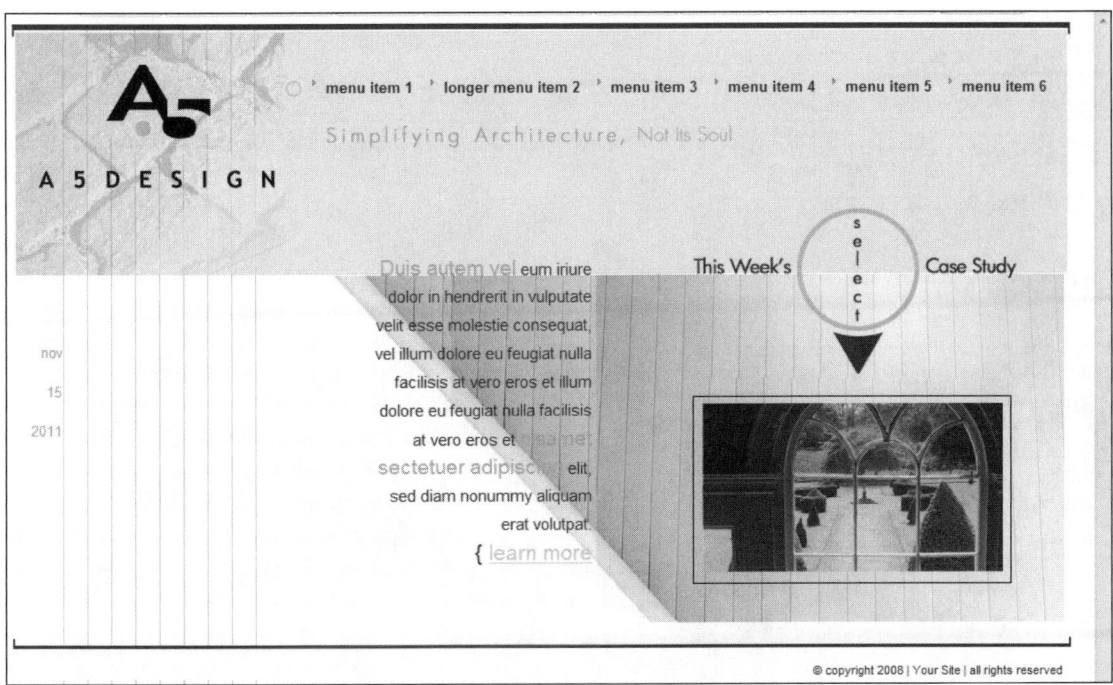

Homepage design.

Photoshop source file names: Designs—Third Edition/121-160-css/design_143/main.psd, bg-body.psd

XHTML pages: index.htm, menu-item-2.htm, menu-item-3.htm

Photo credits: ronsternimages.com, J&N Photography

Design 142

Homepage design.

Photoshop source file names: Designs—Third Edition/121-160-css/design_142/main.psd, main-sl.psd

XHTML pages: index.htm, menu-item-2.htm, menu-item-3.htm

Photo credits: ronsternimages.com

Design 141

Homepage design.

Photoshop source file names: Designs—Third
Edition/121-160-css/design_141/main.psd, main-bg-sl.psd

XHTML pages: index.htm, menu-item-2.htm, menu-item-3.htm

Photo credits: ronsternimages.com

Design 140

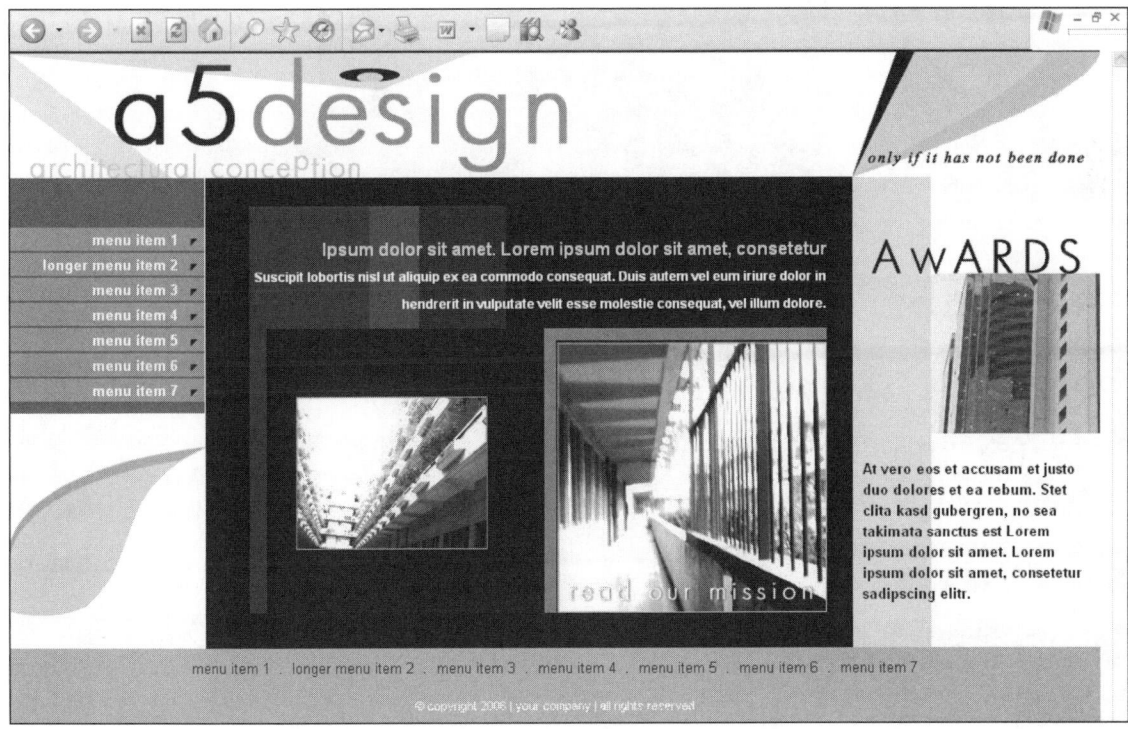

© 2014 Cengage Learning.

Homepage design.

Photoshop source file names: Designs—Third
Edition/121-160-css/design_140/main.psd, main_sl.psd

XHTML pages: index.htm, menu_item_2.htm, menu_item_3.htm

Photo credits: Justin Discoe

Design 139

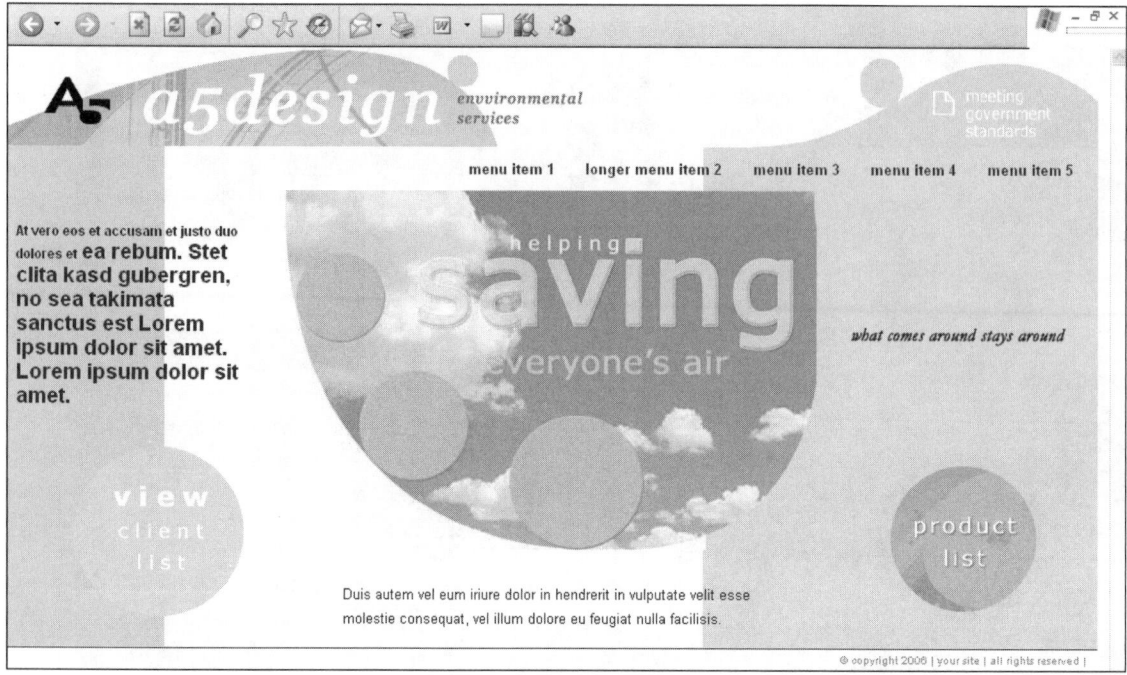

Homepage design.

Photoshop source file names: Designs—Third Edition/121-160-css/design_139/design_139.psd

XHTML pages: index.htm, menu_item_2.htm, menu_item_3.htm, menu_item_4.htm

Photo credits: idlerphotography.com

Design 138

Homepage design.

Photoshop source file names: Designs—Third
Edition/121-160-css/design_138/design_138.psd, bg_design_138.psd

XHTML pages: index.htm, menu_item_2.htm, menu_item_3.htm

Photo credits: idlerphotography.com

Design 137

Homepage design.

Photoshop source file names: Designs—Third Edition/121-160-css/design_137/design_137.psd

XHTML pages: index.htm, menu_item_2.htm, menu_item_3.htm

Photo credits: idlerphotography.com

Design 136

Homepage design.

Photoshop source file names: Designs—Third Edition/121-160-css/design_136/design_136.psd

XHTML pages: index.htm, menu_item_2.htm, menu_item_3.htm

Photo credits: idlerphotography.com

Design 135

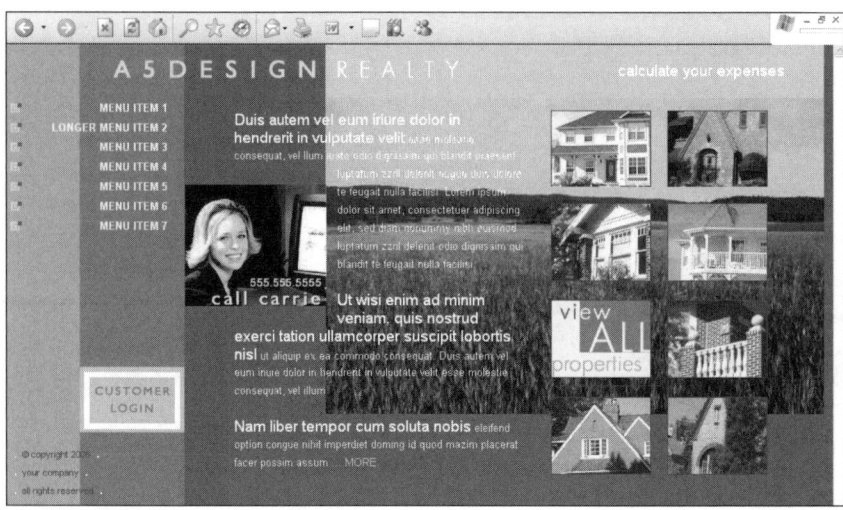

Homepage design.

Photoshop source file names: Designs—Third Edition/121-160-css/design_135/design_135.psd, bg_design_135.psd

XHTML pages: index.htm, menu_item_2.htm, menu_item_3.htm

Photo credits: idlerphotography.com

Design 134

Homepage design.

Photoshop source file names: Designs—Third
Edition/121-160-css/design_134/design_134.psd

XHTML pages: index.htm, menu_item_2.htm, menu_item_3.htm

Photo credits: idlerphotography.com

Design 133

© 2014 Cengage Learning.

Homepage design.

Photoshop source file names: Designs—Third
Edition/121-160-css/design_133/design_133.psd

XHTML pages: index.htm, menu_item_2.htm, menu_item_3.htm

Photo credits: idlerphotography.com

Design 132

Homepage design.

Photoshop source file names: Designs—Third Edition/121-160-css/design_132/design_132.psd, bg_132.psd, bg_132_sl.psd

XHTML pages: index.htm, menu_item_2.htm, menu_item_3.htm

Photo credits: Justin Discoe

Design 131

Homepage design.

Photoshop source file names: Designs—Third Edition/121-160-css/design_131/design_131.psd

XHTML pages: index.htm, menu_item_2.htm, menu_item_3.htm

Photo credits: idlerphotography.com

Design 130

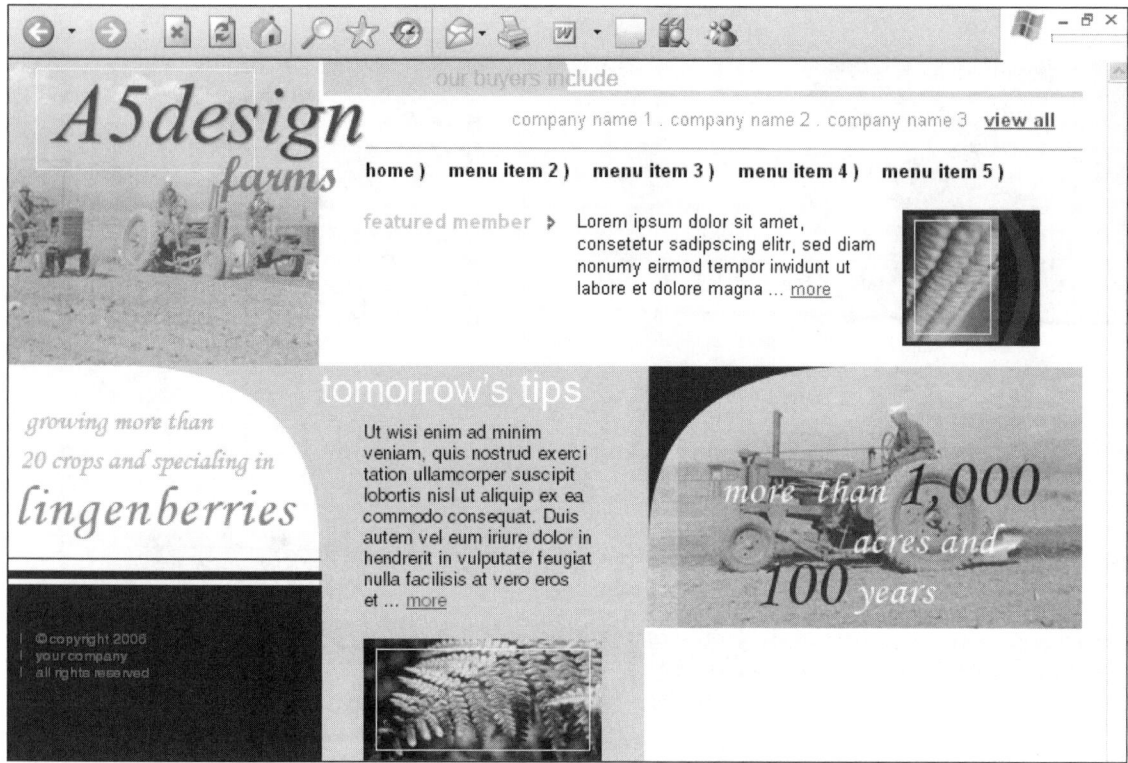

Homepage design.

Photoshop source file names: Designs—Third
Edition/121-160-css/design_130/design_130.psd

XHTML pages: index.htm, menu_item_2.htm, menu_item_3.htm

Photo credits: idlerphotography.com, Joe Eccher

Design 129

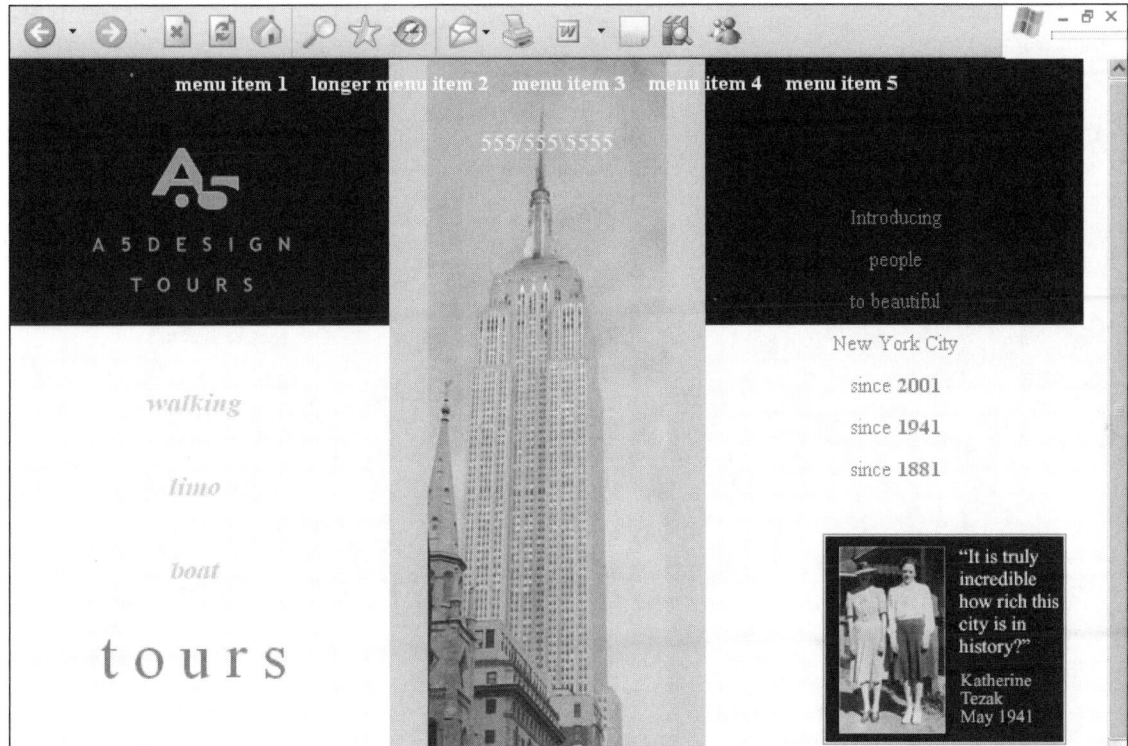

© 2014 Cengage Learning.

Homepage design.

Photoshop source file names: Designs—Third Edition/121-160-css/design_129/design_129.psd, bg_design_129.psd

XHTML pages: index.htm, menu_item_2.htm, menu_item_3.htm, menu_item_4.htm

Photo credits: Justin Discoe, Lori Discoe

Design 128

Homepage design.

Photoshop source file names: Designs—Third Edition/121-160-css/design_128/design_128.psd

XHTML pages: index.htm, menu_item_2.htm, menu_item_3.htm

Photo credits: A5design

Design 127

Homepage design.

Photoshop source file names: Designs—Third
Edition/121-160-css/design_127/design_127.psd, bg_design_127.psd

XHTML pages: index.htm, menu_item_2.htm, menu_item_3.htm

Photo credits: idlerphotography.com

Design 126

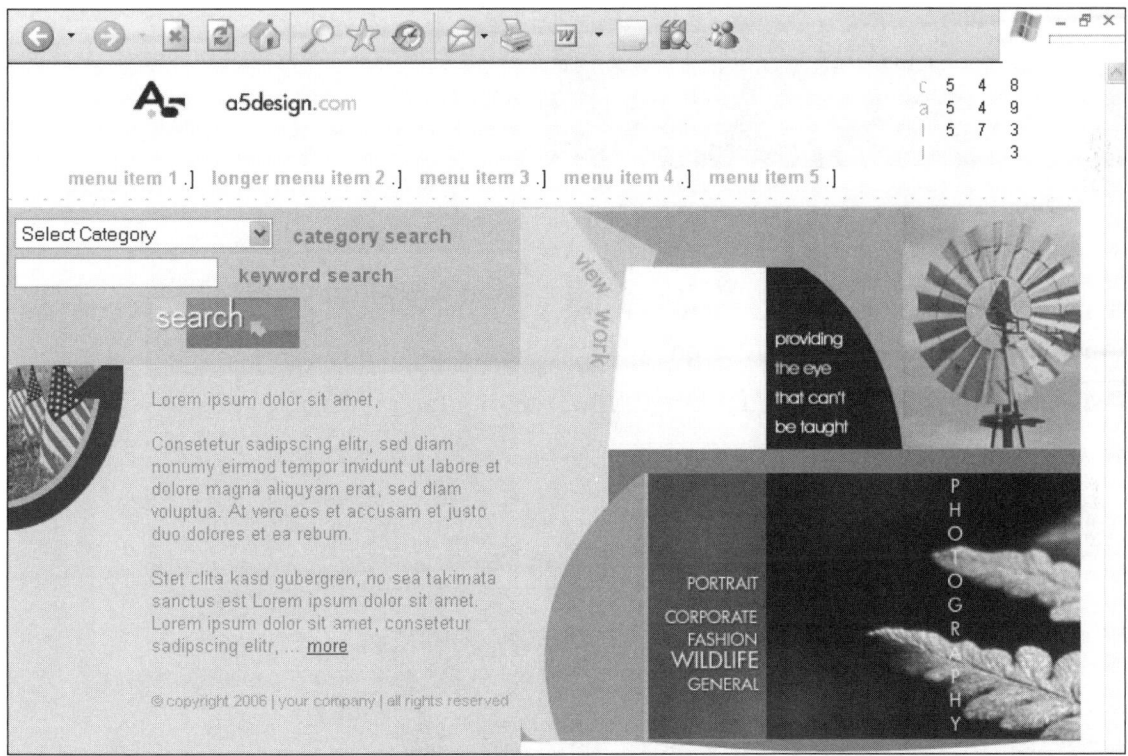

Homepage design.

Photoshop source file names: Designs—Third
Edition/121-160-css/design_126/design_126.psd

XHTML pages: index.htm, menu_item_2.htm, menu_item_3.htm, menu_item_4.htm

Photo credits: idlerphotography.com

Design 125

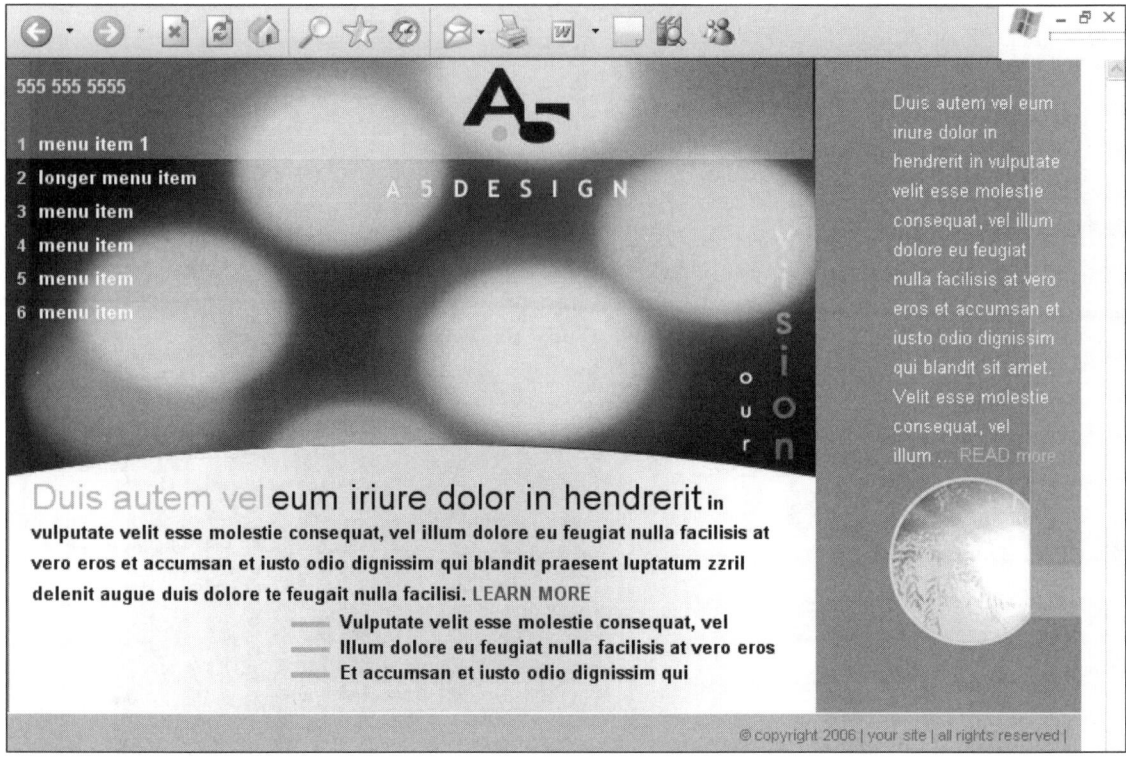

Homepage design.

Photoshop source file names: Designs—Third Edition/121-160-css/design_125/design_125.psd

XHTML pages: index.htm, menu_item_2.htm, menu_item_3.htm

Photo credits: A5design

Design 124

© 2014 Cengage Learning.

Homepage design.

Photoshop source file names: Designs—Third Edition/121-160-css/design_124/design_124.psd, bg_design_124.psd

XHTML pages: index.htm, menu_item_2.htm, menu_item_3.htm

Photo credits: Joe Eccher

Design 123

Homepage design.

Photoshop source file names: Designs—Third Edition/121-160-css/design_123/design_123.psd, bg-left-column.psd

XHTML pages: index.htm, menu_item_2.htm, menu_item_3.htm

Photo credits: idlerphotography.com

Design 122

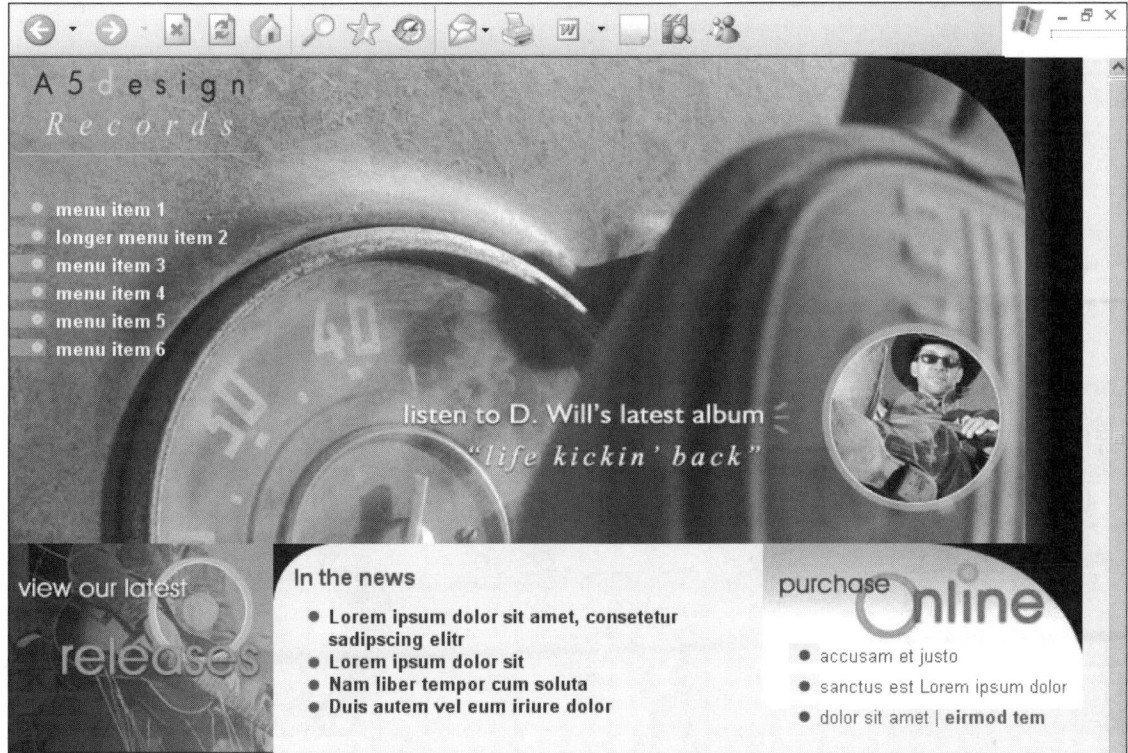

Homepage design.

Photoshop source file names: Designs—Third Edition/121-160-css/design_122/design_122.psd, design_122_sl.psd

XHTML pages: index.htm, menu_item_2.htm, menu_item_3.htm

Photo credits: idlerphotography.com

Design 121

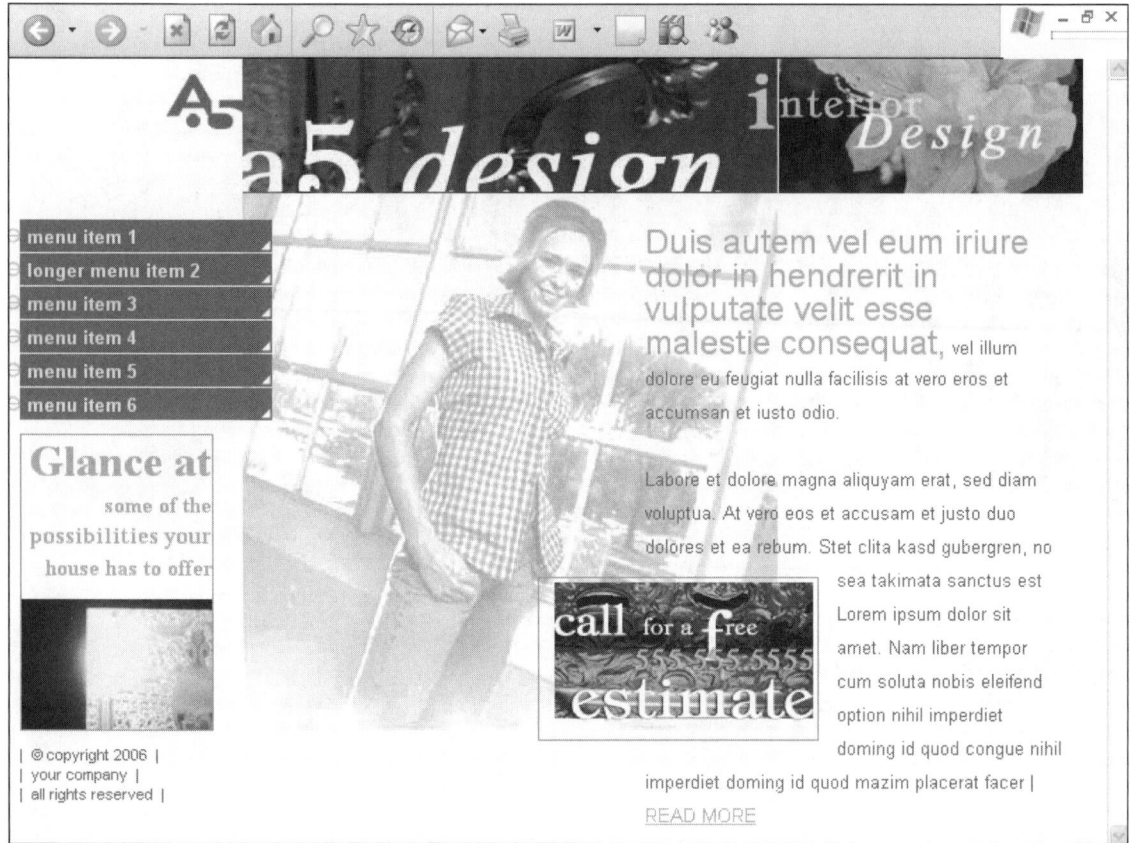

Homepage design.

Photoshop source file names: Designs—Third Edition/121-160-css/design_121/design_121.psd, design_121_sl.psd, bg_body_figure.psd

XHTML pages: index.htm, menu_item_2.htm, menu_item_3.htm

Photo credits: idlerphotography.com

Design 120

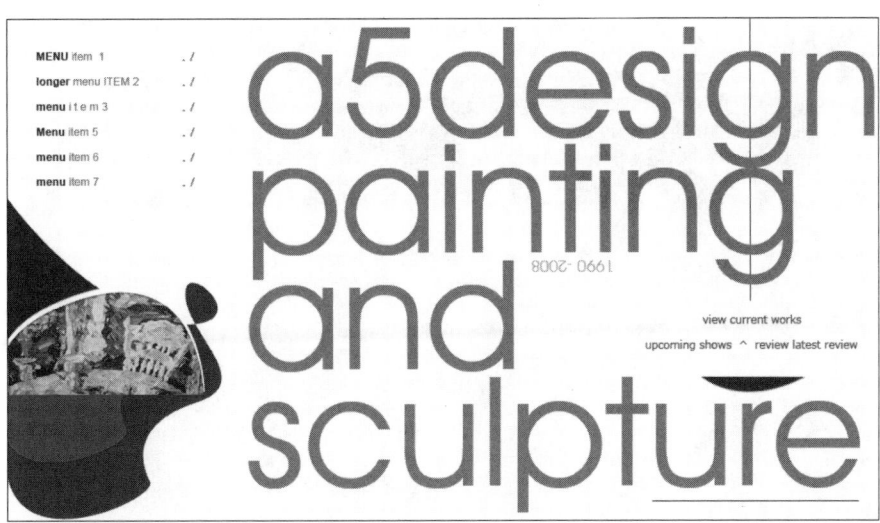

Homepage design.

Photoshop source file names: Designs—Third Edition/101-120-photoshop/design_120/design_120.psd

Photo credits: A5design

Design 119

Homepage design.

Photoshop source file names: Designs—Third Edition/101-120-photoshop/design_119/design_119.psd

Photo credits: idlerphotography.com

Design 118

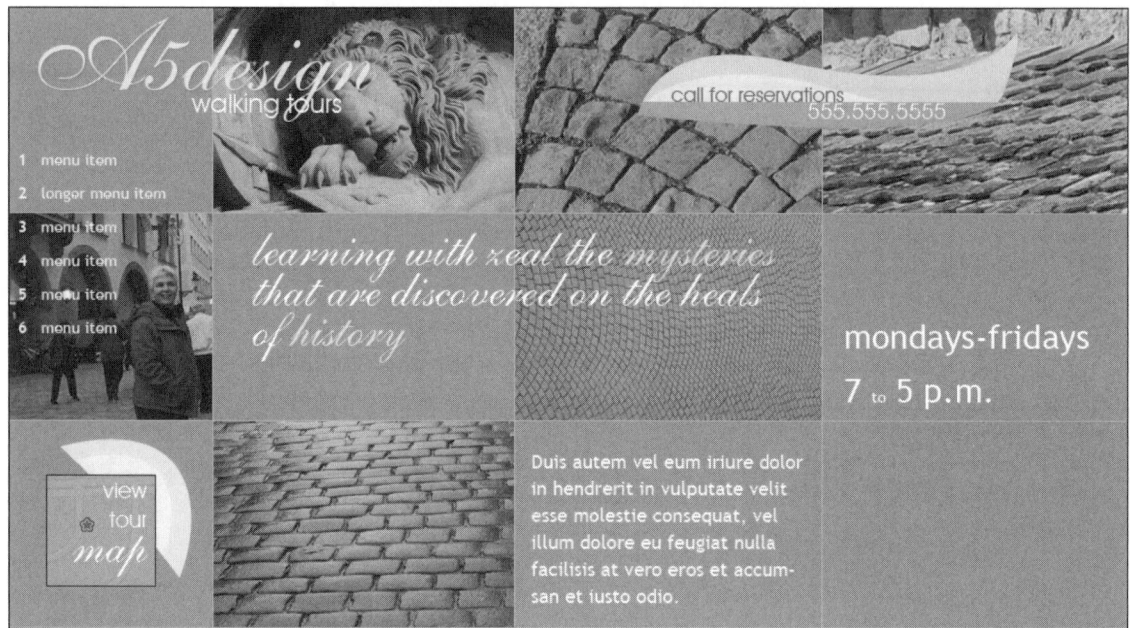

© 2014 Cengage Learning.

Homepage design (Photoshop only).

Photoshop source file names: Designs—Third Edition/101-120-photoshop/design_118/design_118.psd

Photo credits: Joe Eccher

Design 117

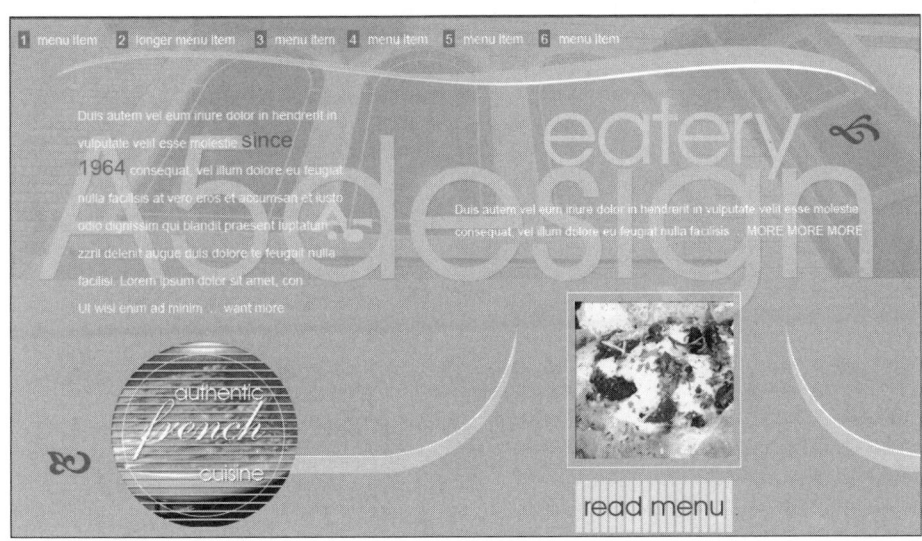

Homepage design (Photoshop only).

Photoshop source file names: Designs—Third Edition/101-120-photoshop/design_117/design_117.psd

Photo credits: idlerphotography.com

Design 116

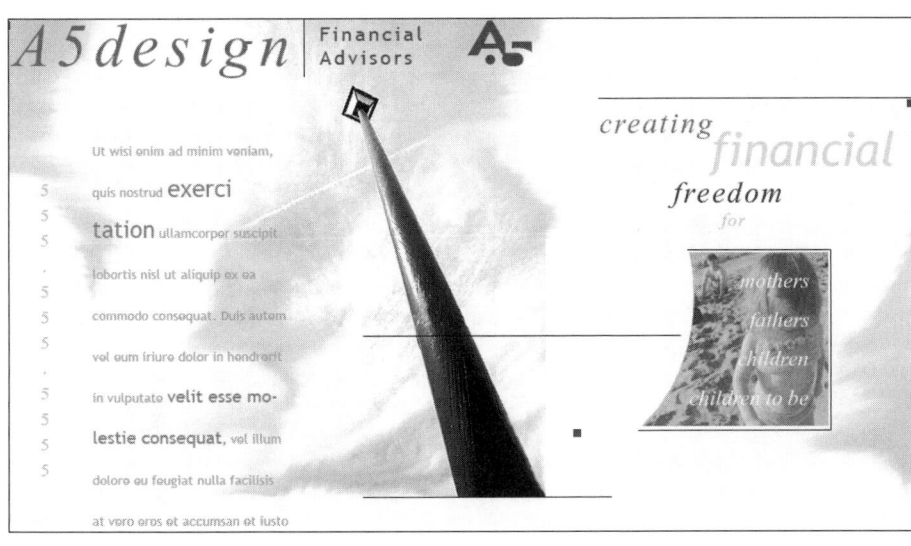

Homepage design (Photoshop only).

Photoshop source file names: Designs—Third Edition/101-120-photoshop/design_116/design_116.psd

Photo credits: idlerphotography.com, Joe Eccher

Design 115

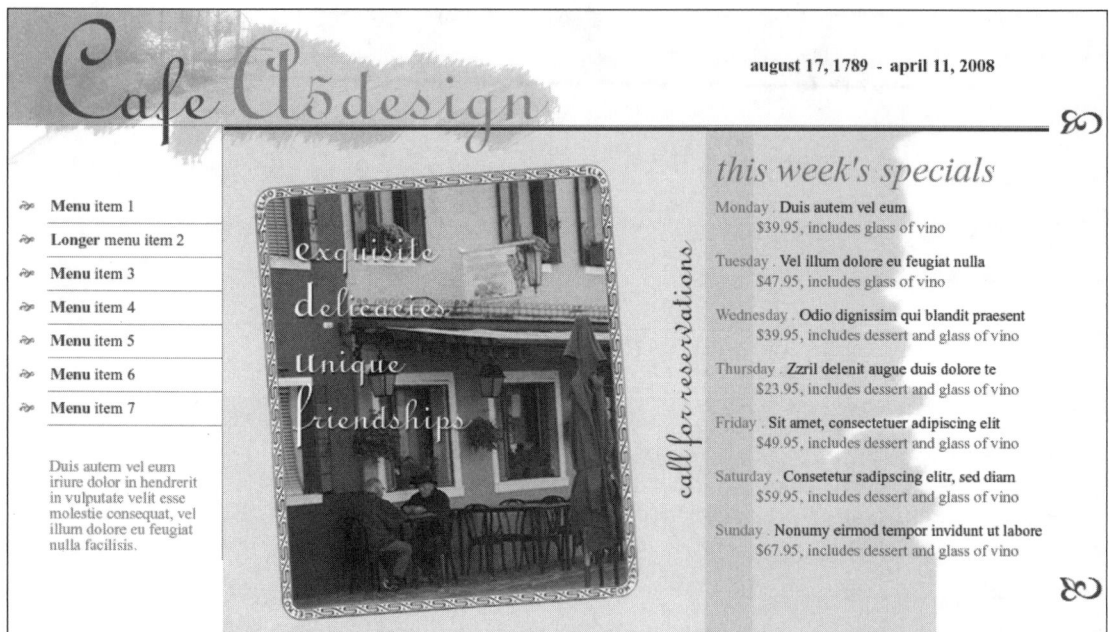

© 2014 Cengage Learning.

Homepage design (Photoshop only).

Photoshop source file names: Designs—Third Edition/101-120-photoshop/design_115/design_115.psd

Photo credits: Joe Eccher

Design 114

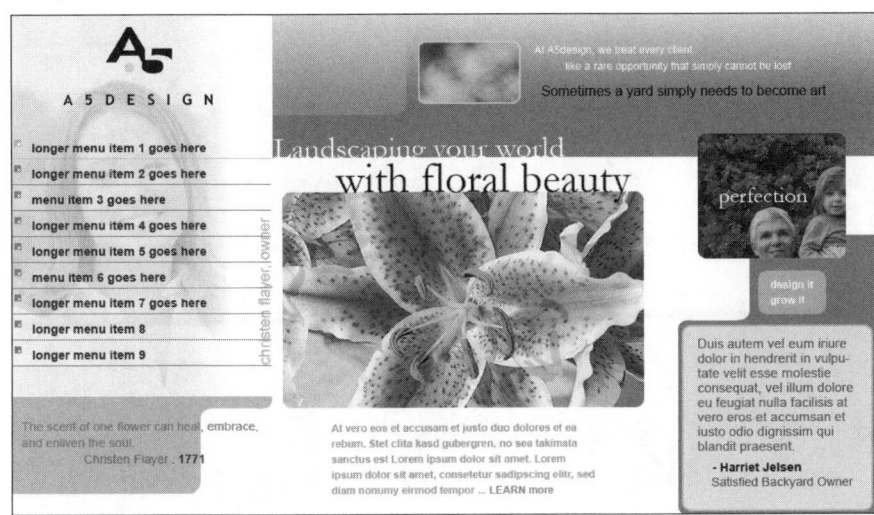

© 2014 Cengage Learning.

Homepage design (Photoshop only).

Photoshop source file names: Designs—Third Edition/101-120-photoshop/design_114/design_114.psd

Photo credits: idlerphotography.com, Joe Eccher

Design 113

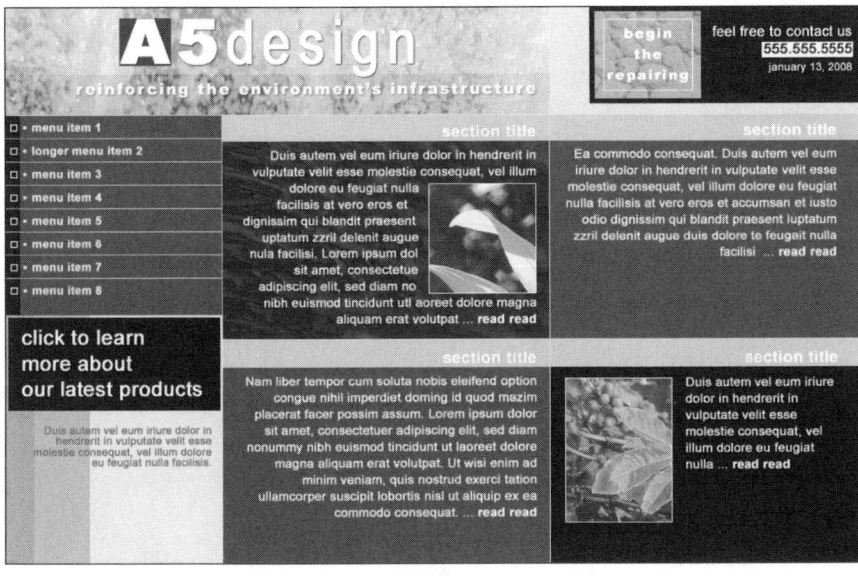

© 2014 Cengage Learning.

Homepage design (Photoshop only).

Photoshop source file names: Designs—Third Edition/101-120-photoshop/design_113/design_113.psd

Photo credits: Joe Eccher

Design 112

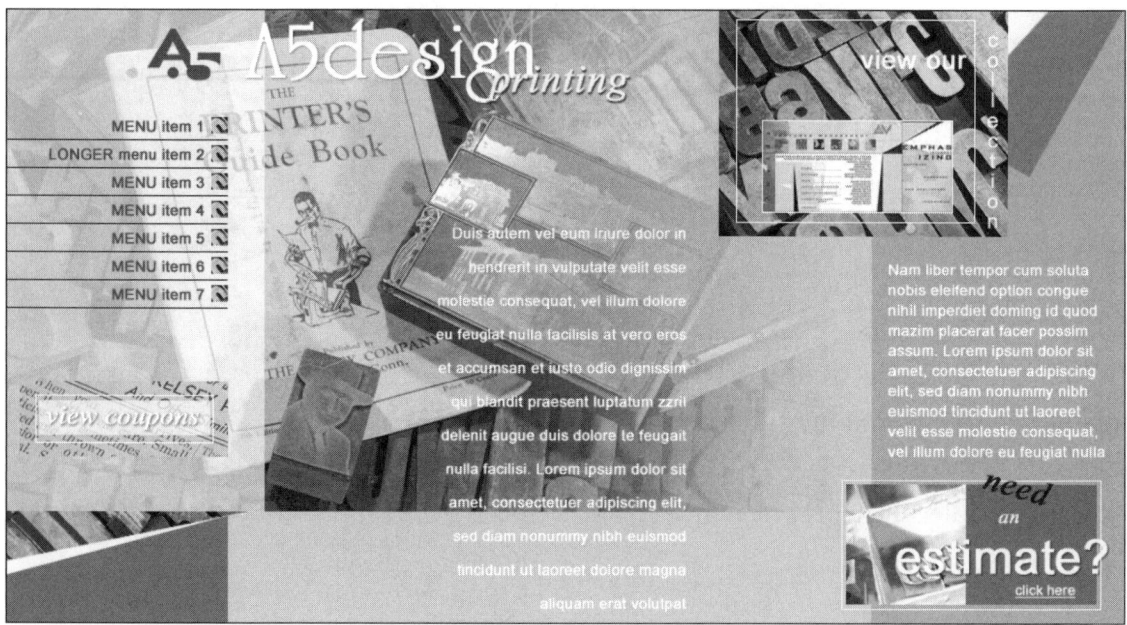

Homepage design (Photoshop only).

Photoshop source file names: Designs—Third Edition/101-120-photoshop/design_112/design_112.psd

Photo credits: idlerphotography.com

Design 111

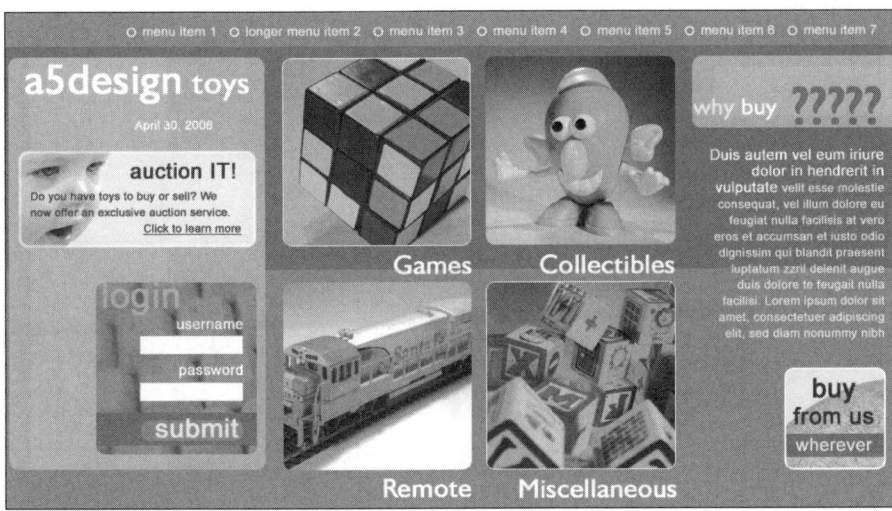

Homepage design (Photoshop only).

Photoshop source file names: Designs—Third Edition/101-120-photoshop/design_111/design_111.psd

Photo credits: idlerphotography.com

Design 110

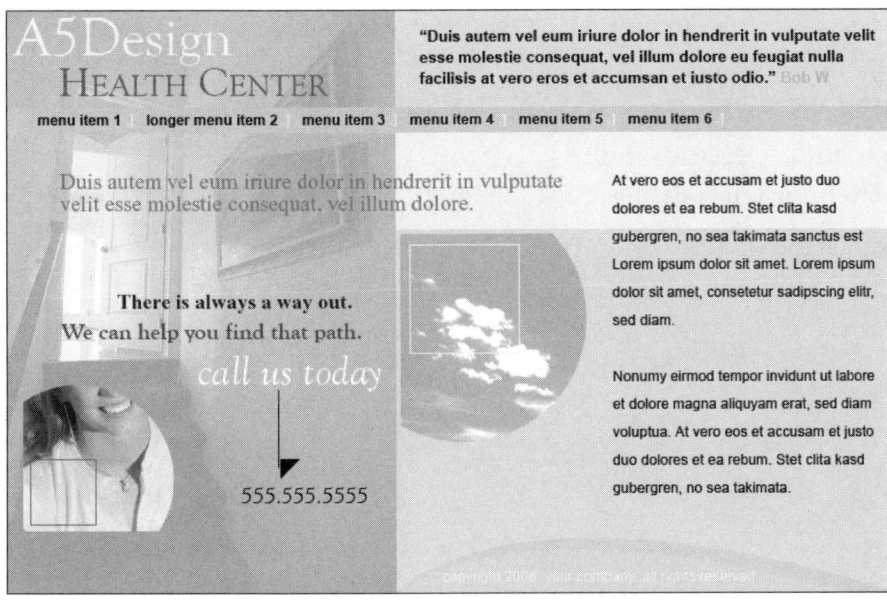

Homepage design (Photoshop only).

Photoshop source file names: Designs—Third Edition/101-120-photoshop/design_110/design_110.psd

Photo credits: idlerphotography.com

Design 109

Homepage design (Photoshop only).

Photoshop source file names: Designs—Third Edition/101-120-photoshop/design_109/design_109.psd

Photo credits: idlerphotography.com, Joe Eccher

Design 108

© 2014 Cengage Learning.

Homepage design (Photoshop only).

Photoshop source file names: Designs—Third Edition/101-120-photoshop/design_108/design_108.psd

Photo credits: idlerphotography.com

Design 107

Homepage design (Photoshop only).

Photoshop source file names: Designs—Third Edition/101-120-photoshop/design_107/design_107.psd

Photo credits: Lisa Murillo, Joe Eccher

Design 106

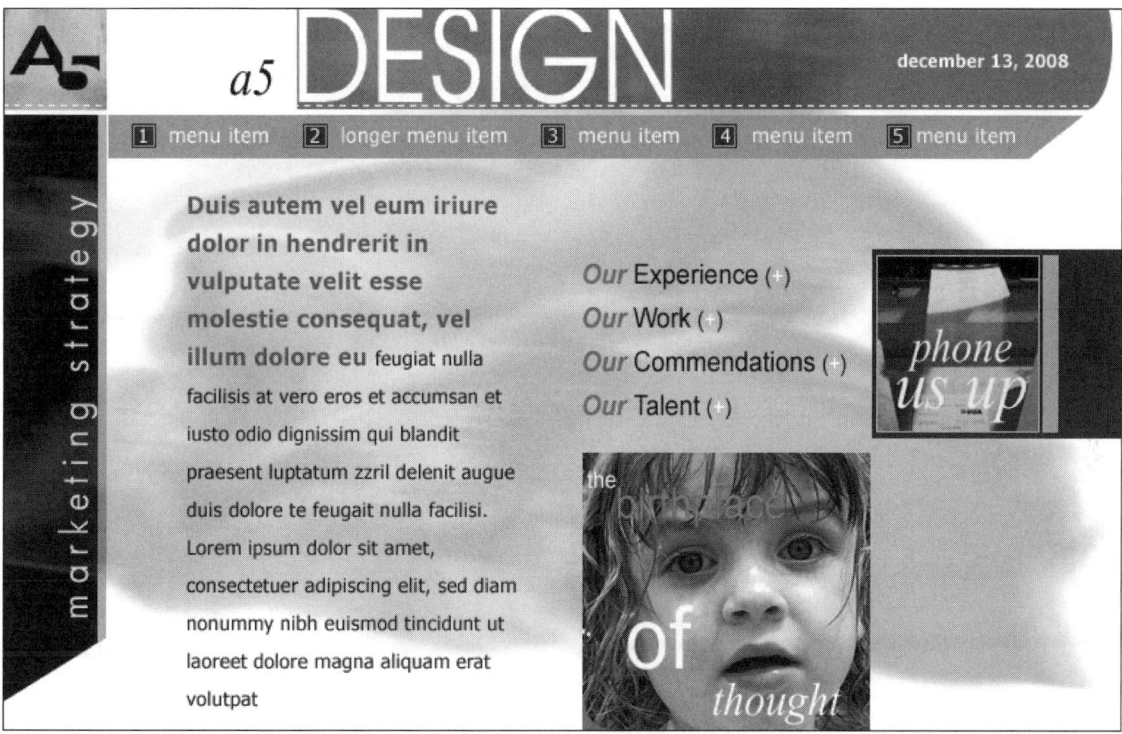

© 2014 Cengage Learning.

Homepage design (Photoshop only).

Photoshop source file names: Designs—Third Edition/101-120-photoshop/design_106/design_106.psd

Photo credits: A5design

Design 105

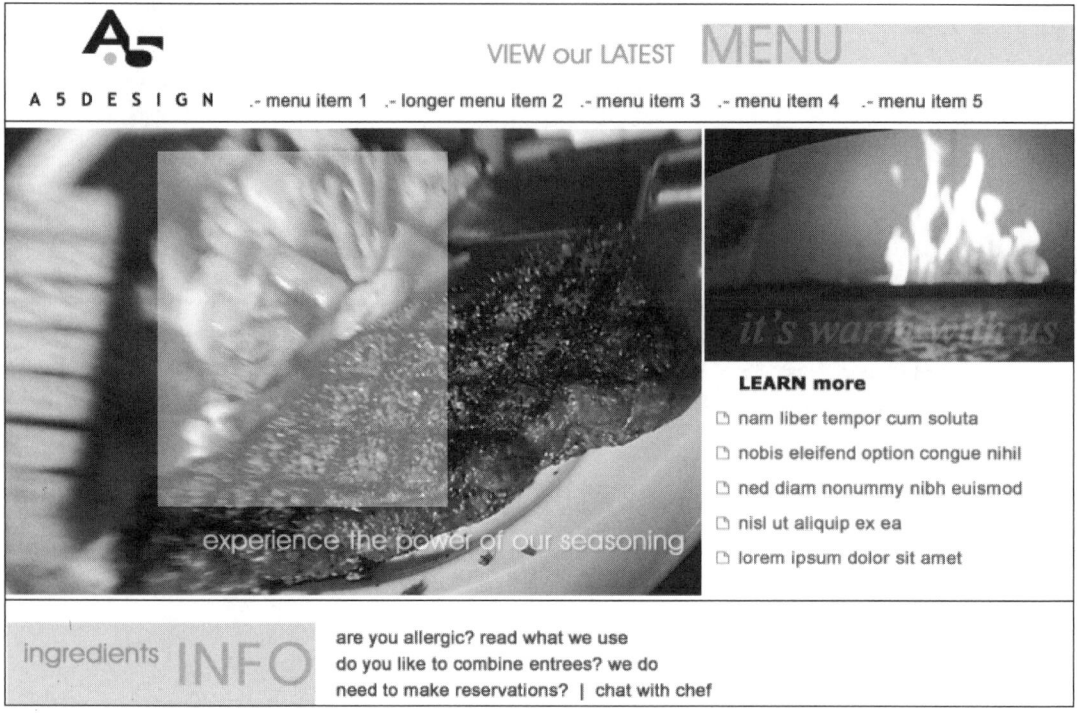

Homepage design (Photoshop only).

Photoshop source file names: Designs—Third Edition/101-120-photoshop/design_105/design_105.psd

Photo credits: idlerphotography.com

Design 104

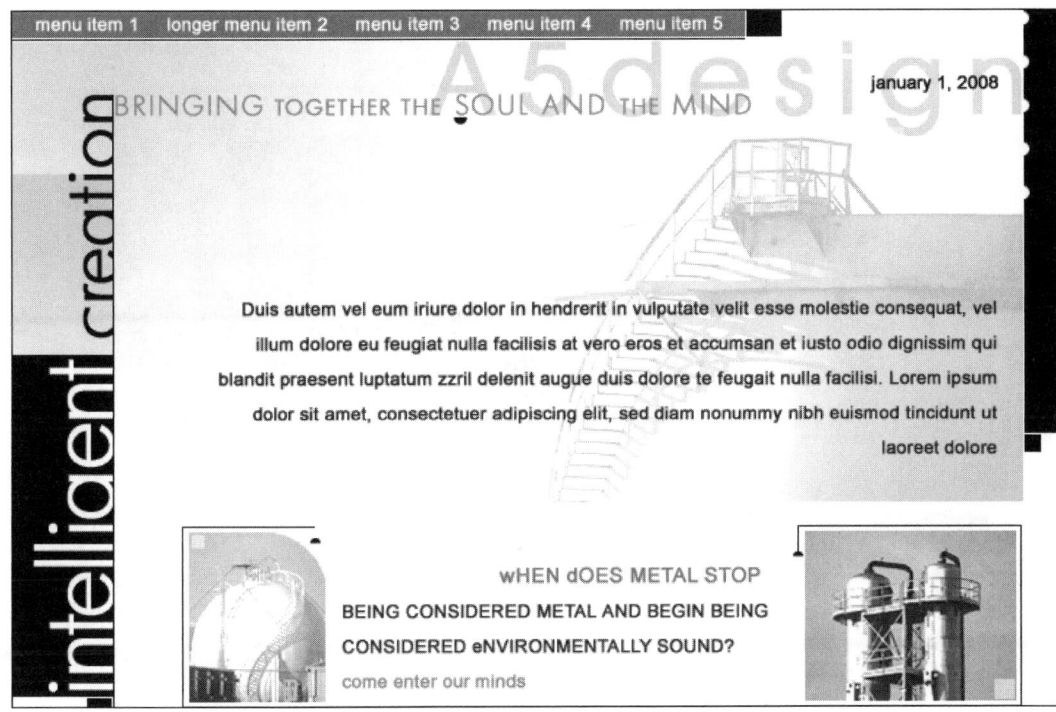

Homepage design (Photoshop only).

Photoshop source file names: Designs—Third Edition/101-120-photoshop design_104//design_104.psd

Photo credits: idlerphotography.com

Design 103

Homepage design (Photoshop only).

Photoshop source file names: Designs—Third Edition/101-120-photoshop/design_103/design_103.psd

Photo credits: idlerphotography.com

Design 102

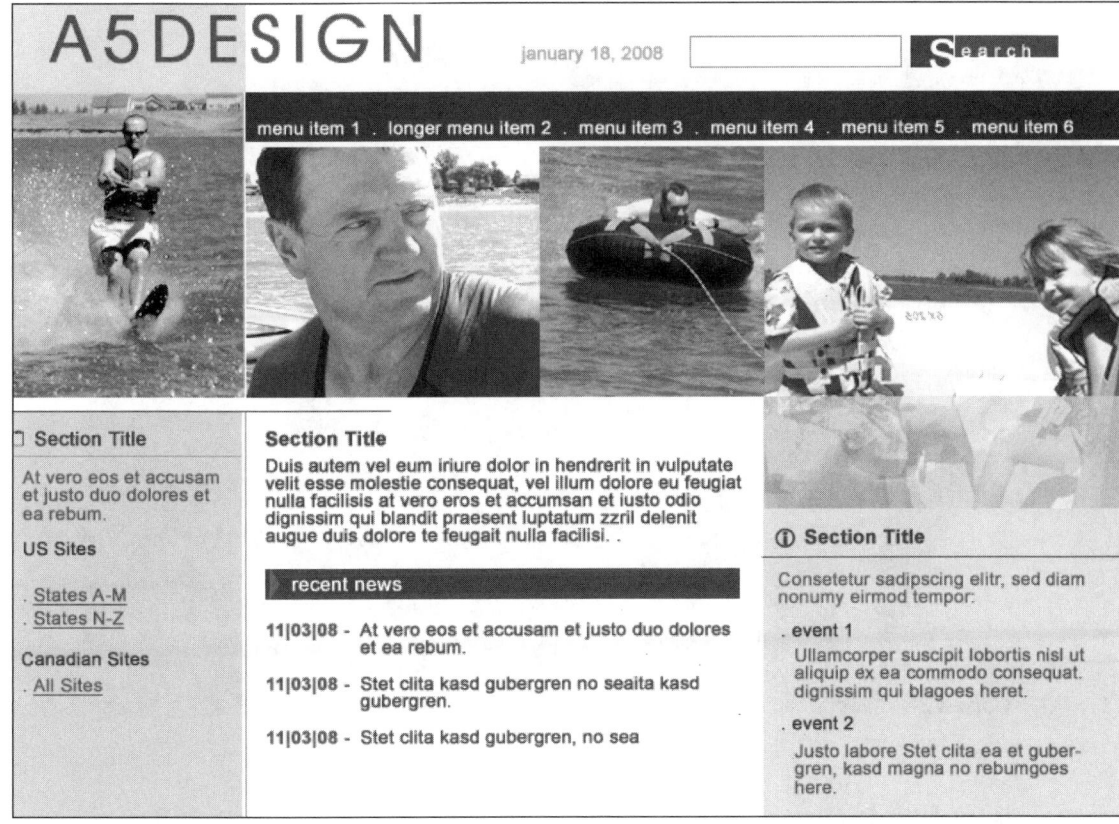

© 2014 Cengage Learning.

Homepage design (Photoshop only).

Photoshop source file names: Designs—Third Edition/101-120-photoshop/design_102/design_102.psd

Photo credits: Joe Eccher, Justin Discoe

Design 101

Homepage design (Photoshop only).

Photoshop source file names: 101-120-photoshop/design_101/design_101.psd

Photo credits: A5design

Design 100

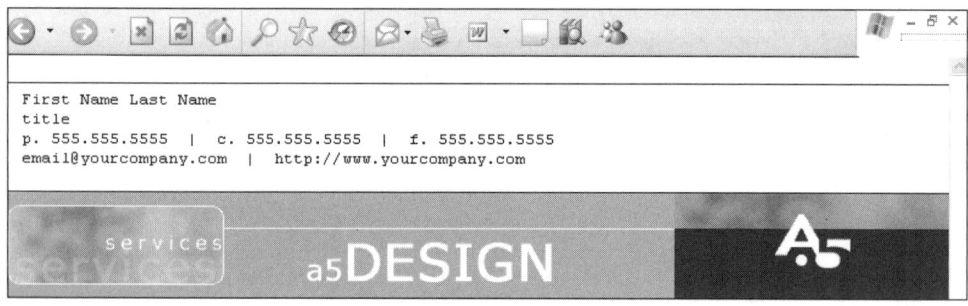

Signature design.

Photoshop source file names: Designs—Third Edition/91-100-signatures/design_100/design_100.psd

Photo credits: Joe Eccher

Design 99

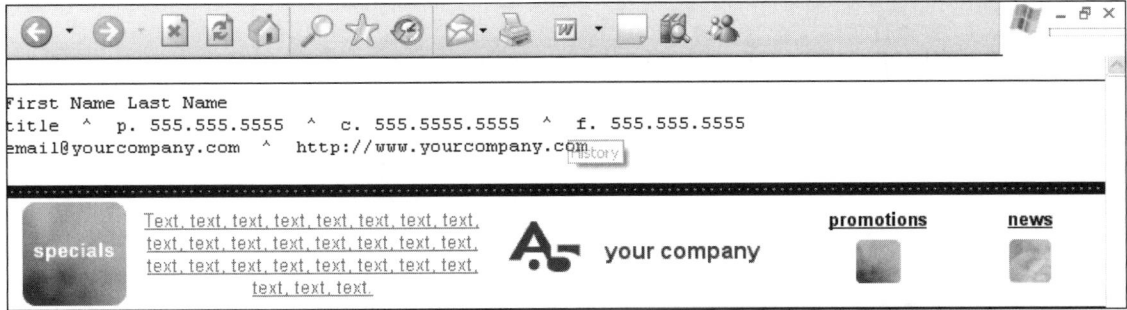

Signature design.

Photoshop source file names: Designs—Third Edition/91-100-signatures/design_99/design_99.psd

XHTML pages: index.htm

Photo credits: A5design

Design 98

Signature design.

Photoshop source file names: Designs—Third Edition/91-100-signatures/design_98/design_98.psd

XHTML pages: index.htm

Photo credits: Lisa Murillo

Design 97

Signature design.

Photoshop source file names: Designs—Third Edition/91-100-signatures/design_97/design_97.psd

XHTML pages: index.htm

Photo credits: Lisa Murillo, A5design

Design 96

Signature design.

Photoshop source file names: Designs—Third Edition/91-100-signatures/design_96/design_96.psd

XHTML pages: index.htm

Photo credits: Lisa Murillo

Design 95

Signature design.

Photoshop source file names: Designs—Third Edition/91-100-signatures/design_95/design_95.psd

XHTML pages: index.htm

Photo credits: A5design

Design 94

Signature design.

Photoshop source file names: Designs—Third Edition/91-100-signatures/design_94/design_94.psd

XHTML pages: index.htm

Photo credits: A5design

Design 93

Signature design.

Photoshop source file names: Designs—Third Edition/91-100-signatures/design_93/design_93.psd

XHTML pages: index.htm

Photo credits: Lisa Murillo

Design 92

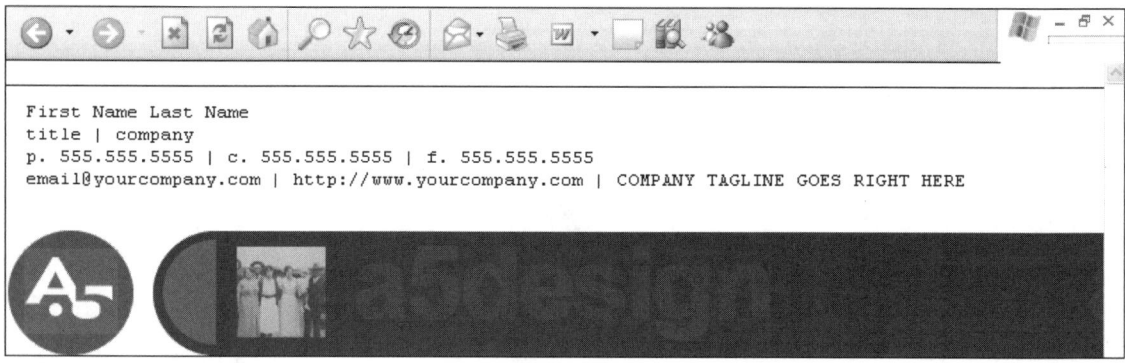

Signature design.

Photoshop source file names: Designs—Third Edition/91-100-signatures/design_92/design_92.psd

XHTML pages: index.htm

Photo credits: Lori Discoe

Design 91

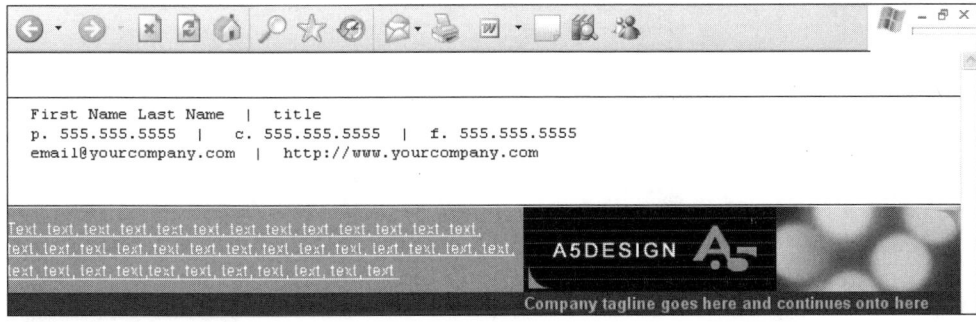

Signature design.

Photoshop source file names: Designs—Third Edition/91-100-signatures/design_91/design_91.psd

XHTML pages: index.htm

Photo credits: A5design

Design 90

E-newsletter design.

Photoshop source file names: Designs—Third Edition/81-90-enewsletters/design_90/design_90.psd

XHTML pages: index.htm

Photo credits: A5design

Design 89

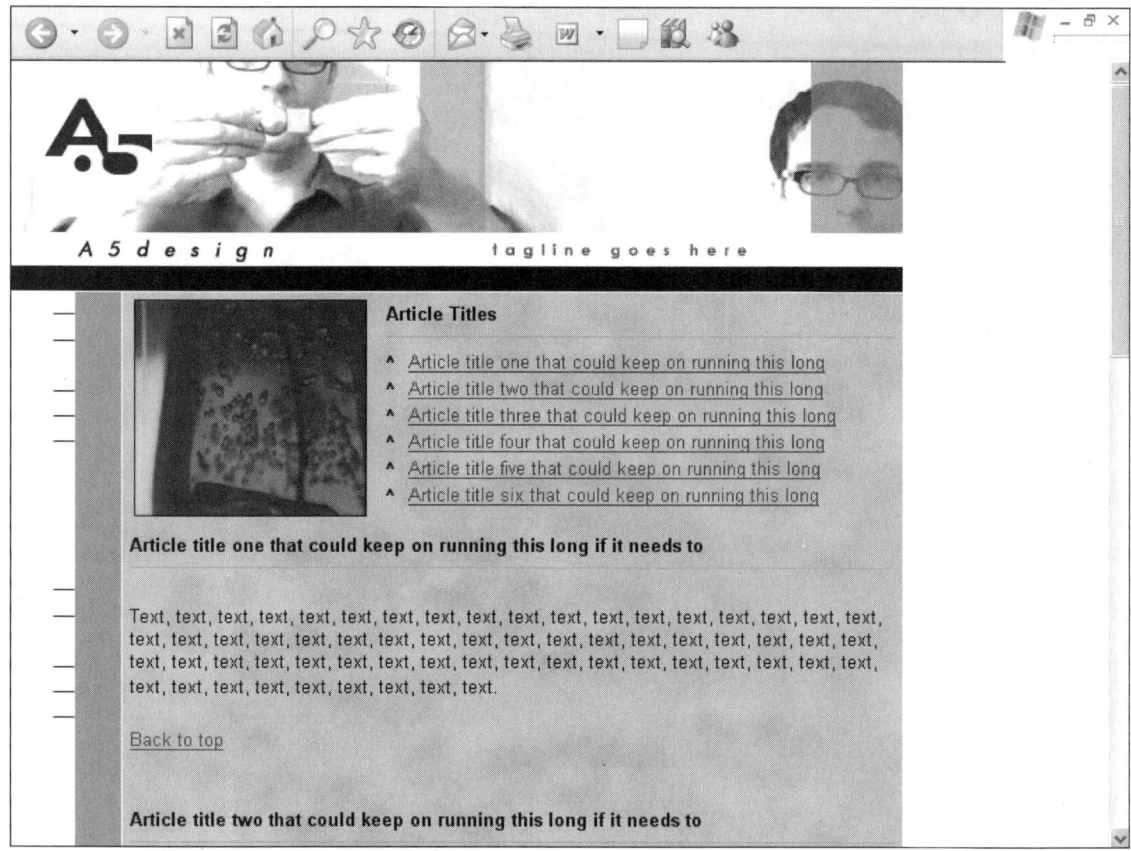

© 2014 Cengage Learning.

E-newsletter design.

Photoshop source file names: Designs—Third Edition/81-90-enewsletters/design_89/design_89.psd

XHTML pages: index.htm

Photo credits: A5design

Design 88

© 2014 Cengage Learning.

E-newsletter design.

Photoshop source file names: Designs—Third Edition/81-90-enewsletters/design_88/design_88.psd

XHTML pages: index.htm

Photo credits: Lisa Murillo

Design 87

© 2014 Cengage Learning.

E-newsletter design.

Photoshop source file names: Designs—Third Edition/81-90-enewsletters/design_87/design_87.psd

XHTML pages: index.htm

Photo credits: Lisa Murillo, Joe Eccher, A5design

Design 86

E-newsletter design.

Photoshop source file names: Designs—Third Edition/81-90-enewsletters/design_86/design_86.psd

XHTML pages: index.htm

Photo credits: Lisa Murillo, A5design

Design 85

E-newsletter design.

Photoshop source file names: Designs—Third Edition/81-90-enewsletters/design_85/design_85.psd

XHTML pages: index.htm

Photo credits: Lisa Murillo, A5design

Design 84

© 2014 Cengage Learning.

E-newsletter design.

Photoshop source file names: Designs—Third Edition/81-90-enewsletters/design_84/design_84.psd

XHTML pages: index.htm

Photo credits: A5design

Design 83

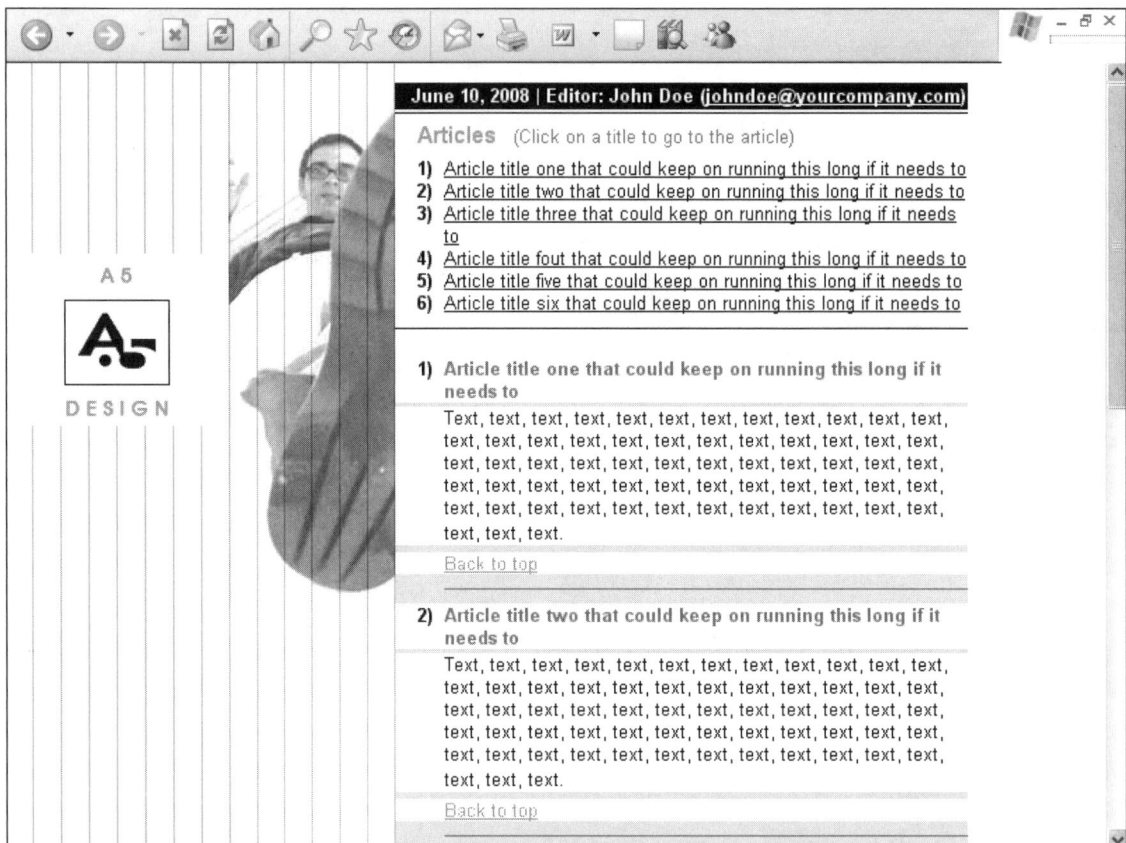

E-newsletter design.

Photoshop source file names: Designs—Third Edition/81-90-enewsletters/design_83/design_83.psd

XHTML pages: index.htm

Photo credits: A5design

Design 82

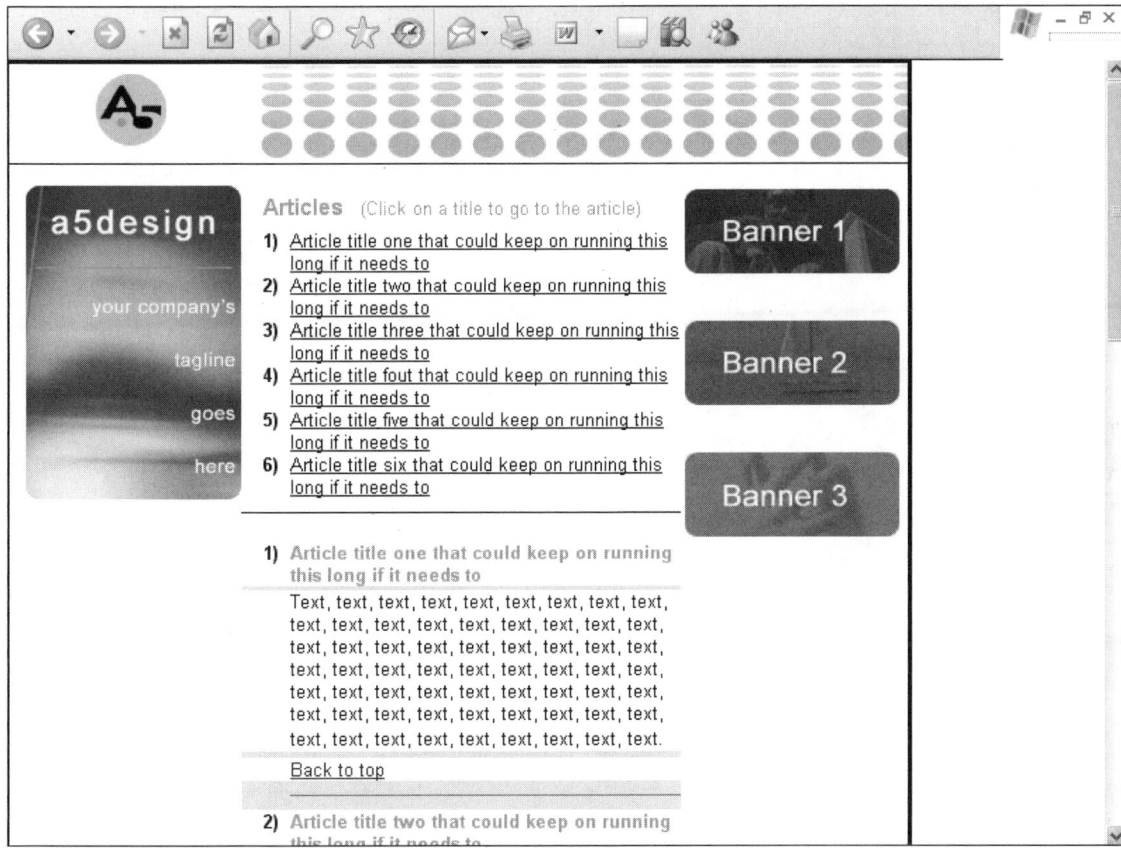

© 2014 Cengage Learning.

E-newsletter design.

Photoshop source file names: Designs—Third Edition/81-90-enewsletters/design_82/design_82.psd

XHTML pages: index.htm

Photo credits: A5design

Design 81

E-newsletter design.

Photoshop source file names: Designs—Third Edition/81-90-enewsletters/design_81/design_81.psd

XHTML pages: index.htm

Photo credits: A5design

Design 80

Homepage design.

Photoshop source file names: Designs—Third Edition/1-80-xhtml/design_80/design_80.psd

XHTML pages: index.htm, menu_item_2.htm, menu_item_3.htm

Photo credits: A5design

Design 79

Homepage design.

Photoshop source file names: Designs—Third Edition/1-80-xhtml/design_79/design_79.psd

XHTML pages: index.htm, menu_item_2.htm, menu_item_3.htm

Photo credits: Joe Eccher

Design 78

© 2014 Cengage Learning.

Homepage design.

Photoshop source file names: Designs—Third Edition/1-80-xhtml/design_78/design_78.psd

XHTML pages: index.htm, menu_item_2.htm

Photo credits: Lori Discoe

Design 77

Homepage design.

Photoshop source file names: Designs—Third Edition/1-80-xhtml/design_77/design_77.psd

XHTML pages: index.htm, menu_item_2.htm, menu_item_3.htm

Photo credits: Joe Eccher, A5design

Design 76

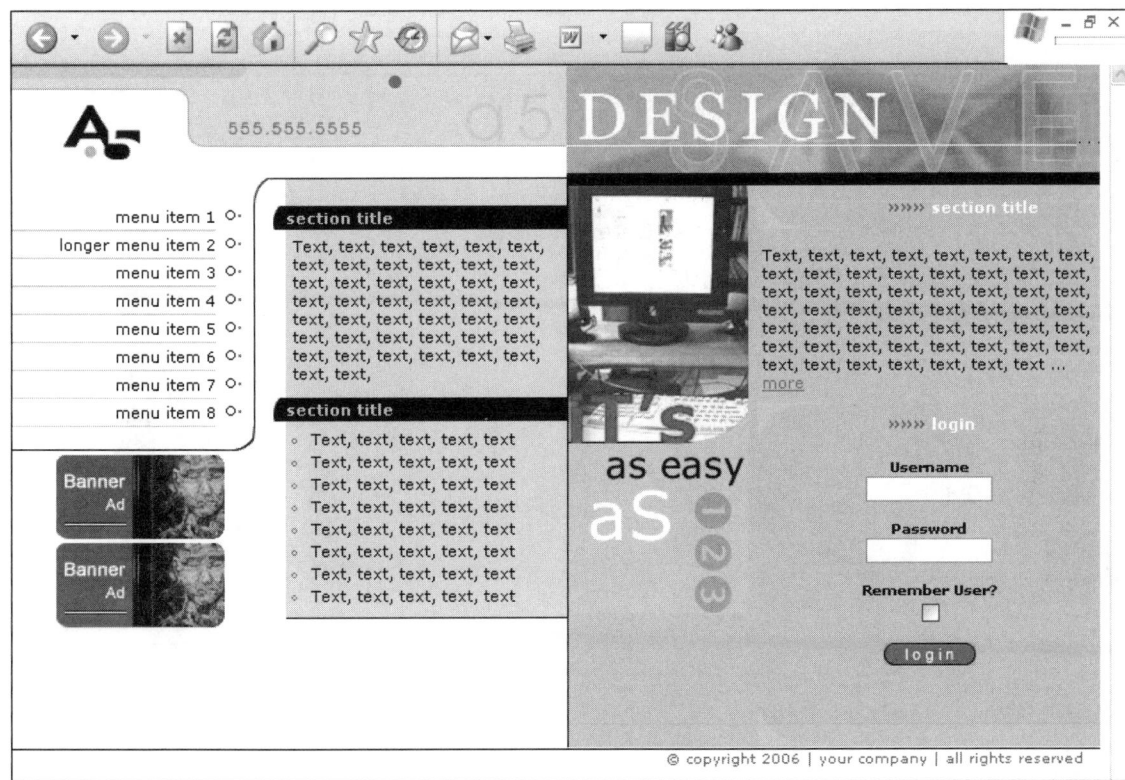

© 2014 Cengage Learning.

Homepage design.

Photoshop source file names: Designs—Third Edition/1-80-xhtml/design_76/design_76.psd

XHTML pages: index.htm, menu_item_2.htm, menu_item_3.htm

Photo credits: A5design

Design 75

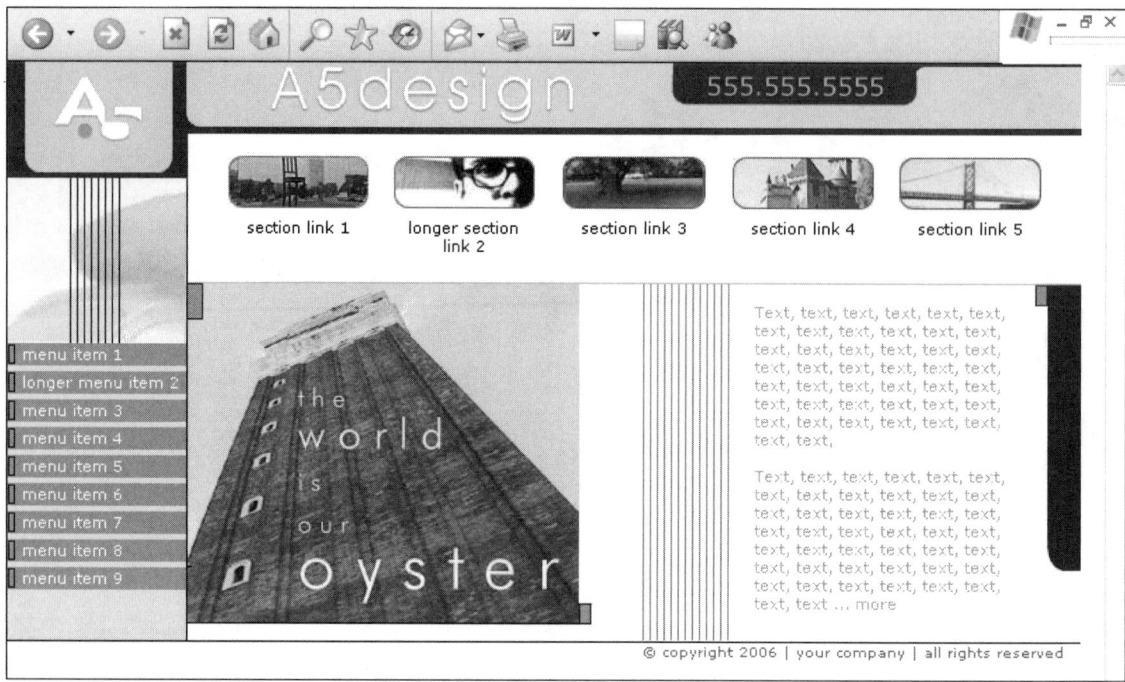

Homepage design.

Photoshop source file names: Designs—Third Edition/1-80-xhtml/design_75/design_75.psd

XHTML pages: index.htm, menu_item_2.htm, menu_item_3.htm, menu_item_4.htm

Photo credits: Joe Eccher, A5design

Design 74

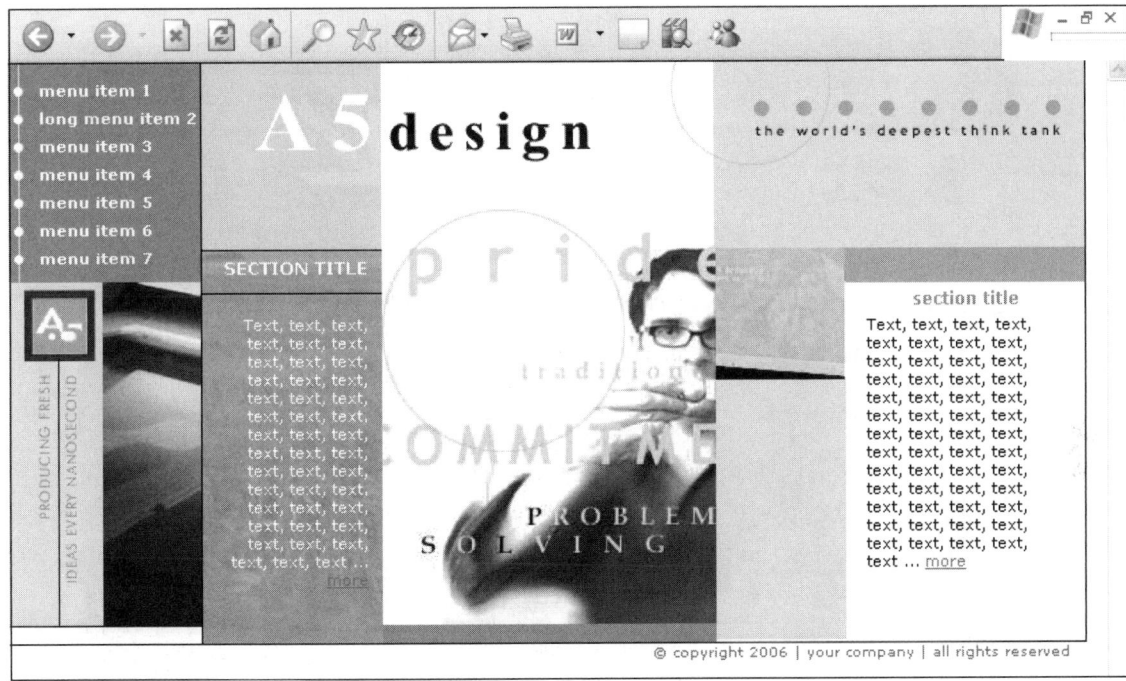

Homepage design.

Photoshop source file names: Designs—Third
Edition/1-80-xhtml/design_74/design_74.psd, bg_images.psd

XHTML pages: index.htm, menu_item_2.htm, menu_item_3.htm, menu_item_4.htm

Photo credits: A5design

Design 73

© 2014 Cengage Learning.

Homepage design.

Photoshop source file names: Designs—Third Edition/1-80-xhtml/design_73/design_73.psd

XHTML pages: index.htm, menu_item_2.htm, menu_item_3.htm, menu_item_4.htm

Photo credits: A5design

Design 72

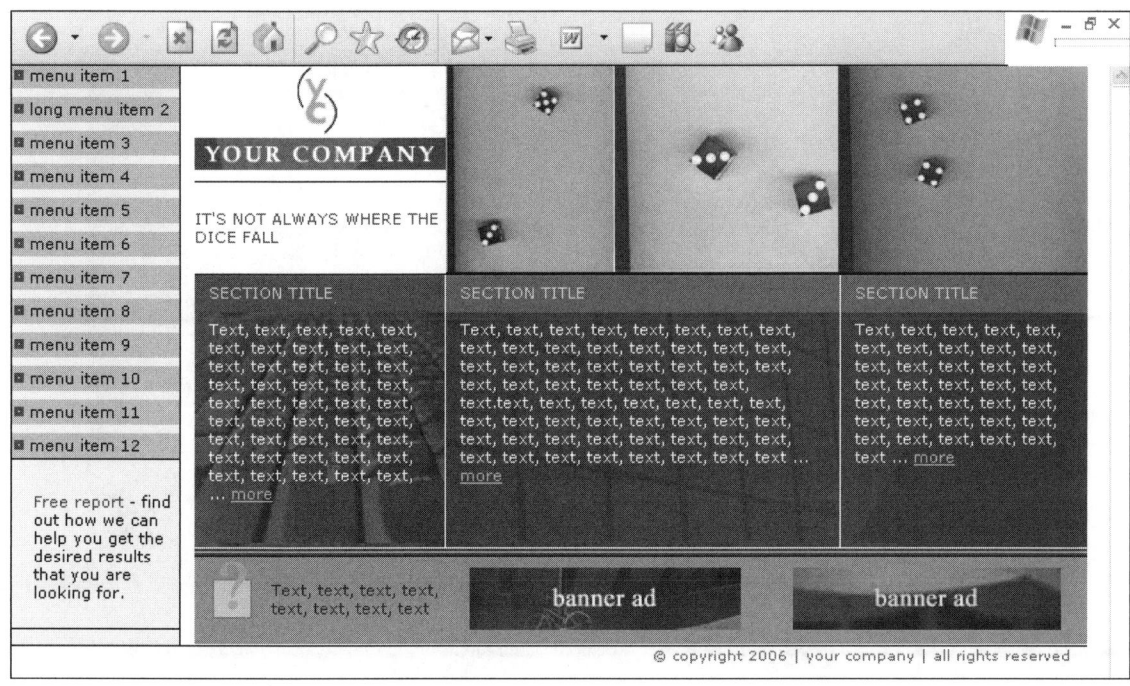

Homepage design.

Photoshop source file names: Designs—Third
Edition/1-80-xhtml/design_72/design_72.psd

XHTML pages: index.htm, menu_item_2.htm, menu_item_3.htm, menu_item_4.htm

Photo credits: A5design

Design 71

Homepage design.

Photoshop source file names: Designs—Third Edition/1-80-xhtml/design_71/design_71.psd

XHTML pages: index.htm, menu_item_2.htm, menu_item_3.htm, menu_item_4.htm

Photo credits: Joe Eccher

Design 70

Homepage design.

Photoshop source file names: Designs—Third Edition/1-80-xhtml/design_70/design_70.psd

XHTML pages: index.htm, menu_item_2.htm, menu_item_3.htm

Photo credits: A5design

Design 69

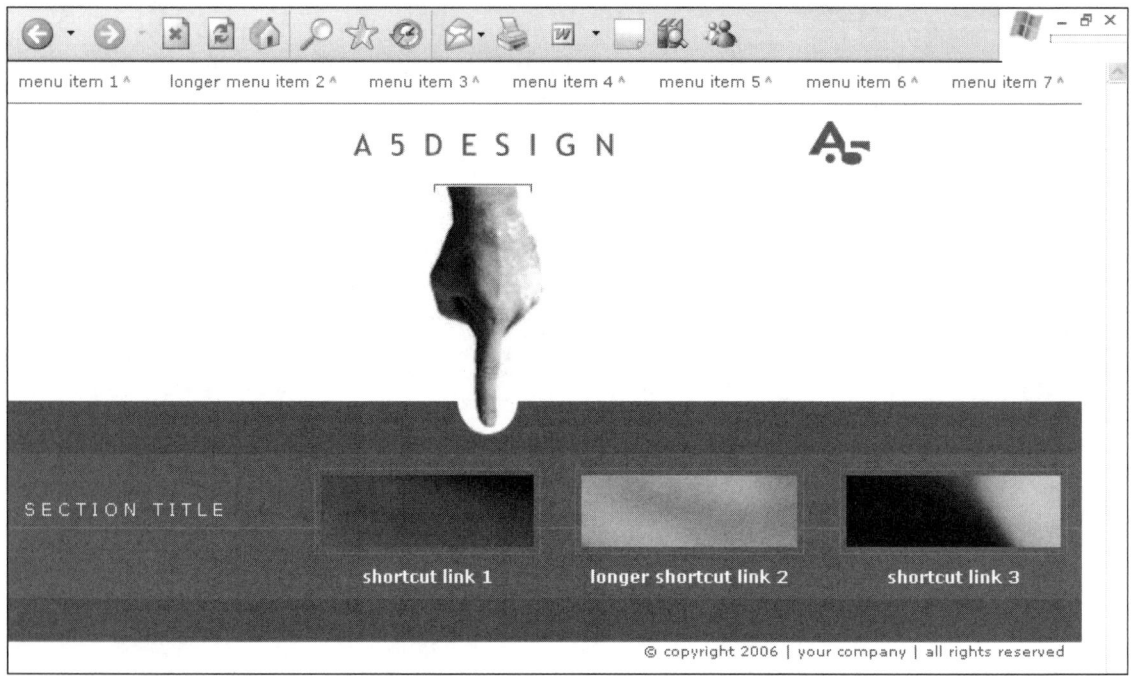

Homepage design.

Photoshop source file names: Designs—Third
Edition/1-80-xhtml/design_69/design_69.psd

XHTML pages: index.htm, menu_item_2.htm, menu_item_3.htm

Photo credits: A5design

Design 68

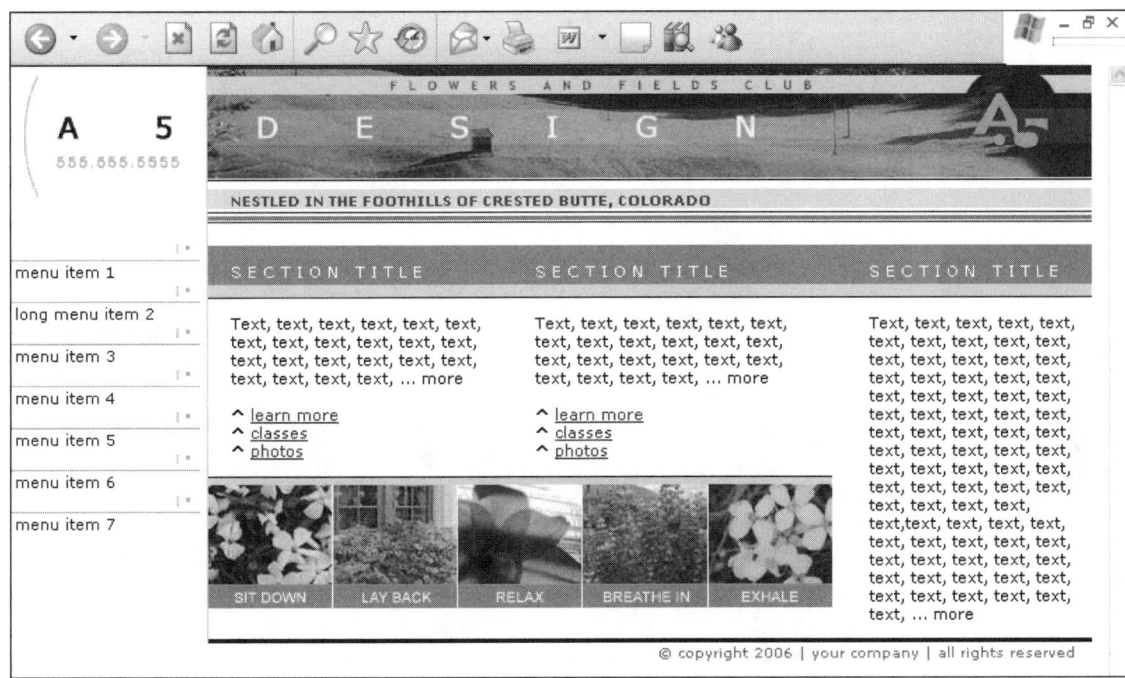

Homepage design.

Photoshop source file names: Designs—Third Edition/1-80-xhtml/design_68/design_68.psd

XHTML pages: index.htm, menu_item_2.htm, menu_item_3.htm

Photo credits: Joe Eccher

Design 67

Homepage design.

Photoshop source file names: Designs—Third Edition/1-80-xhtml/design_67/design_67.psd, bg_images.psd

XHTML pages: index.htm, menu_item_2.htm, menu_item_3.htm, menu_item_4.htm

Photo credits: Lisa Murillo, A5design

Design 66

Homepage design.

Photoshop source file names: Designs—Third
Edition/1-80-xhtml/design_66/design_66.psd

XHTML pages: index.htm, menu_item_2.htm, menu_item_3.htm, menu_item_4.htm,
menu_item_5.htm

Photo credits: Joe Eccher

Design 65

Homepage design.

Photoshop source file names: Designs—Third Edition/1-80-xhtml/design_65/design_65.psd

XHTML pages: index.htm, menu_item_2.htm, menu_item_3.htm, menu_item_4.htm, menu_item_5.htm

Photo credits: Lisa Murillo, A5design, Justin Discoe

Design 64

Homepage design.

Photoshop source file names: Designs—Third Edition/1-80-xhtml/design_64/design_64.psd

XHTML pages: index.htm, menu_item_2.htm, menu_item_3.htm

Photo credits: Joe Eccher

Design 63

Homepage design.

Photoshop source file names: Designs—Third Edition/1-80-xhtml/design_63/design_63.psd

XHTML pages: index.htm, menu_item_2.htm, menu_item_3.htm

Photo credits: Joe Eccher

Design 62

© 2014 Cengage Learning.

Homepage design.

Photoshop source file names: Designs—Third
Edition/1-80-xhtml/design_62/design_62.psd

XHTML pages: index.htm, menu_item_2.htm, menu_item_3.htm

Photo credits: A5design

Design 61

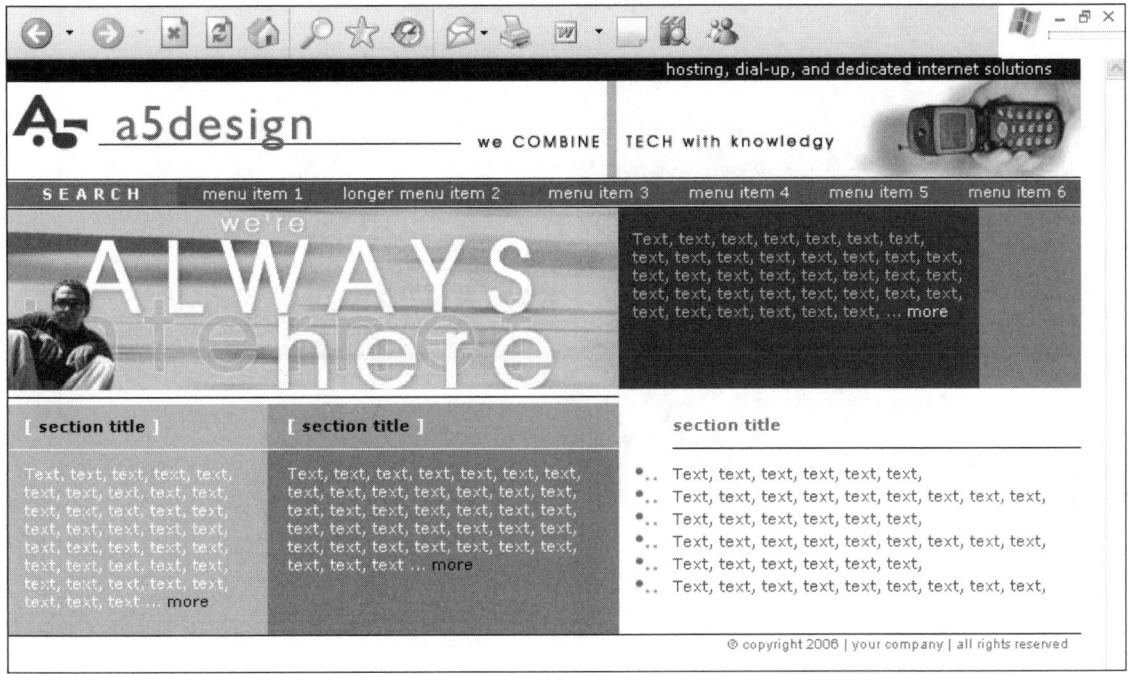

Homepage design.

Photoshop source file names: Designs—Third Edition/1-80-xhtml/design_61/design_61.psd

XHTML pages: index.htm, menu_item_2.htm, menu_item_3.htm

Photo credits: A5design

Design 60

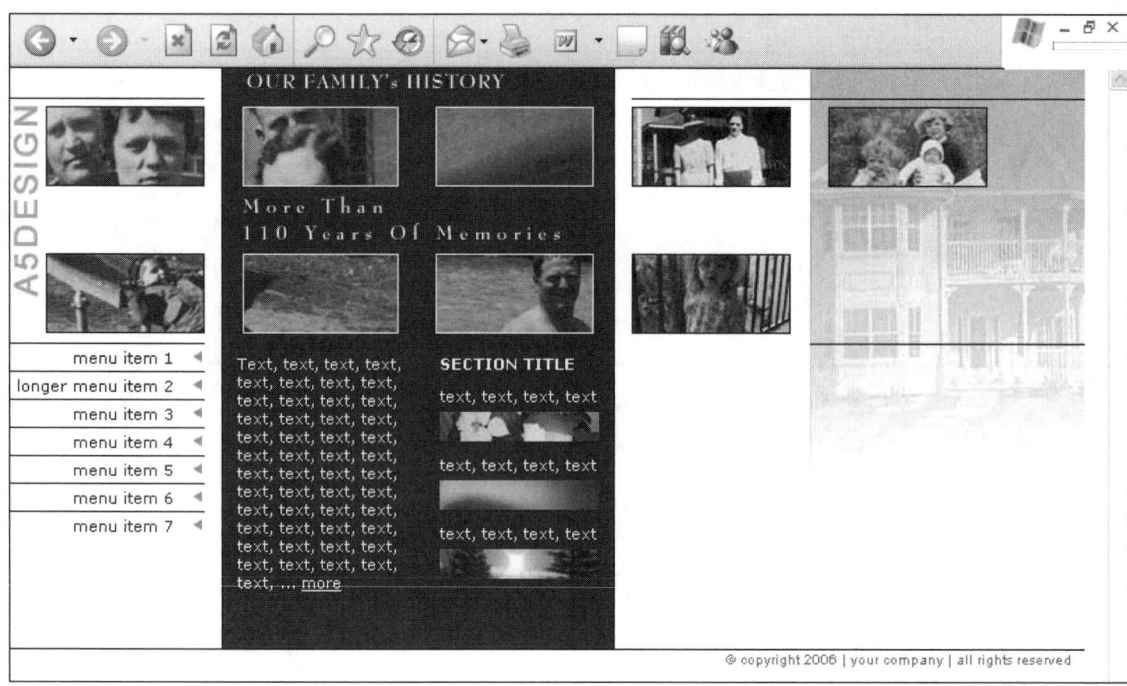

Homepage design.

Photoshop source file names: Designs—Third
Edition/1-80-xhtml/design_60/design_60.psd

XHTML pages: index.htm, menu_item_2.htm, menu_item_3.htm, menu_item_4.htm

Photo credits: Joe Eccher, Lori Discoe, A5design

Design 59

Homepage design.

Photoshop source file names: Designs—Third Edition/1-80-xhtml/design_59/design_59.psd

XHTML pages: index.htm, menu_item_2.htm, menu_item_3.htm

Photo credits: A5design

Design 58

© 2014 Cengage Learning.

Homepage design.

Photoshop source file names: Designs—Third
Edition/1-80-xhtml/design_58/design_58.psd, bg_images.psd

XHTML pages: index.htm, menu_item_2.htm, menu_item_3.htm

Photo credits: A5design

Design 57

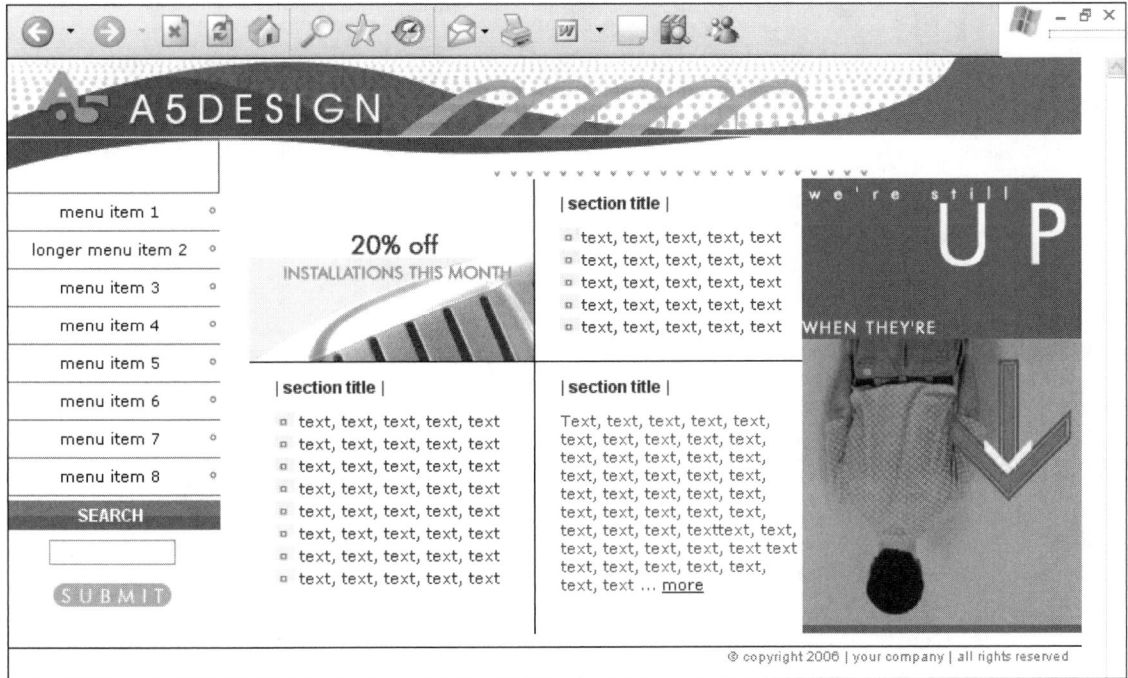

Homepage design.

Photoshop source file names: Designs—Third
Edition/1-80-xhtml/design_57/design_57.psd

XHTML pages: index.htm, menu_item_2.htm, menu_item_3.htm

Photo credits: Lisa Murillo, A5design

Design 56

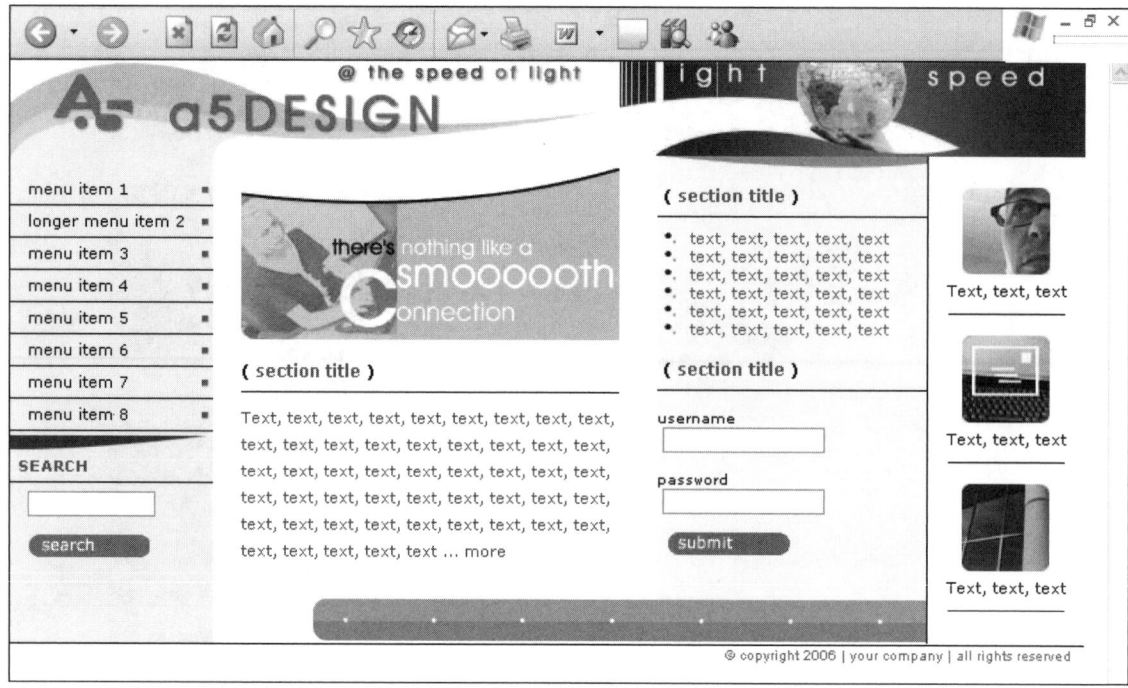

© 2014 Cengage Learning.

Homepage design.

Photoshop source file names: Designs—Third
Edition/1-80-xhtml/design_56/design_56.psd

XHTML pages: index.htm, menu_item_2.htm, menu_item_3.htm

Photo credits: Lisa Murillo, A5design

Design 55

Homepage design.

Photoshop source file names: Designs—Third
Edition/1-80-xhtml/design_55/design_55.psd

XHTML pages: index.htm, menu_item_2.htm, menu_item_3.htm

Photo credits: A5design

Design 54

Homepage design.

Photoshop source file names: Designs—Third
Edition/1-80-xhtml/design_54/design_54.psd, design_54_sl.psd

XHTML pages: index.htm, menu_item_2.htm, menu_item_3.htm

Photo credits: Joe Eccher, A5design

Design 53

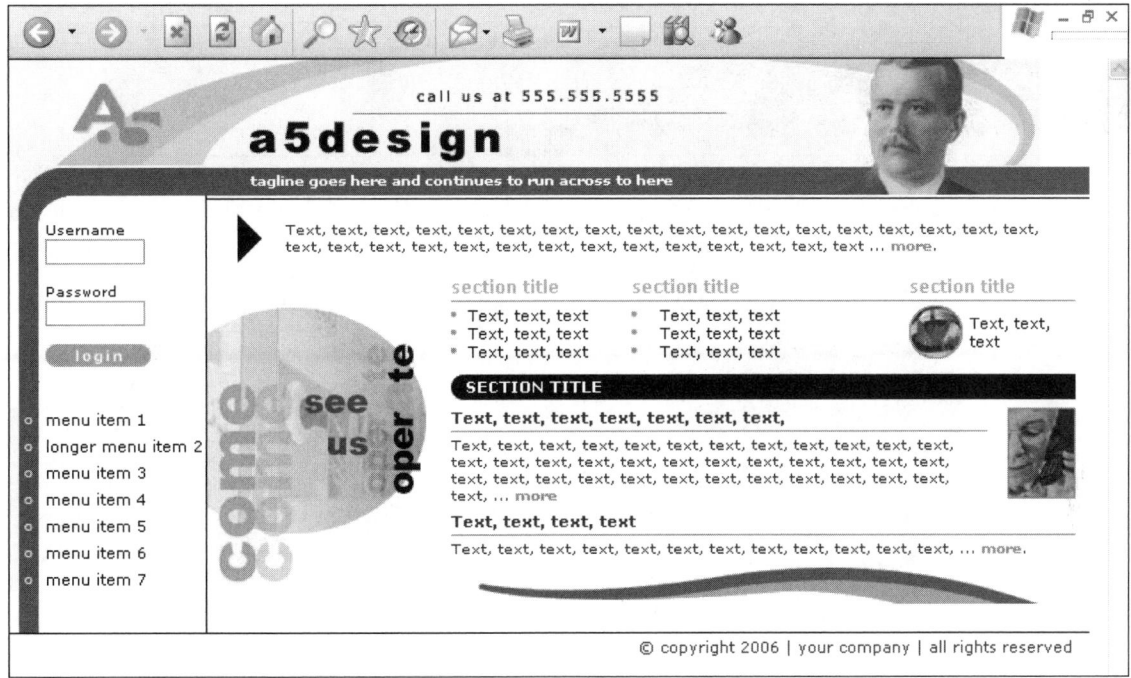

Homepage design.

Photoshop source file names: Designs—Third
Edition/1-80-xhtml/design_53/design_53.psd

XHTML pages: index.htm, menu_item_2.htm, menu_item_3.htm

Photo credits: Lori Discoe

Design 52

© 2014 Cengage Learning.

Homepage design.

Photoshop source file names: Designs—Third Edition/1-80-xhtml/design_52/design_52.psd

XHTML pages: index.htm, menu_item_2.htm, menu_item_3.htm

Photo credits: Justin Discoe, Lori Discoe

Design 51

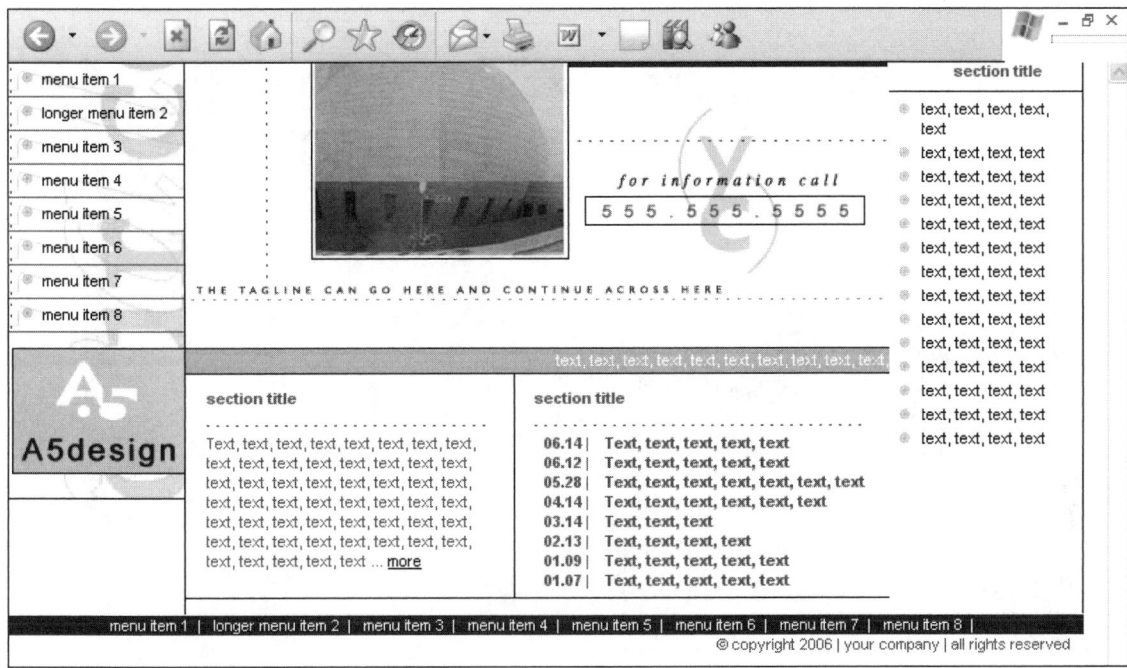

Homepage design.

Photoshop source file names: Designs—Third Edition/1-80-xhtml/design_51/design_51.psd, bg_images.psd

XHTML pages: index.htm, menu_item_2.htm, menu_item_3.htm

Photo credits: Joe Eccher

Design 50

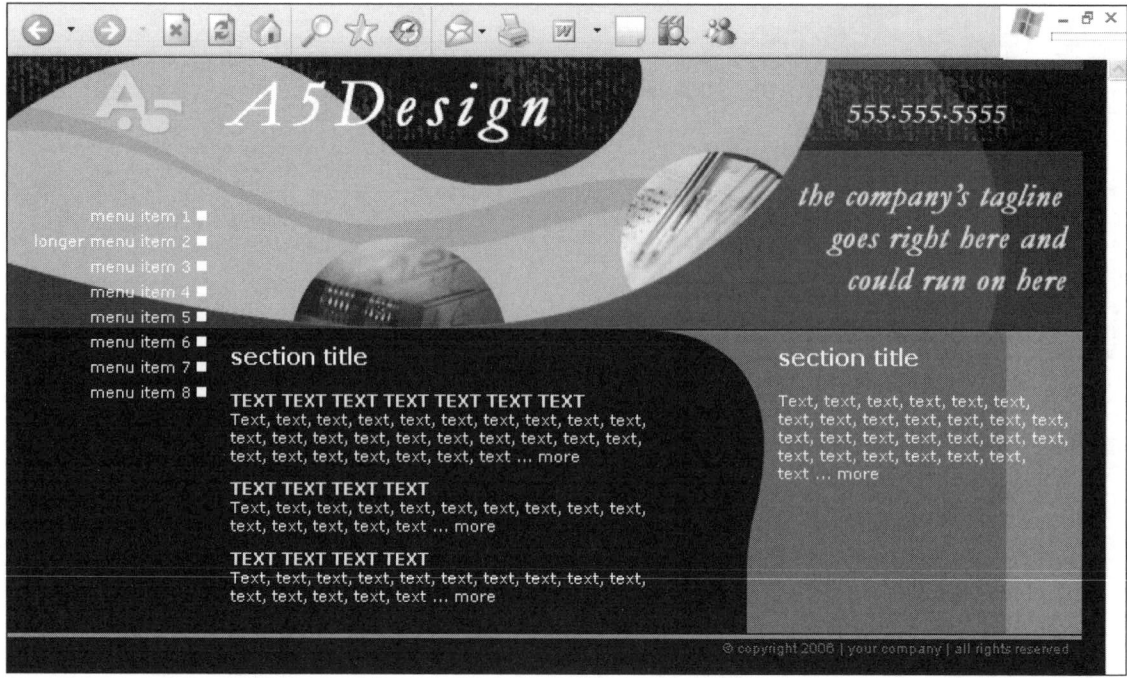

© 2014 Cengage Learning.

Homepage design.

Photoshop source file names: Designs—Third Edition/1-80-xhtml/design_50/design_50.psd, bg_images.psd

XHTML pages: index.htm, menu_item_2.htm, menu_item_3.htm

Photo credits: A5design

Design 49

Homepage design.

Photoshop source file names: Designs—Third Edition/1-80-xhtml/design_49/design_49.psd, bg_images.psd

XHTML pages: index.htm, menu_item_2.htm, menu_item_3.htm, menu_item_4.htm

Photo credits: A5design

Design 48

Homepage design.

Photoshop source file names: Designs—Third
Edition/1-80-xhtml/design_48/design_48.psd

XHTML pages: index.htm, menu_item_2.htm, menu_item_3.htm

Photo credits: A5design

Design 47

© 2014 Cengage Learning.

Homepage design.

Photoshop source file names: Designs—Third
Edition/1-80-xhtml/design_47/design_47.psd

XHTML pages: index.htm, menu_item_2.htm, menu_item_3.htm

Photo credits: Joe Eccher

Design 46

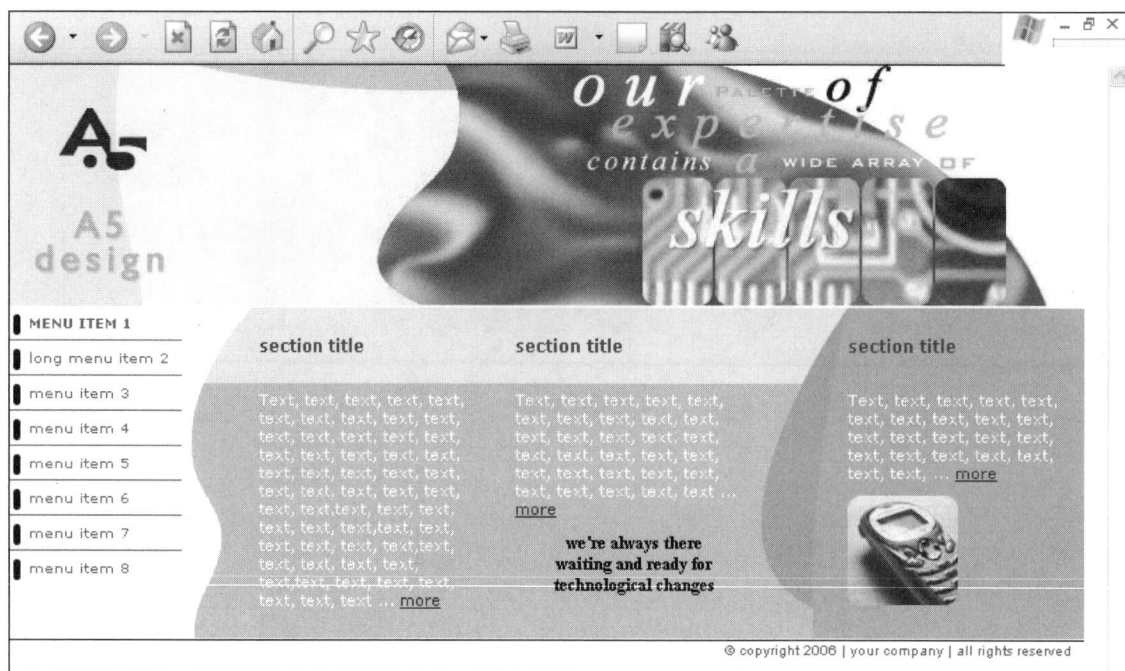

© 2014 Cengage Learning.

Homepage design.

Photoshop source file names: Designs—Third
Edition/1-80-xhtml/design_46/design_46.psd, sl_image.psd

XHTML pages: index.htm, menu_item_2.htm, menu_item_3.htm

Photo credits: Lisa Murillo, A5design

Design 45

Homepage design.

Photoshop source file names: Designs—Third Edition/1-80-xhtml/design_45/design_45.psd

XHTML pages: index.htm, menu_item_2.htm, menu_item_3.htm

Photo credits: Joe Eccher, Lori Discoe

Design 44

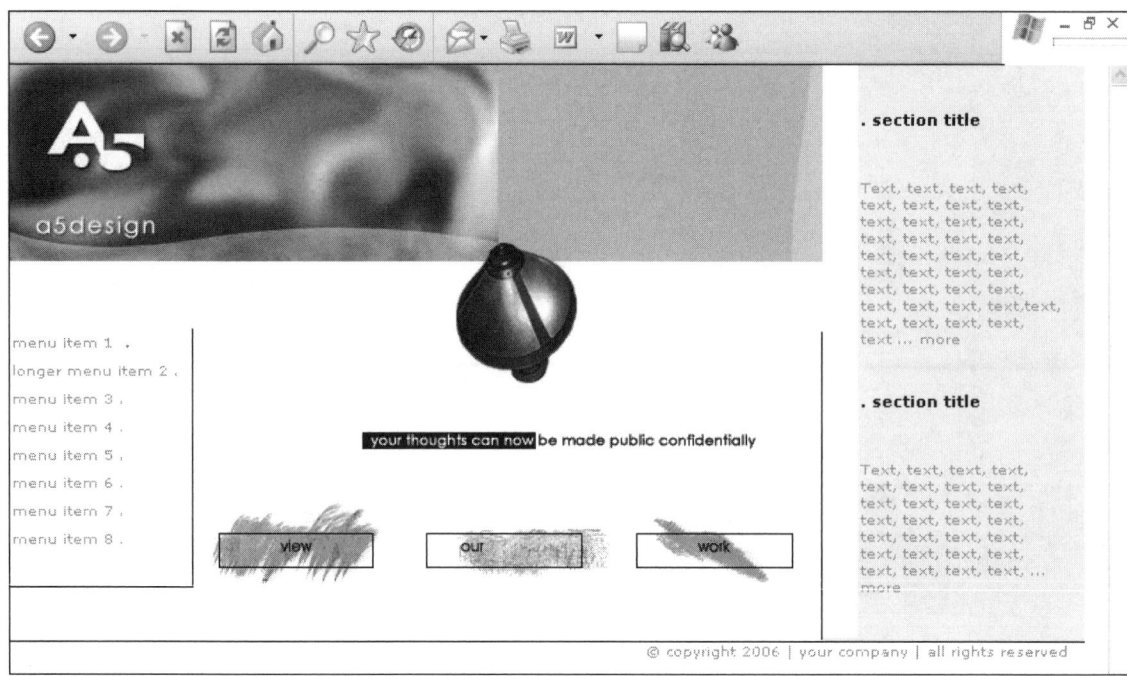

© 2014 Cengage Learning.

Homepage design.

Photoshop source file names: Designs—Third Edition/1-80-xhtml/design_44/design_44.psd

XHTML pages: index.htm, menu_item_2.htm, menu_item_3.htm

Photo credits: A5design

Design 43

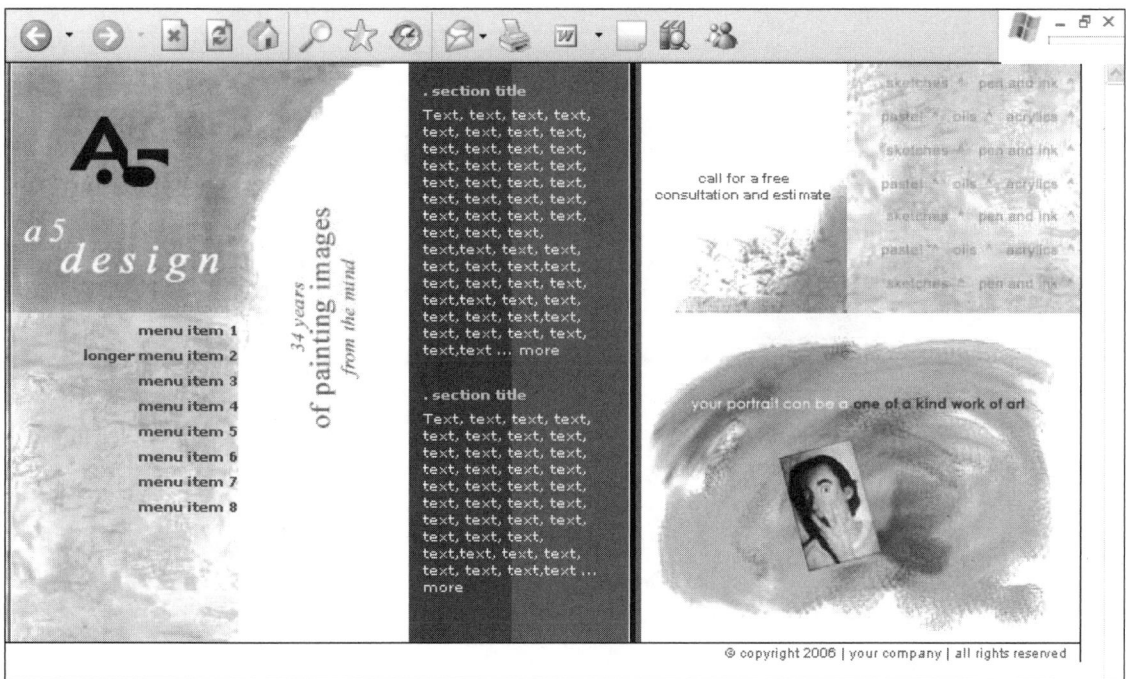

Homepage design.

Photoshop source file names: Designs—Third
Edition/1-80-xhtml/design_43/design_43.psd

XHTML pages: index.htm, menu_item_2.htm, menu_item_3.htm

Photo credits: Lori Discoe

Design 42

© 2014 Cengage Learning.

Homepage design.

Photoshop source file names: Designs—Third
Edition/1-80-xhtml/design_42/design_42.psd

XHTML pages: index.htm, menu_item_2.htm, menu_item_3.htm

Photo credits: Lori Discoe

Design 41

Homepage design.

Photoshop source file names: Designs—Third
Edition/1-80-xhtml/design_41/design_41.psd

XHTML pages: index.htm, menu_item_2.htm, menu_item_3.htm

Photo credits: Lisa Murillo

Design 40

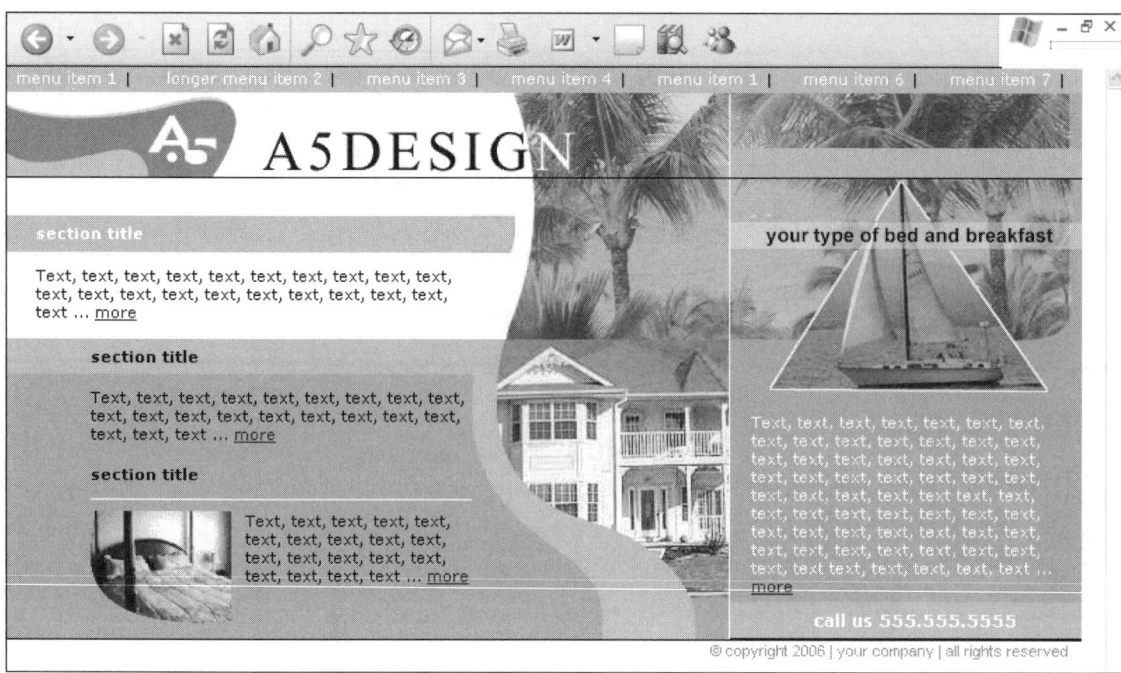

© 2014 Cengage Learning.

Homepage design.

Photoshop source file names: Designs—Third Edition/1-80-xhtml/design_40/design_40.psd

XHTML pages: index.htm, menu_item_2.htm, menu_item_3.htm

Photo credits: A5design

Design 39

© 2014 Cengage Learning.

Homepage design.

Photoshop source file names: Designs—Third
Edition/1-80-xhtml/design_39/design_39.psd

XHTML pages: index.htm, menu_item_2.htm, menu_item_3.htm, menu_item_4.htm

Photo credits: Lori Discoe

Design 38

© 2014 Cengage Learning.

Homepage design.

Photoshop source file names: Designs—Third Edition/1-80-xhtml/design_38/design_38.psd

XHTML pages: index.htm, menu_item_2.htm, menu_item_3.htm

Photo credits: A5design

Design 37

Homepage design.

Photoshop source file names: Designs—Third
Edition/1-80-xhtml/design_37/design_37.psd, design_37_sl.psd

XHTML pages: index.htm, menu_item_2.htm, menu_item_3.htm

Photo credits: Lori Discoe

Design 36

© 2014 Cengage Learning.

Homepage design.

Photoshop source file names: Designs—Third Edition/1-80-xhtml/design_36/design_36.psd, bg_images.psd

XHTML pages: index.htm, menu_item_2.htm, menu_item_3.htm

Photo credits: Justin Discoe, A5design

Design 35

Homepage design.

Photoshop source file names: Designs—Third Edition/1-80-xhtml/design_35/design_35.psd, bg_images.psd

XHTML pages: index.htm, menu_item_2.htm, menu_item_3.htm

Photo credits: Joe Eccher

Design 34

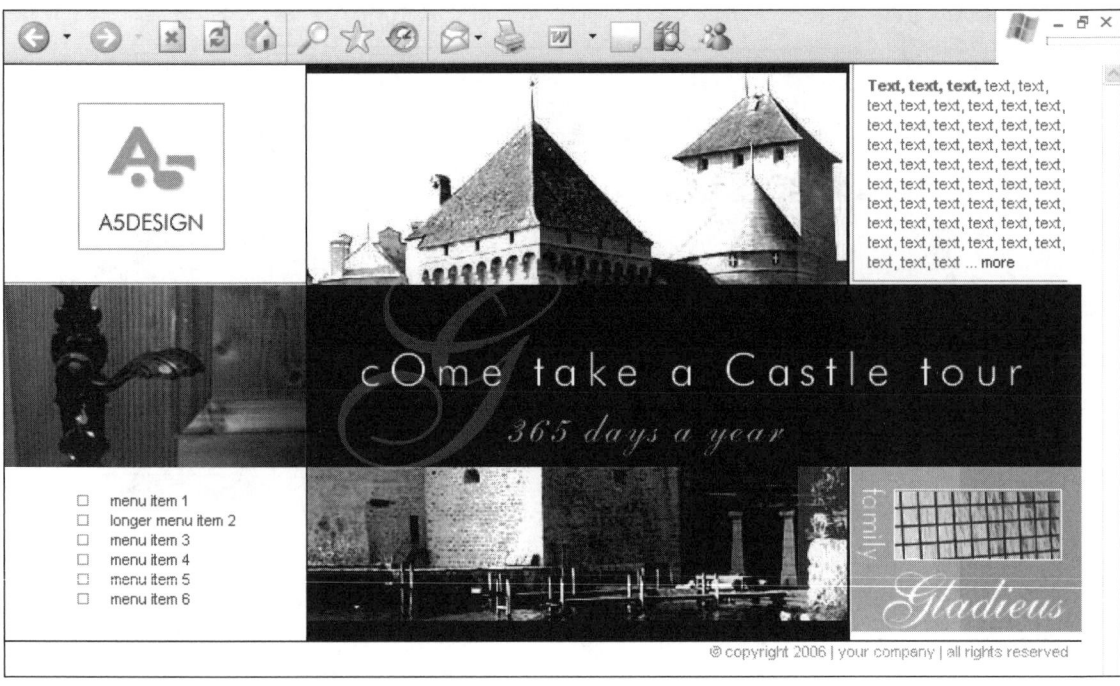

© 2014 Cengage Learning.

Homepage design.

Photoshop source file names: Designs—Third Edition/1-80-xhtml/design_34/design_34.psd, sl_header.psd

XHTML pages: index.htm, menu_item_2.htm, menu_item_3.htm

Photo credits: Joe Eccher

Design 33

Homepage design.

Photoshop source file names: Designs—Third Edition/1-80-xhtml/design_33/design_33.psd, bg_images.psd

XHTML pages: index.htm, menu_item_2.htm, menu_item_3.htm

Photo credits: A5design

Design 32

© 2014 Cengage Learning.

Homepage design.

Photoshop source file names: Designs—Third Edition/1-80-xhtml/design_32/design_32.psd

XHTML pages: index.htm, menu_item_2.htm, menu_item_3.htm

Photo credits: A5design

Design 31

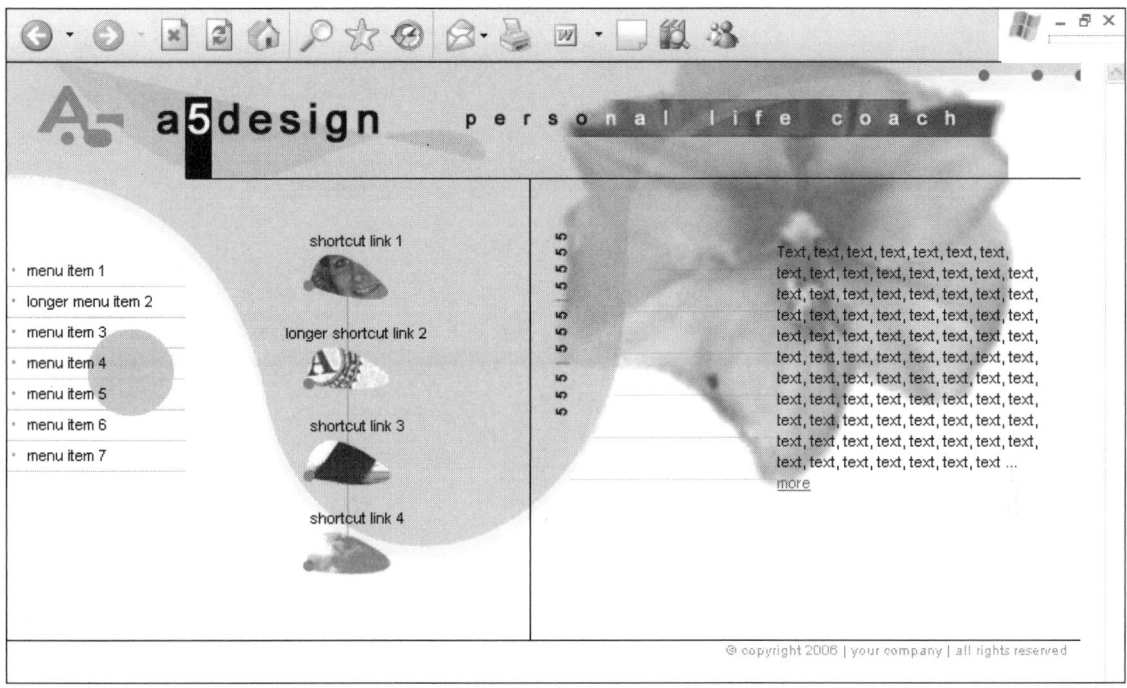

Homepage design.

Photoshop source file names: Designs—Third Edition/1-80-xhtml/design_31/design_31.psd, bg_images.psd

XHTML pages: index.htm, menu_item_2.htm, menu_item_3.htm, menu_item_4.htm

Photo credits: Joe Eccher, Justin Discoe

Design 30

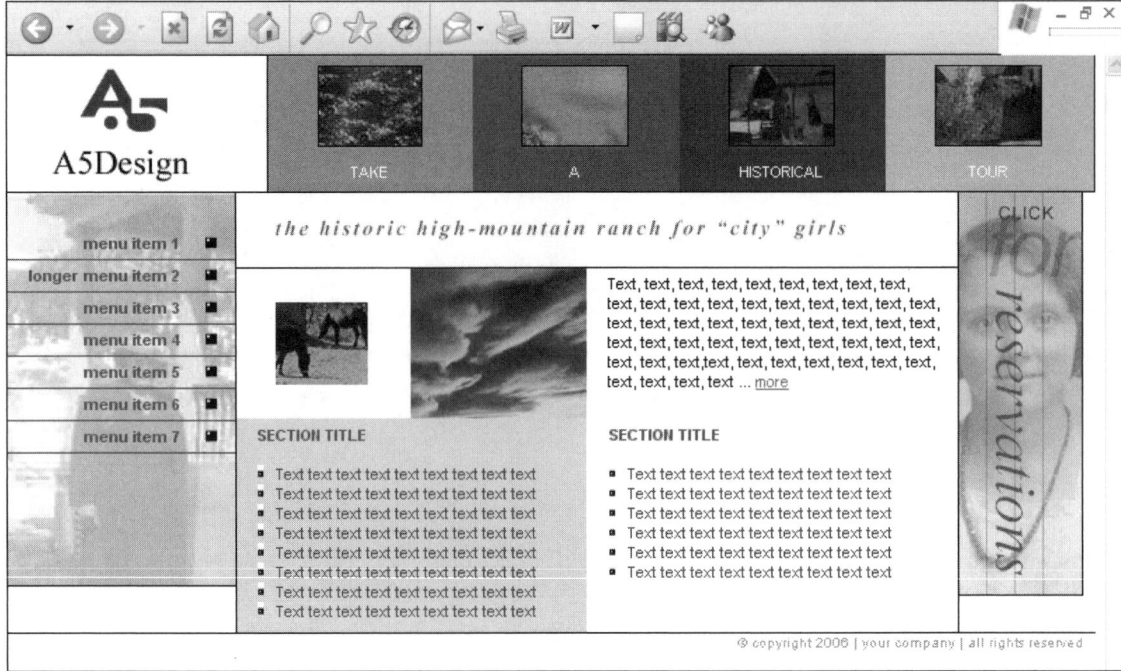

Homepage design.

Photoshop source file names: Designs—Third Edition/1-80-xhtml/design_30/design_30.psd, bg_menu.psd

XHTML pages: index.htm, menu_item_2.htm, menu_item_3.htm

Photo credits: Joe Eccher

Design 29

Homepage design.

Photoshop source file names: Designs—Third Edition/1-80-xhtml/design_29/design_29.psd

XHTML pages: index.htm, menu_item_2.htm, menu_item_3.htm

Photo credits: Joe Eccher

Design 28

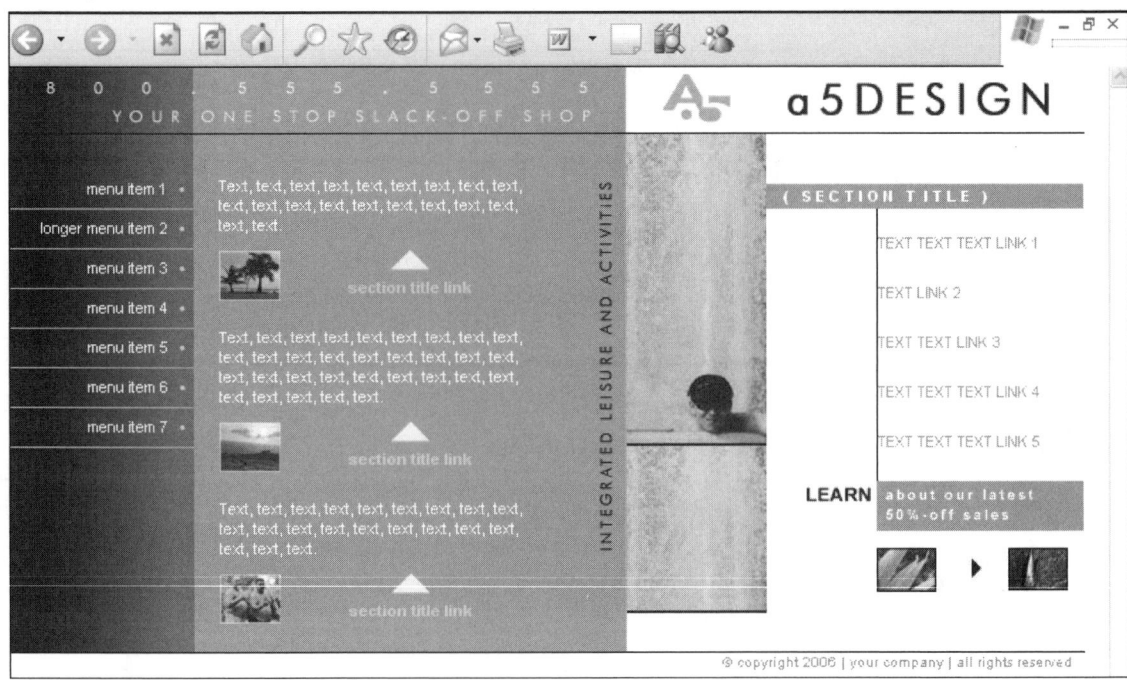

© 2014 Cengage Learning.

Homepage design.

Photoshop source file names: Designs—Third
Edition/1-80-xhtml/design_28/design_28.psd

XHTML pages: index.htm, menu_item_2.htm, menu_item_3.htm

Photo credits: Joe Eccher

Design 27

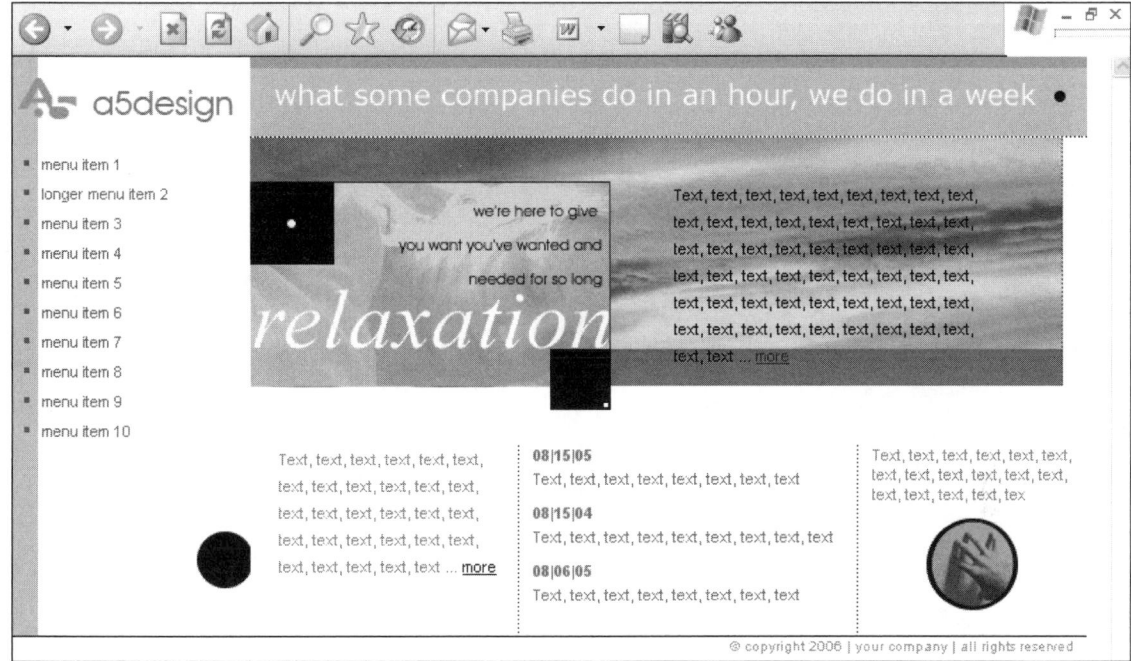

Homepage design.

Photoshop source file names: Designs—Third Edition/1-80-xhtml/design_27/design_27.psd

XHTML pages: index.htm, menu_item_2.htm, menu_item_3.htm

Photo credits: Joe Eccher, A5design

Design 26

© 2014 Cengage Learning.

Homepage design.

Photoshop source file names: Designs—Third
Edition/1-80-xhtml/design_26/design_26.psd

XHTML pages: index.htm, menu_item_2.htm, menu_item_3.htm

Photo credits: Justin Discoe, A5design

Design 25

© 2014 Cengage Learning.

Homepage design.

Photoshop source file names: Designs—Third Edition/1-80-xhtml/design_25/design_25.psd

XHTML pages: index.htm, menu_item_2.htm, menu_item_3.htm, menu_item_4.htm

Photo credits: Lisa Murillo, A5design

Design 24

© 2014 Cengage Learning.

Homepage design.

Photoshop source file names: Designs—Third Edition/1-80-xhtml/design_24/design_24.psd

XHTML pages: index.htm, menu_item_2.htm, menu_item_3.htm

Photo credits: Lisa Murillo, A5design

Design 23

Homepage design.

Photoshop source file names: Designs—Third Edition/1-80-xhtml/design_23/design_23.psd

XHTML pages: index.htm, menu_item_2.htm, menu_item_3.htm, menu_item_4.htm

Photo credits: A5design

Design 22

© 2014 Cengage Learning.

Homepage design.

Photoshop source file names: Designs—Third Edition/1-80-xhtml/design_22/design_22.psd, bg_menu.psd

XHTML pages: index.htm, menu_item_2.htm, menu_item_3.htm, menu_item_4.htm, menu_item_5.htm

Photo credits: A5design

Design 21

Homepage design.

Photoshop source file names: Designs—Third Edition/1-80-xhtml/design_21/design_21.psd

XHTML pages: index.htm, menu_item_2.htm, menu_item_3.htm

Photo credits: Joe Eccher

Design 20

Homepage design.

Photoshop source file names: Designs—Third Edition/1-80-xhtml/design_20/design_20.psd

XHTML pages: index.htm, menu_item_2.htm, menu_item_3.htm

Photo credits: A5design

Design 19

Homepage design.

Photoshop source file names: Designs—Third Edition/1-80-xhtml/design_19/design_19.psd

XHTML pages: index.htm, menu_item_2.htm, menu_item_3.htm

Photo credits: A5design

Design 18

© 2014 Cengage Learning.

Homepage design.

Photoshop source file names: Designs—Third
Edition/1-80-xhtml/design_18/design_18.psd, bg_left_column.psd

XHTML pages: index.htm, menu_item_2.htm, menu_item_3.htm

Photo credits: A5design

Design 17

Homepage design.

Photoshop source file names: Designs—Third Edition/1-80-xhtml/design_17/design_17.psd

XHTML pages: index.htm, menu_item_2.htm, menu_item_3.htm

Photo credits: A5design

Design 16

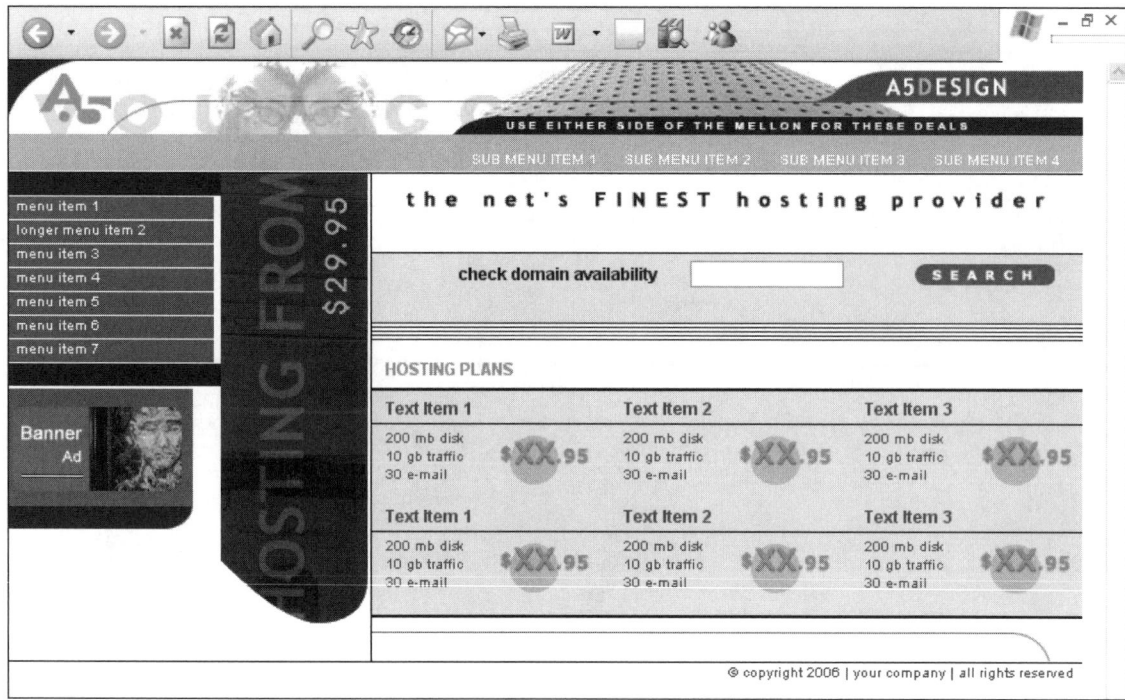

Homepage design.

Photoshop source file names: Designs—Third Edition/1-80-xhtml/design_16/design_16.psd

XHTML pages: index.htm, menu_item_2.htm, menu_item_3.htm

Photo credits: A5design

Design 15

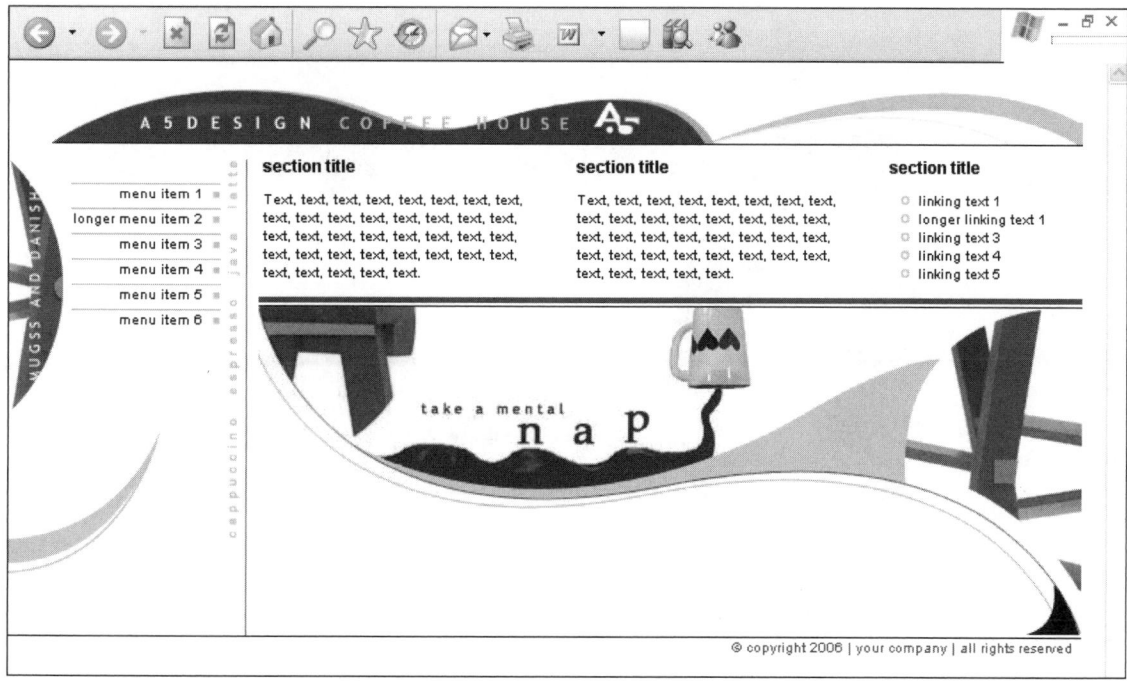

Homepage design.

Photoshop source file names: Designs—Third
Edition/1-80-xhtml/design_15/design_15.psd

XHTML pages: index.htm, menu_item_2.htm, menu_item_3.htm

Photo credits: A5design

Design 14

Homepage design.

Photoshop source file names: Designs—Third Edition/1-80-xhtml/design_14/design_14.psd

XHTML pages: index.htm, menu_item_2.htm, menu_item_3.htm

Photo credits: A5design

Design 13

Homepage design.

Photoshop source file names: Designs—Third Edition/1-80-xhtml/design_13/design_13.psd

XHTML pages: index.htm, menu_item_2.htm, menu_item_3.htm

Photo credits: A5design

Design 12

Homepage design.

Photoshop source file names: Designs—Third Edition/1-80-xhtml/design_12/design_12.psd

XHTML pages: index.htm, menu_item_2.htm, menu_item_3.htm

Photo credits: Joe Eccher, A5design

Design 11

Homepage design.

Photoshop source file names: Designs—Third Edition/1-80-xhtml/design_11/design_18.psd

XHTML pages: index.htm, menu_item_2.htm, menu_item_3.htm

Photo credits: Lisa Murillo, A5design

Design 10

Homepage design.

Photoshop source file names: Designs—Third
Edition/1-80-xhtml/design_10/design_10.psd

XHTML pages: index.htm, menu_item_2.htm, menu_item_3.htm

Photo credits: Lisa Murillo, A5design

Design 9

Homepage design.

Photoshop source file names: Designs—Third Edition/1-80-xhtml/design_9/design_9.psd

XHTML pages: index.htm, menu_item_2.htm, menu_item_3.htm

Photo credits: Joe Eccher

Design 8

Homepage design.

Photoshop source file names: Designs—Third
Edition/1-80-xhtml/design_8/design_8.psd

XHTML pages: index.htm, menu_item_2.htm, menu_item_3.htm

Photo credits: Lisa Murillo

Design 7

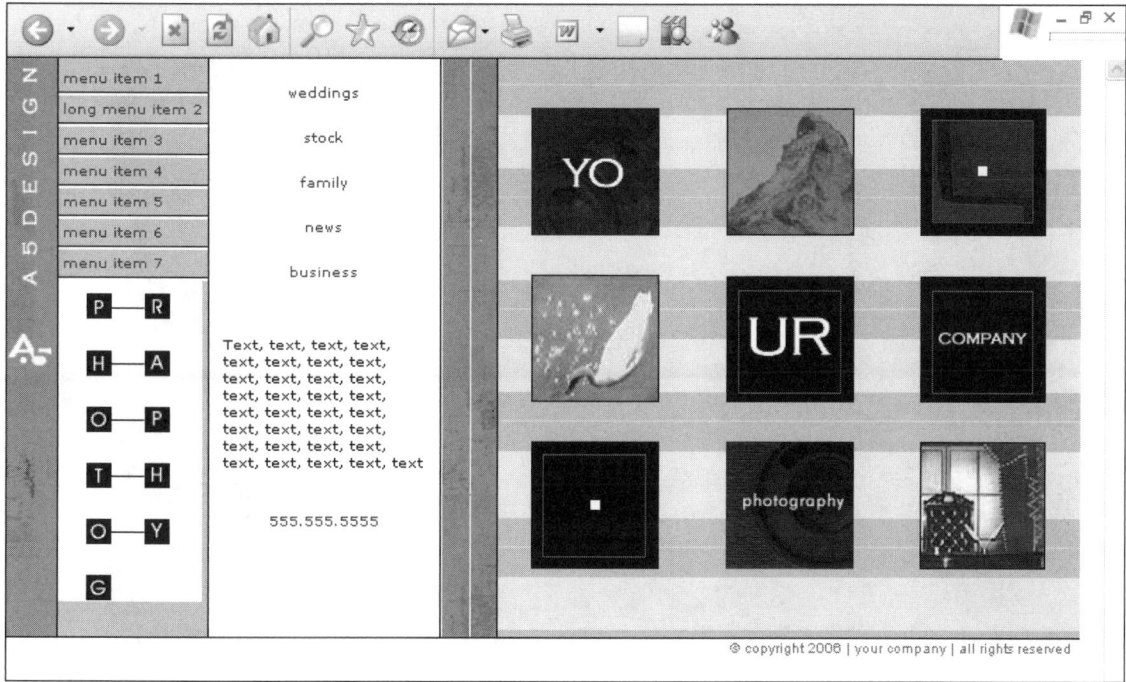

Homepage design.

Photoshop source file names: Designs—Third
Edition/1-80-xhtml/design_7/design_7.psd

XHTML pages: index.htm, menu_item_2.htm, menu_item_3.htm

Photo credits: Joe Eccher

Design 6

© 2014 Cengage Learning.

Homepage design.

Photoshop source file names: Designs—Third Edition/1-80-xhtml/design_6/design_6.psd

XHTML pages: index.htm, menu_item_2.htm, menu_item_3.htm, menu_item_4.htm

Photo credits: Joe Eccher

Design 5

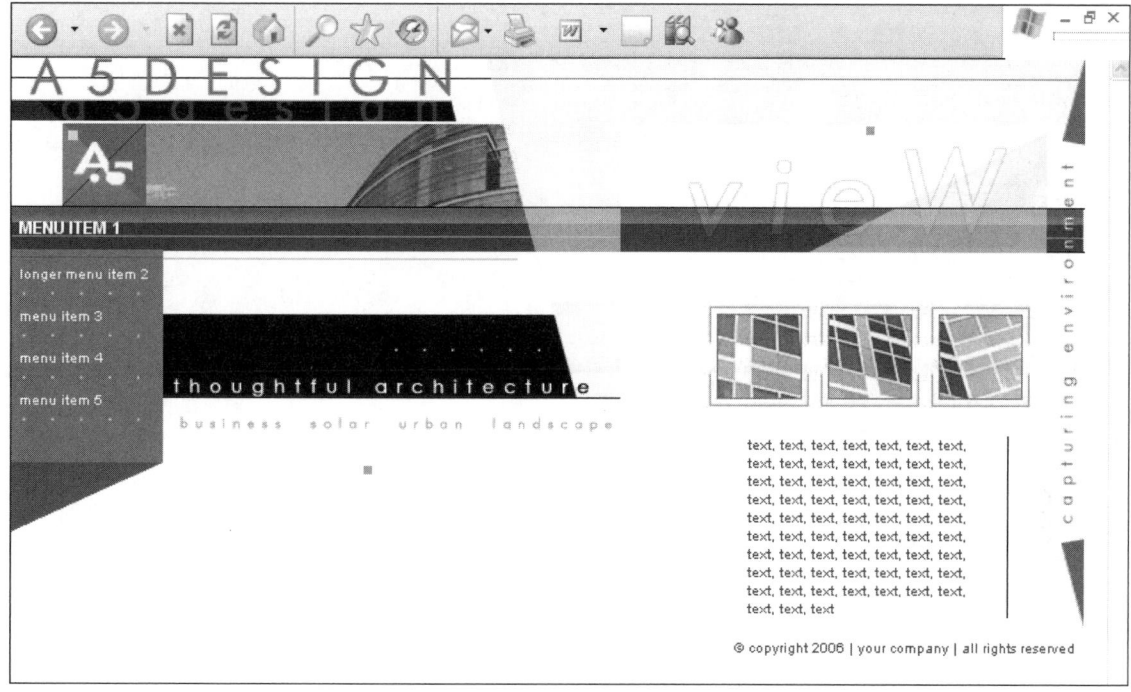

Homepage design.

Photoshop source file names: Designs—Third Edition/1-80-xhtml/design_5/design_5.psd

XHTML pages: index.htm, menu_item_2.htm, menu_item_3.htm

Photo credits: A5design

Design 4

© 2014 Cengage Learning.

Homepage design.

Photoshop source file names: Designs—Third
Edition/1-80-xhtml/design_4/design_4.psd, bg_top_photo.psd

XHTML pages: index.htm, menu_item_2.htm, menu_item_3.htm

Photo credits: A5design

Design 3

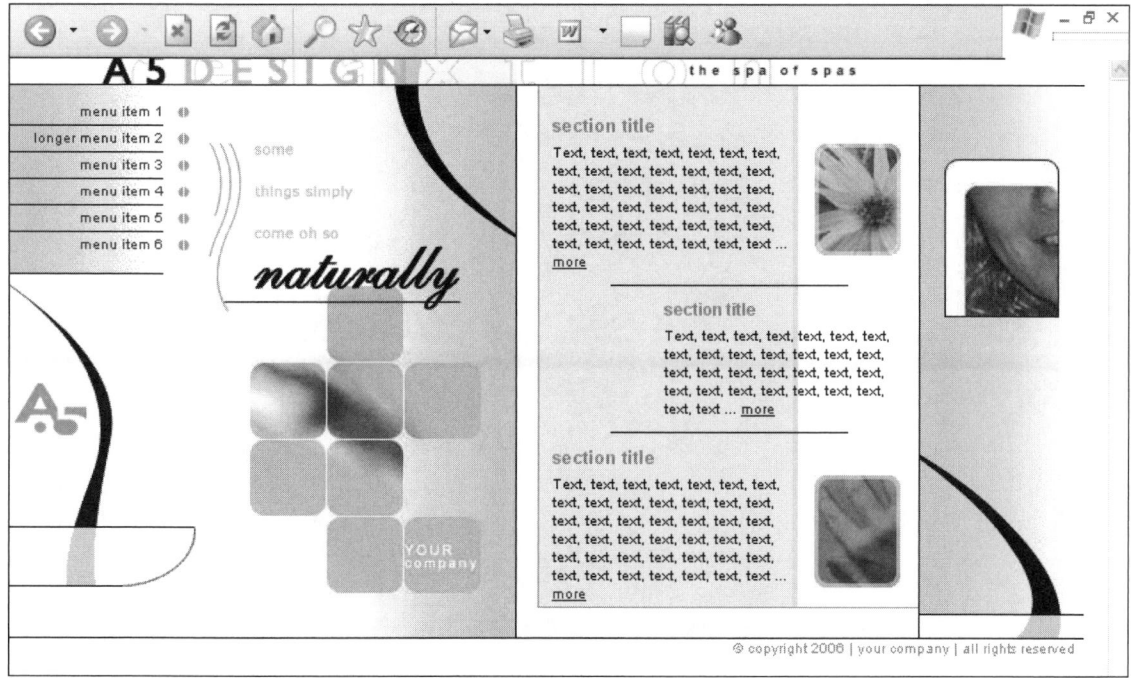

© 2014 Cengage Learning.

Homepage design.

Photoshop source file names: Designs—Third
Edition/1-80-xhtml/design_3/design_3.psd, bg_center_column.psd

XHTML pages: index.htm, menu_item_2.htm, menu_item_3.htm

Photo credits: Justin Discoe

Design 2

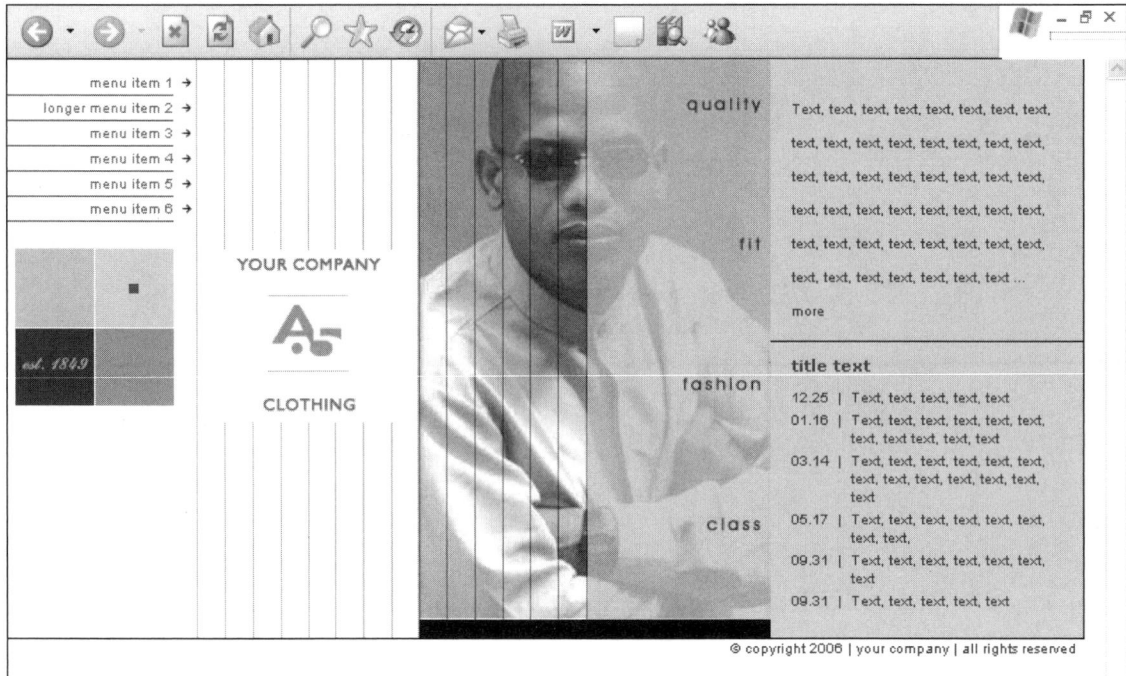

Homepage design.

Photoshop source file names: Designs—Third
Edition/1-80-xhtml/design_2/design_2.psd

XHTML pages: index.htm, menu_item_2.htm, menu_item_3.htm, menu_item_4.htm

Photo credits: Lisa Murillo

Design 1

© 2014 Cengage Learning.

Homepage design.

Photoshop source file names: Designs—Third
Edition/1-80-xhtml/design_1/design_1.psd

XHTML pages: index.htm, menu_item_2.htm, menu_item_3.htm

Photo credits: A5design

DESIGNS—FIRST EDITION FOLDER

Following are the designs that were included with the first edition of this book. While the resolution and coding method are not appropriate for today's designer, the work can still be used for inspiration when creating a site.

Design 50 (First Edition)

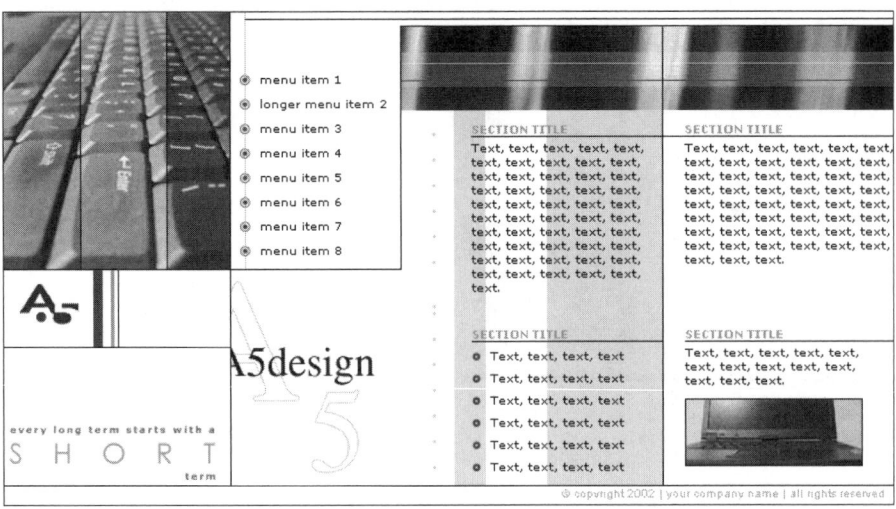

Homepage design.

Photoshop source file names: Designs—First Edition/design_50/design_50.psd

HTML Pages: index.htm, menu_item_2.htm, menu_item_3.htm, menu_item_4.htm (second-level page for nearly full content)

Photo credits: A5design

Design 49 (First Edition)

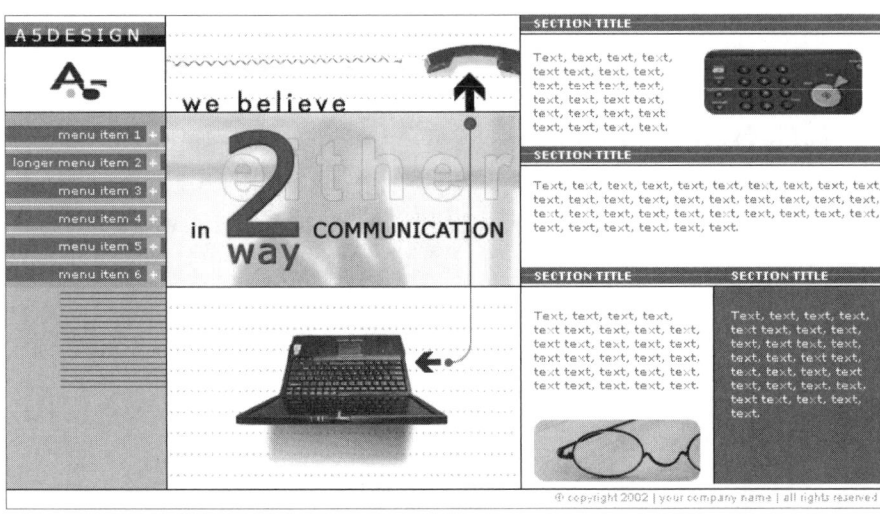

Homepage design.

Photoshop source file names: Designs—First Edition/design_49/design_49.psd

HTML Pages: index.htm, menu_item_2.htm, menu_item_3.htm

Photo credits: Cameracaptured, A5design

Design 48 (First Edition)

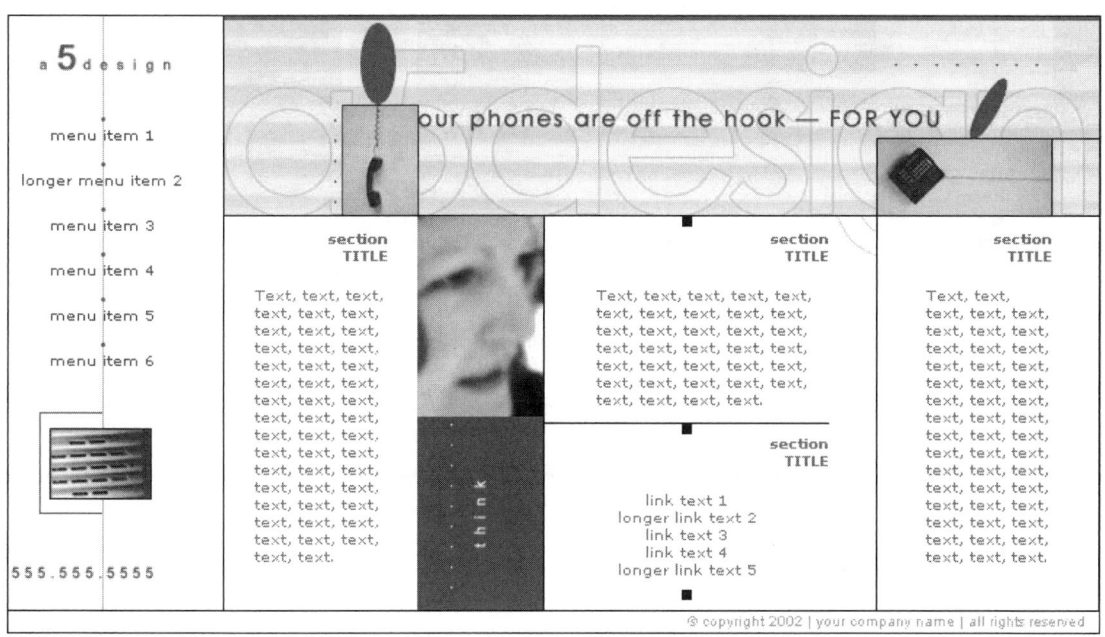

© 2014 Cengage Learning.

Homepage design.

Photoshop source file names: Designs—First Edition/design_48/design_48.psd

HTML Pages: index.htm, menu_item_2.htm, menu_item_3.htm

Photo credits: Onepartart, Cameracaptured

Design 47 (First Edition)

Homepage design.

Photoshop source file names: Designs—First Edition/design_47/design_47.psd

HTML Pages: index.htm, menu_item_2.htm, menu_item_3.htm

Photo credits: Onepartart, Cameracaptured

Design 46 (First Edition)

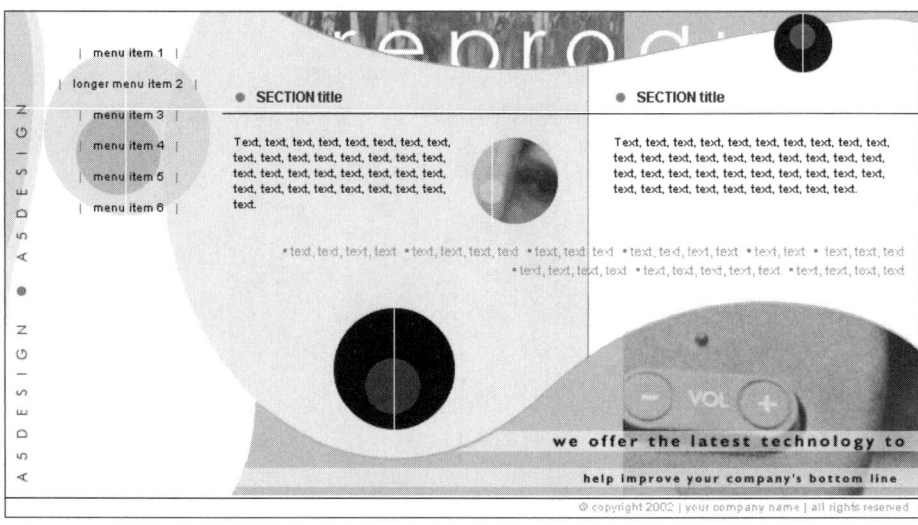

Homepage design.

Photoshop source file names: Designs—First Edition/design_46/design_46.psd

HTML Pages: index.htm, menu_item_2.htm

Photo credits: Cameracaptured, A5design

Design 45 (First Edition)

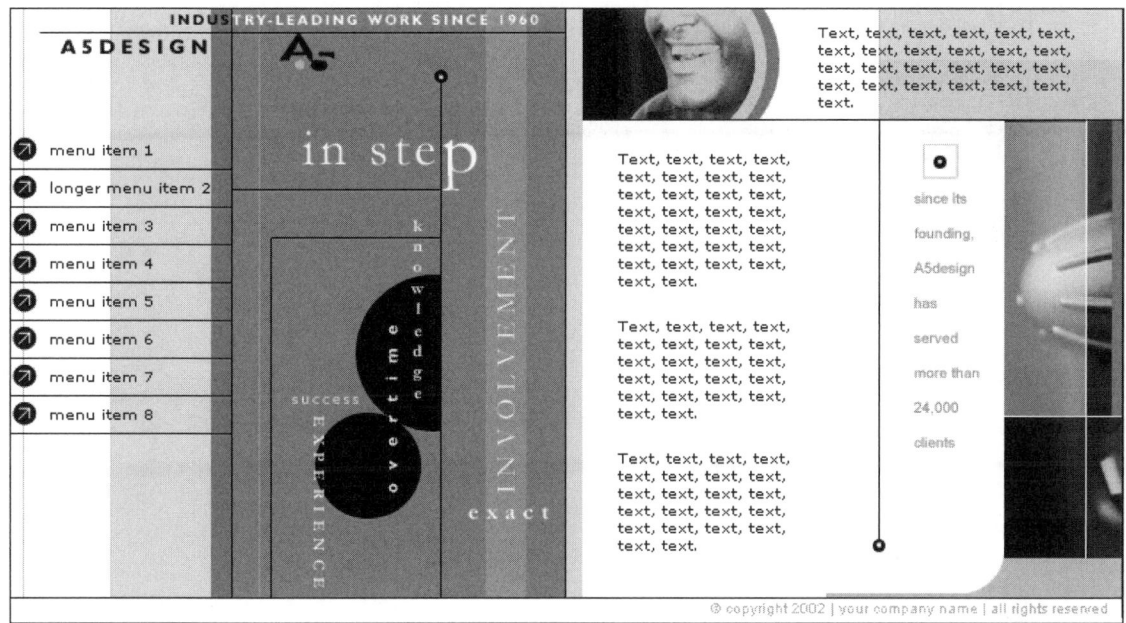

© 2014 Cengage Learning.

Homepage design.

Photoshop source file names: Designs—First Edition/design_45/design_45.psd

HTML Pages: index.htm, menu_item_2.htm, menu_item_3.htm

Photo credits: Cameracaptured

Design 44 (First Edition)

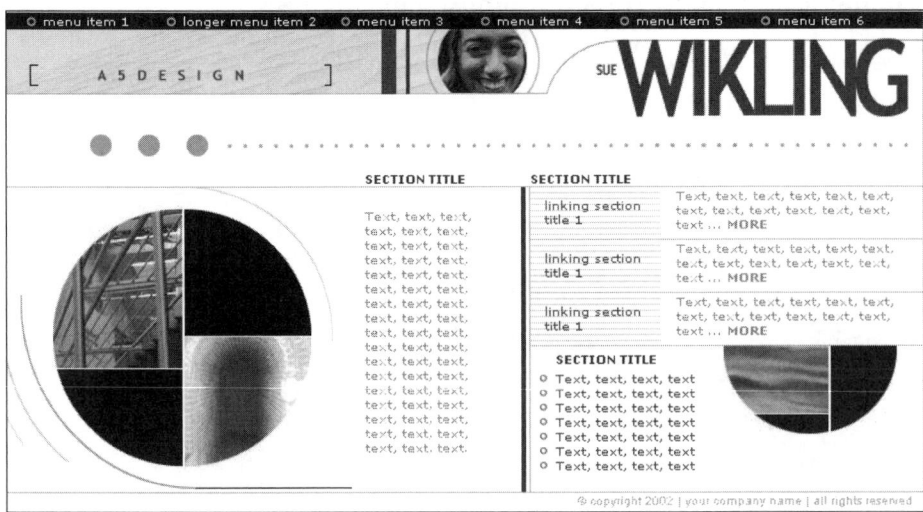

Homepage design.

Photoshop source file names: Designs—First Edition/design_44/design_44.psd

HTML Pages: index.htm, menu_item_2.htm

Photo credits: Onepartart, A5design

Design 43 (First Edition)

Homepage design.

Photoshop source file names: Designs—First Edition/design_43/design_43.psd

HTML Pages: index.htm, menu_item_2.htm, menu_item_3.htm

Photo credits: A5design

Design 42 (First Edition)

© 2014 Cengage Learning.

Homepage design.

Photoshop source file names: Designs—First Edition/design_42/design_42.psd

HTML Pages: index.htm, menu_item_2.htm, menu_item_3.htm

Photo credits: Cameracaptured

Design 41 (First Edition)

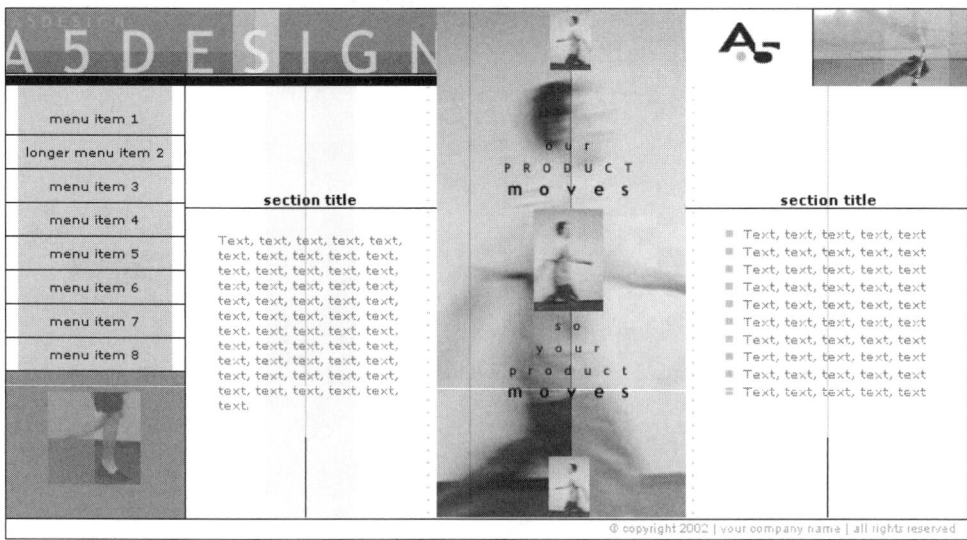

Homepage design.

Photoshop source file names: Designs—First Edition/design_41/design_41.psd

HTML Pages: index.htm, menu_item_2.htm

Photo credits: Cameracaptured

Design 40 (First Edition)

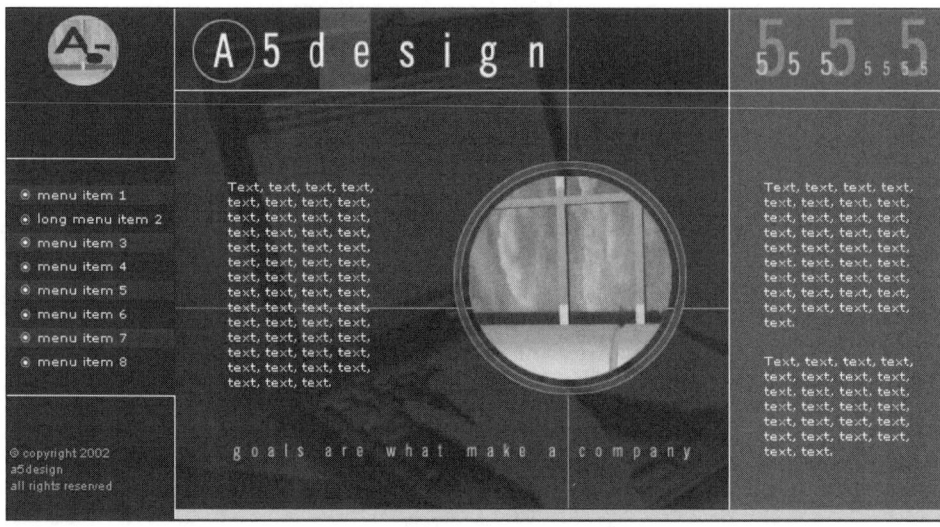

Homepage design.

Photoshop source file names: Designs—First Edition/design_40/design_40.psd

HTML Pages: index.htm, menu_item_2.htm

Photo credits: Cameracaptured, A5design

Design 39 (First Edition)

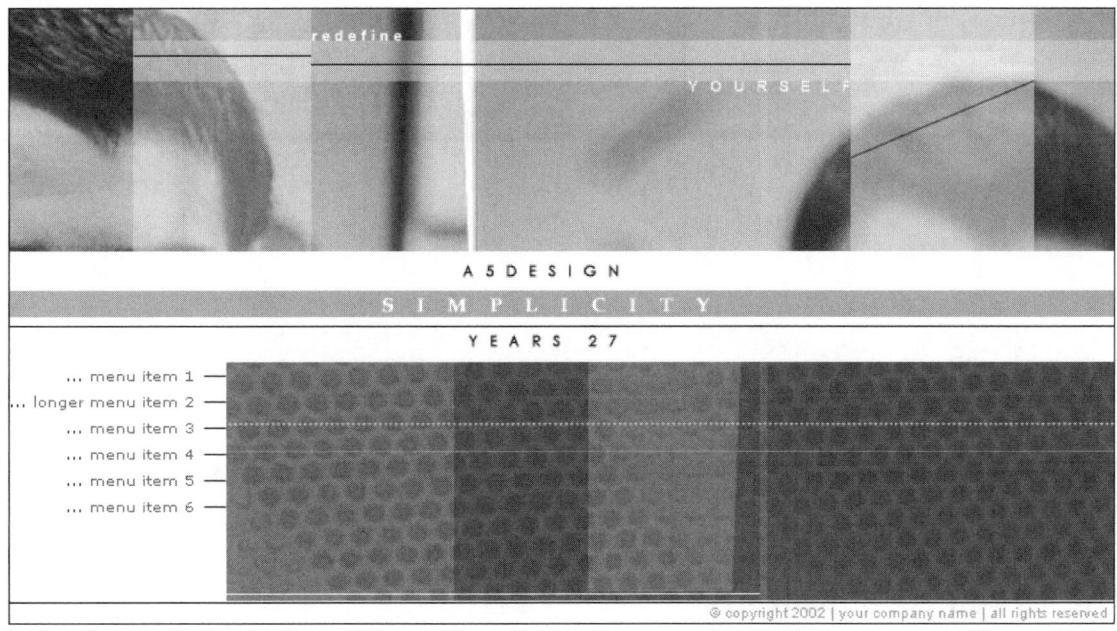

Homepage design.

Photoshop source file names: Designs—First Edition/design_39/design_39.psd

HTML Pages: index.htm, menu_item_2.htm

Photo credits: Cameracaptured

Design 38 (First Edition)

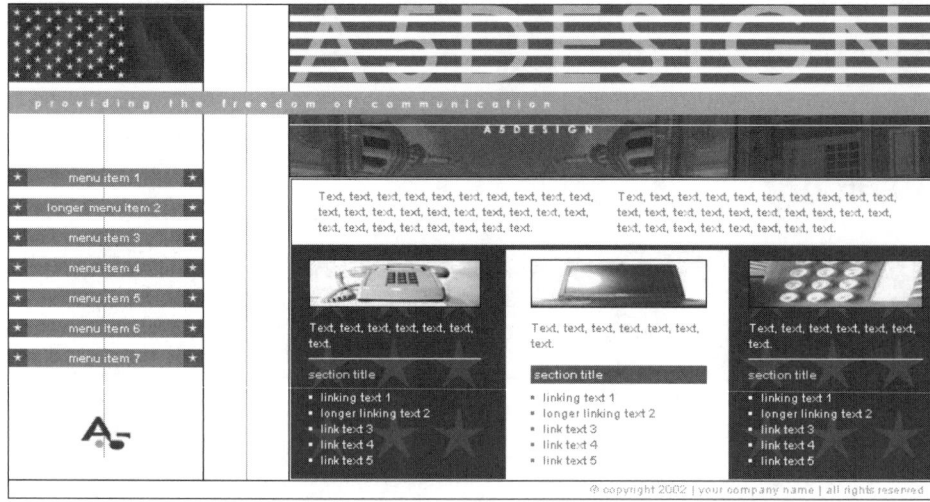

Homepage design.

Photoshop source file names: Designs—First Edition/design_38/design_38.psd

HTML Pages: index.htm, menu_item_2.htm

Photo credits: Cameracaptured, Onepartart, A5design

Design 37 (First Edition)

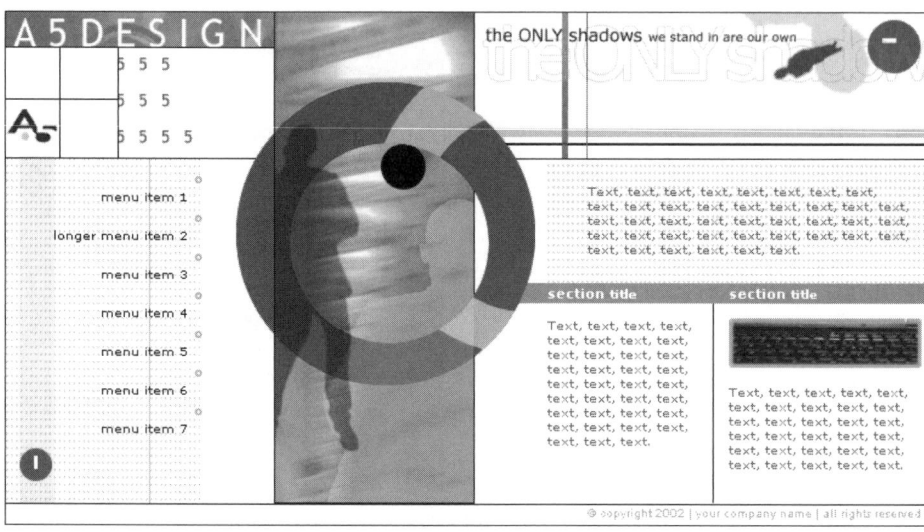

Homepage design.

Photoshop source file names: Designs—First Edition/design_37/design_37.psd

HTML Pages: index.htm, menu_item_2.htm

Photo credits: Cameracaptured, Onepartart

Design 36 (First Edition)

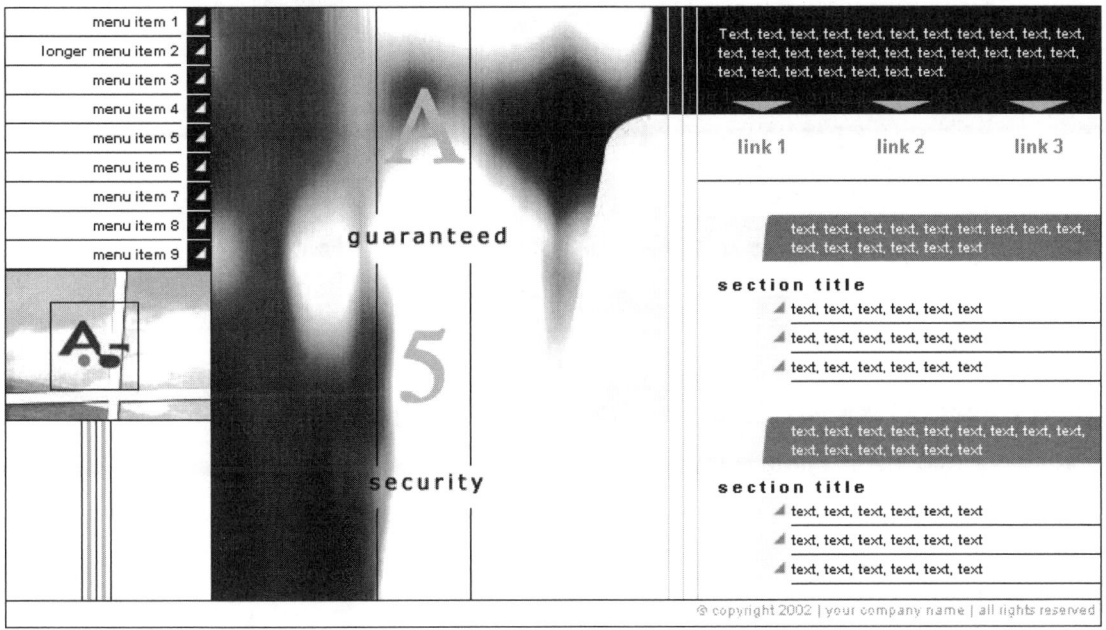

© 2014 Cengage Learning.

Homepage design.

Photoshop source file names: Designs—First Edition/design_36/design_36.psd

HTML Pages: index.htm, menu_item_2.htm, menu_item_3.htm, menu_item_4.htm (second-level page for nearly full content)

Photo credits: A5design

Design 35 (First Edition)

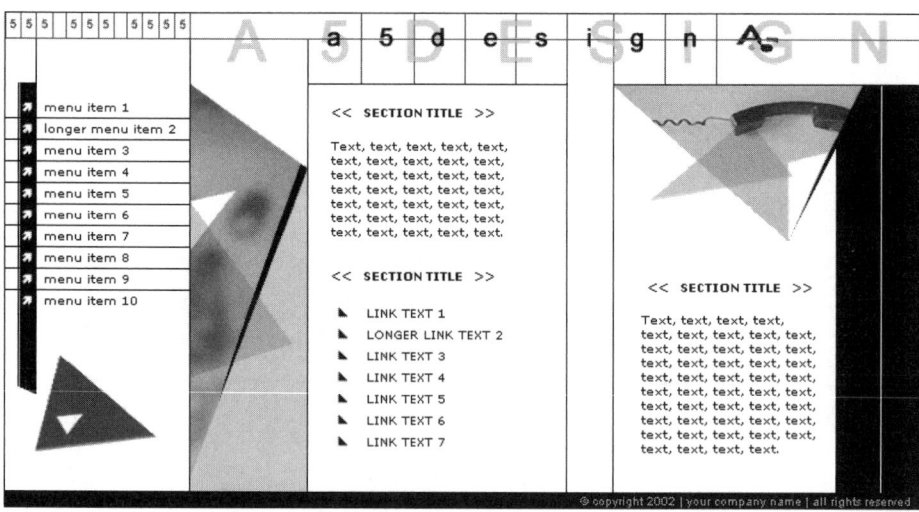

© 2014 Cengage Learning.

Homepage design.

Photoshop source file names: Designs—First Edition/design_35/design_35.psd

HTML Pages: index.htm, menu_item_2.htm, menu_item_3.htm

Photo credits: A5design

Design 34 (First Edition)

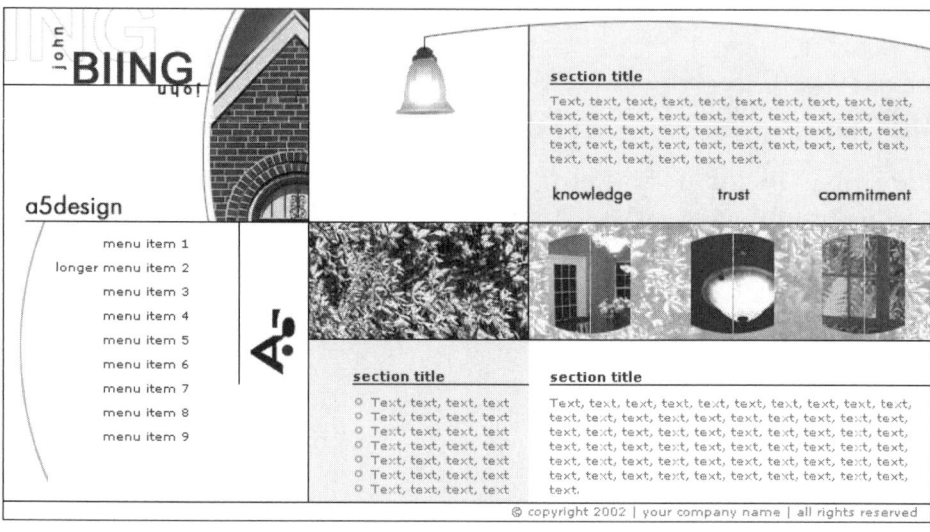

© 2014 Cengage Learning.

Homepage design.

Photoshop source file names: Designs—First Edition/design_34/design_34.psd

HTML Pages: index.htm, menu_item_2.htm

Photo credits: A5design

Design 33 (First Edition)

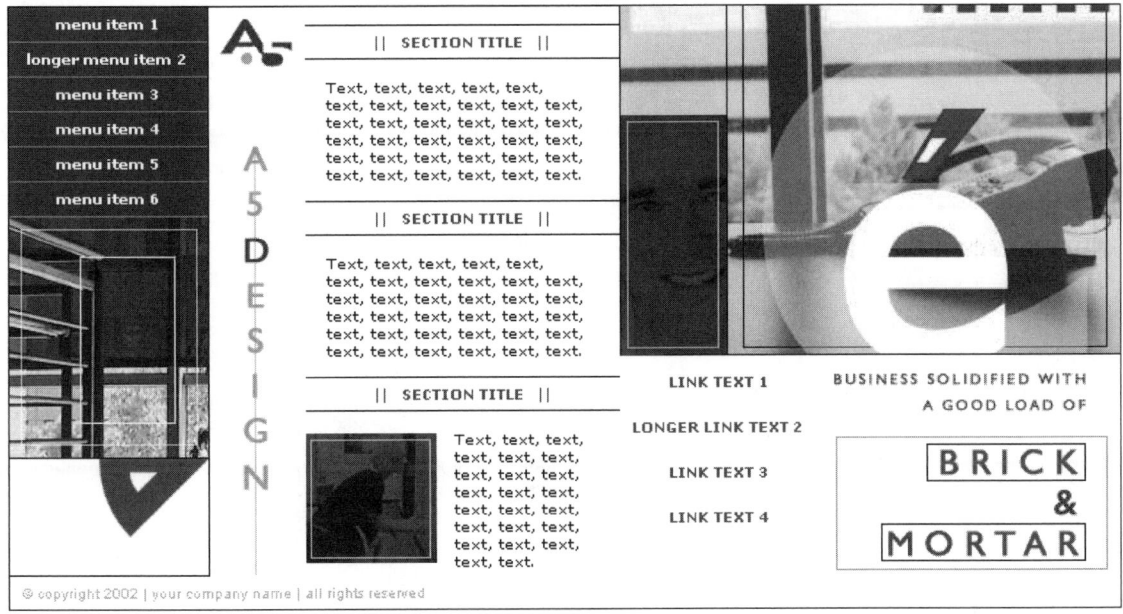

© 2014 Cengage Learning.

Homepage design.

Photoshop source file names: Designs—First Edition/design_33/design_33.psd

HTML Pages: index.htm, menu_item_2.htm

Photo credits: Cameracaptured, Onepartart, A5design

Design 32 (First Edition)

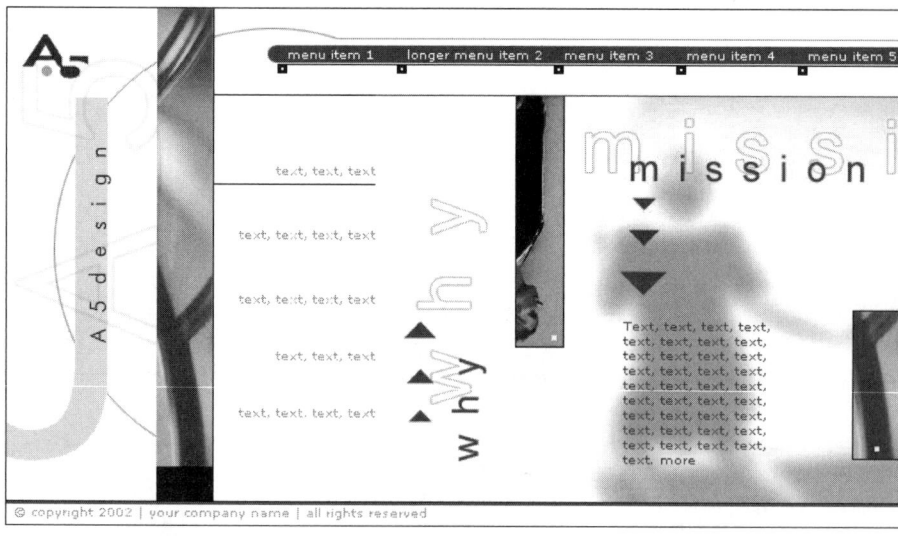

Homepage design.

Photoshop source file names: Designs—First Edition/design_32/design_32.psd

HTML Pages: index.htm, menu_item_2.htm, menu_item_3.htm

Photo credits: Cameracaptured

Design 31 (First Edition)

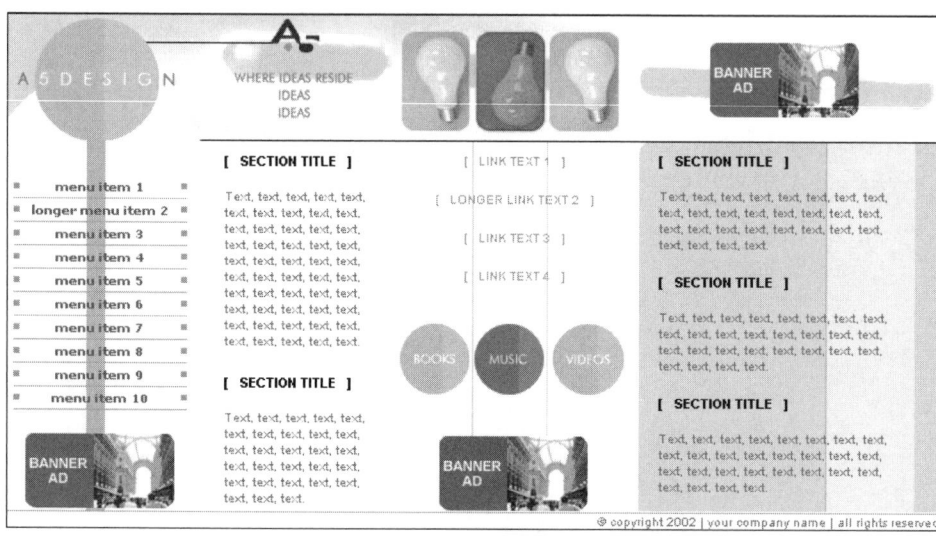

Homepage design.

Photoshop source file names: Designs—First Edition/design_31/design_31.psd, title_curve.psd

HTML Pages: index.htm, menu_item_2.htm, menu_item_3.htm

Photo credits: Cameracaptured

Design 30 (First Edition)

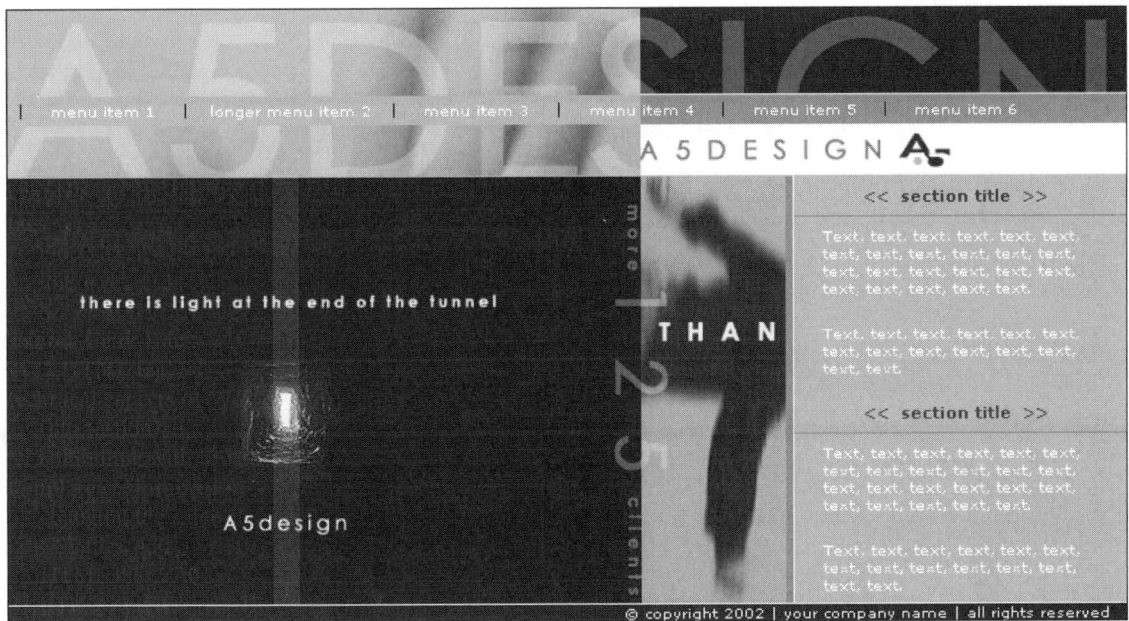

© 2014 Cengage Learning.

Homepage design.

Photoshop source file names: Designs—First Edition/design_30/design_30.psd, bullets.psd, bg_menu.psd

HTML Pages: index.htm, menu_item_2.htm, menu_item_3.htm, menu_item_4.htm (second-level page for full content)

Photo credits: Cameracaptured, A5Design

Design 29 (First Edition)

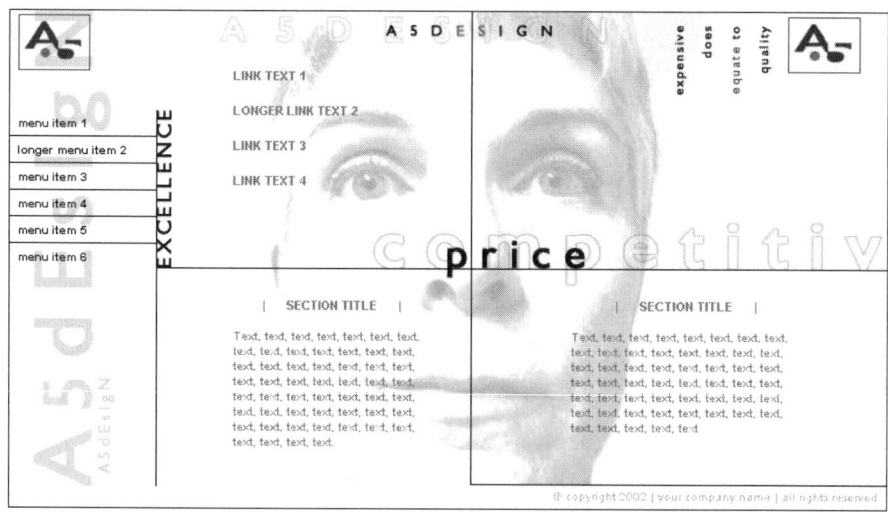

Homepage design.

Photoshop source file names: Designs—First Edition/design_29/design_29.psd, design_29_sl.psd, bg_menu.psd

HTML Pages: index.htm, menu_item_2.htm, menu_item_3.htm

Photo credits: A5Design

Design 28 (First Edition)

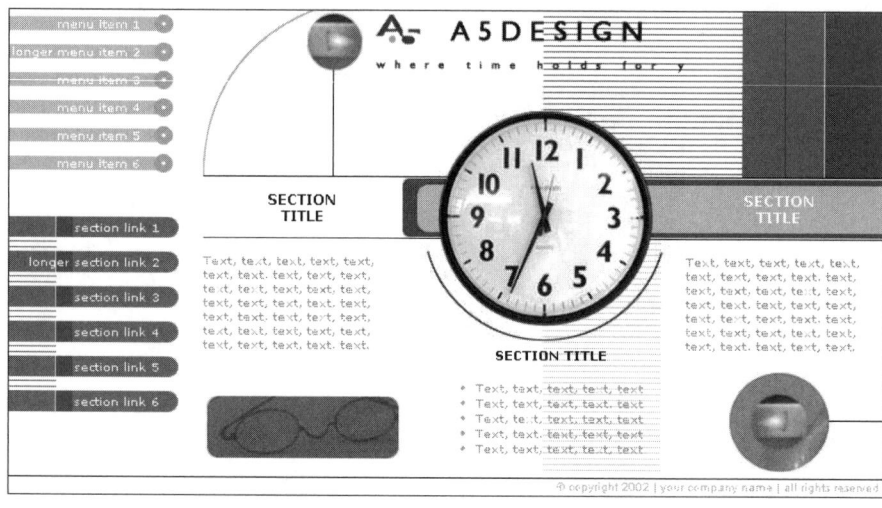

Homepage design.

Photoshop source file names: Designs—First Edition/design_28/design_28.psd

HTML Pages: index.htm, menu_item_2.htm

Photo credits: Onepartart

Design 27 (First Edition)

Homepage design.

Photoshop source file names: Designs—First Edition/design_27/design_27.psd

HTML Pages: index.htm, menu_item_2.htm, menu_item_3.htm

Photo credits: Cameracaptured

Design 26 (First Edition)

Homepage design.

Photoshop source file names: Designs—First Edition/design_26/design_26.psd

HTML Pages: index.htm, menu_item_2.htm

Photo credits: Cameracaptured

Design 25 (First Edition)

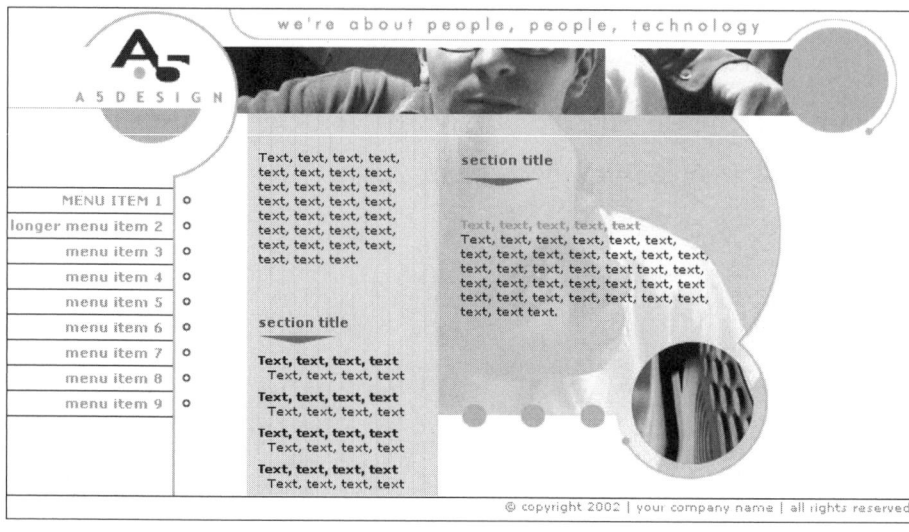

Homepage design.

Photoshop source file names: Designs—First Edition/design_25/design_25.psd

HTML Pages: index.htm, menu_item_2.htm

Photo credits: Cameracaptured, A5design

Design 24 (First Edition)

© 2014 Cengage Learning.

Homepage design.

Photoshop source file names: Designs—First Edition/design_24/design_24.psd

HTML Pages: index.htm, menu_item_2.htm, menu_item_3.htm

Photo credits: Onepartart, Cameracaptured

Design 23 (First Edition)

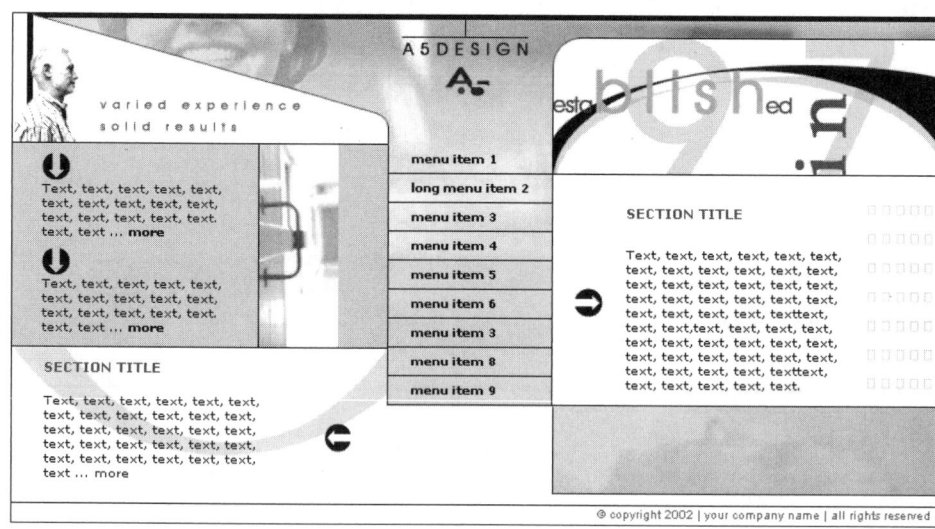

Homepage design.

Photoshop source file names: Designs—First Edition/design_23/design_23.psd

HTML Pages: index.htm, menu_item_2.htm, menu_item_3.htm

Photo credits: A5design

Design 22 (First Edition)

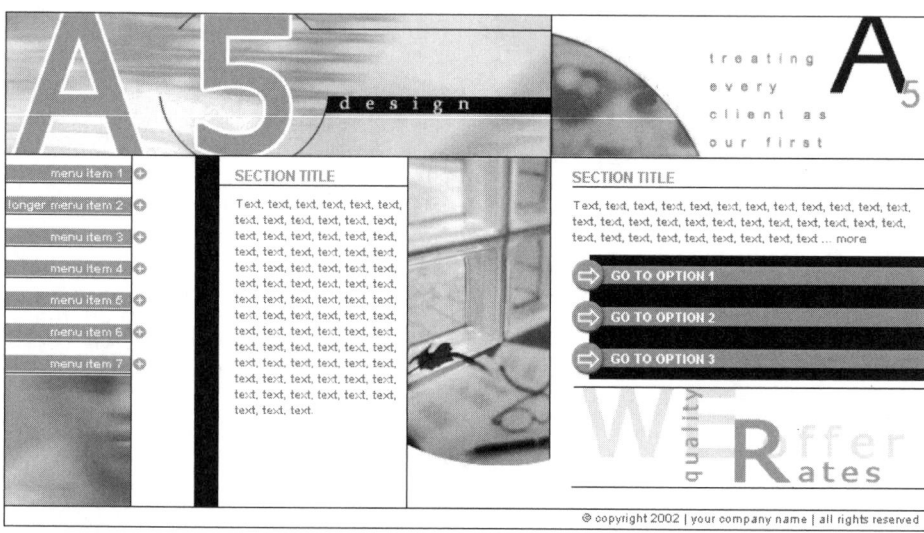

Homepage design.

Photoshop source file names: Designs—First Edition/design_22/design_22.psd

HTML Pages: index.htm, menu_item_2.htm, menu_item_3.htm

Photo credits: Cameracaptured

Design 21 (First Edition)

© 2014 Cengage Learning.

Homepage design.

Photoshop source file names: Designs—First Edition/design_21/design_21.psd

HTML Pages: index.htm, menu_item_2.htm, menu_item_3.htm

Photo credits: Cameracaptured, A5design

Design 20 (First Edition)

Homepage design.

Photoshop source file names: Designs—First Edition/design_20/design_20.psd

HTML Pages: index.htm, menu_item_2.htm, menu_item_3.htm, menu_item_4.htm (second-level page for full content)

Design 19 (First Edition)

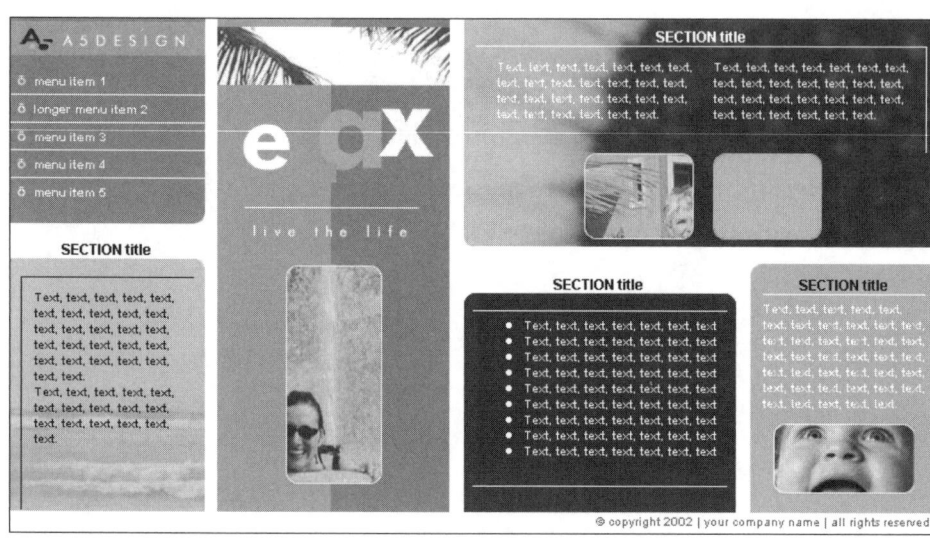

Homepage design.

Photoshop source file names: Designs—First Edition/design_19/design_19.psd

HTML Pages: index.htm, menu_item_2.htm, menu_item_3.htm

Photo credits: J&N Photography

Design 18 (First Edition)

Homepage design.

Photoshop source file names: Designs—First Edition/design_18/design_18.psd

HTML Pages: index.htm, menu_item_2.htm, menu_item_3.htm, menu_item_4.htm (second-level page for full content)

Photo credits: J&N Photography

Design 17 (First Edition)

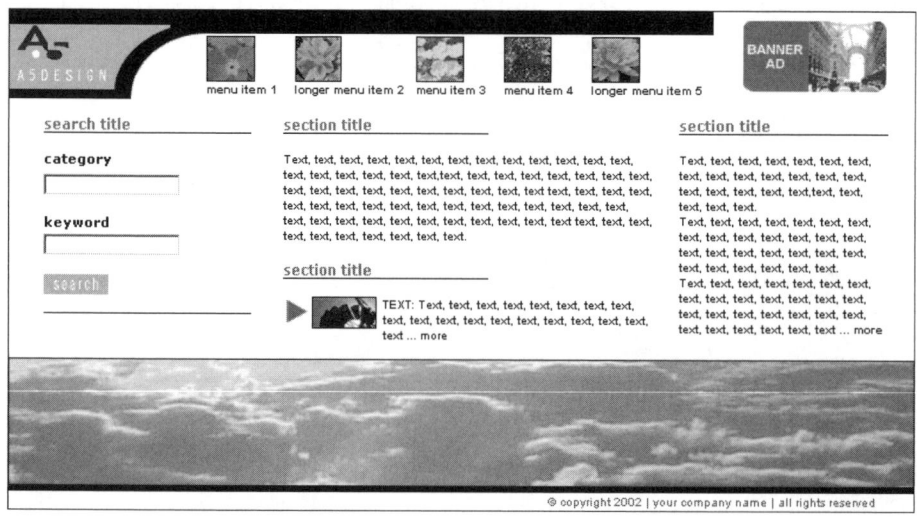

Homepage design.

Photoshop source file names: Designs—First Edition/design_17/design_17.psd, menu_item_text.psd

HTML Pages: index.htm, menu_item_2.htm

Photo credits: J&N Photography

Design 16 (First Edition)

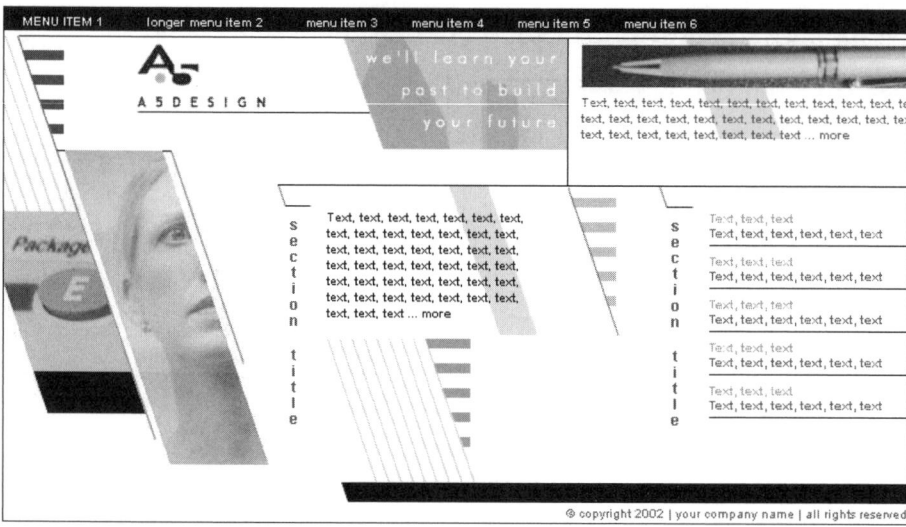

Homepage design.

Photoshop source file names: Designs—First Edition/design_16/design_16.psd

HTML Pages: index.htm, menu_item_2.htm, menu_item_3.htm

Photo credits: Cameracaptured

Design 15 (First Edition)

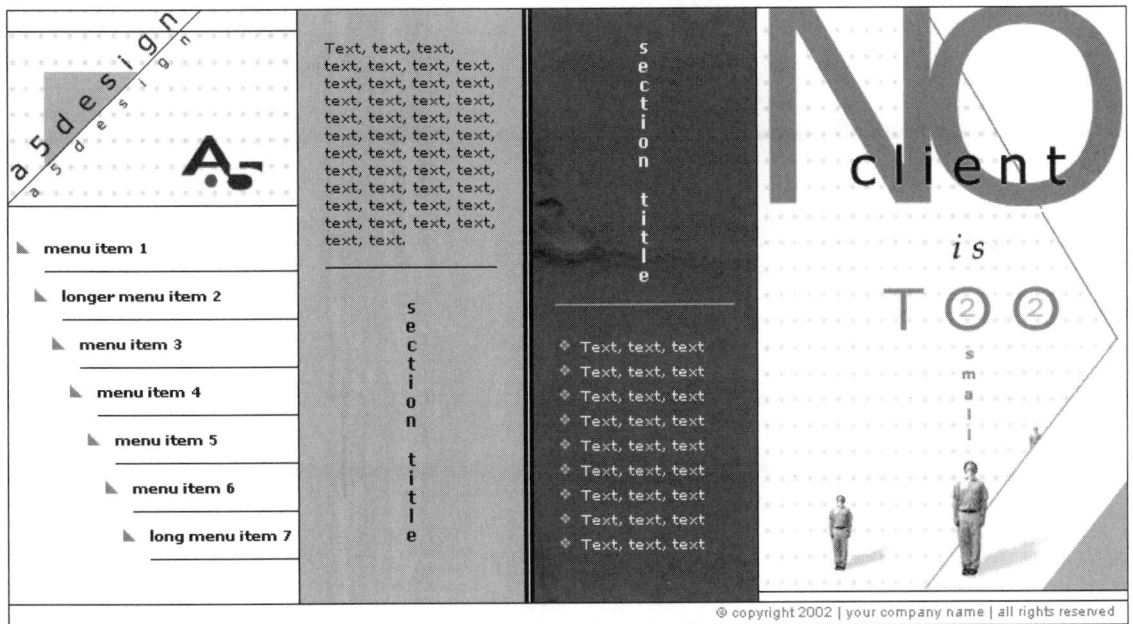

© 2014 Cengage Learning.

Homepage design.

Photoshop source file names: Designs—First Edition/design_15/design_15.psd

HTML Pages: index.htm, menu_item_2.htm, menu_item_3.htm

Photo credits: A5design

Design 14 (First Edition)

© 2014 Cengage Learning.

Homepage design.

Photoshop source file names: Designs—First Edition/design_14/design_14.psd

HTML Pages: index.htm, menu_item_2.htm, menu_item_3.htm

Photo credits: A5design

Design 13 (First Edition)

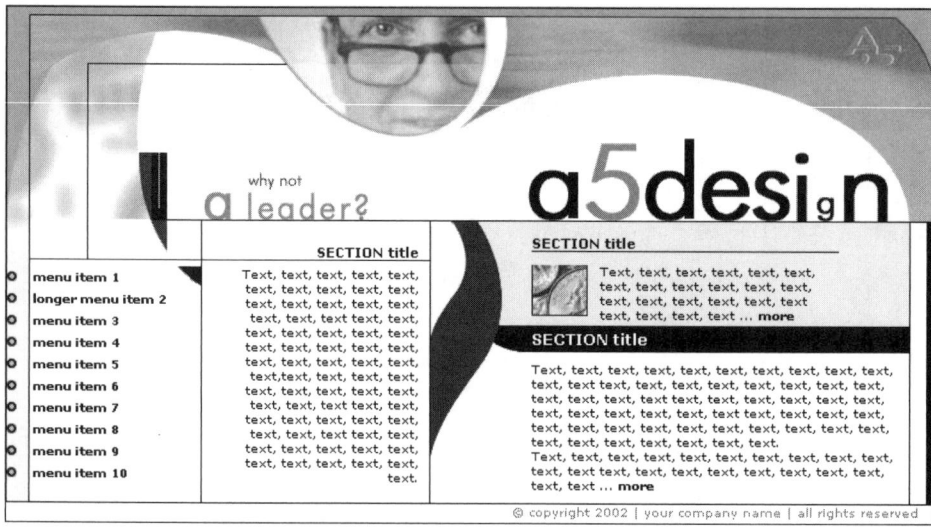

© 2014 Cengage Learning.

Homepage design.

Photoshop source file names: Designs—First Edition/design_13/design_13.psd, design_13_sl.psd

HTML Pages: index.htm, menu_item_2.htm, menu_item_3.htm

Photo credits: Cameracaptured, A5design

Design 12 (First Edition)

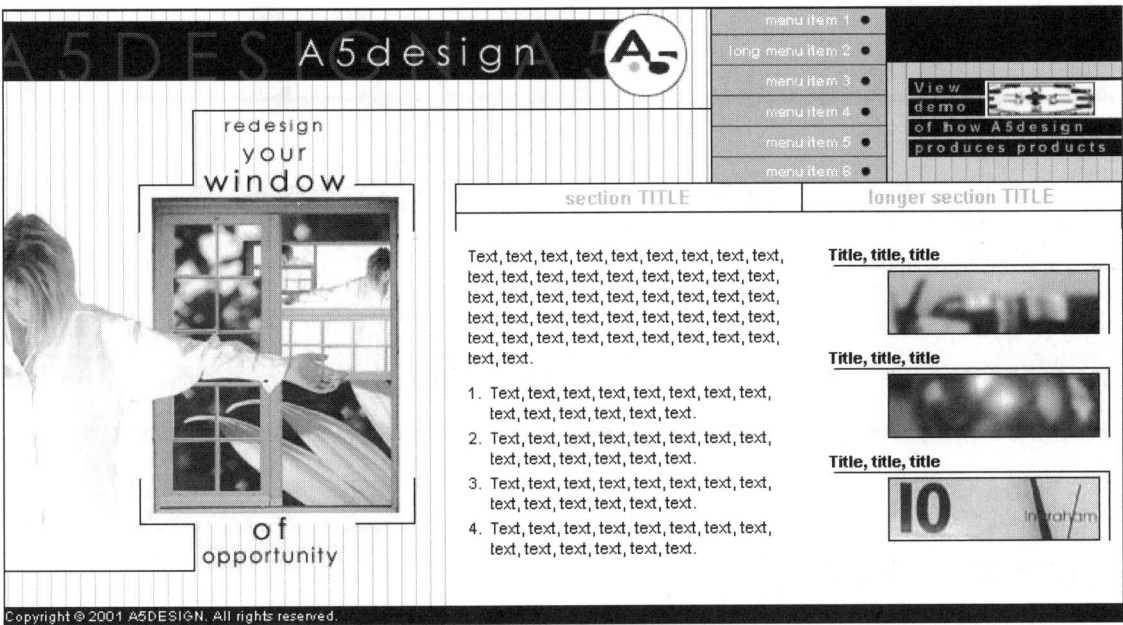

Homepage design.

Photoshop source file names: Designs—First Edition/design_12/design_12.psd, design_12_sl.psd, photo_on.psd

HTML Pages: index.htm, menu_item_2.htm, menu_item_3.htm

Photo credits: J&N Photography, Onepartart, A5design

Design 11 (First Edition)

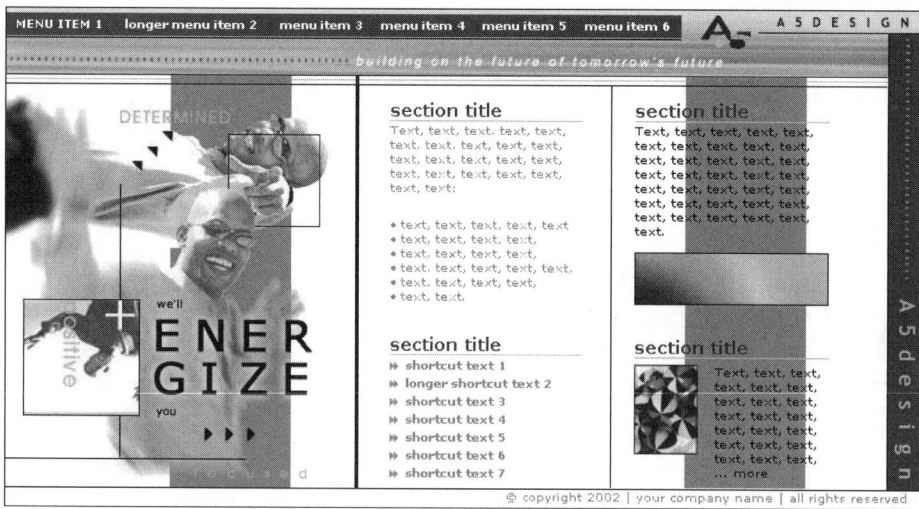

Homepage design.

Photoshop source file names: Designs—First Edition/design_11/design_11.psd

HTML Pages: index.htm, menu_item_2.htm

Photo credits: Cameracaptured

Design 10 (First Edition)

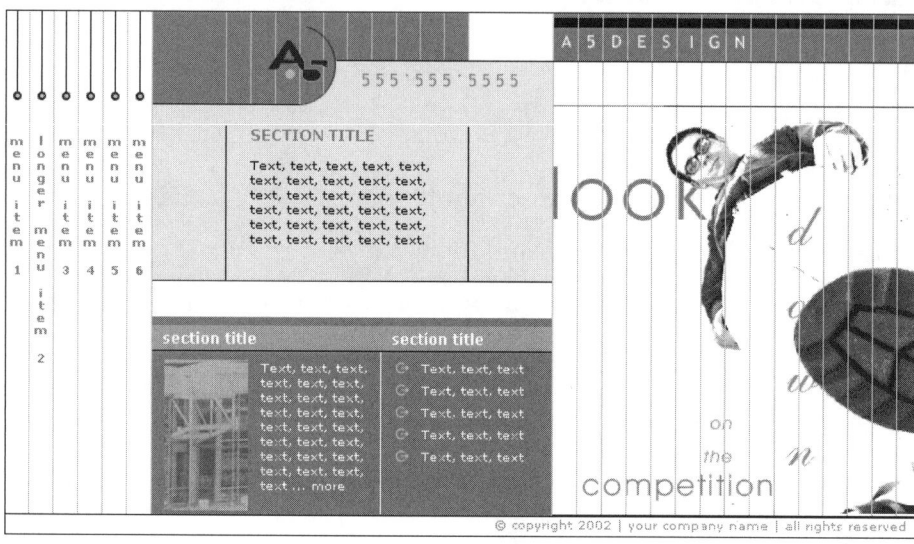

Homepage design.

Photoshop source file names: Designs—First Edition/design_10/design_10.psd

HTML Pages: index.htm, menu_item_2.htm, menu_item_3.htm

Photo credits: Onepartart

Design 9 (First Edition)

Homepage design.

Photoshop source file names: Designs—First Edition/design_9/design_9.psd, design_9_sl.psd

HTML Pages: index.htm, menu_item_2.htm

Photo credits: Onepartart

Design 8 (First Edition)

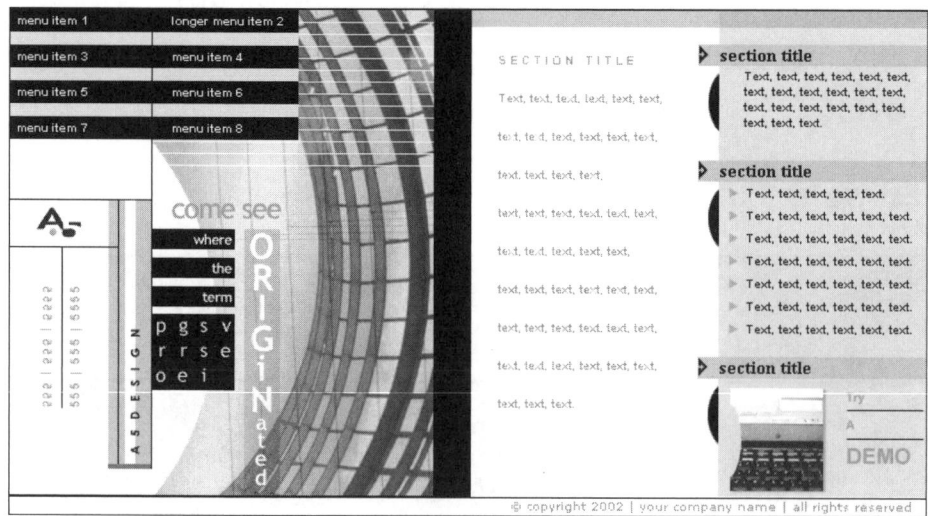

© 2014 Cengage Learning.

Homepage design.

Photoshop source file names: Designs—First Edition/design_8/design_8.psd

HTML Pages: index.htm, menu_item_2.htm, menu_item_3.htm

Photo credits: Cameracaptured

Design 7 (First Edition)

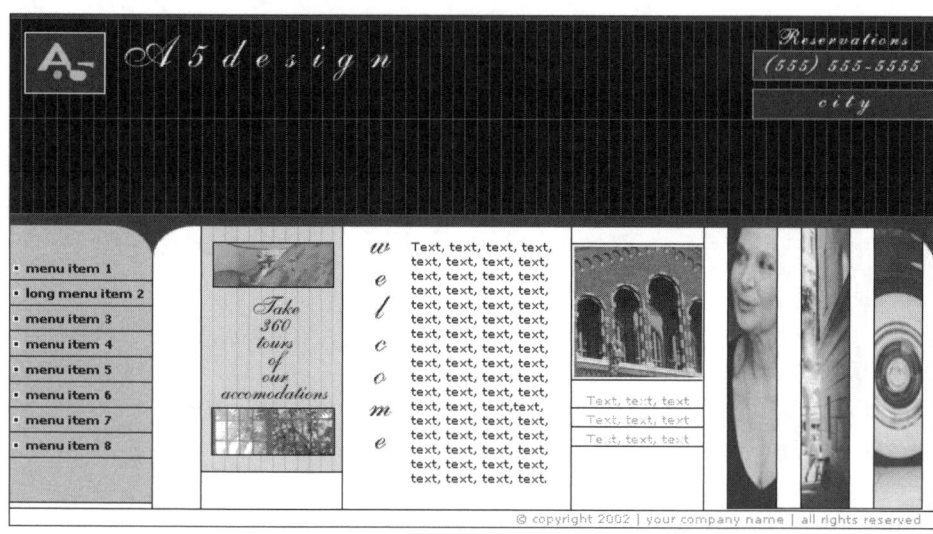

© 2014 Cengage Learning.

Homepage design.

Photoshop source file names: Designs—First Edition/design_7/design_7.psd

HTML Pages: index.htm, menu_item_2.htm, menu_item_3.htm

Photo credits: Cameracaptured, A5design

Design 6 (First Edition)

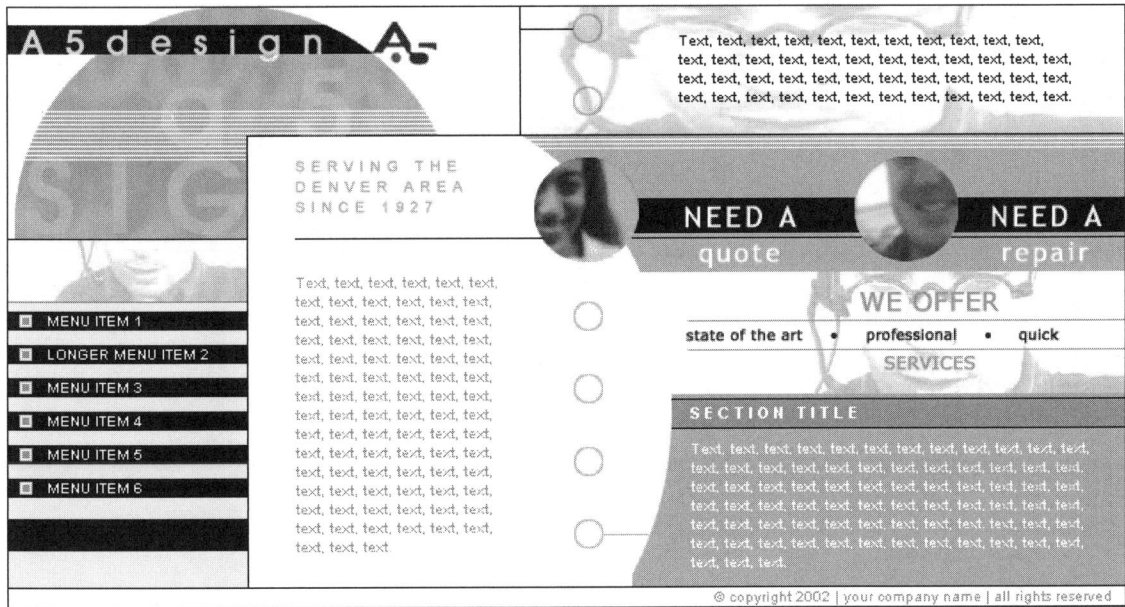

Homepage design.

Photoshop source file names: Designs—First Edition/design_6/design_6.psd

HTML Pages: index.htm, menu_item_2.htm

Photo credits: Onepartart, A5design

Design 5 (First Edition)

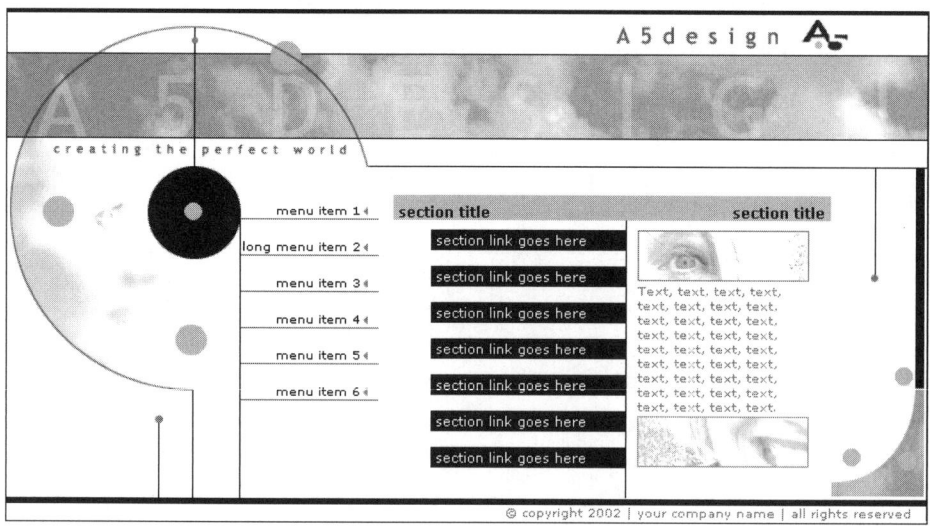

Homepage design.

Photoshop source file names: Designs—First Edition/design_5/design_5.psd

HTML Pages: index.htm, menu_item_2.htm, menu_item_3.htm

Photo credits: A5design

Design 4 (First Edition)

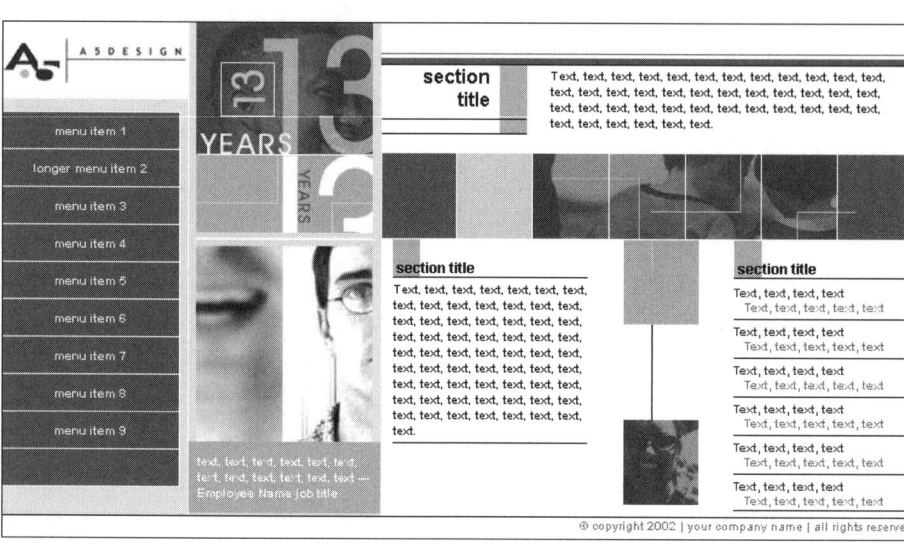

Homepage design.

Photoshop source file names: Designs—First Edition/design_4/design_4.psd

HTML Pages: index.htm, menu_item_2.htm, menu_item_3.htm

Photo credits: Cameracaptured, A5design

Design 3 (First Edition)

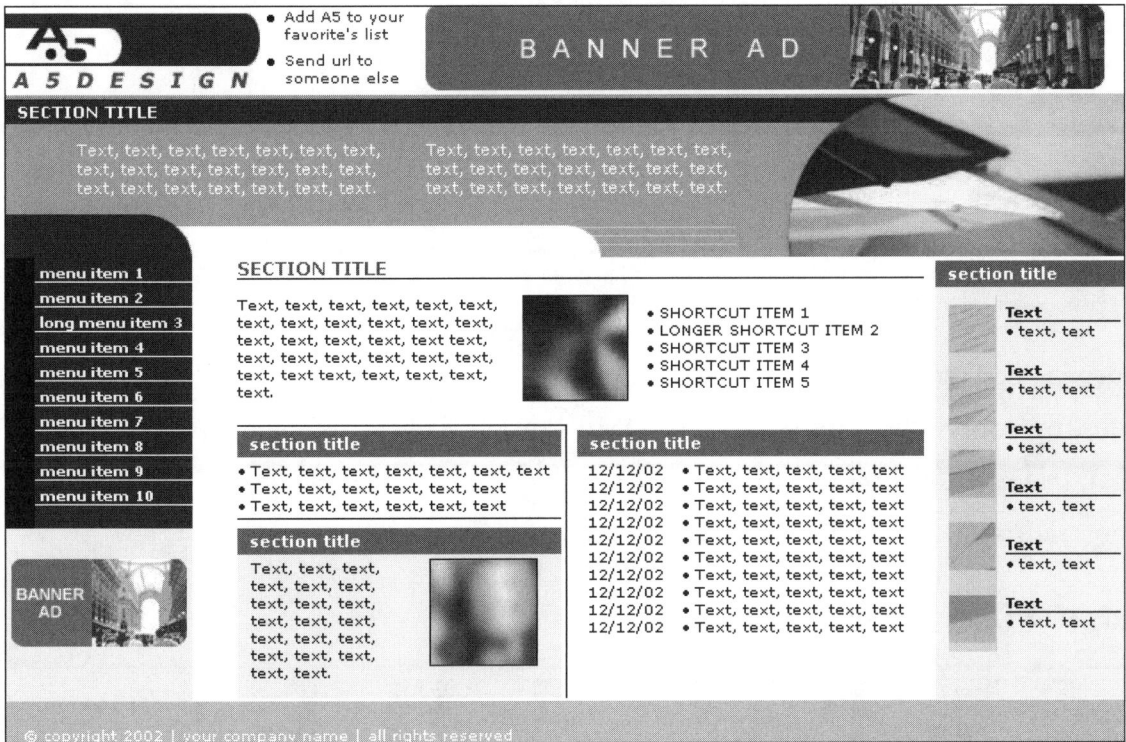

Homepage design.

Photoshop source file names: Designs—First Edition/design_3/design_3.psd

HTML Pages: index.htm, menu_item_2.htm, menu_item_3.htm

Photo credits: Cameracaptured

Design 2 (First Edition)

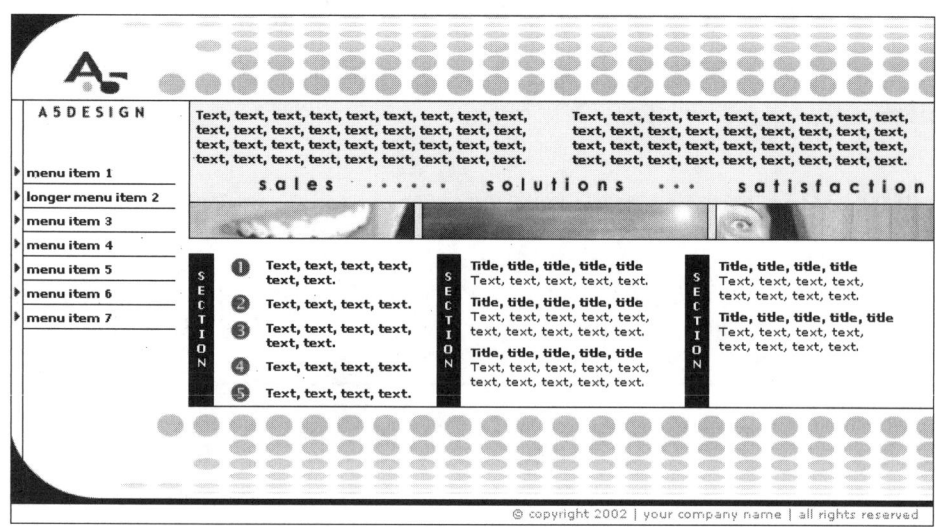

Homepage design.

Photoshop source file names: Designs—First Edition/design_2/design_2.psd

HTML Pages: index.htm, menu_item_2.htm

Photo credits: Onepartart, A5design

Design 1 (First Edition)

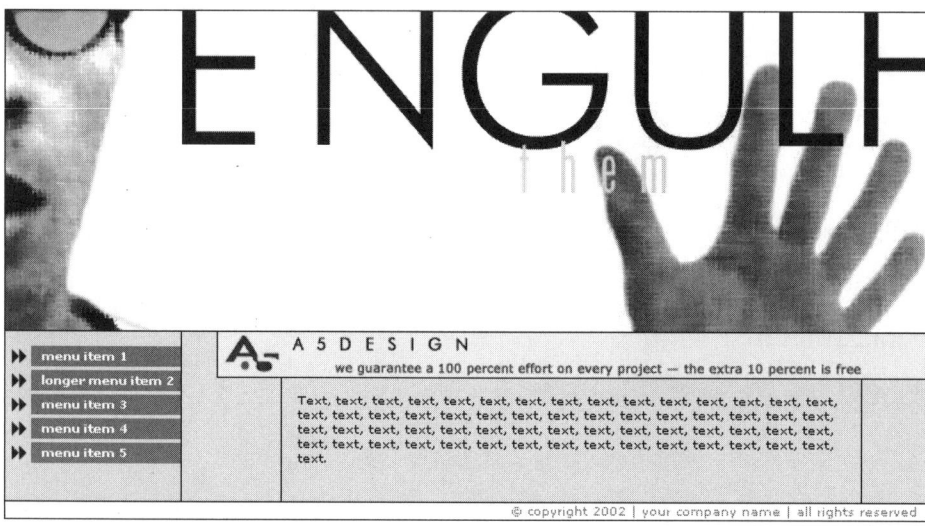

Homepage design.

Photoshop source file names: Designs—First Edition/design_1/design_1.psd

HTML Pages: index.htm, menu_item_2.htm

Photo credits: A5design

SUMMARY

The designs available online for this book offer a variety of options for the reader. The types of designs include XHTML table-based coded websites, e-newsletters, signatures, Photoshop-only designs, and CSS-coded designs. This not only offers the reader a variety of designs that can be quickly customized and used, but they can be used for inspiration as well.

INDEX

Numbers

8-bit PNGs and GIFs, saving images as, 125–129
8-bit resolution, using, 55–56
16-bit resolution, using, 55–56
32-bit resolution, using, 55, 57
800 × 600 resolution, 48
1024 × 768 resolution, 49
1280 × 800 resolution, 49

A

<a href=> HTML tag, 94
a5-bottom-row container, adding, 233–239
accessibility, designing for, 11, 75
aesthetic aspects of Web design, 2, 4–5
Allos Therapeutics, Inc. site, 81–83
animated GIFs, saving, 144
anti-aliasing
    explained, 121
    providing smooth curves with, 172
architecture
    cascading versus flat, 66–67
    consistent naming convention, 64–65
    explained, 63
    limiting clicking, 65
    linking users out of sections, 65
    site map, 64
    using breadcrumbs, 65
artistic aspects of Web design, 2, 4–5
audio
    bad quality, 404–405
    perceiving, 418
    See also editing sound; sound editing

audio editing hardware
    audio interface cards, 402
    microphones, 402
    mixing boards, 402
    speakers, 402
audio file formats, 401–402
audio levels metering
    clipping and distortion, 394–395
    dB (decibels), 393–394
    loudness, 393
Avid Pro Tools, 399

B

background color, using with mortised images, 105
background images
    positioning in CSS design, 182
    using, 331–332
    See also graphics; images
background-based design
    body content, 344–353
    CSS containers, 335
    CSS framework, 336–339
    footer, 344–353
    guides, 333–335
    header area for framework, 339–344
    second-level pages, 354–355
    slices in Photoshop, 333–335
    structure, 332–336
    XHTML framework, 336–339
banding, occurrence with graphics, 125